Television
Production
Handbook

Television
Production
Handbook

T E N T H   E D I T I O N

Herbert Zettl

San Francisco State University

WADSWORTH
CENGAGE Learning™

Australia • Brazil • Japan • Korea • Mexico • Singapore • Spain • United Kingdom • United States

Television Production Handbook, Tenth Edition
Herbert Zettl

Publisher: Michael Rosenberg

Managing Editor, Development: Karen Judd

Assistant Editor: Christine Halsey

Senior Editorial Assistant: Megan Garvey

Technology Project Manager: Jessica Badiner

Marketing Manager: Erin Mitchell

Marketing Assistant: Mary Anne Payumo

Marketing Communications Manager:
  Shemika Britt

Content Project Manager: Georgia Young

Creative Director: Rob Hugel

Art Director: Maria Epes

Print Buyer: Susan Carroll

Permissions Editor: Mollika Basu

Production Service: Ideas to Images

Cover and Text Designer: Gary Palmatier,
  Ideas to Images

Photo Researcher: Cheri Throop

Copy Editor: Elizabeth von Radics

Illustrator and Compositor: Ideas to Images

For product information and technology assistance, contact us at
Cengage Learning Customer & Sales Support, 1-800-354-9706

For permission to use material from this text or product, submit all requests online at **www.cengage.com/permissions**
Further permissions questions can be emailed to
permissionrequest@cengage.com

Library of Congress Control Number: 2007943882
ISBN-13: 978-0-495-50188-6
ISBN-10: 0-495-50188-3

Wadsworth
25 Thomson Place
Boston, MA 02210
USA

Cengage Learning is a leading provider of customized learning solutions with office locations around the globe, including Singapore, the United Kingdom, Australia, Mexico, Brazil and Japan. Locate your local office at: international.cengage.com/region

Cengage Learning products are represented in Canada by Nelson Education, Ltd.

For your course and learning solutions, visit **academic.cengage.com**

Purchase any of our products at your local college store or at our preferred online store **www.ichapters.com**

Printed in China

2 3 4 5 6 7   11 10 09 08

For Erika

Brief Contents

Contents

Part 1   Introduction: Process and System   1

CHAPTER 1   The Television Production Process   2

SECTION 1.1   What Television Production Is All About   4

THREE PRODUCTION PHASES   4
Preproduction   4
Production   4
Postproduction   4

PRODUCTION MODEL   4
Effect-to-cause Model   5
Medium Requirements   5
Process Message Shaping Medium Requirements   5

PRODUCTION PEOPLE   6
Nontechnical Production Personnel   6
Technical Personnel and Crew   8

NEWS PRODUCTION PERSONNEL   10

SECTION 1.2   Technical Production Systems   12

BASIC TELEVISION SYSTEM   12
How a Program Host Appears on the Television Receiver   12

EXPANDED TELEVISION SYSTEM   12
Multicamera Studio System   12

Part II   Preproduction   23

CHAPTER 11   Techniques of Television Lighting   214

SECTION 11.1   Lighting in the Studio   216

Part IV   Postproduction   419

CHAPTER 19   Postproduction Editing: How It Works   420

Photo Credits

360 systems, 9.10

Edward Aiona, 1.5, 1.6, 1.13, 1.18, 4.13, 4.14, 5.4, 5.15, 5.16, 5.17, 6.1, 6.2, 6.5, 6.15, 6.18, 6.20, 6.21, 6.22, 6.23, 6.24, 6.25, 6.30, 6.31, 7.1, 7.11, 7.12, 7.15, 7.16, 7.17, 7.18, 7.19, 7.20, 7.21, 7.28, 7.29, 7.30, 7.31, 7.32, 7.33, 7.34, 7.35, 7.36, 7.37, 7.38, 7.39, 7.40, 7.41, 7.44, 7.45, 7.48, 7.49, 7.50, 7.51, 8.1, 8.7, 8.8, 8.9, 8.14, 8.15, 8.16, 8.17, 8.22, 8.33, 9.1, 9.3, 9.5, 9.7, 9.15, 10.4, 10.5, 10.20, 10.24, 10.25, 10.26, 10.30, 10.31, 10.33, 10.34, 10.35, 10.36, 10.40, 10.41, 10.43, 11.3, 11.4, 11.5, 11.6, 11.8, 11.9, 11.11, 11.16, 11.17, 11.18, 11.19, 11.20, 11.21, 11.22, 11.23, 11.24, 11.27, 11.30, 12.8, 12.10, 12.18, 13.2, 13.5, 13.6, 13.7, 13.8, 13.9, 13.10, 13.11, 13.12, 13.13, 13.14, 13.15, 13.16, 13.20, 13.25, 13.27, 13.30, 13.31, 13.32, 13.33, 13.37, 13.39, 14.6, 14.7, 14.11, 14.15, 14.16, 14.25, 15.2, 15.2, 15.2, 15.2, 15.3, 15.6, 17.1, 17.1, 17.1, 17.6, 18.1, 19.2, 19.7, 19.10, 19.14, 20.1, 20.2, 20.3, 20.4, 20.5, 20.6, 20.10, 20.11, 20.12, 20.13, 20.17, 20.18, 20.19, 20.21, 20.22

AKG Acoustics, 8.6, 8.23, 8.32

Alesis, 9.13

Autoscript, 1.9

Broadcast and Electronic Communication Arts Department at San Francisco State University, 2.6, 8.27, 11.7, 13.29, 14.24, 19.13

beyerdynamic, Inc., 8.32

Canon, 1.10

Renee Child, 13.36

Chimera, 10.18, 10.22

Echolab, LLC, 1.16

Electro-Voice, 8.32

Focus Enhancements, 12.9, 12.11

Fujinon, Inc., 6.17

Glidecam, 7.10

Ikegami, 1.11, 5.10, 5.11

JVC, 5.13

Leviton, Colortran Division, 10.1, 10.32

Loud Technologies, Inc., 1.14

Lowel-Light Mfg., Inc., 10.8, 10.9, 10.11, 10.12, 10.14, 10.16, 10.17, 10.19, 10.21, 10.23

Manfrotto, 7.6

MobiTV, 4.10

Mole-Richardson Company, 10.3, 10.6, 10.7, 10.10, 10.13

Neumann USA, 8.32

NewTek, 13.19

Nikon, Inc., 6.16

Nokia, 4.10

Gary Palmatier, 5.18, 5.19, 7.26, 11.26, 12.19, 13.34, 18.2, 20.20

Panasonic Broadcast & Digital Systems Co., 1.17, 6.3, 12.6, 19.11

Professional Sound Corporation, 8.32

QTV, 15.4

Relflecmedia, www.reflecmedia.com, 13.26

Ross Video Limited, 13.17

Sachtler, 7.2

Samson (Zoom), 9.12

Selco Products Company, 9.4

Sennheiser Electronic Corporation, 8.13, 8.19, 8.32, 9.11

Shure, Inc., 1.15, 8.20, 8.21, 8.32, 9.17

Sony Electronics, Inc., 5.3, 5.12, 5.14, 8.32, 12.5, 12.7

Strand Lighting, 10.37

TASCAM Corporation, 9.9

Telescript, Inc., 15.5

The Tiffen Company, LLC, 7.9. Steadicam® is a registered trademark of The Tiffen Company, LLC.

Vinten, Inc., 7.3, 7.4, 7.7, 7.8, 7.13, 7.14

Vizrt, 14.20, 14.21

Alex Zettl, 6.28

Herbert Zettl, 1.12, 5.8, 5.9, 5.23, 6.12, 6.13, 6.19, 6.26, 6.27, 6.29, 7.22, 7.23, 7.24, 7.25, 7.27, 7.42, 7.43, 7.46, 7.47, 8.5, 8.10, 8.11, 8.12, 8.18, 8.29, 8.30, 8.31, 10.15, 10.27, 10.28, 10.29, 10.38, 10.39, 13.1, 13.21, 13.28, 13.35, 14.14, 14.23, 14.26, 14.28, 14.33, 18.4, 18.6, 18.19, 19.8, 20.7, 20.8, 20.9, 20.15, 20.16

The CNN logo (14.1) is courtesy of Cable News Network.

The hand-drawn storyboard (16.9) is courtesy of Bob Forward, Detonation Films.

The computer-generated storyboard (16.10) is courtesy of PowerProduction Software.

About the Author

Herbert Zettl is a professor emeritus of the Broadcast and Electronic Communication Arts Department at San Francisco State University (SFSU). He taught there for many years in the fields of video production and media aesthetics. While at SFSU he headed the Institute of International Media Communication. For his academic contributions, he received the California State Legislature Distinguished Teaching Award and, from the Broadcast Education Association, the Distinguished Education Service Award.

Prior to joining the SFSU faculty, Zettl worked at KOVR (Stockton-Sacramento) and as a producer-director at KPIX, the CBS affiliate in San Francisco. While at KPIX he participated in a variety of CBS and NBC network television productions. Because of his outstanding contributions to the television profession, he was elected to the prestigious Silver Circle of the National Academy of Television Arts and Sciences (NATAS), Northern California Chapter. He is also a member of the Broadcast Legends of the NATAS Northern California Chapter.

In addition to this book, Zettl has authored *Television Production Workbook, Sight Sound Motion,* and *Video Basics.* All of his books have been translated into several languages and published overseas. His numerous articles on television production and media aesthetics have appeared in major media journals worldwide. He has lectured extensively on television production and media aesthetics at universities and professional broadcast institutions in the United States and abroad and has presented key papers at a variety of national and international communication conventions.

Zettl developed an interactive DVD-ROM, *Zettl's VideoLab 3.0,* published by Wadsworth Cengage. His previous CD-ROM version won several prestigious awards, among them the *Macromedia* People's Choice Award, the *New Media* Invision Gold Medal for Higher Education, and Invision Silver Medals in the categories of Continuing Education and Use of Video.

Preface

The big buzzwords in television are *digital* and *high-definition*. You have probably heard many times that digital television and high-definition television (HDTV) revolutionized how we produce and watch not only television images but cinema as well. In one way such claims are true; in another way, HDTV influences certain production techniques only minimally.

For example, whereas the electronic characteristics of a digital camcorder differ considerably from those of the traditional analog one, its operation is pretty much the same. All types of camcorders—analog or digital, standard definition or high-definition—require that you look through a viewfinder and point the lens in a certain direction to get the desired image. On the other hand, the switch to a wide HDTV screen, or a large movie screen or tiny cell-phone display, requires different ways of framing a shot. Changing from a linear editing system to a nonlinear one calls for not only expanded operational skills but also a whole new concept of what editing is all about. Analog television can use only linear editing systems; digital television can work with both.

ALL-NEW ORGANIZATION FOR THE TENTH EDITION

With every new model of digital equipment getting more technically complex, digital technology is nevertheless also becoming more user-friendly. The focus in this Tenth Edition of the *Television Production Handbook* has therefore shifted from a primarily technical explanation of how television tools work to how they are used and what people do in the preproduction, production, and postproduction phases. Such an approach helps bring teaching and learning television production more in line with how professional television production is actually done.

This new edition of the *Television Production Handbook* has been radically reorganized. It is divided into four parts, reflecting the natural flow of television production:

- Part I Introduction: Process and System
- Part II Preproduction
- Part III Production
- Part IV Postproduction

PART I INTRODUCTION: PROCESS AND SYSTEM

Part I introduces the student to the three production phases: preproduction, production, and postproduction. It presents a production model that gives structure and reliability to the whole process of moving from the initial idea to the final screen image, and it demonstrates how production people and machines interact according to a strict protocol. Part I also introduces students to the primary responsibilities of nontechnical and technical personnel.

The problem of learning and teaching television production is that to really understand a single production element or piece of equipment, students should ideally know the function of all others. To help students cope with this problem and to understand television production as a system, part I includes a brief overview of all major production equipment.

PART II PREPRODUCTION

Part II stresses the importance of preproduction. Most beginning production students, armed with a digital camcorder and a laptop computer loaded with special effects, are itching to run outside and shoot an Emmy award–caliber documentary after the first class. They are, understandably, reluctant to spend any time on thinking about what exactly it is they want to say and how best to say it. But even the most eager students will soon find out that the success or failure of a production is largely determined in the preproduction phase. Part II therefore emphasizes how to move through the entire preproduction process, starting with generating worthwhile ideas, developing the program proposal, and, finally, writing the script.

The fully revised section on scripts includes the standard script formats as well as a brief introduction to dramatic and nondramatic story structures. The discussion of preproduction includes major information resources and introduces students to unions, legal matters, and audience ratings.

PART III PRODUCTION

Not surprisingly, this is the most comprehensive part of the text and includes a detailed explanation of what digital is all about, the various scanning systems, the aspect ratios, the major production tools and their effective use, and what the talent, director, and floor manager do during the actual production. Part III also includes hints for directing single- and multicamera productions for television and digital cinema in the studio and in the field. It includes detailed camera and mic setups for major sporting events.

PART IV POSTPRODUCTION

Postproduction editing was once a highly specialized occupation requiring expensive equipment; today the laptop computer and relatively inexpensive editing software have made editing simply another phase of even the most modest video productions. The aesthetic principles of how to make a sequence of images look seamless or especially dramatic, however, have not changed with the new technology. Production students still have to learn how and why various shots cut together well regardless of whether they use an old linear cuts-only system or the most elaborate nonlinear software. The last two chapters explain not only how nonlinear and linear editing work but also the principles of continuity and complexity editing and how to effectively apply them.

PEDAGOGICAL FEATURES

To facilitate optimal student learning, this edition of the *Handbook* again incorporates important pedagogical principles.

Attention   Each chapter is broken down into relatively short sections marked by separate headings. I hope that such a layout will keep the reader's attention and counteract reading fatigue without fracturing chapter content.

Two-tier approach   The *Handbook* is designed to serve beginning students as well as those who are more adept at television production. To prevent the less advanced students from getting bogged down by the multitude of technical details, each chapter is divided into two sections. Section 1 contains the basic information about a specific topic; section 2 presents more-detailed material. The two sections can be assigned and read together or independently.

Reinforcement   As we all know from advertising, a certain amount of repetition is essential for making a product name stick. The same redundancy principle holds true when learning the language and the production concepts of television. The key terms of each chapter are first listed after the chapter introduction; they appear in **bold italic** in the text and again in the extensive glossary at the back of the book. To benefit from this learning aid, students should read the key terms *before* committing to the chapter and use the chapter summaries as a checklist of what they are expected to know.

Illustrations   The numerous full-color pictures and diagrams are intended to bridge the gap between description and the real thing. All appropriate illustrations that simulate TV images are in the 16 × 9 HDTV aspect ratio. This is done to help students visualize shots in the wide-screen aspect ratio. In most cases the pictures of equipment represent a generic type rather than a specific preferred model.

ACCOMPANYING RESOURCES: AN EXCLUSIVE TEACHING AND LEARNING PACKAGE

As with previous editions, the Tenth Edition of the *Television Production Handbook* offers a wealth of support materials for both students and instructors.

TELEVISION PRODUCTION WORKBOOK

The *Television Production Workbook* is intended primarily to test students' comprehension of various equipment and production concepts. Each chapter contains a review of key terms and the basic content covered as well as a true/false quiz. The problem-solving applications are intended mainly for in-class discussion. I have often used the *Workbook* as a diagnostic tool by having students answer some of the questions in class. This way I could quickly determine who knows what about television production, and the students had immediate feedback about what they needed to know.

All *Workbook* problems except for the problem-solving applications are based on a binary system, which means that the questions can be answered by filling in the appropriate bubbles. This approach makes checking the answers relatively easy, even without the aid of a computer, and provides a basis for objective evaluation.

INSTRUCTOR'S MANUAL WITH ANSWER KEY TO WORKBOOK

The *Instructor's Manual* is intended primarily for the instructor who may be quite experienced in television production but relatively new to teaching. Even experienced instructors, however, may find information that makes the difficult job of teaching television production just a little easier. The *Instructor's Manual* comprises four parts:

- Part I, General Approach to Teaching Television Production, presents information on teaching approaches and ideas about how to teach television production most effectively.

- Part II, Key Concepts, Activities, and Tests, contains expanded definitions of the key concepts introduced in each chapter, appropriate activities for reinforcing them, and multiple-choice problems to test student retention of the material.

- Part III, Additional Resources, is a compact reference that recommends additional teaching and learning resources.

- Part IV consists of the answer key to all the *Television Production Workbook* problems.

ZETTL'S VIDEOLAB 3.0 DVD-ROM

This Windows- and Mac-compatible DVD-ROM contains an interactive program of camera operation, studio and field lighting, audio capture and control, switching, linear and nonlinear editing, and the major parts of the production process. It is intended to give students virtual hands-on practice and a proven shortcut from reading about production techniques to actually applying them in the studio and in the field.

Finally, instructors and students may benefit from a number of resources offered by the publisher.

THE TELEVISION PRODUCTION HANDBOOK COMPANION WEB SITE

academic.cengage.com/rtf/zettl/tvproductionhandbook10e

This site features chapter resources, such as crossword puzzles, flash cards, and a glossary pertaining to the content of the selected chapter. It also lists various media departments and media employment services for people who seek to further their media education or look for jobs in electronic media.

WADSWORTH'S EXAMVIEW® COMPUTERIZED TESTING

ExamView offers both a *Quick Test Wizard* and an *Online Test Wizard* that guide you step-by-step through the process of creating tests, while its "what you see is what you get" interface allows you to see the test you are creating onscreen exactly as it will print or display online. For additional information please contact your local Wadsworth Cengage Learning representative or the Wadsworth Academic Resource Center at 1-800-423-0563.

ACKNOWLEDGMENTS

Once again I was privileged to have Wadsworth Cengage Learning call upon the expertise of its "A-team" to produce this Tenth Edition of the *Television Production Handbook*: Michael Rosenberg, publisher; Karen Judd, managing development editor; Ed Dodd, development editor; Christine Halsey, assistant editor; Megan Garvey, assistant editor; Erin Mitchell, marketing manager; Maria Epes, executive art director; Georgia Young, content project manager; Cheri Throop, photo researcher; and Mollika Basu, permissions editor.

Gary Palmatier of Ideas to Images, art director and project manager; Elizabeth von Radics, copy editor; Mike Mollett, proofreader; and Ed Aiona, photographer, are the principals who actually made this handsome book out of the many loose pages, notes, and sketches I handed them. The highest praise I can give them is to say that they are all true professionals and incredibly dedicated people who are fun to work with.

Once again, a number of committed instructors were kind enough to review the Ninth Edition of the *Handbook* and made numerous valuable suggestions for this edition: Peter B. Gregg, University of Minnesota; Michael F. Korpi, Baylor University, Waco, Texas; Tom O'Hanlon, Lehman

College/City University of New York, Bronx, New York; and Fred Weiss, San Antonio College, San Antonio, Texas. My gratitude goes to all of them, especially because I know well how much effort goes into such a review.

Paul Rose, University of Utah, deserves my special thanks. He is chiefly responsible for having me rethink the organization of the book, and he patiently nudged me into the final chapter flow you see in this edition. He also read the entire draft and made many valuable suggestions for technical and production updates. Here it is, Paul: a special thank-you!

Fortunately, I have colleagues and friends from various universities, television stations, and media production companies who are always ready and willing to share their expertise with me on a moment's notice. For this edition I need to single out Marty Gonzales, Hamid Khani, Phil Kipper, Steve Lahey, Vinay Shrivatava, and Winston Tharp of San Francisco State University; Stanley Alten, Syracuse University; Manfred Muckenhaupt, Media Studies, University of Tuebingen, Germany; Manfred Wolfram, University of Cincinnati; Rudolf Benzler of T.E.A.M., Lucerne, Switzerland; John Beritzhoff and Greg Goddard of Snader and Associates; Ed Cosci, Jeff Green, Jim Haman, and Steve Shlisky of KTVU; and Elan Frank and Reed Maidenberg of Elan Productions.

Special thanks also to Bridget at FedEx/Kinko's in San Rafael, California, who, always with great patience and a smile on her face, helped me numerous times to get the copy machines unstuck or reprogrammed again after I had hopelessly jammed them for one reason or another.

I am, of course, much indebted to all the people who gave a considerable amount of their time to volunteer as on-camera talent during our photo sessions: Talia Aiona, Karen Austin, Ken Baird, Jerome Bakum, Rudolf Benzler, Tiemo Biemueller, Monica Caizada, William Carpenter, Andrew Child, Laura Child, Rebecca Child, Renee Child, Skye Christensen, Ed Cosci, Carla Currie, Sabrina Dorsey, Tammy Feng, Jedediah Gildersleeve, Cassandra Hein, Poleng Hong, Sangyong Hong, Akiko Kajiwara, Hamid Khani, Philip Kipper, Christine Lojo, Orcun Malkoclar, Michael Mona, Johnny Moreno, Anita Morgan, Jacqueline Murray, Tuan Nguyen, Richard Piscitello, Matthew Prisk, Marlin Quintero, Kerstin Riediger, Suzanne Saputo, Alisa Shahonian, Steve Shlisky, Talisha Teague, Takako Thorstadt, and Yanlan Wu.

Finally, my wife, Erika, deserves two big thank-you hugs: one for being so patient with me during my struggles to make the Tenth Edition of the *Handbook* the best yet, and the other for having my study refurbished. The new arrangement helped me not only become more efficient but also stay relatively cheerful throughout the writing process.

Herbert Zettl

I

Introduction: Process and System

1

The Television Production Process

When watching television, somebody's vacation videos, a blogger's video podcast on the Internet, or even a movie, you probably feel that you could do just as well or even better than what's on the screen. This may be true, but it is more likely that you will be surprised to find how difficult it is to match the high production values of the average television show, even if the content begs for improvement. The automatic features of most equipment may even fool you into believing that television production is relatively easy—until your luck runs out. Even if your short vacation video looks pretty good to you, it may need much more effort and production skills to make it look good to somebody else. A seemingly simple 55-second chat between a news anchor in Portland and a soccer star in Madrid presents a formidable challenge even for experienced production personnel. This book will help you meet such a challenge.

The digital era has brought a general convergence of digital video and the necessary production processes, regardless of whether you are working in broadcast television, digital cinema, or independently on small video projects. Fortunately, this convergence has a common base: multicamera and single-camera television production. Learning the ins and the outs of television production allows you to readily adapt to other forms of digital video production.

The major problem with learning television production is that to understand the function of one piece of equipment or production phase, you should already know all of the others. Chapter 1 is designed to help you with this chicken-and-egg problem. It provides you with an overview of the initial production process, the people involved in small and large productions, and the necessary tools to generate the screen images and sound—the standard television equipment. Later chapters provide more-detailed descriptions and explanations of equipment and production processes.

Section 1.1, What Television Production Is All About, walks you through the three phases of production, demonstrates a useful production model, and introduces you to the major nontechnical and technical production personnel.

Section 1.2, Technical Production Systems, introduces you to the technical television systems and their major production equipment.

KEY TERMS

effect-to-cause model Moving from idea to desired effect on the viewer, then backing up to the specific medium requirements to produce such an effect.

EFP Stands for *electronic field production*. Television production outside of the studio that is normally shot for postproduction (not live). Part of field production.

ENG Stands for *electronic news gathering*. The use of portable camcorders or cameras with separate portable video recorders, lights, and sound equipment for the production of daily news stories. ENG is usually not planned in advance and is often transmitted live or immediately after postproduction.

linear editing Analog or digital editing that uses tape-based systems. The selection of shots is nonrandom.

medium requirements All content elements, production elements, and people needed to generate the defined process message.

news production personnel People assigned exclusively to the production of news, documentaries, and special events.

nonlinear editing (NLE) Allows instant random access to shots and sequences and easy rearrangement. The video and audio information is stored in digital form on computer hard drives or read/write optical discs.

nontechnical production personnel People concerned primarily with nontechnical production matters that lead from the basic idea to the final screen image.

postproduction Any production activity that occurs after the production. Usually refers to either video editing or audio sweetening (a variety of quality adjustments of recorded sound).

preproduction The preparation of all production details.

process message The message actually perceived by the viewer in the process of watching the television program.

production The actual activities in which an event is recorded and/or televised.

technical production personnel People who operate the production equipment.

television system Equipment and people who operate the equipment for the production of specific programs. The basic television system consists of a television camera and a microphone, which convert pictures and sound into electrical signals, and a television set and a loudspeaker, which convert the signals back into pictures and sound.

1.1

What Television Production Is All About

As a painter it is relatively easy to get your idea onto the canvas. All you need is something to paint on, some paints, a brush, and, of course, a little technique. You are the only one involved in the translation process from idea to image. Such a translation process for even a simple television production, however, is considerably more complex. You are seldom alone in the production process, face strict deadlines, and are always forced to work with a variety of complex equipment. This section gives a brief overview of the three phases of production—preproduction, production, and postproduction—suggests a production model that will streamline the use of people and equipment, and charts the major nontechnical and technical personnel. **ZVL1** PROCESS→ Process introduction

▶ **THREE PRODUCTION PHASES**
Preproduction, production, and postproduction

▶ **PRODUCTION MODEL**
Effect-to-cause model, medium requirements, and process message shaping medium requirements

▶ **PRODUCTION PEOPLE**
Nontechnical production personnel, technical production personnel, and news production personnel

THREE PRODUCTION PHASES

Regardless of whether you are part of the nontechnical or technical personnel, or whether you work with a big production team or all by yourself, you will inevitably be involved in one or all of the three production phases: preproduction, production, and postproduction.

PREPRODUCTION

Preproduction includes all the preparations and activities before you actually move into the studio or the field on the first day of production. It usually happens in two stages. Stage 1 consists of all the activities necessary to transform the basic idea into a workable concept or script. In stage 2 all the necessary production details, such as location, crews, and the necessary equipment for a single-camera or multicamera production, are worked out.

PRODUCTION

As soon as you open the studio doors for rehearsal or a video-recording session, or load a camcorder into the van for a field shoot, you are in *production*. Except for rehearsals, production involves equipment and normally a crew—people who operate the equipment. It includes all activities in which an event is video-recorded or televised.

POSTPRODUCTION

The major activity of *postproduction* consists of video and audio editing. It may also include color correction of the various video clips (so that the red shirt of an actor looks the same from one shot to the next), the selection of appropriate background music, and the creation of special audio effects. When using a single camera film-style, which means that a scene is built by recording one shot after another with only one camera, the postproduction activities may take longer than the actual production. **ZVL2** PROCESS→ Phases→ preproduction | production | postproduction

PRODUCTION MODEL

Like any other model, a production model is meant to help you move from the original idea to the finished production as efficiently as possible. It is designed to help you decide on the most effective approach the first time around, evaluate each major production step, and finish on time. Its function is similar to that of a road map: you don't have to follow it to get from here to there, but it makes finding your way much easier. If you feel that it is restrictive and cramps your creativity or style, don't use it.

EFFECT-TO-CAUSE MODEL

Like most other production models, the **effect-to-cause model** starts with a basic idea, but instead of moving from the basic idea directly to the production process, it jumps to the desired communication effect on the target audience—the general program objective. This program objective can be reached through a specific message that, ideally, the viewer will actually receive, internalize, or act on. Because this all-important message is generated by the process of the viewer's watching the video and audio content of your television program and attaching meaning to it, we call it the **process message**. This process requires that you as a producer should have a fairly clear idea of what you want the target audience to learn, do, and feel before you think about the necessary technical requirements. The model suggests that you move from the general idea directly to the desired effect and then back up and think about how to bring about—cause—this effect. **ZVL3** PROCESS→ Effect-to-cause→ basic idea | desired effect | cause | actual effect

The more the actual process message (viewer effect) matches the defined one, the more successful the communication. **SEE 1.1**

Defined process message   Rather than being driven by the initial idea, the production process is now driven by the

defined process message—the desired effect on the target audience. At this point you could proceed to the **medium requirements**—the people, facilities, and equipment necessary for the preproduction, production, and postproduction phases. To further streamline the production process, you should find a useful angle.

Angle   As you undoubtedly know, the angle is a specific story focus, a point of view from which to look at and describe an event. It can lead to an obvious bias of who tells the story, or it can be subtler and make a story more interesting to watch.

If a dog bites the letter carrier, the dog owner's story angle might be the rising crime in the neighborhood and the dog's attempt to protect his master. The letter carrier, on the other hand, may have quite a different view of the same event. He may well focus on the viciousness of the neighborhood dogs and the need for stricter leash laws. Both angles contain a strong and unacceptable bias. But you can also use an angle that gives the story a specific approach without introducing a strong bias. For example, you could document a popular singing star by watching her give a concert for a large enthusiastic audience or by observing her during a studio recording session. The first version would be a more public "looking-at" point of view, the second a more private "looking-into" point of view. This would not only change what equipment you need (a multicamera setup with live switching or extensive postproduction for the first version) but also your shooting style (many more close-ups for version 2 than for version 1).

MEDIUM REQUIREMENTS

The advantage of this model is that the precise definition of the process message and a specific angle will help the content and production people work as a team and facilitate selecting the necessary production personnel and equipment. By first carefully defining the desired effect on the audience, you can then decide quite easily on the specific people you need to do the job (content expert, writer, director, and crew), on where to do the production most effectively (studio or field), and on the necessary equipment (studio or field cameras, types of mics, and so forth).

PROCESS MESSAGE SHAPING MEDIUM REQUIREMENTS

Let's assume that you are to produce a 15-minute segment of a live morning show. You are told by the show's executive producer to get a lawyer who is willing to talk about an ongoing high-profile murder trial.

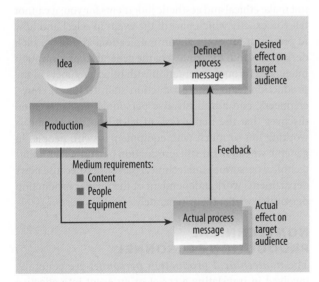

1.1 EFFECT-TO-CAUSE PRODUCTION MODEL

The effect-to-cause production model jumps from the initial idea and story angle directly to the desired effect—the process message. Then it backs up to the medium requirements that suggest the production elements and processes necessary to produce the defined process message.

The usual and intuitive way to approach this assignment would be to contact a well-known criminal lawyer and have the art director design a set that looks like a well-to-do lawyer's office, with an elegant desk, leather chairs, and lots of law books in the background. You would then have to arrange for the recording date, studio time, transportation for the guest, talent fees, and other such details.

When using the effect-to-cause model, on the other hand, you might come up with two different angles: one that shows the intellectual brilliance of a defense lawyer and her skill to engender reasonable doubt in the jurors, and another that reveals the emotional makeup and the inner conflict of a lawyer defending a suspect despite the overwhelming evidence that he is guilty.

Here's how the two different angles might influence the resulting process messages, and, in turn, dictate different production approaches:

Process message 1: The viewer should gain insight into some of the major defense strategies used by the guest.

In this case the questions would revolve around some of the lawyer's former cases and the reasons for their success or failure. Would you need an interviewer who understands the law? Yes. The interviewer could interpret the legal language for the audience or immediately challenge the lawyer's ethics within the framework of the law. The elaborate studio set resembling the lawyer's office would also be appropriate. You may even consider conducting this interview on-location in the lawyer's actual office.

Process message 2: The viewer should gain deeper insight into the conscience and the feelings of the lawyer when handling an especially difficult case as well as how she deals with personal ethics when applying specific defense strategies.

Do you now need a host who is a legal expert? Not at all. In fact, a psychologist would probably be better suited to conduct this interview. You might opt for close-ups of the lawyer throughout most of the show. You may even stay on a close-up of the guest when the host asks questions. Reaction shots (the lawyer listening to questions) are often more telling than action shots (the lawyer answering). Does this interview require an elaborate set? No. Because the interview deals primarily with the lawyer as a person rather than the person as a lawyer, you can conduct it in any environment. Two comfortable chairs on an interview set are all you would need.

Some unsolicited advice: There has been a great reluctance in television production to show "talking heads"—people talking on close-ups without any supporting visual material, special effects, or a constant dribble of background music. Do not blindly adopt this prejudice. So long as the heads talk well, there is no need for additional visual or aural clutter. **ZVL4** PROCESS→ Effect-to-cause→ basic idea | desired effect | cause

As you can see, in this case the angle was not stated separately but rather embedded in the defined process message. But would you need a process message if you were to write a play? Of course not. Even a nicely formulated process message would not help you write a more effective drama. Any dramatic presentation has its own internal structure that does not benefit from stating its desired effect on the audience. It is more important to think about character development and conflict than defining whether you want the audience to cry or laugh. More goal-directed program forms, however, such as instructional shows, interviews, documentaries, and certainly advertising, can benefit greatly from a precisely stated process message.

PRODUCTION PEOPLE

Even the most sophisticated television production equipment and computer interfaces will not replace *you* in the television production process; you and those working with you still reign supreme—at least so far. The equipment cannot make ethical and aesthetic judgments for you; it cannot tell you exactly which part of the event to select and how to present it for optimal communication. You make such decisions within the context of the general communication intent and through interaction with other members of the production team—the production staff, technical crews, engineers, and administrative personnel. You may soon discover that the major task of television production is working not so much with equipment as with people. In general, we can divide the production personnel into nontechnical personnel and technical personnel. Because news departments work independent of the regular production personnel, we list them separately.

NONTECHNICAL PRODUCTION PERSONNEL

The *nontechnical production personnel* are generally involved in translating a script or an event into effective television images. They are also called above-the-line personnel because they fall under a different budget category from the technical crew, who are called below-the-line personnel. The above- and below-the-line distinction is anything but absolute or even uniform, however, and it changes depending on the crewmembers' union affiliations and the budgetary practices of the production company. We therefore use here the more self-evident division of nontechnical and technical personnel. Figure 1.2 shows the principal functions of the major nontechnical production personnel. **SEE 1.2**

You should realize, however, that in smaller television operations one person might carry out several different functions. For example, the producer may also write and direct the show, and the floor manager may take on the responsibilities of the line producer. You may find an AD (associate director) in the production of soap operas or an electronic movie but rarely during most routine television shows. The art director may also function as a graphic artist, and most medium-sized or smaller production companies have little use for a permanent costume designer,

1.2 NONTECHNICAL PRODUCTION PERSONNEL

PERSONNEL	FUNCTION
NONTECHNICAL PRODUCTION PERSONNEL	
Executive producer	In charge of one or several large productions or program series. Manages budget and coordinates with client, station management, advertising agencies, financial supporters, and talent and writers' agents.
Producer	In charge of an individual production. Responsible for all personnel working on the production and for coordinating technical and nontechnical production elements. Often serves as writer and occasionally as director.
Associate producer (AP)	Assists producer in all production matters. Often does the actual coordinating jobs, such as telephoning talent and confirming schedules.
Line producer	Supervises daily production activities on the set.
Field producer	Assists producer by taking charge of remote operations (away from the studio). At small stations function may be part of producer's responsibilities.
Production manager	Schedules equipment and personnel for all studio and field productions. Also called *director of broadcast operations.*
Production assistant (PA)	Assists producer and director during actual production. During rehearsal takes notes of producer's and/or director's suggestions for show improvement.
Director	In charge of directing talent and technical operations. Is ultimately responsible for transforming a script into effective video and audio messages. At small stations may often be the producer as well.
Associate director (AD)	Assists director during the actual production. In studio productions does timing for director. In complicated productions helps "ready" various operations (such as presetting specific camera shots or calling for a video recorder to start). Also called *assistant director.*
Floor manager	In charge of all activities on the studio floor. Coordinates talent, relays director's cues to talent, and supervises floor personnel. Except for large operations, is responsible for setting up scenery and dressing the set. Also called *floor director* and *stage manager.*
Floor persons	Set up and dress sets. Operate cue cards and other prompting devices, easel cards, and on-camera graphics. Sometimes help set up and work portable field lighting instruments and microphone booms. Assist camera operators in moving camera dollies and pulling camera cables. At small stations also act as wardrobe and makeup people. Also called *grips, stagehands,* and *utilities personnel.*

1.2 NONTECHNICAL PRODUCTION PERSONNEL *(continued)*

PERSONNEL	FUNCTION
ADDITIONAL PRODUCTION PERSONNEL	
In small operations these production people are not always part of the permanent staff or their functions are fulfilled by other personnel.	
Writer	At smaller stations and in corporate television, the scripts are often written by the director or producer. Usually hired on a freelance basis.
Art director	In charge of the creative design aspects of show (set design, location, and/or graphics).
Graphic artist	Prepares computer graphics, titles, charts, and electronic backgrounds.
Makeup artist	Does the makeup for all talent. Usually hired on a freelance basis.
Costume designer	Designs and sometimes even constructs various costumes for dramas, dance numbers, and children's shows. Usually hired on a freelance basis.
Wardrobe person	Handles all wardrobe matters during production.
Property manager	Maintains and manages use of various set and hand properties. Found in large operations only. Otherwise, props are managed by the floor manager.
Sound designer	Constructs the complete sound track (dialogue and sound effects) in postproduction. Usually hired on a freelance basis for large productions.

wardrobe person, property manager, or sound designer. Television talent—the performers and actors who work in front of the camera—are usually considered part of the nontechnical production personnel (discussed in chapter 15). **ZVL5** PROCESS→ People→ nontechnical

TECHNICAL PERSONNEL AND CREW

The *technical production personnel* consist of people who are primarily concerned with operating equipment. They are usually part of the crew. The technical personnel include camera operators, audio and lighting people, video-recording operators, video editors, C.G. (character generator) operators, and people who set up communication and signal transmission equipment. The term *technical* does not refer to electronic expertise but rather to operating the equipment with skill and confidence. The true engineers, who understand electronics and know where to look when something goes wrong with a piece of equipment, usually do not operate equipment; rather they ensure that the whole system runs smoothly, supervise its installation,

and maintain it. You may find that in larger professional operations, however, the technical production people are still called engineers, mainly to satisfy the traditional job classification established by the labor unions.

The DP (director of photography) is sometimes listed as part of the nontechnical personnel and sometimes as part of the technical team. The term, borrowed from film production, has found its way into television. In standard theatrical film production, the DP is mainly responsible for lighting and the proper exposure of the film rather than for running the camera. In smaller electronic film productions and EFP (electronic field production), the DP operates the camera as well as does the lighting. So when you hear that an independent television producer/director is looking for a reliable and creative DP, he or she is primarily referring to an experienced EFP camera operator. **SEE 1.3** **ZVL6** PROCESS→ People→ technical

As mentioned, many of the functions of technical and nontechnical production people overlap and even change, depending on the size, location, and relative complexity

1.3 TECHNICAL PERSONNEL

PERSONNEL	FUNCTION
ENGINEERING STAFF	
These people are actual engineers who are responsible for the purchase, installation, proper functioning, and maintenance of all technical equipment.	
Chief engineer	In charge of all technical personnel, budgets, and equipment. Designs system, including transmission facilities, and oversees installations and day-to-day operations.
Assistant chief engineer	Assists chief engineer in all technical matters and operations. Also called *engineering supervisor*.
Studio or remote engineer-in-charge	Oversees all technical operations. Usually called *EIC*.
Maintenance engineer	Maintains all technical equipment and troubleshoots during productions.
NONENGINEERING TECHNICAL PERSONNEL	
Although skilled in technical aspects, the following technical personnel do not have to be engineers but usually consist of technically trained production people.	
Technical director (TD)	Does the switching and usually acts as technical crew chief.
Camera operators	Operate the cameras; often do the lighting for simple shows. When working primarily in field productions (ENG/EFP), they are sometimes called *videographers* and *shooters*.
Director of photography (DP)	In film productions, in charge of lighting. In EFP, operates EFP camera.
Lighting director (LD)	In charge of lighting; normally found mostly in large productions.
Video operator (VO)	Adjusts camera controls for optimal camera pictures (shading). Sometimes takes on additional technical duties, especially during field productions and remotes. Also called *shader*.
Audio technician	In charge of all audio operations. Works audio console during the show. Also called *audio engineer*.
Video-record operator	Runs the videotape recorder and/or disk-based recording devices.
Character generator (C.G.) operator	Types and/or recalls from the computer the names and other graphic material to be integrated with the video image.
Video editor	Operates postproduction editing equipment. Often makes or assists in creative editing decisions.
Digital graphic artist	Renders digital graphics for on-air use. Can be nontechnical personnel.

of the production. For example, you may initially have acted as a producer when setting up the video recording of the semiannual address of a corporation president; then, on the day of the shoot, you may find yourself busy with such technical matters as lighting and running the camera. In larger productions, such as soap operas, your job responsibility is much more limited. When acting as a producer, you have nothing to do with lighting or equipment operation. When working the camera, you may have to wait patiently for the lighting crew to finish, even if the production is behind schedule and you have nothing else to do at the time.

NEWS PRODUCTION PERSONNEL

Almost all television broadcast stations produce at least one daily newscast; in fact, the newscasts are often the major production activity at these stations. Because news departments must be able to respond quickly to a variety of production tasks, such as covering a downtown fire or a protest at city hall, there is generally little time to pre-

pare for such events. News departments therefore have their own *news production personnel*. These people are dedicated exclusively to the production of news, documentaries, and special events and perform highly specific functions. **SEE 1.4**

A relatively new job designation in the news production personnel is the video journalist (VJ), who must combine the functions of reporter, videographer, writer, and editor. This rather demanding job was obviously not instituted to improve news coverage but to save money. Nevertheless you can see that you can no longer afford a narrowly focused training but must be fluent in all aspects of television production.

As in any other organization, television and corporate video involve many more people than what you see listed in this section, such as clerical personnel and the people who answer phones, schedule events, sell commercial time, negotiate contracts, build and paint the sets, and clean the building. Because these support personnel operate outside of the basic production system, their functions aren't discussed here.

1.4 NEWS PRODUCTION PERSONNEL

PERSONNEL	FUNCTION
News director	In charge of all news operations. Bears ultimate responsibility for all newscasts.
Producer	Directly responsible for the selection and the placement of the stories in a newscast so that they form a unified, balanced whole.
Assignment editor	Assigns reporters and videographers to specific events to be covered.
Reporter	Gathers the stories. Often reports on-camera from the field.
Video journalist	Reporter who shoots and edits his or her own footage.
Videographer	Camcorder operator. In the absence of a reporter, decides on what part of the event to cover. Also called *news photographer* and *shooter*.
Writer	Writes on-the-air copy for the anchors. The copy is based on the reporter's notes and the available video.
Video editor	Edits video according to reporter's notes, writer's script, or producer's instructions.
Anchor	Principal presenter of newscast, normally from a studio set.
Weathercaster	On-camera talent, reporting the weather.
Traffic reporter	On-camera talent, reporting local traffic conditions.
Sportscaster	On-camera talent, giving sports news and commentary.

MAIN POINTS

▶ The three production phases are preproduction, production, and postproduction.

▶ Preproduction includes the preparation of a show before the actual production activities take place. It usually happens in two stages: the first is the move from the basic idea to the script; the second is the designation of the necessary equipment (cameras, microphones, and so forth), facilities (studio or field production), and people to transform the script into a television show.

▶ Production includes all the activities in which equipment and the crew operating it create the actual program or program segments. The program can be video-recorded or put on the air; the segments are usually video-recorded for postproduction.

▶ Postproduction involves mostly video and audio editing. The various program sections that were recorded in the production phase are put into the proper sequence. It can also include the enhancement of the pictures and the sound.

▶ The effect-to-cause model facilitates the production approach. It moves from the basic idea to the process message (the desired effect on the viewer) and from there to the medium requirements (content, people, and equipment) necessary to actually cause the process message. The closer the defined and actual process messages match, the more successful the program.

▶ The nontechnical personnel include a variety of people who design the program (writers, art director, sound designer, and so forth) and execute the program (producers, director, floor manager, and assistants).

▶ The technical personnel include the engineers, who install and maintain the equipment, and the nonengineering technical personnel, who operate the equipment.

▶ The news department has its own production personnel, which consist of a variety of producers, writers, assignment editors, graphic artists, reporters, and videographers as well as video journalists, who report, operate the camera, and write and edit the story.

1.2

Technical Production Systems

To make sense of the various pieces of television equipment and how they interact in a multicamera or single-camera production, you should consider them as part of a system. This way you can relate how they function together, even if they are presented here piecemeal. This section gives an overview of the studio and field production systems and an introduction to the major equipment.

▶ **BASIC TELEVISION SYSTEM**
  How a program host appears on the television receiver

▶ **EXPANDED TELEVISION SYSTEM**
  Multicamera studio system

▶ **FIELD PRODUCTION SYSTEMS**
  ENG (electronic news gathering) and EFP (electronic field production) systems

▶ **MAJOR EQUIPMENT**
  Camera, lighting, audio, switcher, video recorder, and postproduction editing

BASIC TELEVISION SYSTEM

A system is a collection of elements that work together to achieve a specific purpose. Each element depends on the proper functioning of the others, and none of the individual elements can do the job alone. The *television system* con-

sists of equipment and people who operate that equipment for the production of specific programs.

HOW A PROGRAM HOST APPEARS ON THE TELEVISION RECEIVER

Whether the production is simple or elaborate or originates in the studio or in the field—that is, on-location—the television system works on the same basic principle: the television camera converts whatever it "sees" (optical images) into electrical signals that can be temporarily stored or directly reconverted by the television set into visible screen images. The microphone converts whatever it "hears" (actual sounds) into electrical signals that can be temporarily stored or directly reconverted into sounds by the loudspeaker. In general, the basic television system transduces (converts) one state of energy (optical image, actual sound) into another (electrical energy). **SEE 1.5** The picture signals are called video signals, and the sound signals are called audio signals. Any small consumer camcorder represents such a system.

EXPANDED TELEVISION SYSTEM

The expanded system includes more equipment in a variety of configurations. Productions such as news, interviews, game shows, and soap operas use the multicamera studio system.

MULTICAMERA STUDIO SYSTEM

The multicamera studio system in its most elementary stage includes two or more cameras, camera control units (CCUs), preview monitors, a switcher, a line monitor, one or more video recorders, and a line-out that transports the video signal to the video recorder and/or the transmission device. **SEE 1.6**

Usually integrated into the expanded system are computer servers or videotape machines for playback, character or graphic generators that produce various forms of lettering or graphic art, and an editing system.

The audio portion of the expanded system consists of one or more microphones, an audio mixer or console, an audio monitor (speaker), and a line-out that transports the sound signal to the video recorder or server and/or the transmitter (see figure 1.6).

FIELD PRODUCTION SYSTEMS

Except for big-remote telecasts that are used for the transmission of live sports or special events, the field production

1.5 BASIC TELEVISION SYSTEM
The basic television system converts light and sounds into electrical video and audio signals that are transmitted (wirelessly or by cable) and reconverted by the television receiver and loudspeaker into television pictures and sound.

systems are much less complex than even a simple studio show. These field productions usually consist of *ENG (electronic news gathering)* or the more elaborate *EFP (electronic field production)*.

ENG SYSTEM
Electronic news gathering is usually done with a camcorder, which houses an entire video system in an amazingly small box. It contains all the elements needed to capture and record an event. The expanded system uses a second microphone in addition to the built-in one and may use a small transmitter that routes the signal to the television station or an ENG van. **SEE 1.7**

EFP SYSTEM
The EFP system normally consists of a single portable EFP camera and an external recording device or camcorder to record various segments of an event for postproduction editing. In more-elaborate productions, several cameras or camcorders are used simultaneously to capture an event from various viewpoints. **SEE 1.8**

MAJOR EQUIPMENT
With the expanded television system in mind, we briefly explore six basic production elements: camera, lighting, audio, switcher, video recorder, and postproduction editing. When learning about television production equipment, always try to see each piece and its operation within the larger context of the television system, that is, in relation to all the other equipment. Then tie the equipment to the people who operate it—the production personnel. It is, after all, the skilled and prudent use of the television equipment by the production team, and not simply the smooth interaction of the machines, that gives the system its value.

CAMERA
The most obvious production element—the camera—comes in all sizes and configurations. Some cameras are so small that they fit easily into a coat pocket; others are so heavy that you have to strain yourself to lift them onto a camera mount. The camera mount enables the operator

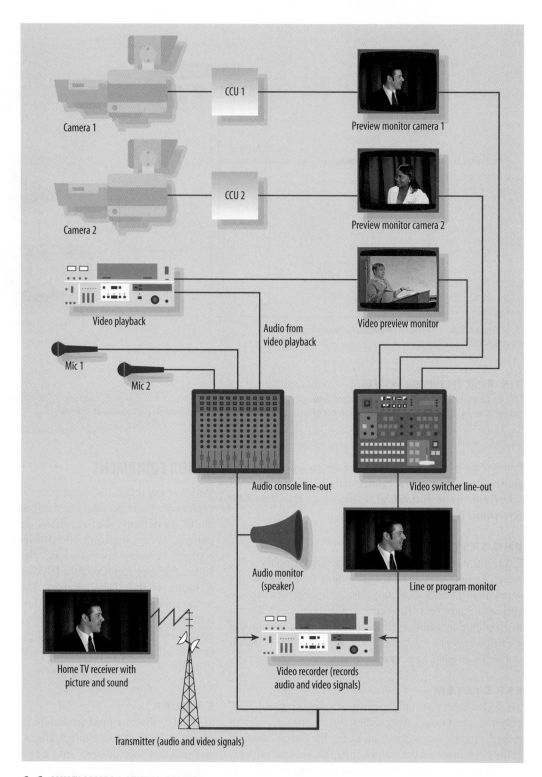

1.6 MULTICAMERA STUDIO SYSTEM
The multicamera studio system contains quality controls (CCU and audio console), selection controls (switcher and audio console), and monitors for previewing pictures and sound.

1.7 ENG SYSTEM
The ENG system consists of a camcorder and a microphone. The camcorder includes all video and audio quality controls as well as video- and audio-recording capabilities. A portable transmitter is necessary to send a live field pickup to the studio.

Microphone

Camcorder Transmitter

1.8 EFP SYSTEM
The EFP system is similar to that for ENG, but it may use more than one camera to feed the output to separate video recorders.

Camera 1 with attached or separate video recorder

Camera 2 with attached or separate video recorder

Video recorder 1

Video recorder 2

1.9 STUDIO CAMERA WITH PEDESTAL
High-quality studio cameras are mounted on a studio pedestal for smooth and easy maneuverability.

to move a heavy camera/lens/teleprompter assembly on the studio floor with relative ease. **SEE 1.9**

ENG/EFP camcorders are portable cameras that use a variety of recording media—videotape, hard drives, optical discs, and memory cards (also called flash drives). They operate much like consumer models except that they have better lenses (which can be exchanged), better imaging devices (which transduce the light coming from the lens into video signals), and more controls that help produce optimal pictures, even under less-than-ideal conditions. In fact, some of the new HDV (high-definition video) camcorders are simply upgrades of high-end consumer models. **SEE 1.10**

Many high-end ENG/EFP camcorders use tapeless recording devices, which store pictures and sound on hard drives, optical discs, or memory cards. The advantage of such tapeless recording media is that they

1.10 HDV CAMCORDER
This high-definition video camcorder delivers video that comes close to that of the much more expensive HDTV (high-definition television) camcorders. It records on MiniDV cassette tapes.

1.11 HDTV CAMCORDER
This high-end camcorder can record on a hard-drive field pack or flash memory card. Both can be transferred directly to an HDTV nonlinear editing system.

can be directly transferred into a digital editing system. SEE 1.11 ZVL7 CAMERA→ Camera introduction ZVL8 CAMERA→ Camera moves

LIGHTING

Like the human eye, the camera cannot see well without a certain amount of light. Because it is actually not objects we see but the light that is reflected off of the objects, manipulating the light falling on objects influences the way we perceive them on-screen. The purposeful control of light is called lighting.

Types of illumination   All television lighting basically involves two types of illumination: directional and diffused. Directional light has a sharp beam and produces harsh shadows. You can aim the light beam to illuminate a precise area. A flashlight and car headlights produce directional light. In television and motion pictures, these lights are called spotlights. Diffused light has a wide, indistinct beam that illuminates a relatively large area and produces soft, translucent shadows. The fluorescent lamps in a department store produce diffused lighting. Television and motion pictures use floodlights to achieve such a general nondirectional lighting. ZVL9 LIGHTS→ Lights introduction

Lighting instruments   In the television studio, the various types of spotlights and floodlights are usually suspended on battens that can be raised close to the ceiling and lowered close to the floor. This gives the lighting people a chance to place the various instruments in the desired positions on the battens. When the battens are raised, the cameras and crewmembers can move freely about the studio floor without interfering with the lighting. SEE 1.12

ENG and EFP use much smaller, portable instruments that can be set up quickly and plugged into ordinary household outlets. ZVL10 LIGHTS→ Instruments→ studio | field

Lighting techniques   As mentioned, lighting is the manipulation of light and shadows that influences the way we perceive how things on-screen look and feel. All television lighting is based on a simple principle: to illuminate specific areas, mold shadows, and bring the overall light on a scene to an intensity level at which the cameras can produce optimal pictures and create a certain mood. *Optimal pictures* means that the colors are faithfully reproduced even in the shadow areas, that there is a certain number of brightness steps between the darkest and brightest spot in the scene, and that you can still see some detail in the brightest and darkest areas. For some shows the lighting is deliberately

1.12 STUDIO LIGHTS SUSPENDED FROM MOVABLE BATTENS
Typical studio lighting uses spotlights and floodlights. All instruments are suspended from battens that can be lowered close to the studio floor and raised well above the scenery.

flat, which means that there is little contrast between light and shadows. Such lighting is frequently used on news and interview sets, for game shows and situation comedies, and in many field productions. Crime and mystery shows often use high-contrast lighting. This creates dense shadows and intensifies the dramatic tension. **ZVL11** LIGHTS→ Falloff→ fast | slow | none

AUDIO
Although the term *television* does not include audio, the sound portion of a television show is nevertheless one of its most important elements. Television audio not only communicates precise information but also contributes greatly to the mood and the atmosphere of a scene. If you were to turn off the audio during a newscast, even the best news anchors would have difficulty communicating their stories through facial expressions, graphics, and video images alone.

The aesthetic function of sound (to make us perceive an event or feel in a particular way) becomes obvious when you listen to the background sounds during a crime show. The squealing tires during a high-speed chase are real enough, but the exciting, rhythmically fast background music that accompanies the scene is definitely artificial.

We have grown so accustomed to such devices, however, that we would probably perceive the scene as less exciting if the music were missing. In fact, some crime shows and commercials carry a continuous music track with a highly rhythmic beat even through the dialogue. Frequently, sound communicates the energy of an event more readily than pictures do.

Even if you don't intend to become a sound designer, you need to learn as much as possible about the major sound production elements: microphones, sound control equipment, and sound recording and playback devices. **ZVL12** AUDIO→ Audio introduction

Microphones All microphones convert sound waves into electric energy—the audio signals. The sound signals are amplified and sent to the loudspeaker, which reconverts them into audible sound. The myriad microphones available today are designed to perform different tasks. Picking up a newscaster's voice, capturing the sounds of a tennis match, and recording a rock concert—all may require different microphones or microphone sets.

Some microphones, called lavalier mics (pronounced "mikes") are quite small and are clipped to the performer's clothing. Hand mics are larger and carried by the performer

1.13 FISHPOLE MICROPHONE
This highly directional shotgun mic is
suspended from a fishpole held by the
boom operator.

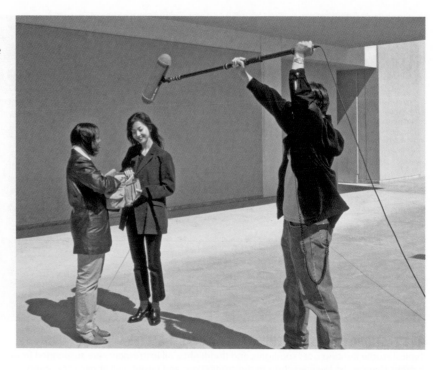

or attached to a mic stand. Boom, or long-distance, mics are either suspended from a small boom (called a fishpole, which is carried by the operator) or from a large boom, whose operator sits on a movable platform. SEE 1.13 **ZVL13** AUDIO→ Microphones→ mic types

Sound control equipment In studio productions the most important piece of sound control equipment is the audio console. At the audio console, you can select a specific microphone or other sound input, amplify a weak signal from a mic or other audio source for further processing, control the volume and the quality of the sound, and mix (combine) two or more incoming sound sources. In relatively simple productions, such as a newscast or an interview, you are mostly concerned with keeping the audio within a certain volume level. If it is too low, the viewer/listener can't hear the sound very well; if it is too high, the sound is not only hard on the ears but distorts so much that it may be impossible to fix in postproduction. SEE 1.14

In ENG and EFP, the sound is normally controlled by the camera operator, who wears a small earphone that carries the incoming sound. Because the camera operator is busy running the camera, the sound controls on the camcorder are often switched to the automatic setting. In the

1.14 AUDIO CONSOLE
Even a relatively simple audio console
has many controls to adjust the volume
and the quality of incoming sound signals
and to mix them in various ways.

1.15 AUDIO MIXER
The portable mixer has a limited number of inputs and volume controls.

1.16 VIDEO PRODUCTION SWITCHER
The production switcher has rows of buttons and other controls for selecting and mixing various video inputs and creating transitions and special effects. It then sends the selected video to the line-out.

more critical EFP, the volume of incoming sounds is usually controlled by a portable mixer. **SEE 1.15** **ZVL14** AUDIO→ Consoles and mixers

Sound recording and playback devices
When an event is recorded for postproduction, most of the dialogue and environmental sounds are recorded simultaneously with the picture.

In large and complex studio productions in which a single camera shoots a scene piecemeal, much in the way films are made, the audio track is subjected to much manipulation in postproduction. The sounds of explosions, sirens, and car crashes, for example, are normally dubbed in (added) during the postproduction sessions. Even parts of the original dialogue are occasionally recreated in the studio, especially when the dialogue occurs outdoors. As you undoubtedly know and have probably experienced, wind is a constant hazard to clean sound pickup. **ZVL15** AUDIO→ Systems

SWITCHER
The switcher works on a principle similar to that of pushbuttons on a car radio, which allow you to choose different radio stations. The switcher lets you select various video inputs, such as cameras, video recorders, and titles or other special effects, and join them through a great variety of transitions while the event is in progress. In effect, the switcher allows you to do instantaneous editing.

Any switcher, simple or complex, can perform three basic functions: select an appropriate video source from several inputs, perform basic transitions between two video

sources, and create or retrieve special effects, such as split screens. **SEE 1.16**

If you now go back to figure 1.6, you can see that three video inputs—camera 1, camera 2, and a video recorder—are routed to the switcher. From these three inputs, camera 1 is selected to go on the air. **ZVL16** SWITCHING→ Switching introduction

VIDEO RECORDER
One of the unique features of television is its ability to transmit a telecast live, which means capturing the pictures and the sounds of an ongoing event and distributing them instantly to a worldwide audience. Most television programs, however, originate from playback of previously recorded material. There are two basic recording systems: videotape recorders and tapeless recorders.

Videotape recorders Despite the great progress made almost daily to develop digital recording systems that are more efficient than videotape, videotape recorders (VTRs) will still be in use for some time to come, so don't throw away your old VCR, videotape collection, or tape-based camcorder just yet. Videotape is still widely used in large and small camcorders, including high-end HDV and HDTV systems. Note that you can use videotape for analog as well as digital recordings.

Videotape recorders are usually classified by the electronic system used for the recording (DVCPRO, S-VHS, or VHS) and sometimes by the tape format (the width of the videotape in the videocassette). Several old VTR systems still use ½-inch videocassettes (digital Betacam

1.17 HDTV VIDEOTAPE RECORDER
This high-definition studio VTR can use a
variety of cassettes (MiniDV and the larger
formats) for recording and playback of
high-definition footage, including digital
cinema material.

SX, S-VHS, and VHS). Most digital systems use ¼-inch
cassettes (6.35mm) for SDTV (standard digital television),
HDV, or HDTV. They come in a larger size, which allows
for longer recording and playback, as well as in the smaller
MiniDV cassettes. **SEE 1.17**

Tapeless systems   Great and rapid progress is being
made toward a tapeless environment wherein all video recording, storage, and playback is done with non-tape-based
systems. Such tapeless systems make use of hard drives,
optical discs, and memory cards or flash drives.

High-capacity hard drives are used extensively for the
storage, manipulation, and retrieval of video and audio
information by desktop computers and dedicated editing
systems (specially manufactured editors) for postproduction. Hard drives with a very large storage capacity (in the
multi-terabyte range—a terabyte equals 1,000 gigabytes)
are called servers and have all but replaced videotape as
the storage and playback device of daily programming in
most television stations.

POSTPRODUCTION EDITING

In principle, postproduction editing is relatively simple:
you select the most effective shots from the original source
material and join them with transitions in a specific sequence. In practice, however, postproduction editing can
be quite complicated and time-consuming, especially if it
also involves extensive audio manipulation. **ZVL17** EDIT-
ING→ Editing introduction

Nonlinear editing   A *nonlinear editing (NLE)* system does not use videotape. Before editing can begin,
all recorded material must first be transferred to the
hard drive of an editing system, which can be a laptop, a
desktop computer, or a workstation especially designed
for postproduction editing. Once they're on the hard
drive of the editing system, you can manipulate the video
and audio clips pretty much as you would edit text with
a word-processing program. You can call up, move, cut,
paste, and join the various shots or audio segments much
like words, sentences, and paragraphs when editing a
document. This method is called nonlinear because you
can call up any shot or frame regardless of the sequence
in which it was captured.

Most nonlinear software programs let you produce
high-resolution full-frame, full-motion video and audio sequences. You can also decide to first produce a
low-resolution preliminary rough-cut, from which you
develop an EDL (edit decision list). This list is then your
guide for the final high-resolution edit master recording, which is used for program duplication or broadcast.
SEE 1.18 **ZVL18** EDITING→ Nonlinear editing→ system

Linear editing   Whenever you use digital or analog videotape for your postproduction, you are engaged in *linear
editing*. Linear editing normally requires two source VTRs,
which contain the original material that you recorded with
the camera, and the record VTR, which produces the final
edit master tape.

Available clips   Preview monitor   Program monitor

Editing tools

Audio levels

Video track   Audio tracks

1.18 NONLINEAR EDITING COMPUTER INTERFACE

The interface of most nonlinear editing systems shows a list of available clips, a preview monitor of the upcoming shot that is to be edited to the shot shown on the program monitor, a video track (blue track with thumbnail images), two or more audio tracks (green tracks), and other information such as available transitions.

All three machines are synchronized by the edit controller, also called an editing control unit. This unit helps you find a particular scene quickly and accurately, even if it is buried midtape. It starts and stops the source and record machines and tells the record VTR to perform the edit at the precise point you have designated. **ZVL19** EDITING→ Linear editing→ system

Regardless of the editing system you are using, it cannot make the creative decisions for you. Thinking about postproduction as early as the shooting stage facilitates considerably your editing chores. Always consider postproduction an extension of the creative process, not a salvage operation.

MAIN POINTS

▶ The basic television system consists of the equipment and the people who operate the equipment to produce specific programs. In its simplest form, the system comprises a television camera that converts what it sees into a video signal, a microphone that converts what it hears into an audio signal, and a television set and loudspeaker that reconvert the two signals into pictures and sound.

▶ The expanded television system adds equipment and procedures to the basic television system to make possible a wider choice of sources, better quality control of pictures and sound, and the recording and/or transmission of video and audio signals.

▶ The ENG (electronic news gathering) system consists basically of a camcorder and a microphone. The EFP (electronic field production) system may include multiple camcorders or field cameras, some lighting, and audio and video control equipment.

▶ The major production elements are the camera, lighting, audio, switcher, videotape recorder, and postproduction editing.

▶ There are several types of video cameras: large studio cameras that need a special support to be moved about the studio floor; ENG/EFP cameras that are small enough to be carried by the operator; and camcorders, which have the recording device either built into the camera or attached to it.

▶ Lighting is the manipulation of light and shadows that influences the way we perceive objects on-screen and how we feel about the screen event.

▶ The two types of illumination are directional light, produced by spotlights, and diffused light, produced by floodlights.

▶ Audio, the sound portion of a television show, is necessary to give specific information about what is said and to set the mood of a scene.

▶ Audio production elements include microphones, sound control equipment, and sound recording and playback devices.

▶ The switcher enables you to do instantaneous editing by selecting a specific picture from several inputs and performing basic transitions between two video sources.

▶ There are a variety of analog and digital tape-based recorders as well as digital tapeless video recorders.

▶ Non-tape-based systems include hard drives, optical discs, and memory cards or flash drives. Large-capacity hard-drive systems, called servers, are used for the recording, storage, and playback of program material.

▶ Postproduction editing consists of selecting various shots from the source material and putting them in a specific sequence. In nonlinear editing, the digital video and audio material is stored on a hard drive and manipulated using computer software. Nonlinear editing systems can produce high-quality video and audio sequences for broadcast or duplication, a rough-cut of lesser video quality, or an EDL (edit decision list), which serves as a guide for the final high-quality edit.

ZETTL'S VIDEOLAB

For your reference or to track your work, the *Zettl's VideoLab* program cues in this chapter are listed here with their corresponding page numbers.

II

Preproduction

2

The Producer in Preproduction

One morning you wake up with an idea for a documentary that will surely blow away the one you saw the night before. You grab your camera and start shooting. After a week of collecting miles of footage, you put the box with the recorded material aside until you have time for editing. When you finally look at it again, the shots don't look so good anymore, and the whole idea has somehow lost its punch. You finally scrap the whole project.

Of course, this is a fictitious scenario. But it is used to underline the importance of carefully thinking about and preparing the whole production process before ever getting into the actual production. This step is the all-important preproduction phase.

You will notice that when studying this text, you cannot simply remain a passive reader. You will be required to wear several hats and assume a variety of production roles. Sometimes you will have to act as producer, and then, a few chapters later, function as a director or as a specific member of the technical crew.

In this chapter you are the producer—a person who not only comes up with a great idea but, contrary to the introductory scenario, also carries it successfully to and through the actual production phase. In section 2.1 you are responsible for the first step of preproduction planning—to move from idea to script—and how to move from there to the production phase. Section 2.2 is concerned with information resources, unions and legal matters, and audience and ratings—just in case you want to be an actual producer.

KEY TERMS

demographics Audience research factors concerned with such data as age, gender, marital status, and income.

production schedule The calendar that shows the preproduction, production, and postproduction dates and who is doing what, when, and where.

program proposal Written document that outlines the process message and the major aspects of a television presentation.

psychographics Audience research factors concerned with such data as consumer buying habits, values, and lifestyles.

rating Percentage of television households tuned to a specific station in relation to the total number of television households.

share Percentage of television households tuned to a specific station in relation to all households using television (HUT); that is, all households with their sets turned on.

target audience The audience selected or desired to receive a specific message.

time line A breakdown of time blocks for various activities on the actual production day, such as crew call, setup, and camera rehearsal.

treatment A brief narrative description of a television program.

2.1

What Producing Is All About

PREPRODUCTION PLANNING: FROM IDEA TO SCRIPT

Although each production has its own creative and organizational requirements, there are nevertheless techniques, or at least approaches, that you can apply to television and digital cinema production in general. Once you know the producer's basic preproduction activities, you can transfer those skills to whatever position you occupy on the production team. To help you become maximally efficient and effective in your preproduction activities, we focus here on program ideas, program proposal, budget, and script.

GENERATING PROGRAM IDEAS

Everything you see and hear on television or in the movie theater started with an idea. As simple as this may sound, developing good and especially workable show ideas on a regular basis is not easy. As a professional television producer, you cannot wait for the occasional divine inspiration but must generate worthwhile ideas on demand.

Despite the volumes of studies written on the creative process, exactly how ideas are generated remains a mystery. Sometimes you will find that you have one great idea after another; at other times you cannot think of anything exciting regardless of how hard you try. You can break through this idea drought by engaging several people to do brainstorming or clustering.

You certainly know what group brainstorming is all about: everybody is allowed to toss out wild ideas in the hope that someone may break through the conceptual blocks and bring an end to the idea drought. The key to successful brainstorming is to not pass judgment on any comments, however far-fetched they may be. Anything goes. When playing back the audio-recorded comments, you may find that the totally unrelated comment may just trigger a new approach.

Another, more personalized and structured idea generator is clustering. This technique is a kind of brainstorming whereby you write down your ideas rather than say them aloud. To begin you write a single keyword, such as *cell phone,* and circle it. You then spin off idea clusters that somehow relate to the initial keyword. **SEE 2.1**

Producing means seeing that a worthwhile idea gets to be a worthwhile television presentation. You are chiefly responsible for all preproduction activities and for completing the various tasks on time and within budget. You are responsible for the concept, financing, hiring, and overall coordination of production activities—not an easy job by any means! But even if you happen to take on the creation of a show all by yourself, you still have to act as your own producer.

As a producer you may have to act as a psychologist and a businessperson to persuade management to buy your idea, argue as a technical expert for a certain piece of equipment, or search as a sociologist to identify the needs and the desires of a particular social group. After some sweeping creative excursions, you may have to become pedantic and double- and triple-check details, such as whether there is enough coffee for the guests who appear on your show.

Considering the painstaking work you have to do before ever getting into the production stage, you may not want to become a producer. But as a professional in television and digital cinema production, you cannot escape the all-important planning details of the preproduction phase. Even as a video journalist, you will have to make preproduction decisions while on the run.

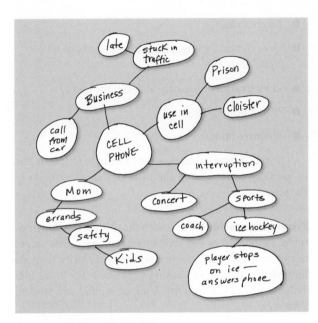

2.1 PARTIAL IDEA CLUSTER

Clustering is a form of written brainstorming. You start with a central idea and branch out to whatever associations come to mind.

As you can see, clustering is a more organized means of brainstorming, but it is also more restrictive. Because clustering shows patterns better than brainstorming does, it serves well as a structuring technique. Although clustering is usually done by individuals, you can easily have a group of people engage in clustering and then collect the results for closer scrutiny. **ZVL1** PROCESS→ Ideas

EVALUATING IDEAS

The evaluation of the ideas is probably the most important step in the preproduction process. The two key questions you need to ask are: Is the idea worth doing? and Is the idea doable? If you can answer both with an honest "yes," proceed to the formulation of a process message.

If your answer to either or both questions is "maybe" or "no," stop right there and find better idea. **SEE 2.2**

Is the idea worth doing?   Whatever you do should make a difference. This means that regardless of whether you produce a brief news package, a longer feature, or a major motion picture, it should have a positive influence on somebody's life (ideally on all people watching your program).[1]

---

1. Stuart W. Hyde has lectured and written about significant vision for more than half a century. See his *Idea to Script: Storytelling for Today's Media* (Boston: Allyn and Bacon, 2003), pp. 58–64. Nancy Graham Holm, an Emmy award–winning journalist and head of the TV Journalism Department at the Danish School of Journalism, says, "Any story worth telling has *significant vision*" [her emphasis]. She defines significant vision as "a problem to be solved, a challenge to be met, an obstacle to be overcome, a threat to be handled, a decision or choice to be made, a pressure to be relieved, a tension to be eased, a victory to be celebrated, a kindness to be acknowledged." See her *Fascination: Viewer Friendly TV Journalism* (Århus, Denmark: Ajour Danish Media Books, 2007), p. 51.

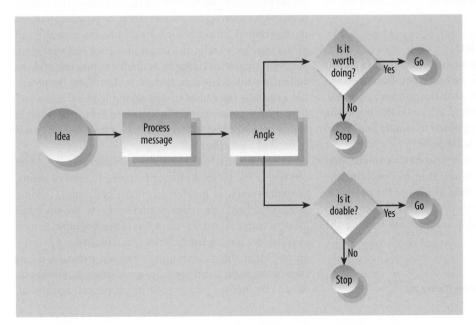

2.2 IDEA EVALUATION

Once you have translated the idea into a process message and found a useful angle, you need to ask two crucial evaluation questions: Is the idea worth doing? and Is the idea doable?

Fortunately, your idea passed the evaluation test, which means that you can progress to the formulation of the process message and the angle. Recall from chapter 1 that the process message is the basic program objective—what you would ideally like the viewers of your target audience to learn, do, and feel when watching your program. The angle is the specific focus or twist you give the story to get and keep the viewers' attention and have the actual process message come as close as possible to the defined one. The clearer you are about what your program should be and achieve, the easier it will be to write the program proposal, develop the script, prepare the budget, and decide on the remaining preproduction steps—but there remains one more question to ask.

Is the idea doable?   This is determined by whether you have the necessary budget, time, and facilities available to proceed to the production phase. You may have a relevant idea that has significant vision, but if you don't have the money to pay for the necessary production people, equipment, and facilities, you had better abandon the project at this point. If you have only two weeks to produce a story, you can't do a documentary that depicts the hard life of a Sherpa in the Himalayas. The availability of three small camcorders will not suffice for a live telecast of a high-school basketball game if you don't also have a switcher, its associated equipment, and transmission facilities. Whether a project is doable can hinge on less obvious deficiencies as well, such as bad weather, an inexperienced crew, or the lack of permits for a location or union affiliation of the talent.

PROGRAM PROPOSAL

Once you pass the two feasibility criteria and have a clear idea of the process message and how you want to communicate it, you are ready to write the program proposal. Don't take this proposal lightly; it is a key factor in getting your program on the air as opposed to simply ending up in a "good idea" file on your hard drive.

A *program proposal* is a written document that stipulates what you intend to do. It briefly explains the program objective and the major aspects of the presentation. Although there is no standard format for a program or series proposal, it should at a minimum include the following information:

- Program or series title
- Program objective (process message)

- Target audience
- Show format (a single TV show or series or a digital movie)
- Show treatment (usually includes the angle)
- Production method
- Tentative budget

If you propose a series, attach a sample script for one of the shows and a list of the titles of the other shows in the series.

Program or series title   Keep the title short but memorable. Perhaps it is the lack of screen space that forces television producers to work with shorter titles than do filmmakers. Instead of naming your show *The Trials and Tribulations of a University Student,* simply say *Student Pressures.*

Program objective   Compared with the process message, this is a less academic description of what you want to do. For example, rather than say, "The process message is to have high-school students exposed to at least five major consequences of running a stop sign," you may write that the program's objective is "to warn teenage drivers not to run stop signs."

Target audience   The *target audience* is whom you would primarily like to have watch the show—the elderly, preschoolers, teenagers, homemakers, or people interested in traveling. A properly formulated process message will give a big clue of who the target audience is. Even when you want to reach as large an audience as possible and the audience is not defined, be specific in describing the potential audience. Instead of simply saying "general audience" for a proposed comedy series, describe the primary target audience as "the 18-to-30 generation" or the "over-60 crowd in need of a good laugh."

Once you are in the actual preproduction phase, you can define the target audience further in terms of *demographics*—such as gender, ethnicity, education, income level, household size, religious preference, or geographical location (urban or rural)—as well as of *psychographics*, such as consumer buying habits, values, and lifestyles. Advertisers and other video communicators make extensive use of such demographic and psychographic descriptors, but you needn't be that specific in your initial program proposal.

Show format   Do you propose a single show, a new series, or part of an existing series? How long is the intended show? An example would be a two-part one-hour program dealing with the various uses of helicopters around the world. This information is vital for planning a budget or, for a station or network, to see whether the show fits into the program schedule.

Show treatment   A brief narrative description of the program is called a *treatment*. Some of the more elaborate treatments have storyboard-like illustrations. The treatment should not only say what the proposed show is all about but also explain its angle and reflect in its writing the style of the show. The style of a treatment for an instructional series on computer-generated graphics, for example, should differ considerably from that of a drama or situation comedy. Do not include production specifics such as types of lighting or camera angles; save this information for the director. Keep the treatment brief and concise, but do not skip important aspects of a plot. A treatment should give a busy executive a fairly good idea of what you intend to do. **SEE 2.3** `ZVL2` PROCESS→ Proposals→ treatment

Production method   A well-stated process message indicates where the production should take place and how you can do it most efficiently. Should you do a multiple- or single-camera studio production or a single-camera EFP? Is the show more effectively shot in larger segments with three or four cameras switched and in iso positions, or shot single-camera film-style for postproduction? What performers or actors do you need? What additional materials (costumes, props, and scenery) are required? `ZVL3` PROCESS→ Methods→ location | studio | single-camera | multicamera

Tentative budget   Before preparing the tentative budget, you must have up-to-date figures for all production services, rental costs, and wages in your area. Independent production and postproduction houses periodically issue rate cards that list the costs for services and the rental of major production items; such information is also usually available on their Web sites. Stay away from high-end services unless video quality becomes your major concern.

PREPARING A BUDGET

When working for a client, you need to prepare a budget for all preproduction, production, and postproduction costs regardless of whether the cost is, at least partially, absorbed by the salaries of regularly employed personnel or the normal operating budget. You need to figure the costs not only for obvious items—script, talent, production personnel, studio and equipment rental, and postproduction editing—but also for items that may not be so apparent, such as videotape or other recording media (memory cards can be quite expensive), props, food, lodging, entertainment, transportation of talent and production personnel, parking, insurance, and clearances or user fees for location shooting.

There are many ways to present a budget, but the usual way is to divide it into preproduction (for example, script, travel to locations and meetings, location scouting, and storyboard), production (talent, production personnel, and equipment or studio rental), and postproduction (editing and sound design). Most production companies show their overall charges in this tripartite division so that the client can more easily compare your charges with those of the other bidders.

When you first present your proposal, the client may be interested not so much in how you broke down the expenses but more in the bottom-line figure. It is therefore critical that you think of all the probable expenses regardless of whether they occur in preproduction, production, or postproduction. Computer software can be of great assistance, helping you detail the various costs and recalculating them effortlessly if you need to cut expenses or if the production requirements change.

An example of a detailed budget of an independent production company is shown in the following figure. It is structured according to preproduction, production, and postproduction costs. **SEE 2.4**

Whenever you prepare a budget, be realistic. Do not underestimate costs just to win the bid—you will probably regret it. It is psychologically, as well as financially, easier to agree to a budget cut than to ask for more money later on. On the other hand, do not inflate the budget to ensure enough to get by even after severe cuts. Be realistic about the expenses, but do not forget to add at least a 15 to 20 percent contingency. `ZVL4` PROCESS→ Proposals→ budget | try it

WRITING THE SCRIPT

Unless you write the script yourself, you'll need to hire a writer. Contrary to books and magazine articles, which are published in printed form, a media script is not intended as literature. Even the most literate and sophisticated script is only an intermediary in the production process. Analyzing scripts in the context of literature may be an interesting academic exercise, but it says as little about the actual

TREATMENT FOR A ONE-HOUR SPECIAL ON THE HOMELESS

Title: HOMELESS

Proposed Actual Program Length: 45 min.

This program is intended to make the audience feel rather than watch the plight of being homeless. It will not show the customary degrading living conditions of the homeless, such as a homeless woman pushing a shopping cart past elegant shopping windows or seeking shelter in an abandoned box next to a garbage container. In fact, it will not show any footage of homeless people. Instead, it will trace a young college professor's ill-fated trip from Boston to a convention on the West Coast.

When he arrives in San Francisco, his suitcase does not show up on the baggage carousel. Only one suitcase keeps circling—and it's not his. When he gets to the baggage claims office, it is crowded. He is nervous because all the conference information and his presentation material are in the suitcase. He finally gets to the claims desk, and the stressed official asks him for the tags and hotel. Yes, his bags will be delivered to the hotel. Yes, he has the claim tags. He finds them in his wallet. Which hotel? He can't remember the exact name. It's in the folder, and the folder is in the suitcase. An impatient, not-so-friendly man behind him curses and jostles him, trying to get out of the queue.

The downtown airport bus does not go to his hotel. He takes a taxi. The cabbie circles a block, takes out his map, and finally drops off the professor in a neighborhood that doesn't seem to be an appropriate convention venue. Was he taken for a ride? When he tries to pay the expensive fare,

2.3 TREATMENT
The treatment tells the reader in narrative form what a program is all about.

his wallet is missing: cash, driver's license, credit cards, everything—gone. The cab driver radios his boss: call the cops or let him go. He lets him go.

The lobby smells. His cell phone doesn't work. Yeah, he can use the phone. But it will cost him. No money, no phone. He again interrupts the lady behind the counter with his story. "Yeah, sure! Can't you think of a better one? There is a phone outside." The graffiti-sprayed booth has only wires hanging out where the phone is supposed to be. The phone book is missing, replaced by an empty liquor bottle. Urine smell. It gets dark and starts to rain. He walks and walks and finally finds a working phone. But he has no money. The few people he approaches on the street walk faster or ask him for money. Finally, a friendly woman with a skirt that is much too tight and much too short listens to his story and gives him a dollar bill. Laughing: "I am usually the one who gets paid." He changes the bill in a bar, is allowed to use the public phone, and calls his friend on the East Coast. He reaches the answering machine.

He is outside again, in the rain, in a place he doesn't know. Hungry. Tired. He is homeless.

He finally flags down a police car and is taken to the station. No, they don't have any information about his convention. But, eventually, a police officer does a computer search and finds the name of the convention hotel. The officer, off-duty now, takes him there. Thanks! Very much! On the way in, he encounters a man, begging for coffee money. "I don't have any money." "Oh yeah?" He gets to the lobby and finds one of his colleagues with a drink in his hand and a slightly crooked nametag on his jacket. Home! Safe!

2.3 TREATMENT *(continued)*

2.4 DETAILED PRODUCTION BUDGET

These detailed budget categories are structured according to preproduction, production, and postproduction costs. Ignore the categories that are not applicable.

PRODUCTION BUDGET

CLIENT:
PROJECT TITLE:
DATE OF THIS BUDGET:
SPECIFICATIONS:

NOTE: This estimate is subject to the producer's review of the final shooting script.

SUMMARY OF COSTS	ESTIMATE	ACTUAL
PREPRODUCTION		
Personnel	_____	_____
Equipment and facilities	_____	_____
Script	_____	_____
PRODUCTION		
Personnel	_____	_____
Equipment and facilities	_____	_____
Talent	_____	_____
Art (set and graphics)	_____	_____
Makeup	_____	_____
Music	_____	_____
Miscellaneous (transportation, fees)	_____	_____
POSTPRODUCTION		
Personnel	_____	_____
Facilities	_____	_____
Recording media	_____	_____
INSURANCE AND MISCELLANEOUS	_____	_____
CONTINGENCY (20%)	_____	_____
TAX	_____	_____
GRAND TOTAL	_____	_____

television show or film as does a city map about the way the city looks and sounds. Nevertheless, a script represents an essential production element of any film and of all but the most routine television presentations. Besides telling the talent what to say, a script indicates how a scene should be played and where and when it takes place; it also contains important preproduction, production, and postproduction information. The script is such a critical production component that if a show does not need a script, a scriptlike notice is distributed, indicating the name of the show, the

**2.4 DETAILED
PRODUCTION BUDGET**
(continued)

BUDGET DETAIL	ESTIMATE	ACTUAL
P R E P R O D U C T I O N		
Personnel		
Writer (script)	———	———
Director (day)	———	———
Art director (day)	———	———
PA (day)	———	———
SUBTOTAL	———	———
P R O D U C T I O N		
Personnel		
Director	———	———
Associate director	———	———
PA	———	———
Floor (unit) manager	———	———
Camera (DP)	———	———
Sound	———	———
Lighting	———	———
Video recording	———	———
C.G.	———	———
Grips (assistants)	———	———
Technical supervisor	———	———
Prompter	———	———
Makeup and wardrobe	———	———
Talent	———	———
Equipment and facilities		
Studio/location	———	———
Camera	———	———
Sound	———	———
Lighting	———	———
Sets	———	———
C.G./graphics	———	———
Video recorder	———	———
Prompting	———	———
Remote van	———	———
Intercom	———	———
Transportation, meals, and housing	———	———
Copyrights	———	———
SUBTOTAL	———	———

date, the director, and the remark "No script." (The basic structural ingredients of a television and film script and the various types of scripts are covered in chapter 3.)

When hiring a writer, make sure that he or she understands the program objective and, more specifically, the defined process message. If a writer disagrees with your approach and does not suggest a better one, find another writer. Agree on a fee in advance—some writers charge enough to swallow up your whole budget. **ZVL5** PROCESS→ Ideas→ scripts

**2.4 DETAILED
PRODUCTION BUDGET**
(continued)

POSTPRODUCTION	ESTIMATE	ACTUAL
Personnel		
Director	_____	_____
Editor	_____	_____
Sound editor	_____	_____
Facilities		
Dubbing	_____	_____
Window dubs	_____	_____
Off-line linear	_____	_____
Off-line nonlinear	_____	_____
On-line linear	_____	_____
On-line nonlinear	_____	_____
DVE	_____	_____
Audio sweetening	_____	_____
ADR/Foley	_____	_____
Recording media	_____	_____
SUBTOTAL	_____	_____
MISCELLANEOUS		
Insurance	_____	_____
Public transportation	_____	_____
Parking	_____	_____
Shipping/courier	_____	_____
Wrap expenses	_____	_____
Security	_____	_____
Catering	_____	_____
SUBTOTAL	_____	_____
GRAND TOTAL	_____	_____

PREPRODUCTION PLANNING: COORDINATION

Before you begin coordinating the various production elements—assembling a production team, procuring studios, or deciding on location sites and equipment—ask yourself once again whether the planned production is possible within the given time and budget and, if so, whether the method (medium translation of defined process message) is indeed the most efficient.

For example, if you are doing a documentary on the conditions of the various residence hotels in your city, it is certainly easier and more cost-effective to go there and video-record an actual hotel room than to re-create one in the studio. On the other hand, if you are doing a magazine-style show on the history of your high school, you could stage the major part of the production in the studio and shoot only a minimum portion on-location. For a drama a specific scene might be shot more advantageously in a friend's kitchen than in a complicated studio kitchen setup. Keep in mind that the studio affords optimal control but that EFP (electronic field production) offers a limitless variety of scenery and locations at little additional cost. Most field productions, however, lack the production control you enjoy in the studio and require extensive use of postproduction time and facilities.

Once you have made a firm decision about the most effective production approach, you must deliver what you promised to do in the proposal. You begin this coordination phase by establishing clear communication channels among all the people involved in the production, and you take care of the facilities request, the production schedule, permits and clearances, and publicity and promotion. Again, it is not your occasional flashes of inspiration that make you a good producer but your meticulous attention to detail. Preproduction is not the most exciting part of creating a show, but, from a producer's point of view, it is the most important one.

PEOPLE AND COMMUNICATION

Whom to involve in the post-script planning stages depends, again, on your basic objective, the process message, and whether you are an independent producer who has to hire additional personnel or whether you are working for a station or large production company that has most essential creative and crew people already on its payroll and available at all times.

As producer you are the chief coordinator among the production people. You must be able to contact every team member quickly and reliably. Your most important task is to establish a database with such essential information as names, positions, e-mail addresses, home addresses, business addresses, and various phone, beeper, and fax numbers. **SEE 2.5**

Don't forget to let everyone know how you can be contacted, as well. Don't rely on secondhand information. Your communication is not complete until you hear back from the party you were trying to reach. A good producer triple-checks everything.

FACILITIES REQUEST

The facilities request lists all pieces of production equipment and often all properties and costumes needed for a production. The person responsible for filling out such a

```
Production Personnel Contact Information
Sight Sound Motion Instructional Video
Program 4
```

Name E-mail	Position	Home address Work address	Home phone Work phone	Home fax Work fax	Cell phone Pager
Herbert Zettl hzettl@best.com	Producer	873 Carmenita, Forest Knolls SFSU, 1600 Holloway, SF	(415) 555-3874 (415) 555-8837	(415) 555-8743 (415) 555-1199	(415) 555-1141
Gary Palmatier bigcheese@ideas-to-images.com	Director	5343 Sunnybrook, Windsor 5256 Aero #3, Santa Rosa	(707) 555-4242 (707) 555-8743	(707) 555-2341 (707) 764-7777	(707) 555-9873
Robaire Ream robaire@mac.com	AD	783 Ginny, Healdsburg Lightsaber, 44 Tesconi, Novato	(707) 555-8372 (415) 555-8000	(415) 555-8080	(800) 555-8888
Sherry Holstead 723643.3722@compuserve.com	PA	88 Seacrest, Marin SH Assoc, 505 Main, Sausalito	(415) 555-9211 (415) 555-0932	(415) 555-9873 (415) 555-8383	(415) 555-0033
Renee Wong rn_wong2@earthlink.com	TD	9992 Treeview, San Rafael P.O. Box 3764, San Rafael	(415) 555-____ ____ 555-8273		(415) 555-3498 ___555-8988
___ Talent		253 Robert___			

2.5 DATABASE: PRODUCTION PERSONNEL
To be able to quickly contact each production team member, the producer needs reliable contact information.

2.6 COMPUTER-BASED FACILITIES REQUEST

This facilities request lists all equipment needed for the production. Usually, the equipment permanently installed in a studio does not have to be listed again, but it must be scheduled.

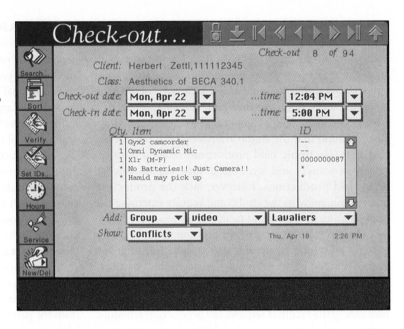

request varies. In small-station operations and independent production companies, it is often the producer or director; in larger operations it is the production manager or director of broadcast operations.

The facilities request usually contains information concerning date and time of rehearsal, recording sessions, and on-the-air transmission; title of production; names of producer and director (and sometimes talent); and all technical elements, such as cameras, microphones, lights, sets, graphics, costumes, makeup, video recorders, video and audio postproduction facilities, and other specific production requirements. It also lists the studio and control room needed or the remote location. If you do EFP, you need to add the desired mode of transportation for yourself and the crew and the exact on-site location. If the production involves an overnight stay, communicate the name and the location of the accommodations, including the customary details, such as phone numbers, when and where to assemble the next morning, and so forth.

Like the script, the facilities request is an essential communication device; be as accurate as possible when preparing it. Late changes will invite costly errors. If you have a fairly accurate floor plan and light plot, attach them to the facilities request. Such attachments will give the crew a fairly good idea of what production problems they may have to face. Facilities requests are usually distributed as "soft copy" via the internal computer system as well as on hard copy. **SEE 2.6**

Regardless of which type of production you do, always try to get by with as little equipment as possible. The more you use, the more people you need to operate it and the more that can go wrong. Do not use equipment just because it is available. Review your original process message and verify that the chosen equipment is indeed the most efficient and that the necessary equipment is actually available and within the scope of the budget. Consult the technical staff, which may include your favorite DP or TD (director of photography or technical director, respectively), on the use of specific equipment and other production tasks.

PRODUCTION SCHEDULE

The ***production schedule*** should tell everybody involved in the production who is doing what, when, and where over the course of the three production phases. It is different from a ***time line***, which is a breakdown of time blocks for each production day. Create a realistic production schedule and stick to it. Assigning too little time will result not in a higher level of activity but usually in a higher level of anxiety and frustration. It is almost always counterproductive. On the other hand, allowing too much time for a production activity will not necessarily improve the production. Besides being costly, wasting time can make people apathetic and, surprisingly enough, fail to meet deadlines.

One of the producer's most important responsibilities is to monitor the progress of each activity and know where everyone stands relative to the stipulated deadlines.

If you don't care whether deadlines are met, you might as well do away with them. If schedules aren't kept, find out why. Again, do not rely on secondhand information. Call the people who are behind schedule and find out what the problem is. It is your job to help solve the problem and get everyone back on track or to change the schedule if necessary. Always inform all production people of all changes—even if the changes seem irrelevant or insignificant.

PERMITS AND CLEARANCES

Most productions involve people and facilities that ordinarily have no connection with your station or production company. These production elements need extra attention. Get the necessary permits for your crew to gain admission to a meeting or sporting event, as well as a parking permit close to the event. You may also need a permit from city hall (the mayor's media coordinator and the police department) or an insurance policy to shoot downtown. Do not ignore such requirements! "Better safe than sorry" applies to all field productions—not just to actual production activities but also to protecting yourself from legal action if a production assistant stumbles over a cable or a bystander slips on a banana peel while watching your shoot. (Copyright and union clearances are discussed in section 2.2.)

PUBLICITY AND PROMOTION

The best show is worthless if no one knows about it. Meet with the publicity and promotions departments (usually combined in one office or even a single person) and inform them of the upcoming production. Even if the target audience is highly specific, you must aim to reach as many viewers as possible. The job of the publicity people is to narrow the gap between the potential and the actual audience.

Regardless of what your specific producing job may be—managing ideas and production schedules or coordinating nontechnical and technical production facilities and teams—don't leave anything to chance. Like a good pilot, triple-check everything, even though you may have done it a hundred times.

Finally, you should remember and act on the following brief sermon.

ETHICS

Whatever you do as a producer, realize that your decisions, however trivial they might seem at the time, always affect a very large number of people: your audience.

Always respect, and have compassion for, your audience. Do not believe critics or colleagues who proclaim that all television audiences have an average intelligence of a five-year-old. In fact, you and I are part of the television audience, and neither of us would appreciate having our intelligence downgraded in this way by a disgruntled producer.

Never breach the prevailing ethical standards of society and the trust the audience has—and inevitably must—put in you. This doesn't mean that you should play censor to a writer who occasionally breaks the mold with frank ideas and a bold vision. It means that you and your production team should not lie to your audience. Do not fake a news story to rev up a slow news day; do not have a speech edited so that it favors your political candidate.

While realizing that producing is always connected with compromise, ask yourself if, and if so to what extent, your show will contribute to the quality of life of your audience.

I suspect you noticed that such a code of conduct concerns not just the producer but everyone working in television.

MAIN POINTS

▶ Producing means seeing to it that a worthwhile idea becomes a worthwhile television show. The producer manages a great number of people and coordinates an even greater number of production activities and details.

▶ Generating program ideas on schedule is facilitated by brainstorming and clustering.

▶ Preproduction includes planning how to move from the idea to the script.

▶ Important preproduction items are the program proposal, the treatment, the budget, and the script.

▶ The coordination tasks in preproduction are establishing communication among all production personnel involved, filing a facilities request, creating a realistic production schedule, securing permits and clearances, and taking care of publicity and promotion.

▶ Everything you do must live up to the prevailing ethical standards.

SECTION

2.2

Information Resources, Unions, and Ratings

As a producer you need quick access to a variety of accurate information resources, an understanding of broadcast guilds and unions, and some basic knowledge of copyrights and other legal matters. Finally—like it or not—you must be conversant with the rudiments of ratings.

▶ **INFORMATION RESOURCES**
The Internet, telephone directories, and other resources

▶ **UNIONS AND LEGAL MATTERS**
Unions, copyrights and clearances, and other legal considerations

▶ **AUDIENCE AND RATINGS**
Target audience, and ratings and share

INFORMATION RESOURCES

As a producer you must be a researcher as well as somewhat of a scrounger. On occasion you may have only a half hour to get accurate information, for example, about a former mayor who is celebrating her ninetieth birthday. Or you may have to procure a skeleton for your medical show, a model of a communications satellite for your documentary on telecommunications, or an eighteenth-century wedding dress for your history series.

The Internet   Fortunately, the vast resources on the Internet put the world's information at your fingertips. And if you know the site address, it is practically instantaneous. Although Google is one of the most prominent and efficient search engines, there are others that can lead you to more-specialized information: Yahoo!, Ask, Alta-Vista, Lycos, Netscape Search, Excite, Mamma Metasearch, MetaCrawler, and People Search. Still others have more-specialized information but often rely on the information of the larger ones. All equipment manufacturers have extensive Web sites with the most up-to-date information about their products. Amazon.com is often faster for locating a specific book than a library. And there is always Wikipedia for kick-starting your research.

You may find, however, that the sheer volume of online information makes it difficult to find a specific item quickly. It may sometimes be faster and more convenient to use readily available printed sources or to call the local library. For example, a call to the local hospital or high-school science department may procure the skeleton more quickly than initiating a Web search. You could ask the community college science department or perhaps even the local cable company for the satellite model, and contact the historical society or the college theater arts department for the wedding dress.

Besides Internet sources, the following are some additional references and services you should have on hand.

Telephone directories   There is a great deal of information in a telephone book. Get the directories of your city and the outlying areas. Also try to get the directories of the larger institutions with which you have frequent contact, such as city hall, the police and fire departments, other city and county agencies, federal offices, city and county school offices, newspapers and radio stations, colleges and universities, and museums. On the Internet you can obtain in seconds the telephone number of practically any phone user in the world.

Other resources   The local chamber of commerce usually maintains a list of community organizations and businesses. A list of the major foundations and their criteria for grants may also come in handy.

UNIONS AND LEGAL MATTERS

Most directors, writers, and talent belong to a guild or union, as do almost all technical people. As a producer you

AFTRA	**American Federation of Television and Radio Artists.** This is the major union for television talent. Directors sometimes belong to AFTRA, especially when they double as announcers and on-the-air talent. AFTRA prescribes basic minimum fees, called scale, which differ from area to area. Most well-known talent (such as prominent actors and local news anchors) are paid well above scale.
DGA	**Directors Guild of America.** A union for television and motion picture directors and associate directors. Floor managers and production assistants of large stations and networks sometimes belong to "the Guild."
WGA	**Writers Guild of America.** A union for writers of television and film scripts.
SAG	**Screen Actors Guild.** A union for all actors in television and digital cinema. Also includes talent for commercials and larger video productions.
SEG	**Screen Extras Guild.** A union for extras participating in major film or video productions.
AFM	**American Federation of Musicians of the United States and Canada.** Relevant only if live musical performances are scheduled in the production.

must be alert to the union regulations in your production area. Most unions stipulate not only salaries and minimum fees but also specific working conditions, such as overtime, turnaround time (stipulated hours of rest between workdays), rest periods, who can legally run a studio camera and who cannot, and so forth. If you use nonunion personnel in a union station, or if you plan to air a show that has been prepared outside the station with nonunion talent, such as a play you produced with your fellow students, check with the respective unions for proper clearance.

UNIONS

There are two basic types of unions: those for nontechnical personnel and those for technical personnel. Nontechnical unions are mainly those for performers, writers, and directors. **SEE 2.7** Technical unions include all television technicians, engineers, and some production personnel such as microphone boom operators, ENG/EFP camera operators, and floor personnel. **SEE 2.8**

Be especially careful about asking studio guests to do anything other than answer questions during an interview. If they give a short demonstration of their talents, they may be classified as performers and automatically become subject to AFTRA fees (see figure 2.7). Likewise, do not request the floor crew to do anything that is not directly connected

IBEW	**International Brotherhood of Electrical Workers.** A union for studio, master control, and maintenance engineers and technicians. May also include ENG/EFP camera operators and floor personnel.
NABET	**National Association of Broadcast Employees and Technicians.** An engineering union that may also include floor personnel and nonengineering production people, such as boom operators and dolly operators.
IATSE	**International Alliance of Theatrical Stage Employees, Moving Picture Technicians, Artists and Allied Crafts of the United States, Its Territories and Canada.** A union for stagehands, grips (lighting technicians), and stage carpenters. Floor managers and even film camera and lighting personnel can also belong.

2.8 TECHNICAL UNIONS

with their regular line of duty, or they too may collect talent fees. Camera operators usually have a contract clause that ensures them a substantial penalty sum if they are willfully shown by another camera on the television screen. Acting students who appear in television plays produced at a high school or college may become subject to AFTRA fees if the play is shown on the air by a broadcast station, unless you clear their on-the-air appearance with the station and/or the local AFTRA office.

COPYRIGHTS AND CLEARANCES

If you use copyrighted material on your show, you must procure proper clearances. Usually, the year of the copyright and the name of the copyright holder are printed right after the © symbol. Some photographs, reproductions of famous paintings, and prints are copyrighted as are, of course, books, periodicals, short stories, plays, and music recordings. Shows or music that you record off the air or download from the Internet as well as many CD-ROMs and DVDs also have copyright protection.

Paradoxically, when you as an artist are trying to protect your rights, you may find that the copyrights are vague; but when you as a producer use copyrighted material, you are bound by stringent laws and regulations. When in doubt, consult an attorney about copyright clauses and public domain before using other people's material in your production.

OTHER LEGAL CONSIDERATIONS

Check with legal counsel about up-to-date rulings on libel (written and broadcast defamation), slander (lesser oral defamation), plagiarism (passing off as one's own the ideas or writings of another), the right to privacy (not the same in all states), obscenity, and similar matters. In the absence of legal counsel, the news departments of major broadcast stations or university broadcast departments generally have up-to-date legal information available.

AUDIENCE AND RATINGS

As a producer in a television station, you will probably hear more than you care to about television audiences and ratings. Ratings are especially important for commercial stations because the cost for commercial time sold is determined primarily by the estimated size of the target audience. Even when working in public or corporate television, you will find that audience "ratings" are used to gauge the relative success of a program.

TARGET AUDIENCE

Broadcast audiences, like those for all mass media, are usually classified by demographic and psychographic characteristics. The standard demographic descriptors include gender, age, marital status, education, ethnicity, and income or economic status. The psychographic descriptors pertain to lifestyle, such as consumer buying habits and even personality and persuasiveness variables. When you fill out the registration card that comes with a new electronic product, you are supplying highly valuable psychographic information.

Despite sophisticated techniques of classifying audience members and determining their lifestyles and potential acceptance of a specific program or series, some producers simply use a neighbor as a model and gear their communication to that particular person and his or her habits. Don't be surprised if an executive producer turns down your brilliant program proposal with a comment such as, "I don't think my neighbor Cathy would like it." For many entertainment programs, such a subjective approach to prejudging the worth of a program might be acceptable. If you are asked to do a goal-directed program such as driver education or a commercial on the importance of water conservation, however, you need to identify and analyze the target audience more specifically. The more you know about the target audience, the more precise your defined process message and, ultimately, the more effective that message will be.

RATINGS AND SHARE

An audience *rating* is the percentage of television households tuned to a specific station in a given population (total number of television households). You get this percentage by dividing the projected number of households tuned to your station by the total number of television households:

$$\frac{number\ of\ TV\ households\ tuned\ in}{total\ number\ of\ TV\ households} = rating\ figure$$

For example, if 75 households of your rating sample of 500 households are tuned to your show, your show will have a rating of 15 (the decimal point is dropped when the rating figure is given):

$$\frac{75}{500} = 0.15 = 15\ rating\ points$$

A *share* is the percentage of television households tuned to your station in relation to all households using television (HUT). The *HUT* figure represents the total pie—or 100 percent. Here is how a share is figured:

$$\frac{\textit{TV households tuned to your station}}{\textit{all households using television (HUT)}} = \textit{share}$$

For example, if only 200 of the sample households have their sets actually in use (HUT = 200 = 100 percent), the 75 households tuned into your program constitute a share of 38:

$$\frac{75}{200} = 0.375 = \textit{share of 38}$$

Rating services such as A. C. Nielsen carefully select representative audience samples and query these samples through diaries, telephone calls, and meters attached to their television sets.

The problem with the rating figures is not so much the potential for error in projecting the sample to a larger population but rather that the figures do not indicate whether the household whose set is turned on has any people watching and, if so, how many. The figures also do not indicate the impact of a program on the viewers (the actual process message). Consequently, you will find that your show is often judged not by the significance of your message, the impact it has on the audience, or how close the actual effect of the process message came to the defined effect, but simply by how many people are assumed to have watched your show in relation to other shows. As frustrating as the rating system in broadcast television is, you must realize that you are working with a mass medium that by definition bases its existence on large audiences.

MAIN POINTS

▶ A producer needs quick and ready access to a great variety of resources and information. The Internet is an almost instantaneous and total information resource. Telephone directories and local business and community resources are also helpful.

▶ Most nontechnical and technical production personnel belong to guilds or unions, such as the Directors Guild of America (DGA) and the National Association of Broadcast Employees and Technicians (NABET).

▶ The usual copyright laws apply when copyrighted material (such as video and audio material, printed information, CD-ROMs, and DVDs) is used in a television production.

▶ An audience rating is the percentage of television households tuned to a specific station in a given sample population owning TV sets. A share is the percentage of households tuned to a specific station in relation to all other households using television (HUT).

ZETTL'S VIDEOLAB

 For your reference or to track your work, the *Zettl's VideoLab* program cues in this chapter are listed here with their corresponding page numbers.

ZVL1 ▶ PROCESS→ Ideas   **27**

ZVL2 ▶ PROCESS→ Proposals→ treatment   **29**

ZVL3 ▶ PROCESS→ Methods→ location | studio | single-camera | multicamera   **29**

ZVL4 ▶ PROCESS→ Proposals→ budget | try it   **29**

ZVL5 ▶ PROCESS→ Ideas→ scripts   **33**

3

The Script

The *script* is one of the most important communication devices in all three production phases; a good one tells you what the program is about, who is in it, what each person says, what is supposed to happen, and how the audience should see and hear the event. Whatever position you hold on the production team, you must be familiar with the basic structure of dramatic and nondramatic scripts and the various script formats.

Section 3.1 explains the basic script formats. Section 3.2 addresses dramatic and nondramatic story structures.

KEY TERMS

A/V format Another name for the two-column AV (audio/video) script.

classical dramaturgy The technique of dramatic composition.

event order The way event details are sequenced.

fact sheet Lists the items to be shown on-camera and their main features. May contain suggestions of what to say about the product. Also called *rundown sheet*.

goal-directed information Program content intended to be learned by the viewer.

partial two-column A/V script Describes a show for which the dialogue is indicated but not completely written out.

script Written document that tells what the program is about, who says what, what is supposed to happen, and what and how the audience should see and hear the event.

show format Lists the show segments in order of appearance. Used in routine shows, such as daily game or interview shows.

single-column drama script Traditional script format for television and motion picture plays. All dialogue and action cues are written in a single column.

two-column A/V script Traditional script format with video information on page-left and audio information on page-right for a variety of television scripts, such as for documentaries and commercials. Also called *A/V (audio/video) script*.

3.1

Basic Script Formats

Whether you work in television or digital movie making, you will encounter different script formats. The more common are the single-column drama script, the two-column A/V script, the partial two-column A/V script, the news script, the show format, and the fact sheet.

▶ **SINGLE-COLUMN DRAMA SCRIPT**
Standard format for writing plays for television and digital cinema

▶ **TWO-COLUMN A/V SCRIPT**
Fully scripted A/V format and partial two-column A/V script

▶ **NEWS SCRIPT**
One of the more widely used news script formats

▶ **SHOW FORMAT**
Guide to routine show segments

▶ **FACT SHEET**
List of items to be mentioned and shown on the air

SINGLE-COLUMN DRAMA SCRIPT

The *single-column drama script* includes every word of the actors' dialogue, who is doing what when and where, and frequently how the action should play. Dramas, situation comedies, skits, and soap operas use this script format. **SEE 3.1**

TWO-COLUMN A/V SCRIPT

This popular script type is also known as the *A/V (audio/video) format* because the right column contains the audio information and the left column contains the video information. Most documentary writers prefer the convenient *two-column A/V script* and therefore call it the *documentary format.* Fortunately, all three names refer to the same thing: a script that shows what is being heard on page-right and what is being seen on page-left. The A/V format can be fully scripted, which means that everything that is spoken appears in the audio column, or partially scripted, which shows only parts of the dialogue.

FULLY SCRIPTED A/V FORMAT

Many fully scripted documentaries use the two-column A/V format. Because a documentary is intended to record an event rather than reconstruct one, scripts are frequently written *after* the field production. Documentary scripts therefore guide the postproduction phase rather than the actual production. The major video cues are listed in the video column, and all spoken words and sound effects are written in the audio column. The script tells the editor which sound bites to use and which video to choose for the voice-over segments. In this format it is important to indicate specific in- and out-cues that tell the director when to insert a video clip, key a title, or move the cameras to another set area. **SEE 3.2**

One word of caution to prospective documentary writers: writing a detailed script before going out to record the event makes no sense. Instead of documenting the event, you would merely be looking for event details that fit your prejudices. **ZVL1** ▶ PROCESS→ Ideas→ scripts

PARTIAL TWO-COLUMN A/V SCRIPT

The *partial two-column A/V script* indicates only part of the dialogue. In general, the opening and closing remarks are fully scripted, but the bulk of what people say is only alluded to, such as: "Dr. Hyde talks about new educational ideas. Dr. Seel replies." This kind of script is almost always used for interviews, product demonstrations, educational program series, variety shows, and other program types that feature a great amount of ad-lib commentary or discussion. **SEE 3.3**

NEWS SCRIPT

Newscasts are always fully scripted. The script must include every word the anchors speak as well as instructions for

SCENE 6

A FEW DAYS LATER. INTERIOR. CITY HOSPITAL EMERGENCY WAITING
ROOM. LATE EVENING.

YOLANDA is anxiously PACING back and forth in the hospital
hallway in front of the emergency room. She has come straight
from her job to the hospital. We see the typical hospital
traffic in an emergency room. A DOCTOR (friend of CHUCK'S)
PUSHES CARRIE in a wheelchair down the hall toward YOLANDA.

                        CARRIE

             (in wheelchair but rather cheerful)

Hi, Mom!

                        YOLANDA

                (anxious and worried)

Carrie—are you all right? What happened?

                        CARRIE

I'm OK. I just slipped.

                DOCTOR (simultaneously)

She has a sprained right wrist. Nothing serious . . .

                        CARRIE

Why is everybody making such a big deal out of it?

                        YOLANDA

        (cutting into both CARRIE'S and DOCTOR'S lines)

Does it hurt? Did you break your arm?

3.1 SINGLE-COLUMN DRAMA SCRIPT

The single-column drama script contains every word of the dialogue and descriptions of primary character action.
It gives minimal visualization and sequencing instructions.

```
GROUP 5

AIR DATE: 07/15 4:00 P.M.
```

VIDEO	AUDIO
OPENING MONTAGE SERV 02 CLIP 9 SOS [sound on source] **00:25**	IN-CUE: "When you drive through this valley..." OUT-CUE: "...Group 5, a remarkable union of five world-renowned artists."
JULIA in Woodacre studio **00:15**	<div align="center">JULIA (on-camera)</div>The founding members of Group 5—a painter, a singer, a potter, a documentary videographer, and a poet—did not know one another and certainly not that they all lived in the San Geronimo Valley in Marin County.
SERV 02 CLIP 10 PACKAGE 1 Julia V/O Valley shots **3:38**	<div align="center">JULIA (V/O)</div>They moved there to get away from city life, to trade the city's nervousness for the calm of rolling hills, ancient oaks, and redwoods. An artists' guild was definitely not on their minds.
TALIA in studio SOS	IN-CUE: "No agents, no obligations..." OUT-CUE: "...until I ran into Mr. Video at the Forest Knolls post office."
JULIA in Woodacre studio	<div align="center">JULIA (on-camera)</div>The Mr. Video is Phil Arnone, an award-winning documentary producer and video artist who sees the world with a child's curiosity and an artist's intensity. His world consists not of spectacular vistas but, much like Talia's paintings, high-energy close-up details.
SERV 02 CLIP 11 PACKAGE 2 SOS Phil in editing room **2:47**	IN-CUE: "Yes, I am a child when it comes to looking at things, at events happening..." OUT-CUE: "...Talia and I are definitely soul brother and sister."

3.2 STANDARD TWO-COLUMN A/V SCRIPT

In a two-column A/V script, the video instructions are page-left, and the audio instructions (including the dialogue) are page-right.

```
        VIDEO                           AUDIO

                                        KATY:
   CU of Katy                  But the debate about forest fires is still
                               going on. If we let the fire burn itself
                               out, we lose valuable timber and kill
                               countless animals, not to speak of the
                               danger to property and the people who live
                               there. Where do you stand, Dr. Hough?


                                        DR. HOUGH:
   Cut to CU of               (SAYS THAT THIS IS QUITE TRUE BUT THAT
   Dr. Hough                   THE ANIMALS USUALLY GET OUT UNHARMED AND
                               THAT THE BURNED UNDERBRUSH STIMULATES
                               NEW GROWTH.)


                                        KATY:
   Cut to                      Couldn't this be done through controlled
   two-shot                    burning?


                                        DR. HOUGH:
                              (SAYS YES BUT THAT IT WOULD COST TOO MUCH
                               AND THAT THERE WOULD STILL BE FOREST FIRES
                               TO CONTEND WITH.)
```

3.3 PARTIAL TWO-COLUMN A/V SCRIPT
This script shows the video information in the left (VIDEO) column but only partial dialogue in the right (AUDIO) column. The host's questions are usually fully scripted, but the answers are only briefly described.

what visuals or prerecorded segments the director must call up and when. Such segments include news features (called packages) and live events, such as an on-location reporter describing some disaster in progress. **SEE 3.4**

SHOW FORMAT

The *show format* lists only the order of particular show segments, such as "interview from Washington," "commercial 2," and "book review." It also lists the set areas in which the action takes place (or other points of origination) as well as the clock and running times for the segments. A show format is frequently used in studio productions that have

established performance routines, such as a daily morning show, a panel show, or a quiz show. **SEE 3.5**

FACT SHEET

A *fact sheet*, or rundown sheet, lists the items that are to be shown on-camera and indicates roughly what should be said. **SEE 3.6** The fact sheet is sometimes written in the A/V format, but no specific video or audio instructions are given. It is most often supplied by a manufacturer or an advertiser who wants the talent to ad-lib about the product.

If the demonstration of the item is complicated, the director may rewrite the fact sheet and indicate key camera

```
Hunter's Point Package        Noon News 04/15


Studio: KRISTI          ((Kristi))


                        A LANDLORD IN HUNTER'S POINT IS UNDER FIRE
                        FOR DANGEROUS LIVING CONDITIONS IN HIS
                        BUILDINGS. RESIDENTS COMPLAIN OF RASHES...
                        HEADACHES AND NOSEBLEEDS.


                        MARTY GONZALES ASKS SEVERAL TENANTS WHO SAY
                        THAT ALL OF THIS IS DUE TO TOXIC MOLD.


                        ------------------------------------------------

Package 1               ((In-cue: "There is no official confirmation
Video and Audio         that these buildings are infested with toxic
Server 03               mold, but it sure looks like it...))
Clip 023                PACKAGE            0:42
                        ((Out-cue:  "...I wish somebody would
                        do something about it."))


Studio: KRISTI          ((Kristi))


                        THE LANDLORD DENIES THESE CHARGES AND SAYS
                        IT MUST BE THE FOGGY WEATHER. WE'LL TALK TO
                        THE LANDLORD AND HEALTH OFFICIALS RIGHT
                        AFTER THESE MESSAGES.
                        ------------------------------------------------

Server 03
Clip 112                BUMPER
Clip 005                COMMERCIAL (California Cheese)
Clip 007                COMMERCIAL (Winston Enterprises)
```

3.4 NEWS SCRIPT

The news script contains every word spoken by the anchor (Kristi), except for the occasional chitchat, and instructions for all video sources used. A package is a previously shot and edited story that contains an on-location reporter and the people interviewed.

```
PEOPLE, PLACES, POLITICS SHOW FORMAT   (Script attached)

PRODUCTION DATE: 2/3   FACILITIES REQUEST:  BECA 415
AIR DATE: 2/17         RUNNING TIME:  25:30
DIRECTOR: Whitney      HOST:  Kipper

                          OPEN

VIDEO                 AUDIO

STANDARD OPENING      SOS [sound on source]
SERVER 1, CLIP #ST1   ANNOUNCER: The Television Center of
EFFECTS 117           the Broadcast and Electronic Communication
                      Arts Department, San Francisco State
                      University, presents "People, Places, Politics"
                      --a new perspective on global events.

KEY C.G. TOPIC TITLE  Today's topic is:
-------------------------------------------------------------
SERVER 1, CLIP #033 PSAs 1 & 2
-------------------------------------------------------------

OPENING STUDIO SHOT   PHIL INTRODUCES GUESTS

KEY C.G.              NAMES OF GUESTS

CUs OF GUESTS         GUESTS DISCUSS TOPICS

CU OF PHIL            CLOSES SHOW
-------------------------------------------------------------
SERVER 1, CLIP #034 PSAs 3 & 4
-------------------------------------------------------------
                         CLOSE

KEY C.G. ADDRESS      ANNOUNCER: To obtain a copy of today's
                      program, write to "People, Places, Politics,"

                      BECA Dept., San Francisco State University,
                      San Francisco, CA 94132
                      E-mail: BECA@sfsu.edu

KEY C.G. NEXT WEEK    Tune in next week when we present:

                      THEME MUSIC UP AND OUT
```

3.5 SHOW FORMAT

The show format contains only essential video information in the left (VIDEO) column and the standard opening and closing announcements in the right (AUDIO) column.

```
VIDEO PRO CD-ROM COMMERCIAL
SHOW:
DATE:

PROPS:
Desktop computer running Zettl's VideoLab 3.0. Triple-I Web page.
Video Pro poster and multimedia awards in background.
Video Pro package with disc as hand props.

1.   New multimedia product by Image, Imagination, Incorporated.

2.   Sensational success. Best Triple-I product yet.

3.   Based on ZVL 2.1, which won several awards for excellence,
     including the prestigious Invision Gold Medal.

4.   Designed for the production novice and the video professional.

5.   Truly interactive. Provides you with a video studio in your
     home. Easy to use.

6.   You can proceed at your own speed and test your progress
     after each exercise.

7.   Will operate on Windows or Macintosh platform.

8.   Special introductory offer. Expires Oct. 20. Hurry. Available
     in all major software stores. For more information or the
     dealer nearest you, visit Triple-I's Web page at
     http://www.triple-i.tv.
```

3.6 FACT SHEET

The fact sheet lists the major points to be made about the demonstrated product. No specific video or audio information is given. The talent ad-libs the demonstration, and the director follows the talent's action with the camera.

shots to help coordinate the talent's and the director's actions. Unless the demonstration is extremely simple, such as holding up a book by a famous novelist, directing solely from a fact sheet is not recommended. Ad-libbing by both director and talent rarely works out satisfactorily, even if the video recording is intended for postproduction editing.

MAIN POINTS

▶ The script is one of the most important communication devices in all three production phases.

▶ The most common script formats are the single-column drama script, the two-column A/V (audio/video) script, the partial two-column A/V script, the news script, the show format, and the fact, or rundown, sheet.

SECTION

3.2

Dramatic Structure, Conflict, and Dramaturgy

Even if you are not a writer, you must be able to judge the quality of a script. There are several classic books on dramatic and nondramatic scriptwriting, so the information in this section is purposely kept to a minimum.[1]

▶ **BASIC DRAMATIC STORY STRUCTURE**
  Structural components

▶ **CONFLICT AND CLASSICAL DRAMATURGY**
  Types of dramatic conflict, classical dramaturgy, and event order

▶ **NONDRAMATIC STORY STRUCTURE**
  Goal-directed programs; from idea to process message: feature story; and from idea to process message: goal-directed program

---

1. As cited in chapter 2, the two most valuable books I've found on the art of writing for the media are: Stuart W. Hyde, *Idea to Script: Storytelling for Today's Media* (Boston: Allyn and Bacon, 2003); and Nancy Graham Holm, *Fascination: Viewer Friendly TV Journalism* (Århus, Denmark: Ajour Danish Media Books, 2007). The Hyde book contains an exceptionally lucid approach to conceptualizing a story and the various structures of dramatic and nondramatic scripts. The small Graham Holm book is a journalistic jewel. Written with conviction and wit, it conveys an amazing amount of solid information that goes way beyond the average "how-to-do-news" approach.

BASIC DRAMATIC STORY STRUCTURE

A good drama operates on many conscious and unconscious levels, all of which must be made explicit by the writer and, especially, the actors.

STRUCTURAL COMPONENTS

All dramas for the stage or screen have four basic elements:

- Theme—what the story is about

- Plot—how the story moves forward and develops

- Characters—how one person differs from the others and how each reacts to the situation at hand

- Environment—where the action takes place

The plot can develop from outside-in or from inside-out. A from-outside-in story has the characters react to outside influences, such as natural disasters, nasty neighbors, or the loss of a job. A from-inside-out story has the characters' behavior and choices determine the way the plot progresses. Large-screen cinema is generally driven by spectacular from-outside-in plots but has also proved that it can deal with character-based stories. Plot-based stories often emphasize outer action (such as car chases, explosions, and fights). Character-based stories thrive on inner action—the characters' psychological makeup and subsequent behavior.

Although you may not see much evidence in the daily program fare, by its very nature the television medium is ideally suited to explicate low-key, character-based, from-inside-out stories. We usually watch television alone or with family members in our home and consider the small screen a welcome and familiar—if not intimate—communication partner. This is why politicians and advertisers spend so much money on using television to deliver their messages to your home.

CONFLICT AND CLASSICAL DRAMATURGY

All drama thrives on conflict. Without conflict you have no drama. In fact, all good stories are based on some form of conflict. In a drama series, such as a soap opera or crime show, each episode solves a number of large and small problems but always ends with a new conflict to be solved in a subsequent show. Granted, this is a rather clichéd way of luring the audience back week after week, but it works.

TYPES OF DRAMATIC CONFLICT

In the plot-based approach, the conflict grows out of circumstances that make the viewer react in a specific way.

For example, person A becomes a politician because, having been a football star, he has wide name recognition and, after marrying into a wealthy family, is urged by his father-in-law to run for an open Senate seat. His wife makes a compelling argument for how he can single-handedly change the Senate majority and bring the country back to honesty and family values. He wins but is horrified by the way the Senate makes decisions. When trying to clean up their act, he runs into a series of conflicts, gets into a mysterious car accident, and loses his arm, job, wife, friends, and self-confidence—in that order.

In the character-based approach, the character's initial decisions create the conflict with which he or she must deal. When looking at a script of a good teleplay or movie, you should be able to identify several layers of conflict—some more subtle, others quite conspicuous.

For example, person B, a physician, becomes more and more frustrated with the way the Senate ignores the wishes of its constituency, and she decides to do something about it. She quits her hospital job, starts a grassroots senatorial election campaign, and gives speeches about universal healthcare. She wins by a slim margin, and, like person A, is horrified by the way the Senate makes decisions. She is immediately chastised for voting not by party lines but by what she believes to be best for people. She too has a mysterious car accident and finds herself in her former hospital, this time as a patient. She is confronted in various ways by former colleagues, who suspect that her motivation for changing professions was power rather than altruism. When she is finally well again, she wants to return to the medical profession, but her loyal husband convinces her that she is needed in the Senate and that she has already made a big difference for the people she represents. So she reenters politics, uses the media to expose some of the ways senators operate, cleans up their act, introduces a new world healthcare system, and lives happily ever after.

As you can see, person A's conflicts were basically caused by external circumstances (what other people told him to do or arranged for him), whereas person B's conflicts arose from her own decisions and convictions.

When you look at television plays and movies more carefully and identify the conflicts and how they come about, you will discover that the conflicts and how they are introduced are quite similar. You can probably come up with a few pages of conflicts with little effort, so consider the following list of possible dramatic conflicts merely examples. **SEE 3.7**

3.7 DRAMATIC CONFLICTS

Though not exhaustive by any means, this list of conflicts is intended as an aid in recognizing possible conflict formulas in scripts and as a stimulus for coming up with similar lists.

GENERAL AREAS OF CONFLICT

- Cultural and ideological differences
- Ideal versus rational worldviews
- Feeling versus reason
- Wishful thinking versus reality
- Society versus the individual
- Honesty versus corruption
- Rich and poor

SPECIFIC AREAS OF CONFLICT

The conflict between the protagonist (who could be you) and:

- Various circumstances
- Environment
- Nature
- Himself/herself (yourself)
- Family members
- Relatives
- Friends
- Neighbors
- Peer pressure
- Classmates
- Conformity
- Lifestyle
- Authority
- Bureaucracy
- Power
- Faith
- Principles
- Morals
- Beliefs
- Religion
- Social system
- Government

CLASSICAL DRAMATURGY

Effective storytelling hasn't really changed much over the centuries. We still use all or most of the ingredients of the ***classical dramaturgy***—the techniques of dramatic composition:

- Exposition—which sets the context in which the action occurs
- Point of attack—the first crisis
- Rising action—more conflicts and trouble brewing
- Climax—major crisis or turning point
- Falling action and resolution (hero runs into more trouble and either wins or loses) **SEE 3.8**

Go back to the treatment of the story in chapter 2 (figure 2.3) and see how, if at all, this treatment conforms to the classical dramatic structure.

Exposition and context: airport, professor on way to conference

Point of attack (first crisis): suitcase missing

Rising action (series of minor conflicts): forgets name of hotel, has to take a cab to hotel in bad neighborhood

Climax: wallet missing

Falling action: several more conflicts—difficulty getting help, trouble finding a telephone, reaches only friend's answering machine, lost in strange city

Resolution: police come to the rescue, finds colleague in lobby of conference hotel

As you can see, the five major criteria of the classical dramaturgy are included in the proposed dramatic pro-gram—and it has a good ending (the hero is rescued). If you wanted to make a tragedy out of it, you could have him get mugged and then beaten up because the villains could not find any money on him, miss his conference, and, as a result, lose his promotion. For good measure, his new marriage is also getting stressed. The hero is doomed.

This classical dramaturgy applies to good storytelling in all media—television and movies included. These media, however, have drastically altered the traditional idea of event order.

EVENT ORDER

The ease with which we can shift past, present, and future through editing has obliterated the myth that a good story must have a neat beginning, middle, and end and has redefined the concept of ***event order*** in storytelling.

Through flashbacks you can "flash" past events on-screen while showing the present; and with flash-forwards, you can begin a story with how it ended and then follow up with what led to the final event. Even during a live telecast of a baseball game, you can interrupt the present and recall past moments with instant replays. Such instant replays have become an important dramaturgical ingredient in television drama. And, as you well know, soap operas and crime series never have a clean ending but entice you with an unresolved crisis to tune in again.

NONDRAMATIC STORY STRUCTURE

Nondramatic stories include everything from a news report and a documentary to a product commercial and a complex

3.8 CLASSICAL DRAMATURGY

The classical dramaturgy moves from the exposition (context) to the point of attack (first crisis) through rising action and a climax (major crisis) to the resolution.

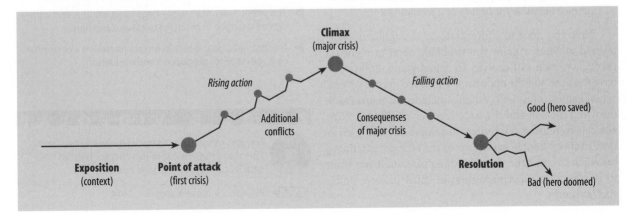

instructional video on some medical procedure. All are nonfiction and principally informational.

GOAL-DIRECTED PROGRAMS

Whereas news stories and documentaries are based on the canons of storytelling and a simplified dramaturgy, commercials and instructional programs purposely comprise ***goal-directed information*** that is not bound by storytelling conventions. They are constructed by motivational and learning objectives and are calculated to have an observable, if not measurable, effect on the viewer. All programs benefit from a process message, but goal-directed programs depend on one.

FROM IDEA TO PROCESS MESSAGE: FEATURE STORY

Here are two examples of how different process messages can influence the concept of a feature that is not goal-directed. The basic idea is to do a story on your favorite football team. But exactly how do you want to show it? What is it you want viewers to see and feel? Let's write two process messages that will streamline your approach to what you show and how you show it.

Process message 1: The program should make viewers feel the immense physical power of a football game.

When translating this process message into actual medium requirements, you will need to show very tight shots of tackles. Can you do this during a regular game? Probably not. You would be better off doing it during a practice session, where you can use portable camcorders and work at close distances. Sound becomes very important. Hearing the impact will make us feel the power more than just seeing the two players crash into each other. The event order is unimportant—you simply show highlights.

Process message 2: The program should make the viewer admire the inherent beauty of a football game.

Now you need to concentrate on the agility of well-trained athletes. Again, you probably need to record a practice session rather than an actual game, unless you have the time and the opportunity to video-record several actual games. Shots will certainly include the quarterback throwing the ball and the wide receiver catching it. Now you can even use special effects in postproduction, such as slow motion, double exposures of the receiver extending his reach to catch the game-winning pass, or, if you want to go all out, a superimposition of ballet dancers doing similar jumps.

FROM IDEA TO PROCESS MESSAGE: GOAL-DIRECTED PROGRAM

This type of program needs a highly precise process message that, much like instructional objectives, must be stated so that the results can be observed and verified.

Here is a process message for a fictional *Sesame Street* episode:

Process message: After having watched this program, preschool children will be able to count from 1 to 5.

The program must now fulfill a specific learning task. You can proceed with preproduction and think of content that fulfills the three credos of advertising: attention, redundancy, and variety. You need to be brief, show something that catches immediate attention (such as a cartoon character), and repeat the numbers in a variety of ways—have somebody scratch them in the sand, have them appear in the squares of a sidewalk game, have five toy cars pop up sequentially, and so forth.

In an actual instructional program in school, the message received by the students can be verified through a test and then compared with the defined process message. The closer they match, the more successful the program.

M A I N   P O I N T S

▶ The four basic components of a drama are theme, plot, characters, and environment.

▶ All drama thrives on conflict. Conflict can be primarily outer-oriented, or plot-based, in which the circumstances prompt the character's reaction; or it can be inner-oriented, or character-based, in which the character causes the circumstances.

▶ The five components of the classical dramaturgy are exposition (context), point of attack (first crisis), rising action, climax (major crisis), and falling action and resolution.

▶ The event order of a story—beginning, middle, and end— can be changed in recorded television and film.

▶ Nondramatic goal-directed programs require a clear process message for production and evaluation.

Z E T T L' S   V I D E O L A B

 For your reference or to track your work, the *Zettl's VideoLab* program cue in this chapter is listed here with its corresponding page number.

ZVL1   PROCESS→ Ideas→ scripts   **44**

Production

CHAPTER

4

Analog and Digital Television

Digital television (DTV) has led to not only dramatically improved television pictures and sound but also a convergence of various media: television is becoming interactive; large, centralized digital databases offer television news organizations instant access to news files; and computers stream audio and video content over the Internet. You can use your cell phone to video-record your friends or to watch television programs while walking to campus. More and more large-scale motion pictures use ***high-definition television (HDTV)*** television cameras rather than traditional film cameras for their studio and field productions. But even if the original footage is captured on photographic film stock rather than videotape or some other digital recording media, all subsequent production steps involve similar (or the same) equipment and processes you encounter in major television productions. Once transformed into digital data, electronic movies can be just as easily distributed via cable, microwave, or satellite, as are HDTV signals. As you can see, learning about digital processes is no longer a luxury; it has become essential for anyone involved in television and even film production.

Section 4.1, Analog and Digital Processes, explains what digital processes are all about and how they differ from analog systems. Section 4.2, Scanning Systems, introduces you to the basics of the creation of a color television image, interlaced and progressive scanning, the current digital scanning systems, and flat-panel displays.

480p The lowest-resolution scanning system of digital television. The *p* stands for *progressive,* which means that each complete television frame consists of 480 visible, or active, lines that are scanned one after the other (out of 525 total scanning lines).

720p A progressive scanning system of high-definition television. Each frame consists of 720 visible, or active, lines (out of 750 total scanning lines).

1080i An interlaced scanning system of high-definition television. The *i* stands for *interlaced,* which means that a complete frame is formed from two interlaced scanning fields, each carrying half of the picture information. Each field consists of 540 visible, or active, lines (out of 1,125 total scanning lines). Just like the standard NTSC television system, the digital HDTV 1080i system produces 60 fields, or 30 complete frames, per second.

analog A signal that fluctuates exactly like the original stimulus.

aspect ratio The width-to-height proportions of the standard television screen and therefore of all standard television pictures: 4 units wide by 3 units high. For HDTV the aspect ratio is 16×9. The small portable media (cell-phone) screens have various aspect ratios.

binary A number system with the base of 2.

binary digit (bit) The smallest amount of information a computer can hold and process. A charge is either present, represented by a *1,* or absent, represented by a *0.* One bit can describe two levels, such as on/off or black/white. The standard decimal system has 10 digits: 0–9. The binary system has only two: 0 and 1.

codec Short for *compression/decompression.* A specific method of compressing and decompressing digital data.

coding To change the quantized values into a binary code, represented by 0's and 1's. Also called *encoding.*

compression Reducing the amount of data to be stored or transmitted by using coding schemes (codecs) that pack all original data into less space (*lossless* compression) or by throwing away some of the least important data (*lossy* compression).

decoding The reconstruction of a video or an audio signal from a digital code.

digital Usually means the binary system—the representation of data in the form of binary digits (on/off pulses).

digital television (DTV) Digital television systems that generally have a higher image resolution than STV (standard television). Also called *advanced television (ATV).*

downloading The transfer of files that are sent in data packets. Because these packets are often transferred out of order, the file cannot be seen or heard until the downloading process is complete.

field One-half of a complete scanning cycle, with two fields necessary for one television picture frame. There are 60 fields, or 30 frames, per second in standard NTSC television.

frame A complete scan from top to bottom of all picture lines by the electron beam, or one single frame of a motion series.

high-definition television (HDTV) Has at least twice the picture detail of standard (NTSC) television. The 720p uses 720 visible, or active, lines that are normally scanned progressively each $\frac{1}{60}$ second. The 1080i standard uses 60 fields per second, each field consisting of 540 visible, or active, lines. In interlaced scanning, a complete frame consists of two scanning fields of 540 visible lines. The *refresh rate* (complete scanning cycle) for HDTV systems can vary.

interlaced scanning In this system the electron beam skips every other line during its first scan, reading only the odd-numbered lines. After the beam has scanned half of the last odd-numbered line, it jumps back to the top of the screen and finishes the unscanned half of the top line and continues to scan all even-numbered lines. Each such even- or odd-numbered scan produces a *field.* Two fields produce a complete *frame.* Standard NTSC television operates with 60 fields per second, which translates to 30 frames per second.

progressive scanning In this system the electron beam starts with line 1, then scans line 2, then line 3, and so forth, until all lines are scanned, at which point the beam jumps back to its starting position to repeat the scan of all lines.

quantizing A step in the digitization of an analog signal. It changes the sampling points into discrete values. Also called *quantization.*

refresh rate The number of complete digital scanning cycles (frames) per second.

RGB Stands for *red, green, and blue*—the basic colors of television.

sampling The process of reading (selecting and recording) from an analog electronic signal a great many equally spaced, tiny portions (values) for conversion into a digital code.

streaming A way of delivering and receiving digital audio and/or video as a continuous data flow that can be listened to or watched while the delivery is in progress.

SECTION

4.1

Analog and Digital Processes

Before you submerge yourself in the world of digital television and digital cinema, you should know the basics of analog and digital systems and how the standard scanning process works. You will also get some answers to why we converted to digital processes, especially because analog television had been doing a pretty good job all along.

▶ **WHAT DIGITAL IS ALL ABOUT**
  Why digital?, the difference between analog and digital, and the process of digitization

▶ **BENEFITS OF DIGITAL TELEVISION**
  Quality, computer compatibility and flexibility, signal transport, and compression

▶ **ASPECT RATIO**
  The 4 × 3, 16 × 9, and mobile multimedia aspect ratios

▶ **DIGITAL SCANNING STANDARDS**
  480p, 720p, and 1080i

WHAT DIGITAL IS ALL ABOUT

All *digital* computers and digital video are based on a *binary* code that uses the either/or, on/off values of 0's and 1's to interpret the world. The *binary digit, or bit*, acts like a light switch: it is either on or off. If it is on, it is assigned a 1; if it is off, it is assigned a 0.

WHY DIGITAL?

At first glance this either/or system of binary digits may seem clumsy. For example, the simple and elegant decimal number 17 translates into the cumbersome 00010001 in binary code. The binary system uses the base-2 numbering system.[1]

The overwhelming advantage of the binary system is that it has great resistance to data distortion and error. In binary code, a light is either on or off. If the light flickers or burns at only half intensity, the digital system simply ignores such aberrations and reacts only if the switch triggers the expected on/off actions. It also permits any number of combinations and shuffling around—an extremely important feature when manipulating pictures and sound. We elaborate on the benefits of digital signals later in this chapter.

DIFFERENCE BETWEEN ANALOG AND DIGITAL

Before getting too technical, let's use a simple metaphor to explain the difference between analog and digital signal processing. The analog signal is like a ramp that leads continuously from one elevation to another. When walking up this ramp, it matters little whether you use small or big steps; the ramp gradually and inevitably leads you to the desired elevation. **SEE 4.1**

To carry on the metaphor, in the digital domain you would have to use steps to get to the same elevation. This is much more an either/or proposition. The elevation has now been quantized (divided) into a number of discrete units—the steps. You either get to the next step or you don't. There is no such thing as standing on a half or quarter step. **SEE 4.2**

The *analog* system processes and records a continuous signal that fluctuates exactly like the original signal (the line of the ramp). Digital processing, however, changes the ramp into discrete values. This process is called digitization. In the digital process, the analog signal is continuously sampled at fixed intervals; the samples are then quantized (assigned a concrete value) and coded into 0's and 1's.

---

1. The number 17 is represented by an 8-bit binary code. All values are mathematically represented by either 0's or 1's. An 8-bit representation of a single color pixel or sound has 2^8, or 256, discrete values. For more-detailed information on the binary system, see Arch C. Luther and Andrew F. Inglis, *Video Engineering*, 3rd ed. (New York: McGraw-Hill, 1999), pp. 45–47.

4.1 ANALOG SIGNAL
The analog signal can be represented by a ramp that leads continuously to a certain height.

4.2 DIGITAL SIGNAL
The digital signal can be represented by a staircase that leads in discrete steps to a certain height.

4.3 DIGITIZATION
The digitization of an analog signal is a four-step process: anti-aliasing, sampling, quantizing, and coding (short for *encoding*).

DIGITIZATION PROCESS

Digitizing an analog video signal is a four-step process: anti-aliasing, sampling, quantizing, and coding. **SEE 4.3**

Anti-aliasing   In this step extreme frequencies of the analog signal that are unnecessary for its proper sampling are filtered out.

Sampling   In the *sampling* stage, the number of points along the ramp (analog signal) is selected for building the steps (digital values). The higher the sampling rate, the more steps chosen and the more they will look like the original ramp (analog signal). Obviously, a high sampling rate (many smaller steps) is preferred over a low one (fewer but larger steps). **SEE 4.4 AND 4.5** The sampling rate of a video signal is usually expressed in megahertz (MHz).

QUANTIZING

At the *quantizing* digitization stage, we are actually building the steps so that we can reach the top of the staircase (which was previously the predetermined high end of the ramp) and assigning them numbers. Technically, *quantizing* means to separate a continuously variable signal into defined levels (steps) and fitting them into the desired sample range (the height of the ramp). For example, an 8-bit quantizing has a maximum number of 256 (2^8) levels. (In our metaphor we cannot use more than 256 steps). **SEE 4.6**

Coding   The process of *coding* (also called encoding) changes the quantization numbers of each step to binary numbers, consisting of 0's and 1's, and the various grouping of the bits (for us, steps). **SEE 4.7**

BENEFITS OF DIGITAL TELEVISION

Why go through all these processes? Wouldn't it be easier to simply walk up the (analog) ramp instead of climbing thousands or even millions of (digital) steps per second? Why do we prefer a partial—sampled—signal if we have

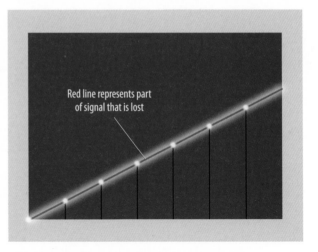

4.4 HIGH SAMPLING RATE

Sampling selects points of the original analog signal. A high sampling rate selects more points of the original signal. The digital signal will be made of more, smaller steps, making it look more like the original ramp. The higher the sampling rate, the higher the signal quality.

4.5 LOW SAMPLING RATE

A low sampling rate selects fewer points of the original analog signal. The digital signal will be composed of a few large steps. Much of the original signal is lost.

4.6 QUANTIZING

Quantizing assigns the selected signal samples a fixed position. This is the step-building stage. Each step gets a particular number assigned. **A** High sampling rate: many small steps. **B** Low sampling rate: fewer large steps.

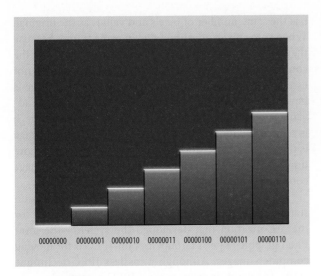

00000000 00000001 00000010 00000011 00000100 00000101 00000110

4.7 CODING
Coding, or encoding, assigns each step a binary number and groups the steps in a specific way.

the real thing—the complete analog signal—readily available? The simple answer is that the digital format has major advantages over the analog one: quality, computer compatibility and flexibility, signal transport, and compression.

QUALITY

Since long before the advent of digital video and audio systems, picture and sound quality have been a major concern of equipment manufacturers and production personnel. Such high-resolution picture quality is especially important for extensive postproduction. In the days of analog video production, complex editing and the rendering of special effects required many tape generations (the number of dubs—copies—away from the original). Unfortunately, the higher the number of generations in analog recordings, the greater the loss of quality. This is not unlike making progressive copies of a letter by photocopying each previous copy. Before long the print has deteriorated so much that you can hardly read it.

But this is where digital recordings shine. First, even small inexpensive camcorders deliver high-quality pictures and sound. Second, and more important, with digital recordings there is hardly any noticeable quality loss even after dozens of generations; the fiftieth generation looks as sharp as the original recording. In fact, through some digital wizardry you can make a copy look even better than the original. Another important quality factor is that the simple binary code is relatively immune to extraneous electronic

signals—noise or artifacts—that infiltrate and distort analog signals. With digital signal processing, electronic noise is held to a minimum if not eliminated altogether.

There is a trade-off, however. High-fidelity video is often criticized for its sharpness and "in-your-face" quality by film people, who lament the lack of the softer "film look." Similarly, digital music recordings sometimes sound so crisp and clean that they lack the warmth and the texture of the original piece—or even of an analog recording. You may remember the monotone sounds of synthesized computer speech; it was missing all the complexity and subtleties (overtones) of actual speech. Audio professionals are using higher sampling rates and more-complex digital signal combinations to make up for this deficiency. Paradoxically, video filters are available to make HDTV pictures less high-definition, and in digital audio a certain amount of noise is reintroduced to contribute to the "warmth" of sound.

COMPUTER COMPATIBILITY AND FLEXIBILITY

Another big advantage of digital television is that its signals can be transferred directly from the camera to the computer without the need for digitization. The elimination of this step is especially welcome to news departments, whose members work under tight deadlines. It is also a great relief to postproduction editors, who can now devote more time to the art of editing rather than sitting idle during the digitizing process.

The flexibility of the digital signal is especially important for creating special effects and computer-generated images. Even a simple weathercast or a five-minute newscast features a dazzling display of digital effects that was all but impossible with analog equipment. The opening animated title, the scene that expands full-screen from the box over the newscaster's shoulder, and the graphical transition from one story to the next where one picture peels off to reveal another underneath—all show the variety and the flexibility of digital effects. The multiple screens-within-the-screen and the various lines of text that run along the bottom, sides, or top of the main television screen are possible only through digital video effects (DVE). Computer software that allows the alteration or even the synthetic creation of audio and video images has become an essential digital production tool.

SIGNAL TRANSPORT

Digital signals can be distributed through a variety of wires (coaxial and fiber-optic cables) or wirelessly (through a broadband router or via wireless fidelity, or WiFi). If you get impatient while waiting for a large computer file to up- or download, think about the incredible amount of data that needs to be pushed through the conduit you are using. A download speed of only 1 megabyte per second (MBps) means the computer is processing well over 8 million on/off choices (8,388,608 bits) per second.

There is often confusion about the difference between downloading and data streaming. When you are ***downloading***, you are receiving data that are sent in packets. Because these data packets are usually sent out of order to make full use of the available transmission line, you cannot call up the entire file until the downloading process is complete. With ***streaming***, you receive digital audio and/or video data as a continuous data flow. Because the data stream is continuous and not converted into out-of-order packets, you can listen to the music or watch the initial video frames while the files for the subsequent frames are still being transferred.

But even broadband (multichannel) and Ethernet (single-channel) coaxial conduits lack the capacity to stream fast enough the huge amount of data of high-definition television, and, even more so, interactive digital television. This is where compression comes in.

COMPRESSION

Compression is the temporary rearrangement or elimination of redundant information for easier storage and signal transmission. Remember the interlaced scanning process? Cutting each picture (frame) into two incomplete halves (fields) is done because half of a picture can be transported more easily than a whole one. Technically, a field takes up less bandwidth (data transmission capacity) than a frame. This is a crude but ingenious way of compressing an otherwise untouchable analog signal for quicker transport.

Fortunately, digital signals are much more flexible in this respect and can be compressed in many different ways, called ***codecs*** (an acronym of *compression/decompression*). One such system does it by regrouping the original data without throwing any away. Once at the destination, the data can be restored to their original positions—a process called ***decoding***—for an output that is identical to the original input. We do this frequently when "zipping" (on a Windows PC) or "stuffing" (on a Mac) large computer texts for storage and transmission and then "unzipping" them when opening the file. Or you can simply delete all data that are redundant.

Compression that results from rearranging or re-packaging data is called lossless—the regenerated image has the same number of pixels and values as the original. When some pixels are eliminated in some frames because they are redundant or beyond our ordinary perception, the compression is called lossy. Even if the lost pixels are not essential for the image creation, the regenerated image is nevertheless different from the original. The obvious advantage of lossless compression is that the original image is returned without diminished quality. The disadvantage is that it takes more storage space and usually takes more time to transport and bring back from storage. Most image compression techniques are therefore the lossy kind.

One of the most widely used digital compression standards for still images is JPEG ("jay-peg"), named for the organization that developed the system—the Joint Photographic Experts Group; motion-JPEG is for moving computer images. Although a lossless JPEG technique exists, to save storage space most JPEG compressions are lossy. Another compression standard for high-quality video is MPEG-2 ("em-peg two"), named and developed by the Moving Picture Experts Group. MPEG-2 is also a lossy compression technique, based on the elimination of redundant information. MPEG-4 and MPEG-7 differ from MPEG-2 in that they are intended more as standardized systems for streaming data. (See chapter 12 for more on MPEG formats).

ASPECT RATIO

One of the most visible differences between traditional (analog) and digital television systems is the horizontally stretched television picture of HDTV. The new television ***aspect ratio***—the width-to-height proportions of the screen—resembles more a small motion picture screen than the traditional television screen. Aspect ratios are covered more thoroughly in chapter 7, but we'll take a brief look here at the main characteristics of the two principal aspect ratios.

4 × 3 ASPECT RATIO

Dating back to the earliest motion picture screens, the aspect ratio of the traditional television screen and of computer screens is 4 × 3, which means that its frame is 4 units wide by 3 units high, regardless of whether the units are inches or feet. This aspect ratio is also expressed as 1.33:1. For every unit in screen height, there are 1.33 units in width. **SEE 4.8**

The advantage of this classic aspect ratio is that the difference between the screen width and the screen height is

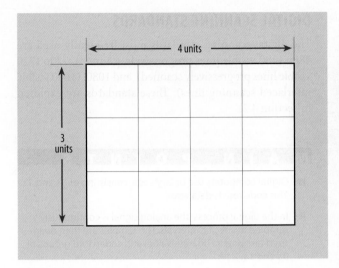

4.8 4 × 3 ASPECT RATIO

The traditional aspect ratio of the television screen is 4 × 3 (4 units wide by 3 units high). It can also be expressed as 1.33:1 (1.33 units in width for each unit of height).

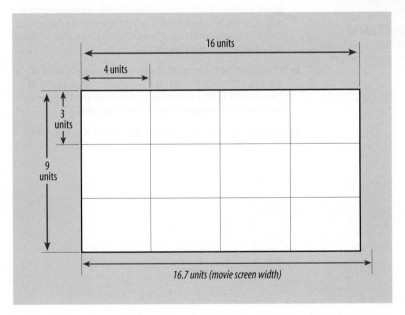

4.9 16 × 9 ASPECT RATIO

The aspect ratio of HDTV is 16 × 9 (16 units wide by 9 units high), which is a multiple of the 4 × 3 ratio ($4^2 × 3^2$). Its horizontally stretched aspect ratio of 1.78:1 resembles that of the movie screen (1.85:1).

not pronounced enough to unduly emphasize one dimension over the other. A close-up or an extreme close-up of a face fits well in this aspect ratio as does a horizontally stretched landscape.[2] The disadvantage is that it does not accommodate wide-screen movies that have the much more horizontally stretched aspect ratio of 1.85:1.

---

2. See Herbert Zettl, *Sight Sound Motion: Applied Media Aesthetics,* 5th ed. (Belmont, Calif.: Thomson Wadsworth, 2008), pp. 81–91.

16 × 9 ASPECT RATIO

The horizontally stretched aspect ratio of HDTV systems is 16 × 9; that is, the screen is 16 units wide by 9 units high, or 1.78:1. As you can see, this aspect ratio resembles that of a movie screen. **SEE 4.9**

MOBILE MULTIMEDIA ASPECT RATIOS

The small screens of mobile multimedia, such as cell phones, iPhones, and iPods, vary from the traditional 4 × 3 format to square and even vertical. **SEE 4.10**

4.10 MOBILE MULTIMEDIA ASPECT RATIO

This cell phone has a vertical aspect ratio, which can be masked when showing television shows or film.

DIGITAL SCANNING STANDARDS

The digital scanning standards most frequently used are 480p (480 visible lines progressively scanned), 720p (720 visible lines progressively scanned), and 1080i (1080 visible interlaced scanning lines). These standards are explored in section 4.2.

MAIN POINTS

▶ Digital computers use binary code, consisting of 0's and 1's. This code resists data error.

▶ In the digital process, the analog signal is continuously sampled at specific intervals. The samples are then quantized (assigned a discrete value) and coded into groups of 0's and 1's.

▶ Digital television produces pictures and sound of superior quality, allows many copies with virtually no signal deterioration, provides great flexibility in image manipulation and creation, and permits data compression codecs for efficient signal transport and storage.

▶ Compared with the traditional television aspect ratio of 4×3 (1.33:1), HDTV systems have a wider aspect ratio of 16×9 (1.78:1). The screens of mobile multimedia have a variety of horizontal and vertical aspect ratios.

▶ The digital scanning standards are 480p, 720p, and 1080i.

SECTION

4.2

Scanning Systems

This section takes a closer look at how the basic color video image is created, interlaced and progressive scanning, major digital scanning systems, and flat-panel displays.

▶ **BASIC IMAGE CREATION**
The travel of the electron beam forming the television image and basic colors

▶ **BASIC COLORS OF THE VIDEO DISPLAY**
Red, green, and blue as the primary colors

▶ **INTERLACED AND PROGRESSIVE SCANNING**
Interlaced scanning, progressive scanning, and retrace and blanking

▶ **DIGITAL SCANNING SYSTEMS**
The 480p, 720p, and 1080i systems

▶ **FLAT-PANEL DISPLAYS**
Plasma display panels and liquid crystal displays

BASIC IMAGE CREATION

To demonstrate how the basic video image is created in a television camera, we will put the cart before the horse and show how the video image is re-created on the CRT (cathode ray tube) of a standard (old-fashioned) television set during playback.

The video image is literally drawn onto the television screen by an electronic pencil—the electron beam. Emitted by the electron gun, the electron beam scans the inside surface of the television screen line by line, from left to right, much as we read. The inside of the television screen is dotted with thousands of light-sensitive picture elements, or pixels (round dots, tiny rectangles, or diamond-shaped), that light up when hit by the beam. If the beam is powerful, the dots light up brightly. If the beam is weaker, the dots light up only partially. If the beam is really weak, the dots don't light up at all. The process is similar to the large displays that use light bulbs for outdoor advertising, except that the light bulbs on the television screen are extremely tiny. **SEE 4.11**

BASIC COLORS OF THE VIDEO DISPLAY

All the beautiful images that you see on television—even the black-and-white pictures—are a mixture of three basic colors: red, green, and blue. Depending on how hard the pixels are hit by an electron beam, they light up at different intensities. Mixing these intensities produces all the other colors. Each line consists of groups of *RGB* (red, green, and blue) pixels. But how can a single electron beam hit each RGB group (the three dots that are grouped together) with various intensities? It can't. There must be a separate electron beam for each basic color: one for the red dots, a second for the green dots, and a third for the blue ones. Each electron beam hits its assigned color with various intensities, producing the different color mixes. Just how these three colors create all the others is explored in chapter 5. **SEE 4.12**

4.11 SCANNING PRINCIPLE
The electron gun in the back of the picture tube produces an electron beam that scans the many light-sensitive pixels (picture elements) located on the inside of the tube's face.

65

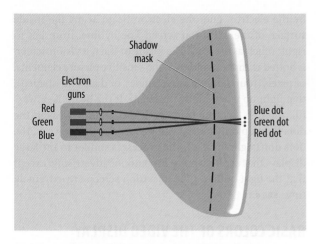

4.12 IMAGE FORMATION FOR COLOR TELEVISION
The color receiver has three electron guns, each responsible
for either a red, a green, or a blue signal. Each of the beams is
assigned to its color dots or rectangles. The shadow mask keeps
the beams from spilling into the adjacent dots.

INTERLACED AND PROGRESSIVE SCANNING

There are basically two ways of creating a video image: one
is through interlaced scanning, and the other is through
progressive scanning.

INTERLACED SCANNING

To produce an image through *interlaced scanning*, the
electron beam scans the odd-numbered lines first; then
it jumps back to the top of the screen and scans the even-
numbered lines. The complete scan of all odd-numbered
or even-numbered lines, which takes ¹⁄₆₀ second, is called a
field. A complete scan of all odd- *and* even-numbered lines
is called a *frame*. In the traditional NTSC system, there are
30 frames per second. The two fields are combined—interlaced—for each frame. In effect, interlaced scanning
combines low-quality pictures to make a higher-quality
one. Because the beam is such a speed-reader and lights
up the pixels at a pretty fast clip, we perceive the two scans
as a complete video image. **SEE 4.13**

PROGRESSIVE SCANNING

The *progressive scanning* system scans every line from top
to bottom just as we read. A single scan produces a complete frame. The electron beam in the progressive system
starts at the top left of the screen and scans the first line,
then jumps back to the left at the start of the second line,
scans the second line, jumps back to the third line, scans the
third line, and so on. As soon as the scanning of a frame is
complete, the beam jumps back to its original starting point

at the top left of the screen and starts scanning the second
frame, and so forth. As you can see, the beam scans all lines
progressively, hence the name of the system. **SEE 4.14**

In the progressive system, the *refresh rate*—how often
the beam jumps back to scan another frame—is usually 60
frames per second, but can be higher or lower.

RETRACE AND BLANKING

Both the interlaced and the progressive scanning systems
use retrace and blanking. The repositioning of the beam
from the end of the scanned line to the starting point of the
next is called horizontal retrace. When the beam reaches
the end of the last line and jumps back to the starting point
of line 1, it is referred to as vertical retrace. To avoid any
picture interference during the horizontal and vertical retraces, the beam is automatically "starved" so that it won't
light up any pixels that might interfere with the original
scan; this process is called blanking. Hence, horizontal
blanking occurs during the horizontal retrace, and vertical
blanking is during the vertical retrace. Let's apply the two
scanning systems to DTV and see how they fare.

DIGITAL SCANNING SYSTEMS

After years of wrangling over the former ATV (advanced
television) and DTV (digital television) scanning standards, the industry seems to have settled on three systems:
480p, 720p, and 1080i.

480P SYSTEM

The *480p* system uses 480 active lines that are scanned
progressively every ¹⁄₆₀ second. Let's take a closer look at
these numbers. As you can see, the 480p system has the
same number of scanning lines as does standard television,
but because the beam in progressive scanning reads all the
lines before it jumps back to begin reading the next screen,
progressive scanning generates a complete frame in each
scanning cycle. Instead of the 60 fields, or 30 frames, per
second of standard television, the 480p system generates
60 complete frames per second. The main reason for the
higher refresh rate of this and all other progressive scanning systems is to improve picture definition and avoid
noticeable flicker.

720P SYSTEM

Both the 720 visible, or active, lines (of 750 actual scanning lines) that are scanned progressively in the *720p*
system and its refresh rate of 60 (all lines are scanned every
¹⁄₆₀ second) contribute to true high-definition television
images. This means that the pictures have superior resolution and color fidelity.

4.13 INTERLACED SCANNING

A The electron beam first scans all odd-numbered lines, from left to right and from top to bottom. This first scanning cycle produces the first field.

B The electron beam jumps back to the top and scans all even-numbered lines. This second scanning cycle produces the second field.

C The two fields make up a complete television picture, called a frame.

4.14 PROGRESSIVE SCANNING
In progressive scanning, the beam reads every line from top to bottom. Each complete scan produces a television frame. Retrace lines (shown as dashed in the figure) are blanked so that they don't appear on-screen.

1080I SYSTEM

The *1080i* system (1,080 visible lines of 1,125 total lines) uses interlaced scanning. Much like with standard NTSC scanning, each field of 540 visible lines is scanned every $\frac{1}{60}$ second, producing 30 frames per second. The high number of scanning lines of the 1080i system dramatically improves the resolution of the television picture—at the cost of requiring a large bandwidth for signal transport. But in the end, it depends on how much of the original picture quality is maintained during the entire production process and, especially, during signal transmission.

The problem with all these scanning standards is that what you get is not necessarily what you see. Because the signals are digital, the digital display (what the television receiver shows) does not have to mirror exactly what is being sent. For example, a DTV receiver may receive an interlaced frame but show it as a progressive scan. It can also show the frames at a different refresh rate from what was delivered to the set.

To make things even more complicated, each of the scanning formats (480p, 720p, and 1080i) can have a variety of refresh rates. You may, for example, assign an HDTV camera to shoot at a frame rate of 24p (24 frames per second) but send it as a 60i (60 fields, or 30 frames per second) sequence. To fool you into an even higher resolution, the receiver may decide to double the refresh rate and show the sequence at 60 frames instead of 60 fields per second. It all boils down to giving you as sharp a picture as possible without taking up too much transmission space and time to deliver it.

Regardless of the relative picture quality of the three standards, like any other system all are ultimately dependent on the program content. A bad program remains bad even when received in digital HDTV; a good program is good even if the picture quality is slightly inferior. Note, however, that picture quality becomes a real issue when using an HDTV system for instructional or training purposes, such as medical programs, and, not too surprisingly, commercials.

FLAT-PANEL DISPLAYS

Because there is a limit to the size of the cathode ray tube of the traditional television receiver, the industry has turned to flat-panel displays, such as the one on a laptop computer. The advantage of flat-panel displays over regular television receivers is that flat panels can be made very large without getting thicker or losing their resolution. In fact, a flat-panel display resembles a large painting with a modest frame. Even large flat panels can be hung on a wall like a painting.

As always with video technology, there are two different, incompatible types of flat-panel displays that can reproduce high-definition video images: the plasma display and the liquid crystal display.

PLASMA DISPLAY PANEL

The plasma display panel (PDP) uses two transparent (usually glass) wired panels that sandwich a thin layer of gas. When the gas receives the voltages of the video signal, it activates the RGB pixels that are arranged very much like those of the standard television receiver.

The advantages of a plasma display are that is has an excellent contrast ratio (more than 1,000:1, which means the brightest picture spot can be at least a thousand times brighter than the darkest spot) and superior color renditions. And you can watch a plasma screen even when standing way to the side without any color or contrast deterioration. The plasma screen shows little or no lag when quick motion is displayed.

One of the disadvantages of a plasma screen is that still pictures have a tendency to "burn in" when left on the screen too long. This means that the static image will remain on the screen as a faint image ("burn" or "ghost") even when other images are displayed. Depending on the manufacturer, some burn in relatively quickly (in less than an hour); others take several hours. If left on even longer, such a burn becomes permanent—in effect ruining the display. To ensure that a plasma panel maintains its quality, a static image should not be left on-screen for more than 15 minutes. Over time the pixels will not light up as brightly as before, which will cause the whole display to look dimmer. You can prevent this premature aging by not setting the brightness and contrast levels too high and by turning off the set when not in use.

LIQUID CRYSTAL DISPLAY

The liquid crystal display (LCD) panels also use two transparent sheets, but instead of gas the panels sandwich a liquid whose crystal molecules change when an electric current is applied. Depending on the electric charge, the crystals either block the light shining through the glass or let certain colors shine through. Laptop computers, digital clocks, telephones, and many other consumer electronics use an LCD.

The advantages of LCD panels are that the display is very bright, they do not deteriorate as fast as plasma screens, they do not burn in, and they are more economical than plasma screens in power consumption. If you look really closely, you may see that LCDs have a slightly sharper image than plasma screens of the same size.

A disadvantage is a limited viewing angle: you cannot stand or sit too far to the side of the panel or tilt it back too far without having the dark areas of the picture appear somewhat washed out. Other minor disadvantages are that very-fast-moving objects seem slightly blurred (aesthetically not really a disadvantage) and that, at least technically, the colors are not quite as subtle and accurate as in a plasma display.

Despite the slight differences between the two display systems, both are capable of producing stunning high-definition pictures.

MAIN POINTS

▶ To create a video image on a television set, the electron beam scans the color pixels on the inside of the CRT (cathode ray tube). The harder the pixels are hit, the brighter they light up.

▶ The basic colors used in television are red, green, and blue (RGB). Each of the 480 visible lines on the face of the display tube consists of groups of red, green, and blue pixels (very tiny round, rectangular, or diamond-shaped dots). Three electron beams activate these dots—one beam for the red pixels, one for the green, and one for the blue. The varying intensities of the three beams produce the colors we see on television.

▶ With interlaced scanning, the beam skips every other line during its first scan, reading only the odd-numbered lines. After the beam has scanned half of the last odd-numbered line, it jumps back to the top of the screen and finishes the unscanned half of the top line and continues to scan all the even-numbered lines. Each such even- or odd-numbered scan produces a field. Two fields produce a complete video frame.

▶ In the progressive scanning system, the electron beam scans each line, starting with line 1, then line 2, then line 3, and so on. When all lines have been scanned, the beam jumps back to its starting point to repeat the sequential scanning of all lines. Each scan of all lines results in a video frame.

▶ During the horizontal and vertical retraces, the beam is "starved" so that it will not activate the pixels and thus interfere with the clarity of the picture.

▶ The most common refresh rate of the 480p and 720p systems is 60 frames per second, whereas for the 1080i system it is 30 frames per second. Many high-definition television (HDTV) systems have a variable frame rate.

▶ Digital television (DTV) employs three principal scanning formats: the 480p (480 lines progressively scanned), the 720p (720 lines progressively scanned), and the 1080i (1,080 lines with interlaced scanning). All have a 16×9 aspect ratio but can be switched to the traditional 4×3 aspect ratio.

▶ The two flat-panel video displays are the plasma display panel (PDP), which sandwiches gas between two transparent panels, and the liquid crystal display (LCD), which sandwiches a liquid between two transparent panels.

▶ The PDP activates RGB (red, green, and blue) dots; the LCD activates a number of tiny transistors that let light shine through according to the charge they receive.

5

The Television Camera

The television camera is still the single most important piece of production equipment. In fact, you can produce and show an impressive short video piece solely with a camcorder that is small enough to fit in your shirt pocket. Almost all other production equipment and techniques revolve around the camera or are greatly influenced by its technical and performance characteristics.

For example, to develop the ubiquitous camcorder, the video recorder had to be made so small that it would fit inside a camera. Because all video cameras and camcorders have become more light sensitive, we can now get by with fewer and smaller studio and field lighting instruments. The studio lights are suspended from the ceiling to facilitate the unrestricted travel of cameras during a multicamera show. Microphones are now so small that they are hardly visible when clipped on people's clothing. Scenery must now be constructed with more care and show more detail because high-definition (HD) cameras deliver a sharper picture than their **standard television (STV)** cousins.

To maximize the full potential of the camera, you need to know how it works.

Section 5.1, How Television Cameras Work, identifies the parts, types, and electronic and operational features of cameras. Section 5.2, Resolution, Contrast, and Color, elaborates on image resolution, image contrast, and the basics of color.

beam splitter Compact internal optical system of prisms within a television camera that separates white light into the three primary colors: red, green, and blue (RGB). Also called *prism block.*

brightness The color attribute that determines how dark or light a color appears on the monochrome television screen or how much light the color reflects. Also called *lightness* and *luminance.*

camcorder A portable camera with the videotape recorder or some other recording device built into it to form a single unit.

camera chain The television camera (head) and associated electronic equipment, including the camera control unit, sync generator, and power supply.

camera control unit (CCU) Equipment, separate from the camera head, that contains various video controls, including color fidelity, color balance, contrast, and brightness. The CCU enables the video operator to adjust the camera picture during a show.

charge-coupled device (CCD) The imaging sensor in a television camera. It consists of horizontal and vertical rows of tiny image-sensing elements, called *pixels,* that translate the optical (light) image into an electric charge that eventually becomes the video signal.

CMOS A camera imaging sensor similar to a CCD but which operates on a different technology. It translates light into an electronic video charge that eventually becomes the video signal.

contrast ratio The difference between the brightest and the darkest portions in the picture (often measured by reflected light in foot-candles). The contrast ratio for low-end cameras and camcorders is normally 50:1, which means that the brightest spot in the picture should be no more than 50 times brighter than the darkest portion without causing loss of detail in the dark or light areas. High-end digital cameras can greatly exceed this ratio and can tolerate a contrast ratio of 1,000:1 or more.

digital cinema camera A high-definition television camera that has a native frame rate of 24 frames per second and a variable frame rate for slow and accelerated motion. Most digital cinema cameras use high-quality CCDs or CMOS sensors, state-of-the-art lenses, and high-definition viewfinders.

EFP camera High-quality portable, shoulder-mounted field production camera that must be connected to an external video recorder.

ENG/EFP camcorder High-quality portable field production camera with the recording device built-in.

high-definition television (HDTV) camera Video camera that delivers pictures of superior resolution, color fidelity, and light-and-dark contrast; uses high-quality imaging sensors and lenses.

high-definition video (HDV) A recording system that produces images of the same resolution as high-definition television (720p and 1080i) with equipment that is similar to standard digital video camcorders. The video signals are much more compressed than those of HDTV, however, which results in lower overall video quality.

hue One of the three basic color attributes; hue is the color itself—red, green, yellow, and so on.

imaging device The imaging element in a television camera. Its sensor (CCD or CMOS) transduces light into electric energy that becomes the video signal. Also called *camera pickup device, chip,* and *sensor.*

pixel Short for *pic*ture *el*ement. (1) A single imaging element (like the single dot in a newspaper picture) that can be identified by a computer. The more pixels per picture area, the higher the picture quality. (2) The light-sensitive elements on a CCD that contain a charge.

resolution The measurement of picture detail, expressed in the number of pixels per scanning line and the number of visible scanning lines. Resolution is influenced by the imaging device, the lens, and the television set that shows the camera picture. Often used synonymously with *definition.*

saturation The color attribute that describes a color's richness or strength.

sensor The CCD or CMOS imaging device in a video camera.

standard television (STV) A system based on the NTSC scanning system of 525 (480 visible) interlaced lines.

studio camera High-quality camera with a large zoom lens that cannot be maneuvered properly without the aid of a pedestal or some other camera mount.

sync generator Part of the camera chain; produces an electronic synchronization signal.

white balance The adjustments of the color circuits in the camera to produce a white color in lighting of various color temperatures (relative reddishness or bluishness of white light).

5.1

How Television Cameras Work

Although the electronics of the television camera have become increasingly complex, the cameras have also become more user-friendly. As you probably know from operating your own camcorder, you don't have to be a skilled electronics engineer to produce an optimal image—all you need to do is press the right buttons. Nevertheless, pressing the right buttons implies that you know how a television camera basically works. This section will help you maximize the potential of the camera and understand the specific functions of various camera types.

▶ **PARTS OF THE CAMERA**
The lens, the camera itself, and the viewfinder

▶ **FROM LIGHT TO VIDEO SIGNAL**
Imaging device, beam splitter, and color filter array

▶ **CAMERA CHAIN**
Camera control unit, sync generator, and power supply

▶ **TYPES OF CAMERAS**
Studio cameras, EFP cameras, ENG/EFP camcorders, and digital cinema

▶ **ELECTRONIC FEATURES**
Imaging device, scanning, resolution, aspect ratio and essential area, gain, electronic shutter, white balance, and audio channels

▶ **OPERATIONAL FEATURES**
Power supply, camera cables and connectors, filter wheel, viewfinder, tally light, and intercom

PARTS OF THE CAMERA

When you take vacation pictures with your camcorder, probably the last thing on your mind is what makes a video camera work. But if you were to open up a camera (not recommended) and see the myriad electronic elements and circuits, you would probably wonder how it functions at all. Despite their electronic complexity, all television cameras (including consumer video cameras) consist of three main parts.

The first is the lens, which selects a certain field of view and produces a small optical image of it. The second part is the camera itself, with its imaging device that converts into electrical signals the optical image as delivered by the lens. The third is the viewfinder, which shows a small video image of what the lens is seeing. Some cameras have an additional foldout screen that enables you to forgo looking through an eyepiece to see the camera picture.

SEE 5.1 **ZVL1** CAMERA→ Camera introduction

FROM LIGHT TO VIDEO SIGNAL

All television cameras, big or small, work on the same basic principle: the conversion of an optical image into electrical signals that are reconverted by the viewfinder and the television set into visible screen images. **SEE 5.2**

Specifically, the light that is reflected off of an object is gathered by a lens and focused on the imaging device. The imaging device is the principal camera element that transduces (converts) the light into an electric charge, which, when amplified and processed, becomes the video signal. The television set uses this signal to produce the images you see on your set. With these basic camera functions in mind, we can examine the major elements and the processes involved in the transformation of light images into color television images. Specifically, we look at the imaging device, the beam splitter, and the color filter array.

IMAGING DEVICE

The principal electronic component that converts light into electricity is called the *imaging device* (also called pickup device and *sensor*). In tech lingo it is commonly known as the chip. There are two types of sensors in use: a *charge-coupled device (CCD)* and a *CMOS* (complementary metal-oxide semiconductor). Although technically differ-

5.1 PARTS OF THE CAMERA
The main parts of a television (video) camera are the lens, the camera itself with the imaging device, and the viewfinder.

5.2 BASIC CAMERA FUNCTIONS: LIGHT TO VIDEO SIGNAL
The light reflected off of the object is gathered by the lens and focused on the beam splitter, which splits the white light of the image into red, green, and blue pictures. These beams are directed toward their respective sensors (CCD or CMOS), which transform the RGB light into electrical RGB charges; these are amplified, processed, and then reconverted by the viewfinder into video pictures.

ent, they look alike and perform the same function: both convert the optical image into electrical impulses. **SEE 5.3**

Both the CCD and the CMOS contain hundreds of thousands or, for a high-quality chip, millions of image-sensing elements, called *pixels* (a compound of *pix*, for picture, and *els* for elements) that are arranged in horizontal and vertical rows. Each pixel is a discrete image element that transforms its color and brightness information into a specific electric charge. In digital cameras each pixel has a unique computer address. The electric charges from all of the pixels eventually become the video signal.

Pixels function very much like tiles that compose a complete mosaic image. A certain number of such elements is needed to produce a recognizable image. If there are

5.3 CHARGE-COUPLED DEVICE
The CCD sensor holds many rows of thousands of pixels, each of which transforms light that enters through the window into an electric charge. The CMOS sensor looks similar but works on a different electronic principle.

5.4 PIXELIZED SUBJECT

Pixels function much like tiles that make up a complete mosaic image. An image comprising relatively few mosaic tiles—pixels—contains little detail. The more and the smaller the tiles, the sharper the image will be.

relatively few mosaic tiles, the object may be recognizable but the picture will contain no detail. **SEE 5.4** The more and the smaller the tiles in the mosaic, the more detail the picture will have. The same is true for the sensor: the more pixels it contains, the higher the resolution of the video image. Larger sensors can contain more pixels and therefore produce a sharper image than small ones. This is not unlike the negative of a photo. The larger the negative, the sharper the printed image.

BEAM SPLITTER AND COLOR FILTER ARRAY

Before the pixels on the sensors can do their translating from light to electricity, the light image coming through the lens must be split into the three primary colors of light—red, green, and blue. This color separation is done by the beam splitter or the color filter array.

The ***beam splitter*** contains prisms that divide the light coming from the lens into the three primary light beams—red, green, and blue, usually referred to as RGB. The prisms guide the three colored beams into their designated sensors, which are attached to the prisms. High-end "prosumer" and professional cameras and camcorders normally use three sensors (CCDs or CMOS)—one for each primary light color. The three primary colors are then electronically "mixed" into the many colors you see on the television screen. Because these prisms are contained in a small block, the beam splitter is often called the prism block. **SEE 5.5**

Most small consumer camcorders and, paradoxically, some very-high-end high-definition television (HDTV) and digital cinema cameras don't have a prism block because they use only a single sensor as an imaging device. The splitting of the colors of the optical lens image into RGB is done by a single filter array that is attached to the sensor. **SEE 5.6**

CAMERA CHAIN

When looking at a high-quality studio camera, you can see that its cable is plugged into a dedicated outlet. This cable connects the camera to a chain of equipment necessary to produce pictures. The major parts of the ***camera chain*** are the actual camera, called the camera head because it is at the head of the chain; the camera control unit; the sync generator, which provides the synchronization pulses to keep the scanning of the various pieces of television equipment in step; and the power supply. **SEE 5.7**

5.5 BEAM SPLITTER

The beam splitter, or prism block, splits the incoming white light (representing the picture as seen by the lens) into RGB (red, green, and blue) light beams and directs them to their respective sensors (CCDs or CMOS).

5.6 STRIPED AND MOSAIC FILTERS
Cameras with only one image sensor use a striped or mosaic-like filter instead of a prism block to divide the white light into RGB color beams. Each colored beam is then transduced by the single sensor into electric charges that eventually become the RGB signals.

Striped RGB filter   Mosaic RGB filter

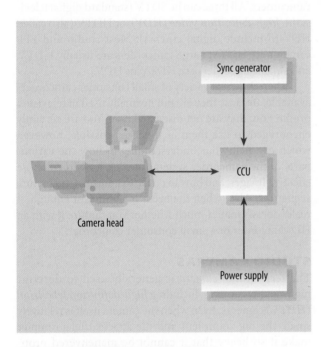

5.7 STANDARD STUDIO CAMERA CHAIN

The standard camera chain consists of the camera head (the actual camera), the camera control unit (CCU), the sync generator, and the power supply. Portable cameras contain all these functions in the camera housing.

CAMERA CONTROL UNIT

Each studio camera has its own *camera control unit (CCU)*. The CCU performs two main functions: setup and control. During setup each camera is adjusted for the correct color rendition, the white balance (manipulating the three color signals so that they reproduce white correctly

under a variety of lighting conditions), the proper contrast range between the brightest and the darkest areas of a scene, and the brightness steps within that range.

Assuming that the cameras are set up properly and have fair stability (which means that they retain their setup values), the video operator (VO) usually need control only "master black" or "pedestal" (adjusting the camera for the darkest part of the scene) and the "white level" (adjusting the iris of the lens so that it will permit only the desired amount of light to reach the imaging device). **SEE 5.8**

Portable CCUs, usually called RCUs (remote control units), can be connected to cameras operating in the field (remote location). In critical field productions, RCUs allow the video operator to "shade" the pictures (maintain optimal picture quality) according not only to technical standards but also to the aesthetic requirements of the production.

SYNC GENERATOR AND POWER SUPPLY

The *sync generator* produces electronic synchronization pulses—sync pulses—that keep in step the scanning of the various pieces of equipment (cameras, monitors, and video recorders). A genlock provides a general synchronization pulse, called house sync. Through the genlocking process, the scanning of video signals of a variety of equipment is perfectly synchronized, allowing you to switch among and intermix the video signals of various cameras and/or video recorders (VRs) without the need for additional digital equipment.

The power supply generates the electricity that drives the camera. In a studio the power supply converts AC (alternating current) to DC (direct current) power and feeds it to the cameras via the camera cable.

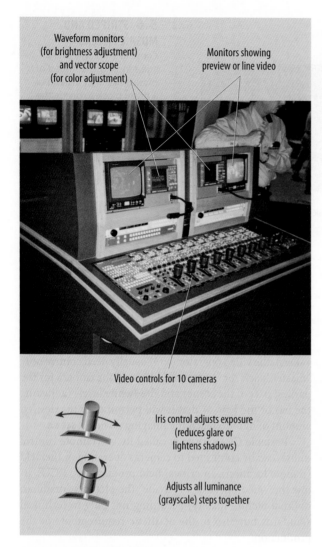

Waveform monitors
(for brightness adjustment)
and vector scope
(for color adjustment)

Monitors showing
preview or line video

Video controls for 10 cameras

Iris control adjusts exposure
(reduces glare or
lightens shadows)

Adjusts all luminance
(grayscale) steps together

5.8 CAMERA CONTROL UNIT

The CCU adjusts the camera for optimal color and brightness and for varying lighting conditions.

Field (ENG/EFP) cameras and **camcorders** are self-contained, which means that the camera itself holds all the elements of the chain to produce and deliver acceptable images to the video recorder. The only part of the camera chain that can be detached from the camera head (the actual camera or camcorder) is the power supply—the battery. All ENG/EFP cameras and camcorders have built-in control equipment that can execute the CCU functions automatically. But if an ENG/EFP camera or camcorder can have a built-in control that can perform all or most CCU functions, why bother with an external CCU? Because the automated controls cannot exercise aesthetic judgment; that is, they cannot adjust the camera to deliver pictures that also suit the artistic rather than the routine technical requirements.

TYPES OF CAMERAS

Television cameras are classified by the way they are used and by their electronic makeup. Some camera types are better suited for studio use, others for the coverage of a downtown fire or the production of a documentary on pollution, and still others for taking along on vacation to record the more memorable sights. When based on their primary function, there are three types: studio cameras, EFP (electronic field production) cameras, and ENG/EFP camcorders. All three can be SDTV (standard digital television), **high-definition video (HDV)**, or HDTV (also called HD—to include digital cinema). Most studio and EFP cameras are HDTV. Large camcorders are usually HDTV, and small camcorders are HDTV or HDV.

There is a great variety of small consumer camcorders available. Because they are not normally used in television production, they are not discussed here. You are certainly encouraged to use them as much as possible, however, which can help your understanding of how the various parts of the camcorder system interact, how to compose effective images, and how to construct meaningful picture sequences. Also, when the event is significant enough, it really doesn't matter much whether you capture it with an HD camcorder or a small consumer camcorder.

STUDIO CAMERAS

The term *studio camera* is generally used to describe high-quality cameras, including **high-definition television (HDTV)** cameras. Even when the camera itself is relatively small, the big zoom lens and the attached teleprompter make it so heavy that it cannot be maneuvered properly without the aid of a pedestal or some other camera mount. SEE 5.9

Studio cameras are used for multicamera studio productions, such as news, interviews, and panel shows, and for commercials, situation comedies, daily serial dramas, and instructional shows that require high-quality video. You can also see these cameras used in such "field" locations as tennis courts, medical facilities, concert and convention halls, and football and baseball stadiums.

Considering that you can get pretty good pictures from a camera that fits in your pocket, why bother with such heavy cameras and the rest of the camera chain? The

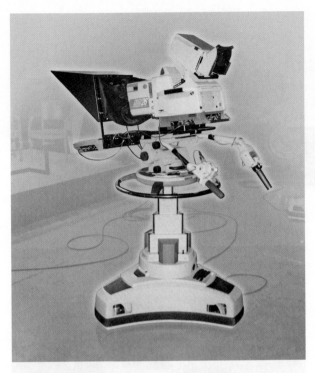

5.9 STUDIO CAMERA ON STUDIO PEDESTAL
Studio cameras have high-quality lenses and sensors. They are quality-controlled by the CCU. Studio cameras are too heavy to be carried and are mounted on a sturdy tripod or studio pedestal.

overriding criteria for the use of studio cameras are picture quality and control. We usually judge picture quality by the amount of sharp picture detail the camera and the monitor can generate, the fidelity of the colors, and the number of contrast steps from the darkest to the lightest picture area. The virtue of HDV and HDTV (480p, 720p, and 1080i) is that both systems can produce high-resolution pictures and a subtle color palette.

But *quality* is a relative term. In many productions the extra quality and control achieved with studio cameras is not worth the additional time and expense necessary for operating such equipment. For example, if you are to get a picture of an approaching tornado, you are probably not thinking about optimum picture quality. Your attention is on getting the shot and then getting out of harm's way as quickly as possible. But if picture quality is paramount, such as in the production of commercials, medical shows, and daytime serials, you would undoubtedly choose a high-end studio camera. Quality is usually a key factor when choosing a television camera for producing digital cinema.

Other factors that ensure quality are the lens, the zoom and focus controls, and the viewfinder.

Lens   The lens of the studio camera is usually larger (and often more expensive) than the ones used for ENG/EFP cameras and camcorders (see figure 5.9). The large studio lenses come with different zoom ranges (from the widest to the closest view). You can use a shorter range for studio work than for a sports pickup, where you might have to zoom in to a tight close-up of the quarterback's face with a camera located high in the stands. The quality of the lens, and especially its zoom range, are the major cost factors when buying a camcorder.

Digital cinema cameras sometimes use prime lenses, which deliver a slightly sharper picture than zoom lenses. You can't zoom with a prime lens because it has a fixed focal length. (Prime lenses are discussed in chapter 6.)

Zoom and focus controls   These controls are attached to the panning handles of the studio pedestal and are driven by a servo (motorized) system. Normally, the rocker-type zoom control is on the right handle and the twist control for the focus is on the left. (Various lenses and their controls are discussed in chapter 6.)

Viewfinder   When using a small camcorder, you've probably wished that you had a larger, more accurate viewfinder. Even fairly large foldout screens wash out in bright sunlight and make it hard to see whether you are in focus. When switching to the eyepiece viewfinder, everything looks awfully small. This is why studio cameras have a large (5- to 7-inch), high-resolution viewfinder that can be tilted and swiveled sideways. Some camera operators clamp an additional flat-panel viewfinder onto the camera, especially when they can't operate the camera from their shoulder.

EFP CAMERAS

The *EFP camera* is a portable, shoulder-mounted camera that must be connected to an external video recorder. Generally, EFP cameras are high-quality cameras that can be carried on the shoulder or put on a tripod. **SEE 5.10**

EFP cameras are almost never used for ENG (electronic news gathering) but rather for demanding documentary productions and outdoor scenes shot single-camera film-style (where all shots are intended for postproduction editing). Because of the high quality of most EFP cameras, they are often used in the studio instead of the more expensive studio cameras.

5.10 EFP CAMERA
The EFP camera is a high-quality camera that can be carried and handled by the operator. It can also be converted into a studio camera.

When used in the studio, the EFP camera is placed in a specially made camera frame, a large external tally light is added, and the small eyepiece viewfinder is replaced with a larger viewfinder attached to the camera housing. The zoom and focus controls are moved to the panning handles and connected to the lens via servo cables. The ENG/EFP lens is usually replaced with a zoom lens that is more suitable to the studio environment. The whole camera assembly is then mounted on a studio pedestal. In a studio configuration, the EFP camera is usually controlled via a CCU. **SEE 5.11**

ENG/EFP CAMCORDERS

ENG/EFP camcorders are high-quality portable field production cameras with the recording device built-in. There are basically two types: large, high-end HDTV camcorders and much smaller HD and HDV camcorders.

LARGE SDTV AND HD CAMCORDERS

The full-sized standard-definition television and high-definition digital camcorder looks much like its analog predecessor and is operated in much the same way. All large camcorders have high-quality, interchangeable zoom lenses, a high-quality imaging device with three large CCD or CMOS sensors in the megapixel range, a relatively large eyepiece viewfinder, and, on some models, an additional foldout flat-panel display. It has a high-quality videotape recorder (VTR) or a nontape recording device (hard drive, optical disc, or flash drive) built-in. **SEE 5.12**

SMALL HD AND HDV CAMCORDERS

Smaller ENG/EFP digital camcorders operate on the same basic principle as the digital consumer models. In fact, the

5.11 EFP CAMERA IN STUDIO CONFIGURATION
The same camera as in figure 5.10 is shown here in a studio configuration. It is placed in a housing and has a large studio lens, a 16 × 9 monitor, and external zoom and focus controls.

digital consumer models produced such high-quality video that their manufacturers upgraded them by adding a better lens, a higher-quality imaging device, and a few more video and audio controls. Because these smaller, lighter, and much less expensive models were used so frequently in professional ENG and EFP, they were called *prosumer* models (a compound of *pro*fessional and con*sumer*). Now that these smaller so-called prosumer camcorders can produce high-definition video, they are rapidly replacing the larger camcorders in news and documentary productions. The prosumer digital camcorder has finally shed its consumer stigma and become a professional workhorse.

Most good HDV camcorders contain a prism block with three CCDs or high-resolution CMOS sensors

5.12 ENG/EFP CAMCORDER
This high-quality HD camcorder has three HD CCDs and a built-in optical disc recorder.

5.13 SMALL HDV CAMCORDER
These high-end HDV camcorders are considerably smaller and lighter than standard camcorders yet they produce excellent high-definition images and sound. They record in 1080i and 720p formats at 60, 30, and 24 frames per second.

attached to it. Some have a large, single sensor that divides the light coming through the lens into RGB via a striped or mosaic RGB filter array (see figure 5.6). Most small HDTV and HDV camcorder use a high-definition VTR that records on ¼-inch full-sized or mini-cassettes just like the larger digital VTR camcorders. **SEE 5.13** The nontape HDV camcorders use flash drives (memory cards) or optical discs as recording media.[1]

Like a large HDTV camcorder, HDV camcorders can be switched between 720p (720 progressively scanned lines) and 1080i (1080 interlaced scanning lines) and various frame rates, usually 24, 30, and 60 frames per second. Does this mean that the HDV pictures look as good as the HDTV ones? Yes and no. Under normal circumstances, you will have a hard time seeing a big difference between the two, especially if the HDV images are displayed on a high-resolution monitor. Thanks to the unique signal processing of HDV, which detects and corrects possible video signal errors and artifacts, the HDV pictures look amazingly sharp.

Most HDV camcorders, however, have a built-in lens. There are adapters that allow you to attach a lens that gives you a wider view than the regular lens, but such an arrangement is less satisfactory during production than is the slightly less flexible built-in lens. Most Canon HDV camcorders come with interchangeable lenses.

---

1. Some ENG/EFP camcorders do not have a built-in video recorder but can be docked with one. The VR is simply plugged into the rear of the camera head.

The single factor that compromises the quality of the HDV picture the most is the system's compression. The higher the compression, the more the picture quality suffers. You notice the negative compression effects especially when the picture has fine detail, when there is a great deal of object and/or camera motion, and when you shoot a scene with high brightness contrast.

Nevertheless, you will find that in most situations a small HDV camera will produce stunning images that approach, or are virtually equal to, the quality of the much more expensive HDTV systems.

DIGITAL CINEMA
In the context of cameras, *digital cinema* means that you use a television camera or camcorder to make movies. Generally, high-end HD cameras with high-quality external video recorders or high-end HD (HDTV) camcorders are used for the acquisition of footage. When used for cinema, the television camera is modified to facilitate the specific requirements of the filmic production process. **SEE 5.14**

The HD *digital cinema cameras* have large, multimillion-pixel CCDs or CMOS sensors and generally operate in the 1080i or 1080p scanning mode. For digital cinema the native frame rate is usually the filmic standard of 24 frames per second (fps). Most camcorders used for electronic movie making have a variable frame rate and can be "overcranked" or "undercranked." Just like with an actual film camera, overcranking in HD cameras means that the scene

5.14 HD CAMCORDER USED FOR DIGITAL CINEMA

This high-end camcorder is designed to function as a digital cinema camera. It has three high-resolution CCDs and records video on an HD VTR in 1080i and 1080p at 60, 30, and 24 frames per second. Note the added high-resolution viewfinder and lens attachments standard for cinema cameras.

is recorded at a much higher-than-normal (24 fps) frame rate, which, when played back at the standard 24 fps speed, displays a slow-motion effect. Undercranking means that the acquisition of the video is much slower than 24 frames per second, which, when played back at the regular 24 fps speed, shows up as accelerated motion. These cameras also have a wide contrast ratio that can be adjusted for high- or low-contrast effects.

An important feature of the camera is its lenses, which are specially manufactured for HDTV cameras. Some cameras have provisions for attaching large studio zoom lenses or a variety of prime lenses, which are similar to the fixed-focal-length lenses used with a still camera. A fixed-focal-length lens will not allow you to zoom. Additional items that facilitate the use of HDTV cameras for film use are a matte box (a lens attachment for optical special effects) and a relatively large high-resolution monochrome viewfinder.

As mentioned in chapter 4, you may hear some committed film people complain about the "in-your-face" look of HDTV images and lament the loss of the mysterious "film look." The film look has been erroneously attributed to high-resolution images and is probably the result of the high contrast ratio and the blackouts that occur when one frame of the film changes over to the next. This constant

going-to-black between frames makes us perceive a softer image. To copy this blackout sensation, some digital cinema systems use filters to reintroduce a variety of artifacts that occur in older film prints. Unfortunately, all such attempts result in a lower-quality image but not in the softer frame-by-frame cushions. As with all art, however, it is not necessarily the equipment that makes a good film but ultimately your creative mind and skill. In fact, some remarkable movies have been made with a small SDTV camcorder.[2]

ELECTRONIC FEATURES

Some electronic video features are typically part of every professional camera or camcorder, including the imaging device, scanning, resolution, aspect ratio and essential area, gain, electronic shutter, and white balance. The audio features concern the number of channels (tracks) and the quality of the sound.

---

2. Some big-screen documentaries and major motion pictures have been shot with a small digital camcorder. For example, David Lynch shot almost all the footage for *Inland Empire* (2006) with a Sony DSR-PD 150 with most of the controls set on automatic. See Jon Silberg, "Inland Empire—David Lynch's DV Dream," *Digital Cinematography* 2, no. 6 (2006), 26–28.

IMAGING DEVICE

Most high-quality cameras and camcorders have three CCDs or CMOS sensors as the imaging device. As mentioned earlier, some camcorders and even some top digital cinema cameras have a single large sensor, but these are the exception.

SCANNING

When shooting in HDTV or HDV, you should be able to switch among the 480p, 720p, and 1080i scanning systems; 720p and 1080i are considered true high-definition.

RESOLUTION

Resolution refers to how sharp a picture looks. It is the measurement of picture detail—the number of distinguishable details. HDTV and HDV produce higher-resolution pictures than STV. Video resolution is determined by the number of scanning lines (vertical resolution) and by the number of pixels that make up each line (horizontal resolution). For example, a 720p video has 720 visible lines that are scanned progressively (one after the other), and each line is made up of 1,280 pixels. This obviously produces a sharper picture than the standard TV resolution of about 480 visible lines, each of which is made up of 640 pixels. (See section 5.2 for more on scanning and resolution.)

ASPECT RATIO AND ESSENTIAL AREA

All HDTV and HDV viewfinders have an aspect ratio of 16 × 9, which means they are 16 units wide by 9 units high. Most cameras that allow you to switch from 16 × 9 to a 4 × 3 aspect ratio have provisions to indicate in the viewfinder the 4 × 3 area. Most viewfinders of HDTV and HDV camcorders have markers to help you frame a shot, such as the safe title area (the area that will definitely show on a home television set), a center cross, and the 4 × 3 area within the 16 × 9 aspect ratio. Even without such markers, it is a good idea to keep the main event within the 4 × 3 area on a 16 × 9 screen. That way you don't lose the essential parts of the event when it is shown on a standard 4 × 3 monitor.

GAIN

When there is not enough light for the imaging device to produce optimal video, the gain comes to the rescue. It is an electric charge that tricks the sensors into believing that they are getting more light than they actually receive from the lens. The higher the gain, however, the lower the picture quality. Gain is measured in decibels (db). Most

Gain control switch

5.15 MANUAL GAIN CONTROL

The gain control compensates for low light levels. The higher the gain, the lower the light level can be. High gain causes video noise.

cameras can be switched from 0 dB (no gain) to 18 dB or more (high gain). **SEE 5.15**

ELECTRONIC SHUTTER

The electronic shutter in a television camera functions just like the mechanical one in an old still camera that uses actual film. The faster the object moves, the faster the shutter speed must be to avoid a blurred image. But instead of the highest shutter speed of about $\frac{1}{1,000}$ second in the mechanical shutter, the electronic shutter can go from $\frac{1}{8}$ second to $\frac{1}{10,000}$ second. The reason for the higher shutter speed is that the CCDs and the CMOS sensors take some time to get fully charged and therefore blur a fast-moving object unless the shutter speed is quite high. The downside, as with a regular still camera, is that the faster the shutter speed, the more light the camera requires. For example, if a bright yellow tennis ball moves from camera-left to camera-right at high speed and the camera is set at a slow shutter speed, it looks blurred and even leaves a trail. But when you increase the shutter speed so that the blur is virtually eliminated, the ball looks considerably darker.

WHITE BALANCE

To guarantee that a white object looks white under slightly reddish (candle or normal light bulb) or bluish (bright sunlight or fluorescent lamp) light, you need to tell the camera to compensate for the reddish or bluish light and to pretend that it is dealing with perfectly white light. This compensation in the camera is called *white balance*. When a camera engages in white-balancing, it adjusts the RGB video signals in such a way that the white object looks white on-screen regardless of whether it is illuminated by reddish or bluish light (see chapter 11).

AUDIO CHANNELS

Good digital cameras provide two audio channels for high-quality (16 bit/48 kHz [kilohertz]) sound, or four audio channels of lower-quality (12 bit/32 kHz) sound. Most digital cameras allow switching between the two quality standards.

OPERATIONAL FEATURES

At first glance, a camcorder with the fewest buttons and a large menu of available electronic functions on its foldout screen seems to be the most desirable—until you use it outdoors in bright sunlight. It is hard enough to dig for a specific menu item when it is buried under two or three layers of submenus; but when the sun washes out the screen display, you are in real trouble. This is why you still see some switches, buttons, and dials on the outside of the camcorder. Unfortunately, not all camcorders have the switches in convenient places. For example, you should be able to press the record button with the same hand that operates the zoom control; and the switch that puts the camera into manual or auto-focus should be near the manual focus ring on the lens. Experienced videographers usually prefer a camera that has the switches in the right place over one whose controls are buried in multi-tiered menus, even if the latter's video quality is slightly superior.

But there are a few more operational features of studio cameras and camcorders that need your attention: power supply, cables and connectors, filter wheel, viewfinder, tally light, and intercom.

POWER SUPPLY

When operating a studio camera, you don't have to worry about the power supply. The necessary electricity to power the camera is supplied by the camera cable. When using an EFP camera or camcorder in the field, however, the power supply becomes a major concern. All EFP cameras and camcorders use battery power. While we herald the progress in digital technology, we tend to overlook the equally dramatic development of the batteries that drive portable cameras and their associated equipment.

Most large camcorders are powered by a 12V (volt) DC battery; small camcorders use batteries that generate between 7V and 8V DC. Batteries can be clipped to the back of the camera or, in some cases, to the bottom. How long a battery lasts depends on how much recording you do and what else you are powering besides the camera/recording unit. For example, a battery will last longer if you refrain from powering with it such items as the camera light (the small light on top of the camera), the foldout flat-panel viewfinder, the steady-shot feature, the playback of the video recorder through the foldout screen, and the teleprompter.

Don't keep the camera turned on between takes; switch it to the standby mode as much as possible. This allows you to have everything up and running at the flip of a switch while preserving the battery between takes. (CMOS sensors, incidentally, draw much less power than the customary CCDs.) Always carry a fully charged spare battery with you, and exchange it a few minutes before the expiration of its life span as advertised by the manufacturer. The most reliable indicator of the remaining battery charge is the one in the camera viewfinder or menu.

Substitute power supplies are household AC current and car batteries, both of which require adapters. Use a car battery only in an emergency; car batteries are hazardous to the operator as well as to the equipment.

CABLES AND CONNECTORS

Camera cables and connectors differ significantly in how they carry electronic signals to and from the camera.

Cables   When requesting cable runs, you need to know which cable the camera can accept and, especially, how long a run you need.

Triaxial (triax) cables are thin and have one central wire surrounded by two concentric shields. Fiber-optic cables contain thin, flexible, glass strands and can transport a great amount of information over relatively long distances. A triax cable allows a maximum distance of almost 5,000 feet (about 1,500 meters); a fiber-optic cable can reach twice as far, to almost 2 miles (up to 3,000 meters).[3] Such a reach is adequate for most remote operations. Some cameras use a multicore cable, which contains a great number of thin wires. Multicore cables are relatively heavy and have a limited reach, but they are extremely reliable.

---

3. One meter (m) is a little more than 3 feet. More accurately, 1 meter = 3.28 feet. If, for example, you need a rough idea of how long a 1,000-meter cable run is in feet, multiply 1,000 by 3, which is approximately 3,000-plus feet. If you need an accurate foot reading, multiply 1,000 by 3.28, which comes to 3,280 feet.

Connectors Before going to the field location, carefully check that the connectors on the cables actually fit into the camera jacks (receptacles) and the jacks of the auxiliary equipment. Little is more annoying than having the whole production held up for an hour or more simply because a connector on a cable does not match the jack on the camera.

Short-run video connections are done with cables that use S-video, RCA phono, FireWire (IEEE 1394), and HDMI (high-definition multimedia interface) connectors; BNC connectors are for longer-run coaxial cables. All but S-VHS cables and connectors can also be used for audio signals. Professional audio cables, which are especially resistant to interference, use XLR connectors. Other audio cables may use ¼-inch phone plugs or mini plugs. Although there are adapters for all plugs (whereby you can change a BNC connector into an RCA phono plug, for example), avoid them when possible. Every adapter introduces a potential trouble spot. **SEE 5.16**

When in the studio, the camera cable is generally left plugged into the camera and the camera wall jack (outlet). When using studio or EFP cameras in the field, you need to carefully check whether the cable connectors fit the receptacles of the remote truck or the RCUs.

FILTER WHEEL
The filter wheel is located between the lens and the imaging device. It normally holds two or three neutral density (ND) filters (referred to as ND-1, ND-2, and ND-3) and two or more color-correction filters.

The ND filters function like good sunglasses: they reduce the amount of light transmitted to the imaging device without affecting the color of the scene too much. You use them for shooting in overly bright sunlight when the smallest aperture (highest f-stop) of the lens still lets too much light through or when the contrast is too high for the camera to handle.

The color-correction filters compensate for the relative bluishness of outdoor and fluorescent light and the relative reddishness of indoor and candlelight (see chapter 11). You can activate these filters with an ND switch near the lens barrel of the camcorder.

VIEWFINDER
A good viewfinder is obviously important because it shows you the exact pictures the camera is taking. Studio cameras have a relatively large (5- or 7-inch) viewfinder that can be swiveled and tilted so that you can see what you are doing even if you are not standing directly behind the camera. **SEE 5.17**

Unless converted to the studio configuration, all EFP cameras and camcorders have a small (1½- to 2½-inch) high-resolution monochrome (black-and-white) or color viewfinder. It is shielded from outside reflections by a flexible rubber eyepiece that you can adjust to your eye. As pointed out earlier, some EFP cameras and most small

BNC   S-video   RCA phono plug   HDMI connector   XLR plug   Phone plug   Mini plug

5.16 VIDEO AND AUDIO CONNECTORS
The most common connectors in television production are pictured here. All have adapters that let you change the plugs to fit other types of jacks. Note, however, that many pieces of equipment have unique cables and connectors.

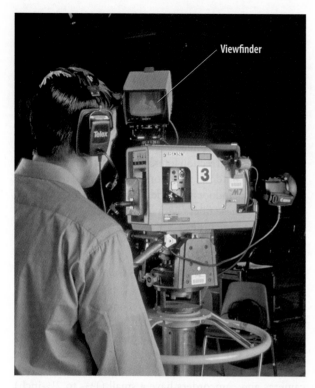

Viewfinder

5.17 STUDIO CAMERA VIEWFINDER
The 7-inch studio camera viewfinder can be swiveled and tilted so that the screen faces the camera operator regardless of the camera position.

camcorders have an additional foldout flat-panel display. This screen is handy for menu displays and for framing shots when in a hurry or under pressure. In bright sunlight these panels wash out and make it hard, or impossible, to see enough of an image for focusing or even framing a shot.

External viewfinder   Despite the two viewfinders on the camera, you will find that in many situations they still seem to be in the wrong place. This is why many videographers use an additional, larger LCD (liquid crystal display) panel that is mounted on top of the camera handle via a flexible arm. This way you can clearly see what you are shooting even if the camera sits on the ground. Similarly, if the camera is on a tripod and locked into a specific location (such as for an interview or a wedding), you can connect it to a small monitor next to the tripod and operate the camera by watching the monitor rather than the small viewfinder.

Color and monochrome   All LCD panels display a color picture, but the eyepiece viewfinders of camcorders and even some large viewfinders on studio cameras are often monochrome. The advantages of color viewfinders are, of course, that you see the colors the camera delivers, and you can compose your shots not only by placing objects in the right spots but also by seeing how the colors are distributed on the screen. The disadvantage is that LCD color viewfinders are often not detailed enough to allow for critical focus.

Focus-assist   Even with a monochrome viewfinder, HD and HDV cameras are hard to focus: the image is so high-definition that everything looks sharp and clear even if the picture is slightly out of focus. To help you focus, some high-end HDTV and HDV camcorders have a focus-assist feature in the viewfinder, which simply enlarges the center section of the image. This enlarged image will show more readily when the shot is out of focus. **SEE 5.18**

Communication center   The viewfinder and/or the foldout screen of EFP cameras and camcorders serves as an important communications center. It displays the menu for various camera and video-recording functions. When it's superimposed over the viewfinder image, you can monitor the control functions in use. **SEE 5.19** Because menus differ from camera to camera, you need to study the manuals and test the options before taking the camera on an important shoot.

Try to activate the setup functions when you are indoors and the menu is clearly visible on the foldout screen. Once you are outside in bright sunlight (or at night), searching the menu for a specific function is difficult; you will appreciate the buttons and the switches that control the most essential camera operations.

TALLY LIGHT AND INTERCOM
All studio cameras have a tally light, which is a small red light on top of the viewfinder (see figure 5.17). Tally lights are especially important for multicamera productions. When the tally light is on, you know that that camera is "hot," that is, on the air. This signals the other cameras (whose tally lights are off) that they are free to line up their next shots. It also helps the talent address the correct camera. As an aid to the camera operator, a small tally light inside the viewfinder hood also lights up. When two cameras are used simultaneously, such as for a split-screen effect or a superimposition (see chapter 13), the tally lights of both cameras are on. When operating a single camera,

Focus-assist off   Focus-assist on

5.18 FOCUS-ASSIST

The focus-assist feature enlarges the center of the image to facilitate focusing. The enlarged picture segment lets you see more readily whether the whole scene as displayed in the viewfinder is in sharp focus.

5.19 FLAT-PANEL FUNCTION DISPLAY

The flat-panel display on a camcorder serves as a communication center. It displays a menu of vital camera functions. During camera operation, specific information is superimposed on the viewfinder picture.

you don't need a tally light. In this case, a flashing red light inside the viewfinder and sometimes on the front of the camera indicates when it is actually recording the event.

The intercom, or intercommunication system, is especially important for multicamera productions because the director and the technical director have to coordinate the cameras' operations. All studio cameras and several high-end field cameras have at least two channels for intercommunication—one for the production crew and the other for the technical crew. Some studio cameras have a third channel that carries the program sound. (Intercoms are explained further in chapter 18.)

MAIN POINTS

▶ The television camera is the single most important piece of production equipment. Other production equipment and techniques are influenced by what the camera can and cannot do.

▶ The major parts of the camera are the lens, the camera itself with the imaging device, and the viewfinder.

▶ The beam splitter separates the entering white light into the three additive light primaries: red, green, and blue (RGB).

▶ The imaging device converts the light entering the camera into electric energy, which when amplified and processed becomes the video signal. This transducing is done by the imaging sensor, a charge-coupled device (CCD) or a CMOS sensor, both of which consist of a solid-state chip containing rows of a great many light-sensitive pixels.

▶ The standard studio camera chain consists of the camera head (the actual camera), the CCU (camera control unit), the sync generator, and the power supply.

▶ When classified by function, the three types of television cameras are studio cameras, EFP cameras, and ENG/EFP camcorders. All three can be SDTV (standard digital television), HDV (high-definition video), and HDTV (high-definition television).

▶ HDV camcorders have a similar resolution (horizontal and vertical lines) to HDTV cameras but much higher compression.

▶ Digital cinema cameras are HDTV cameras or camcorders with modifications to facilitate the specific requirements of the filmic production process.

▶ The electronic features of every professional camera or camcorder include the imaging device, scanning, resolution, aspect ratio and essential area, gain, electronic shutter, and white balance. The audio features concern the number of channels (tracks) and the quality of the sound.

▶ The operational features of studio cameras, EFP cameras, and ENG/EFP camcorders include power supply, cables and connectors, filter wheel, viewfinder and focus-assist, tally light, and intercom.

▶ Studio cameras are powered through the camera cable. ENG/EFP camcorders normally operate off a battery. Large EFP cameras and camcorders use a 12V battery; small camcorders use batteries that can supply between 7V and 8V.

▶ Certain features of a camera that put an additional drain on the battery include the camera light, foldout viewfinder panel, steady shot feature, video-recording playback through the foldout panel, and teleprompter.

▶ Triaxial (triax) and fiber-optic cables can carry video and audio information over relatively long distances.

▶ The filter wheel has one or more neutral density (ND) filters to cut excess light and reduce contrast as well as color-correction filters to facilitate white-balancing.

▶ Black-and-white viewfinders show more detail than color viewfinders and are therefore preferred for critical focusing. The viewfinder can also display menus of camera functions.

▶ Tally lights indicate when a camera is "hot" (on the air). This is important only in multicamera productions.

5.2

Resolution, Contrast, and Color

When you listen to experienced videographers or eager equipment salespeople, you always hear them debate the relative merits of a camera's resolution, contrast, and color attributes. This section explains how these three concepts influence the video image.

▶ **IMAGE RESOLUTION**
Spatial and temporal resolution

▶ **IMAGE CONTRAST**
Contrast ratio and contrast control

▶ **COLOR BASICS**
Color attributes and additive and subtractive color mixing

▶ **LUMINANCE AND CHROMINANCE CHANNELS**
The essential components of a color video signal

IMAGE RESOLUTION

The resolution of a video image is determined by how many pixels there are in each frame and how many frames per second we see. The pixel count is called the spatial resolution; the frames-per-second count is the temporal resolution.

SPATIAL RESOLUTION

The spatial resolution of a video image is determined by how many scanning lines are used for each frame and how many pixels are squeezed on a single scanning line. The stack of scanning lines makes up the vertical detail, and the pixels of each scanning line make up the horizontal detail. **SEE 5.20 AND 5.21**

The more scanning lines the vertical stack contains and the more pixels each line contains, the higher the resolution. As you can see, the vertical resolution is pretty much determined by the scanning system. If you have 480 visible lines (as in the SDTV system), you have 480 lines of vertical resolution. The 720 and 1080 scanning systems have a vertical stack of 720 and 1,080 lines, respectively, and therefore a vertical resolution of 720 and 1,080. The confusion is brought about when we omit the vertical stack of scanning lines and simply refer to the number of horizontal scanning lines as "vertical lines of resolution."

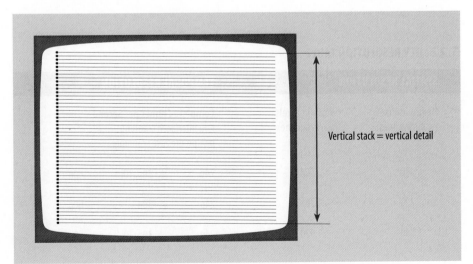

Vertical stack = vertical detail

5.20 VERTICAL DETAIL (LINES OF RESOLUTION)

To measure vertical detail, we count the first pixel of each vertically stacked scanning line. The more lines the vertical stack contains, the more pixels and the higher the resolution. The number of lines is fixed by the system: the NTSC system has 525 lines, of which only about 480 are visible on-screen; HDV and HDTV systems can display 720 and 1,080 active (visible) lines.

5.21 HORIZONTAL DETAIL (LINES OF RESOLUTION)

To measure horizontal detail, we count the pixels of each horizontal line. When we connect vertically the horizontal dots of each line, we get a horizontal stack of lines, hence the horizontal "lines" of resolution. For the 1080 HDTV system, each line comprises 1,920 pixels, or 1,920 horizontal lines of resolution.

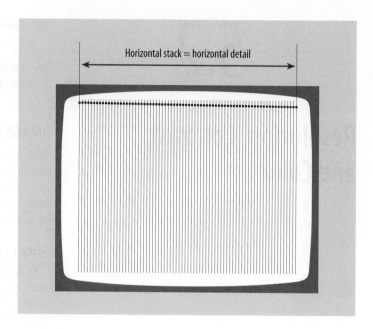

Horizontal stack = horizontal detail

TEMPORAL RESOLUTION

The temporal resolution becomes an issue when something moves on-screen. A high temporal resolution makes movement look smooth without blurring the moving object; a low resolution does the opposite. In video the temporal resolution is measured by the relative frame density, that is, the number of frames per second. When the video frame is interlaced *(i)*, it takes two scanning cycles for each complete frame. When it is scanned progressively *(p)*, each scan produces a complete frame. This is why a progressively scanned image has a higher temporal resolution than an interlaced one. For example, a 480p image looks much better than a 480i image even though the spatial resolution (number of scanning lines and number of pixels per line) is identical. The following table lists the spatial and temporal resolutions of the most common SDTV and HDTV systems. **SEE 5.22** Of course, you should realize that the figures in this table are what the camera system produces, not necessarily what you get on your home screen. Most HD flat panels must down-convert the HD signal to fit the pixel array of their display.

5.22 DTV RESOLUTION TABLE

SPATIAL RESOLUTION		TEMPORAL RESOLUTION		
Height in Pixels (scanning lines)	**Width in Pixels** (pixels per line)	**Complete Frames per Second** i = interlaced scanning p = progressive scanning		
480	704	24p	30p, 30i	60p
720	1,280	24p	30p	60p
1,080	1,920	24p	30p, 30i	60p

IMAGE CONTRAST

The range of contrast between the brightest and the darkest picture areas that the video camera can accurately reproduce is limited. That limit, called contrast range, is expressed as a ratio.

CONTRAST RATIO

Despite their manufacturers' overly optimistic claims, even the better cameras have trouble handling high contrast in actual shooting conditions. You will run into this problem every time you video-record a scene in bright sunlight. When you adjust the camera for the extremely bright sunlit areas, the shadow becomes uniformly dark and dense. When you then adjust the lens (open its iris), you will promptly overexpose—or, in video lingo, "blow out"—the bright areas. It is best to limit the contrast and stay within a *contrast ratio* of about 50:1, meaning that for optimal pictures the brightest picture area can be only 50 times brighter than the darkest area. Digital cameras with high-quality sensors can tolerate much higher contrast ratios (1,000:1 or even higher), but don't be misled by the camera's specifications. It is always a good idea to avoid extreme contrasts.

CONTRAST CONTROL

By watching a waveform monitor, which graphically displays the white and black levels of a picture, the video operator uses the CCUs to control contrast and adjusts the picture to the optimal contrast range, an activity called shading. **SEE 5.23**

To adjust a less-than-ideal picture, the VO tries to "pull down" the excessively bright values to make them match the established white level (which represents a 100 percent video signal strength). But because the darkest value cannot get any blacker and move down with the bright areas, the darker picture areas are "crushed" into a uniformly muddy, noisy dark color. If you insist on seeing detail in the dark picture areas, the video operator can "stretch the blacks" toward the white end, but, except for top-of-the-line cameras, stretching the shadow areas causes the bright areas to lose their definition and take on a uniformly white and strangely flat and washed-out color. In effect, the pictures look as though the contrast is set much too low with the brightness turned too high. Again, before the VO can produce optimal pictures through shading, you must try to reduce the contrast in the scene to tolerable limits.

In digital cinema, the contrast ratio is less a concern than the brightness steps between the limits of the contrast range. This is explained in the following section.

White level 100

Black level 7.5
Zero level

5.23 WAVEFORM MONITOR

The waveform monitor shows a graph of the luminance (black-and-white) portion of the video signal. It also shows the white level (the upper limit of the signal) and the black level (the lower limit of the signal).

COLOR BASICS

When you look at a red ball, its color is not part of the ball but simply light reflected off of it. The red paint of the ball acts as a color filter, absorbing all colors except red, which it bounces back. Thus the ball is stuck with the only color it has rejected: red.

COLOR ATTRIBUTES

When you look at colors, you can easily distinguish among three basic color sensations, called attributes: hue, saturation, and brightness. **SEE 5.24**

Hue   *Hue* describes the color itself, such as a red ball, a green apple, or a blue coat.

Saturation   *Saturation* indicates the richness or strength of a color. The bright red paint of a sports car is highly saturated, whereas the washed-out blue of your jeans or the beige of the sand on a beach are of low saturation.

Brightness   *Brightness* (also called lightness or luminance) is how dark or light a color appears on a black-and-white monitor or, roughly, how dark or light a color appears. The various brightness steps of a television image are usually shown as a grayscale (see figure 14.17). When you see black-and-white television pictures on-screen, you see brightness variations only; the pictures have no hue or

5.24 COLOR ATTRIBUTES

Hue is the term used for the base color—blue, green, yellow, and so on. *Saturation* refers to the purity and the intensity of the color. *Brightness, lightness,* or *luminance* describes the degree of reflectance—how light or dark a color appears on the grayscale.

saturation. In television the hue and saturation properties of color are sometimes named chrominance (from *chroma,* Greek for "color"), and the brightness properties are called luminance (from *lumen,* Latin for "light"). The chrominance, or C, signals and the luminance, or Y, signal are discussed later in this section.

COLOR MIXING

When you think back to your finger-painting days, you probably had three pots of paint: red, blue, and yellow. When mixing blue and yellow, you got green; when mixing red and blue, you got purple; and when smearing red and green together, you got, at best, a muddy brown. An expert finger painter could achieve almost all colors by simply mixing the primary paint colors of red, blue, and yellow. Not so when mixing colored light. The three primary light colors are not red, blue, and yellow but rather red, green, and blue—in television language, RGB.

Additive mixing   Assume that you have three individual slide projectors with a clear red slide (filter) in the first projector, a clear green one in the second, and a clear blue one in the third. Hook up each of the projectors to a separate dimmer. When the three dimmers are up full and you shine all three light beams together on the same spot of the screen, you get white light (assuming equal light transmission by all three slides and projector lamps). Because you *add* various quantities of colored light in the process, it is called additive color mixing. This is not surprising because we can split white light into these three primaries.

When you turn off the blue projector and leave on the red and green ones, you get yellow. If you then dim the green projector somewhat, you get orange or brown. If you turn off the green one and turn on the blue one again, you get a reddish purple, called magenta. If you then dim the red projector, the purple becomes more bluish. **SEE 5.25**

Because the color camera works with light rather than paint, it needs the three additive color primaries (red,

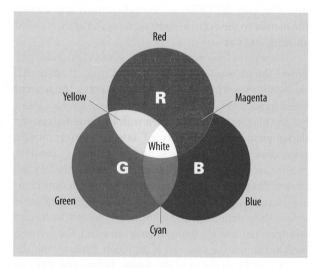

5.25 ADDITIVE COLOR MIXING

When mixing colored light, the additive primaries are red, green, and blue (RGB). All other colors can be achieved by mixing certain quantities of red, green, and blue light. For example, the additive mixture of red and green light produces yellow.

green, and blue) to produce all the colors you see on the television screen. You can make all other colors by adding the three light beams—primaries—in various proportions, that is, in various light intensities.

Subtractive mixing   When using paint instead of colored light, the primary colors are red, blue, and yellow, or, more accurately, magenta (a bluish red), cyan (a greenish blue), and yellow. In subtractive mixing, the colors filter each other out. Because the television camera works with light rather than paint, we skip subtractive mixing at this point.

LUMINANCE AND CHROMINANCE CHANNELS

We tend to see more detail when the picture is in black-and-white than in color. Recall that this is one of the reasons why HDTV cameras have an additional black-and-white viewfinder even if they have a high-quality color one. As stated earlier, chrominance deals with the hue and saturation attributes of a color, luminance with its brightness information. The chrominance channel in a camera and a video recorder carries the color signals, and the luminance channel carries the black-and-white signals.

LUMINANCE CHANNEL

The luminance channel, or Y channel, is responsible for the brightness information of the color pictures. To get the Y signal, we combine a portion of the RGB signals again, which we had just so laboriously split in the prism block. But, as you just read, when mixed in equal proportions, we get white (and a series of steps of progressively darker grays all the way to black). The luminance signal fulfills two basic functions: it translates the brightness variations of the colors in a scene into black-and-white pictures for black-and-white receivers, and it provides color pictures with the necessary crispness and definition, just like the black dots in a four-color print. Because it has such a great influence on the sharpness of the picture, the Y signal is favored in the digital domain. Even in high-end digital cameras, the color signals are normally sampled only half as often as the luminance signal—or only one-fourth as often in HDV camcorders.

CHROMINANCE CHANNEL

The chrominance channel, or C channel, transports all hue attributes. It consists of the three "slide projectors" that produce red, green, and blue light beams of varying intensities, except that in the television camera the "slide

projectors" consist of the sensors that produce an electrical signal of varying intensity (voltage) for each of the three primary RGB colors. The RGB signals are usually modified and combined with the Y signal for the color video you see on the TV screen. How they are modified and combined is explained in chapter 12.

M A I N   P O I N T S

▶   The resolution of video is determined by how many pixels there are in each frame and how many frames per second we see. The pixel count is called the spatial resolution; the frames-per-second count is the temporal resolution.

▶   The range of contrast between the brightest and the darkest picture areas that the video camera can accurately reproduce is limited. That limit, called contrast range, is expressed as a ratio. It is best to limit the contrast and stay within a contrast ratio of about 50:1, meaning that for optimal pictures the brightest picture area can be only 50 times brighter than the darkest area.

▶   By watching a waveform monitor, which graphically displays the white and black levels of a picture, the video operator (VO) uses the CCUs to control contrast and adjusts the picture to the optimal contrast range, an activity called shading.

▶   The three basic color sensations, called attributes, are hue (the color itself), saturation (the purity and the intensity of the color), and brightness (the degree of reflectance, also called lightness and luminance).

▶   Color television operates on additive mixing of the three color primaries of light: red, green, and blue (RGB).

▶   Color cameras contain a chrominance and a luminance channel. The chrominance channel processes the color signals—the C signals—and the luminance channel processes the black-and-white (brightness) signal, called the Y signal. The Y signal contributes to the sharpness of the picture.

Z E T T L ' S   V I D E O L A B

For your reference or to track your work, the *Zettl's VideoLab* program cue in this chapter is listed here with its corresponding page number.

ZVL1   CAMERA→ Camera introduction   **72**

CHAPTER

6

Lenses

Lenses are used in all fields of photographic art. Their primary function is to project a clear image of the viewed scene on the film or, in the case of digital photography and television, on the electronic imaging device. As discussed in chapter 5, the lens is one of the three major parts of the camera. In studio cameras the lens is often considerably larger than the camera itself. Section 6.1, What Lenses Are, covers the basic optical characteristics of lenses and their primary operational controls. The performance characteristics of lenses, that is, how they see the world, are explored in section 6.2, What Lenses See.

aperture Iris opening of a lens, usually measured in f-stops.

auto-focus Automated feature whereby the camera focuses on what it senses to be the target object.

calibrate To preset a zoom lens to remain in focus throughout the zoom.

compression The crowding effect achieved by a narrow-angle (telephoto) lens wherein object proportions and relative distances seem shallower.

depth of field The area in which all objects, located at different distances from the camera, appear in focus. Depth of field depends on the focal length of the lens, its f-stop, and the distance between the object and the camera.

digital zooming Simulated zoom by cropping the center portion of an image and electronically enlarging it. Digital zooms lose picture resolution.

digital zoom lens A lens that can be programmed through a built-in computer to repeat zoom positions and their corresponding focus settings.

fast lens A lens that permits a relatively great amount of light to pass through at its maximum aperture (relatively low f-stop number at its lowest setting). Can be used in low-light conditions.

field of view The portion of a scene visible through a particular lens; its vista. Expressed in symbols, such as *CU* for close-up.

focal length The distance from the optical center of the lens to the front surface of the camera's imaging device at which the image appears in focus with the lens set at infinity. Focal lengths are measured in millimeters or inches. *Short-focal-length lenses* have a wide angle of view (wide vista); *long-focal-length (telephoto)* lenses have a narrow angle of view (close-up). In a *variable-focal-length (zoom)* lens, the focal length can be changed continuously from wide-angle (zoomed out) to narrow-angle (zoomed in) and vice versa. A *fixed-focal-length (prime)* lens has a single designated focal length.

focus A picture is in focus when it appears sharp and clear on-screen (technically, the point at which the light rays refracted by the lens converge).

f-stop The calibration on the lens indicating the aperture, or iris opening (and therefore the amount of light transmitted through the lens). The larger the f-stop number, the smaller the aperture; the smaller the f-stop number, the larger the aperture.

iris Adjustable lens-opening that controls the amount of light passing through the lens. Also called *diaphragm* and *lens diaphragm*.

macro position A lens setting that allows it to be focused at very close distances from an object. Used for close-ups of small objects.

minimum object distance (MOD) How close the camera can get to an object and still focus on it.

narrow-angle lens Gives a close-up view of an event relatively far away from the camera. Also called *long-focal-length* and *telephoto lens*.

normal lens A lens or zoom lens position with a focal length that approximates the spatial relationships of normal vision.

rack focus To change focus from one object or person closer to the camera to one farther away or vice versa.

range extender An optical attachment to the zoom lens that extends its focal length. Also called *extender*.

selective focus Emphasizing an object in a shallow depth of field through focus while keeping its foreground and/or background out of focus.

servo zoom control Zoom control that activates motor-driven mechanisms.

slow lens A lens that permits a relatively small amount of light to pass through at its maximum aperture (relatively high f-stop number at its lowest setting). Can be used only in well-lighted areas.

wide-angle lens A short-focal-length lens that provides a broad vista of a scene.

z-axis An imaginary line representing an extension of the lens from the camera to the horizon—the depth dimension.

zoom lens A variable-focal-length lens. It can gradually change from a wide shot to a close-up and vice versa in one continuous move.

zoom range The degree to which the focal length can be changed from a wide shot to a close-up during a zoom. The zoom range is often stated as a ratio; a 20:1 zoom ratio means that the zoom lens can increase its shortest focal length 20 times.

6.1

What Lenses Are

The lens determines what the camera can see. One type of lens can provide a wide vista even though you may be relatively close to the scene; another type may provide a close-up view of an object that is quite far away. Different types of lenses also determine the basic visual perspective—whether you see an object as distorted or whether you perceive more or less distance between objects than there really is. They also contribute to a large extent to the quality of the picture and how much you can zoom in or out on an object without moving the camera. This section examines what lenses can do and how to use them.

▶ **TYPES OF ZOOM LENSES**
  Studio and field lenses, zoom range, prime lenses, and lens format

▶ **OPTICAL CHARACTERISTICS OF LENSES**
  Focal length, focus, light transmission (iris, aperture, and f-stop), and depth of field

▶ **OPERATIONAL CONTROLS**
  Zoom control, digital zoom lens, and focus control

TYPES OF ZOOM LENSES

When listening to production people talk about *zoom lenses*, you will most likely hear one person refer to a studio rather than a field zoom, another to a 20× (20 times) lens, and yet another to a zoom lens that fits a ⅔-inch image

format. And all may be talking about the same zoom lens. This section looks at these classifications.

STUDIO AND FIELD LENSES

As the name indicates, studio zoom lenses are normally used with studio cameras. Field zooms include large lenses mounted on high-quality cameras that are used for remote telecasts, such as parades and sporting events. They also include the zoom lenses attached to ENG/EFP cameras. The lenses of small camcorders usually come with the camera and cannot be exchanged. Some high-end models, however, allow you to attach a variety of zoom lenses, or they have adapters for mounting various lenses. Because you can, of course, use a field lens in the studio and vice versa, a better and more accurate way to classify zoom lenses is by their zoom range and lens format, that is, what cameras they fit.

ZOOM RANGE

If a zoom lens provides an overview, for example, of the whole tennis court and part of the bleachers when zoomed all the way out and (without moving the camera closer to the court) a tight close-up of the player's tense expression when zoomed all the way in, the lens has a good zoom range. The *zoom range* is the degree to which you can change the focal length of the lens (and thereby the angle of view, or vista) during the zoom.

The zoom range of a lens is often stated as a ratio, such as 10:1 or 40:1. A 10:1 zoom means that you can increase the shortest focal length 10 times; a 40:1, 40 times. To make things easier, these ratios are usually listed as 10× (10 times) or 40× (40 times), referring to the maximum magnification of the image of which the lens is capable. **SEE 6.1**

The large (studio) cameras that are positioned on top of the bleachers for sports coverage may have zoom ranges of 40× and even 70×. In the studio the cameras are well served by a 20× zoom lens. The smaller and lighter ENG/EFP camcorder lenses rarely exceed a 15× zoom range.

Optical and digital zoom ranges You may have noticed that the zoom range on a small camcorder is rather limited; an optical zoom range of 15× is considered excellent even for high-end camcorders. This is why most small camcorders offer the option of increasing the zoom range digitally. During an optical zoom to a tighter shot, the image magnification is achieved by moving elements within the lens. In effect, you are continually changing the focal length during the zoom-in or zoom-out. In *digital zooming* such a change in focal length does not occur.

6.1 MAXIMUM ZOOM POSITIONS OF A 10× LENS

The 10× zoom lens can increase its focal length 10 times. It magnifies a portion of the scene and seems to bring it closer to the camera and ultimately the viewer.

For a digital zoom-in, the electronics of the camera simply select the center portion of the long shot and enlarge the cropped area to full-screen size. The problem with digital zooming is that the enlarged picture portions noticeably reduce the image resolution (recall the mosaic tiles in chapter 5). At one point in digital zooming, the "mosaic tiles" can get so large that they look more like a special effect than a magnification of the original image. Some cameras have a digital zoom that is remarkably good, although even the best digital zoom does not achieve the crispness of the optical zoom.

All studio, field, and ENG/EFP lenses of large camcorders are detachable and interchangeable with lenses of a different zoom range. Most small camcorders, however, have a built-in lens that cannot be detached. This is a major handicap, especially because the wide-angle positions of these lenses are usually not wide enough. **SEE 6.2 AND 6.3**

Studio and large field lenses   Note that a 20× studio lens becomes a field lens if it is used "in the field," that is, for a production that happens outside the studio. Generally, field lenses have a much greater zoom range (from

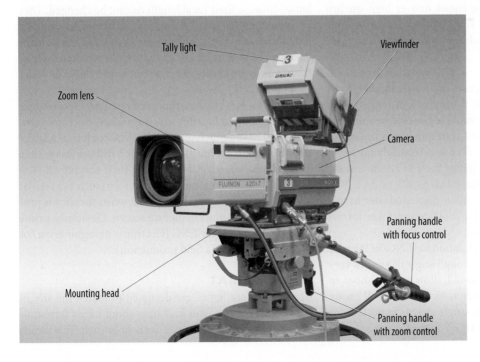

Tally light

Viewfinder

Zoom lens

Camera

FUJINON A20×7

Panning handle
with focus control

Mounting head

Panning handle
with zoom control

6.2 STUDIO ZOOM LENS

High-quality studio lenses are heavy and often larger than the camera itself.

6.3 ENG/EFP ZOOM LENS

The ENG/EFP camera lens is considerably lighter and smaller than studio zoom lenses. Although ENG/EFP lenses are not as high quality as studio lenses, they nevertheless have many of the studio zoom's features, such as servo and manual zoom controls, automatic iris control, and sometimes an auto-focus feature.

40× to 70×) than studio cameras. Some field lenses have an even greater zoom range, allowing the camera operator to zoom from a wide establishing shot of the football stadium to a tight close-up of the quarterback's face. Despite the great zoom range, these lenses deliver high-quality pictures even in relatively low light levels. For studio use such a zoom range would be unnecessary and even counterproductive.

ENG/EFP lenses   These lenses are much smaller, to fit the portable cameras. Their normal zoom range varies between 11× and 20×. A 15× zoom lens would be sufficient for most ENG/EFP assignments, but sometimes you might want a closer view of an event that is relatively far away. You would then need to exchange the 15× zoom lens for one with a higher zoom range—such as 20× or even 30×. You can also use a range extender (discussed later in this chapter), which would let you zoom beyond the normal zoom range into a tighter shot.

A more important consideration for ENG/EFP lenses is whether they have a wide enough angle of view (a very short focal length), which would allow you to shoot in highly cramped quarters, such as in a car, a small room, or an airplane. Also, the wide-angle view is important for shooting in the wide-screen 16 × 9 format.

Many lenses have digital or mechanical stabilizers that absorb at least some of the picture wiggles resulting from camera operation, especially when in a narrow-angle (zoomed-in) position. Realize, however, that such stabilizers cause an additional drain on the battery. Use this feature only when you don't have a tripod or are unable to stabilize the camera in any other way.

Range extenders   If a zoom lens does not get you close enough to a scene from where the camera is located, you can use an additional lens element called a *range extender*, or simply an extender. This optical element, usually available only for lenses on professional cameras, does not actually extend the range of the zoom but rather shifts the magnification—the telephoto power—of the lens toward the narrow-angle end of the zoom range. Most lenses have 2× extenders, which means that they double the zoom range in the narrow-angle position, but they also reduce the wide-angle lens position by two times. With such an extender, you can zoom in to a closer shot, but you cannot zoom back out as wide as you could without the extender. There is another disadvantage to range extenders: they cut down considerably the light entering the camera, which can be problematic in low-light conditions.

PRIME LENSES

You have probably used prime lenses on a single-reflex still camera. Prime lenses are also called fixed-focal-length lenses because their focal length cannot be changed. They are used on HD (high-definition) camcorders used for digital cinema. You cannot zoom in or out with a prime lens, so you have to physically move the camera closer or farther away from the object if you want a closer or wider shot of it.

Prime lenses are sometimes preferred over zoom lenses in critical filmmaking. But why use a relatively clumsy lens when you have a much more versatile zoom lens available? Because a good primary lens delivers a sharper image than a zoom lens, especially under low-light conditions. You won't see this difference on a small screen (such as a regular TV set), but you can probably see it when the shot is projected on a large motion picture screen. Obviously, prime lenses are not used for ENG (electronic newsgathering) or even EFP (electronic field production).

LENS FORMAT

Because camera lenses are designed to match the size of the imaging device, you may hear about a lens format or an image format of ⅓-inch, ½-inch, or ⅔-inch. This means

6.4 FOCAL LENGTH
The focal length is the distance from the optical center of the lens to the front surface of the imaging device.

that you can use only a lens that fits the corresponding size of the sensor chip. Most large camcorders use the ½-inch format. The term *lens format* may also refer to whether a lens is used for standard NTSC cameras or HD cameras.

OPTICAL CHARACTERISTICS OF LENSES

Effective use of a camera depends to a great extent on your understanding of four optical characteristics of lenses: focal length; focus; light transmission—iris, aperture, and *f*-stop; and depth of field.

FOCAL LENGTH

Technically, *focal length* refers to the distance from the optical center of the lens to the point where the image the lens sees is in focus. This point is the camera's imaging device. **SEE 6.4** Operationally, the focal length determines how wide or narrow a vista a particular camera can display and how much and in what ways objects appear magnified.

When you zoom all the way out, the focal length of the lens is short and at the maximum wide-angle position; the camera will provide a wide vista. When you zoom all the way in, the focal length is long and at the maximum narrow-angle (telephoto) position; the camera will provide a narrow vista or field of view—a close-up view of the scene. **SEE 6.5** When you stop the zoom approximately halfway between these extreme positions, the lens has the normal focal length. This means that you will get a "normal" vista that approximates your actually looking at the scene. Because the zoom lens can assume all focal lengths from its maximum wide-angle position (zoomed all the way out) to its maximum narrow-angle position (zoomed all the way in), it is called a variable-focal-length lens. **ZVL1** CAMERA→
Zoom lens→ normal | wide | narrow | try it

6.5 WIDE-ANGLE AND NARROW-ANGLE ZOOM POSITIONS
A The wide-angle zoom position (zoomed out) has a wider vista (field of view) than **B**, the narrow-angle zoom position (zoomed in). Note that zooming in magnifies the subject.

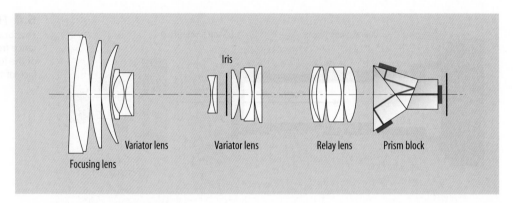

6.6 ELEMENTS OF A ZOOM LENS
A zoom lens consists of many sliding and stationary lens elements that interact to maintain focus throughout the continuous change of focal length. The front elements control the focus; the middle elements control the zoom.

On the television screen, a zoom-in appears as though the object is gradually coming toward you. A zoom-out seems to make the object move away from you. Actually, all that the moving elements within the zoom lens do is gradually magnify (zoom-in) or reduce the magnification (zoom-out) of the object while keeping it in focus, but the camera remains stationary during both operations. **SEE 6.6**

Minimum object distance and macro position   You will find that there is often a limit to how close you can physically move a camera (and a lens) to the object to be photographed and still keep the picture in focus. This is especially problematic when trying to get a close-up of a very small object. Even when zoomed in all the way, the shot may still look too wide. Moving the camera closer to the object will make the shot tighter, but you can no longer get the picture in focus. Range extenders help a little; but while they provide you with a tighter close-up of the object, they force you to back off with the camera to get the shot in focus.

One way to solve this problem is to zoom all the way out to a wide-angle position. Contrary to normal expectations, the wide-angle zoom position often allows you to get a tighter close-up of a small object than does the extended narrow-angle zoom position (zoomed all the way in with a 2× extender). But even with the lens in the wide-angle position, there is usually a point at which the camera will no longer focus when moved too close to the object. The point where the camera is as close as it can get and still focus on the object is called the *minimum object distance (MOD)* of the lens.

Many field lenses on ENG/EFP cameras have a *macro position*, which lets you move the camera even closer to an object without losing focus. When the lens is in the macro position, you can almost touch the object with the lens and still retain focus; you can no longer zoom, however. The macro position changes the zoom lens from a variable-focal-length lens to a fixed-focal-length, or prime, lens. The fixed focal length is not a big disadvantage because the macro position is used only in highly specific circumstances. For example, if you need to get a screen-filling close-up of a postage stamp, you would switch the camera to the macro position, but then you cannot use the camera for zooming until you switch back to the normal zoom mechanism.

FOCUS

A picture is "in focus" when the projected image is sharp and clear. The *focus* depends on the distance from the lens to the film (as in a nondigital still or movie camera) or from the lens to the camera's imaging device (beam splitter with sensors). Simply adjusting the distance from the lens to the film or imaging device brings a picture into focus or takes it out of focus. In television zoom lenses, this adjustment is accomplished not by moving the lens or the prism block (beam splitter) but by moving certain lens elements relative to each other through the zoom focus control (see figure 6.6).

Focus controls come in various configurations. Portable cameras have a focus ring on the lens that you turn; studio cameras have a twist grip attached to the panning handle (see figure 6.18). Most small camcorders have an automatic focus feature, called auto-focus, which is discussed in the context of operational controls later in this section.

If properly preset, a zoom lens keeps in focus during the entire zoom range, assuming that neither the camera nor the object moves very much toward or away from the other. But because you walk and even run while carrying an ENG/EFP camera, you cannot always prefocus the zoom. In such cases you would do well by zooming all the way out to a wide-angle position, considerably reducing the need to focus. This is examined more thoroughly in the discussion on depth of field later in this section.

Presetting (calibrating) the zoom lens   There is a standard procedure for presetting, or *calibrating*, the zoom lens so that the camera remains in focus throughout a zoom: Zoom all the way in on the target object, such as a newscaster on a news set. Focus on the newscaster's face (the eyes or the bridge of the nose) by turning the focus control. When zooming back out to a long shot, you will notice that everything remains in focus. The same is true when you zoom in again. You should now be able to maintain focus over the entire zoom range. If you move the camera, however, or if the talent moves after you preset the zoom lens, you need to calibrate the lens again.

For example, if you had preset the zoom on the news anchor but then the director instructed you to move the camera a little closer and to the left so that the anchor could more easily read the teleprompter, you would not be able to maintain focus without presetting the zoom again from the new position. If, after presetting the zoom, you were asked to zoom in on the map behind the news anchor, you would have to adjust the focus while zooming past her—not an easy task for even an experienced camera operator.

If the camera moves are predetermined and repeated from show to show, as in a daily newscast, you can use the preset features of the digital zoom lens. The lens then remembers the various zoom positions and performs them automatically with the push of a button. This is especially important when using robotic cameras that are run by computers rather than human beings.

Unless you have an automatic focus control, you must preset the zoom lens even when covering a news event in the field. You may have noticed that unedited video of a disaster (such as a tornado or fire) often contains brief out-of-focus close-ups followed by focusing and quick zoom-outs. Despite the precarious situations, the camera operator was calibrating the zoom lens so that it would stay in focus during subsequent zoom-ins.

LIGHT TRANSMISSION: IRIS, APERTURE, AND *f*-STOP

Like the pupil in the human eye, all lenses have a mechanism that controls how much light is admitted through them. This mechanism is called the *iris*, or lens diaphragm. The iris consists of a series of thin metal blades that form a fairly round hole—the *aperture*, or lens opening—of variable size. **SEE 6.7**

If you "open up" the lens as wide as it will go, or, technically, if you set the lens to its maximum aperture, it admits the maximum amount of light. **SEE 6.8A** If you close the lens somewhat, the metal blades of the iris form a smaller

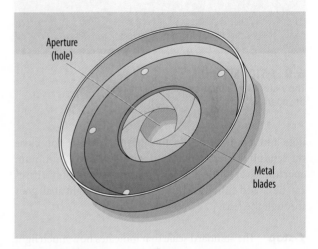

6.7 LENS IRIS
The iris, or lens diaphragm, consists of a series of thin metal blades that form, through partial overlapping, an aperture, or lens opening, of variable size.

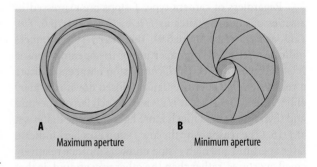

6.8 MAXIMUM AND MINIMUM APERTURES
A At the maximum aperture, the iris blades form a large opening, permitting a great amount of light to enter the lens. **B** At the minimum setting, the blades overlap to form a small hole, admitting only a small amount of light.

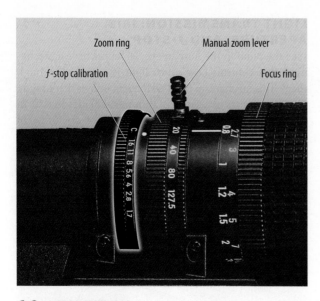

Zoom ring   Manual zoom lever

f-stop calibration   Focus ring

6.9 *f*-STOP SETTINGS
The *f*-stop is a calibration that indicates the size of the aperture.

hole and less light passes through the lens. If you close the lens all the way—that is, if you set it to its minimum aperture—very little light is admitted. **SEE 6.8B** Some irises can be closed entirely, which means that no light at all goes through the lens.

f-stop   The standard scale that indicates how much light goes through a lens, regardless of the lens type, is the *f-stop*. **SEE 6.9** If, for example, you have two cameras—a camcorder with a 10× zoom lens and a field camera with a large 50× lens—and both lenses are set at *f*/5.6, the imaging devices in both cameras will receive an identical amount of light.

Regardless of camera type, *f*-stops are expressed in a series of numbers, such as *f*/1.7, *f*/2.8, *f*/4, *f*/5.6, *f*/8, *f*/11, and *f*/16 (see figure 6.9). The *lower f*-stop numbers indicate a relatively *large* aperture or iris opening (lens is relatively wide open). The *higher f*-stop numbers indicate a relatively *small* aperture (lens is closed down considerably). A lens that is set at *f*/1.7 has a much larger aperture and therefore admits much more light than one that is set at *f*/16. (The reason why the low *f*-stop numbers indicate large apertures and high *f*-stop numbers indicate relatively small apertures, rather than the other way around, is that the *f*-stop numbers actually express a ratio. In this sense *f*/4 is actually *f*/¼; that is, *f* one over four.) Most lenses produce the sharpest pictures between *f*/5.6 and *f*/8. Some lenses extend the optimal focus to *f*/11.

Lens speed   The "speed" of a lens has nothing to do with how fast it transmits light but with how much light it lets through. A lens that allows a relatively great amount of light to enter is called a *fast lens*. Fast lenses go down to a small *f*-stop number (such as *f*/1.4). Most good studio zoom lenses open up to *f*/1.6, which is fast enough to make the camera work properly even in low-light conditions.

A lens that transmits relatively little light at the maximum iris aperture is called a *slow lens*. A studio lens whose lowest *f*-stop is *f*/2.8 is obviously slower than a lens that can open up to *f*/1.7. Range extenders render the zoom lens inevitably slower. A 2× extender can reduce the lens speed by as much as two "stops" (higher *f*-stop numbers), for instance, from *f*/1.7 to *f*/4 (see figure 6.9). This reduction in light transmission is not a big handicap because range extenders are normally used outdoors, where there is enough light. The more serious problem is a slight deterioration of the original picture resolution.

Remote iris control   Because the amount of light that strikes the camera's imaging device is so important to picture quality, the continuous adjustment of the iris is a fundamental function of video control. Studio cameras have a remote iris control, which means that the aperture can be continuously adjusted by the video operator (VO) from the camera control unit (CCU). If the set is properly lighted and the camera properly set up (electronically adjusted to the light/dark extremes of the scene), all that the VO has to do to maintain good pictures is work the remote iris control—open the iris in low-light conditions and close it down somewhat when there is more light than needed.

Auto-iris switch   Most cameras, especially ENG/EFP camcorders, can be switched from the manual to the auto-iris mode. **SEE 6.10** The camera then senses the light entering the lens and automatically adjusts the iris for optimal camera performance. This auto-iris feature works well so long as the scene does not have too much contrast.

There are circumstances in which you may want to switch the camera over to manual iris control. For example, if you took a loose close-up shot of a woman wearing a white hat in bright sunlight, the automatic iris would adjust to the bright light of the white hat, not to the darker (shadowed) face under the hat. The auto-iris control would therefore give you a perfectly exposed hat but an underexposed face. In this case you would have to switch to manual iris control, zoom in on the face to eliminate most of the white hat, then adjust the iris to the light reflecting off of the face rather than the hat. When switching to manual iris control,

6.10 AUTO-IRIS SWITCH
The auto-iris switch lets you change the aperture control from manual to automatic. You can quickly change back to manual simply by pressing the auto-iris switch without interrupting your shot.

however, you will find that even a fairly good ENG/EFP camera can't handle such an extreme contrast. In this case you might try a neutral density (ND) filter, which would lower the extreme brightness without making the dense shadow areas any darker. (Other ways to handle extreme contrast are explained in chapter 11.) **ZVL2** CAMERA→
Exposure control→ aperture | f-stop | auto iris | try it

DEPTH OF FIELD

If you place objects at different distances from the camera, some will be in focus and others will be out of focus. The area in which the objects are in focus is called *depth of field*. The depth of field can be shallow or great, but it is always greater behind the object than in front of it. **SEE 6.11**

If you have a shallow depth of field and you focus on an object in the foreground, the middleground and background objects will be out of focus. **SEE 6.12** If the depth of field is great, all objects (foreground, middleground, and background) will be in focus, even though you focus on the middleground object only. **SEE 6.13**

With a great depth of field, there is a large "sharp zone" in which people or objects can move toward or away from the camera without going out of focus and without any need for adjusting the camera focus. If they move in a shallow depth of field, however, they can quickly become blurred unless you adjust the focus. A similar thing happens when you move the camera. A great depth of field makes it

6.11 DEPTH OF FIELD
The depth of field is the area within which all objects, although located at different distances from the camera, are in focus.

6.12 SHALLOW DEPTH OF FIELD
With a shallow depth of field, the area in which an object is in focus is limited.

6.13 GREAT DEPTH OF FIELD
With a great depth of field, almost everything in the camera's field of view appears in focus.

relatively easy to move the camera toward or away from the object because you do not have to work any controls to keep the picture in focus. If you move the camera similarly in a shallow depth of field, you must adjust the focus continuously to keep the target object sharp and clear.

Operationally, the depth of field depends on the coordination of three factors: the focal length of the lens, the aperture, and the distance between the camera and the object.

Focal length   The focal length of the lens is the factor that most influences the depth of field. In general, wide-angle lenses and, of course, wide-angle (short-focal-length) zoom positions (zoomed out) have a great depth of field. Narrow-angle lenses and narrow-angle (long-focal-length) zoom positions (zoomed in) have a shallow depth of field. You may want to remember a simple rule of thumb:

■ *Depth of field increases as focal length decreases.*

When running after a fast-moving news event, should you zoom all the way in or all the way out? All the way out. Why? Because, first, the wide-angle position of the zoom lens will at least show the viewer what is going on. Second, and most important, the resulting great depth of field will help keep most of your shots in focus, regardless of whether you are close to or far from the event or whether you or the event is on the move.

Aperture   Here are rules of thumb for apertures and depth of field:

■ *Large f-stop numbers (such as f/16 or f/22) contribute to a great depth of field.*

■ *Small f-stop numbers (such as f/1.7 or f/2) contribute to a shallow depth of field.*

The following is an example of how everything in television production seems to influence everything else: If you

have to work in low-light conditions, you need to open up the iris to get enough light for the camera. But this large aperture (low f-stop number) reduces the depth of field. Thus, if you are to cover a news story when it is getting dark and you have no time or opportunity to use artificial lighting, focus becomes critical—you are working in a shallow depth of field. This problem is compounded when zooming in to tight close-ups. On the other hand, in bright sunlight you can stop down (decrease the aperture) and thereby achieve a great depth of field. Now you can run with the camera or cover people who are moving toward or away from you without too much worry about staying in focus—provided the zoom lens is in a wide-angle position.

Camera-to-object distance   The closer the camera is to the object, the shallower the depth of field. The farther the camera is from the object, the greater the depth of field. Camera-to-object distance also influences the focal-length effect on depth of field. For example, if you have a wide-angle lens (zoom lens in a wide-angle position), the depth of field is great. But as soon as you move the camera close to the object, the depth of field becomes shallow. The same is true in reverse: If you work with the zoom lens in a narrow-angle position (zoomed in), you have a shallow depth of field. But if the camera is focused on an object relatively far from the camera (such as a field camera located high in the stands to cover an automobile race), you work in a fairly great depth of field and do not have to worry too much about adjusting focus, unless you zoom in to an extreme close-up. **SEE 6.14** **ZVL3** CAMERA→ Focusing→ focus ring | depth of field | great depth | shallow | rack focus | auto focus | try it

■ *Generally, the depth of field is shallow when you work with close-ups and low-light conditions. The depth of field is great when you work with long shots and high light levels.*

6.14 DEPTH-OF-FIELD FACTORS

DEPTH OF FIELD	FOCAL LENGTH	APERTURE	f-STOP	LIGHT LEVEL	SUBJECT-TO-CAMERA DISTANCE
Great	Short (wide-angle)	Small	Large f-stop number (f/22)	High (bright light)	Far
Shallow	Long (narrow-angle)	Large	Small f-stop number (f/1.4)	Low (dim light)	Near

OPERATIONAL CONTROLS

You need two basic controls to operate a zoom lens: the zoom control, which lets you zoom out to a wide shot or zoom in to a close-up, and the focus control, which slides the lens elements that lie close to the front of the zoom lens back and forth until the image or a specific part of the image is sharp. Both controls can be operated manually or through a motor-driven servo control mechanism.

ZOOM CONTROL

Zoom lenses are equipped with a servo mechanism whose motor activates the zoom, but they also have a mechanical zoom control that can override the servo zoom at any time.

Servo zoom control   All types of professional cameras (studio and ENG/EFP) have a *servo zoom control* for their lenses. The servo zoom control for studio cameras is usually mounted on the right panning handle, and you zoom in and out by moving the thumb lever, similar to a rocker switch. When pressing the right side of the lever, you zoom in; when pressing the left side, you zoom out. The farther you move the lever from the central position, the faster the zoom will be. **SEE 6.15**

The automation lets you execute extremely smooth zooms. Most servo mechanisms for studio cameras offer a choice of at least two zoom speeds: normal and fast. The fast zoom setting is used when fast zoom-ins are required for emphasis. For example, the director may call for a very fast zoom-in on a ringing telephone or a contestant's face. Normal zoom speeds are simply not fast enough to highlight such events.

The servo zoom control for ENG/EFP camcorders is directly attached to the lens; for small camcorders it is sometimes built into the camera housing. The rocker switch, which controls the zoom, is usually marked with a *W* (for wide) and a *T* (for tight or telephoto). To zoom in press the *T* side of the switch; to zoom out press the *W* side. The servo control housing has a strap attached, which lets you support the shoulder-mounted or handheld camcorder while operating the zoom control. This way your other hand is free to operate the manual focus control. **SEE 6.16**

Manual zoom control   ENG and EFP often require extremely fast zoom-ins to get fast close-ups or to calibrate the zoom lens as quickly as possible. Even fast servo settings are usually too slow for such maneuvers. Camcorder lenses therefore have an additional manual zoom control, which is activated by a ring on the lens barrel. **SEE 6.17** By moving the ring clockwise (to zoom in) or counterclockwise

6.15 SERVO ZOOM CONTROL FOR STUDIO CAMERA
This zoom control is attached to the camera panning handle. By moving the rocker switch with your thumb to the right or left, you zoom in or out, respectively. The farther you move the lever from the central position, the faster the zoom will be.

6.16 SERVO ZOOM CONTROL FOR ENG/EFP CAMERA
For ENG/EFP cameras and camcorders, the servo zoom control is part of the lens assembly.

6.17 MANUAL ZOOM CONTROL ON LENS
The ring behind the focus control on ENG/EFP and prosumer camera lenses activates a manual zoom control.

(to zoom out), you can achieve extremely fast zooms not possible with the servo control. Some zoom rings have a small lever attached to facilitate mechanical zooming (see figure 6.9). In addition to news coverage, this manual zoom option is especially important for sports, where getting quick close-ups is the rule rather the exception.

DIGITAL ZOOM LENS

Do not confuse a digital zoom lens with digital zooming. A **digital zoom lens** is a fancy (and often confusing) name for a lens that can preset certain zoom positions and then trigger the operation with the push of a button. This preset device, which also remembers focus calibration, is highly accurate, provided the camera and the subject are in exactly the same positions as during setup. It is most practical when using robotic cameras (cameras whose movements are controlled by computer and not by an operator), such as during studio newscasts.

FOCUS CONTROL

The focus control activates the focus mechanism in a zoom lens. The focus mechanism on studio cameras differs from those on ENG/EFP cameras or camcorders.

Studio cameras   For studio cameras the focus control ordinarily consists of a twist grip similar to a motorcycle throttle, or a knob, usually mounted on the left panning handle. Two or three turns are sufficient to achieve focus over the full zoom range. As with the servo zoom control, the focus operations are transferred by the drive cable from the panning-handle control to the lens, but the lens executes the focusing though an electric motor. **SEE 6.18**

ENG/EFP cameras   EFP cameras and all camcorders have a focus ring near the front of the zoom lens, much like a prime lens for a regular still camera (see figure 6.9). You focus the lens by turning the focus ring clockwise or counterclockwise until the viewfinder shows the image sharply and clearly.

Digital cinema cameras   When using prime lenses on HDV (high-definition video) or HDTV (high-definition television) camcorders used for digital cinema, a flexible cable is attached to the focus ring on the lens. A twist-knob at the end of the cable allows the assistant camera operator to "pull focus," which means to keep in focus when somebody approaches the camera or when the camera moves toward a person or an event.

6.18 SERVO FOCUS CONTROL FOR STUDIO CAMERA
The twist grip of the servo focus control for a studio zoom lens turns clockwise and counterclockwise for focusing.

Remote control   Robotic or fixed cameras, such as the ones mounted in classrooms, have various types of focus controls that can be operated from a remote control station.

Focus-assist   As mentioned, focusing an HDTV image is not always easy because the high resolution can fool you into believing that the picture is in focus when it is not. To help HDTV camera operators focus and stay in focus, some cameras enlarge part of the viewfinder image. Once you get the enlarged portion into focus, the whole image will be crisp.

Servo focus   The servo focus control lets you preset the lens so that it keeps focus during carefully rehearsed camera and/or subject movements. Because even the smartest servo focus control will not help you stay in focus if the camera or subject movements have not been carefully rehearsed, most camera operators prefer to use the manual focus controls.

Auto-focus   The **auto-focus** feature essentially tries to sense which part of the image you want in focus. It works well in most conventional shots but will cause a problem when the principal object to be focused on is not obvious. The auto-focus usually settles for the object that is more or less in the center of the frame and closest to the camera. If you want to focus on part of a scene that is farther in the background and off to one side, the auto-focus will not comply. Unless you are running after a news story, switch to the manual focus. Don't be swayed by "professionals" who reject outright any auto-focus feature, however. So long as the camera gives you the desired focus, use the automatic feature. In many cases the auto-focus is faster and more accurate than a hasty manual one.

M A I N   P O I N T S

▶ The primary function of the lens is to produce a sharp optical image on the front surface of the camera's imaging device.

▶ There are various ways to classify zoom lenses: as studio and field lenses and according to zoom range and lens format.

▶ A range extender (an additional lens element) extends the telephoto power of a zoom lens (permits a closer shot) but reduces the range at the wide-angle end.

▶ All television cameras are equipped with zoom (variable-focal-length) lenses.

▶ Some HDTV (high-definition television) camcorders can be modified to accept prime lenses.

▶ The major optical characteristics of lenses are focal length, focus, light transmission (iris, aperture, and f-stop), and depth of field.

▶ The focal length of a lens determines how wide or narrow a vista the camera can show and how much and how close or far away the object seems to be from the camera (viewer). Zoom lenses have a variable focal length, whose major positions are wide-angle, normal, and narrow-angle (telephoto).

▶ A wide-angle lens (zoomed out) gives a wide vista. A narrow-angle lens (zoomed in) gives a narrow vista but magnifies the object so that it appears closer to the camera than it actually is. A normal lens (zoom position toward the midrange of the zoom) approximates the angle of human vision.

▶ A picture is in focus when the projected image is sharp and clear.

▶ A zoom lens needs to be preset (calibrated) so that focus is maintained over the zoom range. If a lens is properly focused when zoomed in, it should remain in focus when zoomed out and in again.

▶ The lens iris, or diaphragm, controls the amount of light passing through the lens. It consists of a series of thin metal plates that form a hole known as the aperture, or lens opening.

▶ The f-stop is a standard scale indicating how much light passes through the lens. Low f-stop numbers indicate large apertures; high f-stop numbers indicate small apertures.

▶ Studio cameras have a remote iris control, which is operated by the VO (video operator) from the CCU (camera control unit).

▶ The area in which objects at different distances from the camera are in focus is called depth of field. The depth of field depends on the focal length of the lens, the aperture (f-stop), and the distance from camera to object.

▶ The two basic operational controls for the zoom lens are the zoom control and the focus control. On ENG/EFP cameras and camcorders, both can be operated either manually or automatically by servo control.

▶ Auto-focus is an automated feature whereby the camera focuses on what it senses to be the target object. HDTV lenses have a focus-assist feature whereby the camera operator selects the target area.

The performance characteristics of a lens refer to its vista, what it can and cannot do, and how it generally behaves in common production practice. Because the camera normally processes only visual information that the lens can see, knowledge of the performance characteristics—how it sees the world and how it influences the aesthetic elements of a picture—will aid you greatly in composing effective shots and in many other production tasks. This section explores these concepts.

▶ **HOW LENSES SEE THE WORLD**
Field of view, distortion of objects and perceived distance, movement, and depth of field

▶ **IMAGE STABILIZATION**
Reducing or eliminating minor image wobbles

▶ **DEPTH OF FIELD AND SELECTIVE FOCUS**
Increasing and limiting the area in which things are in focus

HOW LENSES SEE THE WORLD

Although all television cameras use zoom lenses, it might be easier for you to learn how various zoom positions influence what you see in the viewfinder by describing three zoom positions as though they were fixed-focal-length (prime) lenses. Recall that fixed-focal-length lenses have a specific focal length that cannot be changed. They are normally classified as wide-angle, or short-focal-length, lenses; normal, or medium-focal-length, lenses; and narrow-angle, or long-focal-length, lenses, also called telephoto lenses.

Let's adjust a zoom lens to correspond to these standard focal lengths and observe their performance characteristics, which include field of view, object and distance distortion, movement, and depth of field.

WIDE-ANGLE LENS

As you recall, you need to zoom all the way out to achieve the maximum short focal length, or wide angle, of the zoom lens.

Field of view The *wide-angle lens* affords a wide vista. You can have a relatively wide *field of view*—the portion of a scene visible through the lens—with the camera rather close to the scene. When you need a wide vista (long shot) or, for example, when you need to see all five people on a panel in a relatively small studio, a wide-angle lens (wide-angle zoom position) is mandatory. The wide-angle lens is also well suited to provide pictures that fit the horizontally stretched 16 × 9 HDTV aspect ratio. **SEE 6.19**

Object and distance distortion A wide-angle lens makes objects relatively close to the camera look large and objects only a short distance away look small. This distortion—large foreground objects, small middleground, and even smaller background objects—seems to pull objects apart and stretch the perceived distance. The wide-angle lens also influences our perception of perspective. Because parallel lines seem to converge faster with this lens than you ordinarily perceive, it gives a forced perspective that aids the illusion of exaggerated distance and depth. With a wide-angle lens, you can make a small room appear spacious or a hallway seem much longer than it really is.

6.19 WIDE-ANGLE LENS FIELD OF VIEW AND PERSPECTIVE
The wide-angle lens expands space, stretching the row of columns.

6.20 WIDE-ANGLE LONG SHOT
The wide-angle lens (zoom position) gives you a wide vista. Although the camera is relatively close to the news set, we can see the whole set.

6.21 WIDE-ANGLE DISTORTION: TRUCK
The wide-angle lens intensifies the raw power of this truck. Note that the apparent size of the front grill is greatly exaggerated through the wide-angle lens.

6.22 WIDE-ANGLE DISTORTION: EMPHASIS ON FOREGROUND OBJECT
The importance of this telephone call in the video adaptation of a famous crime novel is emphasized by the wide-angle distortion.

6.23 WIDE-ANGLE DISTORTION: DEPTH ARTICULATION
Shooting through a permanent foreground piece with the wide-angle lens creates a spatially articulated, forceful picture.

6.24 WIDE-ANGLE DISTORTION: LINEAR PERSPECTIVE
The length of this hallway is greatly exaggerated.

6.25 WIDE-ANGLE DISTORTION: FACE
This face is greatly distorted because the shot was taken with a wide-angle lens at a close distance.

SEE 6.20–6.24 Such distortions can also work against you. If you take a close-up of a face with a wide-angle lens, the nose, or whatever is closest to the lens, will look unusually large compared with the other parts of the face. **SEE 6.25** Such distortions are often used purposely, however, for emphasizing stress or psychological conditions or for stylistic special effects.

Movement The wide-angle lens is also a good dolly lens. Its wide field of view de-emphasizes camera wobbles and bumps during dollies, trucks, and arcs (see chapter 7), but because the zoom lens makes it so easy to move from a long shot to a close-up and vice versa, dollying with a zoom lens has almost become a lost art.

Most of the time, a zoom will be perfectly acceptable as a means of changing the field of view (moving to a wider or closer shot). You should be aware, however, that there is a significant aesthetic difference between a zoom and a dolly. Whereas the zoom seems to bring the scene to the viewer, a dolly seems to take the viewer into the scene. Because the camera does not move during the zoom, the spatial relationships among objects remain constant. The objects appear to be glued into position—they simply get bigger (zoom-in) or smaller (zoom-out). In a dolly, however, the relationships among objects change constantly. You seem to move past them when dollying in or out.[1] Be sure to recalibrate the zoom lens when you reach the end of the dolly so you can zoom in and out from the new position without losing focus. **ZVL4** CAMERA→ Camera moves→ dolly | zoom | try it

When people or objects move toward or away from the camera, their speed appears greatly accelerated by the wide-angle lens. The wide-angle zoom position is often used to accelerate the speed of a car or a dancer moving toward or away from the camera.

When covering a news event that exhibits a great deal of movement or that requires you to move rapidly, you should put the zoom lens in its extreme wide-angle position, as this will reduce camera wobbles to a great extent and make it much easier to keep the event in the viewfinder. Also, the great depth of field helps you keep the pictures in focus. The disadvantage of the extreme wide-angle position is that you need to move the camera quite close to the action if you want a closer look.

Depth of field   The wide-angle lens generally has a great depth of field. When zoomed all the way out, you should have few focus problems, unless you work in low-light conditions (which require a large aperture) or are extremely close to the object.

NORMAL LENS

The zoom position for a normal focal length lies somewhere in the midrange of a zoom lens, perhaps a little more toward the wide-angle position.

Field of view   The *normal lens* offers a field of view (focal length) that approximates that of normal vision. It gives you the perspective between foreground and middleground that you actually see.   **SEE 6.26**

1. See Herbert Zettl, *Sight Sound Motion: Applied Media Aesthetics,* 5th ed. (Belmont, Calif.: Thomson Wadsworth, 2008), pp. 272–74.

6.26 NORMAL LENS FIELD OF VIEW AND PERSPECTIVE
The normal lens gives a field of view that approximates normal vision.

Object and distance distortion   Whereas the wide-angle lens makes objects seem farther apart and rooms seem larger than they actually are, the normal lens or the midrange zoom positions make objects and their spatial relationships appear more like our normal vision. When shooting graphics such as charts that are positioned on an easel, you should put the zoom lens in the midrange position.

Movement   With the normal lens (midrange zoom positions), you have a much more difficult time keeping the picture in focus and avoiding camera wobbles, even when the camera is mounted on a studio pedestal. When carrying an ENG/EFP camera or camcorder, this lens position makes it hard to avoid camera wobbles even when standing still. If you must have such a field of view, put the camera on a tripod.

Because the distance and the object proportions approximate our normal vision, the dolly speed and the speed of objects moving toward or away from the camera also appear normal. But again, such movement may cause focus problems, especially when the object gets fairly close to the camera.

Depth of field   The normal lens has a considerably shallower depth of field than the wide-angle lens under similar conditions (same *f*-stop and object-to-camera distance). You might think that a very great depth of field would be the most desirable condition in studio operations because it shows everything in focus. But a medium depth of field is often preferred in studio work and EFP because the in-focus objects are set off against a slightly out-of-focus background. The objects are emphasized, and a busy background or the inevitable smudges on the television scenery receive less attention. Most important, foreground, middleground, and background are better defined.[2]

Of course, a large depth of field is necessary when there is considerable movement of camera and/or subjects. Also, when two objects are located at widely different distances from the camera, a great depth of field enables you to keep both in focus simultaneously. Most outdoor telecasts, such as sports remotes, require a large depth of field.

NARROW-ANGLE, OR TELEPHOTO, LENS

When you zoom all the way in, the lens is in the maximum narrow-angle, long-focal-length, or telephoto, position.

Field of view   The *narrow-angle lens* not only reduces the vista but also magnifies the background objects. Actually, when you zoom in, all the zoom lens does is magnify the image. You get a view as though you were looking through binoculars, which, in effect, act as telephoto lenses. **SEE 6.27**

Object and distance distortion   Because the enlarged background objects look big in comparison with the foreground objects, an illusion is created that the distance between foreground, middleground, and background has decreased. The long lens seems to compress the space between the objects, in direct contrast to the effect created by the wide-angle lens, which exaggerates object proportions and therefore seems to increase relative distance between objects. A narrow-angle lens, or telephoto zoom position, crowds objects on-screen. This crowding effect, called aesthetic *compression,* can be positive or negative. If you want to show how crowded the freeways are during rush hour, for example, use the zoom lens in the telephoto position. The long focal length shrinks the perceived distance between the cars and makes them appear to be bumper-to-bumper. **SEE 6.28**

But such depth distortions by the narrow-angle lens also work to a disadvantage. You are certainly familiar with the deceptive closeness of the pitcher to home plate on the television screen. Because television cameras must remain at a considerable distance from the action in most sporting events, the zoom lenses usually operate at their extreme telephoto positions (zoomed in all the way) or with powerful range extenders. The resulting compression effect makes it difficult for viewers to judge actual distances. **SEE 6.29**

2. See Zettl, *Sight Sound Motion,* pp. 165–68.

6.27 NARROW-ANGLE LENS FIELD OF VIEW AND PERSPECTIVE
The narrow-angle (telephoto) lens compresses space.

6.28 POSITIVE AESTHETIC COMPRESSION WITH NARROW-ANGLE LENS
With a narrow-angle lens, the background is greatly enlarged and the distance between the cars seems reduced. The feeling of a traffic jam is intensified.

Movement   The narrow-angle lens gives the illusion of reduced speed of an object moving toward or away from the camera. Because the narrow-angle lens changes the size of an object moving toward or away from the camera much more gradually than does the wide-angle lens, the object seems to move more slowly than it actually does; in fact, an extreme narrow-angle lens virtually eliminates such movement. The object does not seem to change size perceptibly even when traveling a considerable distance relative to the camera. Such a slowdown is especially effective if you want to emphasize the frustration of someone running toward the camera but not getting any closer. Added to the compression effect (figure 6.28), the drastic reduction of the perceived speed of traffic will certainly emphasize the congestion. **ZVL5** CAMERA→ Picture depth→ perspective and distortion | try it

6.29 NEGATIVE AESTHETIC COMPRESSION WITH NARROW-ANGLE LENS
This shot was taken with a zoom lens in an extreme long-focal-length position. Note how the pitcher, batter, catcher, and umpire all seem to stand only a few feet apart from one another. The actual distance between the pitcher and the batter is 60½ feet.

You cannot dolly with a narrow-angle lens or with a zoom lens in the telephoto position (zoomed in); its magnifying power makes smooth camera movement impossible. If you work outdoors, even wind can be a problem. A stiff breeze may shake the camera to such a degree that the greatly magnified vibrations become clearly visible on-screen.

In the studio the telephoto position may present another problem. The director may have you zoom in on part of an event, such as the lead guitarist in a rock performance, and then, after you have zoomed in, ask you to truck (move the camera sideways) past the other members of the band. But the telephoto position makes any wobble-free camera movement extremely difficult, if not impossible. What you can do is zoom out before trucking to minimize the wobbles.

IMAGE STABILIZATION

The best way to keep an image steady is to put the camera on a tripod or studio pedestal. If you are operating a shoulder-mounted camera or carrying it in your hands, the image stabilizer may come to your rescue.

IMAGE STABILIZER

Some lenses have an image stabilization device built into the lens or the camera. The lens stabilization is mostly mechanical; the stabilization inside the camera is usually electronic. Both systems reduce and often eliminate subtle image shifts caused by minor camera shakes. But even

with the best image stabilizer, the pictures will be rendered useless by the inevitable camera wobbles when moving the camera in the telephoto position.

DEPTH OF FIELD AND SELECTIVE FOCUS

Unless the object is far away from the camera, long-focal-length lenses have a shallow depth of field. You can use a shallow depth of field effectively to draw attention to certain parts of an event that is staged along the *z-axis*—an imaginary line representing an extension of the lens from the camera to the horizon (the depth dimension). One of the most popular shallow-depth-of-field effects is selective focus.

SELECTIVE FOCUS

Let's assume that you are about to take a quick close-up of a medium-sized object, such as a can of soup. You do not have to bother putting up a background for it—all you need to do is move the camera back and zoom in on the display. With the zoom lens in a telephoto (narrow-angle) position, decreasing the depth of field to a large extent, the background is sufficiently out of focus to prevent undesirable distractions. This technique is called *selective focus*, meaning you can focus either on the foreground, with the middleground and the background out of focus; on the middleground, with the foreground and the background out of focus; or on the background, with the foreground and the middleground out of focus. **SEE 6.30 AND 6.31**

You can also use selective focus to easily shift emphasis from one object to another. For example, you can zoom in on a foreground object, thus reducing the depth of field, and focus on it with the zoom lens in the telephoto position. Then, by refocusing on the person behind it, you can quickly shift the emphasis from the foreground object to the person (middleground). This technique is called racking focus or, simply, *rack focus*. **ZVL6** CAMERA→ Focusing→ rack focus | try it

The advantage of a shallow depth of field also applies to unwanted foreground objects. In a high-school baseball pickup, for example, the camera behind home plate may have to shoot through the chain-link backstop. But because the camera is most likely zoomed in on the pitcher, or on other players a considerable distance from the camera, you work with a relatively shallow depth of field. Consequently, everything fairly close to the camera, such as the chain-link fence, is so out of focus that it becomes virtually invisible. The same principle works for shooting through birdcages, prison bars, or similar foreground objects.

6.30 SELECTIVE FOCUS: FOREGROUND IN FOCUS
In this shot the camera-near person is in focus, drawing attention away from the two people in the background.

6.31 SELECTIVE FOCUS: BACKGROUND IN FOCUS
Here the focus and attention are shifted from the camera-near person (foreground) to the two people farther away.

M A I N   P O I N T S

▶ The performance characteristics of wide-angle, normal, and narrow-angle lenses (zoom lenses adjusted to these focal lengths) include field of view, object and distance distortion, movement, and depth of field.

▶ A wide-angle lens (zoom lens in the wide-angle position, zoomed all the way out) offers a wide vista. It gives a wide field of view with the camera relatively close to the scene.

▶ A wide-angle lens distorts objects close to the lens and exaggerates proportions.

▶ A wide-angle lens is ideal for camera movement. It minimizes camera wobbles and makes it easy to keep the picture in focus during camera movement.

▶ The normal lens gives a field of view that approximates that of normal vision. The normal lens (zoom lens in the mid-range position) does not distort objects or the perception of distance.

▶ When a camera is moved with the lens in the midrange zoom position, camera wobbles are emphasized considerably more than with a wide-angle lens. The shallower depth of field makes it harder to keep the picture in focus.

▶ A narrow-angle lens (zoom lens in the telephoto position, zoomed all the way in) has a narrow field of view and enlarges the objects in the background. Exactly opposite of the wide-angle lens, which increases the perceived distance between objects, the narrow-angle lens seems to compress the space between objects at different distances from the camera. It slows the perception of object speed toward and away from the camera.

▶ The magnifying power of a narrow-angle lens prevents any camera movement while on the air. Narrow-angle lenses have a shallow depth of field, which makes keeping in focus more difficult but allows for selective focus.

Z E T T L ' S   V I D E O L A B

For your reference or to track your work, the *Zettl's VideoLab* program cues in this chapter are listed here with their corresponding page numbers.

ZVL1 ▶ CAMERA→ Zoom lens→ normal | wide | narrow | try it   **97**

ZVL2 ▶ CAMERA→ Exposure control→ aperture | *f*-stop | auto-iris | try it   **101**

ZVL3 ▶ CAMERA→ Focusing→ focus ring | depth of field | great depth | shallow | rack focus | auto-focus | try it   **102**

ZVL4 ▶ CAMERA→ Camera moves→ dolly | zoom | try it   **108**

ZVL5 ▶ CAMERA→ Picture depth→ perspective and distortion | try it   **109**

ZVL6 ▶ CAMERA→ Focusing→ rack focus | try it   **110**

7

Camera Operation and Picture Composition

Digital cameras with their automated features have become so user-friendly that anybody can run a camera, right? Wrong! Although you may see entire television series that are shot by amateurs, professional camera work still requires practice and a basic knowledge of how to move the camera with or without a special camera support—and especially how to compose effective pictures.

There is nothing wrong with using the automated features of an electronic camera so long as the conditions allow it. But even the smartest automated camera has no way of knowing what part of the event you consider important and how best to clarify and intensify the selected event details through maximally effective shots. Nor can it exercise aesthetic judgment—how to frame an extreme close-up, for example. This is why it is important to learn as much as possible about camera operation before trying to do your blockbuster documentary.

Section 7.1, Working the Camera, discusses the basic camera movements, the standard mounting equipment, and the do's and don'ts of camera operation. Section 7.2, Framing Effective Shots, focuses on some of the aesthetic aspects of picture composition in various aspect ratios.

arc To move the camera in a slightly curved dolly or truck.

aspect ratio The width-to-height proportions of the standard television screen and therefore of all standard television pictures: 4 units wide by 3 units high. For HDTV the aspect ratio is 16 × 9. The small portable media (cell-phone) screens have various aspect ratios.

camera stabilizing system Camera mount whose mechanism holds the camera steady while the operator moves.

cant Tilting the shoulder-mounted or handheld camera sideways.

close-up (CU) Object or any part of it seen at close range and framed tightly. The close-up can be extreme (extreme or big close-up—*ECU*) or rather loose (medium close-up—*MCU*).

closure Short for *psychological closure*. Mentally filling in spaces of an incomplete picture.

crane (1) Motion picture camera support that resembles an actual crane in both appearance and operation. The crane can lift the camera from close to the studio floor to more than 10 feet above it. (2) To move the boom of the camera crane up or down. Also called *boom*.

cross-shot (X/S) Similar to the over-the-shoulder shot except that the camera-near person is completely out of the shot.

dolly (1) Camera support that enables the camera to move in all horizontal directions. (2) To move the camera toward (dolly in) or away from (dolly out or back) the object.

extreme close-up (ECU) Shows the object with very tight framing.

extreme long shot (ELS) Shows the object from a great distance. Also called *establishing shot*.

field of view The portion of a scene visible through a particular lens; its vista. Expressed in symbols, such as *CU* for close-up.

headroom The space left between the top of the head and the upper screen edge.

jib arm Similar to a camera crane. Permits the jib arm operator to raise, lower, and tongue (move sideways) the jib arm while titling and panning the camera.

leadroom The space left in front of a person or an object moving toward the edge of the screen.

long shot (LS) Object seen from far away or framed loosely. Also called *establishing shot* and *full shot*.

medium shot (MS) Object seen from a medium distance. Covers any framing between a long shot and a close-up. Also called *waist shot*.

monopod A single pole onto which you can mount a camera.

mounting head A device that connects the camera to the tripod or studio pedestal to facilitate smooth pans and tilts. Also called *pan-and-tilt head*.

noseroom The space left in front of a person looking or pointing toward the edge of the screen.

over-the-shoulder shot (O/S) Camera looks over a person's shoulder (shoulder and back of head included in shot) at another person.

pan To turn the camera horizontally.

pedestal (1) Heavy camera dolly that permits raising and lowering the camera while on the air. (2) To move the camera up and down via a studio pedestal.

quick-release plate A mounting plate used to attach camcorders and ENG/EFP cameras to the mounting head.

robotic pedestal Motor-driven studio pedestal and mounting head. It is guided by a computerized system that can store and execute a great number of camera moves. Also called *robotic*.

studio pan-and-tilt head A camera mounting head for heavy cameras that permits extremely smooth pans and tilts.

tilt To point the camera up or down.

tongue To move the boom or jib arm with the camera from left to right or right to left.

tripod A three-legged camera mount. Can be connected to a dolly for easy maneuverability.

truck To move the camera laterally by means of a mobile camera mount. Also called *track*.

two-shot Framing of two people.

z-axis An imaginary line representing an extension of the lens from the camera to the horizon—the depth dimension.

zoom To change the lens gradually to a narrow-angle position (zoom-in) or to a wide-angle position (zoom-out) while the camera remains stationary.

7.1

Working the Camera

Although it may be fun to take your small camcorder and hold it out of the window of a moving car or swing it through the air like a butterfly net, such moves rarely produce satisfactory pictures. Like painting, good camera work is more difficult than it looks, but the learning curve can be considerably flattened by mastering a few basics of camera operation.

▶ **STANDARD CAMERA MOVEMENTS**
Pan, tilt, pedestal, tongue, crane or boom, dolly, truck or track, arc, cant, and zoom

▶ **CAMERA SUPPORTS**
Monopod, tripod and tripod dolly, studio pedestal, mounting (pan-and-tilt) heads, and special camera mounts

▶ **WORKING THE CAMCORDER AND THE EFP CAMERA**
Some basic camera "don'ts"; and camera setup, operation, and care—the basic operational steps before, during, and after a field production

▶ **WORKING THE STUDIO CAMERA**
Camera setup, operation, and care—the basic operational steps before, during, and after a studio production

STANDARD CAMERA MOVEMENTS

Before learning to operate a camera, you should become familiar with the most common camera movements. *Left* and *right* always refer to the camera's point of view. The camera

mounting equipment has been designed solely to help you move the camera smoothly and efficiently. The major camera movements are pan, tilt, pedestal, tongue, crane or boom, dolly, truck or track, arc, cant, and zoom. **SEE 7.1**

■ *Pan* means turn the camera horizontally, from left to right or from right to left. When the director tells you to "pan right," which means point the lens and the camera to the right (clockwise), you must push the panning handles to the left. To "pan left," which means swivel the lens and the camera to the left (counterclockwise), you push the panning handles to the right.

■ *Tilt* means point the camera up or down. When you "tilt up," you make the camera point up gradually. When you "tilt down," you make the camera point down gradually.

■ *Pedestal* means elevate or lower the camera on a studio pedestal. To "pedestal up," you raise the camera; to "pedestal down," you lower the camera.

■ *Tongue* means move the whole camera from left to right or from right to left with the boom of a camera crane. When you tongue left or right, the camera usually points in the same general direction, with only the boom moving left (counterclockwise) or right (clockwise).

■ *Crane*, or boom, means move the whole camera up or down on a camera crane or jib arm. The effect is somewhat similar to an up or down pedestal except that the camera swoops over a much greater vertical distance. You either "crane [or boom] up" or "crane [or boom] down."

■ *Dolly* means move the camera toward or away from the scene in more or less a straight line by means of a mobile camera mount. When you "dolly in," you move the camera closer to the scene; when you "dolly out" or "dolly back," you move the camera farther away from the scene.

■ *Truck*, or track, means move the camera laterally by means of a mobile camera mount. To "truck left" means to move the camera mount to the left with the camera pointing at a right angle to the direction of travel. To "truck right" means to move the camera mount to the right with the camera pointing at a right angle to the direction of travel.

■ *Arc* means move the camera in a slightly curved dolly or truck movement with a mobile camera mount. To "arc left" means to dolly in or out in a camera-left curve or to truck left in a curve around the object; to "arc right" means to dolly in or out in a camera-right curve or to truck right in a curve around the object.

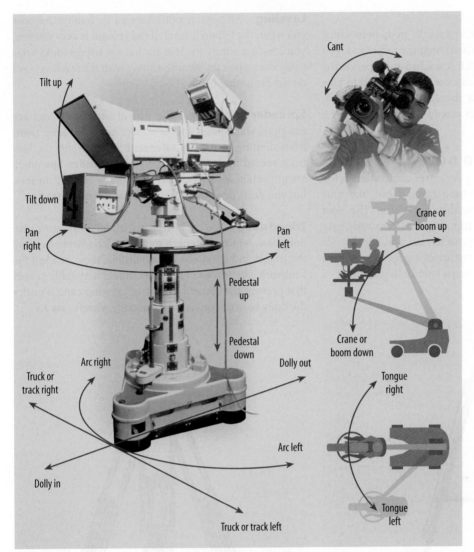

7.1 CAMERA MOVEMENTS
Major camera movements include pan, tilt, pedestal, tongue, crane or boom, dolly, truck or track, arc, and cant.

■ ***Cant*** means tilting the shoulder-mounted or hand-held camera sideways. The result, called a canting effect, is a slanted horizon line, which puts the scene on a tilt. Through the skewed horizon line, you can achieve a highly dynamic scene.

■ ***Zoom*** means changing the focal length of the lens through the use of a zoom control while the camera remains stationary. To "zoom in" means to change the lens gradually to a narrow-angle position, thereby making the scene appear to move closer to the viewer; to "zoom out" means to change the lens gradually to a wide-angle position, thereby making the scene appear to move farther away from the viewer. Although not a camera movement per se,

the zoom effect looks similar to that of a moving camera and is therefore classified as such. **ZVL1** CAMERA→ Camera moves→ dolly | zoom | truck | pan | tilt | pedestal | try it

CAMERA SUPPORTS

Even if your camera is small and lightweight enough to carry in your hands, you should mount it on a camera support whenever possible. Using a camera support will reduce fatigue and especially prevent unnecessary and distracting camera motion. Unless motivated, as in some commercials and MTV shows, wild and rapid camera movement draws too much attention to itself and is one of the sure signs of amateur camera handling.

MONOPOD

The *monopod* is a single pole, or a single "pod," onto which you can mount a camera. When using the monopod, you must balance the support with one hand and operate the camera with the other. You can use the monopod to take some of the weight off your shoulder-mounted camera, but then you must be able to extend the monopod just a bit beyond shoulder-height.

TRIPOD AND TRIPOD DOLLY

The most common mounting device for camcorders is the *tripod*. You certainly know what a tripod is, but, like cameras, tripods can be good, passable, and useless. The most important criteria for a good tripod are that it is sturdy, easy to set up and level on any type of terrain, and, ideally, not too heavy. The other major feature of a good tripod is its mounting head, which we discuss later in this section.

Leveling   All good tripods have an air bubble that tells you when the tripod is level. If the ground is very uneven, you can first adjust the legs so that the tripod looks relatively even, then do the fine-tuning with the leveling bowl on the mounting head.

Spreader and dolly   The tips of the tripod legs are equipped with spikes and/or rubber cups that keep them from slipping. A further safeguard that prevents the legs from spreading is, paradoxically, the spreader. Spreaders are important for tripods that support heavy camcorders, but you don't need them for small camcorders. **SEE 7.2**

Tripod dolly   You can also place a tripod on a three-caster dolly base, which is simply a spreader with wheels. Because the tripod and the dolly are collapsible, they are ideal for fieldwork. The wheels of the dolly should have cable guards that prevent the camera cable from getting caught under the dolly base or run over by the dolly wheels. **SEE 7.3**

7.2 TRIPOD WITH BUILT-IN SPREADER
The tripod is one of the most basic camera supports and is used extensively in field productions. This tripod has a built-in spreader at midlevel.

7.3 COLLAPSIBLE TRIPOD MOUNTED ON DOLLY BASE
The tripod can be mounted on a tripod dolly, which permits quick repositioning of the camera.

STUDIO PEDESTAL

With a studio pedestal, you can move a camera in all directions (assuming there is a smooth floor) and elevate and lower the camera while on the air. This up-and-down movement adds an important dimension to the art of television and cinema photography. You can not only adjust the camera to a comfortable working height but also change the eye level from which you look at an event. For example, if you are in danger of overshooting the set, you can always pedestal up (raise the camera) and look down on the scene. To make a person look more imposing, you can pedestal down (lower the camera) and look up at him or her. This also heightens the perceived energy of the event, such as when shooting the lead singer of a rock group.

All studio pedestals have similar operating features. You can pedestal up and down as well as steer the pedestal smoothly in any direction with a large horizontal steering wheel. The telescoping pedestal column can be locked at any horizontal position.

Like tripod dollies, studio pedestals need a cable guard to keep from running over cables. Always check that the adjustable skirt of the pedestal base is low enough to push the cable out of the way rather than roll over it. **SEE 7.4**

Generally, you work the pedestal in the parallel, or crab, steering position, which means that all three casters point in the same direction. **SEE 7.5A** If you want to rotate the pedestal itself, to move it closer to a wall or piece of scenery, for example, you can switch it from the crab to the tricycle steering position. **SEE 7.5B**

MOUNTING (PAN-AND-TILT) HEADS

The *mounting head* connects the camera to the tripod or studio pedestal. The mounting head (not to be confused with the camera head, which represents the actual camera) allows you to tilt and pan the camera extremely smoothly. This is why the mounting heads are also called pan-and-tilt heads.

Most professional *studio pan-and-tilt heads* have four controls: a tilt and pan drag and a tilt and pan lock. The drag controls give various degrees of resistance to panning and tilting to make the camera movements optimally smooth. The lock controls immobilize the pan-and-tilt mechanism to keep the camera from moving when left unattended. **SEE 7.6**

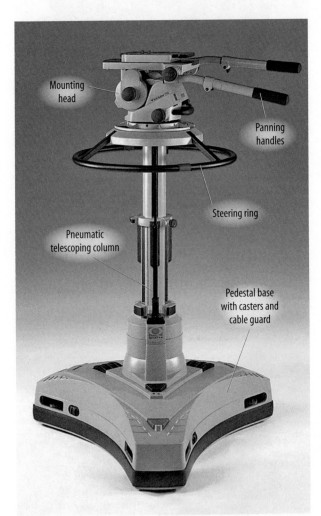

Mounting head

Panning handles

Steering ring

Pneumatic telescoping column

Pedestal base with casters and cable guard

7.4 STUDIO PEDESTAL
The studio pedestal permits smooth dollies and trucks and has a telescoping center column that pedestals the camera from a low of 2 feet to a maximum height of about 6 feet above the studio floor.

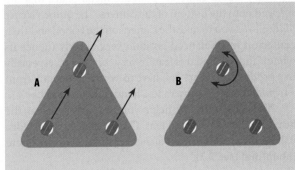

A   B

7.5 PARALLEL (CRAB) AND TRICYCLE STEERING
A In the parallel, or crab, position, all three casters point in the same direction. **B** In the tricycle position, only one wheel is steerable. A foot pedal allows a quick change from parallel to tricycle steering.

7.6 ENG/EFP CAMERA MOUNTING HEAD
This mounting head is designed for mounting and operating ENG/EFP cameras and camcorders on tripods. It has a limited weight capacity.

Pan-and-tilt heads, designed to connect heavy studio or field cameras, have a counterbalance mechanism that permits smooth pans and keeps the heavy load balanced during tilts so that the camera does not tip forward or backward. **SEE 7.7**

Whatever mounting head you use, do not tighten the drag control to lock the pan-and-tilt mechanism or use the lock control to adjust the drag. Using the drag control to lock the camera will ruin the mounting head in a very short time; and trying to use the locking device for tilt and pan drag controls will almost always result in jerky and uneven camera movements.

Quick-release plate and wedge mount   Attaching the camera to the mounting head is done with a quick-release plate for most camcorders and with a wedge mount for heavy studio cameras. Both are metal plates that are screwed onto the bottom of the camera. The *quick-release plate* allows you to take the camera off the tripod and then reattach it in a balanced position very quickly (hence its name). You will find this feature very convenient, especially in a production where you have to switch frequently from a tripod-mounted camera to a handheld one. **SEE 7.8**

The wedge mount helps you properly balance the heavy studio camera and lens. Once balanced, the wedge will keep the camera in a balanced position on subsequent mountings (see 7.7).

SPECIAL CAMERA MOUNTS
These camera mounts are designed for specific camera operations. They include camera stabilizing systems, jib arms, and robotics.

Wedge mount attaches to camera and slides into place on the mounting head

7.7 STUDIO CAMERA MOUNTING HEAD
This studio mounting head is designed for heavier cameras. It is normally used for mounting studio cameras with big lenses and teleprompters onto studio pedestals. Note the wedge mount, which makes it easy to connect the studio camera to the mounting head in a balanced position.

Quick-release plate (attaches to camera base)

Locks into mounting head receptacle

7.8 QUICK-RELEASE PLATE
The quick-release plate enables you to reattach the camera to the mounting head in a balanced position without time-consuming readjustment.

Body harness

Counter-balanced camera

Video monitor

Gimbal

Counterweights

Handle

7.10 STABILIZER FOR LIGHTWEIGHT CAMCORDERS

Stabilizer systems such as this one are designed so that the operator can carry the mount with camera in one hand.

7.9 STABILIZER FOR HEAVY CAMCORDERS

This type of stabilizing system, called a Steadicam, allows you to walk or run with the camera while keeping the pictures perfectly steady. The heavy spring-balanced mechanism is connected to a body harness.

Camera stabilizing systems   A *camera stabilizing system* is a mount that allows the camera operator to walk, run, and even jump while keeping the image steady. One of the most popular camera stabilizing systems is the Steadicam.

For heavy camcorders, the spring-loaded and gimbals-equipped mechanism (which allows the camera to remain level even when its support is tipped) is attached to a harness that supports the vertical monopod and the camera. **SEE 7.9** For small and lightweight camcorders, the camera is connected via gimbals to a handgrip and a counterweight below the camera. **SEE 7.10**

But don't expect to get perfectly smooth pictures the first time you try using such a device. All these stabilizing systems take practice before you make full use of their potential.

When mounting a camcorder to a moving car, you can use a simple beanbag. This camera mount consists of

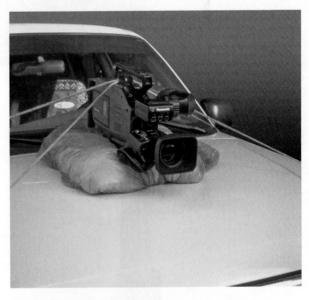

7.11 BEANBAG

This canvas bag filled with synthetic material adjusts to any camera and any object on which it is mounted. Both bag and camera can be easily secured with nylon rope.

a canvas bag filled with high-tech foam that molds itself to the shape of any camcorder. All you do is set the camera on the bag and then strap the bag with the camera to the object that acts as a camera mount. You can use this bag mount on cars, boats, mountain ledges, bicycles, or ladders. **SEE 7.11**

7.12 JIB ARM
The jib arm lets the camera operator dolly, truck, and boom the camera up and down and simultaneously pan, tilt, focus, and zoom.

Camera with pan-and-tilt mechanism

Monitor

Boom

Counterweights and camera operation controls

7.13 ROBOTIC PEDESTAL
The robotic pedestal is fully automated and needs no camera operator. All necessary camera movements and functions are computer-controlled.

Jib arm   The *jib arm* is a cranelike device that lets you—by yourself—lower the camera practically to the studio floor, raise it 12 feet or even higher, tongue the jib arm and swing it a full 360 degrees, dolly or truck the whole assembly, and, at the same time, tilt, pan, focus, and zoom the camera. Obviously, all these movements require practice if they are to look smooth on the air. The camera and the jib arm are balanced by a monitor, the battery pack, remote camera controls, and, for good measure, actual counterweights. **SEE 7.12**

Robotic camera mounts   Automated pedestals and mounting heads, usually called robotics, are used more and more for shows with rigid production formats, such as newscasts, teleconferences, and certain instructional programs. The *robotic pedestal* consists of a motor-driven studio pedestal and a mounting head. **SEE 7.13**

Several studio pedestals can be programmed so that they move their cameras into position for specific shots, such as a two-shot and then close-ups (CUs) of the news anchors followed by a wide shot of the meteorologist and the weather map—all without camera operators. For teleconferencing and classrooms, smaller robotic camera

7.14 OPERATOR CONTROL PANEL FOR ROBOTIC PEDESTAL
With such computer control panels, you can preprogram and control several robotic cameras.

systems often operate from fixed positions, with their pan-and-tilt mechanisms controlled by a single operator in the control room. **SEE 7.14**

WORKING THE CAMCORDER AND THE EFP CAMERA

Similar to learning how to ride a bike, working the camcorder or studio camera cannot be learned from a book (even this one!). You simply need to do it. Knowing some camera "don'ts," however, as well as what to do before, during, and after the shoot can greatly speed up your learning how to operate the camera. When caught up in a large studio production or covering a hot news story, it's easy to forget that the camera is an extremely complex piece of machinery. Although it may not be as precious or fragile as your grandmother's china, it still needs careful handling and a measure of respect. The following "don'ts" before learning the "do's" of camera operation are to prevent you from damaging or losing the equipment before you ever get to use it. In this light these taboos represent a positive beginning.

SOME BASIC CAMERA "DON'TS"

■ Do not leave a camcorder in a car—even in the trunk—for an extended period of time unless the car is safely locked in a garage. Like people and animals, electronic equipment tends to suffer from excessive heat. More important, keeping the camera gear with you as much as possible is a fairly simple way of preventing theft.

■ Do not leave a camcorder unprotected in the rain, hot sun, or extreme cold. When you must use a camcorder in the rain, protect it with a "raincoat"—a prefabricated plastic hood—or at least a plastic sheet. A simple but effective means of keeping rain away from a camera is a large umbrella. Some zoom lenses stick in extremely wet or cold weather. Test the lens before using it on-location. Never use wet tapes or wet nontape media.

■ Do not point the lens for an extended period of time at the midday sun. Although the image sensors will not be damaged by the intensity of the sunlight, they may suffer from the heat generated by the focused rays. The same goes for the viewfinder: don't leave it pointed at the sun for an extended period of time; the viewfinder's magnifying lens can collect the sun's rays, melting its housing and electronics.

■ Do not leave camcorder batteries in the sun or, worse, drop them. Although a battery may look rugged from the outside, it is actually sensitive to heat and shock. Some batteries should not be charged in extremely cold temperatures.

■ Do not lay a camcorder on its side. You run the risk of damaging the viewfinder or the clipped-on microphone on the other side. When finished shooting, cap the camera with the external lens cover and, just to make sure, close the aperture to the *C* (cap) or *close* position.

BEFORE THE SHOOT

■ Before doing anything else, count all the pieces of equipment and mark them on an equipment checklist. If you need auxiliary equipment, such as external microphones, camera lights, a power supply, or field monitors, check on the right connectors and cables. Take some extra adapters along.

■ Unless you are running after hot news, first set up the tripod and see whether it is level. Do some panning and tilting to determine the optimal pan and tilt drag. Check the pan and tilt locks. Insert the battery or connect the camcorder to its alternate power supply (AC/DC converter and transformer) and do a brief test recording before taking the camcorder into the field. Make sure the camcorder records video as well as audio.

■ If you are engaged in elaborate field productions using high-quality EFP cameras and separate video recorders, check the connecting cables and the power supplies (usually batteries). You may need a video feed from the camera (or recorder) to a battery-powered field monitor for the director. Do all the plugs fit the intended jacks? In EFP the wrong, or even a loose, connector can mean a lost production day. As with the camcorder, hook up all the equipment you will use in the field and do a test recording before going on-location. Never assume that everything will work merely because it worked in the past.

■ Check that the external microphone (usually a lavalier or hand mic) and the camera mic are working properly. Most camera mics need to be switched on before they become operational. Scratch the top of the mic and listen for whether it makes any noise. Is there sufficient cable for the external mic so that the reporter can work far enough away from the camera? If you are primarily doing news that requires an external mic for the field reporter, you may want to keep the external mic plugged in to save time and minimize costly mistakes.

■ Does the portable camera light work? Don't just look at the lamp. Turn on the light to verify that it works. When using a separate battery for the light, make sure that the battery is fully charged. If you have additional lights, are they all operational? Do you have enough AC extension cords to power the additional lights?

■ When using a separate video recorder for EFP, do a test recording to ensure that the recorder is in good working order. (See chapter 12 for details on video recording.)

■ Double-check that the recording media (videotape, P2 cards or other flash memory devices, hard disks, or optical discs) work in the camcorder you are using. Some small camcorders cannot accept the larger tapes and use only mini-cassettes. Before putting the recording media into the camcorder, do a quick check of whether the record-protect tab is in the *off* position (see chapter 12). Always take along a few more recording media than you think you will need.

■ Although you are not a maintenance engineer, carry some spare fuses for the principal equipment. Some ENG/EFP cameras and camcorders have a spare fuse right next to the active one. Note, however, that a blown fuse indicates a malfunction in the equipment. Even if the camcorder works again with the new fuse, have it checked when you return from the shoot.

■ Like carrying a medical first-aid kit, always have a field production kit that contains the following necessities: several extra videocassettes or appropriate recording media, an audiocassette recorder and several audiocassettes, an

additional microphone and a small microphone stand, one or more portable lights and stands, additional lamps for all lighting instruments, AC cords, spare batteries for all battery-powered equipment, various clips or wooden clothespins, gaffer's tape, a small reflector, a roll of aluminum foil, a small white card for white-balancing, light-diffusing material, various effects filters, a can of compressed air for cleaning lenses, and a camera raincoat.

You should also carry such personal survival items as water and energy bars, a working flashlight, an umbrella, some spare clothes, and, yes, toilet paper. Once you have worked in the field a few times, you will know how to put together your own field production kit.

DURING THE SHOOT

After getting some field production experience, you will probably develop your own techniques for carrying and operating a camcorder or ENG/EFP camera. There are obvious differences between the small, handheld camcorders and the larger ones that are shoulder-mounted. But most of the general operating procedures are the same.

■ First and foremost, put the camera on a tripod whenever possible. You will have more control over framing and steadying the shot. You will also get less tired during a long shoot.

■ Unless you want to use the camcorder's fully automated white-balance feature, you must white-balance before starting to shoot. Be sure to white-balance the camera in the same light that illuminates the scene you are shooting. If you don't have a white card, focus the camera on anything white, such as somebody's shirt or the back of a script. Repeat the white balance each time you encounter new lighting conditions, such as when moving from an interview on a street corner to the interior of a new restaurant. Careful white-balancing may save you hours of color correction in postproduction.

■ Keep the camera as steady as possible. This is especially important when the zoom lens is in the telephoto position. When operating a small camcorder, support it in the palm of your hand and use the other hand to support the camera arm or the camcorder itself. Whenever possible, press your elbows against your body, inhale, and hold your breath during the shot. Bend your knees slightly when shooting, or lean against a sturdy support to increase the stability of the camera. Such camera handling is recommended even if you have the image stabilizer turned on. Note that image stabilizers correct only minor camera wobbles and drain the battery in the process. **SEE 7.15 AND 7.16**

7.15 HOLDING THE SMALL CAMCORDER
Steady the camcorder with both hands, with your
elbows pressed against your body.

7.16 STEADYING THE CAMERA OPERATOR
Lean against a tree or wall to steady yourself and
the camcorder.

■ Use the viewfinder rather than the foldout screen to
compose your shots. The viewfinder makes focusing more
accurate (you get a sharper image) and is a better guide to
proper exposure (*f*-stop) than the flat-panel display. When
shooting outdoors, you will find that the foldout screen is
often rendered useless by the sun shining on it, obliterating
the image. Use the foldout screen only if the camera is in
the automatic mode and you need only a rough guide to
framing a shot.

■ Large and some midsized camcorders are designed to
be shoulder-mounted. There are shoulder pods available
for the midsized camcorders. Assuming that you are right-
handed, carry the camera on your right shoulder and slip
your right hand through the support strap on the zoom
lens. This helps you steady the camera while allowing you
to operate the zoom and auto-focus controls. Your left
hand is free to operate the manual focus ring. If you are
left-handed, reverse the procedure and switch the lens grip
and the viewfinder to the left side. **SEE 7.17**

7.17 SHOULDER-MOUNTED CAMCORDER
Carry the larger camcorder on your shoulder. One hand slips
through the strap on the lens to steady the camcorder and
operate the zoom. Your other hand is free to operate the focus
ring at the front of the zoom lens and provide further support
for the camcorder.

■ When moving the camcorder, zoom all the way out. Because of the great depth of field, you have fewer problems keeping the event in focus even if you or the subject moves. Even in the wide-angle position, move the camera as smoothly as possible.

■ Before zooming, calibrate the zoom lens by zooming in all the way on the target object, focusing, and then zooming back out to the desired shot. Your subsequent zooms will remain in focus unless the camcorder or the object gets closer or farther away from each other. Then you need to recalibrate the lens.

■ If the target object is obvious, put the camcorder on auto-focus. When in a hurry, the auto-focus gives you better-focused pictures than if you are not careful focusing with the manual one.

■ Achieving optimal focus is especially difficult with HDV (high-definition video) and HDTV (high-definition television) because the high-resolution picture looks in focus even if it is slightly out of focus. If the scene is steady, put the camera on auto-focus. Otherwise, rack through the focus a few times to see where the optimal focus lies. Look through the viewfinder rather than at the foldout screen when focusing. Switch to the focus-assist feature if the camcorder has one.

■ To pan the small—and the large—camcorder, move it with your whole body rather than just your arms. First, point your knees in the direction of the *end* of the pan. Then twist your body with the camera aimed toward the *beginning* of the pan. During the pan you are like a spring that is uncoiling from the start of the action to the finish. Always bend your knees slightly when shooting; as in skiing, your knees act as shock absorbers. Don't panic if you lose the subject temporarily in the viewfinder. Keep the camera steady, look up to see where the subject is, and aim the camera smoothly in the new direction. **SEE 7.18**

When moving with people who are walking, get in front of them with the camera and walk backward at the same speed. This way you can see their faces rather than their backs. Moving backward also forces you to walk on the balls of your feet, which are better shock absorbers than your heels. Watch that you do not bump into or stumble over something while walking backward—a quick check of your proposed route can prevent unexpected mishaps. With the zoom lens in the wide-angle position, you are often closer to the object than the viewfinder image indicates. Be careful not to hit something or someone with

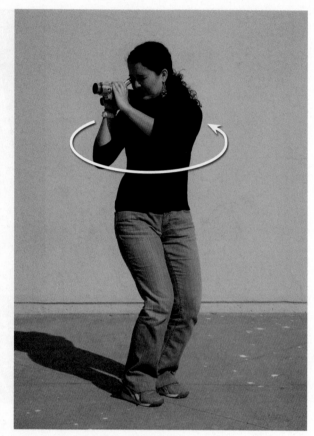

7.18 PANNING THE CAMCORDER
Before panning, point your knees in the direction of the end of the pan, then uncoil your upper body during the pan.

the camera, especially if you walk forward with it into a crowd. **SEE 7.19**

■ Under normal conditions put the camera in the auto-iris mode. "Normal conditions" means that the lighting does not produce a high contrast (such as the midday sun) or that you don't have to create special effects, such as a very shallow depth of field. Despite the objections of some especially critical camera operators, using auto-iris on an overcast day will often yield better-exposed video than doing it manually, especially during ENG.

■ Don't forget the audio. Use earbuds or headphones to listen to the sound. All camcorders record on two audio tracks. Whenever possible, check the audio level before and during recording. When working in relatively quiet surroundings, record with the automatic gain control (AGC). Otherwise, you need to switch to manual gain control, take

7.19 WALKING BACKWARD
When moving with something or somebody, walk backward rather than forward. The balls of your feet act like shock absorbers.

a sound level, and record. (See chapters 8 and 9 for more on ENG sound.)

■ Always record sound with the camera mic, even if you are using an external mic for the primary sound pickup. This ambient sound is important for achieving continuity in postproduction editing. When the reporter is holding the external mic, do not start to run away from him or her to get a better shot of the event. Either you both run together, or you must stay put.

■ Whenever you use a camcorder in the field, use common sense. Be mindful of your and other people's safety. Always ask yourself whether the risk is worth the story. In ENG reliability and consistency are more important than sporadic feats, however spectacular. Do not risk your neck and the equipment to get a shot that would simply embellish a story. Leave that type of shooting to the gifted amateurs.

AFTER THE SHOOT

■ Unless you have just shot a really hot story that must air immediately, even unedited, take care of the equipment before delivering the recording media. If you are properly organized, it should take just a few minutes.

■ Close the lens iris to the *C* or *close* position and replace the lens cap.

■ Put all the switches in the *off* position, unless you are running after another story, in which case put the camera on standby.

■ Extract the recording media (tape, disc, flash drive) from the camera, label it and its box, and put it in a safe place.

■ As soon as you return from the assignment, recharge all batteries. If the camcorder got wet, wait until everything has dried out before putting the camcorder into its case. Moisture is one of the most serious threats to camcorders. If you have time, check all the portable lights so they will work for the next assignment. Coil all AC extension cords—you will not have time to untangle them during an ongoing event.

WORKING THE STUDIO CAMERA

In one way a studio camera is easier to operate than a portable camera: it is mounted on some kind of camera support, and the video operator (VO) makes all the electronic adjustments, "shading" the camera at the CCU (camera control unit). In another way, however, you may find operating the studio camera more difficult because you have to steer the heavy pedestal to truck, arc, dolly, and pedestal up and down. You have to zoom in and out and adjust the focus while composing effective pictures, listening to the director's commands, and watching the studio traffic around you. Obviously, a smooth coordination of all these factors takes practice. The following steps for before, during, and after a show will facilitate your operating the studio camera.

BEFORE THE SHOW

■ Put on your headset and check that the intercom system is functioning. You should hear at least the director, the technical director (TD), and the video operator.

■ Unlock the pan-and-tilt mechanism on the mounting head and adjust the horizontal and vertical drag, if necessary. Check that the camera is balanced on the mounting head. Unlock the pedestal, then pedestal up and down.

■ See how much camera cable you have and whether there are any obstacles that may interfere with the cable run. Check that the pedestal skirt or other type of cable guard is low enough to move the cable out of the way rather than roll over it.

■ Ask the VO to uncap the camera from the CCU, and ask if you can remove the lens cap. You can then see in the viewfinder the pictures the camera actually takes. Is the viewfinder properly adjusted? Like a home television set, the viewfinder can be adjusted for brightness and contrast. If you need framing guides, flip the switch that shows the essential area (safe title area) and the screen-center mark The center mark is especially important if you have to keep the principal action in the 4 × 3 screen area on a 16 × 9 viewfinder (see chapter 14).

■ Check the zoom lens. Zoom in and out. Get a feel for how close you can get to the main event from a certain position. Is the lens clean? If it is dusty, use a fine camel-hair brush and carefully clean off the larger dust particles. With a small rubber bulb or a can of compressed air, blow off the finer dust. Do not blow on the lens with your mouth: the moisture will fog it up and get it even dirtier.

■ Rack through focus: move the focus control from one extreme position to the other. Can you move easily and smoothly into and out of focus, especially when in a narrow-angle, zoomed-in position?

■ Calibrate the zoom lens by zooming all the way in and focusing on the target object. You should now remain in focus throughout the zoom, provided neither the object nor the camera moves toward or away from each other.

■ If you have a shot sheet (also called a shot list), this is a good time to practice the more complicated zoom and dolly or truck shots. A shot sheet is a list of every shot a particular camera has to get. It is attached to the camera to help the operator remember the shot sequence.

■ If a teleprompter is attached to the camera, check all the connections.

■ Lock the camera again (the pedestal and the pan-and-tilt mechanism) before leaving it. Don't ever leave a camera unlocked, even for a short while. Some pedestals have a parking brake. Set the brake on the pedestal before leaving the camera.

■ Cap the camera if you leave it for a prolonged period of time.

DURING THE SHOW

■ Put on the headset and establish contact with the director, TD, and VO. Unlock the camera and recheck the pan and tilt drag and the pedestal movement.

■ Calibrate the zoom at each new camera position. Ensure that you can stay in focus over the entire zoom range.

■ When checking the focus for a new shot, rack through focus a few times to determine at which position the picture is the sharpest. When focusing on a person, the hairline usually gives you enough detail to determine the sharpest focus. In extreme close-ups (ECUs), focus on the bridge of the nose. Achieving and remaining in proper focus is more difficult with an HDV or HDTV camera. If available, use the focus-assist feature.

■ If you anticipate a dolly, set the zoom lens to the wide-angle position. With the zoom lens in the extreme wide-angle position, the depth of field should be large enough so that you need to adjust focus only when you are very close to the object or event.

■ If you have a difficult truck or arc to perform, have a floor person help you move and steer the camera. You can then concentrate on the camera operation.

■ In a straight dolly, you can keep both hands on the panning handles. If you have to steer the camera, steer with your right hand, keeping your left hand on the focus control.

■ When you pedestal up or down, try to brake the camera before it hits the stops at the extreme pedestal positions. Generally, keep your shots at the talent's eye level unless the director instructs you to shoot from either a high (pedestal up and look down) or a low (pedestal down and look up) angle.

■ When you operate a freewheel camera dolly, always preset the wheels toward the intended camera movement to prevent the dolly from starting off in the wrong direction. Check that the cable guards are low enough to prevent the camera from running over the cables on the studio floor instead of pushing them out of the way.

■ Use masking tape on the studio floor to mark the critical camera positions.

■ At all times during the show, be aware of the activity around you. Where are the other cameras? The microphone boom? The floor monitor? It is your responsibility to keep out of the view of the other cameras and not hit anything (including floor personnel and talent) during your moves. Rugs are a constant hazard to camera movement. When dollying into a set that has a rug, watch the floor so that you do not suddenly dolly up onto the rug.

■ Watch for the tally light to go out before calibrating the zoom or moving the camera to a new shooting position. This is especially important if your camera is engaged in special effects. With effects involving two cameras (such as a superimposition), the tally lights of both cameras are on (see chapter 13).

■ In general, keep your eyes on the viewfinder. If the format allows, look around for something interesting to shoot between shots. The director will appreciate good visuals in an ad-lib show (in which the shots have not been rehearsed). If you have a shot sheet, though, stick to it, however tempting the shot possibilities may be. Do not try to outdirect the director. Mark all shot changes on the shot sheet.

■ If you work without shot sheets, try to remember the type and the sequence of shots from the rehearsal. A good camera operator has the next shot lined up before the director calls for it. If you work from a shot sheet, go to the next shot immediately after the preceding one—don't wait until the last minute.

■ Listen carefully to what the director tells all camera operators (not just you) so that you can coordinate your shots with those of the other cameras. Also, you can avoid wasteful duplication of shots by knowing approximately what the other cameras are doing.

■ Avoid unnecessary chatter on the intercom.

AFTER THE SHOW

■ At the end of the show, wait for the "all clear" signal before you lock the camera. Ask the VO whether you can cap the lens.

■ Lock the mounting head and the pedestal in a low position. Push the camera to its designated parking place in the studio. Coil the cable as neatly as possible in the customary figure-eight loops.

▮ M A I N   P O I N T S

▶ The standard camera movements are pan, turning the camera horizontally; tilt, pointing the camera up or down; pedestal, lowering or elevating the camera on a studio pedestal; tongue, moving the whole camera from left to right or from right to left with the boom of a jib arm; crane or boom, moving the whole camera up or down on a camera jib arm; dolly, moving the camera toward or away from the scene; truck or track, moving the camera laterally; arc, moving the camera in a slightly curved dolly or truck movement; cant, tilting the camera sideways; and zoom, changing the focal length of the lens while the camera is stationary.

▶ The basic camera mounts are handheld and shoulder-mounted, the monopod, the tripod and the tripod dolly, the studio pedestal, stabilizing systems, the jib arm, and the robotic pedestal.

▶ The mounting head connects the camera to the tripod or studio pedestal and allows the camera to be smoothly tilted up and down and panned horizontally.

▶ The quick-release plate is used to attach a camcorder to a mounting head. The wedge mount facilitates attaching the heavier cameras to the mounting head in a balanced position.

▶ Before using a camcorder, check that the batteries are fully charged and that you have enough videotape or other recording media for the assignment. Do an audio check with the camera mic and the external mic.

▶ When working a camcorder or portable camera, handle it with the utmost care. Do not leave it unprotected in the sun or uncovered in the rain.

▶ At all times pay particular attention to white balance, pre-setting the zoom, and recording ambient sound. Switch to auto-controls if the conditions are right.

▶ After the production put everything back carefully so that the equipment is ready for the next assignment.

7.2

Framing Effective Shots

▶ **DEPTH**
Creating the illusion of a third dimension in both aspect ratios: choice of lens, positioning of objects, depth of field, and lighting and color

▶ **SCREEN MOTION**
Z-axis motion (movement toward and away from the camera) and lateral movement in both aspect ratios

SCREEN SIZE AND FIELD OF VIEW

Screen size and field of view are closely related. On the large movie screen, you can show a relatively large vista with a great amount of event detail. When the same scene is shown on television or on the small cell-phone screen, however, you will not only have difficulty making out the smaller event details but, more important, you will lose the aesthetic impact of the shot. This is why some film critics suggest seeing a particular film "on the big screen."

SCREEN SIZE

To reveal event details on the relatively small television screen, you must show them in close-ups rather than long shots. In other words, the field of view must generally be tighter on television than on the motion picture screen. Such a close-up approach necessitates choosing and emphasizing those details that contribute most effectively to the overall event and that add aesthetic energy.

FIELD OF VIEW

Field of view refers to how far or how close the object appears relative to the camera, that is, how close it will appear to the viewer. It is basically organized into five steps: *extreme long shot (ELS)*, also called establishing shot; *long shot (LS)*, also called full shot or establishing shot; *medium shot (MS)*, also called waist shot; *close-up (CU)*; and *extreme close-up (ECU)*. **SEE 7.20** **ZVL2** CAMERA→ Composition→ field of view

Four other ways of designating conventional shots are: bust shot, which frames the subject from the upper torso to the top of the head; knee shot, which frames the subject from just above or below the knees; *two-shot*, with two people or objects in the frame; and three-shot, with three people or objects in the frame. Although more a blocking arrangement than a field of view, you should also know two additional shots: the over-the-shoulder shot and the cross-shot. In the *over-the-shoulder shot (O/S)*, the camera looks at someone over the shoulder of the camera-near person. In a *cross-shot (X/S)*, the camera looks alternately

The basic purpose of framing a shot is to show images as clearly as possible and to present them so that they convey meaning and energy. Essentially, you clarify and intensify the event before you. When working a camcorder, you are the only one who sees the images before they are video-recorded. You therefore cannot rely on a director to tell you how to frame every picture for maximum effectiveness.

The more you know about picture composition, the more effective your clarification and intensification of the event will be. But even if you are working as a camera operator during a multicamera studio show or a large remote where the director can preview all the camera pictures, you still need to know how to compose effective shots. The director might be able to correct some of your shots, but he or she will certainly not have time to teach you the fundamentals of good composition.

This section describes the major compositional principles and explains how to frame a shot for maximum clarity and impact.

▶ **SCREEN SIZE AND FIELD OF VIEW**
Operating with close-ups and medium shots rather than long shots and extreme long shots

▶ **FRAMING A SHOT: STANDARD TV AND HDTV ASPECT RATIOS**
Dealing with height and width, framing close-ups, headroom, noseroom and leadroom, and closure

Extreme long shot (ELS),
or establishing shot

Long shot (LS), or full shot

Medium shot (MS),
or waist shot

7.20
FIELD-OF-VIEW STEPS
The shot designations range
from ELS (extreme long shot)
to ECU (extreme close-up).

Close-up (CU)

Extreme close-up (ECU)

at one or the other person, with the camera-near person completely out of the shot. **SEE 7.21**

Of course, exactly how to frame such shots depends not only on your sensitivity to composition but also on the director's preference.

FRAMING A SHOT: STANDARD TV AND HDTV ASPECT RATIOS

Many high-end studio cameras, EFP cameras, and most camcorders have a switch for changing the *aspect ratio* from the standard 4 × 3 format to the HDTV 16 × 9. Although the aspect ratios of STV (standard television) and

HDTV are quite different and require different technical manipulations, many of the aesthetic principles of good picture composition apply to both. Nevertheless, in framing effective shots some aesthetic principles must be adjusted to the specific requirements of the aspect ratio. This section takes a closer look at dealing with height and width, framing close-ups, headroom, noseroom and leadroom, and closure.

DEALING WITH HEIGHT AND WIDTH

You will find that the 4 × 3 aspect ratio is well suited to framing a vertical scene, such as a high-rise building, as well as a horizontally oriented vista. **SEE 7.22 AND 7.23** It is

Bust shot

Knee shot

Two-shot (two persons
or objects in frame)

Three-shot (three persons
or objects in frame)

Over-the-shoulder shot (O/S)

Cross-shot (X/S)

7.21 OTHER
SHOT DESIGNATIONS
Other common shot designations are the bust shot, knee shot, two-shot, three-shot, over-the-shoulder shot, and cross-shot. Note that the bust shot is similar to the MS and that the knee shot is similar to the LS.

7.22 FRAMING A VERTICAL VIEW
The 4 × 3 aspect ratio allows you to frame a vertical scene without having to use extreme camera distance or angles.

7.23 FRAMING A HORIZONTAL VIEW
The 4 × 3 aspect ratio readily accommodates a horizontal vista.

7.24 FRAMING HEIGHT AND WIDTH IN A SINGLE SHOT
The 4 × 3 aspect ratio easily accommodates both horizontal and vertical vistas.

7.25 FRAMING A HORIZONTAL VIEW IN THE HDTV ASPECT RATIO
The 16 × 9 format is ideal for framing wide horizontal vistas.

7.26 FRAMING A VERTICAL VIEW IN THE HDTV ASPECT RATIO
The 16 × 9 format makes it difficult to frame a vertical object. One way to frame a tall object is to shoot it from below and cant the camera.

7.27 NATURAL MASKING OF THE SCREEN SIDES IN THE HDTV ASPECT RATIO
You can use parts of the natural environment to block the sides of the wide 16 × 9 screen to create a vertical space in which to frame the vertical object. In this shot the foreground buildings create a vertical aspect ratio for the high-rise building.

also relatively easy to accommodate a scene that has both wide and high elements. **SEE 7.24**

Although the horizontally stretched 16 × 9 aspect ratio makes horizontal scenes look spectacular, it presents a formidable obstacle to framing a vertical view. **SEE 7.25** You can either tilt the camera up to reveal the height of the object or shoot from below and cant the camera to make the subject fit into the diagonal screen space. **SEE 7.26** Another frequently used film technique for dealing with vertical objects is to have other picture elements block the sides of the screen and, in effect, give you a vertical aspect ratio in which to frame the shot. **SEE 7.27**

FRAMING CLOSE-UPS

Close-ups and extreme close-ups are common elements in the visual language of television because, compared with the large motion picture screen, even large televi-

7.28 FRAMING A CLOSE-UP
The normal close-up shows the head of the
person and part of the shoulders.

7.29 FRAMING AN EXTREME CLOSE-UP
In an extreme close-up, you should crop the
top of the head while keeping the upper part
of the shoulders in the shot.

7.30 FRAMING A CLOSE-UP IN THE HDTV ASPECT RATIO
When framing the same close-up in the 16 × 9 format, both
screen sides look conspicuously empty.

**7.31 FRAMING AN EXTREME
CLOSE-UP IN THE HDTV ASPECT RATIO**
In the 16 × 9 format, the extreme close-up of the person seems
oddly squeezed between the upper and lower screen edges.

sion screens are relatively small. The 4 × 3 aspect ratio
and the small screen of the standard television receiver
are the ideal combination for CUs and ECUs of people's
heads. **SEE 7.28**

As you can see, the normal CU shows the customary
headroom and part of the upper body. The ECU is somewhat trickier to frame: the top screen edge cuts across the
top part of the head, and the lower edge cuts just below
the top part of the shoulders. **SEE 7.29 ZVL3 CAMERA→**
Composition→ close-ups

When you try to frame the same shot in the HDTV
16 × 9 aspect ratio, however, you are left with a great
amount of leftover space on both sides of the subject's
face. The close-up looks somewhat lost in the wide-
screen format, and the extreme close-up looks as though
it is squeezed between the top and bottom screen edges.
SEE 7.30 AND 7.31 You can solve this problem relatively easily

by including some visual elements in the shot that fill the
empty spaces on either side. **SEE 7.32**

Some directors simply tilt the camera or the talent
somewhat so that the shot occupies more of the horizontal
space. On the other hand, the HDTV aspect ratio lets you
easily frame close-ups of two people face-to-face. Such an
arrangement is difficult in the traditional format because
the two dialogue partners must stand uncomfortably close
to each other. **SEE 7.33**

HEADROOM
Because the edges of the television frame seem to attract
like magnets whatever is close to them, leave some space
above people's heads—called **headroom**—in normal long
shots, medium shots, and close-ups. **SEE 7.34** Avoid having
the head "glued" to the upper edge of the frame. **SEE 7.35**

7.32 NATURAL MASKING OF A CLOSE-UP IN THE HDTV ASPECT RATIO
To avoid excessive empty space when framing a screen-center close-up of a person in the 16 × 9 format, you can mask the sides with objects from the actual environment.

7.33 FACE-TO-FACE CLOSE-UPS IN THE HDTV ASPECT RATIO
The 16 × 9 format makes it relatively easy to have two people face each other on a close-up without having to stand uncomfortably close together.

7.34 NORMAL HEADROOM
Headroom counters the magnetic pull of the upper frame. The person appears comfortably placed in the frame.

7.35 TOO LITTLE HEADROOM
With no, or too little, headroom, the person looks cramped in the frame. The head seems to be glued to the upper screen edge.

7.36 TOO MUCH HEADROOM
With too much headroom, the pull of the bottom edge makes the picture bottom-heavy and strangely unbalanced.

Because you lose a certain amount of picture area in video recording and transmission, you need to leave a little more headroom than feels comfortable. Leaving too much headroom, however, is just as bad as too little. **SEE 7.36** If the camera is so equipped, you can use the frame guide in the viewfinder to see the picture area that actually appears on the television screen. The headroom rule applies equally to both aspect ratios. **ZVL4** CAMERA→ Composition→ headroom

NOSEROOM AND LEADROOM
Somebody looking or pointing in a particular direction other than straight into the camera creates a screen force called an index vector. You must compensate for this force by leaving some space in front of the vector. When someone looks or points screen-left or screen-right, the index vector needs to be balanced with **noseroom**. A lack

of noseroom or leadroom makes the picture look oddly out of balance; the person seems to be blocked by the screen edge. **SEE 7.37 AND 7.38**

All motion creates a motion vector. When someone or something moves in a screen-right or screen-left direction, you must leave **leadroom** to balance the force of the motion vector. **SEE 7.39** Even in a still photo, you can see that without proper leadroom the cyclist seems to be crashing into the left screen border. **SEE 7.40**

To avoid such crashes, you must always lead the moving object with the camera rather than follow it. After all, we want to see where the moving object is going, not where it has been. Note, however, that neither of the leadroom examples here represents actual motion vectors because they are still pictures. In a still picture, they do not move but simply point in a specific direction and are, therefore, index vectors. **ZVL5** CAMERA→ Composition→ leadroom

7.37 PROPER NOSEROOM
To absorb the force of the strong index vector created by the person's looking toward the screen edge, you need to leave some noseroom.

7.38 LACK OF NOSEROOM
Without noseroom the person seems to be blocked by the screen edge, and the picture looks unbalanced.

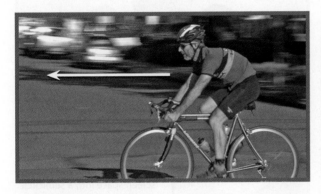

7.39 PROPER LEADROOM
Assuming that the cyclist is actually moving, his motion vector is properly neutralized by the screen space in front of him. We like to see where the person is heading, not where he has been. Note that a still picture cannot show a motion vector. What you see here is an index vector.

7.40 LACK OF LEADROOM
Without leadroom the moving person or object seems to be hindered or stopped by the screen edge.

CLOSURE

Closure, short for *psychological closure,* is the process by which our minds fill in information that we cannot actually see. Take a look around you: you see only parts of the objects that lie in your field of vision. There is no way you can ever see an object in its entirety unless the object moves around you or you move around the object. Through experience we have learned to mentally supply the missing parts, which allows us to perceive a whole world although we actually see only a fraction of it. Because close-ups usually show only part of an object, your psychological closure mechanism must work overtime.

Positive closure   To facilitate closure you should always frame a shot in such a way that the viewer can easily extend the figure beyond the screen edges and perceive a sensible whole. **SEE 7.41** To organize the visual world around us, we also automatically group things together so that they form a sensible pattern. **SEE 7.42 AND 7.43** You would be hard-pressed *not* to perceive figure 7.42 as a triangular pattern and figure 7.43 as a semicircle.

Negative closure   This closure automation can also work against good composition. For example, when framing a close-up of a face without giving prominent visual

7.41 FACILITATING CLOSURE BEYOND THE FRAME
In this shot we perceive the whole figure of the person and her guitar although we see only part of them. This shot gives us sufficient clues to project the figure beyond the frame and apply psychological closure in the off-screen space.

7.42 TRIANGLE CLOSURE
We tend to organize things into easily recognizable patterns. This group of similar objects forms a triangle.

7.43 SEMICIRCLE CLOSURE
These objects organize the screen space into a semicircle.

clues to help viewers project the image beyond the screen edges, the head seems oddly cut off from its body. **SEE 7.44** You therefore need to provide enough visual clues to lead the viewers' eyes beyond the frame so they can apply closure and perceive the complete person in off-screen space. **SEE 7.45**

Our mechanism to organize our environment into simple patterns is so strong that it often works against reason. In the excitement of getting a good story and an interesting shot, it is easy to forget to look behind the object of attention, but it is often the background that spoils a good picture composition. **SEE 7.46** As you can see in figure 7.46, we tend to perceive the background as part of the foreground. The reporter seems to be balancing a street sign on his head. Once you are aware of the background, it is relatively easy to avoid illogical closure. **ZVL6** CAMERA→ Composition→ closure

DEPTH

Because television and movie screens are flat, we must create the illusion of a third dimension. Fortunately, the principles for creating the illusion of depth on a two-dimensional surface have been amply explored and established by painters and photographers over the years. The camera lens will do much of the work for you. To create and intensify the illusion of depth on the most basic level, try to establish a clear division of the image into foreground, middleground, and background. **SEE 7.47** To do this you need to consider four factors: choice of lens, positioning of objects, depth of field, and lighting and color.

Choice of lens   A wide-angle zoom position exaggerates depth. Narrow-angle positions reduce the illusion of a third dimension.

7.44 UNDESIRABLE CLOSURE WITHIN THE FRAME
This shot is badly framed because we apply closure within the frame without projecting the rest of the person into off-screen space.

7.45 DESIRABLE CLOSURE IN OFF-SCREEN SPACE
In this ECU there are enough on-screen clues to project the rest of the person's head and body into off-screen space, thus applying closure to the total figure.

7.46 ILLOGICAL CLOSURE
Although we know better, we perceive this reporter as balancing a street sign on his head.

7.47 FOREGROUND, MIDDLEGROUND, AND BACKGROUND
In general, try to divide the z-axis (depth dimension) into a prominent foreground (tree trunks), middleground (embankment of the creek and the bushes), and background (mountains). Such a division helps create the illusion of screen depth.

Positioning of objects   The *z-axis*—the line representing an extension of the lens from the camera to the horizon—has significant bearing on perceiving depth. Anything positioned along the z-axis relative to the camera will create the illusion of depth. To emphasize depth, always try to include a foreground object in the shot. This inevitably pushes everything else farther back.

Depth of field   A slightly shallow depth of field is usually more effective to define depth because the in-focus foreground object is more clearly set off against the out-of-focus background.

Lighting and color   A brightly lighted object with strong (highly saturated) color seems closer than one that is dimly lighted and has washed-out (low-saturation) colors. **ZVL7** CAMERA→ Picture depth→ z-axis | lens choice | perspective and distortion

SCREEN MOTION[1]

Contrary to the painter or the still photographer, who deals with the organization of static images within the picture frame, the television camera operator must almost always cope with framing images in motion. Composing moving images requires quick reactions and full attention throughout the telecast or recording. The study of the

---

1. For an extensive discussion of screen forces and how they can be used for effective picture composition, see Herbert Zettl, *Sight Sound Motion: Applied Media Aesthetics*, 5th ed. (Belmont, Calif.: Thomson Wadsworth, 2008), pp. 101–25, 247-65.

moving image is an important part of learning the fine art of television and film production; here we look at some of its most basic principles.

When framing for the traditional 4 × 3 aspect ratio and small screen, movements along the z-axis (toward or away from the camera) are stronger than any type of lateral motion (from one screen edge to the other). Fortunately, they are also the easiest to frame: you simply keep the camera as steady as possible and make sure that the moving object does not go out of focus as it approaches the camera. Remember that a wide-angle zoom position gives the impression of accelerated motion along the z-axis, whereas a narrow-angle zoom position slows z-axis motion for the viewer.

When working in the 16 × 9 HDTV aspect ratio, lateral movement takes on added prominence. The stretched screen width gives you a little more breathing room when two people face each other (see figure 7.33), and a laterally moving object has more time to travel from one screen edge to the other.

If you are on a close-up and the subject shifts back and forth, don't try to follow each minor wiggle. You might run the risk of making viewers seasick; at the very least, they will not be able to concentrate on the subject for very long. Keep the camera pointed at the major action area or zoom out (or pull back) to a slightly wider shot.

When one of the persons in a two-shot moves out of the frame, do not try to keep both people in the frame—stay with just one of them. **SEE 7.48 AND 7.49** **ZVL8** CAMERA→ Screen motion→ z-axis | lateral | close-ups

If even after extensive rehearsals you find that in an over-the-shoulder shot the person closer to the camera

7.48 TWO PERSONS SAYING GOOD-BYE
If in a two-shot the people walk away from each other toward the screen edges, don't try to keep both people in the shot.

7.49 CAMERA STAYS WITH ONE OF THEM
You must decide which person you will keep in the frame and let the other move off-camera.

7.50 CAMERA-FAR PERSON BLOCKED
In an over-the-shoulder shot, you may find that the camera-near person blocks the camera-far person.

7.51 CAMERA TRUCKS TO CORRECT
To correct this over-the-shoulder shot so that the camera-far person can be seen, simply truck or arc the camera to the right.

blocks the other person, who is farther away from the camera, you can solve the problem by trucking or arcing to the right or left. **SEE 7.50 AND 7.51**

Whatever you do to organize screen motion, do it smoothly. Try to move the camera as little as possible unless you need to follow a moving object or dramatize a shot through motion. Because you can move a camcorder so easily, it may be tempting to animate a basically static scene by moving the camera with great fervor. Don't do it. Excessive camera motion is a telltale sign of an amateur camera operator.

▶ A simple and effective way to organize screen depth is to establish a distinct foreground, middleground, and background.

▶ In creating the illusion of a third dimension (depth), you need to consider the choice of lens, positioning of objects, depth of field, and lighting and color.

▶ In organizing screen motion for the 4 × 3 aspect ratio, z-axis motion (movement toward or away from the camera) is stronger than lateral movement (from one side of the screen to the other). When working in the 16 × 9 aspect ratio, lateral movement becomes more prominent.

MAIN POINTS

▶ Because the television screen size is relatively small, we use more close-ups and medium shots than long shots. When shooting for wide-aspect-ratio, large-screen HDTV, you can use more medium shots and long shots.

▶ Field of view refers to how much of a scene you show in the viewfinder, that is, how close the object appears relative to the viewer. The field of view is organized into five steps: ELS (extreme long shot, or establishing shot), LS (long shot, full shot, or establishing shot), MS (medium shot, or waist shot), CU (close-up), and ECU (extreme close-up).

▶ Alternate shot designations include the bust shot, the knee shot, the two-shot, the three-shot, the over-the-shoulder shot (O/S), and the cross-shot (X/S).

▶ In organizing the screen area for the traditional 4 × 3 and the HDTV 16 × 9 aspect ratios, the major considerations are dealing with height and width, framing close-ups, headroom, noseroom and leadroom, and closure.

ZETTL'S VIDEOLAB

 For your reference or to track your work, the *Zettl's VideoLab* program cues in this chapter are listed here with their corresponding page numbers.

ZVL1 CAMERA→ Camera moves→ dolly | zoom | truck | pan | tilt | pedestal | try it   **115**

ZVL2 CAMERA→ Composition→ field of view   **128**

ZVL3 CAMERA→ Composition→ close-ups   **131**

ZVL4 CAMERA→ Composition→ headroom   **132**

ZVL5 CAMERA→ Composition→ leadroom   **132**

ZVL6 CAMERA→ Composition→ closure   **134**

ZVL7 CAMERA→ Picture depth→ z-axis | lens choice | perspective and distortion   **136**

ZVL8 CAMERA→ Screen motion→ z-axis | lateral | close-ups   **136**

CHAPTER

8

Audio: Sound Pickup

We are usually so engrossed in the barrage of colorful pictures when watching television that we are often totally unaware of the sound—unless there is an audio problem. All of a sudden we realize that without sound we have a hard time following what is going on. But so long as we can hear the sound track, we can turn away from the TV and still know pretty much what's happening on-screen. But isn't a picture worth a thousand words? Apparently not in television. Because so much information is transmitted by someone talking, the infamous "talking head" is not such a bad production technique after all, provided the person talking has something worthwhile to say.

Sound is also important for establishing mood and intensifying an event. A good chase sequence invariably has a barrage of sounds, including agitated music and squealing tires. Some of the crime shows carry sound throughout the dialogue. It is so cleverly done that most of us are hardly aware of the nonverbal track. The sound track helps us structure the quick cuts and the visual fragments of a string of close-ups to form a meaningful whole.

If sound is, indeed, such an important production element, why do we fail to have better sound on television? Even when you produce a short scene as an exercise in the studio, you will probably notice that although the pictures may look acceptable or even spectacular, it is usually the sound portion that could stand some improvement.

It is often assumed, unfortunately, that by sticking a microphone into a scene at the last minute the audio requirements have been satisfied. Don't believe it. Good television audio needs at least as much preparation and attention as the video portion. And, like any other production element, television audio should not simply be added—it should be integrated into the production planning from the very beginning.

Section 8.1, How Microphones Hear, covers the sound pickup portion of **audio** (from the Latin verb *audire*, "to hear"), including the sound-producing and operational types of microphones. In Section 8.2, How Microphones Work, you learn about the more technical aspects of sound-generating elements and the various microphone uses in electronic news gathering (ENG), electronic field production (EFP), and music setups.

KEY TERMS

audio The sound portion of television and its production. Technically, the electronic reproduction of audible sound.

cardioid Heart-shaped pickup pattern of a unidirectional microphone.

condenser microphone A mic whose diaphragm consists of a condenser plate that vibrates with the sound pressure against another fixed condenser plate, called the *backplate*. Also called *electret* or *capacitor microphone*.

direct insertion Recording technique wherein the sound signals of electric instruments are fed directly to the mixing console without the use of speaker and microphone. Also called *direct input*.

dynamic microphone A mic whose sound pickup device consists of a diaphragm that is attached to a movable coil. As the diaphragm vibrates with the air pressure from the sound, the coil moves within a magnetic field, generating an electric current. Also called *moving-coil microphone*.

fishpole A suspension device for a microphone; the mic is attached to a pole and held over the scene for brief periods.

flat response Measure of a microphone's ability to hear equally well over its entire frequency range. Is also used as a measure for devices that record and play back a specific frequency range.

foldback The return of the total or partial audio mix to the talent through headsets or I.F.B. channels. Also called *cue-send*.

frequency response Measure of the range of frequencies a microphone can hear and reproduce.

headset microphone Small but good-quality omni- or unidirectional mic attached to padded earphones; similar to a telephone headset but with a higher-quality mic.

impedance Type of resistance to signal flow. Important especially in matching high- or low-impedance microphones with high- or low-impedance recorders.

lavalier microphone A small mic that can be clipped onto clothing.

omnidirectional Pickup pattern in which the microphone can pick up sounds equally well from all directions.

phantom power The power for preamplification in a condenser microphone, supplied by the audio console rather than a battery.

pickup pattern The territory around the microphone within which the mic can "hear equally well," that is, has optimal sound pickup.

polar pattern The two-dimensional representation of a microphone pickup pattern.

ribbon microphone A mic whose sound pickup device consists of a ribbon that vibrates with the sound pressures within a magnetic field. Also called *velocity mic*.

shotgun microphone A highly directional mic for picking up sounds from a relatively great distance.

system microphone Mic consisting of a base upon which several heads can be attached that change its sound pickup characteristic.

unidirectional Pickup pattern in which the microphone can pick up sounds better from the front than from the sides or back.

wireless microphone A system that transmits audio signals over the air rather than through mic cables. The mic is attached to a transmitter, and the signals are received by a receiver connected to the audio console or recording device. Also called *RF (radio frequency) mic* or *radio mic*.

8.1

How Microphones Hear

The pickup of live sounds is done through a variety of microphones. How good or bad a particular microphone is depends not only on how it is built but especially on how it is used. Section 8.1 focuses on the specific types and uses of microphones.

▶ **MICROPHONE TYPES BY HOW THEY HEAR**
Sound-generating elements (dynamic, condenser, and ribbon), pickup patterns (omnidirectional and unidirectional), and additional microphone features

▶ **MICROPHONE TYPES BY HOW THEY ARE USED**
Mobile microphones (lavalier, hand, boom, headset, and wireless) and stationary microphones (desk, stand, hanging, hidden, and long-distance)

MICROPHONE TYPES BY HOW THEY HEAR

Choosing the most appropriate microphone, or mic (pronounced "mike"), and operating it for optimal sound pickup requires that you know the three basic types of sound-generating elements, their pickup patterns, and some additional microphone features.

SOUND-GENERATING ELEMENTS

All microphones *transduce* (convert) sound waves into electric energy, which is amplified and reconverted into sound waves by the loudspeaker. The initial conversion is accomplished by the microphone's generating element. There are three major types of sound-converting systems,

which are used to classify microphones: dynamic, condenser, and ribbon.

Dynamic microphones   These are the most rugged. *Dynamic microphones,* also called moving-coil microphones, can tolerate reasonably well the rough handling that television mics frequently (though unintentionally) receive. They can be worked close to the sound source and withstand high sound levels without damage to the microphone or excessive input overload (distortion of very high-volume sounds). They can also withstand fairly extreme temperatures. As you can probably guess, they are an ideal outdoor mic.

Condenser microphones   Compared with dynamic mics, *condenser microphones* are much more sensitive to physical shock, temperature change, and input overload, but they usually produce higher-quality sound when used at greater distances from the sound source. Unlike dynamic mics, the condenser has a built-in preamplifier. This preamp strengthens the sound signal so that it does not get lost on the way to the camcorder, mixer, or console. The power supply for condenser mics is usually a battery. Although these batteries last for about a thousand hours, you should always keep spares on hand, especially if you are using condenser mics for ENG/EFP. Many times condenser mic failures can be traced to a dead or wrongly inserted battery. **SEE 8.1**

Condenser mics can also be powered through voltage supplied by the audio console or mixer through the audio

Battery

8.1 POWER SUPPLY BATTERY FOR CONDENSER MICROPHONE
Many condenser microphones are powered by a battery rather than from the console (phantom power); be sure to observe the + and – poles as indicated on the battery housing.

cable. This method of supplying power to the mic's preamp is called ***phantom power***.

Ribbon microphones   Similar in sensitivity and quality to condenser mics, ***ribbon microphones*** produce a warmer sound, frequently preferred by singers. Unlike condenser mics, which you may use outdoors under certain circumstances, ribbon mics are strictly for indoor use. They are sometimes called velocity mics. **ZVL1** AUDIO→ Microphones→ mic choice | transducer

PICKUP PATTERNS

Whereas some microphones, like our ears, hear sounds from all directions almost equally well, others hear sounds better when they come from a specific direction. The territory within which a microphone can hear equally well is called its ***pickup pattern***; its two-dimensional representation is called the ***polar pattern***, as shown in figures 8.2 through 8.4.

In television production you need to use both omnidirectional and unidirectional microphones, depending on what and how you want to hear. The ***omnidirectional*** microphone hears sounds from all (*omnis* in Latin) directions more or less equally well. **SEE 8.2** The ***unidirectional*** microphone hears better in one (*unus* in Latin) direction—the front of the mic—than from its sides or back. Because the polar patterns of unidirectional microphones are roughly heart-shaped, they are called ***cardioid***. **SEE 8.3**

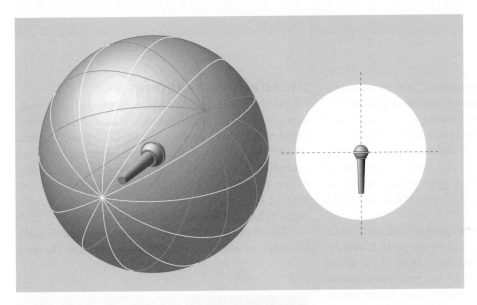

8.2 OMNIDIRECTIONAL PICKUP AND POLAR PATTERNS
The omnidirectional pickup pattern is like a sphere with the mic in its center. All sounds that originate within its pickup pattern are heard by the mic without marked difference.

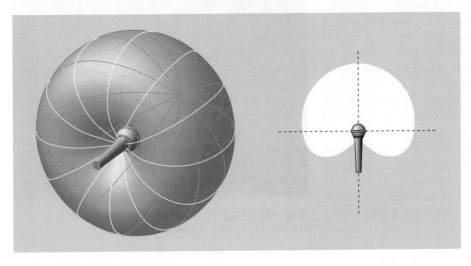

8.3 CARDIOID PICKUP AND POLAR PATTERNS
The heart-shaped pickup pattern makes the mic hear better from the front than from the sides. Sounds to its rear are suppressed.

8.4 HYPERCARDIOID PICKUP AND POLAR PATTERNS

The supercardioid and hyper-cardioid pickup patterns narrow the sound pickup. They have a long but narrow reach in front and eliminate most sounds coming from the sides. They also hear sounds coming from the rear.

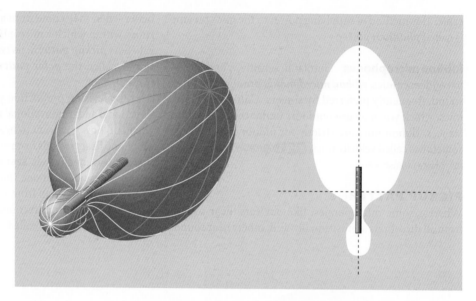

The supercardioid, hypercardioid, and ultracardioid microphones have progressively narrower pickup patterns, which means that their hearing is more and more concentrated in the front. Their claim to fame is that they can hear sounds from far away and make them appear to be relatively close. These mics also hear sounds that are behind them, but because they excel in hearing in one direction (a narrow path in front), they still belong to the unidirectional group. **SEE 8.4**

Which type you use depends primarily on the production situation and the sound quality required. If you are doing a stand-up report (standing in front of the actual scene) on conditions at the local zoo, you would want a rugged, omnidirectional mic that not only favors speech but also picks up some of the animal sounds for authenticity. If, on the other hand, you are video-recording a singer in the studio, you should probably choose a high-quality mic with a more directional cardioid pickup pattern. To record an intimate conversation between two soap opera characters, a hypercardioid shotgun mic is probably best. Unlike the omnidirectional mic, the shotgun mic can pick up their conversation from relatively far away without losing sound presence (the closeness of the sound) while ignoring to a large extent many of the other studio noises, such as people and cameras moving about, the humming of lights, or the rumble of air conditioning. A table of the most common microphones and their characteristics is included in section 8.2 (see figure 8.32). **ZVL2** AUDIO→
Microphones→ pickup patterns

MICROPHONE FEATURES

Microphones that are held close to the mouth have a built-in pop filter, which eliminates the sudden breath pops that might occur when someone speaks directly into the mic. **SEE 8.5** When used outside, all types of microphones are susceptible to wind, which they reproduce as low rumbling noises. To reduce wind noise, put a windscreen made of acoustic foam rubber over the mic. The popular name is zeppelin because it resembles an airship. **SEE 8.6**

To cut the wind noise even more, you need to pull a windsock, or wind jammer, over the windscreen. The wind

8.5 POP FILTER

The built-in pop filter eliminates breath pops.

8.7 **LAVALIER MICROPHONE**
This lavalier mic is properly attached for optimal sound pickup.

8.6 **WINDSCREEN**
The windscreen, normally made of acoustic foam rubber, covers the whole microphone to reduce the low rumble of wind noise.

jammer is made from synthetic material and resembles more a mop than a sophisticated audio device (see figure 8.14). Whatever you use, bear in mind that the rumble of wind noise cannot be totally eliminated. The only way to have no wind noise on the video recording is to shoot when there is no wind. You can, however, use filters in postproduction that can reduce or eliminate some wind noise, or you can cover it up with sound effects or music.

To reduce the need for microphones with different pickup patterns, you can use a *system microphone*, which consists of a base upon which several "heads" can be attached. These heads can change the pickup pattern from omnidirectional to hypercardioid. As convenient as this may be, you will find that most audio engineers favor the individual mics built for specific applications.

MICROPHONE TYPES BY HOW THEY ARE USED

Some microphones are designed and used primarily for sound sources that are moving, whereas others are used for stationary sound sources. When grouped according to how they are used, there are mobile and stationary microphones (see figure 8.32). Of course, any of the mobile mics can be used in a stationary position, and the stationary mics can be moved about if the production situation so requires.

The mobile microphones include lavalier, hand, boom, headset, and wireless mics. The stationary microphones include desk, stand, hanging, hidden, and long-distance mics.

LAVALIER MICROPHONES

The first of the mobile type, the *lavalier microphone*, usually referred to as a lav, is probably the most frequently used on-camera mic in television. The high-quality lavaliers, which range in size from a pushbutton on a pay telephone to the eraser on the end of a pencil, can be fastened to clothing with a small clip. Because of their size, they are unobtrusive and look more like jewelry than a technical device. **SEE 8.7**

Lavalier microphones are dynamic or condenser, with an omnidirectional or cardioid pickup pattern. They are designed primarily for voice pickup. The quality of even the smallest one is amazingly high. Once the lav is properly attached to the performer (approximately 5 to 8 inches below the chin, on top of the clothes, and away from anything that could rub or bang against it), sound pickup is no longer a worry. The audio engineer also has less difficulty riding the gain (adjusting the volume) of the lavalier than the boom mic or hand mic. Because the distance between the mic and the sound source does not change during the performance, an even sound level can be achieved more easily than with other mobile microphones.

The use of lavalier mics frees the lighting people from "lighting around the boom" to avoid shadows. They can concentrate more on the aesthetic subtleties of lighting as required by the scene.

Although the action radius of performers is still limited by the lavalier cable, the cable is flexible enough that they can move quickly and relatively unrestricted in a limited studio area. For greater mobility you can plug the lavalier into a transmitter, which you can clip on a belt or put in a coat pocket, and use it as a wireless mic (see figure 8.21). Despite their small size and high-quality sound pickup characteristics, lavs are durable and relatively immune to physical shock. Because they are so small and lightweight, some production people unfortunately take much less care when handling a lav than with other, larger mics. If you happen to drop a lavalier, or any other mic, check it immediately to see if it is still operational.

When to use lavalier microphones   The following are some typical productions that use lavs as the primary microphone.

News   The lavalier is the most efficacious sound pickup device for all types of indoor news shows and interviews. You can also use it outdoors with a windscreen attached for ENG/EFP.

Interviews   So long as the interview takes place in one location, the wearing of lavalier mics by the interviewer and each guest ensures good, consistent voice pickup.

Panel shows   Rather than use desk mics, which are apt to pick up the unavoidable banging on the table, you can achieve good audio with individual lavaliers. But note that each panel member needs his or her own lavalier mic. With several people on a panel, however, using lavaliers gets unwieldy. Desk mics are, therefore, the better choice.

Instructional shows   In shows with a principal performer or television teacher, the lavalier is ideal. The sound pickup is the same whether the instructor speaks to the class or turns to the whiteboard.

Dramas   Some multicamera studio productions, such as soap operas, use wireless lavaliers for audio pickup. In such productions the lavs are hidden from camera view. If properly attached to the talents' clothing so that the voices do not sound muffled, lavalier mics seem the ideal solution to a traditionally difficult sound pickup problem. Once the levels are set, the audio engineer need do very little to keep the voices balanced. As mentioned earlier, the lighting director (LD) can design the lighting without worrying about boom or camera shadows.

Music   The lavalier has been successfully used for singers (even when accompanying themselves on guitar) and for the pickup of certain instruments, such as a string bass, with the mic taped below the fingerboard. In the realm of music, there is always room for experimentation; do not be too limited by convention. If the lavalier sounds as good as or better than a larger, more expensive mic, stick with the lavalier.

ENG/EFP   The lav is often used for field reports, in which case you need to attach the little windscreen. Wireless lavs are used when the field reporter needs a great deal of mobility. For example, if you talk with a farmer about the drought while walking with him in the parched field, two wireless lavs will solve the audio problem. Wireless lavs can also save you many headaches when picking up the school principal's comments while conducting a tour through the newly completed computer lab.

Disadvantages of lavalier mics   Despite their versatility and high-quality pickup, there are some disadvantages to the lavalier:

■ The wearer cannot move the mic any closer to his mouth; consequently, if there is extraneous noise, it is easily picked up by an omnidirectional mic, although a unidirectional lavalier will usually take care of this problem.

■ The lav is prone to distort very loud input levels. This is especially important when you use a lav for sound inputs other than speech.

■ The lavalier can be used for only one sound source at a time—that of the wearer. Even for a simple interview, each participant must wear his or her own mic.

■ Although the lav allows considerable mobility, a wired lavalier can limit the performer's action radius.

■ Because it is attached to clothing, the lav tends to pick up occasional rubbing noises, especially if the performer moves around a great deal.

■ The voice sounds muffled when the mic is concealed underneath clothing.

■ If the performer's clothes generate static electricity, the mic may pick up the discharge as loud, sharp pops.

■ If two lavaliers are at a certain distance from each other, they may cancel out some frequencies and make the voices sound strangely thin (see figure 8.26).

■ The main problem with using lavs for drama is not operational but aesthetic. Because the lavalier mic is always at the same distance from its sound source, long shots sound exactly the same as close-ups. The unchanging presence does not contribute to a credible sound perspective (whereby close-ups sound closer and long shots sound farther away). This is why most productions of television dramas use a boom mic rather than a lavalier (see chapter 9).

How to use lavalier microphones   Lavaliers are easy to use, but there are some points you need to consider:

■ Be sure to put it on. You would not be the first performer to be discovered sitting on, rather than wearing, the microphone by airtime when getting cued.

■ To put on the mic, bring it up underneath the blouse or jacket and then attach it on the outside. Clip it firmly to the clothing so that it does not rub against anything. Do not wear jewelry in proximity to the mic. If you get rubbing noises, put a piece of foam rubber between the mic and the clothing.

■ Tape the cable to part of the clothing so that it cannot pull the microphone sideways.

■ Loop the cable or even make a loose knot just below the clip to block unwanted pops and rubbing noises.

■ If you hear electrostatic pops, treat the clothes with antistatic laundry spray, available at supermarkets.

■ If you must conceal the mic, do not bury it under layers of clothing; keep it as close to the surface as possible.

■ If you use the dual-redundancy microphone system (which uses two identical mics for the sound pickup in case one fails), fasten both mics securely to a clip designed to hold two lavaliers so that they do not touch each other. Don't use two lavs without a clip, and don't activate both at the same time.

■ Avoid hitting the microphone with any object you may be demonstrating on-camera.

■ If the lav is a wireless and/or condenser mic, check that the battery is in good condition and correctly installed.

■ When using a wireless lav, double-check that the transmitter is turned on (there are normally two switches—one for power and one for the mic) and that it is turned off when leaving the set.

■ If your lavalier was used as a wireless mic, don't walk off with the mic still clipped to your clothing. Turn off the transmitter, take off the mic, and remove the cable from under the clothing before leaving the set. Put the mic down gently.

■ When using a lavalier outdoors, attach the windscreen. You can also make a windscreen by taping a piece of acoustic foam or cheesecloth over the mic. Experienced EFP people claim that by wrapping the mic in cheesecloth

and covering it with the tip of a child's woolen glove, wind noise is virtually eliminated.

HAND MICROPHONES

As the name implies, the hand microphone is handled by the performer. It is used in all production situations in which it is most practical, if not imperative, that the performer exercise some control over the sound pickup. Hand mics are used extensively in ENG, where the reporter often works in the midst of noise and commotion. In the studio or on-stage, hand mics are used by singers and by performers who do audience participation shows. With the hand mic, the performer can approach and talk at random to anyone in the audience.

For singers the hand mic is part of the act. They switch the mic from one hand to the other to visually support a transition in the song, or they caress it during an especially tender passage. The hand mic gives them freedom of movement, especially if it is wireless; they can work the mic during a song, holding it close to the mouth to increase the intimacy during soft passages or farther away during louder, more external ones. You will find that most singers have a preference for the type of mic they use, so you don't have to worry about just what mic to give them.

The wide variety of uses makes heavy demands on the performance characteristics of a hand mic. Because it is handled so much, it must be rugged and capable of withstanding physical shock. And because it is often used extremely close to the sound source, it must be insensitive to plosive breath pops and input overload distortion (see section 8.2). When used outdoors on remote locations, it must withstand rain, snow, humidity, heat, and extreme temperature changes and yet be sensitive enough to pick up the full range and subtle tone qualities of a singer's voice. Finally, it must be small enough to be handled comfortably by the performer.

Of course, no single mic can fulfill all these requirements equally, which is why some hand mics are built for outdoor use, whereas others work best in the controlled studio environment. Normally, you should use dynamic mics for outdoor productions. Their built-in pop filter and sometimes even built-in windscreen produce acceptable audio even in bad weather. **SEE 8.8** Condenser or ribbon mics do not fare as well outdoors but are excellent for more-demanding sound pickup, such as of singers.

The major disadvantage of the hand mic is what we just listed as one of its advantages: the sound control by the performer. If a performer is inexperienced in using a hand mic, he or she might produce more pops and bangs

8.8 DYNAMIC HAND MICROPHONE FOR OUTDOOR USE
The hand mic is rugged, has a built-in windscreen, and is insulated to prevent rubbing sounds from the talent's hands.

8.9 POSITION OF DIRECTIONAL HAND MIC DURING SONG
For optimal sound pickup, the singer holds the microphone close to her mouth, at approximately a 45-degree angle.

than intelligible sounds or may, much to the dismay of the camera operator, cover the mouth or part of the face with the mic. Another disadvantage of most hand mics is that their cables can restrict movement, especially in ENG, when a field reporter is tied to the camcorder. Although wireless hand mics are successfully used in the studio, stay away from them when working outdoors. A cable is still the most reliable connection between the mic and the audio mixer or camcorder.

How to use hand microphones   Working with the hand mic requires dexterity and foresight. Here are some hints:

■ Although the hand mic is fairly rugged, treat it gently. If you need both hands during a performance, do not just drop the mic; put it down gently or wedge it under your arm. If you want to impress on someone the sensitivity of a microphone, especially that of the hand mic, turn up the volume level and feed the clanks and bangs back into the studio for all to hear.

■ Before the telecast check your action radius to see if the mic cable is long enough for your actions and laid out for maximum mic mobility. The action radius is especially important in ENG, where you may be closely tied to the camcorder. If you have to move about a great deal, use a wireless hand mic or lavalier.

■ Always test the microphone before the show or news report by speaking into it or lightly scratching the pop filter or windscreen. Do not blow into it. Have the audio engineer or camcorder operator confirm that the mic is working properly.

■ When using an omnidirectional mic, speak across rather than into it. With a directional hand mic, hold it close to your mouth at approximately a 45-degree angle to achieve optimal sound pickup. Unlike the reporter, who speaks across the omnidirectional hand mic, the singer sings into the directional mic. **SEE 8.9**

■ If the mic cable gets tangled, do not yank on it. Stop and try to get the attention of the floor manager.

■ When walking a considerable distance, do not pull the cable with the mic. Tug the cable gently with one hand while holding the microphone with the other.

■ When in the field, always test the microphone before the show or news report by having the camcorder operator record some of your opening remarks and then play them back for an audio check. Insist on a mic check, especially if the crew tells you not to worry because they've "done it a thousand times before"!

■ When doing a stand-up news report in the field under normal conditions (no excessively loud environment, no strong wind), hold the microphone at chest level. Speak toward the camera, across the microphone. **SEE 8.10** If the background noise is high, raise the mic closer to your mouth while still speaking across it. **SEE 8.11**

■ When interviewing someone, hold the microphone to your mouth whenever you speak and to the guest's whenever he or she answers. Unfortunately, this obvious procedure is sometimes reversed by nervous performers.

■ Do not remain standing when interviewing a child. Crouch down so that you are at the child's eye level; you can then keep the microphone close to the child in a

8.10 HAND MIC POSITION: CHEST
When used in a fairly quiet environment, the hand mic should be held chest high, parallel to the body.

8.11 HAND MIC POSITION: MOUTH
In a noisy environment, the hand mic must be held closer to the mouth. Note that the talent is still speaking across the mic, rather than into it.

natural way. You become a psychological equal to the child and also help the camera operator frame an acceptable picture. **SEE 8.12**

■ Always coil the mic cables immediately after use to protect them and have them ready for the next job.

BOOM MICROPHONES

When a production, such as of a dramatic scene, requires that you keep the microphone out of camera range, you need a mic that can pick up sound over a fairly great distance while making it seem to come from close up and which keeps out most of the extraneous noises surrounding the scene. The *shotgun microphone* fills that bill. It is highly directional (supercardioid or hypercardioid) and has a far reach with little loss of presence. **SEE 8.13**

The directionality of the shotgun mic is achieved by allowing extraneous sounds enter the mic through the many slots on the shotgun barrel. Once trapped, they get canceled. Because it is usually suspended from some kind of boom, or is handheld with your arms acting as a boom, we call it a boom microphone.

How to use shotgun microphones   The external microphones you see attached to camcorders are small shot-

8.12 USE OF HAND MIC WITH CHILD
When interviewing a child, crouch down to the child's eye level. The child is more at ease, and the camera operator is able to frame a better shot.

gun mics. They operate like a lens except that they capture sounds instead of light. Most commonly, shotgun mics are handheld on a mount or suspended from a fishpole boom. Both methods work fairly well for short scenes, where the mic is to be kept out of camera range. The advantages of holding it are threefold: the microphone is extremely flexible—you can carry it into the scene and aim it in any direction without any extraneous equipment; by holding

8.13 SHOTGUN MIC
The shotgun mic has a highly directional (super- or hypercardioid) pickup pattern and a far reach, permitting the pickup of sounds that are relatively far away.

the shotgun, or by working the fishpole, you take up very little production space; and you can easily work around the existing lighting setup to keep the mic shadows out of camera range.

There are, however, disadvantages: you can cover only relatively short scenes without getting tired; you have to be relatively close to the scene to get good sound pickup, which is often difficult, especially if the set is crowded; if the scene is shot with multiple cameras (as in a studio production), you are often in danger of getting in the wide-shot camera view; and the mic is apt to pick up some handling noises, even if you carry it by the shock mount (a suspension device that prevents transmitting handling noises to the mic).

Because there is a great likelihood that you will be asked to handle a shotgun mic, here are some tips:

■ Always wear good-quality earphones or earbuds so that you can hear what the mic is actually picking up. Listen not only to the sound quality of the dialogue but also for unwanted noise. If you hear sounds that are not supposed to be there, tell the director about the interference immediately after the take (from start to stop of the show segment being video recorded). You can plug the earphones into the camera audio jack that usually takes a mini plug.

■ Always carry the shotgun mic by the shock mount. Do not carry it directly or you'll end up with more handling noises than actors' dialogue. **SEE 8.14**

■ Do not cover the ports (openings) at the sides of the shotgun with anything but the windscreen. These ports must be able to receive sounds to keep the pickup pattern directional. Holding the mic by the shock mount minimizes the danger of covering the ports.

■ Watch that you do not hit anything with the mic and that you do not drop it. A short cable can yank it right out of your hands.

■ Aim the mic as much as possible toward whoever is speaking, especially if the mic is fairly close to the sound source.

■ Watch for unwanted mic shadows.

How to use fishpole microphones   A *fishpole* is an extendable metal pole that lets you mount a shotgun mic. It is used mostly outdoors for ENG/EFP but can, of course, be applied to brief scenes in the studio in place of the big perambulator boom. You will find that a short fishpole is

8.14 HANDHELD SHOTGUN MIC
Always hold the shotgun mic by its shock mount. When outdoors a windscreen is mandatory. This mic has an additional wind jammer attached.

relatively easy to handle, whereas working a long or fully extended fishpole can be quite tiring, especially during long, uninterrupted takes.

Short shotgun mics, called pencil mics by audio people, are frequently preferred over the more directional long shotguns when picking up sounds indoors. The obvious advantage of a pencil mic is that it is smaller and therefore lighter; it is also not quite so directional as the long shotgun, so you don't always need to point it directly at the person who is speaking. If, for example, you cover a conversation between two people, you can often position the pencil mic between them for a balanced pickup. To make your job even easier, most pencil mics let you exchange the unidirectional head with one that has a slightly wider cardioid pattern.

When using the fishpole, many of the foregoing points apply. Here are some more:

■ Check that the mic is properly shock-mounted so that it does not touch the pole or the mic cable. The normal shock mount consists of an outside ring within which the mic barrel is suspended with rubber bands.

■ Fasten the mic cable to the pole. Some fishpoles let you feed the mic cable through the pole, much like through a conduit.

■ Hold the fishpole from either above or below the sound source. **SEE 8.15 AND 8.16**

■ If you are recording two people talking to each other, point the mic at whoever is speaking.

8.15 FROM-ABOVE MIC POSITION
The short fishpole is usually held as high as possible and dipped into the scene from above.

8.16 FROM-BELOW MIC POSITION
The fishpole can also be held low, with the mic aimed at the sound source from below.

■ If the actors speak while walking, walk with them at exactly the same speed, holding the mic in front of them during the entire take.

■ Watch for obstacles that may block your way, such as cables, lights, cameras, trees, or pieces of scenery. Because you usually walk backward while watching the actors, rehearse your route a few times.

■ Before each take check that you have enough mic cable for the entire walk.

■ If you have a long fishpole, anchor it in your belt and lower it into the scene as though you were "fishing" for the appropriate sound. **SEE 8.17**

The big perambulator boom   When working with large, multicamera studio productions, such as situation comedies and soap operas, you will find that despite the presence of lavalier mics, the big perambulator boom is very much alive and well. In the controlled environment of the studio, the big boom is still one of the most effective ways of getting a high-quality mic close to the talent while keeping it out of camera view. **SEE 8.18**

There are several reasons why the big boom has not achieved great popularity in routine studio productions: it takes up a large space, it makes lighting difficult, and it is not easy to operate. That said, we haven't come up with anything better for picking up actors' dialogue during long takes. You can extend or retract the boom, simultaneously pan it horizontally, move it up and down

8.17 HANDLING THE LONG FISHPOLE BOOM
The long fishpole can be anchored in a belt and raised and lowered similar to an actual fishing pole.

vertically, and rotate and tilt the mic toward the sound source. During all these operations, the boom assembly can be moved when the fully extended boom cannot reach the sound source.

How to use boom microphones   However and wherever you move the boom, do it smoothly. It is better to be a little off while following the actors than to lose them entirely because you can't stop your wild boom swing in time. Here are some more operational tips:

8.18 BIG PERAMBULATOR BOOM

The big boom can extend to a 20-foot reach, pan 360 degrees, and tilt up and down. The microphone itself can be rotated by about 300 degrees—almost a full circle.

Mic tilt and turn grip

Crank to adjust boom length

Operator's seat

Pan-and-tilt lock screws

Steering control

Control to raise or lower platform

Break and gear change

Platform for operator and TV monitor

■ Try to keep the mic in front of the sound source and as low as possible without getting it in the picture.

■ Do not ride the mic directly above the talent's head—the actor speaks from the mouth, not the top of the head.

■ Watch the studio line monitor or the monitor on your dolly (which shows the picture that goes on the air or is video recorded). Try to ascertain during rehearsal how far you can dip the mic toward the sound source without getting it or the boom in the picture. The closer the mic, the better the sound. In boom mic operation, you will rarely get close enough to violate the minimum distance required of shotgun mics to avoid the proximity effect (breath pops and boomy bass). The optimum distance for boom mics is when the talent can almost touch the mic by reaching up at about a 45-degree angle.

■ If the boom gets in the picture, it is better to pull it back than to raise it. By retracting the boom, you pull the mic out of the camera's view and at the same time keep it in front of, rather than above, the sound source.

■ Watch for shadows. Even the best LD cannot avoid shadows but can only redirect them. If the major boom positions are known before the show, work with the LD to light around them. You may sometimes have to sacrifice audio quality to avoid boom shadows.

■ If you discover a boom shadow when the camera is already on the air, do not suddenly move the mic—everyone will see the shadow travel across the screen. Try to sneak it out of the picture very slowly or, better, just keep the mic and the shadow as steady as possible until a relief shot permits you to move into a more advantageous position.

■ Listen for good audio balance. With a highly directional shotgun mic, you normally must rotate it toward whoever is talking. In fully scripted shows, the audio board operator in the booth may follow the scripted dialogue and signal you (the boom operator) whenever the mic needs to be rotated from one actor to the other. **ZVL3** AUDIO→ Microphones→ mic types | placement

HEADSET MICROPHONES

The *headset microphone* consists of a small but good-quality omni- or unidirectional mic attached to earphones. One of the earphones carries the program sound (whatever sounds the headset mic picks up or is fed from the station), and the other carries the I.F.B. (interruptible foldback or feedback) cues and instructions of the director or producer. Headset mics are used in certain EFP situations, such as sports reporting, or in ENG from a helicopter or convention floor. The headset mic isolates you sufficiently from the outside world so that you can concentrate on your specific reporting job in the midst of much noise and commotion while at the same time keeping your hands free to track players' statistics on a laptop or to buttonhole someone for an interview. **SEE 8.19**

WIRELESS MICROPHONES

In production situations in which complete and unrestricted mobility of the sound source is required, *wireless microphones* are used. If, for example, you are recording a singer who is also doing some dance moves, or if you are

Headset mic

Receiver   Mic with transmitter and built-in antenna

8.20 WIRELESS HAND MIC AND RECEIVER
The wireless hand mic normally has the transmitter built into the housing. The antenna either is built into the mic or sticks out at the bottom. The receiver, which is tuned to the frequency of the hand mic's transmitter, picks up the signal and sends it via mic cable to the audio console or camcorder.

8.19 HEADSET MICROPHONE
The headset mic is similar to an ordinary telephone headset except that it has bigger, padded earphones and a higher-quality microphone.

8.21 WIRELESS LAVALIER MIC AND TRANSMITTER
The wireless lavalier mic has a separate transmitter that is worn by the talent. The receiver picks up the mic's signal and routes it via mic cable to the audio mixer, console, or camcorder.

Belt-pack transmitter

Lavalier mic

asked to pick up a skier's grunts and the clatter of the skis on a downhill course, the wireless mic is the obvious choice. Wireless mics are also used extensively for newscasts, for EFP, and occasionally for multicamera studio productions of dramatic shows. Wireless mics actually broadcast their signals. They are therefore also called RF (radio frequency) mics or radio mics. Most wireless microphones are used as either hand or lavalier mics.

In wireless hand mics, the battery-powered transmitter is built into the microphone itself. Some models have a short antenna protruding from the bottom of the mic, but in most the antenna is incorporated into the microphone housing or cable. **SEE 8.20**

The wireless lavalier mic is connected to a battery-powered transmitter that is either worn in the hip pocket or taped to the body. The antenna is usually tucked into the pocket or strung inside the clothing. **SEE 8.21**

The other important element of the wireless microphone system is the receiver (see figure 8.20). The receiver tunes in to the frequency of the wireless transmitter and can receive the signal from as far as 1,000 feet (approximately 330 meters) under favorable conditions. When conditions are more adverse, the range may shrink to about 100 feet (about 33 meters). To ensure optimal signal reception, you can set up several receiving stations in the studio as well as in the field. When the signal gets too weak for one of the receivers, the other or others will take over. This is called diversity reception.

The wireless mic works best in the controlled environment of a studio or stage, where you can determine the precise range of the performer's movements and find the optimal position for the receiver(s). Most singers prefer working with the wireless hand mic because it affords them unrestricted movement. It is also useful in audience participation shows, where the performer walks into the audience for brief, unscripted interviews. The wireless lavalier mic has been used successfully for musicals and dramatic shows and, of course, in many ENG/EFP situations.

When using any wireless mic, you should watch for these problems:

■ If the transmitter is taped to the body, the performer's perspiration can reduce signal strength, as does, of course, the increasing distance from transmitter to receiver.

■ Large metal objects, high-voltage lines and transformers, X-ray machines, microwave transmissions, and cellular phones—all can interfere with the proper reception of the wireless mic signal.

■ Although most wireless equipment offers several frequency channels, there is still some danger of picking up extraneous signals, especially if the receiver operates in the proximity of someone else's wireless signals or other strong radio signals. Interference is evident by pops, thumps, signal dropouts, and even the pickup of police band transmissions.

■ If you use several wireless mics, they need to be fed into a mixer for proper audio control.

DESK MICROPHONES

As the name implies, desk microphones are usually put on tables or desks. These stationary mics are widely used in panel shows, public hearings, press conferences, and other programs where the performer is speaking from behind a desk, table, or lectern. These mics are used for voice pickup only. Because the performer is usually doing something—shuffling papers, putting things on the desk, accidentally bumping the desk with feet or knees—desk microphones must be rugged and able to withstand physical shock.

Dynamic, omnidirectional mics are generally used as desk mics. If a high separation of sound sources is desired, however, unidirectional mics are an option. Also, when you use a desk mic for a speaker at a lectern, use a unidirectional rather than an omnidirectional mic. The unidirectional mic will make it easier for you to avoid feedback through the speakers in the same room. Once properly positioned the unidirectional mic is less apt to cause feedback. Generally, most hand mics double as desk mics—all you do is place them in a desk stand and position them for optimal sound pickup. **SEE 8.22**

Boundary microphone   One type of desk mic is the boundary microphone or, as it is commonly called, the pressure zone microphone (PZM). These mics look differ-

8.22 MICROPHONE ON DESK STAND
In television production desk mics are usually hand mics clipped to a desk stand.

ent from ordinary microphones and operate on a different principle. **SEE 8.23**

The boundary microphone is mounted or positioned close to a reflecting surface, such as a table or a plastic plate accessory. **SEE 8.24** When placed into this sound "pressure zone," the mic receives both direct and reflected sounds at the same time. Under optimal conditions the boundary microphone produces a clearer sound than do ordinary mics. Its chief advantage is that it can be used for the simultaneous voice pickup of several people with equal fidelity. Boundary mics have a wide, hemispheric pickup pattern and are therefore well suited for large group

**8.23
BOUNDARY
MICROPHONE**
This mic must be mounted or put on a reflecting surface to build up the "pressure zone" at which all sound waves reach the mic at the same time.

8.24 BOUNDARY MIC USED FOR MULTIPLE-VOICE PICKUP
With the boundary mic on a table, the sound pickup is equal
for all people sitting around it.

8.25 DESK MIC PLACEMENT FOR SINGLE PERFORMER
The desk mic should be placed to the side of the talent and
aimed at the talent's collarbone so that he or she speaks across,
rather than into, it. This way the mic is not obstructing the shot
of the talent.

discussions and audience reactions. You can, for example, simply place this mic on a table and achieve a remarkably good pickup of the people sitting within its semicircular pickup pattern. If people are sitting around the table, you need two boundary mics: one to pick up the people on one half of the round table, the second for the people on the other half of the table.

Unfortunately, when used as a table mic, the boundary mic also picks up paper rustling, finger tapping, and the thumps of people knocking against the table; pads for the mic minimize or virtually eliminate such problems. Note that the boundary mic can also be used for miking musical instruments, such as a piano.

How to use desk microphones Desk mics, like peanuts, seem to be irresistible—not that performers want to eat them, but when sitting or standing behind a desk mic they feel compelled to grab it and pull it toward them no matter how carefully you might have positioned it. Polite or not-so-polite requests not to touch the mic seem futile. Sooner or later the talent will move the mic. To counter this compulsion, consider taping the mic stand to the table, or at least tape the microphone cable securely and unobtrusively so that the mic can be moved only a short distance.

■ As with the hand mic, no attempt is made to conceal the desk mic from the viewer. Nevertheless, when placing it on a desktop or lectern, consider the camera picture as well as

optimal sound pickup. Performers certainly appreciate it if the camera shows more of them than the microphone. If the camera shoots from straight on, place the mic somewhat to the side of the performer and point it at his or her collarbone rather than mouth, giving a reasonably good sound pickup while allowing the camera a clear shot of the performer's face. **SEE 8.25**

■ When integrating the mic unobtrusively in the picture, do not forget about concealing the mic cable as best as you can. Even if the director assures you that the mic cable on the floor will never be seen, don't bet on it.

■ When using two desk mics for the same speaker as a dual-redundancy precaution, use identical mics and place them as close together as possible. As noted, *dual-redundancy* is the rather clumsy term for using two mics for a single sound source so that you can switch from one to the other in case one fails. Do not activate them at the same time unless you are feeding separate audio channels. If both mics are on at the same time, you may experience multiple-microphone interference, which means that when the mics receive the same sound at slightly different times, they tend to cancel each other's frequencies. To avoid such interference, place the mics so that they are at least three times as far apart as any mic is from its user. **SEE 8.26**

■ Although almost a lost cause, remind panel members— or anyone working with a desk mic—not to reposition it

8.26 MULTIPLE-MICROPHONE SETUP
When using a multiple-microphone setup, keep the individual mics at least three times as far apart as the distance any mic is from its user.

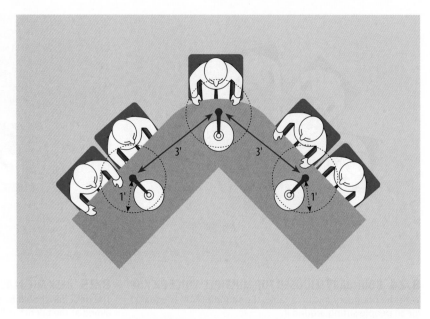

once it is set and to avoid banging on the table or kicking the lectern, even if the discussion gets lively. Tell participants not to lean into the mics when speaking.

STAND MICROPHONES

Stand microphones are used whenever the sound source is fixed and the type of programming permits them to be seen. For example, there is no need to conceal the mics of a rock group; on the contrary, they are an important show element. You are certainly familiar with the great many ways rock performers handle the stand mic. Some tilt it, lift it, lean against it, hold themselves up by it, and, when the music rocks with especially high intensity, even swing it through the air like a sword (not recommended, by the way).

The quality of stand mics ranges from dynamic hand mics clipped to a stand to highly sensitive ribbon or condenser mics used exclusively for music recording sessions.

How to use stand microphones Stand mics are usually placed in front of the sound source—whether it is a singer or the speaker of an amplified electric guitar. **SEE 8.27** Many singers prefer to unclip the mic from the stand for some especially energetic or intimate passages, so you need to ensure that the mic can be easily detached and then re-attached to the stand. For the pickup of a singer using an acoustic guitar, you may attach two mics to a single stand: one for the singer and one a little lower for the guitar.

8.27 STAND MIC FOR SINGER
The singer stands in front of the stand mic and sings directly into it.

HANGING MICROPHONES

Hanging microphones are used whenever any other concealed-microphone method (boom or fishpole) is impractical. You can hang the mics (high-quality cardioid condenser mics but also lavaliers) by their cables over any fairly stationary sound source. Most often, hanging mics are used in dramatic presentations where the action is fully blocked so that the actors are in a precise location for each delivery of lines. A favorite spot for hanging mics is the upstage door (at the back of the set), from which the actors deliver their hellos and good-byes when entering or leaving the major performance area. The boom can generally not reach that far to adequately pick up voices. The actors have

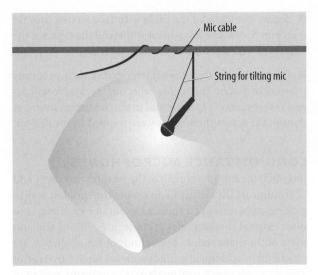

8.28 AUDIO POOL OF HANGING MICROPHONE
Hanging microphones are high-quality unidirectional mics that are normally suspended by their cables from the lighting grid. The talent must remain in the audio pool to be properly heard.

to take care to speak only within the "audio pool" of the hanging mic. Similar to the spotlight pool, where the actors are visible only so long as they move within the limited circle of light, the audio pool allows actors to be heard only when they are within the limited range of the mic. **SEE 8.28**

The sound quality from hanging mics is not always the best. The sound source is often at a distance from the mic, and if the actor is not precisely within the audio pool,

his or her voice is off-mic. In the case of the upstage door, such quality loss is actually an asset because it underscores the physical and psychological distance of the departing person. Unfortunately, hanging mics have the annoying tendency to pick up the shuffling of feet and the rumbling of moving camera pedestals almost as well as the voices. A further disadvantage is that when positioned close to the studio lights, the hanging mic might pick up and amplify their hum. Hanging mics are nevertheless popular in dramas, studio productions, and audience participation shows. They are easy to set up and take down and, when in the right positions, produce acceptable sound.

You may find that a single suspended boundary mic will meet the audio requirements better than several regular hanging mics. Mount the boundary mic on a sound-reflecting board (such as a 3-by-4-foot piece of plastic or plywood), suspend it above and in front of the general sound-generating area (such as an audience area), and angle the reflecting board for optimal pickup. **SEE 8.29** Regardless of whether the sound source is near the mic or farther away, the sounds still have good presence. This positive aspect turns negative in dramatic productions, where sound perspective is an important factor. This is one of the reasons why in complex productions the boom is still preferred over the boundary mic.

When suspending a microphone from the lighting grid, be careful not to place the mic next to a hot lighting instrument. It will inevitably pick up its hum. Separate the mic cables from the studio lights or the AC cables to minimize electronic interference. If that is not possible,

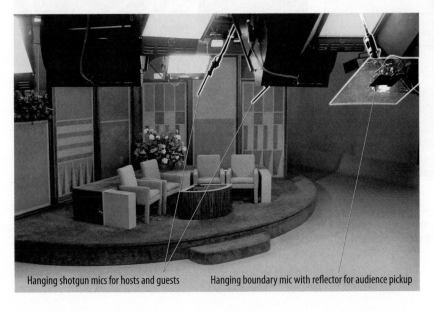

Hanging shotgun mics for hosts and guests   Hanging boundary mic with reflector for audience pickup

8.29 BOUNDARY MIC USED AS HANGING MICROPHONE
When using a boundary mic as a hanging microphone, mount it on an additional sound-reflecting board and angle it toward the sound source for optimal pickup. The shotgun mics are for the host and guests' audio pickup.

cross the mic and power cables at right angles rather than having them run parallel.

HIDDEN MICROPHONES

You may sometimes find that you need to hide a small lavalier mic in a bouquet of flowers, behind a centerpiece, or in a car to pick up a conversation during studio productions or in EFP where microphones should be out of camera range. **SEE 8.30** Realize that it is time-consuming to place a hidden mic so that it yields a satisfactory pickup. Often you get a marvelous pickup of various noises caused by people hitting the table or moving their chairs but only a poor pickup of their conversation.

Again, the boundary mic can serve as an efficient "hidden" mic. Especially because it looks nothing like an ordinary mic, you may get away with not hiding it at all; simply place it on a table among other eclectic objects.

How to use hidden microphones   Hiding mics presents unexpected problems. These tips may minimize or eliminate some of them:

■ Do not try to conceal the mic completely unless there is an extreme close-up of the object to which it is attached.

■ Realize that you must hide not only the microphone but also the cable. If you use a wireless setup, you must hide the transmitter as well.

■ Secure the mic and the cable with tape so that they do not come loose. The setup must withstand the rigors of the rehearsals and the video-recording sessions.

■ Do not hide a mic in enclosed spaces such as empty drawers or boxes. The highly reflecting enclosure will act as a reverberation chamber and make the voices sound as though the actors themselves were trapped in the drawer.

LONG-DISTANCE MICROPHONES

It is often the sounds more than the pictures that carry and communicate the energy of an event. The simplest way to pick up the sounds of a sporting event, for example, is to place normal shotgun mics at strategic positions and aim them at the main action. The sounds of the spectators are picked up by additional omnidirectional mics. Coverage of a single tennis match may involve six or more microphones to pick up the sounds of the players, the judges, the ball, and the crowd. Place a fairly dense windscreen on every mic to eliminate wind noise as much as possible.[1]

An old-fashioned but successful means of picking up distant sounds is the parabolic reflector microphone, which consists of a parabolic dish (similar to a small satellite dish)

---

1. You will find highly useful suggestions for how to mic a variety of sports for ambient sound in Stanley R. Alten, *Audio in Media*, 8th ed. (Belmont, Calif.: Thomson Wadsworth, 2008), pp. 209–27.

8.30 LAVALIER AS HIDDEN MIC
This "hidden" lavalier microphone is attached to the rear-view mirror to pick up the conversation inside the car. Note that the mic is not covered, to ensure optimal sound pickup.

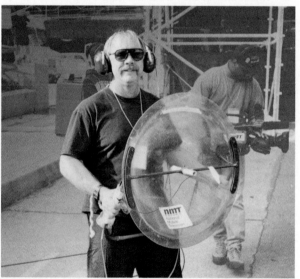

8.31 PARABOLIC REFLECTOR MICROPHONE
The parabolic reflector mic is used primarily for sound pickup over long distances, such as crowd noises in a stadium.

that has an omnidirectional microphone facing inward at its focal point. All incoming sounds are reflected toward and concentrated at the mic. **SEE 8.31** A popular use of the parabolic mic is to pick up the sounds of the bands during a parade, the collisions of football players, and the enthusiastic chanting of a group of home-team fans. Because the parabolic reflector directs the higher sound frequencies to the mic better than the lower ones, the sounds take on a slight telephonic tone. We tend to ignore this impaired sound quality, however, when the mic is used primarily for ambient (environmental) sounds that communicate the feel of an event (such as a football game) rather than precise information.

M A I N   P O I N T S

▶ Audio is the sound portion of a television show. It transmits information (such as a news story), helps establish the specific time and locale of the action, contributes to the mood, and provides continuity for the picture portions.

▶ The three major types of microphones are dynamic, condenser, and ribbon. Each type has a different sound-generating element that converts sound waves into electric energy—the audio signal.

▶ Some microphones can hear sounds equally well from all directions (omnidirectional); others hear better from a specific direction (unidirectional or cardioid).

▶ Microphones are classified according to their operation and are either mobile or stationary. The mobile types include lavalier, hand, boom, headset, and wireless mics. The stationary types include desk, stand, hanging, hidden, and long-distance mics.

▶ The lavalier microphone, or lav for short, is most common in normal television operations. It is usually clipped to clothing. Although it is extremely small, it provides high-quality sound reproduction.

▶ Hand microphones are used when the performer needs to exercise some control over the sound pickup.

▶ When the microphone must be kept out of camera range, it is usually handheld or mounted on and operated from a fishpole or microphone boom. All boom mics are highly directional.

▶ The headset mic is used when the talent needs both hands free to take notes or work with scripts or a keyboard. Headset microphones are especially practical for sportscasting and for ENG (electronic news gathering) from a helicopter or convention floor.

▶ When unrestricted mobility of the sound source is required, a wireless, or RF (radio frequency), microphone is used. Also called radio mics, wireless mics need a transmitter and a receiver.

▶ Desk microphones are simply hand mics clipped to a desk stand. They are often used for panel discussions.

▶ Stand microphones are employed whenever the sound source is fixed and the type of programming permits the mics to be seen by the camera, such as in rock concerts.

▶ Hanging microphones are popular in some studio productions because the mics are kept out of camera range without using booms.

▶ Hidden microphones are small lavaliers concealed behind or within set dressings.

▶ Long-distance mics are shotgun or parabolic reflector mics that pick up sound over relatively great distances.

8.2

How Microphones Work

Section 8.1 examined sound pickup and the electronic and operational characteristics of microphones. Although you may never see the inside of a microphone (unless you break one), you should have some idea of how they work. Knowing the differences among the sound-generating elements may help you choose the right mic for a specific sound pickup. This section also includes a list of popular mics and their primary uses, some additional mic features, examples of mic setups for music groups, and microphone use specific to ENG/EFP.

▶ **SOUND-GENERATING ELEMENTS**
The diaphragm and the sound-generating element—and sound quality—of dynamic, condenser, and ribbon microphones

▶ **SPECIFIC MICROPHONE FEATURES**
High and low impedance, frequency response, flat response, balanced and unbalanced mics and cables, and audio connectors

▶ **MIC SETUPS FOR MUSIC PICKUP**
Possible setups for various musical events

▶ **MICROPHONE USE SPECIFIC TO ENG/EFP**
Ambient sounds and line-out tie-in

SOUND-GENERATING ELEMENTS

Simply speaking, microphones convert one type of energy—sound waves—to another—electric energy. All microphones have a diaphragm, which vibrates with the sound pressures, and a sound-generating element, which transduces the physical vibrations of the diaphragm into electric energy; but the particular process each mic uses to accomplish this conversion determines its quality and use.

DYNAMIC MICROPHONES

In the dynamic microphone, the diaphragm is attached to a coil—the voice coil. When someone speaks into the mic, the diaphragm vibrates with the air pressure from the sound and makes the voice coil move back and forth within a magnetic field. This action produces the audio signal. Because of this physical process, dynamic mics are sometimes called moving-coil microphones.

The diaphragm–voice coil element is physically rugged, so the mic can withstand and accurately translate high sound levels and other air blasts close to it with little or no sound distortion.

CONDENSER MICROPHONES

In the condenser microphone, also called electret or capacitor microphone, the movable diaphragm constitutes one of the two plates necessary for a condenser to function; the other, called the backplate, is fixed. Because the diaphragm moves with the air vibrations against the fixed backplate, the capacitance of this condenser is continuously changed, thus creating the audio signal. The condenser mic hears better than the dynamic mic (wider frequency response) but is also more sensitive to high-intensity sound sources (prone to overload distortion).

RIBBON MICROPHONES

In the ribbon, or velocity, microphone, a very thin metal ribbon vibrates within a magnetic field. These vibrations create the electrical audio signal. The ribbon mic hears extremely well and produces warm sounds, but its "ears" are extremely sensitive. The ribbon is so fragile that even moderate physical shocks to the mic, or sharp air blasts close to it, can damage and even destroy the instrument.

SOUND QUALITY

High-quality microphones can hear higher and lower sounds better than can the less expensive models. Other, less definable quality factors are whether a mic produces especially warm or crisp sounds, but don't be misled by specifications or the often very strong personal preferences of singers or sound engineers. What is a good microphone? It's the one that produces the sounds you want. To help you get started on your mic selection for a particular assignment, the table in figure 8.32 lists some of the more popular mics and their most common use. **SEE 8.32**

8.32 TABLE OF MICROPHONES

MICROPHONE	ELEMENT TYPE *PICKUP PATTERN*	CHARACTERISTICS	USE
SHOTGUN MIC — LONG			
Sennheiser MKH 70	Condenser *Supercardioid*	Excellent reach and presence, therefore excellent distance mic. Extremely directional. Quite heavy when held on extended fishpole.	Boom, fishpole, handheld. Best for EFP and sports remotes to capture sounds over considerable distances.
SHOTGUN MICS — SHORT			
Sennheiser MKH 60	Condenser *Supercardioid*	Good reach and wider pickup pattern than long shotguns. Less presence over long distances but requires less precise aiming at sound source. Lighter and easier to handle than long shotgun mics.	Boom, fishpole, handheld. Especially good for EFP indoor use.
Neumann KMR 81i	Condenser *Supercardioid*	Slightly less reach than the MKH 60 but has warmer sound.	Boom, fishpole, handheld. Especially good for EFP. Excellent dialogue mic.
Sony ECM 672	Condenser *Supercardioid*	Highly focused but slightly less presence than long shotguns.	Boom, fishpole, handheld. Especially good for EFP indoor use.
HAND, DESK, AND STAND MICS			
Electro-Voice 635N/D	Dynamic *Omnidirectional*	An improved version of the classic 635A. Has good voice pickup that seems to know how to differentiate between voice and ambience. Extremely rugged. Can tolerate rough handling and extreme outdoor conditions.	Excellent mic (and therefore standard) for all-weather ENG and EFP reporting assignments.

8.32 **TABLE OF MICROPHONES** *(continued)*

MICROPHONE	ELEMENT TYPE *PICKUP PATTERN*	CHARACTERISTICS	USE
HAND, DESK, AND STAND MICS (continued)			
Electro-Voice RE50	Dynamic *Omnidirectional*	Similar to the E-V 635N/D. Rugged. Internal shock mount and blast filter.	Good, reliable desk and stand mic. Good for music pickup, such as vocals, guitars, and drums.
Beyerdynamic M58	Dynamic *Omnidirectional*	Smooth frequency response, bright sound. Rugged. Internal shock mount. Low handling noise.	Good ENG/EFP mic. Especially designed as an easy-to-use hand mic.
Shure SM57	Dynamic *Cardioid*	Good-quality frequency response. Can stand fairly high input volume.	Good for music, vocals, electric guitars, keyboard instruments, and even drums.
Shure SM58	Dynamic *Cardioid*	Rugged. Good for indoors and outdoors.	Standard for vocals and speech.
Shure SM81	Condenser *Cardioid*	Wide frequency response. Also good for outdoors.	Excellent for miking acoustic instruments.
Beyerdynamic M160	Double ribbon *Hypercardioid*	Sensitive mic with excellent frequency response. Can tolerate fairly high input volume.	Especially good for all sorts of music pickup, such as strings, brass, and piano. Also works well as a stand mic for voice pickup.
AKG D112	Dynamic *Cardioid*	Rugged. Specially built for high-energy percussive sound.	For close miking of kick drum.

8.32 TABLE OF MICROPHONES *(continued)*

MICROPHONE	ELEMENT TYPE *PICKUP PATTERN*	CHARACTERISTICS	USE
LAVALIER MICS			
Sony ECM 55	Condenser *Omnidirectional*	Excellent presence. Produces close-up sound. But, because of this excellent presence, does not mix well with boom mics, which are normally farther away from the sound source.	Excellent for voice pickup in a controlled environment (studio interviews, studio news, and presentations).
Sennheiser MKE 102	Condenser *Omnidirectional*	Mixes well with boom mics. Excellent, smooth overall sound pickup. Very sensitive to clothes noise and even rubbing of cable, however. Must be securely fastened to avoid rubbing noises.	Excellent for most lavalier uses. Works well as a concealed mic.
Sony ECM 77	Condenser *Omnidirectional*	Highly directional. Isolates most ambient noise when used for speech pickup in noisy surroundings. High directionality can be a problem when mic shifts from original point. Blends well with boom mic. Mic and cable are sensitive to rubbing on clothes. Must be securely fastened.	Excellent pickup of all sounds. Good for concealed mic use and even for the pickup of some musical instruments.
Professional Sound PSC MilliMic	Condenser *Omnidirectional*	Extremely small yet has excellent pickup quality. Blends well with boom mics. Well shielded against electromagnetic interference.	Excellent as a concealed mic for interviews, dramas, and documentaries. Works well outdoors.

SPECIFIC MICROPHONE FEATURES

When working with audio equipment, you will probably hear some terms that are not self-explanatory: high- and low-impedance mics, flat response, and balanced and unbalanced mics and cables. Although these features are quite technical in nature, you need to know at least their operational requirements.

IMPEDANCE

Impedance is a type of resistance to signal flow. You can have high-impedance (sometimes abbreviated *high-Z*) and low-impedance (*low-Z*) microphones. A high-impedance mic (usually less expensive and lower quality) works only with a relatively short cable, whereas a low-impedance mic (all high-quality professional mics) can be used with several hundred feet of cable. The impedance of the mic and the recorder must match.

If you use a low-impedance recorder with a high-impedance mic or vice versa, you need an impedance transformer. Many electric instruments, such as electric guitars, have a high-impedance output. For them to match up with low-impedance equipment, they must be routed through a direct box—a unit containing the transformer-like electronics that adjust the high-impedance signal to a low-impedance one. You will find, however, that newer equipment is much more tolerant than older equipment to impedance differences and will often match impedances without a transformer.

FREQUENCY RESPONSE

The ability of a microphone to hear extremely high and low sounds is known as the *frequency response*. A good microphone hears better than most humans and has a frequency range of 20 Hz (*hertz,* which measures cycles per second) to a very high 20,000 Hz. Many high-quality mics are built to hear equally well over the entire frequency range, a feature called *flat response*. High-quality mics should therefore have a great frequency range and a relatively flat response.

Balanced and Unbalanced Mics and Cables, and Audio Connectors   All professional microphones have a balanced output that is connected by three-wire microphone cables with three-pronged connectors, called XLR connectors, to recorders and mixers. The balanced line rejects hum and other electronic interference.

Unbalanced mics and cables may work just as well so long as the cables are quite short and there is no interfer-ence. Unbalanced cables carry the audio signal on only two wires. The well-known two-wire connectors include the ¼-inch phone plug, the RCA phono plug, and the mini plug. **SEE 8.33** `ZVL4` AUDIO→ Connectors→ overview

With adapters you can connect an XLR to the unbal-anced connectors and vice versa. Note, however, that every adapter is a potential trouble spot. Always try to find a mic cable with the appropriate connector already attached.

MIC SETUPS FOR MUSIC PICKUP

The following suggestions of how to mike musical events should be taken with a grain of salt. It's hard to find two audio experts who agree on just how a musical event should be miked and what mics to use. Nevertheless, the suggested setups will help you get started.

The sound pickup of an instrumental group, such as a rock band, is normally accomplished with several stand mics. These are placed in front of each speaker that emits the amplified sound of a particular instrument as well as in front of unamplified sound sources, such as singers and drums. The mic to use depends on such factors as studio

8.33 **AUDIO CONNECTORS**
Balanced audio cables use XLR connectors (**A** and **B**); unbalanced cables use the ¼-inch phone plug (**C**), the RCA phono plug (**D**), and the mini plug (**E**).

acoustics, the type and the combination of instruments, and the aesthetic quality of the desired sound.[2]

Generally, the rugged dynamic (omnidirectional or cardioid) mics are used for high-volume sound sources, such as drums, electric guitar speakers, and some singers, whereas condenser or ribbon mics are used for such sound sources as singers, strings, and acoustic guitars. Although many factors influence the type of microphone used and its placement, the figures in this section give some idea of how three different yet typical musical events may be miked. Again, the final criterion is not what everybody tells you but whether the playback loudspeakers give you the sounds you expected.

MICROPHONE SETUP FOR SINGER AND ACOUSTIC GUITAR

For a singer accompanying himself or herself on an acoustic guitar, one cardioid condenser or ribbon mic is sufficient in most cases. Try a Beyerdynamic M160 (ribbon) or a

2. See Alten, *Audio in Media*, pp. 309–28.

Shure SM81 (condenser). You may also try to attach two microphones on a single mic stand—one for the singer, pointing just below the mouth, and another pointing at the guitar. **SEE 8.34**

MICROPHONE SETUP FOR SINGER AND PIANO

If the concert is formal, with the vocalist singing classical songs with piano accompaniment, you should keep the mics out of the picture. You may want to try a Beyerdynamic M160 mic suspended from a small boom. For the piano tape a boundary mic on the lid in the low-peg position or directly on the sounding board. **SEE 8.35** Another way of miking a piano is to have one Shure SM81 mic pointing at the lower half of the strings and another at the upper half. Good results have also been achieved by putting the mic underneath the piano close to the sounding board and about a foot behind the pedals.

If the concert comprises popular songs, such as light classics or rock, a hand mic, such as a Shure SM58, may be a more appropriate choice for the singer. The miking of the piano does not change.

8.34 MICROPHONE SETUP FOR SINGER AND ACOUSTIC GUITAR
The mic setup for a singer with an acoustic guitar is to have one mic for the voice and another lower on the same mic stand for the guitar.

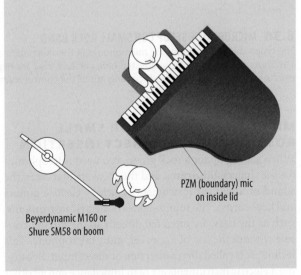

8.35 MICROPHONE SETUP FOR SINGER AND PIANO
If the singer's mic is to be out of camera view, it should be suspended from a boom. The piano is miked separately. For an on-camera mic, the singer can use a hand mic.

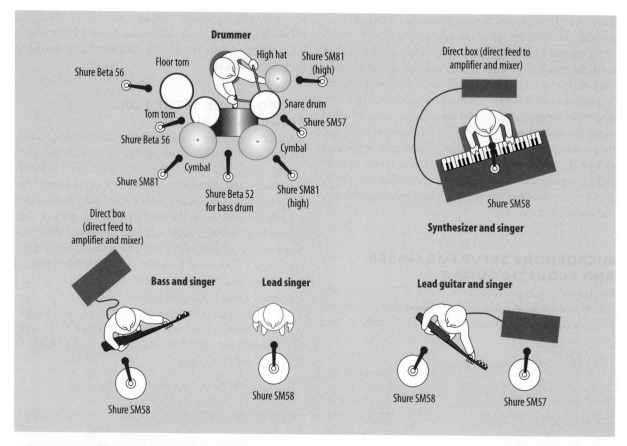

8.36 MICROPHONE SETUP FOR SMALL ROCK BAND
The types and the placement of microphones in this illustration are a general suggestion for how you may start with the mic setup. The Shure microphones are suggested here because they are high-quality mics at a reasonable price. The final criterion for a successful setup is when the sounds coming out of the control room speakers are satisfactory.

MICROPHONE SETUP FOR SMALL ROCK GROUP AND DIRECT INSERTION

When setting up for a rock group, you need microphones for the singers, the drums, and the speakers that carry the sound of amplified instruments (such as electric guitars and keyboards). The sound signals of electric instruments, such as the bass, are often fed directly to the mixing console without the use of a speaker and a microphone. This technique is called *direct insertion* or direct input. Because most electric instruments are high impedance and all other professional sound equipment is low impedance, you need to match impedances through the direct box (unless the input equipment does it for you).

When setting up mics and speakers, watch for feedback and multiple-microphone interference. For the band

members to hear themselves, you must supply the foldback sound mix through either earphones or speakers. *Foldback*, also called cue-send, is the return of the total or partial audio mix from the mixing console to the musicians. Again, note that the microphones in figure 8.36 are merely suggestions. By all means, try the mics you have and listen to the mix.

Generally, use dynamic or ribbon mics for singers, dynamic mics for other instruments, and dynamic mics for high-output sound sources, such as the bass drum. **SEE 8.36**

MICROPHONE USE SPECIFIC TO ENG/EFP

The sound pickup requirements in ENG/EFP do not differ significantly from those in studio operation. In the field as in the studio, your ultimate objective is optimal sound. You will find, however, that sound pickup in the field is much more challenging than in the studio. When outdoors there is the ever-present problem of wind noise and other unwanted sounds, such as airplanes or trucks passing by during a critical scene. The best way to combat wind noise is to use a highly directional mic, cover it with an effective windscreen and a wind jammer, and hold it as close to the sound source as possible without causing a proximity effect (distorted sound when the shotgun mic is too close to the source). Contrary to most studio shows, ambient (environmental) sounds are often needed to support the video. After you are done with the video recording of an indoor event, you need to record room tone—the "silence" of an empty room without speaker or audience and the ambient sounds of the room with the audience present but without the speaker's voice. These ambient sounds are essential for masking cuts in postproduction.

When on an ENG assignment, always have the camera microphone (the shotgun mic, which is built into, or clipped to, the camera) open to record ambient sounds, even when shooting "silent" footage. In fact, when using a hand mic for a stand-up report (with the reporter describing a news event on-location), you must also turn on the camera mic for the ambient sounds. Feed the two mics into separate audio tracks during the recording. As with room tone, such ambient sounds are essential for sound continuity in postproduction editing. The split tracks allow the video editor to control at least somewhat the mix between the reporter's voice and the ambient sounds.

If you have only one microphone, which you must use for voice pickup, record the ambient sounds on a portable audiocassette recorder or on the recording media you are using after finishing the voice work. Again, the editor will appreciate some authentic sounds with which to bridge the edits.

You may find that a seemingly simple audio pickup, such as a speech in a large conference room, can pose a formidable audio problem, especially if you cannot get close enough in the crowded and noisy room for a clean voice pickup. In this case it may be easier to ask the engineer in charge (usually the audiovisual manager of the hotel or convention center) to assist you with a line-out tie-in. In such a setup, you do not need a microphone to pick up the speaker's sound but simply a direct feed from the audio control board of the in-house audio system to the audio input of your camcorder. In effect, you "tie in" to the audio feed from the audio system of the conference room.

MAIN POINTS

▶ All microphones have a diaphragm, which vibrates with sound pressure, and a generating element, which transduces the physical vibrations of the diaphragm into electric energy.

▶ In the dynamic, or moving-coil, mic, the diaphragm is attached to the voice coil. The air pressure moves the voice coil back and forth within a magnetic field. This type of generating element makes the mic quite rugged.

▶ The condenser, or electret, mic has a condenser-like generating element. The movable diaphragm constitutes one of the two condenser plates; a fixed backplate is the other. The moving condenser plate changes the capacitance of the condenser, creating the audio signal. Condenser mics have a wide frequency response.

▶ In the ribbon, or velocity, mic, a thin metal ribbon vibrates within a magnetic field. Because the ribbon is fragile, such mics are generally used indoors under controlled conditions.

▶ Impedance is a type of resistance to signal flow. The impedances of mics and electric instruments must be matched with those of the other electronic audio equipment.

▶ High-quality microphones have a wide frequency range and pick up sounds equally well over the total range—called a flat response.

▶ Microphones can be balanced or unbalanced. Most professional mics have a balanced output. Balanced microphones and mic cables have three-pronged XLR connectors. The balanced audio cable prevents external signals from causing a hum in the audio track. Unbalanced (two-wire) cables have phone plug, RCA phono plug, and mini plug connectors.

▶ Direct insertion, or direct input, involves feeding the sound signal of an electric instrument into a direct box that matches impedances with the input of the console. This eliminates the use of a speaker and a microphone.

▶ Foldback is the return of the total or partial audio mix from the mixing console to the musicians.

ZETTL'S VIDEOLAB

 For your reference or to track your work, the *Zettl's VideoLab* program cues in this chapter are listed here with their corresponding page numbers.

9

Audio: Sound Control

The previous chapter dealt mostly with sound pickup—the types of microphones and their uses. This chapter explores the equipment and the techniques of controlling sound and sound recording in television studio and field production. Section 9.1, Sound Controls and Recording, identifies the major equipment and production techniques for mixing and recording sound in the studio and the field. Section 9.2, Stereo, Surround Sound, and Sound Aesthetics, highlights the principal aesthetic factors of sound.

You should realize that audio production is a highly specialized field in its own right and that this chapter is limited to the major equipment, the basic production techniques, and some fundamental aesthetic considerations. Even if you don't intend to become a sound designer, you need to know what good audio is all about. Whatever you do, the most important prerequisite to successful audio for television is, and will always be, a good pair of ears. **ZVL1** AUDIO→ Audio introduction

ambience Background sounds.

audio control booth Houses the audio, or mixing, console; analog and digital playback machines; a turntable; a patchbay; a computer display; speakers; intercom systems; a clock; and a line monitor.

automatic gain control (AGC) Can regulate sound volume or video brightness and contrast levels.

calibrate To make all VU meters (usually of the audio console and the video recorder) respond in the same way to a specific audio signal.

digital audiotape (DAT) The sound signals are encoded on audiotape in digital form. Includes digital recorders as well as digital recording processes.

digital cart system A digital audio system that uses built-in hard drives, removable disks, or read/write optical discs to store and access audio information almost instantaneously. It is normally used for the playback of brief announcements and music bridges.

equalization Controlling the quality of sound by emphasizing certain frequencies while de-emphasizing others.

figure/ground Emphasizing the most important sound source over the general background sounds.

flash memory device A read/write portable storage device that can download, store, and upload very fast (in a flash) a significant amount of digital information. Also called *flash drive, stick flash, flash stick,* and *flash memory card.*

mini disc (MD) Optical 2½-inch-wide disc that can store one hour of CD-quality audio.

mixing Combining two or more sounds in specific proportions (volume variations) as determined by the event (show) context.

mix-minus Type of multiple audio feed missing the part that is being recorded, such as an orchestra feed with the solo instrument being recorded. Also refers to a program sound feed without the portion supplied by the source that is receiving the feed.

MP3 A widely used compression system for digital audio. Most Internet-distributed audio is compressed in the MP3 format.

peak program meter (PPM) Meter in an audio console that measures loudness. Especially sensitive to volume peaks, it indicates overmodulation.

sound perspective Distant sound must go with a long shot, close sound with a close-up.

surround sound Sound that produces a soundfield in front of, to the sides of, and behind the listener by positioning loudspeakers either to the front and the rear or to the front, sides, and rear of the listener.

sweetening Variety of quality adjustments of recorded sound in postproduction.

volume-unit (VU) meter Measures volume units, the relative loudness of amplified sound.

SECTION

9.1

Sound Controls and Recording

When watching a television program, we are generally not aware of sound as a separate medium. Somehow it seems to belong to the pictures, and we become aware of the audio portion only when it is unexpectedly interrupted. But in your own video recordings, you probably notice that there are always some minor or even major audio problems that tend to draw attention away from your beautiful shots. Although audio is often treated casually, you quickly realize that the sound portion is, indeed, a critical production element that requires your full attention.

▶ **PRODUCTION EQUIPMENT FOR STUDIO AUDIO**
The audio console, the patchbay, and analog and digital tape-based and tapeless audio-recording systems

▶ **AUDIO CONTROL IN THE STUDIO**
The audio control booth and basic audio operation

▶ **PRODUCTION EQUIPMENT AND BASIC OPERATION FOR FIELD AUDIO**
Keeping sounds separate and the audio mixer

▶ **AUDIO CONTROL IN THE FIELD**
Using the automatic gain control in ENG and EFP, using an XLR pad, and EFP mixing

PRODUCTION EQUIPMENT FOR STUDIO AUDIO

The major components of audio equipment are the audio console, the patchbay, and analog and digital tape-based and tapeless audio-recording systems.

AUDIO CONSOLE

Regardless of individual models—analog or digital—all audio consoles, or audio control boards, are built to perform five major functions:

■ *Input:* to preamplify and control the volume of the various incoming signals

■ *Mix:* to combine and balance two or more incoming signals

■ *Quality control:* to manipulate the sound characteristics

■ *Output:* to route the combined signals to a specific output

■ *Monitor:* to listen to the sounds before or as their signals are actually recorded or broadcast **SEE 9.1**

Input Studio consoles have multiple inputs to accept a variety of sound sources. Even small studio consoles may have 16 or more inputs. Although that many inputs are rarely used in the average in-house production or broadcast day, they must nevertheless be available for the program you may have to do the next day.

9.1 AUDIO CONSOLE
Each module of this audio console contains a volume control (slide fader), various quality controls, and assignment switches. It can route several mixes to different destinations.

Sub pot

Input selectors

Equalizers
(quality controls)

Auxiliary
(send) outputs
(headphones, etc.)

Pan pot

Solo monitor

Slide faders

Output selectors

9.2 AUDIO CONSOLE MODULE

The major controls on this module are the slide fader
volume control, equalizers, assignment switches, the mute
switch (silences this input), the pan pot (moves the sound
horizontally from one stereo speaker to the next), and
various other quality controls.

Each input module requires that you select either the
mic-level or the line-level input. Mic-level inputs are for
sound sources that need to be preamplified before they
are sent to the input controls. All microphones need such
preamplification and are therefore routed to the mic input.
Line-level inputs, such as CD players, DVD players, and
digital audiotape (DAT) recorders, have a strong enough
signal to be routed to the line input without preamplification. All incoming audio signals must reach line-level
strength before they can be further adjusted or mixed at
the audio console.

Because not all input levels of microphones or line
signals are the same, they run the risk of becoming over-
amplified. To prevent this you can manipulate the signals
individually with the trim control, which adjusts the input
strength of the mic signals so that they won't become distorted during further amplification.

Regardless of input, the audio signals are then routed
to the volume control, a variety of quality controls, switches
(mute or solo) that silence all the other inputs when you
want to listen to a specific one, and assignment switches
that route the signal to certain parts of the audio console
and to signal outputs. **SEE 9.2**

Volume control All sounds fluctuate in volume (loudness).
Some sounds are relatively weak, so you have to increase
their volume to make them perceptible. Other sounds come
in so loud that they overload the audio system and become
distorted or they outweigh the weaker ones so much that
there is no longer proper balance between the two. The
volume control that helps you adjust the incoming sound
signals to their proper levels is usually called a pot (short
for potentiometer) or a fader (also called attenuator or
gain control).

To increase the volume, turn the knob clockwise or
push the fader up, away from you. To decrease the volume,
turn the knob counterclockwise or pull the fader down,
toward you. **SEE 9.3**

Mix The audio console lets you mix, or combine, the
signals from various inputs, such as two lavalier mics, the
background music, and the sound effect of a phone ring.
The mix bus combines these various audio signals with
the specific volume that you assign. Without the *mixing*
capability of the board, you could control only one input at
a time. The completed mix is then fed to the line-out.

A mix bus is like a riverbed that receives the water
(signals) from several different streams (inputs). These
streams (various sound signals) converge (mixed sound

9.3 SLIDE FADERS

Pushing the fader up increases the volume; pulling it down decreases the volume.

9.4 ANALOG VU METER

The VU meter indicates the relative loudness of a sound. The upper figures ranging from –20 to +3 are the volume units (decibels). The lower figures represent a percentage scale, ranging from 0 to 100 percent signal modulation (signal amplification). Overmodulation (too much signal amplification) is indicated by the red line on the right (0 to +3 VU).

signal) and finally flow downstream along the riverbed (mix bus) to their destination (recorder). **ZVL2** AUDIO→ Consoles and mixers→ parts | signals | control | try it

Solo switch and pan pot The solo switch lets you listen to a particular incoming sound while silencing all other sound signals you are mixing. Every console module has a solo switch. The pan pot shifts the sound or sounds you select horizontally from left to right or vice versa (clockwise or counterclockwise when mixing surround sound).

Quality control   All audio consoles have controls that let you shape the character of a sound (see figure 9.2). Among the most important are equalization, filters, and reverberation (reverb) controls.

The process of controlling the audio signal by emphasizing certain frequencies and de-emphasizing or eliminating others is called *equalization*. It can be accomplished manually or automatically through an equalizer, which works like the tone control on a home stereo receiver. It can boost or reduce selected frequencies and thereby influence the character of the sound. For example, you can make a sound more brilliant by boosting the high frequencies or more solid by boosting the lows, or you can eliminate a low-frequency hum or a high-frequency hiss. Filters eliminate automatically all frequencies above or below a certain point. The reverb controls can add an increasing amount of reverberation to each of the selected inputs.

Output   The mixed and quality-processed signal is then routed to the output, called the line-out. To ensure

that the mixed signals stay within the acceptable volume limits, they are regulated by final volume controls—the master pots—and metered by volume indicators, the most common of which is the *volume-unit (VU) meter*. As the volume varies, the needle of the VU meter oscillates back and forth along a calibrated scale. **SEE 9.4**

If the volume is so low that the needle barely moves from the extreme left, you are riding the gain (or volume) "in the mud." If the needle oscillates around the middle of the scale and peaks at the red line on the right, you are riding the gain correctly. If the needle swings in the red on the right side of the scale, and even occasionally hits the right edge of the meter, the volume is too high—you are "bending the needle," "spilling over," or "riding in the red."

Much like the volume indicator of home stereo systems, the VU meter in many audio consoles consists of light-emitting diodes (LEDs), which show up as thin, colored light columns that fluctuate up and down a scale. When you ride the gain too high, the column shoots up on the scale and changes color. **SEE 9.5**

Some audio consoles have an additional *peak program meter (PPM),* which measures loudness peaks. A PPM reacts more quickly to the volume peaks than does the needle of the VU meter and clearly shows when you are overmodulating.

Output channels We often classify audio consoles by the number of output channels. Older television consoles had several input channels but only one output channel because television sound was monophonic. Today, however, even small television consoles have at least two output chan-

9.5 LED VU METER
The light-emitting diode VU meters indicate overmodulation by lighting up in a different color (usually red).

nels to handle stereophonic sound or to feed two pieces of equipment (such as headphones and a video recorder) simultaneously with two identical but independent signals. With high-definition television (HDTV), the sound requirements also change. Very much like motion pictures, large-screen TV displays require surround sound, which involves multiple discrete output channels and a variety of speakers that are strategically placed in front and in back of the display screen (see figure 9.18). This increasing demand for high-quality audio has led to greater use of multichannel (output) consoles in the audio control booth and especially in the audio postproduction room.

To identify how many inputs and outputs a specific console has, they are labeled with the number of input and output channels, such as an 8 × 1 or a 32 × 4 console. This means that the small 8 × 1 console has eight inputs and one output; the larger 32 × 4 console has 32 inputs and four outputs. With a single output channel, the 8 × 1 board obviously is monophonic.

Most larger television audio consoles have eight or more output channels (with eight master pots and eight VU meters), each of which can carry a discrete sound signal or mix. The advantage of multiple outputs is that you can feed the individual signals onto a multitrack audio recorder for postproduction mixing. If, for example, there are 24 inputs but only two outputs, you need to mix the input signals down to two, which you can then feed to the left and right channels of a stereo recorder. But if you want to keep the various sounds separated to exercise more control in the final postproduction mix, or if you want to feed separate surround-sound speakers, you need more outputs. Even when covering a straightforward rock concert, for example, you may have to provide one mix for the musicians, another for the audience, one for the video recorder, and yet another for the multitrack audiotape recorder (ATR). You will be surprised by how fast you run out of available inputs and outputs even on a big console.

In-line consoles   Some of the more elaborate consoles, called in-line consoles, have input/output, or I/O, modules, which means that each input has its own output. If, for example, there are 24 inputs and each receives a different sound signal, you could send each of them directly to the separate tracks of a 24-track recorder without feeding them through any of the mix buses. That way you use the console to control the volume of each input, but the console does not function as a mixing or quality-control device. In fact, the sound is sent to the audio recorder in its raw state. The mixing and quality control of the various sounds are done in the postproduction and mixdown sessions. The I/O circuits let you try out and listen to all sorts of mixes and sound manipulations without affecting the original signals sent to the recorder.

Phantom power   Don't let the name scare you. As mentioned before, the "phantom" in phantom power is more like "virtual." All it means is that the audio console or some other source, rather than a battery, supplies the preamplification power to condenser mics.

Monitor and cue   All consoles have a monitor system, which lets you hear the final sound mix or allows you to listen to and adjust the mix before switching it to the line-out. A separate audition or cue return system lets you hear a particular sound source without routing it to the mix bus. This system is especially important when you want to cue a digital audiotape or a cassette or when you need to check a specific track of a compact disc (CD) or a digital versatile disc (DVD) while on the air with the rest of the sound sources.

Computer-assisted and digital consoles   Almost all consoles include a computer through which you can preset, store, recall, and activate many of the audio control functions. For example, you can try out a particular mix with specific volume, equalization, and reverberation values for each of the individual sounds, store it all in the computer's memory, try something else, and then recall the original setup with the press of a button.

Digital consoles look like their analog cousins except that they have centralized controls that trigger sound control and routing functions for each input module. These controls are not unlike the delegation controls of a video switcher (see figure 13.7). The advantage is that this routing architecture keeps the console relatively small and workable.

PATCHBAY

The primary function of the patchbay, or patch panel, is connecting and routing audio signals to and from various pieces of equipment. You can accomplish this by using actual wires that establish specific connections or with a computer that rearranges the signals and sends them according to your instructions. Whichever method you use, the principle of patching is the same. Here we use wires, called patch cords, to explain a simple patching procedure.

Assume that you want to have two microphones, a remote feed from a field reporter, and a CD operating during a newscast. Lav 1 and lav 2 are the newscasters' lavaliers. The remote feed comes from the field reporter with a live story. The CD contains the opening and closing theme music for the newscast.

Any one of these audio sources can be patched to individual volume controls (pots or faders) in any desired order. Suppose you want to operate the volume controls in the following order, from left to right: CD, lav 1, lav 2, remote feed. You can easily patch these inputs to the audio console in that order. If you want the inputs in a different order, you need not unplug the equipment; all you do is pull the patch cords and repatch the inputs in the different order. **SEE 9.6**

Wired patchbay   All wired patch panels contain rows of holes, called jacks, which represent the outputs and the inputs. The upper rows of jacks are normally the outputs (which carry the signals from mics, CDs, and so forth). The rows of jacks immediately below the output jacks are the input jacks, which are connected to the audio console. The connection between output and input is made with the patch cord.

To accomplish a proper patch, you must plug the patch cord from one of the upper output jacks into one of

9.6 PATCHING
This patching shows that the signal outputs (audio sources) of two microphones, a remote feed, and a CD are grouped in the following order of fader inputs: CD, lavalier 1, lavalier 2, remote feed.

the lower input jacks. **SEE 9.7** Patching output to output (upper-row jack to another upper-row jack) or input to input (lower-row jack to lower-row jack) will give you nothing but headaches.

To reduce the number of patch cords, certain frequently used connections between outputs (a specific mic, DAT machine, or CD) and inputs (specific volume controls assigned to them) are directly wired, or normaled, to one another. This means that the output and the input of a circuit are connected without a patch cord. By inserting a patch cord into one of the jacks of a normaled circuit, you break, rather than establish, the connection.

Although patching helps make the routing of an audio signal more flexible, it can also cause some problems. Patching takes time; patch cords and jacks get worn out from frequent use, which can cause a hum or an intermittent connection; and many patch cords crisscrossing each

9.7 PATCHBAY WITH PATCHES
All patchbays connect the signal outputs (mics, CDs, video recorder) to specific input modules of the audio console. The patching is accomplished by connecting the audio outputs (top row) to the inputs (bottom row) with patch cords.

other are confusing and look more like spaghetti than orderly connections, making individual patches difficult to trace. Also, when patching with a corresponding fader still set at a reasonably high volume, the pop caused by plugging or unplugging the patch cord can blow even the most robust speaker. Once again, although physical connections are important because you can see which signal goes where, the computer can perform many of the routine patching functions more efficiently.

Computer patching   In computer patching, the sound signals from the many sources, such as mics, direct boxes, CDs, DVDs, or video recordings, are routed to the patch panel programmer, which assigns the multiple signals to specific fader modules of the audio console for further processing. To route lavalier 1 to pot 2, and the CD to pot 1, for example, you don't need any physical patches; you simply enter the routing information into the patch panel programmer, which tells the electronic patch panel to connect the inputs to the desired faders on the console, show the information on the display screen, and store your patching commands for future use. Patching is now as easy as pasting words with a word processor.

AUDIO-RECORDING SYSTEMS

The sound of routine television productions is usually recorded simultaneously with the pictures on one of the audio tracks of the video recorder. There are occasions,

however, when you need to back up your sound recording with a separate audio recording, or record the audio on a separate system for high-end postproduction.

In general, audio-recording systems can be analog or digital. As explained in chapter 4, analog means that the signal fluctuates exactly like the original stimulus, which means that the electrical signal leaving the microphone is analogous to the fluctuations of the microphone's generating element. Digital sound recording translates such analog signals into many discrete digits (on/off pulses expressed as 0's and 1's). Almost all audio recording in professional television is done digitally. As with video, digital audio recordings excel not only in sound quality but also in maintaining that quality in extensive postproduction editing. Because digital systems allow you to see a visual display of the recorded sounds, they make editing much more precise than with analog methods.

But don't dismiss analog audio just yet. Many older camcorders and VHS recorders are analog, and there are extensive analog sound archives that will most likely remain analog even in the digital age. You may still have a collection of analog equipment that most likely includes an analog cassette machine. Some audio purists have returned to analog sound systems because, according to them, analog recordings have a warmer sound than digital ones.

ANALOG AUDIO RECORDERS

All analog recorders are tape-based. Here we briefly touch on the two analog audio systems that are still in use: the open-reel audiotape recorder and the audiocassette recorder.

Open-reel audiotape recorder   The open-reel audiotape recorder is generally used for multitrack recording or for playing back longer pieces of audio material.

Head assembly The tape moves from a supply reel to a takeup reel over at least three heads: the erase head, the record head, and the playback head. **SEE 9.8** This head assembly arrangement is standard for all analog tape recorders. When the ATR is being used for recording, the erase head clears the portions of the tape that receive the recording (tracks) of all audio material that might have been left on the tape from a previous recording; the record head then puts the new audio material on the tape. When the tape is played back, the playback head reproduces the audio material previously recorded. The erase and record heads are not activated during playback.

9.8 ANALOG AUDIOTAPE HEAD ASSEMBLY
The head assembly of an analog reel-to-reel audiotape recorder consists of an erase head, a record head, and a playback head.

Operational controls In addition to the switch for the recording speeds, all professional ATRs, analog and digital, have the well-known five control buttons that regulate the tape motion in all audio as well as videotape recorders: *play,* which moves the tape at the designated speed; *fast-forward,* which advances the tape at high speed; *stop,* which brakes the reels to a stop; *rewind,* which rewinds the tape at high speed; and *record,* which activates both the erase and the record heads. Many tape recorders also have a cue control, which enables you to hear the sound on a tape even when running at fast-forward or rewind speeds.

Audiocassette recorder Professional cassette systems are similar to the one you may have at home except that they have slightly more-sophisticated electronics to reduce noise and more-durable tape transports that allow faster and smoother fast-forward and rewind speeds. As you know from experience, cassettes are easy to store and handle and can play up to 120 minutes of audio material. Despite the narrow tape, cassettes produce good sound, especially if they are the metal-particle-coated variety.

DIGITAL AUDIO RECORDERS
All digital recording is done with either tape-based or tapeless systems.

Tape-based recorders: videotape The tape-based audio-recording devices include videotape used by stand-alone or camcorder videotape recorders (VTRs) and DAT recorders.

Most digital audio recording for video is done simultaneously with the picture on one or two tracks of the videotape (see figure 12.4). High-end camcorders offer four tracks, but if you need multiple tracks, you should feed them into a mixer and route them to a multitrack recorder for postproduction editing.

9.9 PORTABLE DAT RECORDER
This portable DAT recorder can record up to two hours on a single battery charge. It has one balanced stereo input (two XLR jacks) and four unbalanced inputs (RCA phono jacks). Its excellent frequency response lets you make high-fidelity recordings of speech and music.

Tape-based recorders: DAT Normally, a *digital audiotape (DAT)* recorder refers to a digital audiocassette recorder. These machines operate more like videocassette recorders than audiocassette recorders. The heads of the cassette recorders rotate at high speed while the tape is moving past them. **SEE 9.9** Besides recording sound with the customary digital, virtually noise-free high fidelity, high-end DAT recorders include the following features that are especially important for video production:

- High-speed search and extremely accurate cueing

- Verbal slating (identifying a scene or take) through a built-in microphone

- Time code recording simultaneously with the audio material, for cueing and for matching sound and pictures in postproduction

- Display that shows the time remaining on the tape

- Synchronization, if desired, of its internal time code with an external time code (such as the one supplied by the cameras)

But these wonder machines are not problem-free. The high-speed rotary heads are subject to wear and tear, especially if not properly maintained, and the recorders are sensitive to moisture. DAT cassettes cannot have any flaws, or the recording will be equally flawed. Finally, high-end DAT recorders are quite expensive, which is why tapeless recorders have gained in popularity.

9.10 DIGITAL CART

This digital cart system can record, store on its hard drive, and play back instantly a great amount of audio data. You can also edit audio files with it, interface it via Ethernet with digital audio workstations, and exchange audio data with a removable 250 MB (megabyte) Zip disk.

Tapeless recording systems   In television production the more popular tapeless audio-recording systems include: the digital cart system, mini disks and flash memory devices, hard drives with removable or fixed disks, and optical disc systems with a variety of CD and DVD formats.

Digital cart system   A *digital cart system* lets you record a great amount of audio data (literally hundreds of hours), cue up almost instantly any audio file stored in its hard drive, edit audio files, construct a playlist for an automated playback sequence, operate with a remote control, and exchange audio data that were recorded on a separate, small removable disk. **SEE 9.10**

Mini discs and flash memory devices   The *mini disc (MD)* is a small (about 2¾ inch) read-only or read/write optical disc that can store more than an hour of high-quality digital stereo audio. Its small size, large storage capacity, and easy cueing make it a useful playback device for television production. **SEE 9.11**

    The *flash memory device*, or flash drive, is used extensively in digital audio recording. One such flash drive is a small SD (Secure Digital format) memory card, very much like the one you may be using in a digital still camera or camcorder. There are small and relatively inexpensive digital recorders that have two remarkably good condenser mics built-in and can store on a 2 GB (gigabyte) SD card a little more than three hours of high-quality stereo sound. When compressed with the *MP3* system, it can store about 30 hours of music. The advantage over DAT recorders is that SD card recorders have no moving parts. **SEE 9.12**

9.11 PROFESSIONAL MINI DISC RECORDER/PLAYER

Mini disc recorders can store and provide random access to more than an hour of high-quality digital stereo audio. The disc cassette measures only about 2¾ inches and operates much like a small removable disk in a hard drive.

9.12 SD CARD RECORDER

This digital stereo recorder uses an SD flash memory card that can hold up to three hours of high-quality stereo sound. The advantage of flash memory devices is that they have no moving parts.

VU meters for 24 tracks

Display window

Hard disk bay 1

Hard disk bay 2

Operational controls

9.13 DIGITAL MULTITRACK RECORDER/PLAYER

This digital recorder can record 24 tracks on two high-capacity hard drives. Both hard disks are removable and can be swapped from bay to bay.

Hard drives There are large-capacity systems built specifically for audio production and postproduction that store audio information just like you would on a computer hard drive. **SEE 9.13** For example, with this recorder you can record 24 tracks of high-quality audio on two hard drives; do editing with common cut, copy, and paste commands; and move entire tracks from one position to another. You can randomly access and play any audio file almost instantly.

As you know, the ubiquitous Apple iPod is a powerful recording device. The 160 GB model can store thousands of songs and photos or store and display 200 hours of video. If you have the right software, you can transfer the recorded information to your laptop for further processing.

CD and DVD The professional compact disc and digital versatile disc players are often used in television (and radio) stations for playing back commercially produced

music and other audio material. The rewritable CDs and DVDs are used for multiple recording and playback. There are several different CD and DVD formats on the market, all of which perform similar production functions: the storage and playback of a variety of audio material. Some of the more elaborate models let you load several CDs at the same time and select and program separate tracks for automatic playback. **SEE 9.14**

Although CDs and DVDs can theoretically withstand unlimited playback without deterioration, they are nevertheless vulnerable. If you scratch the shiny side or even the label side, the disc won't play past the scratch. And if there are fingerprints on the disc, the laser may try to read the fingerprints instead of the imprinted digits. When handling CDs and DVDs, try to keep your hands off of the surface and always lay the disc down on its label side—not its shiny side.

9.14 PROFESSIONAL CD PLAYER

Professional CD and DVD players allow instant random access to various tracks. The play sequence can be stored and displayed on playback.

AUDIO CONTROL IN THE STUDIO

All television control rooms are divided into an audio control section and a program control section. The *audio control booth* is a soundproof room adjacent to the larger program control room. Most audio booths provide visual access to the control room. Ideally, the audio engineer should be able to see the preview monitors in the program control room so that he or she can anticipate the audio cues.

Generally, the audio control booth houses the audio, or mixing, console and the analog and digital recording and playback equipment, including (largely for nostalgic reasons) a turntable. There is also a physical patchbay (despite the presence of computer patching) and one or more desktop computers. You will also find cue and program speakers, intercom systems, a clock, and a line monitor. The audio engineer (or audio operator or audio technician) operates the audio controls during a show. **SEE 9.15**

BASIC AUDIO OPERATION

Learning to operate all this equipment takes time and practice. Fortunately, in most studio productions your audio tasks consist mostly of making sure that the voices of the news anchors or panel guests have acceptable volume levels and are relatively free of extraneous noise and that the sound appears with the pictures when video recordings are played. Most likely you will not be asked to do intricate sound manipulations during complex recording sessions—at least not right away. Consequently, the focus here is on the basic audio control factors: audio system calibration, volume control, and live studio mixing.

Audio system calibration   Before doing any serious volume adjustment or mixing, you need to make sure that the audio or video recorder hears the same thing. Technically, this means that the input volume (recording level) of the video recorder matches the console output (line-out signal). This process is called audio system calibration or simply calibration. To *calibrate* a system is to make all the VU meters (usually of the audio console and the video recorder) respond in the same way to a specific audio signal—the control tone. (Note that audio calibration has nothing to do with zoom lens calibration, whereby you adjust the zoom lens so that it stays in focus during the entire zoom range.)

To calibrate the audio system, you send a 0 VU tone from the console to the video recorder. The VR (video recorder) operator adjusts the input level on the video recorder so that it also reads 0 VU. When dealing with digital audio, it is a good idea to set the recording level somewhat below 0 VU to avoid distortion of some of the louder bursts; if this is done, however, all other inputs must then be calibrated in the same way. **SEE 9.16** **ZVL3** AUDIO→ Consoles and mixers→ calibration

Window to video control room

Computer display of console functions

Audio console

Studio talkback

9.15 AUDIO CONTROL BOOTH

The television audio control booth contains a variety of audio control equipment, such as the audio console with computer display; the patchbay; CD, DVD, and mini disc players; DAT recorder/players; loudspeakers; intercom systems; and a video line monitor.

VTR input (recording level): 0 VU

Audio console line-out: 0 VU

9.16 AUDIO SYSTEM CALIBRATION
An audio system is calibrated when all VU meters respond in the same way to a specific audio signal—the control tone. Here the line-out of the audio mixer is calibrated with the input (recording level) of the VTR. Both VU meters show the same value.

Volume control   Once the system is calibrated, you can pay attention to the finer points of adjusting the volume of the incoming sound sources. Before starting the video recording, you should always take a level—that is, adjust the input level so that the talent's speech falls more or less within the tolerable volume range (not riding in the mud and not bending the needle). Ask the talent to talk long enough for you to see where the lower and upper limits of the speech volume are, then place the fader between these two extremes. An experienced performer will stay within this volume range even in subsequent takes.

Unfortunately, when asked to give a level, most performers consider it an intrusion on their concentration and simply count rapidly to three or four; then, when they are on the air, their voices rise to the occasion—and also in volume. Always be prepared for this sudden volume increase. Experienced performers give a few of their opening remarks in about as loud a voice as they will use when on the air. But don't bet on it.

When overmodulating speech (riding the gain consistently at too high a level), you end up not with a recording that is slightly too loud but with distorted sound. Although it is relatively easy to boost sound that was recorded at a

slightly lower-than-normal level (even at the risk of amplifying some of the noise with the low-level sounds), it is very difficult and often impossible to fix overmodulated, distorted sound in postproduction. Digital sound is especially susceptible to overmodulation. You should therefore always set the recording levels somewhat lower than for analog recording. (Audio people recommend setting the maximum level for audio at –4 to –6 dB [decibels] rather than at 0 dB.)

Live studio mixing   Live mixing means that you combine and balance sounds while the production is in progress. Studio mixing may range from the relatively simple task of riding gain for the newscaster's lavalier mic or balancing the voices of several panel members during a discussion, to the more complicated job of switching among multiple audio sources during a newscast or recording a rock band or even a dramatic scene for an interactive multimedia program on how to recognize potential shoplifters.

As with the setup of mics for a complex production, there is no formula for how an optimal mix is achieved. When riding gain for the single mic of the news anchor, simply keep his or her level within the acceptable audio range and watch that the anchor is clearly heard. When controlling the audio of the panel discussion, riding gain is easiest if every member wears a lavalier. Once the levels are set, you have little to do except bring down the fader somewhat if one of the members gets excited and starts talking much louder than normal, or bring it up when somebody drifts off mumbling.

When using desk mics, the most important audio job is before the show even starts—the mic setup. Remember to place the mics at least three times as far apart as the distance of any mic to the panel member (as described in chapter 8) to eliminate possible multiple-microphone interference. After taking preliminary levels, adjust the mics for optimal positions and tape them down. Take another level, adjust the faders for all mics, and hope that the panel members' kicking and banging on the table will be kept to a minimum.

The multisource newscast is more challenging. For example, you may need to switch quickly from the anchor's introduction to SOT (sound on tape) or SOS (sound on source) of a video from the video server, and from there to the co-anchor, to the guest in London (remote source), back to the co-anchor, to another SOS clip from the video server, back to the anchor, to a commercial, and so forth. You will find that labeling each audio input will greatly facilitate your audio control: simply put a strip of masking tape below the faders and mark them with a grease pencil. As for volume control, you have to watch the remote sources and the SOT/SOS clips more than the mics of the anchors and the weathercaster (whose voice levels you have set before the newscast).

The mixing for the rock band or dramatic scene for the multimedia project can be quite complicated and is best left to an audio expert. Again, the initial choice of mics and their proper placement is more challenging than the mixing itself. The recording engineer may also have to patch the mics for multiple audio feeds, such as foldback, mix-minus, audience feed, and video feed. A *mix-minus* feed is a type of foldback in which you send into the studio a complete mix (usually the band or orchestra) minus the sound generated in the studio (such as the singer's voice).

Surprisingly enough, the recording of a symphony orchestra is generally simpler. All you have to do is hang two good condenser mics close together in front of and high above the orchestra (about 10 feet or higher). Point them in a V to the left and the right of the orchestra, with the tip of the V facing the audience. Most of the balancing of instruments and volume will be done for you by the conductor.

PRODUCTION EQUIPMENT AND BASIC OPERATION FOR FIELD AUDIO

As with all audio, the better the sound pickup, the easier the sound control during the production or in postproduction. (Refer to chapter 8 for information and advice on what mics to use outdoors and how to achieve optimal sound under various field conditions.)

Unless you are engaged in a big remote (see chapter 18), the audio equipment in the field is much less elaborate than its studio counterparts. This is not because you don't need to produce optimal audio in the field but simply because in electronic news gathering (ENG) the audio requirements are usually more modest. Similarly, in electronic field production (EFP) most of the quality control is done in postproduction in the studio. But don't be fooled into thinking that field audio is somehow easier than studio audio. On the contrary—sound pickup and recording in the field are actually more difficult. In the field you have to worry about wind noise, barking dogs, traffic sounds, airplanes overhead, chattering onlookers, or rooms that produce the dreaded inside-a-barrel sounds.

KEEPING SOUNDS SEPARATE

The key to good field audio is keeping the primary sounds as separate from the environmental sounds as possible. For example, you usually want to record the reporter's mic input on one audio track and the camera mic's input of primarily ambient sounds on the second audio track. There will nevertheless be circumstances in which you need to mix and balance several sound sources in the field. For example, if you have to cover an interview of several people in somebody's living room, you should balance their voices right then and there. This is where the field mixer comes in.

AUDIO MIXER

An audio mixer differs from an audio console in that it normally serves only the input (volume control) and mixing (combining two or more signals) functions. **SEE 9.17**

Most portable mixers have only three or four input channels and one or two outputs. Even then the small mixers require that you distinguish between mic-level (low signal strength) and line-level (high signal strength) input sources. A switch above or below each sound input must be set either to *mic* for low-level inputs, such as all microphones, or to *line* for high-level sources, such as the output of a CD player. Because most of the time you will use

9.17 PORTABLE MIXER

This portable mixer has three inputs and two outputs. The volume controls are rotary knobs. Such big knobs and switches are especially convenient in the field, where digital menus are often hard to see and activate.

the field mixer for mixing microphones, double-check that the input switch is set to *mic.* If you are not sure whether a particular piece of audio equipment produces a mic-level or a line-level signal, do a brief test recording. Don't rely on the VU meter when playing back the test recording—you should actually listen to it with headphones. The VU meter might show the recording to be in the acceptable volume range, but it will not reflect sound distortions.

Even though some digital mixers have more inputs as well as some quality controls, elaborate mixing in the field is not recommended unless you're doing a live telecast.

AUDIO CONTROL IN THE FIELD

You usually do not need a mixer when doing ENG. You can plug the external mic into one of the camcorder audio inputs and plug the camera shotgun mic into the other audio input. Make sure that you record the sound at 16 bits/ 48 kHz, especially if you use a small digital video camcorder. If you record at a lower bit rate (such as 12 bits), the audio will drift away from the video and remain out of sync when you transfer the footage to a DVD or hard drive.

USING THE AGC IN ENG AND EFP

When you are on an ENG assignment and cannot watch the VU meter on the camcorder, switch on the ***automatic gain control (AGC),*** which boosts low sounds and reduces high-volume sounds so that they conform to the accept-

able volume range. Note, however, that the AGC does not discriminate between wanted and unwanted sounds; it faithfully boosts the sound of the passing truck and the coughing crewmember and even the noise of the pauses when the field reporter is thinking of something clever to say. Whenever possible, and especially when in noisy surroundings, switch off the AGC, take a level, and try to watch the audio levels in the camcorder viewfinder or on the VU meter of the mixer. When using DAT, turn down the pot (volume control) a bit from where you had it while taking a level. This way you can be pretty sure not to overmodulate once you are on the air.

USING AN XLR PAD

An XLR pad is a simple and reliable way of preventing overload distortion when the incoming signal is too strong. For all practical purposes, it substitutes for the console's trim control, which you don't find on a portable mixer or camcorder. It looks like an XLR connector, and you use it in a similar way: you plug one end into the XLR connector of the (balanced) cable coming from the sound source; you plug the other end into the XLR connector of the cable going to the mixer, the audio input of the camcorder, or a separate audio recorder. This pad introduces a little bit of noise but is not nearly so detrimental to the field audio as overload distortion.

EFP MIXING

In EFP mixing there are always assignments for which you have to control more audio sources than the two microphones. Even a simple assignment such as covering the opening of the local elementary school's new gym will most likely require that you mix at least three microphones: the field reporter's mic, the lectern mic for the speeches, and a mic to pick up the school choir. If you run out of mic inputs on the mixer, you can always cover the choir with the camera mic.

Despite the number of mics, the mixing itself is relatively simple. Once you have set the level for each input, you probably need to ride gain only for the reporter's mic during interviews and for the various speakers at the lectern. You may also want to bring up (increase the gain of) the choir mic during the performance. Although in an emergency you could try to pick up most of these sounds with the camera mic or by pointing a shotgun mic at the various areas, the multiple-mic setup and the portable mixer afford you better control.

Here are a few basic guidelines for live ENG/EFP mixing:

■ Even if you have only a few inputs, label each one with what it controls, such as field reporter's mic, audience mic, and so forth. You would be surprised at how quickly you forget whose mic corresponds to which pot. If you have to turn over the audio control to someone else, he or she can take over without long explanations.

■ If you do a complicated mix in the field, protect yourself by feeding it not only to the camcorder but also to a separate audio recorder for probable remixing in postproduction.

■ If you work with a separate audio recorder, calibrate the audio output of the camera with the audio input of the audio recorder.

■ If recording for postproduction, try to put distinctly different sound sources on separate audio tracks, such as the reporter's and guests' voices on one track and the speaker's lectern mic and the choir on the other. That way it will be easier during postproduction *sweetening* (getting rid of unwanted noises and improving the sound quality) to balance the reporter's voice with the other sounds.

It is usually easier to do complicated and subtle mixing in postproduction rather than live in the field. This does not mean that you should forgo filtering out as much unwanted sound as possible during the on-location pickup, assuming that the mixer has some basic quality controls available. If it doesn't, don't worry. If any sweetening is to be done, do it in postproduction. Remember that the more attention you pay to good sound pickup in the field, the less time you need in postproduction. A good wireless lavalier is often the best solution to good field audio.

MAIN POINTS

▶ The major production equipment for studio audio includes the audio console; the patchbay; analog and digital tape-based recording systems such as videotape recorders (VTRs) and digital audiotape (DAT); and tapeless recording systems, including the digital cart system, mini discs and flash memory devices, hard drives, and optical disc systems such as CDs and DVDs.

▶ Audio consoles perform five major functions: input—select, preamplify, and control the volume of the various incoming signals; mix—combine and balance two or more incoming signals; quality control—manipulate the sound characteristics; output—route the combined signal to a specific output; and monitor—route the output or specific sounds to a speaker or headphones so that they can be heard.

▶ The audio control area of a television studio includes the basic audio control booth, which is used for the sound control of daily broadcasts.

▶ The basic audio operation includes: the audio system calibration, which means that all volume-unit (VU) meters in the system must respond in the same way to a specific audio signal—the control tone; volume control; and live studio mixing.

▶ Live studio mixing usually involves combining and balancing sounds while the production is in progress.

▶ In EFP the key to good field audio is keeping the various sound sources reasonably separate so that they can be properly mixed in postproduction.

▶ The automatic gain control (AGC) is a convenient means of keeping the volume within acceptable limits, but in its automatic amplification it will not distinguish between desired sounds and unwanted sounds.

▶ The XLR pad is a small device that, much like the trim control on the audio console, prevents input overload.

9.2

Stereo, Surround Sound, and Sound Aesthetics

This section introduces stereo and surround sound and the principal aesthetic sound factors.

▶ **STEREO AND SURROUND SOUND**
Making sound multidimensional

▶ **BASIC AESTHETIC SOUND FACTORS**
Environment, figure/ground, perspective, continuity, and energy

STEREO AND SURROUND SOUND

As you read this brief discussion of stereo and surround sound, imagine the sound not as the only means of expression, such as the songs to which you may be listening, but as part of an audio/video structure.

STEREO SOUND

Stereo sound, which defines especially the horizontal audio field (left-right or right-left positioning of the major audio source) is of little use when played back on a standard television set. Because the horizontal dimension of the screen is so small, any panning (horizontal positioning) of sound will inevitably lead to off-screen space, even if you sit in the sweet spot (the center where you perceive the two or more channels as one). But hearing a conversation happening in off-screen space when seeing both dialogue partners on-screen makes little sense. At best, stereo for standard television will enrich the general shape of the sound, that is, make it more spacious.

With large-screen, home-theater HDTV video projections, however, stereo sound becomes extremely important for keeping up with and balancing the high-energy video. In fact, the movielike experience when watching large-screen video projections will be greatly intensified by a surround-sound system.

SURROUND SOUND

Surround sound is a technology that produces a soundfield in front of, to the sides of, and behind the listener, enabling one to hear sounds from the front, sides, and back. Developed originally for film reproduction, it is now used for HDTV and other large-screen home-theater arrangements. The most prevalent surround-sound system is Dolby 5.1, which positions three speakers in front and two in back for sound reproduction. These five speakers are supported by an additional subwoofer that is usually positioned between the two rear speakers. This .1 speaker can reproduce especially low-frequency, thunderous sounds. Because low frequencies are omnidirectional, the exact placement of the subwoofer is not critical. **SEE 9.18**

Good surround-sound mixing generally restricts on-screen dialogue to the center-front speaker and laterally spreads action to all three front speakers. But if the video shows the hero standing amid downtown traffic, playing in an orchestra, or dodging bombs, all five speakers are active as well as the "thunder box" at rear-center.[1]

BASIC AESTHETIC SOUND FACTORS

As reiterated throughout this chapter, the bewildering array of audio equipment is of little use if you cannot exercise some aesthetic judgment—make decisions about how to work with television sound artistically and not just technically. Yet aesthetic judgment is not arbitrary or totally personal; there are some common aesthetic factors to which we all react similarly.

When dealing with television sound, you should pay particular attention to five basic aesthetic factors: environment, figure/ground, perspective, continuity, and energy.

---

1. See Stanley R. Alten, *Audio in Media,* 8th ed. (Belmont, Calif.: Thomson/Wadsworth, 2008), pp. 414–24.

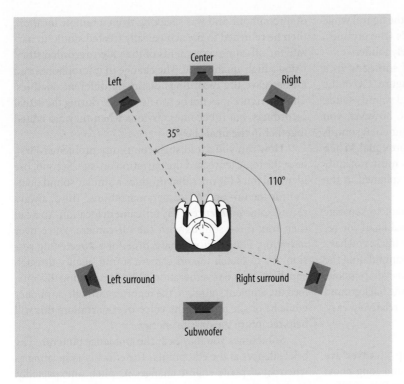

9.18 SURROUND SOUND
The 5.1 Dolby surround-sound system uses six speakers—three in front and three in back. The rear-center (.1) speaker is a sub-woofer for very low sounds.

ENVIRONMENT

In most studio recordings, we try to eliminate as much ambient sound as possible. In the field these sounds, when heard in the background of the main sound source, are often important indicators of where the event takes place or even how it feels. Such sounds help establish the general environment of the event.

For example, when covering a downtown fire, the sirens, the crackling of the fire, the noise of the fire engines and the pumps, the tense commands of the firefighters, and the agitated voices of onlookers are significant in communicating to the television viewer some of the excitement and apprehension on the scene. Now consider the recording of a small orchestra. In a studio recording, the coughing of a crewmember or musician during an especially soft passage would certainly prompt a retake. Not so in a live concert. We have learned to identify occasional coughing and other such environmental sounds as important indicators of the immediacy of the event.

Environmental sounds are especially important in ENG. By using an omnidirectional mic, you pick up the ambient sounds automatically with the main audio source. But, as mentioned before, if you intend to do some postproduction, use a more directional (cardioid) mic for recording the main sound source, such as the reporter or the guest, on audio track 1; use another mic (usually the camera mic) for recording the ambient sounds on audio track 2.

FIGURE/GROUND

One important perceptual factor is the *figure/ground* principle, whereby we tend to organize our visual environment into a relatively mobile figure (a person or a car) and a relatively stable background (a wall, houses, or mountains). We can expand this principle a little and say that we single out an event that is important to us and make it the foreground while relegating all other events to the background—the environment.

For example, if you are looking for your friend and finally discover her in a crowd, she immediately becomes the focus of your attention—the foreground—while the rest of the people become the background, regardless of whether they walk ahead of her or behind her. The same happens in the field of sound. We have the ability to perceive, within limits, the sounds we want or need to hear (the figure) while ignoring to a large extent all other sounds (the ground), even if the background sounds are relatively louder.

When showing a close-up (CU) of someone in a noisy environment, you should make the figure (CU of the person talking) louder and the background sounds softer. When showing the person in a long shot, however, you should increase the volume of the environmental sounds so that the figure/ground relationship is more equal. When emphasizing the foreground, the sounds must not only be louder but also have more presence (explained in the following section).

You can now see why it is so important to separate sounds as much as possible during the recording. If you record background and foreground all on one track, you have to live with whatever the mic picked up; manipulating the individual sounds would be very difficult, if even possible. With the figure sounds on one track and the background sounds on the other, the manipulation is relatively easy.

PERSPECTIVE

Sound perspective means that close-up pictures are matched with relatively nearby sounds, and long shots correspond with sounds that seem to come from farther away. Close sounds have more presence than distant sounds—a sound quality that makes us feel in proximity to the sound source. Generally, background sounds have less presence, and close-ups have more presence. Experienced singers hold the mic close to the mouth during intimate passages but pull it back a little when the song becomes less personal.

Such a desirable variation of sound presence is virtually eliminated when using lavalier mics in a drama. Because the distance between mic and mouth is about the same for each actor, their voices exhibit the same presence regardless of whether they are seen in a close-up or a long shot. The necessary presence must then be achieved in time-consuming and costly postproduction. This is why boom mics are still preferred in many multicamera productions of television plays such as soap operas. The boom mic can be close to an actor during a close-up and moved somewhat farther away during a long shot to stay out of the picture—a simple solution to a big problem.

CONTINUITY

Sound continuity is especially important in postproduction. You may have noticed the sound quality of a reporter's voice change depending on whether he was speaking on- or off-camera. When on-camera the reporter used one type of microphone and was speaking from a remote location; then he returned to the acoustically treated studio to narrate the off-camera segments of the video-recorded story, using a high-quality mic. The change in microphones and locales gave the recordings distinctly different qualities. This difference may not be too noticeable during the actual recordings, but it becomes obvious when they are edited together in the final show.

How can you avoid such continuity problems? First, have the reporter record the narration on-site. Second, use identical mics (or mics that produce a similar sound quality) for the on- and off-camera narrations. Third, always record some ***ambience*** at the on-camera location. You can then mix these sounds with the off-camera, voice-over narration. Fourth, if you have time for a sweetening session, try to match the on-camera sound quality through equalization and reverberation. When producing this mix, feed the ambient sounds to the reporter through earphones while he or she is doing the voice-over narration; this will help recapture the on-site energy.

Sometimes you may hear the ambience punctured by brief silences at the edit points. The effect is as startling as when an airplane engine changes its pitch unexpectedly. The easiest way to restore the background continuity is to cover up these silences with prerecorded ambience. Always record a few minutes of "silence" (room tone or background sounds) before and after videotaping or whenever the ambience changes decisively (such as a concert hall with and without an audience). **ZVL4** EDITING→ Continuity→ sound

Sound is also a chief element in establishing visual continuity. A rhythmically precise piece of music can help a disparate series of pictures seem continuous. Music and sound are often the important connecting link among abruptly changing visual sequences.

ENERGY

Unless you want to achieve a special effect through contradiction, you should match the general energy of the pictures with a similar sound intensity. Energy refers to all the factors in a scene that communicate a certain degree of aesthetic force and power. Obviously, high-energy scenes, such as a series of close-ups of an ice-hockey game or a rock band in action, can stand higher-energy sounds than can a more tranquil scene, such as lovers walking through a meadow. Good television audio depends a great deal on your ability to sense the general energy of the pictures or sequences and to adjust the volume and sound presence accordingly. **ZVL5** AUDIO→ Aesthetics→ continuity | environment | sound perspective | try it

M A I N   P O I N T S

▶ Surround-sound technology uses three speakers placed in front of the listener and three in back to produce a sound-field that surrounds the listener.

▶ The five major aesthetic factors in sound control are: environment—sharpening an event through ambient sounds; figure/ground—emphasizing the most important sound source over the general background sounds; perspective—matching close-up pictures with nearby sounds, and long shots with distant sounds; continuity—maintaining the quality of sound when combining various takes; and energy—matching the force and the power of the pictures with a similar intensity of sound.

Z E T T L ' S   V I D E O L A B

For your reference or to track your work, the *Zettl's VideoLab* program cues in this chapter are listed here with their corresponding page numbers.

ZVL1 ▶ AUDIO→ Audio introduction   **166**

ZVL2 ▶ AUDIO→ Consoles and mixers→ parts | signals | control | try it   **170**

ZVL3 ▶ AUDIO→ Consoles and mixers→ calibration   **177**

ZVL4 ▶ EDITING→ Continuity→ sound   **184**

ZVL5 ▶ AUDIO→ Aesthetics→ continuity | environment | sound perspective | try it   **184**

10

Lighting

Lighting means to control light and shadows for three principal reasons:

■ To help the television camera see well, that is, produce technically optimal pictures

■ To help the viewer see well—to recognize what things and people look like and where they are in relation to one another and to their immediate environment

■ To establish for the viewer a specific mood that helps intensify the feeling about the event

But why bother with lighting when even a small and inexpensive camcorder can see virtually in the dark? This is a valid point so long as the available light in which you are video recording is the right type and in the right place to produce good pictures. Unfortunately, this is rarely the case, and we have to give nature a little help.

Section 10.1, Lighting Instruments and Lighting Controls, describes the tools you need to accomplish the three lighting objectives. Section 10.2, Light Intensity, Lamps, and Color Media, introduces a few more elements about light, how to control and measure it, and how to use colored light.

barn doors Metal flaps mounted in front of a lighting instrument that control the spread of the light beam.

baselight Even, nondirectional (diffused) light necessary for the camera to operate optimally. Normal baselight levels are 150 to 200 foot-candles (1,500 to 2,000 lux) at ƒ/8 to ƒ/16. Also called *base*.

broad A floodlight with a broadside, panlike reflector.

clip light Small internal reflector spotlight that is clipped to pieces of scenery or furniture with a gator clip. Also called *PAR (parabolic aluminized reflector) lamp*.

cookie A popularization of the original term *cucoloris*. Any pattern cut out of thin metal that, when placed inside or in front of an ellipsoidal spotlight (pattern projector), produces a shadow pattern. Also called *gobo*.

dimmer A device that controls the intensity of light by throttling the electric current flowing to the lamp.

ellipsoidal spotlight Spotlight that produces a very defined beam, which can be shaped further by metal shutters.

flag A thin, rectangular sheet of metal, plastic, or cloth used to block light from falling on specific areas. Also called *gobo*.

floodlight Lighting instrument that produces diffused light with a relatively undefined beam edge.

fluorescent Lamps that generate light by activating a gas-filled tube to give off ultraviolet radiation, which lights up the phosphorous coating inside the tube.

foot-candle (fc) The amount of light that falls on an object. One foot-candle is the amount of light from a single candle that falls on a 1-square-foot area located 1 foot away from the light source.

Fresnel spotlight One of the most common spotlights, named after the inventor of its lens. Its lens has steplike concentric rings.

gel Generic term for color filters put in front of spotlights or floodlights to give the light beam a specific hue. *Gel* comes from *gelatin,* the filter material used before the invention of more-durable plastics. Also called *color media*.

HMI light Stands for *hydragyrum medium arc-length iodide.* Uses a high-intensity lamp that produces light by passing electricity through a specific type of gas. Needs a separate ballast.

incandescent The light produced by the hot tungsten filament of ordinary glass-globe or quartz-iodine light bulbs (in contrast to fluorescent light).

incident light Light that strikes the object directly from its source. An incident-light reading is the measure of light in foot-candles (or lux) from the object to the light source. The light meter is pointed directly into the light source or toward the camera.

lumen The light intensity power of one candle (light source radiating isotropically, i.e., in all directions).

luminaire Technical term for a lighting instrument.

luminant Lamp that produces the light; the light source.

lux European standard unit for measuring light intensity. 10.75 lux = 1 fc; usually roughly translated as 10 lux = 1 fc.

neutral density (ND) filter Filter that reduces the incoming light without distorting the color of the scene.

patchboard A device that connects various inputs with specific outputs. Also called *patchbay*.

pattern projector An ellipsoidal spotlight with a cookie (cucoloris) insert, which projects the cookie's pattern as a cast shadow.

quartz A high-intensity incandescent light whose lamp consists of a quartz or silica housing (instead of the customary glass) that contains halogen gas and a tungsten filament. Produces a very bright light of stable color temperature (3,200K). Also called *TH (tungsten-halogen) lamp*.

reflected light Light that is bounced off of the illuminated object. A reflected-light reading is done with a light meter held close to the illuminated object.

scoop A scooplike television floodlight.

scrim A spun-glass material that is put in front of a lighting instrument as an additional light diffuser or intensity reducer.

softlight Television floodlight that produces extremely diffused light.

spotlight A lighting instrument that produces directional, relatively undiffused light with a relatively well-defined beam edge.

10.1

Lighting Instruments and Lighting Controls

When you turn on the light in a room, you are concerned primarily with having enough illumination to see well and get around. Contrary to the lighting in your home, however, lighting for television and digital cinema must also please the camera and fulfill certain aesthetic functions, such as simulating outdoor or indoor light or creating a happy or sinister mood. Studio lighting requires instruments that can simulate bright sunlight, a street lamp at a lonely bus stop, the efficiency of a hospital operating room, and the horror of a medieval dungeon. It must also reflect the credibility of a news anchor, the high energy of a game show, and the romantic mood in a love scene.

When in the field, you need lighting instruments that are easy to transport and set up and flexible enough to work in a great variety of environments for a multitude of lighting tasks. This section describes the major studio and field lighting instruments and the types of lighting controls. Section 10.2 addresses light intensity, types of lamps, and color media. The techniques of lighting are covered in chapter 11.

▶ **STUDIO LIGHTING INSTRUMENTS**
Spotlights and floodlights

▶ **FIELD LIGHTING INSTRUMENTS**
Portable spotlights, portable floodlights, and camera lights

▶ **LIGHTING CONTROL EQUIPMENT**
Mounting devices, directional controls, intensity controls, and the basic principle of electronic dimmers

STUDIO LIGHTING INSTRUMENTS

All studio lighting is accomplished with a variety of spotlights and floodlights. These instruments, technically called *luminaires*, are designed to operate from the studio ceiling or from floor stands.

SPOTLIGHTS

Spotlights produce directional, well-defined light that can be adjusted from a sharp light beam like the one from a focused flashlight or a car headlight to a softer beam that is still highly directional but that lights up a larger area. All studio spotlights have a lens that helps sharpen the beam. Most studio lighting uses two basic types of spotlights: the Fresnel and the ellipsoidal spot.

Fresnel spotlight   Named for the early-nineteenth-century French physicist Augustin Fresnel (pronounced "fra-*nel*") who invented the lens used in it, the *Fresnel spotlight* is widely used in television studio and film production.   **SEE 10.1**   It is relatively lightweight and flexible and has a high output. The spotlight can be adjusted to a "flood" beam position, which gives off a widespread light beam; or it can be "spotted," or focused to a sharp, clearly defined beam.

Panning mechanism controlled by pole-operated knob (see inset)

Gel and scrim holder

Fresnel lens

Other side:

Focus knob   Pan knob   Tilt knob

10.1 FRESNEL SPOTLIGHT
This spotlight is one of the most useful lighting instruments in the studio. Note the pan, tilt, and focus controls, which can be operated from the studio floor with a lighting pole.

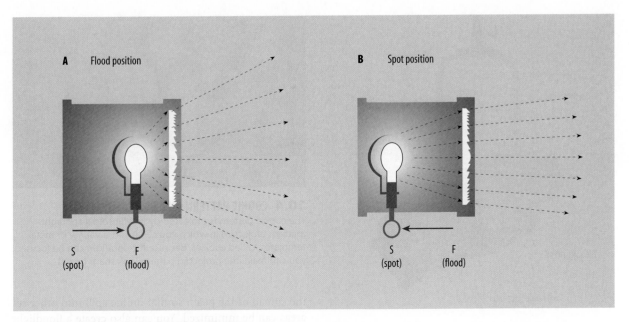

10.2 BEAM CONTROL OF FRESNEL SPOTLIGHT

A To flood (spread) the beam, turn the focus spindle, ring, or knob so that the lamp-reflector unit moves toward the lens.
B To spot (focus) the beam, turn the focus spindle, ring, or knob so that the lamp-reflector unit moves away from the lens.

You manipulate the relative spread of the beam with a beam control that changes the distance between the lamp and the lens. Most Fresnel spotlights have a lamp-reflector unit inside the lighting instrument that slides toward or away from the lens. To spot, or focus, the beam, turn the control so that the lamp-reflector unit moves *away* from the lens. To flood, or spread, the beam, turn the control so that the lamp-reflector unit moves *toward* the lens. Even in the flood position, the beam of the spotlight is still directional and much sharper than that of a floodlight. The flood position softens the beam (and with it the shadows) and simultaneously reduces the amount of light falling on the object. Always adjust the beam gently. When the lamp is turned on, its hot filament is highly sensitive to shock. **SEE 10.2**

Some Fresnel spots have external knobs with which you can also control the pan and the tilt of the instrument without climbing a ladder and doing it manually (see figure 10.1).

Fresnel spotlights come in different sizes, depending on how much light they produce. Obviously, the larger instruments produce more light than the smaller ones. The size of Fresnel spotlights is normally given in the wattage of the lamp. For example, you might be asked to rehang the "1K" (1 kilowatt [kW] = 1,000 watts) Fresnel or change the lamp in the "2K" Fresnel.

In most television studios, the most common Fresnels are the 1kW and the 2kW instruments. For maximum lighting control, technicians usually prefer to operate with as few (yet adequately powerful) lighting instruments as possible. The increased sensitivity of cameras has made the 1kW Fresnel the workhorse in average-sized studios.

Ellipsoidal spotlight   A favorite for theater lighting, the *ellipsoidal spotlight* produces a sharp, highly defined beam. Even when in a flood position, the ellipsoidal beam is still sharper than the focused beam of a Fresnel spot. Ellipsoidal spots are generally used when specific, precise lighting tasks are necessary. For example, if you want to create pools of light reflecting off the studio floor, the ellipsoidal spot is the instrument to use.

As with the Fresnel, you can spot and flood the light beam of the ellipsoidal. Instead of sliding the lamp inside the instrument, however, you focus the ellipsoidal spot by moving its lens in and out. You can even shape the beam into a triangle or rectangle by adjusting the four metal shutters inside the instrument. **SEE 10.3**

Ellipsoidal spotlights come in sizes from 500W (watts) to 2kW, but the most common is 750W. Some ellipsoidal spotlights can also be used as **pattern projectors**. These instruments are equipped with a slot next to the beam-shaping shutters, which can hold a metal pattern called a

10.3 ELLIPSOIDAL SPOTLIGHT
The highly focused beam of the ellipsoidal spotlight can be further shaped by shutters. It produces the most directional beam of all the spotlights.

10.4 COOKIE PATTERN ON CYCLORAMA
The cookie pattern is projected by an ellipsoidal spotlight (pattern projector) in which you can insert a variety of metal templates, called cookies. Because the spotlight can be focused, you can make the projected pattern look sharp or soft.

cucoloris, or ***cookie*** for short. When the spotlight is turned on, the cookie causes a shadow pattern on any surface. Most often it is used to break up flat surfaces, such as the cyclorama (large cloth drape used for backing of scenery) or the studio floor. **SEE 10.4**

To make lighting terminology a little more confusing, some lighting people call these metal templates "gobos." Unfortunately, *gobo* seems to have as ambiguous a meaning as the word *spring*. If a lighting director (LD) asked you to fetch a gobo, he or she could mean a cookie; a flag, which is a rectangular piece of metal, plastic, or cloth to keep light from falling onto certain areas; or even a freestanding piece of scenery, such as prison bars or a picture frame, through which the camera can shoot a related scene.

FLOODLIGHTS
Floodlights are designed to produce great amounts of highly diffused light. They are often used as principal sources of light (key lights) in situations where shadows are to be kept to a minimum, such as news sets and product displays; to slow down falloff (reduce contrast between light and shadow areas); and to provide baselight. With some floodlights, as with some spotlights, you can adjust

the spread of the beam so that undue spill into other set areas can be minimized. You can also create a floodlight effect by flooding the beam of a spotlight and diffusing it further with a ***scrim***—a spun-glass material held in a metal frame—in front of the instrument.

There are four basic types of studio floodlights: the scoop; the softlight and the broad; the fluorescent floodlight bank; and the strip, or cyc, light.

Scoop   Named for its peculiar scooplike reflector, the ***scoop*** is one of the more popular floodlights. Although it has no lens, it nevertheless produces a fairly directional but diffused light beam. **SEE 10.5**

The standard scoop emits a fixed diffused beam of light. You can increase the diffusion of the beam by attaching a scrim (see figure 10.5). Although the light output through the scrim is considerably reduced, some lighting people put scrims on all scoops, not only to produce highly diffused light but also to protect studio personnel in case the hot lamp inside the scoop shatters. Most scoops operate with a 1,500W lamp. **ZVL1** LIGHTS→ Instruments→ studio | field

Softlight and broad   *Softlights* are used for even, extremely diffused lighting. They have large tubelike lamps, a diffusing reflector in the back of the large housing, and a diffusing material covering the front opening to further scatter the light. Softlights are often used for flat (virtually shadowless) lighting setups. You can also use softlights to increase the baselight level without affecting specific lighting where highlights and shadow areas are carefully

10.5 SCOOP
The scoop is a rugged, all-purpose floodlight. Its scooplike reflector gives its beam some directionality. This scoop has a scrim attached to soften the beam.

10.6 INCANDESCENT SOFTLIGHT
The softlight produces extremely diffused light and is used for illumination with slow falloff. It renders a scene almost shadowless.

controlled. For example, if a scene calls for a hallway with alternating bright and dark areas, you can lighten up the dark areas with softlights to provide enough baselight for the camera to see well even in the dark areas. Softlights come in various sizes and use incandescent or HMI lamps, which are discussed in section 10.2. **SEE 10.6**

The **broad** (from *broadside*) is similar to a softlight except that it has a higher light output that causes more-distinct shadows. Broads also have some provision for beam control. They are generally used in digital cinema production to evenly illuminate large areas with diffused light. **SEE 10.7** Smaller broads emit a more directional light beam than do the larger ones, for evenly illuminating smaller areas. To permit some directional control over the beam, some broads have barn doors—movable metal flaps—to block gross light spill into other set areas.

Fluorescent floodlight bank The fluorescent flood-light bank goes back to the early days of television lighting,

10.7 LARGE BROAD
This instrument illuminates a fairly large area with diffused light. Its light output is normally greater than that of a softlight of equal size.

10.8 FLUORESCENT FLOODLIGHT BANK
These floodlight banks act like softlights except that they do not get as hot as incandescent floodlights of equal output. Some floodlight banks use lamps that operate on fluorescent-like principles.

Egg crate

10.9 EGG CRATE ON FLUORESCENT FIXTURE
The egg crate makes the floodlight from a fluorescent fixture more directional without influencing the light's softness.

when the banks were large, heavy, and inefficient. Today's fluorescent banks are relatively lightweight, much more efficient, and can burn close to the standard indoor color temperature (3,200K), giving off reddish light. By simply changing the tubes, you can approximate the standard outdoor color temperature (5,600K) or achieve even higher ones (more-bluish light) that resemble the extremely bluish midday sunlight filtered by a hazy sky. (Color temperature is explained in detail in chapter 11. For now it should suffice to know that a high color temperature refers to white light with a slight bluish tint; a low color temperature refers to white light with a slight reddish tint. Color temperature has nothing to do with how hot a lamp gets.)

Other advantages of fluorescent banks are that they use less power than incandescent lamps and they burn much more coolly—a definite advantage when lighting interiors with poor ventilation. The disadvantages are that fluorescent banks are still quite large and bulky and their color spectrum is sometimes uneven. This means that the light emitted does not reproduce all colors faithfully. Some lamps still cause a persistent and noticeable greenish tint.

Floodlight banks have rows of low-powered fluorescent lamps inside a housing that looks similar to a softlight. **SEE 10.8** Some fluorescent studio lighting fixtures have a gridlike contraption, called an egg crate, attached to make the light beam more directional without losing its softness. **SEE 10.9**

Strip, or cyc, light   This type of instrument is commonly used to achieve even illumination of large set areas, such as the cyclorama (cyc) or some other uninterrupted background. Similar to the border, or cyc, lights of the theater, television strip lights consist of rows of three to 12 quartz lamps mounted in long, boxlike reflectors. The more sophisticated strip lights have, like theater border lights, colored-glass frames for each of the reflector units so that the cyc can be illuminated in different colors. **SEE 10.10**

You can also use strip lights as general floodlights by suspending them from the studio ceiling, or you can place them on the studio floor to separate pillars and other set pieces from the lighted background. Strip lights are sometimes used for silhouette lighting (where the background is evenly illuminated and the foreground objects remain unlit) and special-effects chroma-key lighting (see chapter 11). **ZVL2** LIGHTS→ Design→ silhouette

For relatively static scenes, such as news or interviews, you will find that it is often easier to use the much lighter and more flexible field lighting instruments, even if there are a great variety of studio lights hanging from the lighting grid. There are several advantages to using these lighter

10.10 STRIP, OR CYC, LIGHT
Strip lights are used to illuminate cycloramas and other large areas that need even illumination.

instruments instead of those on the grid: you can place the small instruments anywhere in the studio with a minimum of effort, they can be easily repositioned to get the desired lighting effect, they draw considerably less power than the larger instruments, and they generate less heat. The following section highlights some of the principal portable field lighting instruments.

FIELD LIGHTING INSTRUMENTS

You can use studio lighting instruments on remote locations, but you'll find that most of them are too bulky to move around easily, their large plugs do not fit the normal household receptacles, and they draw too much power. Once in place and operating, they may not provide the amount or type of illumination you need for good field lighting. Unless you do big remotes or a movie scene where the lighting requirements rival studio lighting, you need instruments that are easy to transport and quick to set up and that give you the lighting flexibility you need in the field.

Although many portable lighting instruments fulfill dual spotlight and floodlight functions, you may still find it useful to group them, like studio lights, into those categories. Note, however, that by putting a diffusing scrim in front of the spotlight, or by bouncing its beam off the ceiling, a wall, or a large foam-core board, the spotlight will take on the function of a floodlight. On the other hand, you can use a small floodlight and control its beam with barn doors so that it illuminates a relatively limited area, operating as a spot.

PORTABLE SPOTLIGHTS

Portable spotlights, often called hard lights (as the opposite of softlights), are easy to set up and transport and small enough to be effectively hidden from camera view even in

10.11 SMALL FRESNEL SPOTLIGHT
This low-powered (300W to 650W) Fresnel spotlight is especially effective in lighting for electronic field production (EFP). You can focus or diffuse its beam and attach four-way barn doors and color media (gels).

cramped interiors. They come in different sizes and with or without a lens. Some portable spots have a Fresnel lens, just like the Fresnel spots hanging from the studio lighting grid, and some have no lens and are, therefore, called open-face spots.

Spotlights with lenses These include low-powered (up to 750W) Fresnel spots, the much smaller (125W to 250W) spotlight with a prismatic lens or simply a glass cover, and the HMI spots.

The portable Fresnels are identical to the ones hanging in the studio except that they operate with lower-wattage lamps. They are usually mounted on a tricaster light stand. **SEE 10.11**

The smaller spotlights with a plain (prismatic) lens emit enough light to be used as a key light for an interview in a small area. The beam of these small spotlights can be

10.12 SMALL SPOTLIGHT
This low-powered (125W and 250W) spotlight has an efficient reflector and lens (not a Fresnel) that, despite its small size, make it into a highly effective lighting instrument. It is primarily used for EFP and electronic news gathering (ENG).

10.13 PORTABLE HMI FRESNEL SPOT WITH BALLAST
The HMI Fresnel spotlight burns with the daylight standard (5,600K). It needs considerably less power than does an incandescent light of equal intensity.

spread or focused just like a larger Fresnel, which makes them ideal instruments in tight quarters. **SEE 10.12**

When working in digital cinema, you will be undoubtedly use the portable HMI (200W or higher) Fresnel spots. *HMI lights* are highly efficient, which means that they use very little power to produce a great amount of light. One of the major advantages of these superefficient HMI lights is that you can use up to five 200W instruments simultaneously without overloading a single circuit, assuming that nothing else is plugged into the same circuit. Because you plug most of the lights into household outlets, you can light most interiors with a minimum of time and effort.

HMI lights also have some serious drawbacks, however. They are expensive and need a separate ballast unit to run the lamp. They can cause an audio hum or, when shooting at specific frame rates, a noticeable flicker. The larger instruments are normally used outdoors to fill in

dense shadows caused by the supreme spotlight—the sun. In any case, test them out with the camera before using them on-location. **SEE 10.13**

Open-face spotlights   Mainly because of weight considerations and light efficiency, the open-face spotlight has no lens. This permits a higher light output, but the beam is less even and precise than that of the spots with a lens. In most remote lighting tasks, however, a highly defined beam offers no particular advantage. Because you usually have to work with a minimum of lighting instruments, a fairly general illumination is often better than a highly defined one.

You can spot or spread the beam of the high-efficiency quartz lamp through a focus control lever or knob on the

Metal scrim to
lower intensity

Barn doors

Open-face reflector

10.14 OPEN-FACE SPOT

The open-face (external reflector) spot has no lens. Its beam spread can be adjusted to a spot or moderate flood position. It is one of the most versatile lighting instruments in field production.

10.15 CLIP LIGHT

The clip light, or PAR lamp, consists of a normal internal reflector bulb (such as a PAR 38), a socket with an on/off switch, and a clip for fastening the lamp to a support. You can also get a small metal housing with a two-way barn door for the clip light.

back. **SEE 10.14** Unfortunately, the focused beam is not always even. When you place the spot close to the object, you may notice (and the camera surely will) that the rim of the beam is intense and "hot" while the center of the beam has a "hole"—a low-intensity dark spot. If you place the instrument too close when lighting a face, for example, the hot spot may cause a glowing white area surrounded by red on the lighted face or, at best, a distinct color distortion. But by spreading the beam a little and pulling the instrument farther away from the person, or by placing a scrim in front of the spotlight, you can usually correct the problem. In fact, when using a spot for general indoor lighting, you should routinely place a scrim or similar light-diffusing material in front of the instrument.

Most open-face spots use 300W to 500W lamps and can therefore be plugged into a regular household receptacle without risking a circuit overload. They can also be adapted to run off of 12V (volt) batteries. Most of these instruments have a power switch close to the lamp so that you can turn it off anytime it is not in use. All these small spotlights come as part of a lighting kit—a suitcase containing several such instruments and light stands.

Open-face lights get extremely hot: don't touch the front of the instrument when handling it, and place it far enough away from curtains and other combustible materials to prevent fires. With any lighting instrument, always be careful not to overload the circuit; that is, do not exceed the circuit's rated amperage by plugging in too many instruments per outlet. Extension cords also add their own resistance to that of the lamp, especially when they get warm. Ordinary household outlets can tolerate a load of up to 1,200 watts. You can therefore plug four 300W spots or two 500W instruments into a single circuit without risking an overload (see chapter 11).

Internal reflector spot   Although these lights are not part of the usual arsenal of field lighting equipment, they have been used successfully in many small-area lighting situations. This small spotlight is also known as a *clip light* because it is usually clipped onto things. These lamps are also called PAR lamps for their parabolic aluminized reflector, which is the inside coating of the lamp. **SEE 10.15**

Internal reflector spots come in a variety of beam spreads, from a soft, diffused beam to a hard, precisely shaped beam. For even better beam control, as well as for the protection of the internal reflector bulb, the lamp can be used in a metal housing with barn doors attached.

PORTABLE FLOODLIGHTS

Most ENG/EFP lighting requires a maximum amount of even illumination with a minimum of instruments

10.16 V-LIGHT
This small (500W) lighting instrument is popular in field productions because of its light weight and high output.

10.17 SOFT-BOX
The softlight comes as a single unit of lamp and diffusion tent. It can be folded up for easy transport.

and power requirements. Floodlights are therefore preferred over highly directional spotlights. We look first at the more popular portable floodlights: the V-light, the soft-box, the Chinese lantern, the portable fluorescent bank, and the LED light. We then discuss how you can change portable open-face, and even Fresnel, spots into effective floodlights.

V-light One of the more popular floodlights is the V-light. Although the V-light was originally a specific floodlight manufactured by the Lowel-Light Manufacturing company, it has become the generic name for any small instrument that consists of a large (500W) incandescent quartz lamp mounted in a V-shaped metal reflector. **SEE 10.16** The V-light is highly portable and easy to set up and can light up large areas relatively evenly. Be careful when handling such lights—they get very hot. Don't touch them when they are switched on, and keep them away from combustible materials.

Soft-box The soft-box (250W to 1kW), also called light box or tent, is simply a black heat-resistant cloth bag with a scrim at its opening. It has a built-in lamp, or you can

attach a small Fresnel spot with a ring adapter. Because it is lightweight and can be folded up, it makes an ideal portable softlight. **SEE 10.17**

Chinese lantern A highly effective portable softlight is the Chinese lantern. This softlight is a more durable version of an actual round or bulb-shaped Chinese lantern. It is usually suspended from a mic stand or a microphone fishpole (see chapter 8). You can put various types of low-powered lamps inside the same lantern, such as a 250W clip light, a 200W household light bulb, or even a daylight (5,600K) lamp if you want to match outdoor light. **SEE 10.18**

The Chinese lantern gives off a very soft yet noticeable light that is especially useful for close-up shots. The advantage of using the lantern as a principal light source is that you can follow the subject as you would with a microphone (but you have to secure the lantern to the pole so that it doesn't swing). Because the lantern has an opening on the bottom to vent the heat, keep the bright spot coming from this hole out of the picture. For brief takes, covering it with a light scrim works well. There are huge Chinese lanterns that are used primarily for providing

10.18 CHINESE LANTERN
This floodlight is modeled after an actual Chinese lantern. It can be suspended from a fishpole and illuminates a relatively large area with extremely soft light.

10.19 PORTABLE FLUORESCENT BANK
The portable fluorescent bank can be mounted on a light stand. It has great light output and emits no heat.

even light for large, reflective objects, such as automobiles or major appliances.

Portable fluorescent bank Even small portable fluorescent floodlights are considerably bulkier and heavier than comparable incandescent instruments. But because fluorescent floodlights use much less power and generate practically no heat, they are frequently used for indoor EFP lighting. As mentioned before, the problem with fluorescent lights is that they do not always accurately reproduce all colors, even if the camera has been properly white-balanced. Because fluorescent instruments do not always burn at the standard Kelvin ratings of 3,200K and 5,600K, pay particular attention to white-balancing the camera. Check the colors and especially the skin tones on a well-adjusted field monitor before starting to video record. If highly accurate color reproduction is not a major concern, however, the small fluorescent unit is a valuable EFP lighting tool. **SEE 10.19**

LED light LED lights are like small computer screens or a stretched foldout viewfinder, but instead of displaying an image they simply emit soft white light. The LEDs (light-emitting diodes) of these small panels (about 7 inches wide) put out enough light to illuminate an object sufficiently for

acceptable video images, provided the panel is fairly close to the object. The battery-powered (12V to 24V) panel produces light with the 5,600K daylight color temperature that can be dimmed with a knob on its topside. When shooting in close proximity to the object, the LED panel makes a good camera light because it does not cause any hot spots. When it's not mounted on the camera, you can use it to light up small areas, such as a car interior.

DIFFUSING PORTABLE SPOTLIGHTS
The open-face instruments (discussed at the beginning of this section) can also be used as floodlights: just change the light from a spot to a flood position. You will find that despite the flood control, however, you will not always get the even diffusion you may need. Fortunately, there are several ways to achieve a more diffused light with these instruments.

Bouncing the light The simplest way to diffuse the light is to bounce it off of the wall, the ceiling, or a piece of foam core. Unfortunately, bouncing light drastically reduces its intensity, even if the walls are painted a light

10.20 SCRIM ATTACHED TO BARN DOORS
To further diffuse the beam of an open-face instrument, you can attach a scrim to the barn doors with wooden clothespins.

10.21 DIFFUSION UMBRELLA
The umbrella reflector is a popular diffusion device. Note that the lighting instrument shines into, not away from, the inside of the umbrella.

color. To salvage maximum light intensity, try to get the instrument as close to the wall or ceiling as possible without charring the paint.

Attaching a scrim   The most popular diffusers are scrims and frosted gels. As mentioned, scrims are spun-glass diffusers that you can put in front of small spotlights, floodlights, or open-face spots to achieve maximum diffusion of the light. The simplest way to attach a scrim to an open-face instrument is to clip it to the barn doors with wooden clothespins. Don't use plastic ones: open-face lights get very hot and will melt plastic within a few minutes. **SEE 10.20**

Scrims come in various thicknesses; the thinner ones absorb less light, and the thicker ones absorb more light. You can also convert a scoop into a softlight by attaching a scrim that is trimmed to fit a scrim holder (see figure 10.5). Some lighting people prefer frosted gels as diffusers. Frosted gels are white translucent sheets of plastic that have a semiopaque surface. Like scrims, they come in different densities that diffuse and therefore reduce the intensity of the light beam by varying degrees.

Using a diffusion umbrella   Another highly effective diffusion device is the umbrella. The small, silvery, heat-resistant umbrella is not to protect you from the rain but to reflect and diffuse the light source that shines into it. You can attach the scooplike umbrella to the lighting instrument and/or the light stand and then aim the umbrella's opening in the general direction of illumination. You need to shine the light *into the umbrella opening*, not on the rounded surface. **SEE 10.21**

Attaching a soft-box   As mentioned earlier, you can use a soft-box rather than an umbrella to change an incandescent spotlight into an effective softlight. **SEE 10.22** **ZVL3** LIGHTS→ Instruments→ field

When doing elaborate field productions, such as covering a high-school basketball game, you can try to use high-powered V-lights and umbrellas, but you may need larger floodlights, such as scoops, or floodlight banks. If available, HMI floodlights would probably be the most efficient instruments. A few 1kWs or even 575W HMI instruments in the flood position are all you need to light up a gymnasium. But then you must white-balance the cameras for the 5,600K outdoor color temperature.

CAMERA LIGHTS
Electronic news gathering requires yet another type of light, which can be mounted on top of the camera or handheld

Small floodlights in the flood position

Diffusion tents

10.22 SOFT-BOX ON FRESNEL SPOTLIGHT
You can turn a small Fresnel spot into a softlight by diffusing its beam with a portable soft-box.

10.23 CAMERA LIGHT
This small light is mounted on the camera and powered by the camcorder battery or a separate battery pack. Its beam can be diffused by flipping up a small diffusion filter.

by the camera operator or an assistant. **SEE 10.23** Camera lights have a high light output. They are open-faced and relatively small and have an assortment of diffusion filters and a daylight filter (5,600K), which you can flip over the opening of the small light. Camera lights draw their power either from the camera battery or from a larger battery that can be attached to a tripod or carried by the camera operator.

LIGHTING CONTROL EQUIPMENT

To understand lighting control, you need to be familiar with some specific equipment: mounting devices, directional controls, intensity controls, and electronic dimmers.

MOUNTING DEVICES

Mounting devices let you safely support a variety of lighting instruments and aim them in the desired direction. Good mounting devices are as important as the instruments themselves. The major devices specially designed and intended for studio lights are: the pipe grid and the counterweight batten, the C-clamp, the sliding rod and the pantograph, and floor stands. Portable lights are mounted primarily on collapsible stands. For on-location lighting there are additional mounting devices available, such as small booms, cross braces, and braces that fit over doors and furniture.

Pipe grid and counterweight batten   Studio lights are hung either from a fixed pipe grid or from a counterweight batten. The pipe grid consists of heavy steel pipe strung either crosswise or parallel. The height of the grid is determined by the height of the studio ceiling, but even in rooms with low ceilings the pipe should be mounted approximately 2 feet below the ceiling so that the lighting instruments or hanging devices can be easily attached. The space above the grid is also necessary to dissipate the heat generated by the lights. **SEE 10.24**

10.24 PIPE GRID
This simple pipe grid supports all the necessary lighting for a small performance area, such as a news, interview, or kitchen set.

10.25
COUNTERWEIGHT BATTEN
The counterweight batten can be raised and lowered and locked at a specific operating height.

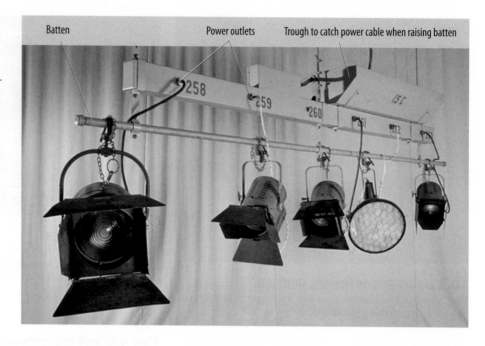

Batten Power outlets Trough to catch power cable when raising batten

Unlike the pipe grid, which is permanently mounted below the ceiling, a counterweight batten can be raised and lowered to any desired position and locked firmly in place. **SEE 10.25** The battens and the instruments are counterweighted by heavy iron weights and moved by means of a rope-and-pulley system or by individual motors. **SEE 10.26** Before unlocking a counterweight rope to move a batten up or down, always check that the batten is properly weighted. You can do this by counting the weights and comparing them with the type and the number of instruments mounted on the batten. The counterweights and the instruments should roughly balance each other.

The obvious advantage of the counterweight battens over the pipe grid system is that the instruments can be hung, adjusted, and maintained from the studio floor. You will find, however, that you cannot do without a ladder entirely. Although you can initially adjust the instruments to a rough operating position, you need to re-aim them once the battens are locked at the optimal height.

By that time, however, the studio floor is generally crowded with sets, cameras, and microphones, which prevent lowering the battens to a comfortable working height, so you use a lighting pole (a long wooden pole with a hook at one end) to aim the lighting instrument at the desired target and focus its beam.

C-clamp The lighting instruments are directly attached either to the batten by a large C-clamp or to hanging devices

Counterweights

Pin rail (rope locks)

10.26 COUNTERWEIGHT RAIL
The battens and the lighting instruments attached to them are counterweighted by heavy iron weights and moved up and down by a rope-and-pulley system from a common rail.

10.27 C-CLAMP
The C-clamp is the connection between the lighting instrument and the batten. Even when the C-clamp is securely tightened to the batten, you can swivel the instrument as necessary.

10.28 SLIDING ROD (TELESCOPE HANGER)
This sliding rod, also called a telescope hanger, allows you to move the instrument up and down and lock it into position. It is used primarily on lighting grids but also on counterweight systems when more vertical control is needed.

(discussed next). You need a wrench or key to securely fasten the C-clamp to the round metal batten. The lighting instrument is attached to the C-clamp and can be swiveled horizontally without loosening the bolt that holds it to the batten. Although the C-clamp will support the lighting instrument and not fall off the batten even if the large bolt becomes loose, you should nevertheless check that all C-clamps on the grid are securely tightened. As an added safety measure, all lighting instruments should be chained or secured to the batten itself by a strong steel cable loop. Similarly, the barn doors must be secured to the lighting instruments. Even if you are under severe time pressure when rehanging lights, *do not neglect to secure each instrument with the safety chain or cable.* **SEE 10.27**

Sliding rod and pantograph   If the studio has a fixed pipe grid, or if you need to raise or lower individual instruments without moving an entire batten, you can use sliding rods. A sliding rod consists of a sturdy pipe attached to the batten by a modified C-clamp; it can be moved and locked into a specific vertical position. For additional flexibility, the more expensive sliding rods have telescopic extensions. **SEE 10.28** Some high-end lighting systems have motor-driven sliding rods whose vertical movement can be remotely activated from the studio lighting control.

Some studios use the pantograph, a spring-loaded hanging device that can be adjusted with a lighting pole to any vertical position within its 12-foot range. Pantographs are most useful for adjusting the height of scoops and other floodlights. **SEE 10.29**

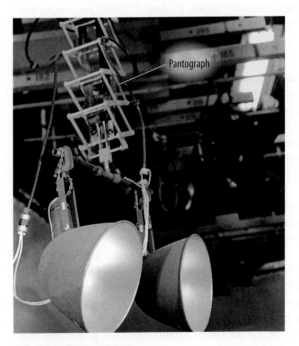

10.29 PANTOGRAPH
You can adjust this spring-loaded pantograph quickly and easily by pushing it up or pulling it down with a lighting pole. The springs act as a counterweight for the lights.

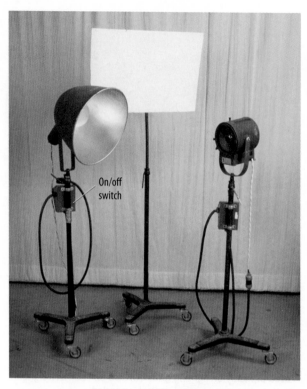

10.30 FLOOR STANDS
A floor stand can support a variety of lighting instruments and can be adapted for an easel or for large reflectors.

10.31 PORTABLE LIGHT STANDS
These light stands are designed for relatively lightweight portable instruments and can be extended to a height of 8 to 10 feet. Because light stands tend to tip over when fully extended, always secure them with sandbags.

Floor stands   You will find that when video-recording a scene film-style with a single camera, there will be many lighting instruments on the studio floor. Mounting the lights on roller-caster floor stands will certainly speed up the lighting job. **SEE 10.30** Such stands can hold all types of instruments: scoops, broads, spots, and even strip lights. The stands usually have a switch to turn the light on and off.

For small lighting instruments, you can use the collapsible light stands in most lighting kits. Just be sure to secure each stand with a sandbag to prevent it and the light from tipping over. **SEE 10.31**

In a pinch, you can always make a simple lighting bridge out of 1 × 3 lumber that will hold one or two portable spotlights for back-lighting. Whatever mounting devices you use—including your own contraptions—see to it that the lighting instrument is securely fastened and sufficiently far from curtains, upholstery, or other combustible materials.

DIRECTIONAL CONTROLS

You are already familiar with the spot and flood beam control on spotlights. Several other devices, such as barn doors, flags, and reflectors, can help you control the direction of the beam.

Barn doors   This admittedly crude beam control method is very effective for blocking certain set areas partially or totally from illumination. *Barn doors* consist of two or four metal flaps that you can fold over the lens of the lighting instrument to prevent the light from falling on certain areas. For example, if you want to keep the upper part of the scenery dark without sacrificing illumination of the lower part, you simply block off the upper part of the beam with

10.32 FOUR-WAY BARN DOOR
This four-way barn door allows you to control the beam spread on all four sides—top, bottom, left, and right.

10.33 FLAG
Flags come in various sizes and densities. You use them to prevent light from hitting specific set areas.

a barn door. Or if you want to eliminate a boom shadow, you can partially close a barn door. **SEE 10.32** `ZVL4` LIGHTS→ Instruments→ beam control

Barn doors are also effective for preventing the back light from shining into the camera lens, which can cause lens flare (an uncontrolled light reflection inside the lens that shows up as superimposed rays of light circles). Because barn doors slide into their holders easily, they have a tendency to slide out of them just as readily. Always secure barn doors to their instruments with the safety chain or cable. Barn doors also get very hot: wear protective gloves while adjusting them when the instrument is turned on.

Flags Rectangular metal frames with heat-resistant cloth or thin metal sheets of various sizes, *flags* act very much like barn doors except that you don't place them directly on the lighting instrument. Flags are mounted on light stands and put anywhere they are needed to block the light from falling on a specific area without being seen by the camera. In movie lingo, flags are also called gobos—yet another definition of *gobo*, this time referring to a flag and

not to a cookie (the metal template that is inserted into an ellipsoidal spotlight to produce a shadow pattern; see figure 10.4). Obviously, you can use flags only if the camera and talent movements have been carefully blocked and rehearsed. **SEE 10.33**

Reflectors Mirrors are the most efficient reflectors. You can position them to redirect a light source (often the sun) into areas that are too small or narrow for setting up lighting instruments. For example, if you had to light up a long, dark hallway that has an exterior door, you could use mirrors to redirect the sunlight into the hall and reflect it off the wall. This technique would save you setup time, equipment, and electricity. Most often, however, you use reflectors to produce highly diffused light to lighten up dense shadows (in media aesthetic language, to slow down falloff) on someone's face or on an object. You don't use mirrors to slow down falloff; rather, you use material that will reflect only a portion of the light and diffuse it at the same time. Most LDs prefer a large sheet of white foam core; it is lightweight, quite sturdy, simple to set up or hold,

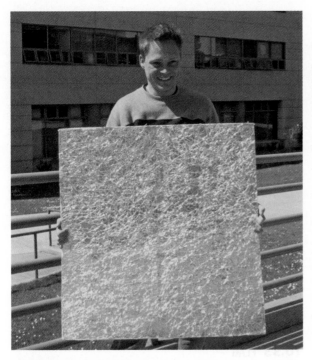

10.34 **FOIL REFLECTOR**
This homemade but highly efficient reflector uses crumpled aluminum foil taped to a piece of cardboard.

10.35 **COLLAPSIBLE REFLECTOR**
This reflector can be folded up for easy transport. It has a silver-colored reflector on one side and a warmer, gold-colored reflector on the other.

and easily replaced if it gets dirty or broken. Any large white cardboard will do almost as well. If you need a more efficient reflector (one that reflects more light), you can crumple up some aluminum foil to get an uneven surface (for a more diffused reflection) and then tape it to a piece of cardboard. **SEE 10.34** **ZVL5** LIGHTS→ Field→ use of reflectors

Commercial reflectors come in white, silver, and gold and can be folded up for easy transport and setup. The silver and white models reflect a higher-color-temperature light than do the gold-colored ones. **SEE 10.35**

INTENSITY CONTROLS: INSTRUMENT SIZE, DISTANCE, AND BEAM

When you are out in the field, you probably won't carry a sophisticated digital dimmer with you, so you must find other ways of controlling light intensity. The three most common methods are selecting an instrument of the proper size, adjusting the distance of lighting instrument to object, and focusing or diffusing the light beam.

Instrument size   The simplest way to control light intensity is obviously to turn on only a certain number

of instruments of a specific size (wattage). Because of the light sensitivity of today's cameras and the high light output of incandescent and fluorescent lamps, you don't need the large instruments you may still see in major motion picture production. The largest instrument used in most television studios is a 2kW Fresnel spotlight. The lights for ENG/EFP rarely exceed 650 watts. In fact, many crime dramas are partially shot in available light—without any lighting instruments.

Distance   When you move the lighting instrument closer to the object, the intensity of the light increases; if you move it farther away, the intensity decreases. You can apply this principle easily so long as the instruments are mounted on light stands and you can move them without too much effort. In many cases this is the most efficient way of controlling light intensity on an ENG/EFP shoot. You can also apply this principle in the studio if the lights are mounted on a movable batten. In general, try to position the instruments as low as possible while keeping them out of camera range. This way you achieve maximum light intensity with minimal power. **ZVL6** LIGHTS→ Instruments→ field

Beam   The more focused the light beam, the higher its intensity; the more diffused the light beam is, the less intensity it has. Note that, except for a laser, even a focused light beam becomes more diffused the farther away the instrument is from its target object.

You have already learned about diffusing the beam using the focus control in the instrument as well as with scrims and reflectors. You can also use a wire-mesh screen to diffuse and block a certain amount of light: You simply slide the metal screen directly into the gel holder in front of the instrument, much like scrims and frosted gels (see figure 10.14). Depending on the fineness of the mesh, the screen dims the light without influencing its color temperature. The problem with wire-mesh screens is that the heat of the quartz lamp tends to burn up the fine metal wires within a relatively short time; the screens become brittle and eventually disintegrate.

BASIC PRINCIPLE OF ELECTRONIC DIMMERS

The most precise light control is the electronic dimmer. With a *dimmer* you can easily manipulate each light, or a group of lights, to burn at a given intensity, from an *off* position to full strength. Regardless of whether you use an old manual dimmer or a sophisticated digital computer dimmer, both operate on the same basic principle: by allowing more or less voltage to flow to the lamp, the lamp burns with a higher or lower intensity. If you want the lighting instrument to burn at full intensity, the dimmer lets all the voltage flow to the lamp. If you want it to burn at a lesser intensity, the dimmer reduces the voltage. To dim the light completely—called a blackout—the dimmer permits no voltage (or at least an inadequate voltage) to reach the lamp.

Manual dimmers   Although few manual dimmers are still in operation, it is easier to explain basic dimmer operation with a manual dimmer than with a complex computerized one. Each individual lighting instrument has its own dimmer control, which in a manual operation is a fader with a specific calibration. As you can see in the following figure, the left fader is moved to 2, which is barely enough to make the lamp glow. The fader on the right is all the way up at 10, which means that its lamp burns at full intensity. **SEE 10.36**

Computerized dimmers   Most larger studio dimmers can control hundreds of lights with a great number of

10.36 MANUAL DIMMER CALIBRATION
The higher you push the lever on this manual dimmer, the more voltage flows to the lamp. At the 0 setting, no voltage flows to the lamp; at a setting of 10, the lamp burns at full intensity. The 2 setting on the left dimmer makes the lamp barely glow; the 10 setting on the right dimmer makes the lamp burn at full intensity.

intensity steps from no light to full burn. Although the actual dimming is done with a computer program, a good computerized dimmer should nevertheless have a number of manual faders that can override the stored dimming program. **SEE 10.37**

The downside of dimming—manual and computerized—is that lowering the voltage will cause incandescent lamps to lower their color temperature to a more reddish light. We discuss this problem in more detail in chapter 11.

Patchboard   The *patchboard*, or patchbay, makes it possible to connect each lighting instrument to a specific dimmer. Let's assume that you have one lamp in your study and another lamp in your bedroom but only one dimmer. Because you can't be in the study and the bedroom at the same time, you can plug lamp 1 into the single dimmer when in the study and then plug in lamp 2 for the bedroom light. What you have done is patched different lighting instruments to a single dimmer. The patchboard of an actual dimmer system works in the same way. Although the computer can patch a great variety of instruments to any one of dozens of dimmers, we again use a manual system to explain the patching principle.

To patch a lighting instrument into a dimmer, you select its designated patch cord and plug it into the dimmer receptacle (called a jack). **SEE 10.38**

10.37 COMPUTERIZED DIMMER CONTROL

This simple but powerful dimmer and lighting effects panel can control 48 channels in a single scene or 24 channels in two scenes. The video display shows the status of submaster settings, lighting effects, and patching data. Large dimmers can control hundreds of channels.

Video display

Scene A faders

Scene B faders

Record button

Blackout button

Preset A master

Preset B master

Lighting effects

Grandmaster

10.38 MANUAL PATCHBOARD

The patchboard enables you to establish power connections between specific lighting instruments and specific dimmers.

Instrument connected to dimmer

Patch cord (connection to lighting instrument)

Power sockets, or jacks (connection to dimmer)

Breakers

Figure 10.39 shows lighting instruments 5 (a Fresnel spot) and 27 (a scoop) patched into dimmer 1. When you bring up dimmer 1 at the dimmer control (move the fader to a designated intensity setting—let's say 8), both instruments—spotlight 5 and scoop 27—should light up simultaneously and be dimmed equally to a number 8 intensity. **SEE 10.39** If you want to control them separately, you would plug spotlight 5 into dimmer 1 and scoop 27 into dimmer 2.

Besides controlling the intensity of the light, patching enables you to change from one type of lighting setup to another quickly and easily. For example, you may change a dining room set from day to night by simply switching from the stored daylight setup to the nighttime one. This way you can light several studio areas at once, store the lighting setup in the dimmer's memory, and activate part of or all the stored information whenever necessary. Some shows may require that you go from one background color to another, such as from red to blue. With the dimmer you can simply fade down all instruments that throw red light onto the background while at the same time bringing up the blue lights.

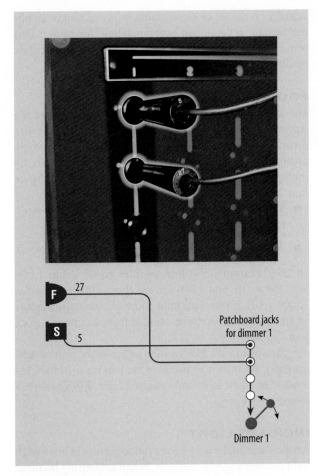

10.39 MANUAL PATCHING

As you can see, the patches for the lighting instruments (spotlight 5 and scoop 27) are both patched to dimmer 1. Consequently, both lighting instruments respond identically to any dimmer 1 setting.

MAIN POINTS

▶ All studio lighting is accomplished by a variety of spotlights and floodlights, technically called luminaires.

▶ Studio spotlights include the Fresnel spot and the ellipsoidal spot.

▶ Studio floodlights include the scoop, the softlight and the broad, the fluorescent floodlight bank, and the strip, or cyc, light.

▶ Field lighting uses the small portable spotlights with lenses (small Fresnel and HMI spotlights), open-face spotlights without a lens, and the internal reflector spot (clip light).

▶ Most portable floodlights are open-faced, which means that they have no lens. Small fluorescent banks are also used as portable floodlights. Soft-box diffusers can turn a spotlight into a floodlight.

▶ ENG lighting is often done with small, versatile camera lights or LED panels that are mounted on the camera or handheld.

▶ Lighting control equipment includes mounting devices, directional controls, intensity controls, and dimmers.

▶ The principal mounting devices are the pipe grid and the counterweight batten, the C-clamp, the sliding rod and the pantograph, and floor stands.

▶ Directional controls include barn doors, flags, and reflectors.

▶ Basic intensity controls are the size of the instrument (lamp wattage), the relative distance of lighting instrument to target object, and the relative focus or diffusion of the beam.

▶ With an electronic dimmer, you can easily manipulate a light, or a group of lights, to burn at a given intensity. The patchboard, or patchbay, makes it possible to connect each lighting instrument to a different dimmer.

10.2

Light Intensity, Lamps, and Color Media

Before learning to do actual lighting in the studio and the field, you need to study a few more elements about light, how to control and measure it, and how to produce colored light. This section adds to the technical details given in section 10.1.

▶ **LIGHT INTENSITY**
Using foot-candles and lux to measure incident and reflected light

▶ **CALCULATING LIGHT INTENSITY**
The lumen and the inverse square law

▶ **OPERATING LIGHT LEVEL: BASELIGHT**
Establishing optimal light levels

▶ **TYPES OF LAMPS**
Basic luminants: incandescent, fluorescent, and HMI

▶ **COLOR MEDIA**
Plastic sheets (gels) that change the color of light

LIGHT INTENSITY

Although some video cameras can produce pictures in almost total darkness, most standard cameras need a certain amount of light for optimal performance. As sensitive as our eyes are, they cannot always tell accurately just how much light an instrument produces, how much light is actually on the set or on-location, how much light an object actually reflects, and how much light the camera lens actually receives. A light meter gives us a more accurate reading of light intensity.

FOOT-CANDLES AND LUX

The standard units of measuring light intensity are the American *foot-candle (fc)* and the European *lux*. Because ordinary television lighting doesn't require extremely precise units of intensity, you can simply figure lux by multiplying foot-candles by a factor of 10, or you can figure foot-candles by dividing lux by 10:

■ To find lux when given foot-candles, multiply foot-candles by 10.

■ To find foot-candles when given lux, divide lux by 10.

For example, 100 foot-candles equal about 1,000 lux (100 × 10), and 2,000 lux are about 200 foot-candles (2,000 ÷ 10). If you want to be more accurate, use a factor of 10.75 to calculate foot-candles from lux or lux from foot-candles.

Equipped with foot-candles or lux as the unit of light intensity, you can now measure the two types of light intensity: incident light and reflected light. **ZVL7** LIGHTS→ Measurement→ meters

INCIDENT LIGHT

An incident-light reading gives you some idea of how much light reaches a specific set area. When measuring *incident light*, you are actually measuring the amount of light that falls on a subject or a performance area but not what is reflected by it. To measure incident light, you must stand in the lighted area or next to the subject and point the incident-light meter toward the camera lens. The meter will give a quick reading of the overall light level that reaches the set area. This general light level is also called baselight. But incident light can also refer to the light produced by a particular instrument. If you want a reading of the intensity of the light coming from specific instruments, you should point the foot-candle (or lux) meter into the lights. **SEE 10.40**

Such measurements may come in handy, especially when you need to duplicate the illumination for a scene shot on the same set over a period of several days. For some reason duplicating the exact lighting from one day to the next is difficult , even with a computer-assisted patchboard that faithfully duplicates the dimmer settings of the previous day. An incident-light check, however, guarantees identical or fairly close intensities.

10.40 **INCIDENT-LIGHT READING**
To read incident light, you point the light meter at the camera or into the lights while standing next to the lighted subject or performance area. Here the LD checks the intensity of a specific light.

10.41 **REFLECTED-LIGHT READING**
To measure reflected light, you point the reflected-light meter (used in still photography) close to the lighted subject or object.

To discover possible holes in the lighting (unlighted or underlighted areas), walk around the set with the light meter pointed at the major camera positions. Watch the light meter: whenever the needle dips way down, it is indicating a hole.

REFLECTED LIGHT

The reading of **reflected light** gives you an idea of how much light is bounced off of the various objects. It is primarily used to measure contrast.

To measure reflected light, you must use a reflected-light meter (most common photographic light meters measure reflected light). Point it closely at the lighted object, such as the dancer's face or blond hair, and then at the dark background—all from the direction of the camera (the back of the meter should face the principal camera position). **SEE 10.41**

Do not stand between the light source and the subject when taking this reading or you will measure your shadow instead of the light actually reflecting off the subject. To measure contrast, point the meter first at the lighted side of the object and then move it to the shadow side. The difference between the two readings gives you the contrast ratio. (Chapter 11 describes contrast ratio and its importance in television lighting.)

Do not be a slave to these measurements and ratios, however. A quick check of the baselight is all that is generally needed for most lighting situations. In especially critical situations, you may want to check the reflectance of faces or exceptionally bright objects. Some people get

so involved in reading light meters and oscilloscopes that visually display the light levels against camera tolerances that they forget to look at the monitor to see whether the lighting looks the way it was intended. If you combine your knowledge of how the camera works with artistic sensitivity and, especially, common sense, you will not let the light meter tell you how to light but rather use it as a guide to make your job more efficient.

CALCULATING LIGHT INTENSITY

Light intensity measures how much light strikes an object. One foot-candle is the amount of light of a single candle that falls on a 1-by-1 foot surface located 1 foot away from the candle (1 lumen). One lux is the light that falls on a surface of 1 square meter (about 3 by 3 feet) generated by a single candle that burns at a distance of 1 meter (roughly 3 feet). The norm for the light intensity of one candle is 1 **lumen**.

Light intensity is subject to the inverse square law. This law states that if a light source radiates isotropically (uniformly in all directions), such as a candle or a single light bulb burning in the middle of a room, the light intensity falls off (gets weaker) at $1/d^2$ where d is the distance from the source. For example, if the intensity of a light is 1 fc at a distance of 1 foot from the source, its intensity at a distance of 2 feet is ¼ fc. **SEE 10.42**

The inverse square law also applies to lux. In this case the light intensity is measured off a surface of 1 m^2 located 1 meter from the light source of 1 lumen.

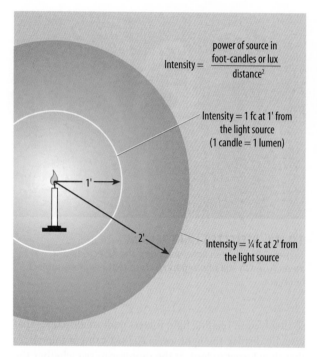

$$\text{Intensity} = \frac{\text{power of source in foot-candles or lux}}{\text{distance}^2}$$

Intensity = 1 fc at 1' from the light source
(1 candle = 1 lumen)

1'

2'

Intensity = ¼ fc at 2' from the light source

10.42 INVERSE SQUARE LAW

Note that the inverse square law applies only to light sources that radiate isotropically (uniformly in all directions). This law applies equally to lux.

This formula tells you that light intensity decreases the farther away you move the lighting instrument from the object, and it increases if you move the light closer. Otherwise, the formula does little to make television lighting more accurate. The beams of a searchlight, a flashlight, car headlights, and a Fresnel or an ellipsoidal spotlight do not radiate light isotropically (like a candle) but are collimated (the light rays are made to run parallel as much as possible) and, therefore, do not obey the inverse square law. Even floodlights radiate their light more in the direction of the reflector opening than its back. The more collimated the light—that is, the more focused its beam—the slower its intensity decreases with distance. This is why we "focus" a spotlight when we want more light on an object and "flood" its beam when we want less light, without changing the distance between the lighting instrument and the object. An example of an extremely well-collimated light is a laser beam, which, as you know, maintains its intensity over a great distance.

OPERATING LIGHT LEVEL: BASELIGHT

To make the camera "see well" so that the pictures are relatively free of video noise (artifacts in the picture, or "snow"), you must establish a minimum operating light level, called baselight or base. As you recall, **baselight** is the general, overall light level on a scene.

BASELIGHT LEVELS

Many an argument has been raised concerning adequate minimum baselight levels for different cameras. The problem is that baselight levels do not represent absolute values but are dependent on other production factors, such as the sensitivity of the camera, the desired lighting contrast, the general reflectance of the scenery, and, of course, the aperture of the lens (f-stop). When shooting outdoors on an ENG assignment, you do not have much control over baselight levels; you must accept whatever light there is. But even there you might be able to use sunlight reflectors to lighten up shadow areas, or additional lighting instruments to boost available light. Most often the problem is inadequate baselight. But there are also situations in which you struggle with controlling too much light.

Not enough baselight   Although you often hear that consumer camcorders can operate in light levels as low as 0.1 fc or even 0.02 fc (10 or even 2 lux), the light levels for optimal camera performance are much higher. Professional ENG/EFP and studio cameras normally need about 150 fc, or approximately 1,500 lux, for optimal picture quality at an aperture setting of f/5.6 to f/8.0. These f-stops produce the highest-resolution images. You will probably read camera specifications that use 200 fc (2,000 lux) as the standard illumination and then give the highest f-stop, such as f/11, at which the camera still delivers optimal pictures.

Most video cameras can work at baselight levels that are considerably lower without noticeable loss of picture quality. By turning on the gain control and switching to a low gain setting (which, as you recall, will electronically boost the video signal), you may get an acceptable image even in low-light conditions. Despite manufacturers' claims to the contrary, high gain can cause increased video noise and occasional color distortion. For home video and even ENG, video quality may be secondary to picture content, but it is of major concern for EFP and studio shows that must tolerate many picture manipulations in postproduction editing. In general, digital cameras tolerate higher gain than do analog cameras, without noticeable picture deterioration.

Here is the rule of thumb: in general, a camera has less trouble producing true colors and crisp, high-quality pictures when the light level is fairly high and the contrast limited than under very low light levels with high-contrast lighting.

Too much baselight   Despite the validity of this general rule for baselight and picture quality, there will be instances when there is simply too much light for the camera to operate properly. You can cope with too much light by reducing the lens aperture, which translates into setting the f-stop to a higher number, such as $f/22$, and/or using an ND filter that is part of the filter wheel inside the camera. Much like a small aperture, a **neutral density (ND) filter** reduces the amount of light falling on a scene or entering the beam splitter in the camera without changing the color temperature of the light. (Color temperature is explained in detail in chapter 11.) Such ND filters will also help you control the extreme contrast between light and shadows when shooting outdoors on a sunny day. **ZVL8** LIGHTS→ Measurement→ baselight

TYPES OF LAMPS

Lighting instruments are classified not only by function (spotlight or floodlight) but also by the lamp they use—technically called a **luminant**. Television lighting generally uses three basic types of luminants: incandescent, fluorescent, and HMI.

INCANDESCENT
The **incandescent** lamp operates on the same principle as the ordinary household light bulb: it generates light by heating up a filament with electricity. The incandescent lamps used in television resemble the ones in home fixtures except that they usually have more wattage and therefore produce higher-intensity light. The disadvantages of regular incandescent lamps are that the higher-wattage lamps are quite large, the color temperature becomes progressively lower (more reddish) as the lamp ages, and they have a relatively short life.

Incandescent luminants include the smaller but hotter **quartz** lamps, also called TH (tungsten-halogen) lamps. The quartz lamp has a tungsten filament that is encased in a quartz bulb filled with halogen gas. The advantages of a quartz lamp over regular incandescent systems are that it is smaller and maintains its color temperature over its entire life. The disadvantage is that it burns at an extremely hot temperature. When changing quartz lights, do not touch the lamp with your fingers. The old lamp may still be hot enough to burn your skin, and your fingerprints will cause the new one to develop weak spots in the quartz housing that may cause the lamp to explode. Always use gloves, a paper towel, or a clean rag when handling lamps.

FLUORESCENT
A **fluorescent** lamp generates light by activating a gas-filled tube to give off ultraviolet radiation. This radiation in turn lights up the phosphorous coating inside the tube, similar to the way the electron beam lights up the television screen. Despite improved fluorescent lamps that produce a fairly even white light, many still have a tendency to give off a slightly greenish light. If accurate color rendering is critical to your assignment, test out a fluorescent light before using it. Check especially whether its color temperature blends with the other lighting instruments.

HMI
HMI (which stands for *hydragyrum medium arc-length iodide*) lamps generate light by moving electricity through various types of gases. This creates a sort of lightning inside the lamp, which is the discharge that creates the light. To create the lightning inside the lamp, you need a ballast—a fairly heavy transformer. HMI lamps produce light with a color temperature of 5,600K, the outdoor standard. (See section 10.1 for the advantages and disadvantages of the HMI when used in production.) As with quartz lamps, do not touch HMI lamps with your hands: your fingerprints will weaken the quartz housing and cause the lamp to burn out in a relatively short time.

COLOR MEDIA

You can produce a great variety of colored light simply by putting different color media, or **gels**, in front of the lighting instrument. (*Gel* is short for *gelatin*, which was the color medium used before the more heat- and moisture-resistant plastic was developed.) Color media are sheets of highly heat-resistant plastic that act as color filters. They are used extensively to color-tint scenic backgrounds or to create color special effects, such as a sunset or dark blue sky, or

10.43 COLOR MEDIA

Color media, or gels, are colored filters that are put in front of lighting instruments to produce colored light.

the color effects in dance programs, rock concerts, or some mystery or outer-space adventure shows. **SEE 10.43**

HOW TO USE COLOR MEDIA

You can cut the color media sheet to fit the frame of the gel holder of the lighting instrument. You then slip the gel holder into brackets in front of the lens of the lighting instrument. If the colored lighting does not have to be too precise, you can use wooden clothespins (plastic ones melt) to hang the color sheets from the barn doors like laundry on a clothesline. The advantages of this method are that it saves you from having to cut the expensive gels and they are farther away from the heat generated by the lamp. Highly focused instruments generate so much heat that they will burn out the center of even the most heat-resistant gels. You can avoid such burns by putting the instrument into more of a flood position (by moving the lamp-reflector unit toward the lens), thereby dissipating some of the heat.

MIXING COLOR GELS

When using gels, you can mix the colors additively or subtractively. For example, if you put a red gel in one instrument and a green gel in the other and then partially overlap their beams, you get yellow in the overlap. Because you added one light on top of the other, this is additive mixing. If, however, you were to put both gels—the red and the green—in front of the same instrument, you would get no light from the instrument. This is because the red gel blocks (subtracts) all the green light, and the green gel negates all the red light.

A similar problem occurs if you shine colored lights on colored objects. We see an apple as red because the color filters in the apple absorb all colors of white light except red,

which is reflected back to our eyes. A green apple absorbs all colors except green, which is reflected back and makes the apple look green. What would happen if you shined a red light on a green apple? Would it turn yellow? No, the apple would look dark brown or black. Why? Because the red light that shines on the green apple contains no green, the apple can't reflect any green. In the same way, you may have a problem using yellow objects under blue "night" illumination: the blue light contains no yellow, and the objects therefore have no yellow to reflect, so they turn dark gray or black.

Most lighting experts advise against using colored lights to illuminate talent and performance areas unless, of course, it's for special effect, such as the greenish tint on crime shows or the multicolored lights on a rock music scene. If colors are critical, try to keep the colored light away from the faces.

M A I N   P O I N T S

▶ Light intensity is measured in foot-candles (fc) or lux. To find lux when given foot-candles, multiply foot-candles by 10. To find foot-candles when given lux, divide lux by 10. If you need to be most accurate, use 10.75 instead of 10 as the conversion factor.

▶ To measure incident light (the light that falls on the scene), point the light meter away from the lighted scene toward the camera or into the lights that are illuminating the subject.

▶ To measure reflected light, use a reflected (standard) light meter and point it closely at various areas of the lighted subject or object. Reflected-light readings measure primarily contrast.

▶ The inverse square law in illumination applies only if the light source radiates isotropically (uniformly in all directions), such as a bare light bulb or a candle. Because most television lighting instruments collimate the light (focus the light rays), the inverse square law does not apply to the same degree. The general principle, however, still holds true: the farther away the light source is from the object, the less intense the light; the closer the light is to the object, the more intense the light.

▶ Baselight is the overall light level on a scene. Cameras require a minimum baselight level for optimal operation.

▶ Lamps are labeled by the type of luminant: incandescent, including quartz; fluorescent; and HMI.

▶ Color media, normally called gels, are colored plastic filters that, when put in front of the lens of a lighting instrument, give the light beam the color of the gel.

▶ Colored light beams mix additively, but overlaying gels mix subtractively.

ZETTL'S VIDEOLAB

For your reference or to track your work, the *Zettl's VideoLab* program cues in this chapter are listed here with their corresponding page numbers.

CHAPTER

11

Techniques of Television Lighting

When watching television, you will probably notice that newscasts, situation comedies, and game shows are brightly lit with a minimum of shadows on faces. But when watching crime shows or soap operas, you will often see more deep shadows on the actors' faces than light, and even the colors are sometimes distorted. The techniques of television lighting suggest how to achieve such different lighting effects and more.

In most video production situations, especially EFP, available space, time, and people are insufficient for you to accomplish motion picture–quality lighting. The time allotted to lighting is often so short that all you can do is flood the studio or location site with highly diffused light, regardless of the nature of the event. Although such a technique may please the camera and probably the video operator (who because of the uniform light levels has little shading to do), it does not always fulfill the aesthetic requirements of the production. A dramatic studio scene that is supposed to play on a dark street corner will not look convincing if everything is brightly and evenly illuminated by softlights. But to light the street corner set so that it looks believable requires not only time but especially that you know the principles of manipulating light and shadows. Lighting for digital cinema requires even more care and time because you normally have to light for every shot or, at best, for every scene.

The ever-present time limitation should not preclude good and creative television lighting, but it does call for a high degree of efficiency. Without a thorough understanding of the basic lighting principles, you can easily spend all your allotted time, and part of the rehearsal time, on trying to achieve a specific lighting effect that, in the end, might look out of place. Efficiency in lighting also means careful preparation.

This chapter will help you with such preparations. Section 11.1, Lighting in the Studio, covers basic and special-effects studio lighting techniques and principles; section 11.2, Location Lighting, addresses lighting techniques for electronic news gathering (ENG), electronic field production (EFP), and on-location digital cinema productions.

KEY TERMS

background light Illumination of the set, set pieces, and back-drops. Also called *set light*.

back light Illumination from behind the subject and opposite the camera.

cameo lighting Foreground figures are lighted with highly directional light, with the background remaining dark.

chroma keying Effect that uses color (usually blue or green) for the backdrop, which is replaced by the background image during a key.

color temperature The standard by which we measure the relative reddishness or bluishness of white light. It is measured on the Kelvin (K) scale. The standard color temperature for indoor light is 3,200K; for outdoor light it is 5,600K. Technically, the numbers express Kelvin degrees.

contrast ratio The difference between the brightest and the darkest portions in the picture (often measured by reflected light in foot-candles). The contrast ratio for low-end cameras and camcorders is normally 50:1, which means that the brightest spot in the picture should be no more than 50 times brighter than the darkest portion without causing loss of detail in the dark or light areas. High-end digital cameras can exceed this ratio and can tolerate a contrast ratio of 1,000:1 or more.

cross-keying The crossing of key lights for two people facing each other.

diffused light Light that illuminates a relatively large area with an indistinct light beam. Diffused light, created by flood-lights, produces soft shadows.

directional light Light that illuminates a relatively small area with a distinct light beam. Directional light, produced by spotlights, creates harsh, clearly defined shadows.

falloff (1) The speed with which light intensity decays. (2) The speed (degree) with which a light picture portion turns into shadow area. *Fast falloff* means that the light areas turn abruptly into shadow areas and there is a great brightness difference between light and shadow areas. *Slow falloff* indicates a very gradual change from light to dark and a minimal brightness difference between light and shadow areas.

fill light Additional light on the opposite side of the camera from the key light to illuminate shadow areas and thereby reduce falloff. Usually done with floodlights.

floor plan A diagram of scenery and properties drawn onto a grid pattern. Can also refer to *floor plan pattern*.

high-key Light background and ample light on the scene. Has nothing to do with the vertical positioning of the key light.

Kelvin (K) Refers to the Kelvin temperature scale. In lighting it is the specific measure of color temperature—the relative reddishness or bluishness of white light. The higher the K number, the more bluish the white light. The lower the K number, the more reddish the white light.

key light Principal source of illumination.

kicker light Usually directional light that is positioned low and from the side and the back of the subject.

light plot A plan, similar to a floor plan, that shows the type, size (wattage), and location of the lighting instruments relative to the scene to be illuminated and the general direction of the beams.

location survey Written assessment, usually in the form of a checklist, of the production requirements for a remote.

low-key Dark background and illumination of selected areas. Has nothing to do with the vertical positioning of the key light.

photographic lighting principle The triangular arrangement of key, back, and fill lights, with the back light opposite the camera and directly behind the object, and the key and fill lights on opposite sides of the camera and to the front and the side of the object. Also called *triangle lighting*.

side light Usually directional light coming from the side of an object. Acts as additional fill light or a second key light and provides contour.

silhouette lighting Unlighted objects or people in front of a brightly illuminated background.

11.1

Lighting in the Studio

SAFETY

In the actual operation of lighting instruments and the associated control equipment, you should heed the rule for all production activities: *safety first.*

■ As mentioned in chapter 10, always wear gloves when working with active lighting instruments. The gloves will protect you from burns when touching hot barn doors or lamps and will give you some protection from electric shock.

■ Always secure the lighting instruments to the battens with safety chains or cables and attach the barn doors and the scrims to the lighting instruments. Check all C-clamps periodically, especially the bolt that connects the lighting instrument to the hanging device.

■ Be careful when plugging in lights and when moving active (switched-on) instruments. Because the hot lamps are especially vulnerable to physical shock, try not to jolt the instrument; move it gently.

■ When replacing lamps, wait until the instrument has cooled somewhat. Always turn off the instrument before reaching in to remove a burned-out lamp. As a double protection, unplug the light at the batten. Do not touch a new quartz lamp with your fingers. Fingerprints, or anything else clinging to the quartz housing of the lamp, cause the lamp to overheat and burn out. Wear gloves or, if you have nothing else, use a tissue or even your shirttail when handling the lamp.

■ Watch for obstacles above and below when moving ladders. Do not take any chances by leaning way out to reach an instrument. Position the ladder so that you can work from behind, rather than in front of, the instrument.

■ When adjusting a light, try not to look directly into it; look instead at the object to be lighted and see how the

Lighting means the control of light and shadows. Both are necessary to show the shape and the texture of a face or an object, to suggest a particular environment, and, like music, to create a specific mood. Regardless of whether you do lighting for dramatic or nondramatic productions, you will find that there are usually many solutions to any one problem. And though there is no universal recipe that works for every possible lighting situation, there are some basic principles that you can easily adapt to a great variety of specific requirements. When faced with a lighting task, do not start with anticipated limitations. Start with how you would like the lighting to look and then adapt to the existing technical facilities and especially the available time.

beam strikes it. If you must look into the light, wear dark glasses and do so only briefly.

■ Before you start patching (assuming that you use a physical patchboard) have all dimmers and breakers in the *off* position. Do not "hot-patch" by connecting the power cord of the instrument to the power outlet on the batten with the breaker switched on. Hot-patching can burn your hand and also pit the patches so that they no longer make the proper connection.

QUALITY OF LIGHT

Whatever your lighting objective, you will be working with two types of light: directional and diffused. Normal white light, which you get from the sun or the light you use while reading, is never pure white but has a slight reddish or bluish tinge. Technically, white light has a certain color temperature.

DIRECTIONAL LIGHT AND DIFFUSED LIGHT

Directional light, produced by spotlights, illuminates a relatively small area with a distinct light beam and produces dense, well-defined shadows. The sun on a cloudless day acts like a giant spotlight, producing dense and distinct shadows. *Diffused light* illuminates a relatively large area with a wide, indistinct beam. It is produced by floodlights and creates soft, transparent shadows. The sun on a cloudy or foggy day acts like an ideal floodlight because the overcast transforms the harsh light beams of the sun into highly diffused light.

Actually, it is the density of the shadows and their falloff that indicates whether the light is directional or diffused. If you looked only at the illuminated side, you would have a hard time telling whether it was directional or diffused light.

COLOR TEMPERATURE

You may have noticed that a fluorescent tube gives off a different "white" light than does a candle. The fluorescent tube actually emits a white light that has a bluish-green tinge, whereas the candle produces a more reddish-white light. The setting sun gives off a much more reddish light than does the midday sun, which is more bluish. These color variations in light are called *color temperature*. Note that color temperature has nothing to do with physical temperature, that is, how hot the lamp actually gets; it is strictly a measure of the relative reddishness or bluishness of white light.

This reddishness and bluishness of white light can be precisely measured; it is expressed in degrees of color temperature, or *Kelvin (K)* degrees. In lighting lingo, the degrees are dropped and a specific color temperature is referred to only as a certain amount of K.

The color temperature standard for indoor illumination is 3,200K, which is a fairly white light with just a little reddish (warm) tinge. All studio lighting instruments and portable lights intended for indoor illumination are rated at 3,200K, assuming they receive full voltage. Lighting instruments used to augment or simulate outdoor light have lamps that emit a 5,600K light. They approximate more the bluish light of the outdoors. **SEE 11.1**

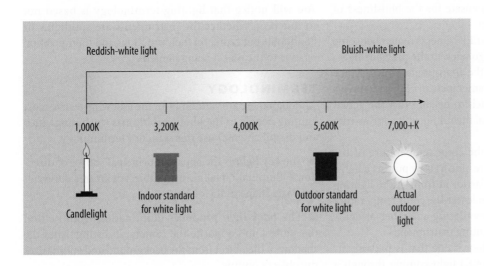

11.1 COLOR TEMPERATURE
Color temperature is measured on the Kelvin scale. It measures the relative reddishness or bluishness of white light. The norm for indoor light is 3,200K; for outdoor light it is 5,600K.

Reddish-white light   Bluish-white light

1,000K   3,200K   4,000K   5,600K   7,000+K

Candlelight   Indoor standard   Outdoor standard   Actual
               for white light   for white light   outdoor
                                                                   light

When you dim a lamp that is rated at 3,200K, the light becomes progressively more reddish, similar to sunlight at sunset. The color camera, when adjusted to seeing white in 3,200K light, will faithfully show this increasing reddishness. For example, the white shirt of a performer will gradually turn orange or pink, and the skin tones will take on an unnatural red glow. Some lighting experts therefore warn against any dimming of lights that illuminate performers or performance areas. The skin tones are, after all, the only real standard viewers have by which to judge the accuracy of the television color scheme. If the skin colors are distorted, how can we trust the other colors to be true? So goes the argument. Practice has shown, however, that you can dim a light by 10 percent or even a little more without the color change becoming too noticeable on a color monitor. Note that dimming the lights by at least 10 percent will not only reduce power consumption but just about double the life of the lamps. **ZVL1** LIGHTS→ Color temperature→ white balance | controlling | try it

How to control color temperature   As you learned in chapter 5, you need to white-balance the camera to ensure the correct color reproduction even if the illumination has different color temperatures. You may find, however, that occasionally the camera will refuse to white-balance although you follow exactly the procedures outlined here. This difficulty may be caused by a color temperature that is too low (light is too reddish) or too high (too bluish) for the automatic white balance to handle. In this case you need to choose one of the color filters on the filter wheel inside the camera (see chapter 5). Light-blue filters compensate for the reddishness of low-color-temperature light; amber or light-orange filters compensate for the bluishness of high-color-temperature light.

Most professional ENG/EFP cameras remember some of these setups, so you can go back to the previous lighting environment and recall the appropriate white balance automatically. Experienced camerapersons, however, prefer to white-balance from scratch to be sure that the actual colors as seen by the camera, including white, are as true as possible.

Another way to raise the color temperature of the reddish light (to make it more bluish) is by putting a light-blue gel (sheet of colored plastic) in front of the lighting instrument's lens; or you can lower the color temperature (to make it more reddish) by placing an amber or light-orange gel in front of the lighting instrument.

When shooting an indoor scene that is partially illuminated by outdoor (5,600K) light coming through a window and by portable indoor (3,200K) lighting instruments, you have two choices: either lower the high outdoor color temperature (bluish light) or raise the indoor color temperature (reddish light) to match the daylight streaming through the window. In elaborate field productions, the usual way is to cover the entire window with amber plastic sheets that act like gigantic filters, lowering the high outdoor color temperature to the lower indoor standard. The advantage of this method is that the whole interior is adjusted to the 3,200K standard. A quicker and cheaper way is to let the high-color-temperature outdoor light stream through the window and put bluish filters in front of the indoor lighting instruments to raise their light to the outdoor standard. **SEE 11.2** **ZVL2** LIGHTS→ Color temperature→ light sources

In certain circumstances, you can get away with mixing lights of different color temperatures so long as one or the other dominates the illumination. For example, if you are in an office that is illuminated by overhead fluorescent tubes and you need to add key and back lights (see the following discussion) to provide more sparkle and dimension to the performer, you can most likely use normal portable lighting instruments that burn at the indoor color temperature standard. This is because the portable instruments provide the dominant light, so they overpower the overhead lights that now act as rather weak fill lights. The camera will have little trouble white-balancing on the strong indoor lights while more or less ignoring the higher color temperature of the overhead fluorescent lights.

LIGHTING FUNCTIONS

You will notice that lighting terminology is based not so much on whether the instruments are spotlights or floodlights but rather on their functions and their position relative to the object being lighted.

TERMINOLOGY

Although there are variations for the following terms, most lighting people in the photographic arts (including video and digital cinema) use this standard terminology.

■ The *key light* is the apparent principal source of directional illumination falling on a subject or an area; it reveals the basic shape of the object.

■ The *back light* produces illumination from behind the subject and opposite the camera; it distinguishes the shadow of the object from the background and emphasizes the object's outline.

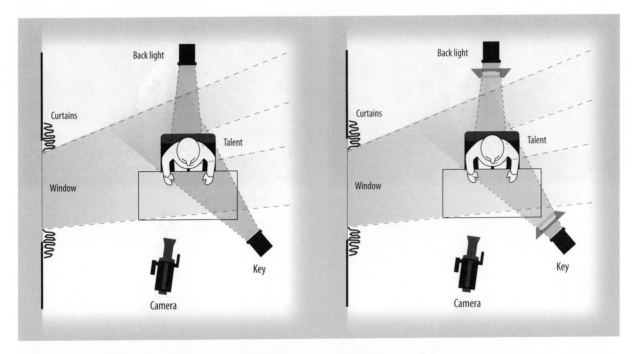

11.2 MATCHING COLOR TEMPERATURES OF DIFFERENT LIGHT SOURCES

A When illuminating an object with indoor light mixed with outdoor light coming through a window, you need to equalize the color temperatures of both light sources to ensure proper white-balancing.

B To equalize the color temperatures, you can put light-blue gels on the indoor lighting instruments to raise their 3,200K color temperature to the more prominent 5,600K daylight coming through the window.

■ The *fill light* provides generally diffused illumination to reduce shadow or contrast range (to slow falloff). It can be directional if the area to be "filled in" is rather limited.

■ The *background light*, or set light, is used specifically to illuminate the background or the set and is separate from the light provided for the performers or performance area.

■ The *side light* is placed directly to the side of the subject, usually on the opposite side of the camera from the key light. Sometimes two side lights are used opposite each other, acting as two keys for special-effects lighting of a face.

■ The *kicker light* is a directional illumination from the back, off to one side of the subject, usually from a low angle opposite the key light. Whereas the back light merely highlights the back of the head and the shoulders, the kicker light highlights and defines the entire side of the person, separating him or her from the background.

SPECIFIC FUNCTIONS OF MAIN LIGHT SOURCES

How do these lights now function in basic lighting tasks? Let's take a look.

Key light   As the principal source of illumination, the major function of the key light is to reveal the basic shape of the subject. **SEE 11.3** To achieve this the key light must produce some shadows. Fresnel spotlights, medium spread, are normally used for key illumination. But you can use a scoop, a broad, or even a softlight for a key if you want softer shadows or, technically, slower falloff. In the absence of expensive softlights, some lighting directors (LDs) take a cue from filmmakers and still photographers and use reflectors as key and fill lights. Instead of diffusing the key and fill lights with diffusion material, such as scrims or frosted gels, you do not aim the key light (a Fresnel spot) directly at the subject but rather bounce it off of white foam core or a large white posterboard. The reflected, highly diffused light nevertheless produces distinct, yet extremely soft, slow-falloff shadows.

11.3 KEY LIGHT
The key light represents the principal light source and reveals the basic shape of the object or person.

11.4 KEY AND BACK LIGHTS
The back light provides more definition to the actual shape of the subject (her hair on camera-left), separates her from the background, and gives her hair sparkle and highlights.

Because during the day we see the principal light source—the sun—coming from above, the key light is normally placed above and to the right or left front side of the object, from the camera's point of view. Look again at figure 11.3, which shows the woman illuminated with the key light only, and notice that the falloff is very fast, blending part of her hair and shoulder with the dark background. To help clarify the outline and the texture of the woman's right (camera-left) side, you obviously need light sources other than the single key light.

Back light Adding illumination from behind helps separate the subject from the background. **SEE 11.4** Note how the back light helps distinguish between the shadow side of the woman and the dark background, emphasizing the outline—the contour—of her hair and shoulders. We have now established a clear figure/ground relationship,

which means that we can easily perceive a figure (the woman) in front of a (dark) background. Besides providing spatial definition, the back light adds sparkle and professional polish.

In general, try to position the back light as directly behind the subject (opposite the camera) as possible; there is no inherent virtue in placing it somewhat to one side or the other unless it is in the camera's view. A more critical problem is controlling the vertical angle at which the back light strikes the subject. If it is positioned directly above the person, or somewhere in that neighborhood, the back light becomes an undesirable top light: instead of revealing the subject's contour to make her stand out from the background and giving the hair sparkle, the light simply brightens the top of her head, causing dense shadows below her eyes and chin. On the other hand, if the back light is positioned too low, it shines into the camera.

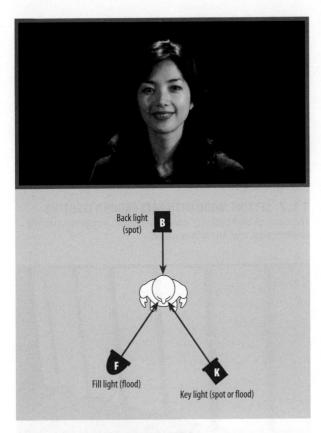

11.5 KEY, BACK, AND FILL LIGHTS
The fill light slows falloff, making the shadow side (camera-left) more transparent and revealing details without eliminating altogether the form-revealing shadows.

To get good back lighting on a set, you need a generous space between the performance areas (the areas in which the talent move) and the background scenery. Therefore you must place "active" furniture, such as chairs, tables, sofas, or beds actually used by the performers, at least 8 to 10 feet away from the walls toward the center of the set. If the talent works too close to the scenery, the back lights must be tilted at very steep angles to reach over the scenery, and such steep angles inevitably cause undesirable top light.

Fill light Now take another look at figure 11.4. Despite the back light, the difference between the light and shadow sides is still extreme, and the light side of the face still changes abruptly to a dense shadow. This change is called falloff. *Falloff* refers to the speed (degree) to which a light picture portion turns into shadow area. If the change is

sudden, as in figure 11.4, it is fast falloff. With fast falloff the shadow side of the subject's face is very dense; the camera sees no shadow detail. To slow down the falloff, that is, to make the shadow less prominent and more transparent, you need some fill light. **SEE 11.5**

Not surprisingly, you place the fill light on the opposite side of the camera from the key light. A highly diffused floodlight or reflected light is generally used as fill. The more fill light you use, the slower the falloff becomes. When the intensity of the fill light approaches or even matches that of the key light, the shadows, and with them the falloff, are virtually eliminated. This gives the subject a flat look—shadows no longer help define shape and texture.

When doing critical lighting in a specific area and not wanting the fill light to spill over too much into the other set areas, you can use a Fresnel spotlight as fill by spreading the beam as much as possible or by putting a scrim in front of the lens. You can then use the barn doors to further control the spill.

The photographic principle, or triangle lighting With the three main light sources (key, fill, and back) in the triangle setup, you have established the basic *photographic lighting principle*, also called triangle lighting (see figure 11.5). But you are not done yet! You must now fine-tune this lighting arrangement. Take a good hard look at the lighted object or, if possible, the studio monitor to see whether the scene (in our case, the close-up of the woman) needs some further adjustment for optimal lighting. Are there any undesirable shadows? Are there shadows that distort rather than reveal the face? How is the light balance? Does the fill light wash out the necessary shadows, or are the shadows still too dense? Is the back light too strong for the key/fill combination?

Background, or set, light To illuminate the background (walls or cyclorama) of the set or portions of the set that are not a direct part of the principal performance area, you use the background light, or, as it is frequently called, the set light. To keep the shadows of the background on the same side as those of the person or object in front of it, the background light must strike the background from the same direction as the key light. **SEE 11.6**

As you can see in the figure, the key light is placed on the camera-right side, causing the shadows on the subject to fall on the camera-left side. Consequently, the background light is also placed on camera-right to make the shadows on camera-left correspond with those of the

11.7 SETTING MOOD WITH BACKGROUND LIGHTING
The colorful background lighting in this set suggests a trendy environment and an upbeat mood.

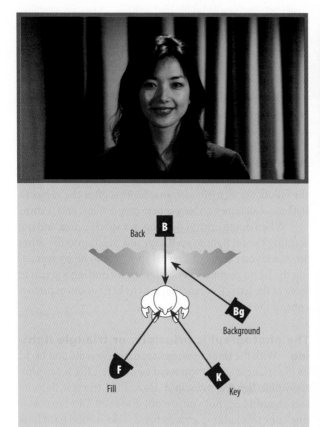

11.6 BACKGROUND LIGHT
The background light illuminates the background area. It must be on the same side of the camera as the key light to keep the background shadows (curtain) on the same side as the foreground shadows (woman).

11.8 SETTING LOCALE WITH BACKGROUND LIGHTING
Background lighting can place an event in a specific locale or environment. Here the background light produces barlike shadows, suggesting that the scene takes place in a prison.

foreground. If you place the background light on the opposite side from the key, the viewer may assume that there are two separate light sources illuminating the scene or, worse, that there are two suns in our solar system. **ZVL3** LIGHTS→
Triangle lighting→ key | back | fill | background | try it

Background light frequently goes beyond its mere supporting role to become a major production element. Besides accentuating an otherwise dull, monotonous background with a slice of light or an interesting cookie, the background light can be a major indicator of the show's locale, time of day, and mood. **SEE 11.7** A cookie projection of prison bars on the wall, in connection with the clanging of cell doors, immediately places the event in a prison. **SEE 11.8**

A long slice of light or long shadows falling across the back wall of an interior set suggests, in connection

with other congruent production clues, late afternoon or evening. In normal background lighting of an interior setting, try to keep the upper portions of the set relatively dark, with only the middle and lower portions (such as the walls) illuminated. This will emphasize the talent's face and shoulders against a slightly darker background and will set off furniture and medium- and dark-colored clothing against the lighter lower portions of the set. Also, the dark upper portions suggest a ceiling. You can darken the upper portions of the set easily by using barn doors to block off any spotlight (including the background lights) that would hit those areas.

Side light   Usually placed directly to the side of the subject, the side light can function as a key or fill light. When used as a key, it produces fast falloff, leaving half

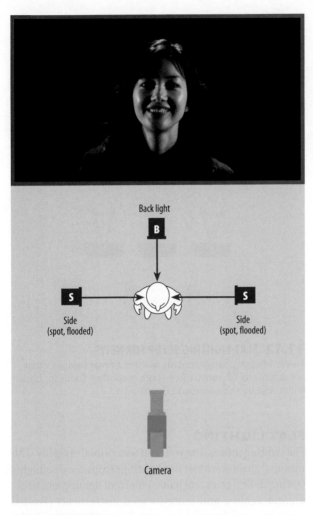

11.9 SIDE LIGHT
The side light strikes the subject from the side. It can act as key and/or fill light. In this case two opposing side lights are used as two keys.

the face in dense shadow. When used as a fill, it lightens up the whole shadow side of the face. When you place side lights on opposite sides of the person, the sides of the face are bright, with the front of the face remaining shadowed. **SEE 11.9**

The side light becomes a major light source if the camera's shooting arc is exceptionally wide. If, for instance, the camera moves around the subject from a 6 o'clock to an 8 o'clock position, the side light takes on the function of the key light and provides essential modeling (lighting for a three-dimensional effect). Although Fresnel spots at a wide-beam setting are generally used for side lighting,

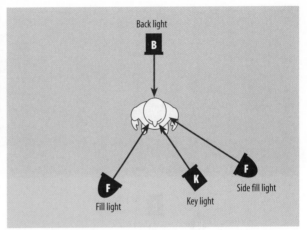

11.10 SIDE FILL-LIGHT SETUP
The side fill light provides soft illumination, with the key (spot) adding sparkle. When the key is turned off, the side fill takes over the function of the key light.

using scoops or broads as side lights can produce interesting effects.

For extrabrilliant lighting, you can support the key light with side fill light. The fill light gives the key side of the subject basic illumination, with the key light providing the necessary sparkle and accent. **SEE 11.10**

Kicker light Generally a sharply focused Fresnel spot, the kicker light strikes the subject from behind and on the opposite side of the camera from the key light (the fill-light side). Its main purpose is to highlight the subject's contour at a place where key-light falloff is the densest and where the dense shadow of the subject opposite the key-lighted side tends to merge with the dark background. The function of the kicker is similar to that of the back light except that the kicker "rims" the subject not at the top-back but at the lower side-back. It usually strikes the subject from below eye level. Kicker lights are especially useful for creating the illusion of moonlight. **SEE 11.11**

SPECIFIC LIGHTING TECHNIQUES

Once you are familiar with how to apply the photographic principle in a variety of lighting situations, you can move on to a few specific lighting techniques. These include: high- and low-key lighting, flat lighting, continuous-action lighting, large-area lighting, high-contrast lighting, cameo lighting, silhouette lighting, chroma-key-area lighting, and controlling eye and boom shadows.

11.11 KICKER LIGHT

The kicker light rims the subject opposite the key, emphasizing contour. Like the back light, the kicker helps separate the foreground subject from the background.

11.12 FLAT-LIGHTING SETUP FOR NEWS

This flat-lighting setup consists of three frontal softlights that act as key and fill lights, three spots or spotted floods for back lights, and three background floodlights.

Accurate lighting is always done with basic camera positions and points of view in mind. It therefore helps immensely to know at least the basic camera positions and the range of all major camera viewpoints before starting with the lighting

HIGH- AND LOW-KEY LIGHTING

A light background, a generous amount of light (high base-light levels), and slow falloff usually constitute a **high-key** scene with an upbeat, happy mood. That is why situation comedies and game shows are much more brightly lighted (higher baselight level and less contrast) than are mystery and police dramas (lower baselight level and more contrast). Selective, fast-falloff lighting with distinct shadows and normally a dark background define a **low-key** scene. It creates a dramatic or mysterious mood. Do not confuse *high-key* and *low-key* with high and low vertical hanging positions of the key light or with the intensity with which it burns.

FLAT LIGHTING

Flat lighting means that you light for optimal visibility with minimal shadows. Most flat-lighting setups use floodlights (softlights or fluorescent banks) for front lighting and background lighting and more-focused instruments (Fresnel spots or small broads) for back lights. This setup is the favorite lighting technique for more or less permanently installed news sets and interview areas. **SEE 11.12** As you can see in the figure, the basic lighting triangle is preserved. In effect, you have three key lights, or, if you wish, three fill lights, evenly illuminating the front area. The back lights add the sparkle and make the flatness of the lighting setup less noticeable. The additional background lights illuminate the set.

The major disadvantage of flat lighting is that it looks like what it is: flat.

CONTINUOUS-ACTION LIGHTING

When watching dramas or soap operas on television, you probably notice that many of them have fast-falloff, low-key lighting, which means prominent shadows and relatively dark backgrounds. In such multicamera productions, the cameras look at a scene from different points of view, and

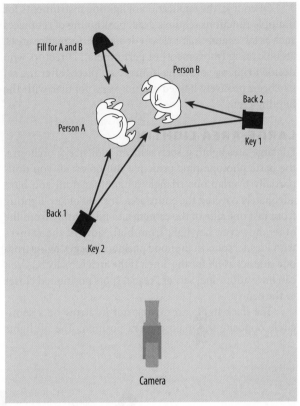

11.13 MULTIPLE-TRIANGLE APPLICATION

In this lighting setup, a separate lighting triangle with its own key, back, and fill light is used for each of the two persons (performance areas). If floodlights are used for the keys, you can probably dispense with the fill lights.

11.14 CROSS-KEYING

In this lighting setup, the key light for person A (the camera-near person) also functions as a back light for person B (the camera-far person); and the back light for person A is the key for person B.

people and cameras are always on the move. Wouldn't it be easier to light "flat," that is, to flood the whole performance area with flat light rather than with spotlights? Yes, but then the lighting would not contribute to the mood of the scene or how we feel about the persons acting in it. Fortunately, the basic lighting triangle of key, back, and fill lights can be multiplied and overlapped for each set or performance area for continuous-action lighting. Even if there are only two people sitting at a table, you have to use a multiple application of the basic lighting triangle. **SEE 11.13**

To compensate for the movement of the performers, you should illuminate all adjacent performance areas so that the basic triangle-lighted areas overlap. The purpose of overlapping is to give the performers continuous lighting as they move from one area to another. It is too easy to concentrate only on the major performance areas and to neglect the small, seemingly insignificant areas in between.

You may not even notice the unevenness of such lighting until the performers move across the set and all of a sudden they seem to be playing a "now you see me, now you don't" game, popping alternately from a well-lighted area into dense shadow. In such situations a light meter comes in handy to pinpoint the "black holes."

If you do not have enough instruments to apply multiple-triangle lighting for several performance areas when lighting for continuous action, you must place the instruments so that each can serve two or more functions. In reverse-angle shooting, for instance, the key light for one performer may become the back light for the other and vice versa. This technique is generally called *cross-keying*. Or you may have to use a key light to serve also as directional fill in another area. Because fill lights have a diffused beam, you can use a single fill light to lighten up dense shadows in more than one area. **SEE 11.14**

Of course, the application of lighting instruments for multiple functions requires exact positioning of set pieces such as tables and chairs, clearly defined performance areas, and blocking (movements of performers). Directors who decide to change blocking or move set pieces after the set has been precisely lighted are not very popular with the lighting crew.

LARGE-AREA LIGHTING

For large-area lighting, such as for an audience or orchestra, the basic photographic principle still holds: all you do is partially overlap one triangle on another until you have adequately covered the entire area. Instead of key-lighting from just one side of the camera and fill-lighting from the other, however, key-light from both sides of the camera with Fresnel spots in the flood position. The key lights from one side act as fill for the other. If the area is really big, you can have additional sets of Fresnel spots positioned closer to the center.

The back lights are strung out in a row or a semicircle opposite the main camera position. The fill lights (broads or scoops) usually come directly from the front. If the cameras move to the side, some of the key lights also function as back lights. You can also use broads or fluorescent banks instead of Fresnel spots for this type of area lighting. **SEE 11.15**

For some assignments, such as lighting a school gym for a basketball game, check first whether the available light is adequate. Turn on a camera and look at the monitor. If you need more light, you can simply flood the gym with highly diffused light. As mentioned, one possibility is to use fairly high-powered open-face instruments with light-diffusing umbrellas. Watch out that you don't mix color temperatures of the house lights and your additional lighting. See to it that all cameras are properly white-balanced.

HIGH-CONTRAST LIGHTING

The opposite of flat lighting is high-contrast lighting, much of which mirrors motion picture lighting techniques. Because of the increased tolerance of today's video cameras to low light levels and higher-contrast lighting, many television plays make extensive use of fast-falloff lighting. You

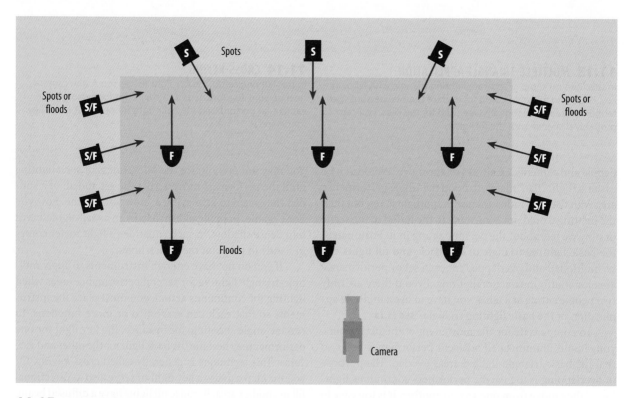

11.15 LARGE-AREA KEYING

In this lighting setup, the Fresnel spots at the left and right sides function as keys and directional fill lights. Fresnel spots are also strung out as regular back lights behind the main action area. If necessary, scoops provide additional fill light from the front.

may have noticed that some series, such as crime or medical shows, use not only extremely fast-falloff lighting (harsh shadows) but also color distortion to intensify the scenes. For example, extremely fast falloff on a face inevitably looks more dramatic than if it were lighted with slow falloff. **SEE 11.16** **ZVL4** LIGHTS→ Design→ high key | low key

Prominent side lighting and fast-falloff lighting can be combined for dramatic effect. **SEE 11.17** And instead of always having the key-lighted side face the camera, you may show the shadow side to establish a certain mood. **SEE 11.18**

In addition to fast-falloff lighting, color distortion can add dramatic impact. In this example the scene is purposely given a green tint. **SEE 11.19**

Realize that such lighting effects require not only skill but also a lot of production time. That said, you should still

11.16 FAST-FALLOFF LIGHTING ON FACE
The fast-falloff lighting increases the dramatic impact of this close-up.

11.17 HARSH SIDE LIGHT
The fast falloff and prominent side lighting intensify the mysterious mood of this scene.

11.18 SHADOW SIDE TOWARD CAMERA
The camera-far person is lighted so that his shadow side, rather than key side, is seen by the camera. This shadow reversal has dramatic impact.

11.19 COLOR DISTORTION
In addition to the fast-falloff lighting, the precariousness of this scene is further emphasized by the green tint.

11.20 CAMEO LIGHTING
In cameo lighting, the background is kept dark, with only the foreground person illuminated by highly directional spotlights.

try to apply some of these lighting techniques whenever possible and when appropriate to the show. If your lighting time is limited, however, stay away from such precision lighting and stick with the classic triangle-lighting approach. You might be pleasantly surprised to find that by turning on a few Fresnel spots and fill lights that are already pointed at the set area, your lighting will look quite acceptable.

CAMEO LIGHTING

Certain television shows, especially those of a dramatic nature, are staged in the middle of an empty studio against an unlighted background. This technique, where the performers are highlighted against a plain dark background, is commonly known as *cameo lighting* (from the cameo art form in which a light relief figure is set against a darker background). **SEE 11.20** Like the close-up, cameo lighting concentrates on the talent and not the environment.

All cameo lighting is highly directional and is achieved most effectively using spotlights with barn doors. In small studios the background areas are carefully shielded

from any kind of distracting spill light with black, light-absorbing draperies.

SILHOUETTE LIGHTING

Lighting for a silhouette effect is the opposite of cameo lighting. In *silhouette lighting* you light the background but leave the figures in front unlighted. This way you see only the contour of objects and people but not their volume and texture. To achieve silhouette lighting, use highly diffused light (usually from softlights, cyc lights, or scoops with scrims) to evenly illuminate the background. Obviously, you light in silhouette only those scenes that gain by emphasizing contour. **SEE 11.21** You can also use silhouette lighting to conceal the identity of a person appearing on-camera. **ZVL5** LIGHTS→ Design→ silhouette

CHROMA-KEY-AREA LIGHTING

The chroma-key set area normally consists of a plain blue or green backdrop. It is used to provide backgrounds that are electronically generated, replacing the blue or green areas during the key—a process called *chroma keying*. A popular

11.21 SILHOUETTE LIGHTING
In silhouette lighting, only the background is lighted, with the figure in front remaining unlighted. It emphasizes contour.

use of the chroma key is a weather report. Although the weathercaster seems to be standing in front of a large weather map, she is in fact standing in front of an empty, evenly lighted blue or green backdrop. When the blue or green areas are electronically replaced by the weather map during the key, the weathercaster must look into a monitor to see the map. **SEE 11.22** (See chapter 13 for an in-depth explanation of the chroma-key process.)

The most important aspect of lighting the chroma-key set area is even background illumination, which means that the blue or green backdrop must be lighted with highly diffused instruments, such as softlights or floodlight banks. If there are unusually dark areas or hot spots (undesirable concentrations of light in one area), the electronically supplied background image looks discolored or, worse, breaks

up. When lighting the weathercaster in the foreground, prevent any of the lights used for the foreground from hitting the backdrop. Such spill would upset the evenness of the chroma-key background illumination and lead to keying problems. In practice this means that the key and the directional fill light (a Fresnel in the flood position) must strike the subject from a steeper-than-normal angle. You may find that using softlights for the key and fill lights on the weathercaster will not affect the chroma key even if they spill onto the backdrop.

If you use a chroma-key light ring on the camera, do not place any reflective objects close to the light source. The light ring is an actual ring that fits over the lens and emits a relatively weak ray of blue or green light (see figure 13.26). This light beam sufficiently illuminates a beaded gray cloth to make it function as a blue or green chroma-key backdrop. Because the talent in front of the backdrop does not wear any reflecting beads and is sufficiently far away from the camera, he or she will not reflect any blue or green light coming from the light ring. If a highly reflecting object is placed near the camera with the light ring, however, the object will take on a blue or green sheen or, worse, let some of the keyed background image show through. We revisit the ring light in section 13.2.

Sometimes the outline of a weathercaster looks out of focus or seems to vibrate during the chroma key. One reason for such vibrations is that especially dark colors or shadows at the contour line take on a blue or green tinge, caused by a reflection from the colored backdrop. During the chroma key, these blue or green spots become transparent and let the background picture show through. To

11.22 CHROMA-KEY EFFECT: WEATHERCAST
A In this weathercast, the blue background is evenly lighted with floodlights. The weathercaster is lighted with the standard triangle arrangement of key, back, and fill lights.

B During the chroma key, the weathercaster seems to stand in front of the satellite view.

11.23 SHADOW CAUSED BY EYEGLASSES
The steep angle of the key light causes the shadow of the woman's glasses to fall right across her eyes.

11.24 KEY LIGHT LOWERED
By lowering the key light, the shadow moves up and is hidden behind the glasses.

counteract a blue reflection, try putting a light-yellow or amber gel on all the back lights or kicker lights. For green reflections, use a light-magenta or soft-pink gel. The back lights then not only separate the foreground subject from the background picture through contour illumination but also neutralize the blue or green shadows with the complementary yellow or pink filters. As a result, the outline of the weathercaster will remain relatively sharp even during the chroma key.

CONTROLLING EYE AND BOOM SHADOWS

Two fairly persistent problems in studio lighting are the shadows caused by eyeglasses and microphone booms. Depending on the specific lighting setup, such unwanted shadows can present a formidable challenge to the lighting crew. Most often, however, you can correct such problems rather quickly.

Key light and eye shadows The key light's striking the subject from a steep angle will cause large dark shadows in any indentation and under any protrusion, such as in the eye sockets and under the nose and the chin. If the subject wears glasses, the shadow of the upper rim of the frames may fall directly across the eyes, preventing the camera (and the viewer) from seeing them clearly. **SEE 11.23**

There are several ways to reduce these undesirable shadows. First try to lower the vertical position of the light itself or move the key light farther away from the subject. When you lower it (with a movable batten or a rod), notice that the eye shadows seem to move farther up the face. As soon as the shadows are hidden behind the upper rim of

the glasses, lock the key light in position. Such a technique works well so long as the subject does not move around too much. **SEE 11.24**

You can also reduce eye shadows by illuminating the person from both sides with similar instruments. Also try repositioning the fill light so that it strikes the subject directly from the front and from a lower angle, thus placing the shadows upward, away from the eyes. Annoying reflections from eyeglasses can be eliminated with the same technique.

Boom shadows Although you may not normally use a large microphone boom in the studio except for some dramatic productions, the principles of dealing with boom shadows also apply to handheld microphone booms, such as fishpoles and even handheld shotgun mics.

When you move a boom mic in front of a lighted scene—in this case a single person—and move the boom around a little, you may notice shadows on the actor or on the background whenever the mic or boom passes through a spotlight beam. (You can easily test for shadows by substituting a broomstick or the lighting pole.) You can deal with boom shadows in two ways: move the lights and/or the mic boom so that the shadow falls out of camera range, or use such highly diffused lighting that the shadow becomes all but invisible.

First you need to find the light that is causing the boom shadow. The easiest way to locate it is to move your head directly in front of the boom shadow and look at the microphone suspended from the boom. The shadow-causing light will now inevitably shine into your eyes. Be careful not to stare into the light for any prolonged period.

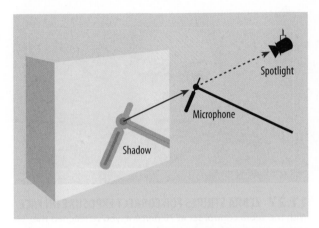

11.25 LOCATING THE SHADOW-CAUSING LIGHT
The instrument that causes the undesirable boom shadow lies at the extension of a line drawn from the shadow to the microphone causing it.

More precisely, the instrument lies at the extension of a line drawn from the shadow to the microphone causing it. **SEE 11.25**

To get rid of the shadow, simply turn off the offending instrument. You may be pleasantly surprised to find that you have eliminated the shadow without impeding the overall lighting. If such a drastic step seriously weakens the lighting setup, try to position the boom so that it does not have to travel through this light. If you use a handheld fishpole boom, walk around the set while pointing the mic toward the sound source. Watch the shadow move on the background wall until it is out of camera range. If the mic is still in a position for optimal sound pickup, you have solved the problem. You may locate such a shadow-safe spot more readily when holding or placing the boom parallel to the key-light beam rather than when crossing it. Some LDs use the key and fill lights close to side-light positions to provide a "corridor" in which to operate the boom.

Another simple way to avoid boom shadows is to light more steeply than usual. You do this by moving the key light closer to the performance area. The closer the lights are to actors, the steeper the lights will have to be angled to hit the target. The boom will now cast its shadow on the studio floor rather than on the talent's face or background scenery and thus be out of camera range. The downside to this technique is that the steep key lights produce dense and prominent shadows under the eyes, nose, and chin.

You can also try to use barn doors to block off the part of the spotlight that causes the boom shadow. Such a

technique is especially useful when the shadow appears in the upper part of the background scenery.

CONTRAST

In chapter 5 you learned about contrast ratio and the way television cameras react to it. Now you'll get acquainted with how lighting affects contrast and how to keep it within tolerable limits. Contrast does not depend so much on how much light comes from the lighting instruments (incident-light reading) as on how much light is reflected by the illuminated objects (reflected-light reading). For example, a white refrigerator, a yellow plastic raincoat, and a polished brass plate reflect much more light than does a dark-blue velvet cloth, even if they are illuminated by the very same source. If you place the brass plate on the velvet cloth, there may be too much contrast for the television camera to handle properly—and you have not even begun with the lighting.

What you must consider when dealing with contrast are the constant relationships among multiple factors, such as how much light falls on the subject, how much light is reflected, and how much difference there is between the foreground and the background or the lightest and darkest spots in the same picture. Because we deal with relationships rather than absolute values, we express the camera's contrast limit as a ratio.

CONTRAST RATIO

As you learned, *contrast ratio* is the difference between the brightest and the darkest spots in the picture (often measured by reflected light in foot-candles). The brightest spot, that is, the area reflecting the greatest amount of light, is called the reference white, and it determines the "white level." The area reflecting the least amount of light is the reference black, which determines the "black level." With a contrast limit of 50:1, the reference white should not reflect more than 50 times the light of the reference black.

MEASURING CONTRAST

As pointed out in chapter 10, you measure contrast with a reflected-light reading—by first pointing the light meter close to the brightest spot (often a white card on the set, which serves as the reference white) and then to the darkest spot. Even if you don't have a light meter or waveform monitor for checking the contrast ratio, you can tell by looking at the camera viewfinder or studio monitor. When the white areas, such as the white tablecloths in a restaurant

11.26 ZEBRA STRIPES ON OVEREXPOSED MOUNTAIN
With the zebra control set at 100 percent, the zebra stripes appear on all overexposed areas.

11.27 ZEBRA STRIPES FOR CORRECT EXPOSURE ON FACE
With the zebra control set at 70 percent, you've reached the proper exposure (*f*-stop) when the zebra stripes appear on the bright areas of the face.

set, look awfully bright, or the dark clothing of the people sitting at the tables is a dense black without any detail, the contrast is obviously great and probably exceeds the optimal ratio. With a little practice, squinting your eyes when taking a brief look at the set will give you a good idea about the contrast ratio even without using the light meter. **ZVL6** LIGHTS→ Measurement→ contrast

Zebra stripes   Most good camcorders show a zebra pattern when a certain white level is achieved or exceeded. If you have only one setting for zebra stripes, they will appear over the areas that exceed the brightness limits. This overexposure level for zebra stripes is sometimes labeled 100 percent zebra. **SEE 11.26**

If you have a choice between 70 percent zebra and 100 percent zebra, choose the 70 percent setting to get the proper exposure for skin tones on a face. When using manual exposure control, you should open up the iris until you see the zebra stripes appear on parts of the close-up of a face (such as the cheekbones, nose, forehead, and chin). This indicates the correct exposure. **SEE 11.27**

CONTROLLING CONTRAST

The problem with contrast occurs when the bright areas reach a certain upper limit and are electronically clipped, very much like an audio signal that is too loud. When this happens, all detail in the bright areas is lost. This clipping is done either automatically or, when using a CCU (camera control unit), by the video operator (VO): when the VO "pulls down the whites," the black areas become crushed into a uniformly dark area without shadow detail. High-end cameras can tolerate a much higher contrast, however,

and they show shadow detail in the dark areas even if the VO, also called the shader, brings extremely bright areas into tolerable limits.

If you feel that the contrast ratio is too high, think about what you can do to reduce it before fussing with the lighting. For example, changing the white tablecloth to a pink or light-blue one will help eliminate the contrast more readily than dimming some of the lights.

Such help is much appreciated by the video operator, who is ultimately responsible for controlling contrast. If there is too much contrast, however, even the best VOs have difficulty unless they're working with top-of-the-line cameras. For example, it is difficult for the camera to reproduce true skin color if the talent is wearing a highly reflective starched white shirt and a light-absorbing black jacket. If the camera adjusts for the white shirt by clipping the white level, the talent's face will go dark. If the camera tries to bring up the black level (making the black areas in the picture light enough to distinguish shadow detail), the face will be overexposed, or, in production slang, "blown out."

One big advantage of shooting in the studio is that you can control the light intensity and, with it, the contrast. Even if the talent wear contrasting clothes, you can always reduce the contrast by adjusting the key and fill lights so that the differences between light and dark areas are somewhat reduced.

Here are a few tips for preventing an overly high contrast ratio.

■ Be aware of the general reflectance of the objects. A highly reflective object obviously needs less illumination than does a highly light-absorbing one.

- Avoid extreme brightness contrasts in the same shot.

- Have the talent avoid clothes whose colors are too contrasting (such as a starched white shirt with a black suit).

Many contrast problems, however, occur when shooting outdoors on a sunny day. These problems and how to solve them are explored in section 11.2.

BALANCING LIGHT INTENSITIES

Even if you have carefully adjusted the position and the beam of the key, back, and fill lights, you still need to balance their relative intensities. For example, it is not only the direction of the lights that orients the viewer in time but also their relative intensities. A strong back light with high-key, slow-falloff front lighting can suggest the early-morning sun; a generous amount of strong back light and very low-intensity front lighting can suggest moonlight.

Because balancing the three lights of the lighting triangle depends on what you intend to convey to the viewer, you can't use precise intensity ratios among key, back, and fill lights as an absolute guide for effective lighting. Nevertheless, there are some ratios that have proved beneficial for a number of routine lighting assignments. You can always start with these ratios and then adjust them to your specific lighting task.

KEY-TO-BACK-LIGHT RATIO

In normal conditions back lights have approximately the same intensity as key lights. An unusually intense back light tends to glamorize people; a back light with an intensity much lower than that of the key tends to get lost on the monitor. A television performer with blond hair and a light-colored suit will need considerably less back light than will a dark-haired performer in a dark suit. The 1:1 key-to-back-light ratio (key and back lights have equal intensities) can go as high as 1:1.5 (the back light has one and a half times the intensity of the key) if you need a fair amount of sparkle or if the talent has dark, light-absorbing textured hair.

KEY-TO-FILL-LIGHT RATIO

The fill-light intensity depends on how fast a falloff you want. If you want fast falloff for dramatic effect, little fill is needed. If you want very slow falloff, higher-intensity fill is

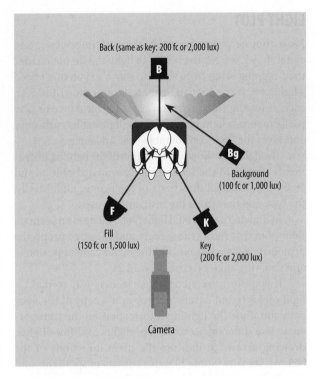

11.28 LIGHTING RATIOS
Lighting ratios differ, depending on the specific lighting task. These ratios are a good starting point.

needed. As you can see, there is no single key-to-fill-light ratio, but for starters you may want to try a fill-light intensity that is half that of the key and go from there. Remember that the more fill light you use, the less modeling the key light is doing but the smoother the texture becomes (such as that of a person's face). If you use almost no fill light, the dense shadows reveal no picture detail.

If you are asked to light for a high-baselight, low-contrast scene (high-key lighting), you may want to use floodlights for both the key and the fill, with the fill burning at almost the same intensity as the key. As you know by now, high-key has nothing to do with the actual positioning of the key light but rather the intensity of the overall light level. The back light should probably burn with a higher intensity than the key or the fill light to provide the necessary sparkle. In a low-key scene, the back light is often considerably brighter than the key and fill lights. **SEE 11.28**

Again, as helpful as light meters are in establishing rough lighting ratios, do not rely solely on them. Your final criterion is how the picture looks on a well-adjusted monitor.

LIGHT PLOT

Most routine programs, such as news, interviews, and panel shows, are relatively easy to light and do not change their lighting setup from show to show, so you don't need a light plot. If you have to light an atypical show, however, such as for the video recording of a college dance or play performance, a light plot makes the lighting less arbitrary and saves the crew considerable time and energy.

The *light plot* shows: the location of the lighting instruments relative to the set and the illuminated objects and areas; the principal directions of the beams; and, ideally, the type and the size of the instruments used.

In drawing a successful light plot, you need an accurate *floor plan* that shows the scenery and the stage props, the principal talent positions, and the major camera positions and shooting angles (see section 14.2).

If you don't use a computer, an easy way to make a light plot is to put a transparency over a copy of the floor plan and draw the lighting information on the transparency. Use different icons for spotlights and floodlights, drawing arrows to indicate the main directions of the beams. **SEE 11.29** Some LDs use cutouts of spotlights and floodlights, which they lay on the floor plan and move to the appropriate positions.

Try to work with the set designer (usually the art director) or the floor manager (who is responsible for putting up the set) as much as possible to have them place the set in the studio where you won't have to move any, or only a few, instruments to achieve the desired lighting. Placing the small set to suit the available lighting positions is much easier than moving the lights to suit the location of a small set.

Studio lighting is successful when you get it done on time. With due respect to creative lighting, don't fuss over a single dense shadow somewhere on the background while neglecting to light the rest of the set. If you are really pressed for time, turn on some floodlights and back lights that hang in approximate positions and hope for the best. More often than not, the lighting will look acceptable.

OPERATION OF STUDIO LIGHTS

When initially hanging lights, divide the studio into major performance areas and hang the appropriate instruments (spotlights and floodlights) in the triangular arrangements of the basic photographic principle.

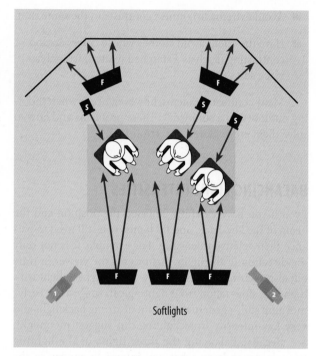

Softlights

11.29 LIGHT PLOT FOR FLAT LIGHTING OF INTERVIEW
This light plot shows the slow-falloff (flat) lighting setup for a simple interview. Ordinarily, such a simple setup would not require a light plot. Note that the sketch is not to scale.

PRESERVING LAMPS AND POWER

Always warm up large instruments through reduced power by keeping the dimmer low for several minutes before supplying full power. This will prolong the lamp life and the Fresnel lenses, which occasionally crack when warmed up too fast. This warm-up period is essential for getting HMI lights up to full operation.

Do not waste energy. Dry runs (without cameras) can be done just as efficiently when illuminated by work lights as by full studio lighting. If you have movable battens, telescope hangers, or pantographs, try to bring the lights down as close as possible to the object or scene to be illuminated. As you know, light intensity drops off considerably the farther the light moves from the object. Bring the lights up full only when necessary.

USING A STUDIO MONITOR

If you intend to use a well-adjusted color monitor as a guide for lighting, you must be ready for some compromise. As noted, the lighting is correct if the studio monitor shows what you want the viewer to perceive. To get to this point, you should use the monitor as a guide to lighting, rather than the less direct light meter. Switch the camera to automatic exposure for the setup and then, if you have a VO operating a CCU, work with the VO to fine-tune the lighting.

M A I N   P O I N T S

▶ Exercise caution during all lighting operations. Do not look directly into the instruments, and wear gloves when handling the hot lights.

▶ All lighting uses directional and/or diffused light.

▶ Color temperature, measured in Kelvin degrees (K), is the relative reddishness or bluishness of white light. The standard color temperature for indoor light is 3,200K; for outdoor light it is 5,600K.

▶ The key light is the principal source of illumination and reveals the basic shape of the object.

▶ The back light provides more definition to the object's out-line, separates it from the background, and gives it sparkle.

▶ The fill light reduces falloff and makes the shadows less dense.

▶ Most television and film lighting setups use the basic photographic principle, or triangle lighting, of key, back, and fill lights.

▶ The background, or set, light illuminates the background of the scene and the set. The side light acts as additional fill or a side key. The kicker light is used to outline the contour of an object that would otherwise blend in with the background.

▶ Specific lighting techniques include high- and low-key lighting, flat lighting, continuous-action lighting, large-area lighting, high-contrast lighting, cameo lighting, silhouette lighting, chroma-key-area lighting, and controlling eye and boom shadows.

▶ Falloff indicates how fast the lighted side of a subject changes to shadow and how dense the shadows are. Fast falloff means that the light and shadow areas are distinct and that the shadows are dense. Slow falloff means that the transition from light to shadow is more gradual and that the shadows are transparent. Generally, fast falloff means high-contrast lighting; slow falloff means low-contrast, or flat, lighting.

▶ A high-key scene has a light background, a generally high baselight level, and usually an upbeat, happy mood. A low-key scene has a dark background with selective fast-falloff lighting and a dramatic or mysterious mood.

▶ The contrast ratio is the difference between the lightest and the darkest areas in a picture, often measured by reflected light in foot-candles. The normal optimal contrast ratio is 50:1. It can be much higher for digital cameras, which means that they can tolerate a higher contrast.

▶ The light plot indicates the location of the lighting instruments, the principal direction of their light beams, and sometimes the type and the size of the instruments used.

11.2

Location Lighting

ing or difficult, excuses you from abandoning safety for expediency or effect.

ELECTRIC SHOCK

Be especially careful with electric power when on-location. A charge of 110V (volts) can be deadly. Secure cables so that people do not trip over them. Every connection—from cable to power outlet, from cable to cable, and from cable to lighting instrument—can cause an electric shock if not properly joined. If you use regular AC (alternating current) extension cables, tape all connections so they won't pull apart accidentally. Be especially careful when using power cords in the rain.

CABLES

String the cables above doorways or tape them to the floor and cover them with a rubber mat or flattened cardboard at points of heavy foot traffic. A loose cable not only can trip somebody but may also topple a lighting instrument and start a fire. See that all light stands are secured with sandbags.

FIRES

As discussed in chapter 10, portable incandescent lighting instruments get very hot when turned on for only brief periods of time. Place them as far as possible from combustible materials, such as drapes, books, tablecloths, wood ceilings, and walls. It pays to double-check. If they must be close to walls or other combustibles, insulate them with aluminum foil.

LOCATION LIGHTING

There is no clear-cut division between lighting for ENG and EFP, except that in electronic news gathering you often have to shoot in available light or with the camera light. But when called upon to do an interview in a hotel room or in the office of a CEO, or when covering a ceremony on the steps of city hall, ENG and EFP lighting techniques are pretty much the same. The big difference is that in electronic field production you have enough lead time to survey the lighting requirements before the event takes place; but then you may be expected to make the office of a corporate president look like the best Hollywood can muster or to illuminate the hearing room of the board of supervisors so that it rivals a courtroom scene in the latest blockbuster movie—all without adequate time or equipment.

When lighting a remote location for digital cinema, you will proceed in pretty much the same way you would

When engaged in location lighting, you are not working in the studio, where all the lighting equipment is in place and ready to go. Every piece of equipment, however large or small, must be hauled to the remote location and set up in places that always seem either too small or too large for good video lighting. You also never seem to get enough time to experiment with various lighting setups to find the most effective one. Whatever the remote lighting task, you need to be especially efficient in the choice of instruments and their use. This section explains the techniques of location lighting and describes some of its essential requirements.

▶ **SAFETY**
   Primary safety concerns: electric shock, cables, and fires

▶ **LOCATION LIGHTING**
   Shooting in bright sunlight, in overcast daylight, in indoor light, and at night

▶ **LOCATION SURVEY**
   Survey checklists and power supply

SAFETY

As in the studio, safety is a primary concern when lighting in the field. In fact, there are more safety hazards in the field than in the studio. No production, however excitto light a set in the studio, except that you need to haul all of the lighting equipment to the location and then set it up in usually cramped quarters.

When engaged in location lighting, you will find yourself confronted with problems both indoors and out. When outdoors you have to work with available light—the illumination already present at the scene. At night you must supplement available light or provide the entire illumination. Although you have a little more time in EFP and certainly in digital cinema than in ENG, you must still work quickly and efficiently to obtain not only adequate lighting but also the most effective lighting possible under the circumstances.

SHOOTING IN BRIGHT SUNLIGHT

Most lighting problems occur when you have to shoot in bright sunlight. A shooter's nightmare is having to cover a mixed choir, with the women dressed in starched white blouses and the men in white shirts and black jackets, with half of them standing in the sun and the rest of them in a deep shadow against a sun-flooded white building. Even a good digital ENG/EFP camcorder would have trouble handling such high contrast.

If you put the camera in the auto-iris mode, it will faithfully read the bright light of the shirts and the light background and close its iris for optimal exposure. The problem is that the drastic reduction of light coming through the lens will darken equally drastically the shadow area and the people standing in it. The black jackets will turn into a dull black and lose all detail. If you switch to manual iris to open the aperture somewhat to achieve some transparency in the shadows and the black jackets, the white shirts and the sunlit background will be overexposed. Worse, the highlights on the perspiring foreheads and occasional bald spots of the choir members will begin to "bloom," turning the skin color into strangely luminescent white spots surrounded by a pinkish rim.

Should you give up? No, even though your options are somewhat limited, here are some potential remedies.

■ Whenever possible, try to position the talent in a shadow area, away from a bright background. You could probably move the whole choir in the shadow and away from the sunlit building. For a single on-camera person, you can always create a shadow area with a large umbrella.

■ Ask whether the male choir members can take off their black jackets. This is worth a try, even though you will probably be turned down.

■ Shoot from an angle that avoids the white building in the background.

■ Stretch a large piece of gauze or other diffusion material between two stands to diffuse the sunlight striking the choir, and use large reflectors to slow down the falloff. Recall that a reflector functions like an effective fill light. **SEE 11.30 AND 11.31**

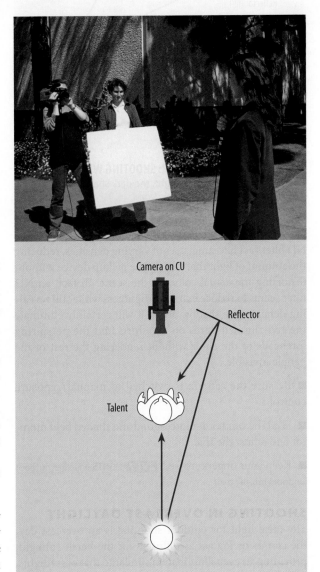

11.30 USING A REFLECTOR: SHOOTING AGAINST THE SUN
When shooting against the sun, reflect as much sunlight as possible back to the talent with a simple reflector (in this case a white card).

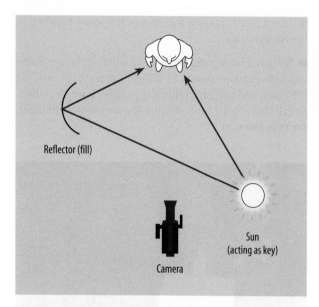

11.31 USING A REFLECTOR: SHOOTING WITH THE SUN
When shooting in bright sunlight, the dark shadows can be easily lightened with a reflector.

■ Use the neutral density (ND) filters in the camera. The ND filters act like sunglasses of varying densities, reducing the amount of light that falls on the pickup device without distorting the actual colors of the scene. In fact, an ND filter seems to reduce extreme brightness while still revealing detail in the shadow areas. It will certainly eliminate the red-rimmed flares on the shirts and the perspiring foreheads of the choir without rendering the rest of the people invisible.

■ Be sure the camera is switched to manual exposure control.

■ Feed the camcorder into a good and shaded field monitor and adjust the iris.

■ Keep your fingers crossed. **ZVL7** LIGHTS→ Field→ outdoor | indoor | mixed | try it

SHOOTING IN OVERCAST DAYLIGHT

The ideal light for outdoor shooting is an overcast day: the clouds or fog act as diffusers for the harsh sunlight, providing an even illumination similar to that of softlights. Do not be surprised if you have to use an ND and/or color-correction filter. The light of a cloudy day is often surprisingly bright and usually has a high color temperature.

Even in diffused lighting, avoid an overly bright background. If you must shoot against a light background,

zoom in on the person, thereby avoiding as much of the background as possible. Be sure that you have manual iris control, and adjust the iris to meet the light requirements of the person rather than of the background. It is better to have an overexposed background than an underexposed person.

SHOOTING IN INDOOR LIGHT

You encounter countless amounts and types of light when shooting indoors. Some interiors are illuminated by the daylight that comes through large windows, others by high-color-temperature fluorescent banks that make up a light ceiling. Still others, such as windowless hotel rooms, have desk and floor lighting that provide a romantic mood but hardly the proper illumination for good television pictures. The major problem here is not so much how to supply additional light but how to place the instruments for optimal aesthetic effect and how to match the various color temperatures.

In all cases try first to set up the lighting triangle of key, fill, and back lights. If this isn't possible, try to adjust the setup so that you maintain at least the effect of triangle lighting. Whenever possible try to get some back-light effect; it is often the back light that distinguishes good lighting from mere illumination.

Let's assume that you are lighting an interview of the CEO of a software company. Except for some cutaway close-ups of the interviewer at the end of the show, the CEO is seen in a close-up for most of the interview. Let's put her in three different environments: in a windowless hotel room, in a hotel room with a window, and in her office with a large picture window behind her desk.

Windowless room   In a room with no windows, you can simply set up portable, open-face lights in a typical triangle fashion. Use a diffused key light, a more focused back light of the same kind, and a reflector or softlight (or diffusion tent) for the fill (see figure 11.5). If you have a fourth instrument, you can use it as a background light. If only two instruments are available, use an open-face spot as a back light and use a diffused light (open-face spot with scrim, tent, or umbrella) as a key, placed so that most of the face is illuminated. The spill of the key will also take care of the background lighting. **SEE 11.32**

If the director insists on cross shooting with two cameras to catch the immediacy of the interviewer's asking questions or reacting to the CEO, you can still get by with two or three instruments. Place two open-face spots or small Fresnel spots with tents, scrims, or umbrella reflectors

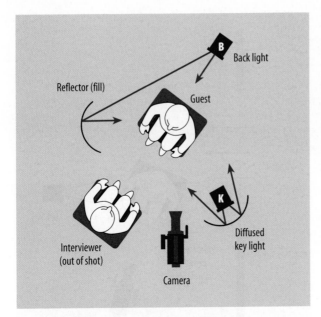

11.32 TRIANGLE LIGHTING FOR INTERVIEW

This one-person lighting setup uses two instruments. The diffused key light is an open-face spot with a scrim, a tent, or an umbrella. The back light is a spread or focused open-face spot. If fill light is necessary, it can be created with a softlight or a reflector. You can use an additional softlight as a background light. Note that the interviewee is looking at the interviewer, who is sitting or standing next to the camera, out of the shot.

so that they shine over the shoulder of the participants sitting opposite each other. In this cross-keying, the two lights now serve as multifunction key and back lights. You can use the third instrument as general fill light. This lighting setup can also be used for an interview in a hallway, living room, or other such location. **SEE 11.33**

Room with window   When there is a window in the room, you can use it as a key or even a back light. If you use the window as a key, you need a reflector or fill light on the opposite side. In any case, you need a strong back light. To match the outdoor color temperature of the window light, both the fill and back lights need either 5,600K lamps or 3,200K lamps with blue gels to raise their color temperature. **SEE 11.34**

The better way of lighting is to position the CEO so that the window acts as a back light—without letting it get into the shot. You can then use a single diffused 5,600K key light (an open-face spot with a 5,600K lamp or a 3,200K lamp with a blue gel) to illuminate most of her face, eliminating the need for a fill light. **SEE 11.35**

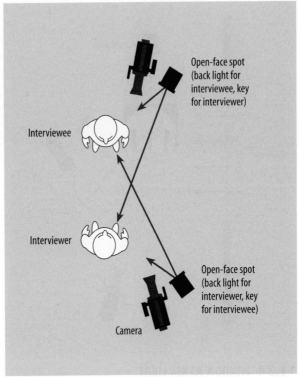

11.33 CROSS-KEYING FOR INTERVIEW

The two portable lights serve multiple functions: key and back lights for the interviewer and the interviewee. If you have a third light, use it as fill.

Panoramic office window   A typical problem is having to shoot against a large window. If, for example, the CEO insists on making her statement from behind her desk that is located in front of a large picture window, your lighting problem is identical to that of shooting a person standing in front of a bright background: If you set the iris according to the background brightness, the person in front tends to appear in silhouette. If you adjust the iris for the person in front, the background is overexposed. Here are some possible solutions.

■ Frame a fairly tight close-up and set the exposure for the face rather than the background. The little you see of the background window will be overexposed but will not render the close-up unusable.

■ Draw the drapes or the blinds and light the person with portable instruments.

■ Move the camera to the side of the desk and have the person face the camera. You can then shoot parallel to the

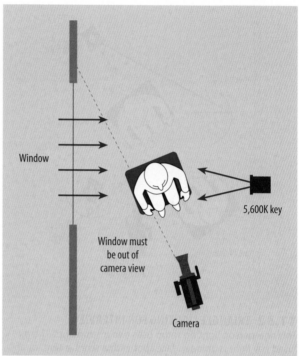

11.34 WINDOW AS KEY LIGHT

The daylight shining through a window can serve as the key light, and a reflector as the fill light. If you use a portable light as the fill and/or back light, you need to bring its color temperature up to the 5,600K daylight standard.

11.35 WINDOW AS BACK LIGHT

You can use a window as a back light so long as you place the talent with the window out of the shot. The key light can be a diffused open-face spot that burns at 5,600K.

window. You can use the light from the window as the key, and fill with a large reflector or an additional light on a stand (see figure 11.34).

■ If the person insists on having the window in the background, you must cover it with large color temperature filters and/or ND filters (plastic sheets) of varying densities. Use two strong but diffused open-face instruments (5,600K) as key and fill, or use a large, highly efficient reflector that bounces the light from the window onto the CEO's face. Bear in mind that these procedures take up a great amount of time and are generally left to EFP.

■ Take a picture of the window view and use it as a chroma-key video source (see chapter 14).

Large-area indoor lighting Sometimes you have to deal with groups of people who are gathered in locations with inadequate illumination. Typical examples are meeting rooms, hotel lobbies, and hallways. Most of the time, the available light or a camera light provides enough illumination to cover the speaker and individual audience

members. If you are to do extensive coverage of such an event, however, you need additional illumination.

The quickest and most efficient way to light such a location is to establish a general, nondirectional baselight level. Use two or three open-face spots or V-lights and bounce the light off of the ceiling or walls. If you have light-reflecting umbrellas, direct the lights into the open part of the umbrellas and place them so that you can cover the event area with the diffused light. You will be surprised by how much illumination you can get out of a single V-light when diffused by an umbrella. If that is not possible, direct the lights on the group but diffuse the light beam with scrims. The most effective method is to use portable HMI, quartz, or fluorescent softlights and flood the active area. Always be sure to white-balance the camera for the light in which the event actually takes place.

As you probably noticed, all these lighting techniques aim to establish a high baselight level. Even when pressed for time, try to place one or two diffused back lights out of camera range. They will provide sparkle and professional polish to an otherwise flat scene. **SEE 11.36**

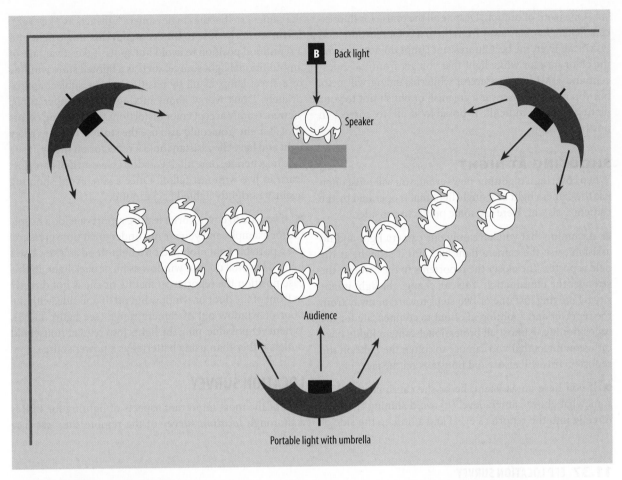

11.36 LARGE-AREA LIGHTING
To establish sufficient baselight over a large area, you need highly diffused light. Here three portable incandescent lights and light-diffusing umbrellas provide maximally diffused light over the entire area. You can, of course, use fluorescent or HMI lights in place of the quartz lights.

Working with fluorescents The basic problem of working with the fluorescent lights used in stores, offices, and public buildings is their color temperature; it is usually higher than the 3,200K indoor standard of incandescent lights. Even if some fluorescent tubes burn at the warmer indoor color temperature, they have a strange greenish blue tint. So if you turn on the camera light for additional illumination, you are confronted with two color temperatures. Some lighting people advise turning off the fluorescents altogether when working with quartz lights (3,200K), but this is unrealistic. If you need to get a fast-breaking story and you shoot in a hallway that is illuminated by fluorescent lights, you certainly do not have time to locate and persuade the building manager to turn off the lights and then to relight the scene before starting to shoot.

If the fluorescent lights give enough illumination, simply select the appropriate color temperature filter in the camera (to bring down the high color temperature of the fluorescents) and white-balance the camera with the available light. If you have to use a camera light for additional illumination, either boost the color temperature of the camera light (by inserting a dichroic filter that often comes with the camera light) or white-balance the camera with the illumination provided by the camera light (3,200K).

As mentioned in chapter 10, the portable incandescent lights—including the camera light—are strong enough to wash out the fluorescent baselight. If available, the better solution, of course, is to use floodlights that burn at the outdoor color temperature of 5,600K or floodlights whose color temperature is raised by light-blue gels.

One word of caution: Despite all the praise for fluorescent field lights, stay away from them if color reproduction is critical. Even the best fluorescent lamps do not give you the color mix for white light that you get from incandescent and HMI lamps. Careful white-balancing will help, but you may still discover a greenish or bluish tint to your pictures that is difficult, if possible at all, to correct in postproduction.

SHOOTING AT NIGHT

When covering a nighttime news event, you will most often use the camera light or a single light that is operated by the camera assistant. Here are some points to consider.

■ Assuming that you have only one camera light and no assistant, use the camera light and aim it straight at the field reporter. The closer the reporter is to the camera, the stronger the illumination. You can change the light intensity by moving just one or two steps toward or away from the reporter and zooming in or out to compensate for the repositioning. Almost all professional camera lights have diffusion filters that you can use to soften the light on the reporter. This will also avoid hot spots on the face.

■ If you have an assistant, he or she can hold the light somewhat above camera level (to avoid shining the light directly into the reporter's eyes) and a little to the side of the camera so that the single camera light acts as a key light. If you are fairly close to the event, put this single light into a semiflood position to avoid hot spots. Take advantage of any additional light source, such as a lighted store window or a street lamp, as fill by positioning the subject appropriately. Don't worry about mixing color temperatures; viewers readily accept color distortions when seeing events shot at night. You could also use the store window as a key light and have the assistant hold a reflector on the opposite side to generate some fill. If you don't have an assistant, just learn to live with fast falloff. Once again, avoid shooting against a brightly lighted background.

■ If you are to cover a brief feature report outside a hospital, for example, and you are not under great time pressure, use a portable light mounted on a light stand as a key. Use a lighted hospital door or window as fill or back light. In this case position the reporter so that he or she is not directly in front of the door or window but off to one side, with the door or window out of camera range (see figure 11.35). Whenever possible, plug the lights into regular household outlets rather than using batteries as a power source.

LOCATION SURVEY

One of the most important aspects of lighting for EFP is a thorough *location survey* of the remote site. **SEE 11.37**

11.37 EFP LOCATION SURVEY

INDOORS	OUTDOORS
AVAILABLE LIGHT	
Is the available light sufficient? If not, what additional lights do you need? What type of available light do you have? Incandescent? Fluorescent? Daylight coming through windows?	Do you need any additional lights? Where is the sun in relation to the planned action? Is there enough room to place the necessary reflectors?
PRINCIPAL BACKGROUND	
Is there any action planned against a white wall? Are there windows in the background? If so, do they have curtains, drapes, or venetian blinds that can be drawn? If you want to use the daylight from the window, do you have lights that match the color temperature of the daylight (5,600K)? If the window is too bright, or if you have to reduce the color temperature coming through the window, do you have the appropriate ND or color filters to attach to the window? You will certainly need some reflectors or other type of fill-light illumination.	How bright is the background? Even if the sun is not hitting the background at the time of the survey, will it be there when the actual production takes place? When shooting at the beach, does the director plan to have people perform with the ocean as the background? You will need reflectors and/or additional lights (HMIs) to prevent the people from being shown in silhouette, unless the director plans on extreme close-ups most of the time.

11.37　EFP LOCATION SURVEY　*(continued)*

INDOORS	OUTDOORS
CONTRAST	
If there are dense shadows or if the event takes place in high-contrast areas (sunlight and shadows), you need extra fill light and/or ND filters to reduce the contrast.	Does the production take place in bright sunlight? Can the scene be moved into the shadow area? If not, you must provide for a generous amount of fill light (reflectors and/or HMI spotlights) to render the shadows transparent, or ND filters to reduce the glare of overly bright areas.
LIGHT POSITIONS	
Can you place the lights out of camera range? What lighting supports do you need (light stands, gaffer grip, clamps)? Do you need special mounting devices, such as battens or cross braces? Are the lighting instruments far enough away from combustible materials? Are the lights positioned so that they do not interfere with the event? People who are not used to television complain mostly about the brightness of the lights.	If you need reflectors or additional lights on stands, is the ground level enough for the stands to be securely placed? Will you need to take extra precautions because of wind? (Take plenty of sandbags along, or even some tent stakes and rope, so that you can secure the light stands in case of wind.)
POWER REQUIREMENTS	
Your main concern will be power and how to get it to the lighting instruments. Is the necessary power available nearby? Do you need a generator? If you can tap available power, make sure you can tell the engineer in charge the approximate power requirement for all lights. (Simply add up the wattage of all the lights you plan to use, plus another 10 percent to ensure enough power.) Do you have enough extension cords to reach all lighting instruments? Do you know exactly where the outlets are, what the capacities of the circuits are, and which outlets are on the same circuit? Make a rough sketch of all outlets and indicate the distance to the corresponding light or lights. What adapters do you need to plug lights into the available outlets? Do you have the necessary cables, extension cords, and power strips so that you can get by with a minimum of cable runs? In the projected cable runs, have you taken all possible safety precautions?	You do not need to use lighting instruments very often when shooting outdoors unless you shoot at night or need to fill in particularly dense shadows that cannot be reached with a simple reflector.

The survey checklists in figure 11.37 are intended for relatively simple productions, as are all other discussions of EFP. (For more-detailed information on location surveys, see Remote Survey in chapter 18.) The lighting for large and complex electronic field productions is more closely related to motion picture techniques and is not addressed here. But even in a relatively simple EFP, you will find that the power supply is one of the key elements for good remote lighting.

POWER SUPPLY

In EFP you have to work with three types of power for lighting instruments: household current (usually from 110 to 120 volts), generators, and 7.2V, 12V, or 30V batteries.

The most frequently used power supply is household current. When using regular wall outlets, be aware of the power rating of the circuits, which is usually 15 or 20 amps (amperes) per circuit. This rating means that you can theoretically plug in a 1,500W (or 2kW) instrument, or any combination of lights that does not exceed 1,500 (or 2,000) watts, without overloading the circuit, provided nothing else is on the same circuit. But that is not always wise to do. Recall the discussion about extension cords that build up additional resistance, especially when warm. To be on the safe side, do not load up a single circuit to full capacity. Otherwise you may find that the lights go out just at the most important part of the shoot.

You can find the capacity of the circuit by checking its fuse or breaker. Each breaker is labeled with the number of amps it can handle. You can now figure the total wattage capacity of each circuit: simply multiply the number of amps of the circuit (15 or 20 amps) by 100 (assuming the household current rates between 110 and 120 volts). This gives you an upper limit: 1,500 watts for a 15-amp breaker (100 volts × 15 amps = 1,500 total wattage) or 2,000 watts for a 20-amp breaker (100 volts × 20 amps = 2,000 watts). But don't press your luck. Try to use lower-wattage instruments per circuit to ensure that the lights will work properly during the entire production. **SEE 11.38**

If you need to power more lights than a single circuit can handle, plug them into different circuits. But how do you know which outlets are on separate circuits?

Determining the circuits   Normally, several double wall outlets are connected to a single circuit. You can determine which outlets are on the same circuit by plugging one low-powered lamp into a particular outlet. Find the specific circuit breaker that turns off the lamp. Switch the

breaker on again. The light should light up again. Now plug the light into the next convenient outlet and switch off the same circuit breaker or fuse. If the light goes out, the plugs are on the same circuit. If the light stays on, it's a different circuit and you are safe to use it.

Safe power extensions   Obviously, you need enough extension cords to get from the outlets to the lighting instruments. You can minimize cable runs by using power strips (multiple-outlet boxes), especially if you use low-wattage instruments. The larger the wires in the extension cords (lower gauge ratings), the more wattage they can handle without getting unduly hot. Have enough and various kinds of adapters available so that lights can be plugged into the existing outlets.

Whenever there is doubt about the availability or reliability of power, use a generator, the responsibility of which falls to the engineering crew. The circuit ratings and the allowable combined wattage of the lights per circuit still apply.

For relatively simple on-location productions, you may power the lights with batteries. First check whether the lamps in the portable lights are appropriate for the voltage of the battery. Obviously, you cannot use a 12V lamp with a 30V battery. Then check that the batteries are properly charged and that there are enough spares for the duration of the production. Turning off the lights whenever possible saves battery power and greatly extends the life of the lamps.

11.38 CALCULATING ELECTRIC POWER REQUIREMENTS

	WATTAGE OF LAMP	NUMBER OF INSTRUMENTS PER 15-AMP CIRCUIT

To find the maximum load (watts) for a single circuit, use the following formula:
 	
    amperes × volts = watts
 	
The ampere rating of a standard household circuit is 15 amps (normally stamped on the circuit breaker). This means that the circuit can theoretically support a maximum load of 15 amps × 110 volts = 1,650 watts.
 	
To be safe always figure 100 volts instead of 110 volts:
 	
    15 amps × 100 = 1,500 watts
 	
To calculate how many instruments to plug into a single circuit, divide their total wattage into 1,500 watts (maximum load). The table lists the number of instruments of a certain wattage that you can safely plug into a single 15-amp circuit.
	100
	150
	175
	200
	350
	500
	750
	1,000
	1,500
		15
		10
		9
		7
		4
		3
		2
		1
		1

MAIN POINTS

▶ Safety is a primary concern when lighting in the field. Never abandon safety for expediency or effect.

▶ When shooting in bright sunlight, try to place the talent in the shade. If you must shoot in the sun, use a reflector and/or a neutral density (ND) filter to reduce contrast.

▶ The best outdoor shooting light is an overcast day. The clouds act as a giant diffusion filter.

▶ Use the basic photographic principle (triangle lighting) when lighting a single-person interview in a windowless room. If you have only two instruments, use a softlight from the front as key and fill and use a second instrument as a back light. When cross shooting use two instruments to fulfill key- and back-light functions.

▶ When a window is present, use it for fill or back light. Any indoor lights must then burn at 5,600K. Gel the 3,200K indoor lights with light-blue media, or use 5,600K lamps. Use a large panoramic window for the key light or cover it with a curtain and use a triangle lighting setup. If the window is in the shot, filter the intensity of the light and lower the color temperature with gels on the window, and add 3,200K key and fill lights.

▶ When shooting under fluorescent lights, use 5,600K lights for additional key and back lights, or "wash out" the fluorescent ceiling lights with incandescent key, back, and fill lights.

▶ When shooting at night, use the camera light as the principal light source if no other light is available. Use a diffusion filter on the camera light and any other available light or a reflector for fill.

▶ Before doing any EFP lighting, conduct a location survey.

▶ The formula for figuring the electric power rating is watt = volt × ampere.

▶ When powering portable lights with household current, check the capacity of the circuits and do not overload them.

ZETTL'S VIDEOLAB

For your reference or to track your work, the *Zettl's VideoLab* program cues in this chapter are listed here with their corresponding page numbers.

ZVL1 LIGHTS→ Color temperature→ white balance | controlling | try it   **218**

ZVL2 LIGHTS→ Color temperature→ light sources   **218**

ZVL3 LIGHTS→Triangle lighting→ key | back | fill | background | try it   **222**

ZVL4 LIGHTS→ Design→ high key | low key   **227**

ZVL5 LIGHTS→ Design→ silhouette   **228**

ZVL6 LIGHTS→ Measurement→ contrast   **232**

ZVL7 LIGHTS→ Field→ outdoor | indoor | mixed | try it   **238**

12

Video-recording and Storage Systems

Although one of television's great assets is its capability to transmit an event "live," that is, while the event is in progress, most programs have been prerecorded on some kind of video-recording device. There is virtually no show on the air, including live newscasts, that does not contain a preponderance of prerecorded material.

The ubiquitous camcorder, like the still camera, made the recording of various slices of life—observed or constructed—even more popular. In fact, it was principally the breakthrough of small recording devices that made the portable camcorder possible and precipitated a revolution in video production. That you can get a high-definition television (HDTV) camcorder small enough to hold in your hand is a sheer miracle. Manufacturers are constantly striving to compress more and more video and audio information onto ever-smaller storage devices while making the retrieval of program material as quick and simple as possible. Despite the rapid move toward a totally tapeless operation, videotape is still the most prominent recording media; it is therefore discussed extensively in this chapter. Note that many of the operational principles of using videotape also apply to nontape media.

As you know by now, there is more to video recording than simply pressing the little red button on a camcorder and waiting for the *rec* light to flash. Section 12.1 explains the principal tape-based and tapeless analog and digital recording systems, and section 12.2 covers how video recording is done.

KEY TERMS

analog recording systems Record the continually fluctuating video and audio signals generated by the video and/or audio source.

codec Short for *compression/decompression*. A specific method of compressing and decompressing digital data.

composite system A process in which the luminance (Y, or black-and-white) signal and the chrominance (C, or color) signal as well as sync information are encoded into a single video signal and transported via a single wire. Also called *NTSC signal*.

compression Reducing the amount of data to be stored or transmitted by using coding schemes that pack all original data into less space (*lossless* compression) or by throwing away some of the least important data (*lossy* compression).

control track The area of the videotape used for recording the synchronization information (sync pulse). Provides reference for the running speed of the videotape recorder, for the reading of the video tracks, and for counting the number of frames.

digital recording systems Sample the analog video and audio signals and convert them into discrete on/off pulses. These digits are recorded as 0's and 1's.

electronic still store (ESS) system An electronic device that can grab a single frame from any video source and store it in digital form. It can retrieve the frame randomly in a fraction of a second.

field log A record of each take during the video recording.

flash memory device A read/write portable storage device that can download, store, and upload very fast (in a flash) a significant amount of digital information. Also called *flash drive, stick flash, flash stick,* and *flash memory card*.

framestore synchronizer Image stabilization and synchronization system that stores and reads out one complete video frame. Used to synchronize signals from a variety of video sources that are not genlocked.

JPEG A video compression method mostly for still pictures, developed by the Joint Photographic Experts Group.

MPEG A compression technique for moving pictures, developed by the Moving Picture Experts Group.

MPEG-2 The compression standard for motion video.

MPEG-4 The compression standard for Internet streaming.

RGB component system Analog video-recording system wherein the red, green, and blue (RGB) signals are kept separate throughout the entire recording and storage process and are transported via three separate wires.

tape-based video recorder All video recorders (analog and digital) that record or store information on videotape. All tape-based systems are linear.

tapeless video recorder All digital video recorders that record or store digital information on media other than videotape.

time base corrector (TBC) Electronic accessory to a video recorder that helps make playbacks or transfers electronically stable.

video leader Visual material and a control tone recorded before the program material. Serves as a technical guide for playback.

video recorder (VR) All devices that record video and audio. Includes videotape, hard disks, read/write optical discs, and flash memory devices.

videotape recorder (VTR) Electronic recording device that records video and audio signals on videotape for later playback or postproduction editing.

videotape tracks Most videotape systems have a video track, two or more audio tracks, a control track, and sometimes a separate time code track.

Y/C component system Analog video-recording system wherein the luminance (Y) and chrominance (C) signals are kept separate during signal encoding and transport but are combined and occupy the same track when actually laid down on videotape. The Y/C component signal is transported via two wires. Also called *S-video*.

Y/color difference component system Video-recording system in which three signals—the luminance (Y) signal, the red signal minus its luminance (R–Y) signal, and the blue signal minus its luminance (B–Y)—are kept separate throughout the recording and storage process.

SECTION

12.1

Tape-based and Tapeless Video Recording

RECORDING SYSTEMS

On your visit to the video-recording section of a television station or video production company, you hear engineers discussing the advantages of tapeless video recorders when compared with videotape recorders and why some analog recorders are still in use. Then they get into such tech-talk as sampling, compression, the quality difference between component and composite video recordings, and so forth. They are basically discussing the types and the functions of video-recording systems and the major electronic features that determine the quality of the video recorders.

TAPE-BASED SYSTEMS

This classification is based on the recording media used rather than how the video recorder works. Obviously, all *tape-based video recorders* use videotape as the recording media. What is not so obvious is that the *videotape recorders (VTRs)* can be either analog or digital.

ANALOG AND DIGITAL SYSTEMS

At this juncture you may ask: why bother with analog tape-recording systems when everything is digital anyway? You've got a point, but the venerable VHS (video home system) you may have is still used in millions of homes for off-the-air recording of favorite programs and playing rental movies. Besides, there are all the favorite tapes of birthdays, weddings, and off-the-air recordings that are still awaiting transfer to a less cumbersome digital media, such as DVDs. So, don't recycle your VHS recorder just yet.

In fact, the higher-quality S-VHS (Super VHS) and the high-end analog Betacam recorders are still produced by their manufacturers, and many consumer and professional analog camcorders are just too good to be thrown away. Their analog output can be easily digitized and imported by digital editing systems—such as a laptop computer.

Analog VTRs   The basic problem with less-than-high-end video recording is that the recordings deteriorate quickly from one generation to the next (a generation is the number of dubs away from the original recording). This shortcoming is especially apparent during editing and the rendering of special effects. Both operations usually require several tape generations.

Without going into too much detail, the following table gives an overview of the major *analog recording systems*. **SEE 12.1**

Despite the great variety of video-recording devices, there are basically two types of systems: tape-based and tapeless. Tape-based systems can record analog or digital signals; tapeless systems can record only digital information. The great advantage of a tapeless operation is that you can store and archive vast amounts of information on media that take up very little space—and you can retrieve the information much faster than if it were stored on videotape.

To help you make sense of the many video-recording systems, section 12.1 gives an overview of tape-based and tapeless recording devices and how they work.

▶ **RECORDING SYSTEMS**
Tape-based systems, analog and digital systems, and tapeless systems

▶ **TAPED-BASED VIDEO RECORDING**
How videotape recording works, operational controls, and time base corrector and frame store synchronizer

▶ **TAPELESS VIDEO RECORDING**
Hard drives, read/write optical discs, and flash memory devices

▶ **ELECTRONIC FEATURES OF VIDEO RECORDING**
Composite and component signals, sampling, and compression

12.1 ANALOG VIDEOTAPE-RECORDING SYSTEMS

SYSTEM	CASSETTE	PRODUCTION CHARACTERISTICS
VHS	½-inch (12.7mm)	Low to fair quality for first generation. Rapid deterioration from one generation to the next.
Hi8	8mm (approx. 0.31-inch)	Sharp images. Good quality for first generation.
S-VHS	½-inch (12.7mm)	Very good quality. Will hold up fairly well for three or four generations.
Betacam SP	½-inch (12.7mm)	Superior quality. Will stand up well over multiple generations.

12.2 DIGITAL VIDEOTAPE-RECORDING SYSTEMS

SYSTEM	CASSETTE	PRODUCTION CHARACTERISTICS
DV	¼-inch (6.35mm) mini	Good digital quality.
Digital8	8mm	Good quality—about the same as DV.
DVCAM	¼-inch (6.35mm) full-sized	Excellent quality.
DVCPRO	¼-inch (6.35mm) full-sized	Excellent quality.
Betacam SX	½-inch (12.7mm) full-sized	Superior quality.
HDV	¼-inch (6.35mm) mini	Excellent quality. HDTV resolution.
HDTV	¼-inch (6.35mm) full-sized	Superior quality. High resolution and color.

Digital VTRs The major advantages of *digital recording systems* are that they are more compact and that even inexpensive models produce high-quality pictures and sound. They maintain their quality through repeated dubs. For all practical purposes, the fiftieth generation looks the same as the original recording. Unlike analog recordings, digital recordings do not need to be converted for computer storage on a hard disk for nonlinear editing and special-effects manipulation. Except for a few older high-end, ½-inch digital recording systems still in use (such as the D5 VTRs), almost all new digital videotape systems use the much smaller ¼-inch cassettes. They do, however, differ in size and range from the mini-cassette you are probably using in your camcorder to larger (but not wider) cassettes that allow longer continuous recording. **SEE 12.2**

TAPELESS SYSTEMS

Tapeless systems record only digital signals and use a variety of recording media: computer hard disks, read/write optical discs, and various flash memory devices, also called memory cards. The latter have no moving parts but are more limited in their recording capacity than are hard drives and optical discs. Because most professional television equipment is digital, the more flexible *tapeless video recorders* are more desirable.

There are four big advantages of a tapeless recording system over videotape: it allows almost instant random access to any frame in the recording, it is much less prone to wear and tear, it facilitates the entire editing process, and the archived material takes up considerably less space.

All tapeless video-recording systems operate on the same principle: they store digital video and audio data in computer files that can be identified and randomly retrieved. If that sounds familiar, it's because disk-based systems are, indeed, nothing but specialized computers. This is why you can use a laptop or desktop computer and appropriate software as the key elements for a disk-based recording and editing system.

TAPED-BASED VIDEO RECORDING

Although there is a great difference in the electronic makeup of analog and digital video recorders, the basic recording and operational principles are quite similar and often identical.

HOW VIDEOTAPE RECORDING WORKS

When recording video and audio signals, the videotape moves past a rotating head assembly that "writes" the video and audio signals on the tape during the recording process and "reads" the magnetically stored video and audio signals off the tape during playback. In the play mode on some VTRs, the same heads used for recording are also used to read the information off the tracks and convert it back into video signals. Others use different heads for the record and playback functions. Some analog VTRs use two or four heads for the record/play (write/read) functions.

Digital VTRs record the coded video and audio signals, which consist of combinations of on/off pulses (0's and 1's). Some digital VTRs have more read/write heads than analog VTRs for various video, audio, control, and cue tracks. For a simple explanation of how video recording works, the following discussion uses an analog VTR with two record/playback heads.

Record/playback heads   As mentioned, during video recording the tape moves past a rotating head assembly that writes the video and audio signals on the tape while recording and reads the information off the tape during playback. Good VTRs use one set of heads for recording

12.3 BASIC VIDEOTAPE-RECORDING METHOD
When recording, the videotape moves past a revolving head drum, which contains recording and playback heads. These heads write the video and audio information onto the tape or read it from the tape.

Videotape head spins...

...producing a slanted video track

the signals and another set for playing back the information. **SEE 12.3**

Videotape tracks   There are many ways in which video and audio signals are written to videotape, but they all use comparable *videotape tracks:* a video track, two or more audio tracks, one or more control tracks, and various data tracks. All video tracks are recorded as helical (slant) tracks, but the audio and control information can be on separate longitudinal tracks or incorporated in the helical tracks of the video signals. In its simplest form, the standard VHS recorder puts four separate tracks on the tape: the video track containing the picture information, two audio tracks containing all sound information, and a control track that regulates the videotape and the rotation speed of the VTR heads.   **SEE 12.4**   **ZVL1** EDITING→ Postproduction guidelines→ tape basics

Video track   When you record the video signal in the normal NTSC composite configuration, one pass of the head records the first field (half of a frame) of video information. The next pass of the head lays down the second field right next to it, completing a single video frame. Because two fields make up a single frame, the two heads must

12.4 BASIC VIDEOTAPE TRACK SYSTEM

The basic videotape track system comprises a slanted video track, two or more audio tracks, and a control track.

write 60 tracks for 60 fields, or 30 frames, for each second of NTSC video.[1] Digital systems use high-speed heads to lay down 20 or more tracks to record a single video fame.

Audio tracks   Analog audio information is generally recorded on longitudinal tracks (stripes) near the edge of the tape. Because of the demand for stereo audio and for keeping certain sounds separate even in monophonic sound, all VTR systems (even VHS recorders) provide at least two audio tracks. Digital VTRs have the multitrack audio information embedded in the video track.

---

1. There are actually only 29.97 fps (frames per second).

Control and cue tracks   The *control track* contains evenly spaced blips or spikes, called the sync pulse, which mark each complete television frame. These pulses synchronize the tape speed (the speed with which the tape passes from the supply reel to the take-up reel in the cassette) and the rotation speed of the record heads so that a tape made on a similar machine can be played back without picture breakup. The control track is also essential for linear videotape editing. Some VTRs have a separate track, called the cue track, for additional data, such as the SMPTE time code. This code marks each frame with a different address—a number that shows elapsed time and number of frames. (You will read more about time code in chapter 19.)

Digital VTR systems have a control track and a separate cue track for time code, and on each pass of the record heads they squeeze yet more coding information into a subcode area on a tape that is half the width of that in a standard VHS cassette.

OPERATIONAL CONTROLS

When merely looking at a high-end analog VTR and a high-end digital one side by side, you will be hard-pressed to tell the difference. Although their electronic make-up is quite different, they look pretty much the same. **SEE 12.5 AND 12.6**

12.5 ANALOG STUDIO VTR

This high-end analog VTR has all of the controls of a standard VTR plus additional audio, shuttle, and editing controls.

12.6 DIGITAL STUDIO VTR
This high-end digital Panasonic
DVCPRO50 VTR has all the controls of
a standard VTR plus additional audio,
shuttle, and editing controls.

A high-end studio VTR has the same controls as your home VCR, but the professional models have additional shuttle, edit, and audio controls. You know the basic VTR functions, so we address them only briefly. All VTRs (or VCRs), low-end or high-end, analog or digital, have these basic controls: the *play, stop, record, fast-forward, rewind,* and *eject* buttons and the audio volume controls. **SEE 12.7**

The more sophisticated VTRs have additional controls for these operations: standby, pause or still, search or shuttle, and audio level.

Standby   In the standby mode, the VTR threads the tape and rotates the video heads, but the tape remains stationary. The rotating video heads are disengaged and not in contact with the tape.

Pause or still   The pause control will stop the tape with the heads still moving. In this mode the rotating video heads are in contact with the tape and continuously scan

the adjacent video fields and produce a still—or freeze—frame on the video monitor or in the camera viewfinder. Do not keep a machine on pause for too long—the heads are apt to scrape the iron-oxide coating off of the tape and leave you with nothing but clogged heads and video noise on the monitor. Most VTRs switch off pause if the tape has had enough abuse. Even so, don't leave a tape too long in pause mode, especially if you want to use it for editing.

Search or shuttle   This control lets you advance or reverse the tape at speeds that may be much faster or slower than the normal record/play speed. The shuttle feature is especially important when searching for a particular shot or scene on the videotape. You can advance the tape frame-by-frame or rattle through a whole scene until you find the right picture. You can also slow down the shuttle enough to get a jogging effect, which shows a frame-by-frame advancement of the videotape. Some high-end recorders keep the original pitch of the recorded audio rather than raise it

**12.7 BASIC
VTR CONTROLS**
Standard VTR controls are
similar to those on a home
videocassette recorder.

Eject

Rewind

Play

Fast-forward

Stop

Record

to the infamous chipmunk voice at high-speed shuttle or lower it to angry growls at a low-speed shuttle.

Audio level   The main audio controls are the volume control and volume-unit (VU) monitoring for each audio channel. Some recorders have separate volume controls for sound recording and playback. The audio dub control lets you record sound information without erasing the pictures already recorded on the video track. Most professional analog VTRs allow to you choose between regular (analog) and hi-fi (digital) audio. Depending on how the sound on the videotape was recorded, you may have to switch to or from hi-fi audio. If the audio doesn't play back properly, try the other mode.

TIME BASE CORRECTOR AND FRAME STORE SYNCHRONIZER

One of the main problems of tape-based video recorders is that you may experience some picture breakup when playing back a tape that has been recorded on a different VTR. If the record and play machines are not perfectly aligned, if the edit points were not perfectly matched, or if you switch live from a remote source to a studio, you may experience a time base error, usually called a sync roll, which will show up as a glitch or a band that slowly moves up or down the screen, separating the upper and lower halves of the picture. **SEE 12.8** This is why all professional videotape recording employs additional stabilizing equipment: the time base corrector or the framestore synchronizer.

Time base corrector   The *time base corrector (TBC)* adjusts the scanning of the play VTR to the one that did the original recording. Such synchronization is especially

12.8 SYNC ROLL
The sync roll is caused by a time base error—a momentary picture breakup at the edit point or when two video sources that have different sync pulses are switched.

important in editing, where one or more source (or play) VTRs supplies the material to be edited, and another VTR (the record VTR) does the actual editing. The TBC makes sure that the scanning clocks of all VTRs are in step. It can be a stand-alone piece of equipment, but most high-end VTRs have a built-in TBC to prevent picture breakup and ensure jitter-free pictures.

Framestore synchronizer   This electronic marvel is an all-digital signal stabilizer that fulfills the same functions as the TBC and then some. The *framestore synchronizer* grabs each frame of the video signal, digitizes it, and stores it momentarily until its scanning is synchronized with the next good video frame it receives. It can be used to stabilize weak signals or signals that are temporarily interrupted. You may have seen a picture freeze momentarily when watching a live news report from a remote location. But how can a live picture freeze? Because the framestore synchronizer was doing its job. As you can see, in the digital age, even live events are temporarily recorded, however fleeting this recording may be.

TAPELESS VIDEO RECORDING

This overview looks at the recording features of hard drives, read/write optical discs, and flash memory devices.

HARD DRIVES

The most prominent hard drive used is the one in your computer. Even today's small laptops have hard drives with enough storage capacity for most simple editing jobs. But there are also specialized hard drives that serve specific recording functions.

Large-capacity hard disks   The simplest way to store and retrieve digital video and audio information for post-production editing is with large-capacity external hard disks. Accelerated hard-drive speeds and highly efficient compression techniques enable you to store hours of video and audio information and call up any frame in a fraction of a second. Unlike videotape, which inevitably degrades after repeated use, the hard disk has no such limitation—its data remains like new even after a great many recordings and erasures. **SEE 12.9**

Video servers   In the ongoing move to an entirely tapeless operation, many television stations use video servers, which are especially sturdy, large-capacity disk arrays that record, store, and play many hours of television programming. These servers function to serve many

12.9 DIGITAL STUDIO VIDEO RECORDER

This tapeless digital studio video recorder has a large-capacity hard drive and provides a wide range of analog and digital video and audio inputs and outputs.

12.10 VIDEO SERVER

The video server comprises large-capacity disk arrays that can store a great number of program segments. It can accommodate multiple users simultaneously.

clients simultaneously—in our case various departments in a television operation. During a news show, the server can be accessed by the technical director (TD) to play a specific news segment, but editors, writers, and producers may also work with the news material stored on them. A server can accommodate multiple users simultaneously and can multitask, meaning it can run more than one program at the same time. **SEE 12.10**

Portable hard drives   These small hard drives are usually built into the camcorder, but some can also be docked with ENG/EFP cameras. Still others can be clipped onto the video camera or belt and connected to the camcorder via FireWire. Such detachable hard drives are often called field packs. All such portable hard drives are rated in gigabytes of storage, and can hold several hours of SDTV, HDV, or HDTV footage.[2] Besides high-quality video, such hard drives can record time code and two- or four-channel audio. The FireWire and Ethernet connections are especially handy when transferring the video recording to the editing system. **SEE 12.11**

Some portable hard drives allow you to do editing in the field with an externally connected laptop—a big advantage in ENG. Some camcorders have a tape-based as well as a disk-based recording system. You can use both simultaneously for recording, or use the tape as a backup in case the hard drive crashes (which is rare).

Electronic still store systems   In effect a large slide collection that allows you to access any slide in a fraction of a second, the *electronic still store (ESS) system* can grab any frame or short clip from various video sources (camera, videotape, or computer) and store it in digital form on a hard disk. Although it used to be a stand-alone

2. Standard digital television, high-definition video, and high-definition television, respectively.

12.11 HARD DISK FIELD PACK

The 80 GB hard disk in this portable video recorder is capable of storing six hours of video and audio data in the DV (Digital Video) and HDTV formats.

piece of equipment that was dedicated to the storage of still frames, the still- and clip-store functions have largely been incorporated into the software of video switchers, servers, or high-capacity character and graphics generators.

READ/WRITE OPTICAL DISCS

There are a variety of read/write optical discs that can record and play back a great amount of digital information. The optical discs most often used for storing video are DVDs (digital versatile discs), although in the true spirit of needless competition, you now must have at least two DVD systems to play all three DVD formats: the standard DVD; the HD DVD, which is downward compatible with the standard DVD (it can play the standard DVD, but the standard DVD player can't play the HD DVD); and the Blu-ray system, which can play only its own Blu-ray discs. The table below describes the standards and the operational characteristics of each system. **SEE 12.12**

Some camcorders use read/write optical discs rather than hard disks as their recording media. The advantages of optical discs are that they are easy to store and they permit extremely fast access time. The disadvantage is that they must be handled very carefully. A single scratch can ruin two days' worth of shooting. Be especially careful with Blu-ray discs; they scratch rather easily despite their plastic coating.

FLASH MEMORY DEVICES

Flash memory devices, also called flash drives and memory cards (among other names), are solid-state digital storage media. They have become effective recording media for ENG/EFP camcorders. Their biggest advantage over hard drives and optical discs is that they have has no moving parts. Much like the memory card in a digital still camera, video flash drives can be used over and over again without any noticeable deterioration. Other advantages are that they are small and lightweight. Some can be inserted directly into the card slot of a laptop computer. The downside is that even the largest cards have a relatively limited storage capacity, especially when recording in high-definition. The real problem with using these cards is not technical but economical. When considering the cost per gigabyte of storage, the cards are outrageously expensive. **SEE 12.13**

12.12 DVD STANDARDS AND OPERATIONAL FEATURES

The maximum playing times are approximate. The capacities (in gigabytes) are given for single-side and double-side recording.

STANDARD	RECORDING	CAPACITY	VIDEO PLAY TIME (IN HOURS)
DVD*	Normally read-only	4.7 GB	3.8
HD DVD	Read and read/write	25 GB; 50 GB	8.5; 17
HDTV	Read and read/write	15 GB; 30 GB	5.1; 10.2
Blu-ray†	Normally read-only	50 GB	9 (HDTV); 23 (SDTV)

*DVD has stereo sound; HD DVD and HDTV have audio tracks for surround sound.
†New experimental Blu-ray discs can hold 200 GB or more.

12.13 PANASONIC P2 CARD RECORDING TIMES

This solid-state flash memory card can be extracted from the camcorder and plugged directly into a computer slot for non-linear editing. The data below show the approximate recording times for the normal 8 MB (megabyte) card as well as the 16 MB and 32 MB cards.

SIZE	RECORDING SYSTEM	RECORDING TIME (IN MINUTES)
8 MB	DVCPRO HD	8
	24p HD	20
	DVCPRO50	32
	DVCPRO	64
16 MB	DVCPRO HD	16
	24p HD	40
	DVCPRO50	64
	DVCPRO	128
32 MB	DVCPRO HD	32
	24p HD	80
	DVCPRO50	128
	DVCPRO	256

ELECTRONIC FEATURES OF VIDEO RECORDING

This discussion of electronic *video recorder (VR)* features concerns primarily the digital recorders and recording processes. If the material is getting a little too technical for your taste, at least try to remember its impact on video recording and editing. Nevertheless all this information is important if you aim to become a video professional or to hone the production skills you already possess. This section addresses composite and component signals, sampling, and compression.

COMPOSITE AND COMPONENT SIGNALS

Analog and digital recording systems can treat their video signals in one of four basic ways: composite, Y/C component, Y/color difference component, and RGB component. Video-recording systems that use composite signals throughout the recording process are not compatible with component systems; and video recording using a composite signal is not as good as one that uses a component signal.

Composite signal The *composite system* combines the color (C, or chrominance) and the brightness (Y, black-and-white, or luminance) information into a single—composite—signal. Only one wire is necessary to transport the composite signal. Because this electronic combination was standardized some time ago by the National Television System Committee (NTSC), the composite signal is also called the NTSC signal or, simply, NTSC. The NTSC system is different from other composite systems, such as the European PAL system. A standard conversion is necessary when systems don't match. Most such standard conversions are done in the satellite that distributes the signal.

The advantage of the composite signal is that it is one way of compressing an analog signal to save bandwidth in the signal transport, video recording, and signal transmission. The major disadvantage of the composite signal is that there is usually some interference between chrominance and luminance information that gets worse and therefore more noticeable with each videotape generation. **SEE 12.14**

Y/C component signal The advantage of the *Y/C component system* is that it produces higher-resolution pictures that will suffer less in subsequent tape generations than do composite tapes. In the Y/C system, also called S-video, the Y (black-and-white) signal and the C (color) signals are kept separate during signal encoding and transport but are combined and occupy the same track when actually laid down on the videotape. The Y/C configuration requires two wires to transport the Y/C component signal. **SEE 12.15**

To maintain the advantages of Y/C component recording, other equipment used in the system, such as monitors, must also keep the Y and C signals separate. This means that you cannot play a Y/C component videotape on a regular VHS recorder but only on an S-VHS recorder.

Y/color difference component signal In the *Y/color difference component system*, the luminance signal, the red signal minus its luminance (R–Y), and the blue signal minus its luminance (B–Y) are transported and recorded as three separate signals. The green signal is matrixed (regenerated) from these three signals. This signal, sometimes called the RGB signal, needs three wires to transport the three separate signals. **SEE 12.16**

RGB component signal In the true *RGB component system*, the red, green, and blue signals are kept sepa-

Composite NTSC signal

Chrominance (C) channel   Luminance (Y) channel

12.14 COMPOSITE SIGNAL
The composite system uses a video signal that combines the color (C, or chrominance) and the luminance (Y, or brightness) information. It needs a single wire to be transported and recorded on videotape as a single signal. It is the standard NTSC system.

12.15 Y/C COMPONENT SYSTEM
The Y/C component system separates the Y (luminance) and C (color) information during signal encoding and transport, but it combines the two signals on the videotape. It needs two wires to transport the separate signals.

12.16 Y/COLOR DIFFERENCE COMPONENT SYSTEM
The Y/color difference component system separates the three RGB signals throughout the recording process. It needs three wires to transport the three component signals: the Y (luminance) signal, the R–Y (red minus luminance) signal, and the B–Y (blue minus luminance) signal. The green signal is then matrixed (regenerated) from these signals.

rate and treated as separate components throughout the recording and storage process. Each of the three signals remains separate even when laid down on the videotape. This signal is actually the most desirable for maintaining video quality. When working with a true RGB component system for HDTV, however, it takes up so much bandwidth, storage space, and retrieval time that it is used only by very high-end recorders and editing and graphics systems. The Y/color difference signal was developed to overcome these problems. **SEE 12.17**

The Y/C, Y/color difference, and RGB component signals eventually must combine the separate parts into a single NTSC composite signal for traditional television broadcast and distribution.

SAMPLING
Although you learned in chapter 4 what sampling is all about, you still may wonder what video and digital cinema experts are talking about when they discuss the relative merits of 4:2:2 over 4:1:1 sampling in video recording.

Red (R)

Green (G)

Blue (B)

12.17 RGB COMPONENT SYSTEM

Like the Y/color difference system, the RGB component system (also called the RGB system) separates the three RGB signals throughout the recording process. It needs three wires to transport the signals. It provides the greatest color quality but takes up an inordinate amount of frequency space.

All that this means is that in the digitizing process, the C (color) signals are sampled less frequently than the Y (black-and-white) signal. In 4:2:2 sampling, the Y signal is sampled twice as often as the C signals. During every period that the Y signal is sampled four times, the C signals are sampled only twice. In a 4:1:1 sampling process, the Y signal is sampled four times, whereas the C signals are sampled only once. The luminance signal receives such privileged treatment because it is a major contributor to picture sharpness.

Most normal productions look stunning with 4:1:1 sampling. If, however, you require high-quality color that must withstand a variety of special effects, such as chroma-key effects (see chapter 13) or a great number of key layers, you will do well to use equipment that employs the higher 4:2:2 sampling ratio.

Here are the most important points to remember about these recording features:

■ The composite video signal of the NTSC composite system is of lower quality than that of the Y/C component system, which is somewhat inferior to the Y/color difference component system and the RGB component system.

■ A 4:2:2 sampling ratio produces better colors than does a 4:1:1 ratio, although the latter certainly produces great images. In fact, you would notice the difference between the two sampling ratios only when using or building complex effects or when trying to maintain color fidelity in extremely high-contrast video images.

COMPRESSION

All digital video pictures are compressed in one way or another. The specific *codec* (short for *compression/decompression*) system is often more important than the sampling ratio a camcorder uses. For example, a cell-phone video is much more compressed than that of a small HDTV camcorder. The less the images are compressed, the better they look.

As you recall from chapter 4, **compression** refers to the rearrangement or elimination of redundant picture information for more-efficient storage and signal transport. Lossless compression means that we rearrange the data so that they take up less space. This technique is similar to repacking a suitcase to make all the stuff fit into it. In lossy compression we throw away some of the unnecessary items and therefore can use a much smaller suitcase. Most codecs are of the lossy kind. The more relevant compression question, however, may well be whether a camcorder uses the intraframe or interframe compression system.

Understanding the difference between these two systems is important when you get to actual editing in the postproduction phase.

Intraframe compression   This compression system was designed primarily for still images but has been adapted to moving images. Intraframe compression looks at each frame and throws away all video information that is unnecessary to perceiving pretty much the same picture as the original. In technical terms it eliminates spatial redundancy for each frame.

Let's consider our overstuffed suitcases again. To save some space, we must look at each of the packed suitcases (each frame) and ask whether we can get along with two shirts instead of six; then we move to the other suitcase to see whether we can take out five of the six sweaters we packed, especially since we are going to go to a warm, sunny location. We continue to check each suitcase (frame) to see what we can leave behind. Pretty soon we will have discarded enough unnecessary clothing (redundant pixels) to get by with much smaller suitcases.

The **JPEG** system—a video compression method used mostly for still pictures—employs this intraframe compression technique. What we did was apply lossy compression to each frame—or, in our case, suitcase—one by one.

The big advantage of the intraframe codec is that each frame contains a usable picture. When editing you can choose any frame as the edit-in or edit-out point and all the ones in between. The initial disadvantage of this system was that repacking each of the suitcases (frames) took time, that is, it was too slow when capturing fast-moving objects; but this drawback has largely been eliminated in most intraframe codecs.

Interframe compression   This system was developed for moving images. Rather than compress each video frame independent of all the others, interframe compression looks for redundancies from one frame to the next in a motion sequence. Basically, the system compares each frame with the preceding and following ones and keeps only the pixels that constitute a change.

For example, if you see a cyclist moving against a cloudless blue sky, the system will not bother with repeating all the information that makes up the blue sky but only with the position change of the cyclist. As you can see, interframe compression looks for temporal redundancy (change from frame to frame) rather than spatial redundancy within a single frame.

Let's use the suitcase example one last time. We now have two people with suitcases. John has already packed his big suitcase, and Ellen is ready to begin packing. Before she starts, however, she checks with John to see what he has packed (full video frame 1). To her delight he has packed a lot of stuff she wanted to take along, so she needs to fit only a few more items into a very small suitcase (interframe-compressed frame 2). *MPEG-2*, the compression standard for motion video, uses the interframe technique. (*MPEG* stands for *Moving Picture Experts Group*.)

The problem with the interframe system is in editing. Because some of the compressed frames are incomplete, they can't be used as the start or end point of an edit. The system therefore periodically sends a full reference frame (say, every fifth or tenth frame), called an I-frame, that is compressed but, unlike the other frames, holds video information for a complete picture. Such I-frames are intraframe compressed and are therefore not influenced by the adjacent frames. Because an I-frame contains the information for a whole picture, an editor can go to the full frame to do the actual cut.

Being restricted to every fifth or tenth frame for a cut, however, does not please an editor who may need to match each frame of lip movement with the corresponding sound; but in most cases a five-frame cutting restriction is not too much of a handicap. This is why systems designed for editing include these reference I-frames as often as feasible. Some more-sophisticated MPEG-2 editing systems can recalculate a complete frame anywhere in the compressed video for critical frame-accurate editing.

The usual compression standard for streaming video is *MPEG-4*. As you know, *streaming* means sending and receiving digital video data as a continuous data flow that can be watched while the delivery is in progress. The more efficient the compression systems are, the faster and smoother the streaming process becomes.

Whatever the compression technique may be, you can always apply a simple compression/quality formula: *the less compression, the better the image quality*. But then there is another, not so happy formula: *the less compression, the more unwieldy the huge amount of information becomes*.

M A I N   P O I N T S

▶ There are two basic types of recording systems: tape-based and tapeless.

▶ Videotape can be used for recording analog or digital information.

▶ All analog recording systems use videotape as the recording media.

▶ Tapeless recording systems can record digital information only.

▶ Digital recordings are virtually immune to deterioration in subsequent dubs.

▶ During the recording, the videotape moves past one or more rotating heads that write video tracks on the tape as it passes. During playback the same or different heads read the video and audio information off the tape.

▶ The basic tracks on a videotape are the video track, two audio tracks, and the control track.

▶ The time base corrector (TBC) and the framestore synchronizer are electronic devices that help stabilize the playback of video recorders (VRs) and synchronize the scanning from remote sources.

▶ Tapeless video recording uses hard drives, read/write optical discs, and flash memory devices as the recording media.

▶ Video recorders can treat their signals in one of four basic ways: composite, Y/C component, Y/color difference component, and RGB component. The composite signal is called NTSC.

▶ The component signal is better than the composite one.

▶ Sampling concerns mainly color fidelity. A sampling ratio of 4:2:2 is slightly better than 4:1:1.

▶ Intraframe compression eliminates all redundant pixels in each video frame.

▶ Interframe compression eliminates redundant pixels from frame to frame.

12.2

How Video Recording Is Done

Now that you know all about video-recording systems, you need to know what to do with them. This section introduces you to the operational uses of video recording and the video-recording procedures in studio production and ENG/EFP.

▶ **USES OF VIDEO RECORDING AND STORAGE**
   Building a show, time delay, program duplication and distribution, and record protection and reference

▶ **VIDEO-RECORDING PRODUCTION FACTORS**
   Recording preparations (schedule and equipment checklist) and production (video leader, recording checks, time code, recordkeeping, and specific aspects of disk-based video recording)

USES OF VIDEO RECORDING AND STORAGE

Video recording is used primarily for building a show, time delay, program duplication and distribution, and the creation of a protection copy of a video recording for reference and study.

BUILDING A SHOW

One of the major uses of video recordings is to build a television show from previously recorded video segments. This construction process is done through postproduction

editing. It may include assembling multiple segments shot at different times and locations, or it may simply involve condensing a news story by cutting out the nonessential parts. It also includes stringing together longer multicamera scenes that were switched (instantaneously edited) and video recorded. A good example of this technique is the recording of relatively long and uninterrupted studio segments of soap operas and then editing them together for the program in a postproduction session.

TIME DELAY

Through video recording, an event can be stored and played back immediately or hours, days, or years after its occurrence. In sports many key plays are recorded and shown right after they occur. Because the playback of the recording happens so quickly after the actual event, they are called instant replays. Network shows that you can watch at the same schedule time in each time zone are time delayed through some type of video recording. For example, by recording in San Francisco a satellite feed at 3 p.m. (Pacific Standard Time, or PST) of an awards show that takes place at 6 p.m. (Eastern Standard Time, or EST) in New York, it can be played back and aired at 6 p.m. (PST) in San Francisco.

PROGRAM DUPLICATION AND DISTRIBUTION

Video recordings can be easily duplicated and distributed to television outlets by mail, courier, telephone line, coax or fiber-optic cable, satellite, or Internet streaming. With satellite or Internet streaming, a single video recording can be distributed simultaneously to multiple destinations around the world with minimal effort. Eventually, digital movies will be similarly distributed to movie houses by satellite or fiber-optic cable rather than by shipping the heavy 35mm film cans.

RECORD PROTECTION AND REFERENCE

To protect the recordings of important events, make protection copies of the original video recording. Make these dubs with equipment that has the same or a better recording quality as that which was used to shoot the original footage. DVDs are an excellent archival recording media. They take up very little space, and the playback equipment is readily available.

The problem with digital recordkeeping is the rapidly changing technology that makes one recording device obsolete in just a few years. You have probably run into this problem with playbacks of DVDs and Blu-ray discs or with the ever-changing systems software. Unless you transfer the digital records periodically to the latest system, your archives are worthless once the playback system becomes obsolete.

VIDEO-RECORDING PRODUCTION FACTORS

Unless you are chasing a hot news story, video recording needs careful preparation and attention to detail. An entire production can be lost if you as the video-record operator forget to push the right button during the recording process. You might do well to follow some checklists for the recording preparation and the actual recording activities.

RECORDING PREPARATIONS

When doing video recordings of a studio show, the wrong cable, connector, or videocassette is no great disaster. But when you are out in the field, a wrong cable or connector may cancel the entire EFP. Let's take a brief look at scheduling, the equipment checklist, and general recording preparations.

Schedule   Double-check that the equipment you need for the recording or dubbing is actually available. Have a backup recorder standing by in case somebody is using "your" (scheduled) machine. Be reasonable in your request. You will find that recording equipment is usually available for the actual studio or field production but not always for your playback demands.

If you are asked to simply check the order of the scenes on a videotape recording or to time some segments, dub the material down to a regular ½-inch VHS format or a DVD so that you can watch the material at home. That way you free up the high-quality machines for more important tasks, and you are not tied to a precise schedule when reviewing the recordings. Once the source footage is in the computer, you can dub it to your notebook and watch it while riding the bus.

Always follow the established routine for equipment checkout and use. If you don't, you not only jeopardize your recording session but possibly some other people's as well. When sharing a server, do you know how to access the material? What are the established safeguards from accidental erasure?

Equipment checklist   Like a pilot who goes through a checklist before every flight, you should have your own

equipment checklist every time you do a production. Such a list is especially important in field productions. This brief checklist is limited to video recording.

■ *Dubbing.* When dubbing you need two recorders: the source machine and the record machine. Try not to use the camcorder as the play VTR. The VTR mechanism in a camcorder is not as rugged as that of a studio VTR.

■ *Correct recorder.* Does the video recorder match the media used in the camcorder? If the camcorder used an optical disc for recording, you obviously can't play it back on a VTR. As obvious as this example is, you may find that some digital VTRs do not have provisions for playing mini-cassettes.

■ *Combine jobs.* Can you combine certain recording jobs, such as doing a window-dub when making a protection copy of the original recording? (As you will read in chapter 19, a window dub is a copy of the recording with the time code address keyed over each frame.)

■ *Video recorder status.* Does the VTR or other recorder actually work? If possible, do a brief test recording to ensure that it functions properly.

■ *Power supply.* Do you have a fully charged battery for the camcorder and/or the external video recorder? Always take an extra fully charged battery along. When using household current for the power supply, you need the appropriate transformer/adapter. Before leaving for the field location, check that the connecting cable from the power supply fits the jack on the video recorder or camcorder. Do not try to make a connector fit if it is not designed for that jack. You may blow more than a fuse if you do.

■ *Correct recording media.* Do you have the correct recording media, that is, the videocassette, disc, or flash drive that fits the camcorder or external VR? Also check that the boxes contain the correct media. Because even same-size cassettes can be loaded with different lengths of tape, check the supply reel to see that it contains the amount of tape indicated on the label. If, for example, the box says that it contains a 184-minute tape but your check shows only a relatively small amount of tape on the supply reel, the box is obviously mislabeled.

■ *Enough media.* Do you have enough recording media for the proposed production? This is especially important when you record HDV or HDTV. High-definition data take up much more storage space than is advertised on the

12.18 DIGITAL VIDEOCASSETTE IN RECORD-PROTECT POSITION
Digital videocassettes have a movable tab that prevents accidental erasure. To record on the cassette, the tab must be in the closed position.

Tab in open, record-protect position

box (which usually shows the recording time for standard digital video).

If the largest media does not hold enough data for the entire event, you need to schedule two machines or you will lose a few minutes during the media change. Especially when doing multiple recordings for instant replay, you need three or four times the normal storage capacity. Always take along more recording media than you think you'll need.

■ *Record protection.* If a VTR refuses to record despite a careful check of the connecting cables, remove the cassette to see whether its recording is enabled. All cassettes have a device, sometimes called the record inhibitor, to protect the videotape from accidental erasure. VHS and S-VHS ½-inch cassettes have a record-protect tab on the back edge at the lower left. When this tab is broken off, the cassette is record-protected. You can enable the cassette again by putting a piece of masking tape or even gaffer's tape over the tab opening. Digital videocassettes have a tab on the back edge that you can move into or out of a record-protect position. If it is in the open position, you cannot record on the cassette. On some cassettes this tab is colored so that you can easily see whether it is in the closed (recording OK) or open (no recording) position. **SEE 12.18**

Routinely check the record-protect tab before using a cassette for recording. Although you cannot record on a record-protected tape, any cassette will play back with or without a record-protect device in place.

PRODUCTION

If you have followed the basic preproduction steps, you should have little trouble during the actual recording, although the following elements still need attention: video leader, recording checks, time code, recordkeeping, and specific aspects of disk-based video recording.

Video leader   When playing back a properly executed video recording, you will notice some front matter at the head of the recording: color bars, a steady tone, an identification slate, and perhaps some numbers flashing by with accompanying audio beeps. These elements, collectively called the *video leader*, help adjust the playback and record machines to standard audio and video levels. Let us look at them one by one. **SEE 12.19** **ZVL2** EDITING→ Postproduction guidelines→ leader

Color bars help the video-record operator match the colors of the playback machine with those of the record machine. It is therefore important that you record the color bars (fed by color-bar generators located in master control or built into ENG/EFP cameras) for a minimum of 30 seconds each time you use a new recording media or begin a new taping session. Some VOs (video operators) prefer to have the color bars run for a full minute or more so that they do not have to rerun the bars if the equipment requires further adjustment; but this may be overdoing it, especially if you have to listen to the test tone for a whole minute.

Most audio consoles and even some field mixers can generate the test tone that you need in calibrating the line-out level of the audio console or mixer with the input (record) level of the video recorder (see chapter 9). You should record this test tone along with the color bars. Obviously, these test signals should be recorded with the equipment that you use for the subsequent video recording; otherwise

12.19 VIDEO LEADER
The video leader helps adjust the playback and record machines to standard audio and video levels.

the playback will be referenced to the recorded color bars and test tone but not to the video-recorded material. The director refers to these test signals as "bars and tone." When doing a studio show, you will hear the director call for bars and tone right after the video recorder has stabilized. In EFP the camera or VTR operator will take care of this reference recording.

The slate and the clapboard give pertinent production information along with some technical details. Normally, the slate indicates the following identification data:

■ Show title and scene number (corresponding to that in the script)

■ Take number (how often you record the same thing)

■ Recording date

Some slates also list the director, the location (especially for EFP), and additional in-house information, such as "reel" numbers (number of the specific media used), editing instructions, name of producer, and so on. The essential information is the name of the show and the scene and take numbers.

You should use the clapboard rather than the slate when video/audio synchronization is a crucial postproduc-

tion element. It is used much like the slate, except that the clapboard is recorded until the floor manager has snapped the clapstick. This way you get a visual marker (the frame where the clapstick meets the board) and an audio marker (the clap) in a single frame. This frame gives the editor a reference point for lining up the slate frame with the audio clap on the visual waveform for exact video/audio synchronization. This frame is also a starting point for the time code if it has to be laid down in postproduction. **SEE 12.20**

In the studio the slate is usually generated by the character generator (C.G.) and recorded right after the color bars. **SEE 12.21** In the absence of a C.G., you can use a small whiteboard with a 4 × 3 or 16 × 9 aspect ratio. Because the information on the slate changes from take to take, the slate surface should be easily cleaned (chalk or dry-erase markers work well). The slate identifies the scene as well as the take, so you must use it every time you record a new take, regardless of how short or how complete the take may be. **ZVL3** EDITING→ Production guidelines→ slate

Assume that you are the director of the weekly *President's Chat* production. You have just videotape-recorded about 10 seconds of the first take when the college president stumbles over the name of the new dean. You stop the tape, keep calm, roll the tape again, and wait for the "in-record"

12.20 CLAPBOARD
The clapboard is used to identify the scene and take numbers and to help synchronize video and audio.

12.21 CHARACTER-GENERATED SLATE
The electronic slate gives pertinent information about the production. It is recorded at the beginning of each take.

Title: **The Chinook Challenge**
Director: **Dan Kahane**
Date: **21 February**
Scene: **6**   Take: **3**

confirmation from the VTR operator. Before repeating the president's introduction, you need to record the slate again. It reads: scene 1, take 1. But shouldn't the slate read: scene 1, take 2? Yes—the C.G. operator obviously forgot to change the slate. Should you go on, or stop the tape again to correct the slate? In this case you might as well keep going. The VTR operator, who keeps the field log, can note the false 10-second start and record the second take as take 1. If, however, you are breaking up the president's "chat" into several short takes to be assembled in postproduction, the slate numbers must be accurate.

Leader numbers are used for the accurate cueing of the videotape during playback. The leader numbers flash at 1-second intervals from 10 to 3 or from 5 to 3 and are

usually synchronized with short audio beeps. The last two seconds are normally kept in black and silent so that they do not accidentally appear on the air if the videotape is punched up early (sometimes the numbers and beeps go down to the last second). The first frame of recorded program material should appear at the zero countdown.

When cueing a videotape for playback, you can stop the tape at a particular leader number, say, 4; or you can advance the tape right to the first video frame. When you stop the tape at leader number 4, you must preroll the tape exactly 4 seconds before the program material is to appear on the air. If, after starting the tape on leader number 4, there is a longer interval between the last leader number 3 (and two seconds of black and silence) and the first video frame, the TD will not know exactly when to punch up the videotape and almost certainly will miss the first second of the playback. If you start the tape on leader number 4, the first video frame should come up after exactly 4 seconds.

When all the footage is on a video server, you can use the leader numbers for cueing the segment right to the first frame. One of the big advantages of using a server over a VTR is that it has an instant start without any video or audio breakup or distortion.

Recording checks   As the video-record operator, you are responsible for seeing that the pictures and the sound are actually recorded. Here are some checkpoints that greatly reduce recording problems.

■ Always do a brief test recording, then play back the tape to ensure that the whole system works properly. Just because you see a picture on the video-record monitor and see the VU meter fluctuate during the test recording, it does not mean that the video and audio signals are actually being recorded. But once the test recording plays back all right, you can trust that the subsequent video and audio feeds will be recorded.

■ Reset the tape counter on the VTR or tapeless VR before starting the actual program recording. If you need to record time code at the actual videotaping, make sure it is recorded with the picture.

■ When using a VTR, wait until the machine has reached operating speed and has stabilized before starting to record. This lockup time may take anywhere from one to four seconds. The VTR has a control light that flashes during the lockup period and remains steady once the system is locked, that is, sufficiently stabilized for recording. As the VTR operator, you should watch the flashing light and, when you see a steady light, call out, "speed" or "in record." The director will then proceed with the actual recording.

■ Watch the audio and video levels during the recording. If you do not have a separate audio setup but instead feed the mic directly to the video recorder, pay particular attention to the audio portion. You may find that some directors become so captivated by the beautiful camera shots that they don't not even hear, for example, the talent giving an African country the wrong name, an airplane noise interrupting the medieval scene shot on-location, or the wireless mic cutting out briefly during an especially moving moment of a song.

■ If you are using an external video recorder in the field, always monitor the audio by wearing headphones.

■ When recording for postproduction, record enough of each segment so that the action overlaps the preceding and following scenes. At the end of each take, record a few seconds of black before stopping the tape. This run-out signal acts as a pad and greatly facilitates editing.

■ Ask the director whether you should video-record the camera rehearsals. Sometimes you get a better performance during rehearsal than during the actual take. The camera rehearsals (when run like full dress rehearsal) can then be edited into the rest of the production.

■ Again, be sure to slate every take, rehearsal or not. When you are in a hurry, audio-slate each take by having the audio operator use the console mic. When in the field, have the floor manager read the brief slate information into the talent's lavalier or fishpole shotgun mic: "President's Chat, take 7." Some directors like an additional brief verbal countdown, such as "five, four, three" with the last two seconds silent before the cue to the talent. Many field productions are slated more extensively only at the beginning of the video recording, with subsequent takes being only verbally slated.

■ Do not waste time between takes. If you are properly prepared, you can keep the intervals to a minimum. Although the playback of each take may occasionally improve the subsequent performance by cast and crew, it often does not justify the time it takes away from the actual production. If you pay close attention during the video-recording, you do not need to review each take. Long interruptions not only waste time but also lower the energy level of the production team and the talent. On the other hand, do not rush through taping sessions at a frenetic pace. If you feel that another take is warranted, do it right then and there. It is far less expensive and time-consuming to repeat a take immediately than to re-create a whole scene later simply because one take turned out to be unusable.

Time code   If you need to record time code simultaneously with each take, verify that the time code is recorded on its designated address track or, if necessary, on a free audio track (but make sure that the audio track is not already used for recording actual audio information). Unless the camera or video recorder has a built-in time code generator, you need a separate time code generator for the address system. Time code can also be laid down later in postproduction (as explained in chapter 19). **ZVL4** ▶EDIT-ING→ Postproduction guidelines→ time code

12.22 FIELD LOG

The field log is kept by the video-record operator during the recording. It normally indicates the media (tape) or reel number, scene and take numbers, approximately where the take is located on the tape, and other information useful in postproduction editing.

CASSETTE NUMBER	SCENE	TAKE	OK or NO GOOD	TIME CODE IN	TIME CODE OUT	EVENT / REMARKS
PRODUCTION TITLE: "impressions"				PRODUCER/DIRECTOR: Hamid Khani		
TAPING DATE: 4/15				LOCATION: BECA Newsroom		
C-005	2	1	NG	01:57:25	02:07:24	Student looks into Camera CU - Z-axis
		(2)	OK	02:09:04	02:14:27	monitor + L news anchor MS getting ready
		(3)	OK	02:14:28	02:34:22	Pan R to reveal anchor in news set
		4	NG	02:34:22	02:45:18	Rack focus from Floor Mgr to L anchor · OUT OF FOCUS
		5	NG	02:48:05	02:55:12	Rack focus Both out of focus
		6	NG	02:58:13	03:05:11	Rack OK LOST Audio
		(7)	OK	03:12:02	03:46:24	Hurrah! Rack OK
	3	(1)	OK	04:16:03	04:28:11	MS Floor Mgr + Camera op from behind
		2	NG	04:35:13	04:49:05	CU of R anchor Lost audio
		(3)	OK	05:50:00	06:01:24	CU of R anchor
		4	NG	06:03:10	06:30:17	CU of L anchor audio problem
		5	NG	06:40:07	07:04:08	LS of both anchors Floor Mgr walks through shot
		(6)	OK	07:07:15	07:28:05	Good! Floor Mgr silhouette against set
		(7)	OK	07:30:29	07:45:12	slow pullout
C-006	4	(1)	OK	49:48:28	51:12:08	MCU Marty talks to anchors
		2	NG	51:35:17	51:42:01	Lav comes off R anchor

Recordkeeping Keeping accurate records of what you video-record and the proper labeling of the recording media may seem insignificant while in the middle of a production, but they are critical when you want to locate a particular scene or a specific tape or disc. You will be surprised at how quickly you can forget the "unforgettable" scene and especially the number and the sequence of takes.

Keeping accurate records during the video recording saves much time in postproduction editing. Although you will most likely log the various takes and scenes when reviewing the video recording after the production, you are still greatly aided by a rough record kept during the production, called a *field log*. As a video-record operator, you should keep a field log even when recording in the studio. A field log is especially useful in more-complex field productions (hence its name) that involve a number of locations. Mark the good takes (usually with a circle) and identify especially those takes that seem unusable at that time. Label each recording media and its box, and mark the field log with the corresponding information. SEE 12.22 **ZVL5** EDITING→ Production guidelines→ field log

Specific aspects of disk-based video recording The preproduction and production elements discussed here apply equally whether you record with an analog or a digital VTR or some tapeless recording device. There are, of course, some different production requirements when you use the disk-based system for editing, which is the subject of chapter 20.

MAIN POINTS

▶ Video recording is used primarily for building a whole show by assembling parts that have been recorded at different times and/or locations; for time delay; for program duplication and distribution; and for records for protection, reference, and study.

▶ The production purpose should determine the type of video recorder (VR) used. Simple material destined for home consumption does not need a top-of-the-line video recorder.

▶ The important preproduction steps for video recording include scheduling, equipment checklists, and specific edit preparations. Take along enough recording media and be sure that it fits the camcorder or separate recording device. Check that the record-protect tab is in the closed (record) position.

▶ The major production factors in video recording are the video leader (color bars, test tone, slate information, and leader numbers and beeps), recording checks, time code, recordkeeping, and specific aspects of disk-based video recording.

▶ Slate all takes, either visually and/or verbally.

▶ The field log is kept during the actual studio or field production. It lists all media numbers, scenes, takes, and comments about shots and audio.

ZETTL'S VIDEOLAB

For your reference or to track your work, the *Zettl's VideoLab* program cues in this chapter are listed here with their corresponding page numbers.

ZVL1 EDITING→ Postproduction guidelines→ tape basics   **250**

ZVL2 EDITING→ Postproduction guidelines→ leader   **262**

ZVL3 EDITING→ Production guidelines→ slate   **263**

ZVL4 EDITING→ Postproduction guidelines→ time code   **265**

ZVL5 EDITING→ Production guidelines→ field log   **266**

13

Switching, or Instantaneous Editing

When watching a television director during a live multicamera show, such as a newscast or a basketball game, you might be surprised to find that the primary activity of the director is not telling the camerapersons what to do but rather selecting the most effective shots from the variety of video sources displayed on a row of preview monitors. In fact, the director is engaged in a sort of editing, except that it's the selection of shots *during* rather than after the production. Cutting from one video source to another or calling for other transitions, such as dissolves, wipes, and fades, while a show is in progress is known as ***switching*** or instantaneous editing.

Unlike postproduction editing, in which you have the time to deliberate exactly which shots and transitions to use, switching demands snap decisions. Although the aesthetic principles of switching are identical to those used in postproduction, the technology involved is quite different. Instead of linear and nonlinear editing systems, the major editing tool is the video switcher or a computer that performs the switcher functions.

Section 13.1, How Switchers Work, acquaints you with the basic functions, layout, and operation of a production switcher in a television control room. Section 13.2, Electronic Effects and Switcher Functions, looks at standard and digital video effects and additional switcher functions.

auto-transition An electronic device that functions like a fader bar.

bus A row of buttons on the switcher.

character generator (C.G.) A dedicated computer system that electronically produces a series of letters, numbers, and simple graphic images for video display. Any desktop computer can become a C.G. with the appropriate software.

chroma keying Effect that uses color (usually blue or green) for the backdrop, which is replaced by the background image during a key.

delegation controls Buttons on the switcher that assign specific functions to a bus.

digital video effects (DVE) Visual effects generated by a computer or digital effects equipment in the switcher.

downstream keyer (DSK) A control that allows a title to be keyed (cut in) over the picture (line-out signal) as it leaves the switcher.

effects buses Program and preview buses on the switcher, assigned to perform effects transitions.

fader bar A lever on the switcher that activates preset transitions, such as dissolves, fades, and wipes, at different speeds. It is also used to create superimpositions.

genlock The synchronization of two or more video sources (such as cameras and video recorders) or origination sources (such as studio and remote) to prevent picture breakup during switching. A house sync will synchronize all video sources in a studio.

key An electronic effect. *Keying* means cutting with an electronic signal one image (usually lettering) into a different background image.

key bus A row of buttons on the switcher, used to select the video source to be inserted into a background image.

key-level control Switcher control that adjusts the key signal so that the title to be keyed appears sharp and clear. Also called *clip control* and *clipper*.

layering Combining two or more key effects for a more complex effect.

matte key Keyed (electronically cut-in) title whose letters are filled with shades of gray or a specific color.

M/E bus Short for *mix/effects bus.* A row of buttons on the switcher that can serve a mix or an effects function.

mix bus Rows of buttons on the switcher that permit the mixing of video sources, as in a dissolve or super.

preview/preset bus Rows of buttons on the switcher used to select the upcoming video (preset function) and route it to the preview monitor (preview function) independent of the line-out video. Also called *preset/background bus.*

program bus The bus on a switcher whose inputs are directly switched to the line-out. Also allows cuts-only switching. Also called *direct bus* and *program/background bus.*

special-effects generator (SEG) An image generator built into the switcher that produces special-effects wipe patterns and keys.

super Short for *superimposition.* A double exposure of two images, with the top one letting the bottom one show through.

switching A change from one video source to another during a show or show segment with the aid of a switcher. Also called *instantaneous editing.*

wipe Transition in which a second image, framed in some geometric shape, gradually replaces all or part of the first image.

13.1

How Switchers Work

When you look at a large production switcher with all the different-colored rows of buttons and the various levers, you may feel as intimidated as when looking into the cockpit of an airliner. But once you understand the basic principles and functions of a switcher, you can learn to operate it faster than running a new computer program. Even the most elaborate digital video-switching system performs the same basic functions as a simple production switcher, except that large switchers have more video inputs and can perform more visual tricks.

This section explores what a production switcher does and how it works.

▶ **BASIC SWITCHER FUNCTIONS**

Monitor display, selecting video sources, performing transitions between them, and creating special effects

▶ **SIMPLE SWITCHER LAYOUT**

Program bus, mix buses, preview bus, effects buses, multifunction switchers, additional switcher controls, and large production switchers

▶ **OTHER SWITCHERS**

Portable switchers, switching software, routing switchers, master control switchers, and genlock

BASIC SWITCHER FUNCTIONS

There are three basic functions of a production switcher: to select an appropriate video source from several inputs, to perform basic transitions between two video sources, and to create or access special effects. Some switchers can automatically switch the program audio with the video.

Each video input on a switcher has a corresponding button. If you have only two cameras and all you want to do is cut from one to the other, two buttons (one for camera 1 and the other for camera 2) are sufficient. By pressing the camera 1 button, you put camera 1 "on the air," that is, route its video to the line-out, which carries it to the video recorder or transmitter. Pressing the camera 2 button will put camera 2 on the air. What if you wanted to expand your switching to include a video recorder, a character generator (C.G.), and a remote feed? You would need three additional buttons—one for the video recorder, one for the C.G., and one for the remote feed. When you want the screen in black before switching to one of the video sources and then to go to black again at the end of the show, you need an additional *BLK* (black) button. The row of buttons, called a **bus**, has increased to six inputs. Production switchers have not only many more buttons but several buses as well. Let's find out why. **ZVL1** SWITCHING→ Switching functions→ select | connect

MONITOR DISPLAY

If you are to select among various video sources, wouldn't you have to see all of them before making your choice? Yes, and this is why a switcher is usually located in front of a monitor bank or a divided monitor panel much like the screen on your laptop computer. **SEE 13.1** As you can see, in this control room of a remote truck, there are preview monitors for all kinds of inputs, from multiple cameras to a variety of special effects. There are three larger monitors in the middle of the display: one for presetting effects (such as titles and split screens), another for previewing the upcoming shot, and the third—the line or program monitor—that shows the pictures going out on the air and/or to a video recorder.

SIMPLE SWITCHER LAYOUT

It may be easier to understand the parts of a switcher by constructing one that fulfills the basic switcher functions:

13.1 MONITOR BANK
This monitor bank, located in a large remote truck, shows preview monitors of a great variety of video sources. Note the larger preview, preset, and program (line) monitors. The switcher is located below the monitor bank. In a production the director and the technical director (TD) sit side by side.

cuts, dissolves, supers, and fades.[1] This switcher should also let you see the selected video inputs or effects before you punch them up on the air. While building a switcher, you will realize that even a simple switcher can get quite complicated and that we need to combine several functions to keep it manageable.

PROGRAM BUS

If all you wanted to do was cut (switch instantaneously) from one video source to another without previewing them, you could do it with a single row of buttons, each one representing a different video input. **SEE 13.2** This row of buttons, which sends everything you punch up directly to the line-out (and from there to the video recorder or transmitter), is called the *program bus*. Also called program/background bus, the program bus represents, in effect, a

selector switch for the line-out. It is a direct input/output link and is therefore also called the direct bus. Note that there is an additional button at the beginning of the program bus, labeled *BLK* or *BLACK*. Instead of calling up a specific picture, the *BLK* button puts the screen to black.

MIX BUSES

If you want the switcher to do dissolves (during which one image gradually replaces the other through a temporary double exposure), supers (a double exposure of two images, with the top one letting the bottom one show through), and fades (the gradual appearance of an image from black or disappearance to black) in addition to simple cuts, you need two more buses—the *mix buses*—and a lever, called the *fader bar*, that controls the speed of the mix (dissolves and fades) and the nature of the super. **SEE 13.3**

When moving the fader bar to the full extent of travel, the picture of one bus is faded in while the picture of the other bus is faded out. The actual dissolve happens when the video images of the two buses temporarily mix. When

---

1. See Stuart W. Hyde, *Television and Radio Announcing,* 4th ed. (Boston: Houghton Mifflin, 1983), pp. 226–35. He explains the workings of an audio console by building one. I am using his construction metaphor with his permission.

13.2 PROGRAM BUS

This switcher has six video inputs: black, camera 1, camera 2, video recorder, character generator, and remote feed. Whatever source is punched up on the program bus (camera 1) goes directly to the line-out.

13.3 PROGRAM BUS WITH MIX BUSES AND FADER BAR

The mix buses A and B enable the mixing of two video sources.

you stop the fader bar somewhat in the middle, you arrest the dissolve and create a superimposition of the two video sources.

How does the program bus get this "mix" to the line-out? You must add still another button to the program bus that can transfer to the line-out the video generated by the mix buses. This *MIX* button is at the far right of the program bus.

PREVIEW BUS

The preview bus is identical to the program bus in the number, type, and arrangement of buttons. The functions of the buttons are also similar, except that the "line-out" of the preview bus does not go on the air or to a recording device but simply to a preview (P/V) monitor. If, for example, you press the camera 2 *(C-2)* button on the preview bus, camera 2's picture appears on the preview monitor without affecting the output of the program bus, such as the *C-1* button in figure 13.2. If you don't like camera 2's picture and want to switch to what the video recorder is showing, you simply press the *VR* button on the preview bus. The preview bus is also called the preset bus if it also functions as a monitor that shows preset effects.

The preview and line monitors are usually side-by-side to show whether two succeeding shots will cut together well, that is, preserve vector continuity and mental map positions (see chapter 20).

As you can see, our simple switcher has grown to 26 buttons, arranged in four buses, and has a fader bar added. **SEE 13.4**

13.4 BASIC SWITCHER LAYOUT

This basic production switcher has a preview bus, two mix buses, and a program bus. Note that the preview bus is identical to the program bus except that its output is routed to the preview monitor rather than to the line-out.

EFFECTS BUSES

If you now wanted your switcher to perform some special effects, such as wipes (one image framed in a geometrical shape gradually replacing the other), *keys* (lettering or an image inserted into a different background picture), and other image manipulations (shape and/or color transformations), the basic design would have to include at least two or more *effects buses* and one additional fader bar. You would probably then want to expand the other video inputs to accommodate several more cameras, two or three video recorders (VRs), electronic still store (ESS) and clip store functions, and remote feeds. In no time your switcher would have so many buttons and levers that operating them would require roller skates to get to all of them in a hurry.

MULTIFUNCTION SWITCHERS

To keep switchers manageable, manufacturers have designed buses that perform multiple functions. Rather than have separate program, mix, effects, and preview buses, you can assign a minimum of buses various mix/effects (M/E) functions. When you assign two such *M/E buses* (A and B) to the mix mode, you can dissolve from A to B or even do a super (by stopping the dissolve midway). By assigning them to the effects mode, you can achieve special effects, such as wipes from A to B. You can even assign the program and preview buses various M/E functions while still preserving their original functions. The buttons with which you delegate what a bus is to do are, logically enough,

called *delegation controls*. The following discussion identifies the different buses and how they interact on a simple multifunction switcher. **SEE 13.5**

Major buses   The switcher in figure 13.5 (Grass Valley 100)[2] has only three buses: a preview/preset bus (lower row of buttons), a program bus (middle row), and a key bus (upper row). It also has a number of button groups that let you create certain effects.

Let's briefly review the functions of the buses. The program bus always directs its output to the line-out. If you don't need to preview the upcoming pictures and your switching is "cuts-only," you can do it all on the program bus. **SEE 13.6** When assigned a mix or an effects function, however, it becomes one of the two M/E buses—in this case M/E bus A.

The *preview/preset bus* (also called preset/background bus) lets you preview the video source that you selected as your next shot. Whenever you press the corresponding button on the preview bus, the selected shot will automatically appear on the preview/preset monitor. But this preview bus can also function as the second M/E bus—on

---

2. The Grass Valley (GV) 100 switcher is a classic that you still find in many smaller professional and educational television studios. Although more-modern digital switchers have greater effects capabilities (which allow the layering of effects through multiple keys, a high-capacity effects memory, and two or more downstream channels to provide separate video feeds), they still operate on the principal M/E architecture of the GV 100.

Joystick

Key controls

Soft wipe

Black buttons

Key bus

Program bus
(M/E bus A)

Preset/preview
bus (M/E bus B)

Wipe selectors

Color background controls

Auto transition rate

Clipper

Downstream keyer

Delegation
controls

DSK fade-to-
black button

Fader bar

Cut button

Auto-transition button

13.5 MULTIFUNCTION SWITCHER
This multifunction switcher (Grass Valley 100) has only three buses: a preview/preset bus, a program bus, and a key bus. You can delegate M/E functions to the program and preview/preset buses.

Program bus | BLK | C-1 | C-2 | VR | CG | REM | *"Take one."*

Program bus | BLK | C-1 | C-2 | VR | CG | REM | *"Take two."*

13.6 SWITCHING ON THE PROGRAM BUS
When switching on the program bus, the transitions will be cuts-only. With camera 1 on the air, you can cut to camera 2 by pressing the *C-2* button.

13.7 DELEGATION CONTROLS

The delegation controls assign the function of the buses and the specific transition mode.

our switcher, M/E bus B. As soon as you activate a certain transition (cut, dissolve, or wipe), this preview picture will replace the on-the-air picture as shown on the line monitor. Despite its dual function, this bus is generally known as the preview bus.

Complicating the terminology a little more, both the program and the preview/preset buses are sometimes called "background" buses because they can serve as background for special effects, such as a title key.

The third (top) row of buttons is the *key bus*. It lets you select the video source, such as lettering supplied by the C.G., to be inserted into the background image, supplied by the program bus. **ZVL2** SWITCHING→ Architecture→ program bus | preview bus | mix buses | fader bar automatic transition | try it

Delegation controls   These controls let you choose a transition or an effect. On this multifunction switcher, they are located to the immediate left of the fader bar. **SEE 13.7**

By pressing the background button (*BKGD*), you activate the program and preview/preset (A and B) buses for cuts-only switching. Whatever you punch up on the program bus (A) will go on the air and, therefore, show up on the line monitor. Whatever you press on the preview/preset bus (B) will show up on the preview monitor, ready to replace—through a cut—the picture from bus A currently on the air. To perform the actual cut from the line picture (on the air) to the new picture selected on the preview bus, you need to press the red *CUT* button. If you press the *CUT* button repeatedly, it will toggle from preview to program and back. This is especially important when switching from one person to another in a fast dialogue. **SEE 13.8 AND 13.9**

By additionally pressing the red *MIX* button in the delegation controls section of the switcher, you expand the

13.8 DUAL FUNCTION OF PROGRAM AND PRESET BUSES

When delegated a background and mix function, the program bus becomes M/E bus A and the preview/preset bus becomes M/E bus B. Here camera 1 is punched up on bus A and is on the air. Camera 2 is preset to replace camera 1 as soon as you press the *CUT* button.

13.9 IMAGE CHANGE AFTER CUT
When the cut is completed, the program bus shows camera 2 on the air, and the preview/preset bus switches automatically to camera 1.

transitions from cuts-only to include dissolves as well. You can now cut from one video source to another or dissolve between them. **SEE 13.10** When you press the red *WIPE* button instead of the *MIX* button, the transition will be a wipe instead of a dissolve.

Fading from black or to black is actually dissolving from black to a picture or from a picture to black. Instead of choosing an actual image on the preview bus, you choose the *BLK* button. **SEE 13.11**

By pressing the *KEY* button, you activate the top (key) bus. On this bus you can select a proper key source, such as the C.G., that is to be inserted into the background picture currently activated on the program bus (A) and therefore on the air.

The advantage of a multifunction switcher is that you can achieve all these effects with only three buses. If you had continued the architecture—the electronic design logic—of the switcher we were building, you would have needed at least five buses, two fader bars, and several additional buttons to achieve the same key effect. **ZVL3** SWITCH-ING→ Switching functions→ transitions | create effects

ADDITIONAL SWITCHER CONTROLS
Now that you are familiar with the basic switcher controls, there are a few more you need to know: auto-transition, wipe controls and wipe patterns, key and key-level controls, the downstream keyer, and color background controls.

At this point don't worry about exactly how these controls are operated. Although all professional production switchers have these additional controls, they often require different means of operation. To become efficient in using a particular switcher, you need to study its opera-

tions manual and, above all, practice, as you would when learning to play a musical instrument.

Realize that these controls do not by themselves create the effect; rather, it is the special-effects generator (SEG) that performs this task. (We discuss special effects in section 13.2.) All production switchers have a built-in SEG. In fact, you will find that the manufacturers of most digital production switchers pride themselves not so much on operational ease but on the many visual tricks their SEGs can perform. The buzzword is **layering**, which means combining several key effects into a more complex one. **ZVL4** SWITCHING→ Transitions→ cut | mix/dissolve | wipe | fade | try it

Auto-transition   The *auto-transition* is an automated fader bar. Instead of your moving the fader bar toward and away from you, the auto-transition control does it automatically. Such a device is especially useful if you must time each dissolve or wipe exactly the same. You can set the number of frames to establish the rate of the transition. With 30 frames per second, a 60-frame setting will give you a two-second (rather slow) dissolve. On our switcher (figure 13.5), the auto-transition control is in the upper-right corner, set at 30, which means a one-second transition. To activate the transition, you press the *AUTO TRANS* button next to the *CUT* button.

Wipe controls and wipe patterns   When pressing the *WIPE* button in the delegation controls section in addition to the *BKGD* button, all transitions will be wipes. During a *wipe* the source video is gradually replaced by the second image that is framed in a geometrical shape. You can select

13.10 DISSOLVE

Once you have assigned the mix function through the mix delegation control, you can dissolve from camera 1 to camera 2. Assuming that camera 1 is on the air on bus A, you need to preset camera 2 on bus B. By moving the fader bar to the full extent of travel (in this case, up), you activate the dissolve from camera 1 to camera 2. Once the dissolve is completed, camera 2 will replace camera 1 on the program bus. Note that you can move the fader bar either up or down for the dissolve.

13.11 FADE TO BLACK

When fading to black from camera 2, you need to punch up the *BLK* button on bus B (preview/preset) and then dissolve into it by moving the fader bar to the full extent of travel (in this case, down).

Joystick positioner   Wipe patterns

13.12 WIPE PATTERNS

The wipe selectors offer a choice of geometrical wipe patterns. The configurations can be placed in a specific screen position using the joystick.

the specific pattern in the group of buttons called wipe mode or pattern selectors. **SEE 13.12**

Common wipe patterns are expanding vertical wipes and horizontal wipes. **SEE 13.13 AND 13.14** When you stop a horizontal wipe midway, you get a split screen. **SEE 13.15** Other popular wipes are diamond wipes and an assortment of box wipes whereby the new image replaces the old image as an expanding box. **SEE 13.16**

On large switchers these controls can be extended to nearly 100 different patterns by inputting a code into the switcher. You can also control the direction of the wipe (whether a horizontal wipe, for example, starts from screen-left or screen-right during the transition). The joystick positioner lets you move patterns on different loca-

13.13 VERTICAL WIPE

In a vertical wipe, one picture is gradually replaced by another from the bottom up or from the top down.

13.14 HORIZONTAL WIPE

In a horizontal wipe, one picture is gradually replaced by another from the side.

13.15 SPLIT SCREEN

A In this horizontal split-screen effect, camera 1 frames in the left side of the viewfinder the image designated to become the left half of the split screen.

B Camera 2 places its image in the right side of the viewfinder.

C In the completed split-screen wipe, the two images appear in the designated sides of the frame.

13.16 DIAMOND WIPE
In a diamond wipe, the second video source is gradually revealed in an expanding diamond-shaped cutout.

tions on-screen. Other controls give the wipes a soft or hard edge and give letters different borders and shadows.

Key and key-level controls   As mentioned, keying lets you insert lettering or other picture elements into the existing, or background, scene. The most common use of keys is to put lettering over people or scenes, or the familiar box over the newscaster's shoulder. With the key bus, you can select the video source to insert into the background image, such as the titles from the C.G. The *key-level control*, also called the clip control or clipper, adjusts the key signal so that the letters appear sharp and clear during the key.

Regardless of the switcher model, you must always first select a background image (the main image into which you want to insert the title) and the key source (the title) and then work with the clip control so that the key has sharp and clear edges.

Downstream keyer   The "downstream" in *downstream keyer (DSK)* refers to the manipulation of the signal at the line-out (downstream), rather than at the M/E (upstream) stage. With a downstream keyer, you can insert (key) a title or other graphic over the signal as it leaves the switcher. This last-minute maneuver, which is totally independent of any of the controls on the buses, is done to keep as many M/E buses as possible available for the other switching and effects functions. Most switchers with a DSK have a master fader, which consists of an additional fader bar or, more commonly, a fade-to-black button, with which you can automatically fade to black the base picture together with the downstream key effect (see figure 13.5).

You may ask why this fade-to-black control is necessary when, as just demonstrated, you can fade to black by simply dissolving to black on the program bus. The reason for the extra fade control is that the effect produced by the DSK is independent of the rest of the (upstream) switcher controls. The *BLK* button on the program bus will eliminate the background but not the key itself. Only the button in the downstream keyer section (to the right of the fader bar) will fade the entire screen to black. **ZVL5** SWITCHING→ Effects→ keys | key types | downstream keyer | special effects

As an example, let's set up a simple DSK effect at the end of a product demonstration of the latest computer model and then fade to black. The final scene shows a close-up (CU) of the computer as the background, with the name of the computer inserted by the DSK. Recall that one way to fade to black is to press the *BLK* button on the preset bus and then dissolve into it by moving the fader bar or pressing the *AUTO TRANS* button. But when you look at the line monitor, the background image (CU of the computer) has been replaced by black as it should be, but the name of the computer remains on-screen. You now know why. The downstream keyer is unaffected by what you do in the upstream part of the switcher—such as going to black on the M/E bus. Totally independent of the rest of the switcher controls, the DSK obeys only those controls in its own (downstream) territory, hence the need for its own black controls.

Color background controls   Most switchers have controls with which you can provide color backgrounds to keys and even give the lettering of titles and other written information colors or colored outlines. Color generators built into the switcher consist of dials that you can use to adjust hue (the color itself), saturation (the color strength), and brightness or luminance (the relative darkness and lightness of the color) (see figure 13.5). On large production switchers, these controls are repeated on each M/E bus.

LARGE PRODUCTION SWITCHERS

Just to give you an idea of how large production switchers look, the following figure shows one with 32 video inputs, 16 separate outputs, and multiple M/E buses that permit complex, multilevel effects, such as running video clips into secondary screens or other graphic frames. Just in case you forgot to key some names over those screens, you can use any one or all four of the downstream keyers. Such complex wonder switchers nevertheless operate on the same basic

13.17 LARGE PRODUCTION SWITCHER
This large production switcher has more of everything. It can handle all standard and high-definition video systems and import more than 30 video sources. You may select any one of 40 buttons for designated wipes and digital video effects, and you can operate four DSKs and an array of additional multilevel effects. This switcher operates on the same principles as a much simpler switcher.

13.18 PORTABLE SWITCHER
This portable switcher, packed in a small suitcase, represents a control room, with six video source monitors, larger preview and program (line) monitors, a fader bar, a six-channel stereo audio mixer, a C.G., and operating controls for remote cameras.

principles you have learned from studying the architecture of the simple multifunction switcher. **SEE 13.17**

OTHER SWITCHERS

Besides studio production switchers, which are also used in large remote trucks for the coverage of sporting events, there are four other types that you may find in television stations or independent production houses: portable switchers, switching software, routing switchers, and master control switchers.

PORTABLE SWITCHERS

Portable switchers are actually small control centers that contain a production switcher, preview monitors for the video sources, larger preview and line monitors, an audio console, a character generator, remote camera controls, and an intercom system—all packed in a small suitcase that weighs less than 18 pounds. **SEE 13.18** In effect, the suitcase holds all the key elements you would need for a moderately complex electronic field production (EFP). The portable switcher in figure 13.18 has the customary layout of preview and program buses, with six video inputs and a seventh one for ESS images. The video inputs are visible on a row of preview monitors, with larger monitors for preview and program sources. It has a special effects generator, a C.G., and pan, tilt, zoom, and focus controls for remote cameras. It also has a six-channel audio mixer with individual faders and a master pot and volume-unit (VU)

13.19 COMPUTER SWITCHER INTERFACE

This software program of the NewTek switcher VT[4] displays and activates all basic production and postproduction switcher functions. It has an amazing array of built-in test and video-quality equipment as well as a multitrack audio console. This switcher can be used for live switching or postproduction work.

meter, an i-link (1394 FireWire) to connect to an external video recorder, and several additional pieces of production control equipment.

SWITCHING SOFTWARE

Some companies have developed software that allows you to use a desktop or even a notebook computer as a switcher. The computer interface displays the customary preview, program, and key buses; a fader bar; a monitor bank; and, among the more advanced systems, various video and audio control equipment. **SEE 13.19**

The switcher in *Zettl's VideoLab* is a simple version of a computer switcher.[3] **ZVL6** SWITCHING→ Architecture→ try it

ROUTING SWITCHERS

Routing switchers route video signals to specific destinations. For example, you would need a routing switcher to switch the line-out or preview video to specific monitors

and then to the satellite video. Or you may assign the line-out signal to the video server instead of video recorder 2 because VR 2 is involved in editing. The buttons on a routing switcher are usually arranged in rows that look very much like the program bus on a production switcher or part of a computer-controlled system.

MASTER CONTROL SWITCHERS

The master control switcher retrieves all the program material stored in the server according to the program log time line; it cues, rolls, and stops video recorders and video cart machines; it calls up any number of still shots from the ESS system; it activates a number of transition sequences; and it switches automatically to remote feeds, such as a network program or live event. **SEE 13.20**

GENLOCK

When switching among various video sources in the studio or among remote sources, you normally need to provide the same synchronization information—a signal called house sync—to all video sources. This procedure guarantees that all video sources march in step to the same drummer—in this case, the same scanning clock—and that there will be

---

3. Although the switcher layout and functions were designed by the author, the software programs were specially developed by the highly creative computer people of THEmedia company, Vancouver, Canada.

13.20 MASTER CONTROL SWITCHER

The computerized master control switcher switches specific video and audio sources automatically. An operator can override the automation if necessary.

no picture breakup during the switching. Locking the synchronization generators from different origination sources is called *genlock*.

When you have to import a video for live switching without genlock (that is, without supplying house sync to all video sources), the framestore synchronizer will take over and help prevent picture breakup during the switching.

MAIN POINTS

▶ Instantaneous editing is the switching from one video source to another, or the combining of two or more sources while the show, or show segment, is in progress.

▶ All switchers, simple and complex, perform the same basic functions: selecting an appropriate video source from several inputs, performing basic transitions between two video sources, and creating or accessing special effects.

▶ The switcher has a separate button for each video input. There is a button for each camera, video recorder (VR), character generator (C.G.), and other video source, such as a remote input. The buttons are arranged in rows, called buses.

▶ The basic multifunction switcher has a preset bus for selecting and previewing the upcoming shot, a program bus that sends its video input to the line-out, a key bus for

selecting the video to be inserted over a background picture, a fader bar to activate mix effects, a delegation control section, and various special-effects controls.

▶ The program bus is a direct input/output link and is therefore also called the direct bus. Whatever is punched up on the program bus goes directly to the line-out. It can also serve as a mix/effects (M/E) bus.

▶ The preview/preset bus is used to select the upcoming video (preset function) and route it to the preview monitor (preview function). It also serves as an M/E bus.

▶ The M/E buses (program and preview buses in a mix/effects mode) can serve a mix (dissolve, super, or fade) or an effects function.

▶ The key bus is used to select the video source to be inserted (keyed) into a background image.

▶ Delegation controls are used to assign the buses specific functions.

▶ The actual transition is activated by moving the fader bar from one limit of travel to the other, or by an auto-transition button that takes on the functions of the fader bar.

▶ Most switchers offer additional effects, such as wipe patterns, borders, background colors, and the possibility of effects layering.

▶ Other types of switchers include portable switchers, switching software, routing switchers, and master control switchers.

13.2

Electronic Effects and Switcher Functions

When watching television you are bombarded with an awesome array of effects. Even in a simple weathercast, the weathercaster stands in front of the weather map with the landscape of your area, zoomed in on the town in which you live. The map may show little suns moving over areas where it is sunny, or show rain and snow falling, depending on what is happening outside. The three-dimensional landscape tilts while the prevailing temperatures pop in and out. What used to be the province of MTV has become commonplace.

Even news presentations are so loaded with video special effects that they often rival, if not surpass, the latest video games. Titles dance across the screen, change color, and zoom in and out. News anchors, field reporters, and guests are squeezed into side-by-side boxes when talking to one another. The brief stories that introduce the latest troubles in the world often end in a freeze-frame and then peel off the screen and tumble out of sight to make room for the next batch of maladies.

The screen is often bursting with simultaneous information. While the anchor's comments about a tragic traffic accident are accompanied by graphic video footage, the stock market quotes crawl across the bottom of the screen, and the side panel reveals the latest sports scores and weather. Throughout it all, the station or network logo is solidly embedded in a corner.

Such electronic wizardry is so easy to use that it may tempt you to substitute effect for content. Do not fall into the trap of camouflaging insignificant content or poorly shot or edited pictures with electronic effects. As dazzling as the effects may be, they cannot replace a basically solid message. When applied judiciously, however, many effects can enhance production considerably and give the message added impact.

Whenever you intend to use a visual effect, ask yourself: *Is it really necessary? Does it help clarify and intensify my message? Is it appropriate?* If the answer to all three questions is yes, such effects are readily available in even modest switchers, and many more can be created with special-effects software.

Some effects can be created during a production, such as title keys and wipes; others need to be built with digital equipment in the pre- or postproduction phase and stored in the switcher or integrated during editing. This section discusses the two major types of visual effects—standard video effects and digital video effects—as well as additional functions of the switcher.

▶ **STANDARD VIDEO EFFECTS**
Superimposition, key, and chroma key

▶ **DIGITAL VIDEO EFFECTS**
Manipulation of image size, shape, light, and color; manipulation of motion; and manipulation of multi-images.

▶ **ADDITIONAL SWITCHER FUNCTIONS**
Character generator, still store, and clip store

STANDARD VIDEO EFFECTS

The *special-effects generator (SEG)* is built into all production switchers. It can produce or recall a dazzling variety of special effects reliably and with ease. Many electronic effects have become so commonplace in television production that they have lost their specialty status and are simply considered part of the standard visual arsenal. These include the superimposition, the key, and the chroma key. You can accomplish all these effects "on the fly" without having to build and store them in the switcher ahead of time.

SUPERIMPOSITION

As you certainly know, a superimposition, or *super* for short, is a form of double exposure. The picture from one video source is electronically superimposed over the picture from another. As explained in section 13.1, the super is easily achieved by activating both mix buses with the fader bar (see figure 13.10b). A distinct characteristic of a super is that you can see through the superimposed image to the one that lies beneath it. You can then vary the strength of either picture (signal) by moving the fader bar toward one mix bus or the other.

Supers are often used for creating the effects of inner events—thoughts, dreams, or processes of imagination. The traditional (albeit overused) super of a dream sequence shows a close-up of a sleeping person, with images superimposed over his or her face. Sometimes supers are used to make an event more complex. For example, you may want to super a close-up of a dancer over a long shot of the same dancer. If the effect is done properly, we are given new insight into the dance. You are no longer photographing a dance but helping create it. **ZVL7** SWITCHING→ Transitions→ mix/dissolve

KEY

Keying means using an electronic signal to cut out parts of a television picture and fill them in with colors or another image. The basic purpose of a key is to add titles to a background picture or to cut another image (the weathercaster) into the background picture (the satellite weather map). (Because chroma keying works on a different principle, we discuss it separately later in this section.) The lettering for the title is generally supplied by a built-in or stand-alone character generator. **SEE 13.21** **ZVL8** SWITCHING→ Effects→ keys

13.21 KEY

When keying a title over a base picture, the key signal cuts a hole into the base picture in the shape of the letters supplied by the C.G.

Matte key   The most common keys are the ***matte keys***, in which one signal is doing the cutting and another is filling the hole with color. To achieve a clean key, in which the letters are cut into the base picture without any tearing or breakup, you may have to first use the key-level (or clip) control, which adjusts the brightness difference between foreground and background, and the gain control, which adjusts the key signal strength. Most switchers have rotary knobs for these key controls. (On the Grass Valley 100 switcher, the gain control is right above the clipper in the key control section; see figure 13.5.) You can preset the key effect and then watch the preview monitor to check that the key shows up and whether the letters are tearing or otherwise fuzzy. On many switchers with downstream keyers, you can push down the key-level control to display the total key effect on the preview monitor.

The most common modes for keying letters are the edge mode, the drop-shadow mode, and the outline mode. In the edge mode, each letter has a black outline around it. **SEE 13.22** In the drop-shadow mode, the letters have a black shadow contour that makes them appear three-dimensional. **SEE 13.23** In the outline mode, the letters themselves appear in outline form, with the base picture filling the inside. **SEE 13.24** These key modes are especially effective in preventing the lettering from getting lost in a busy background.

You may be somewhat bewildered hearing about keys, mattes, and matte keys—all seemingly referring to the same thing. It really doesn't matter what term you use, so long as you are consistent and all members of the production team know what you mean.

You can, of course, also key shapes of objects into the base picture so long as there is enough contrast relative to the base that the edges do not tear. The box over the news anchor's shoulder is an example of a widely used key effect.

CHROMA KEY

Chroma keying is a special effect that uses a specific color (chroma), usually blue or green, as the backdrop for a person or an object that is to appear in front of the background scene. During the key the blue (or green) backdrop is replaced by the background video source without affecting the foreground object. A typical example is the weathercaster in front of a weather map or satellite picture. During the chroma key, the computer-generated weather map or satellite image replaces all blue (or green)

13.22 MATTE KEY IN EDGE MODE
The edge mode matte key puts a black border around the letter to make it more readable than with the normal key.

13.23 MATTE KEY IN DROP-SHADOW MODE
The drop-shadow matte key adds a prominent cast shadow below the letter as though it were illuminated by a spotlight.

13.24 MATTE KEY IN OUTLINE MODE
The outline matte key makes the letter appear in outline form. It shows only the contour of the letter.

13.25 CHROMA-KEY EFFECT: WEATHERCAST

A In this chroma key, the weathercaster stands in front of a blue backdrop.

B During the key the blue backdrop is replaced by the computer-enhanced satellite photo.

C The weathercaster appears to be standing in front of the satellite photo.

areas—but not the weathercaster. The key effect makes the weathercaster appear to be standing in front of the weather map or satellite image. SEE 13.25

Because the chroma key responds to the hue of the backdrop rather than to the brightness (luminance) contrast as in a regular key, be sure that the chroma-key area is uniformly painted (even blue or green with a fairly high saturation throughout the area) and especially evenly lighted. Uneven background lighting will prevent a full replacement of the backdrop by the background video or cause the foreground image to tear.

If the on-camera talent wears something similar to the backdrop color, such as a blue sweater, while standing in front of the blue chroma-key area, the blue of the sweater will also be replaced by the background image during the key. Unless you want to amuse your audience with a special effect in which part of the weathercaster disappears,

don't let him or her wear anything blue in front of the blue chroma-key set. If the talent likes to wear blue, use green as the backdrop color.

If the weathercaster stands too close to the chroma-key backdrop, the blue reflections on part of his or her clothing or hair may cause the key to tear. Such problems may also occur especially if the lighting on the weathercaster has extremely fast falloff. The deep shadows, which are apt to be seen as blue by the camera, may cause the image to tear during the key.

Recall that you can counteract this nuisance to some extent by using yellow or amber gels on the back lights (not the background lights) because the yellow or amber back light neutralizes the blue shadows, thus eliminating the tearing. When using green as the chroma-key color, you need to use a light (desaturated) magenta (bluish red) gel to counteract the green reflections.

13.26 CHROMA-KEY LIGHT RING

This light ring, attached to the front of the lens, emits enough light to have the beaded gray backdrop reflect enough blue (or green) light for a functional chroma key.

Because an even backdrop color and even lighting are critical to getting a clean chroma key, alternative chroma-key methods have been developed. One uses a small light ring that is attached to the front of the camera lens. It emits blue (or green) light that is reflected off of a beaded gray

cloth backdrop. But shouldn't this cloth be blue or green? No—the backdrop has millions of embedded glass beads that reflect enough of the blue (or green) light to enable the switcher to perform the chroma key. **SEE 13.26**

You may wonder why the person standing in front of the reflective backdrop doesn't look blue (or green). It's because the light is simply too weak to reflect off of the skin or clothing. If the person stands too close to the camera and wears a highly reflective shirt, however, you may see a bluish or greenish tint on the person. This coloring process also tends to occur when objects are too close to the camera.

Studio use of chroma key　Despite the availability of highly sophisticated digital video effects, the chroma-key process is used extensively in studio production. The previous discussion focused on one of the most popular uses of the chroma key—for weathercasts—but chroma keying can also be done to enhance the background of an office set, for example, or to place a person in a specific outdoor setting. **SEE 13.27 AND 13.28**　In both cases the key source (skyline or museum pillars) was supplied by the switcher's electronic still store system.

13.27 CHROMA-KEY EFFECT: WINDOW

A In this chroma key, a suitable background view is selected from the ESS system.

B A studio camera focuses on the office set in front of a green chroma-key backdrop.

C Through chroma keying there seems to be a picture window behind the CEO sitting at her desk.

13.28 CHROMA-KEY EFFECT: SIMULATED LOCATION

A The source for the background image is a video frame of the museum exterior from the ESS system.

B The studio camera focuses on the actor playing a tourist in front of a blue chroma-key backdrop.

C All blue areas are replaced by the background image; the actor appears to be a tourist in front of the museum.

EFP chroma key   Chroma keying is also useful during electronic field productions and big remotes, especially if the talent is not able to stand directly in front of the desired background scene, such as a stadium or government building. When using a chroma-key effect during a sports remote, for example, the announcer may even be in the studio, with the remote feed (long shot of the football stadium) serving as the chroma-key background.

If you do chroma keying on-location, with the talent standing outdoors, watch out for blue reflections from the sky. To avoid such problems, switch to green for the chroma-key color and put the talent in front of a green backdrop. Because green is usually less common than blue in skin tones, it is slowly replacing blue as the dominant chroma-key color.

DIGITAL VIDEO EFFECTS

To make sense of the potential of *digital video effects (DVE)*, we divide them into three areas: manipulation of image size, shape, light, and color; manipulation of motion; and creation and manipulation of multi-images.

IMAGE SIZE, SHAPE, LIGHT, AND COLOR

A great variety of effects are available for manipulating the size, shape, light, and color of an image. Some of the more prominent are: shrinking and expanding, perspective, mosaic, and posterization and solarization. Many of these DVE change a realistic picture into a basically graphical image.

Shrinking and expanding   Shrinking refers to decreasing a picture's size while keeping the entire picture and its aspect ratio intact. Unlike cropping, where you actually remove some of the picture information, shrinking simply renders the picture smaller. Because the visual effect is similar to a zoom-out (shrinking) or a zoom-in (expansion), this effect is also called a squeeze-zoom. **SEE 13.29**

Perspective   You can distort an image in such a way that it looks as though it is floating in the three-dimensional video space. When combined with motion, such a 3D video space is greatly intensified. **SEE 13.30**

Mosaic   In the mosaic effect, the video image (static or in motion) is distilled into many discrete, equally sized squares of limited brightness and color. The resulting screen image looks like an actual tile mosaic. Such an image appears to contain greatly enlarged pixels. **SEE 13.31** This

13.29 SHRINKING
Through shrinking, also called a squeeze-zoom, you can reduce the total full-frame image to a smaller frame that contains the same picture information.

13.30 PERSPECTIVE
Through DVE you can distort an image so that it seems to float in the three-dimensional screen space.

13.31 MOSAIC EFFECT
Here the image is reduced to equally sized squares resembling mosaic tiles. In the electronic mosaic, as in a traditional tile mosaic, you can change the size of the tiles.

13.32 POSTERIZATION
In posterization the brightness values are severely reduced. The picture takes on a high-contrast look.

13.33 SOLARIZATION
Solarization is a special effect that is produced by a partial polarity reversal of an image. In a color image, the reversal results in a combination of complementary hues.

13.34 PEEL EFFECT
In a peel, or page-turn, effect, video A seems to curl and peel off a stack of images, revealing video B underneath.

technique is sometimes used to obscure parts of the body or a guest's identity. The mosaiclike distortion shows the person's face but renders the features unrecognizable.

Posterization and solarization   In posterization the brightness values (luminance) and the shades of the individual colors are collapsed so that the image is reduced to a few single colors and brightness steps. For example, the colors on a face show up as though they were painted by number with only a few paints. This image looks like a poster, hence the name of the effect. **SEE 13.32**

Solarization combines a positive and a negative image of the subject. Some solarization effects result in a complete polarity reversal, in which white becomes black, and colors appear as their complementary hue (yellow turns to blue, and red turns to green). When combined such effects often look like highly overexposed images. **SEE 13.33**

MOTION

There are so many possibilities for making effects move that a sensible and common terminology has not yet been developed. Don't be surprised to hear the director in the control room or the editor in the editing room using the sound language of cartoons—"squeeze," "bounce," or "fly"—when calling for motion effects. Some terms have been coined by DVE manufacturers, others by imaginative production personnel. Let's look at a few of the more popular effects: peel effect, rotation and bounce effects, and cube spin.

Peel effect   In the peel, or page-turn, effect, the top (existing) image curls up as though it were peeled off a pad of paper images, revealing the next "page"—a new image that seems to lie underneath. **SEE 13.34**

Rotation and bounce effects   With the rotation effect, you can spin any image on all three axes, individually or simultaneously: the x-axis (representing width), the y-axis (representing height), and the z-axis (representing depth). Although rotation terminology varies, normally a "tumble" refers to an x-axis rotation, a "flip" to a y-axis rotation, and a "spin" to a z-axis rotation. **SEE 13.35**

Cube spin   The rotation can also be applied to three-dimensional effects. The well-known cube spin shows a rotating cube, with each of the three visible sides displaying a different static or moving image. **SEE 13.36**

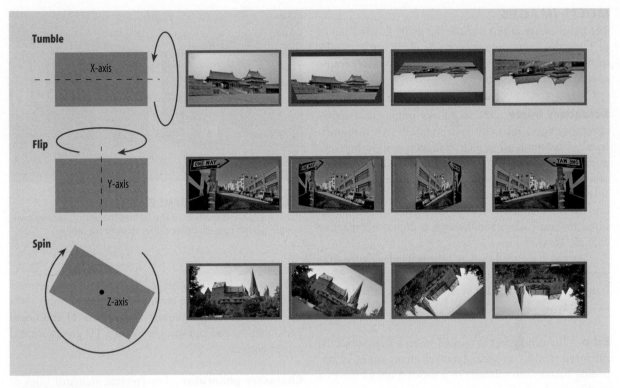

13.35 ROTATION EFFECT
In a rotation effect, the image can be revolved around the x-axis (tumble), the y-axis (flip), and the z-axis (spin).

13.36 CUBE SPIN
In a cube spin, a rotating cube displays a different static or moving image on each of the three visible sides.

MULTI-IMAGES

The multi-image effects include the many possibilities of dividing the screen into sections or of having a specific image update itself. The former we call secondary frame effects; the latter, echo effects.

Secondary frame   The secondary-frame effect shows several images, each clearly contained within its own frame. A common use of such an effect is to show host and guest simultaneously in separate frames, talking to each other from different locations. To emphasize that they are speaking to each other, although both are actually looking into the camera (at the viewer), the frames are sometimes tilted toward each other through a digital perspective change. **SEE 13.37**

As you have seen in many show formats, even dramatic shows, the screen is sometimes divided into multiple frames, each showing a different event occurring at the same time.

Echo   The echo effect is created when a static object is mirrored (similar to seeing yourself many times in opposing barbershop mirrors) or a moving object leaves a continuous trail of previous positions.   **SEE 13.38 AND 13.39**

ADDITIONAL SWITCHER FUNCTIONS

In addition to the standard selection, mix, and effects functions, many switchers incorporate features that effectively make the switcher a small production center. The most common are the character generator, the electronic still

13.37 SECONDARY-FRAME EFFECT
The trapezoidal distortion of the frames makes us perceive two people talking to each other rather than to the viewer.

store system, and clip storage. These features are primarily intended to help the technical director perform tasks that would otherwise require the services of additional personnel. As you can see, the job of a TD gets more and more complex.

Character generator   For creating standard titles or a credit crawl (names that move up the screen), you can plug in a keyboard to activate the built-in *character generator (C.G.)*. You can store these titles and call them up when needed.

Still store   As you recall, the ESS (electronic still store) system lets you grab any video frame, store it in an ESS file, and retrieve it for a news story, background, or key source.

13.38 ECHO EFFECT: STATIC TITLE
In this echo effect, a static image is repeated many times, and the copies are placed in close proximity to one another.

13.39 ECHO EFFECT: MOVING DANCER
In this echo effect, the moving dancer trails her previous movements.

This is much like when you grab a single frame from a motion clip and store it in a still-photo file.

Clip store　With this feature you can import, store, and retrieve a number of video clips without the need for an external server or video recorder. You can store a fair number of video clips (in some models up to two or more hours' worth) and retrieve them for bumpers (short videos announcing upcoming news stories), brief news stories, or animated titles. You can also use them to show events in secondary screens, similar to the multiple screens that show simultaneous events happening in different locations.

M A I N   P O I N T S

▶ The special-effects generator (SEG) is built into all production switchers. It can produce or recall a dazzling variety of special effects reliably and with ease.

▶ The three standard video effects are the super (superimposition), key, and chroma key.

▶ The main purpose of a key is to add titles or objects to a base (background) picture.

▶ In a matte key, one video signal cuts a hole in the base picture, and the other signal fills the cutout with colors generated by the switcher. The standard matte key modes are edge, drop shadow, and outline.

▶ Chroma keying uses a blue or green backdrop, which, during the key, is replaced by the background image.

▶ For a standard chroma key, the blue or green backdrop must be evenly lighted.

▶ To neutralize blue (or green) reflections on the talent standing in front of the chroma-key backdrop, backlights can be used that use complementary color gels: light yellow or amber for a blue background, and light magenta for a green background.

▶ Digital video effects (DVE) show images whose size, shape, light, and motion are manipulated in a predetermined fashion.

▶ The more common DVE include shrinking and expanding; perspective changes; mosaic; posterization and solarization; peel, or page-turn, effect; rotation and bounce effects; and cube-spin effect.

▶ Multi-images are secondary frames that show simultaneous events happening in different locations.

▶ Additional switcher functions include a built-in character generator (C.G.), an electronic still store (ESS) system, and a clip store that holds and plays more than two hours of video clips.

Z E T T L ' S   V I D E O L A B

For your reference or to track your work, the *Zettl's VideoLab* program cues in this chapter are listed here with their corresponding page numbers.

14

Design

Although you are probably very conscious of design and style when buying clothes or an automobile, you may be unaware of specific design elements when watching an opening show title, a news set, or the living room set of a situation comedy. You may be dazzled by an animated title that does everything but pop out of the screen, but you're probably not motivated to analyze its aesthetic qualities. And you probably perceive the living room in the daytime drama as exactly that—a living room—not carefully placed scenery and properties. We all know, of course, that all such design elements are meticulously planned.

In fact, design, or the lack of it, permeates everything a television production company shows on the air and off. It sets the style of the video presentation if not of the production company as a whole. Design includes not only the colors and the letters of a show title and the look of a studio set but also the production company's stationery, office furniture, hallway artwork, and logo. The CNN logo, for example, suggests up-to-date, no-nonsense news. **SEE 14.1**

But a handsome logo does not automatically carry its design qualities over to the programming or the on-air graphics or scenery. It is important to develop a design consciousness for everything you do; a well-executed logo is merely the symbol for such awareness, not its sole cause.

14.1 CNN LOGO

Section 14.1, Designing and Using Television Graphics, stresses the major design considerations of graphics for television. Section 14.2, Scenery and Props, looks at major aspects of television scenery and properties and discusses some elements of scene design.

KEY TERMS

character generator (C.G.) A dedicated computer system that electronically produces a series of letters, numbers, and simple graphic images for video display. Any desktop computer can become a C.G. with the appropriate software.

color compatibility Color signals that can be perceived as black-and-white pictures on monochrome television sets. Generally used to mean that the color scheme has enough brightness contrast for monochrome reproduction with a good grayscale contrast.

essential area The section of the television picture, centered within the scanning area, that is seen by the home viewer regardless of masking or slight misalignment of the receiver. Also called *safe title area* and *safe area*.

flat A piece of standing scenery used as a background or to simulate the walls of a room.

floor plan A diagram of scenery and properties drawn on a grid pattern. Can also refer to *floor plan pattern*.

floor plan pattern A plan of the studio floor, showing the walls, main doors, location of the control room, the lighting grid or battens.

graphics generator Dedicated computer or software that allows a designer to draw, color, animate, store, and retrieve images electronically. Any desktop computer with a high-capacity RAM and a hard drive can become a graphics generator with the use of 2D and 3D software.

grayscale A scale indicating intermediate steps from TV white to TV black. Usually measured with a nine-step scale for standard television.

letterbox The aspect ratio that results from fitting the full width of a 16 × 9 image onto a 4 × 3 screen by blocking the top and bottom screen edges with stripes.

pillarbox The aspect ratio that results from fitting a 4 × 3 image onto a 16 × 9 screen by blocking the sides with stripes.

props Short for *properties*. Furniture and other objects used for set decoration and by actors or performers.

scanning area Picture area that is scanned by the camera pickup device; in general, the picture area usually seen in the camera viewfinder and the preview monitor.

14.1

Designing and Using Television Graphics

When watching television you may be more captivated by the opening titles than the show that follows. Even when the program consists of a no-nonsense interview or a simple product demonstration, we seem obliged to have the title burst onto the scene, make its dancing letters change shape and color, and have at least three different backgrounds moving slowly underneath it. Such titles are usually supported by high-energy sound effects.

You may wonder whether we spend an inordinate amount of time and effort on the graphics compared with the program itself. Even if we don't, video graphics have become a major factor in television production. Because creating such titles requires highly specialized computer skills, rather than competence in television production, we limit our discussion to the following aspects of television graphics.

▶ **SPECIFICATIONS OF TELEVISION GRAPHICS**
Scanning and essential areas, out-of-aspect-ratio graphics, and matching STV and HDTV aspect ratios

▶ **INFORMATION DENSITY AND READABILITY**
Making screen lettering legible

▶ **COLOR**
Color aesthetics and grayscale

▶ **STYLE**
Contemporary look, personal touch, and consistency

▶ **SYNTHETIC IMAGES**
Computer-generated pictures

SPECIFICATIONS OF TELEVISION GRAPHICS

When comparing a television screen with a movie screen, you will see two obvious differences: the standard television (STV) screen is much smaller and much narrower than the movie screen. But even the large and wide flat-panel displays are considerably smaller than even a small movie screen. These two factors have a profound influence on the design specifications of television graphics.

The relatively small size of the STV screen limits the amount of writing you can display and demands fonts (lettering) that can be clearly seen. The limited screen width in relation to its height means that the titles do not have as much room to play across the screen and therefore must be kept closer to the center. Other design requirements of television graphics are common to all graphic design and deal more with readability, color, and style.

This section takes a closer look at the following design requirements and specifications: scanning and essential areas, out-of-aspect-ratio graphics, and matching STV and HDTV (high-definition television) aspect ratios.

SCANNING AND ESSENTIAL AREAS

Unlike the painter or still photographer who has full control over how much of the picture shows within the frame, we cannot be so sure about how much of the video-recorded or broadcast pictures can actually be seen on the home screen. There is an inevitable picture loss during transmission, and sometimes even from one dubbing generation to the next. Also, not all television receivers are as carefully adjusted as the preview monitors in a control room or editing room. Even if you gave the proper headroom when framing a close-up shot in a studio interview, your shots may have lost most or all of the headroom by the time they reach the home receiver. The same is true for titles that are framed too close to the screen edge. Because the edge information is often lost, you may end up with incomplete titles or the first and last digits missing from a telephone number.

How can you ensure that the information you send is actually seen on the home screen? Is there a standard that will more or less guarantee that all essential picture information, such as a title or telephone number, will appear in its entirety? The answer is a qualified yes. Although not mathematically precise, guidelines are available that can help you keep picture information from getting lost during dubbing or transmission. Basically, these guidelines tell you to keep vital information away from the screen edges. This is especially important when framing shots in the wider 16 × 9 ratio that are then broadcast for mainly STV (standard 4 × 3) receivers. Just how far away you should be from the edge when framing a shot is prescribed by the scanning and essential areas.

The *scanning area* includes the picture you see in the camera viewfinder and on preview monitors in the control room. It is the area actually scanned by the camera pickup device (the CCD). The *essential area*, also called safe title area and, simply, safe area, is centered within the scanning area. It is the portion seen by the home viewer regardless of the masking of the set, transmission loss, or slight misalignment of the receiver. **SEE 14.2**

Obviously, information such as titles and telephone numbers should be contained within the essential area. Also, if two people are facing each other from one screen edge to the other (blocked along the x-axis), be sure to place them well within the left and right borders of the essential area. But just how large is the essential area? It is usually smaller than you think—about 70 percent of the total area. Some *character generators (C.G.s)* automatically keep a title within the essential area. The better studio cameras and camcorders have a device that electronically generates a frame outline within the viewfinder, showing the safe area.

If your C.G. or camera does not have such a built-in safety net, you need to create your own. Most word-processing or drawing programs let you create a rectangle and then reduce it by a specific percentage. You could, for example, draw a 4 × 3 or 16 × 9 rectangle that simulates a 100 percent TV screen area and then reduce it to a 70 percent one (exclusive of the lettering, of course). These new borders would then outline the essential area for you. You could use the same method for creating the essential area for a 4 × 3 or 16 × 9 format.[1]

After some practice you will be able to compensate in the camera framing for the picture loss or place a title within the essential area without having to juggle percentages. The surest way to test a title is to project it on the preview monitor. If the letters come close to the edges of the preview monitor, the title extends beyond the essential area and will certainly be cut off when seen by the home viewer. **SEE 14.3**

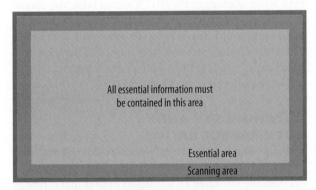

14.2 SCANNING AND ESSENTIAL AREAS
The scanning area is what the camera viewfinder and the preview monitor show. The essential, or safe title, area is what appears on the home television screen.

---

1. Adobe Photoshop software, for example, lets you specify the aspect ratio and the desired area percentage.

14.3 TITLE BEYOND ESSENTIAL AREA
A On the preview monitor, you can still see the complete title, although it comes close to the edges.

B When viewed on the home receiver, the information that lies outside the essential area is lost.

OUT-OF-ASPECT-RATIO GRAPHICS

Although you can change the aspect ratio of pictures within the television screen through various digital video effects (DVE), you can't change the dimensions of the screen itself. You can divide the screen into secondary frames of various aspect ratios, and you can block off areas of the screen and thus simulate different aspect ratios, but you are nevertheless confined to the set aspect ratio of the television display screen.[2]

You will inevitably run into situations in which the pictures to be shown do not fit the requirements of the television aspect ratio and essential area. Most often you encounter this problem when someone brings in an out-of-aspect-ratio chart or poster to pitch an upcoming event during a promotional interview or to illustrate a point in a sales meeting. More often than not, you must cover such a meeting live or record it without much chance for post-production doctoring. Many oversized graphics are vertical and do not adhere to the 4 × 3, much less the 16 × 9, aspect ratio. The problem with an out-of-aspect-ratio graphic is that, when shown in its entirety, the information on the graphic becomes so small that it is no longer readable. **SEE 14.4** By moving the camera close enough that the graphic fits the aspect ratio of the television screen, you inevitably cut out important information. **SEE 14.5**

If the lettering and other visual information are simple and bold enough, you can mount the entire out-of-aspect-ratio chart on a larger card that is in aspect ratio. You simply pull back with the camera and frame up on the

large card, keeping the out-of-aspect-ratio information as screen-center as possible. On a vertically oriented graphic without lettering, you could possibly tilt up and reveal the information bit by bit. If done smoothly, this gradual revelation adds drama. With lettering, however, such a tilt does not add drama but simply makes the graphic more difficult to read.

You encounter the same framing difficulty when trying to show a line of musical notation, a long mathematical formula or flow chart, or writing on a blackboard or whiteboard. If you zoom out all the way to show the entire whiteboard, the text is difficult to read. If you zoom in to a close-up, you can see only part of the writing. **SEE 14.6** The correct way of presenting whiteboard information is to divide the whiteboard into 4 × 3 or 16 × 9 aspect ratio fields and contain the writing within each of these fields. The camera can then get a close-up of the entire sentence. Even when working in the HDTV aspect ratio, you should write the information in blocks rather than across the width of the whiteboard. This is especially important if you work in a situation that uses remotely controlled cameras. It is much easier to zoom in on such a lettering block than to make the camera pan sideways. **SEE 14.7**

MATCHING STV AND HDTV ASPECT RATIOS

You may wonder why digital television did not maintain the traditional 4 × 3 aspect ratio. The main reason for the horizontally stretched 16 × 9 aspect ratio is that it readily accommodates the wide-screen movie format. When showing a movie on a traditional television set, either both sides of the wide frame are crudely amputated or the images are

---

2. See Herbert Zettl, *Sight Sound Motion: Applied Media Aesthetics*, 5th ed. (Belmont, Calif.: Thomson Wadsworth, 2008), pp. 186–93.

14.4 OUT-OF-ASPECT-RATIO GRAPHIC
When trying to frame this out-of-aspect-ratio graphic in its entirety, most of the information becomes difficult to read if not totally illegible.

14.5 INFORMATION LOSS IN CLOSE-UP
When you try to get a closer shot, all information outside the aspect ratio is lost.

14.6 ASPECT RATIO PROBLEM WITH A LONG LINE
Normal writing on a whiteboard can present a typical aspect ratio problem. The camera cannot show a close-up of a message that spans the full width of the whiteboard.

14.7 PROPER USE OF ASPECT RATIO BLOCKS
If the whiteboard is divided into proper aspect ratio fields, the camera can see the entire message even in a close-up.

displayed in the *letterbox* that shows the movie in its full width but necessitates the black stripes at the top and the bottom of the screen. **SEE 14.8**

Sometimes the 16 × 9 frame is digitally squeezed into the 4 × 3 frame, making everything look taller and skinnier than in the original shot. To avoid such picture distortions, some films are subjected to the pan-and-scan process whereby the more important portions of the wide-screen frame are selected to fit the 4 × 3 frame. But this process is quite time-consuming and costly and often violates the integrity of the original shot compositions.

When shown on the 16 × 9 HDTV screen, wide-screen movies suffer only slight picture loss, but what about standard 4 × 3 television programs? We can either stretch or enlarge the STV image so that it fills the full width of the HDTV screen. When we stretch the STV image to fill the

14.8 LETTERBOX
Making the entire frame of a wide-screen movie fit into the 4 × 3 aspect ratio of STV results in empty (black) space at the top and the bottom of the screen. The resulting horizontal aspect ratio is called a letterbox.

14.9 PILLARBOX

When showing a standard 4 × 3 television frame on the 16 × 9 screen, there are empty dead zones, or side bars, on both sides of the screen. The resulting vertical aspect ratio is called a pillarbox.

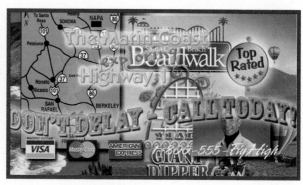

14.10 SCREEN CLUTTER

This screen has so much unrelated information that it is difficult to make sense of it amid the visual clutter.

width of the wide screen, everything looks fat, including the people. When enlarging the STV image so that it fills the 16 × 9 screen, objects and people lose some of their headroom—and sometimes even their heads and feet! You can also place the full 4 × 3 frame in the center of the 16 × 9 screen, leaving black stripes on both sides of the screen, called dead zones or side bars; the resulting aspect ratio is called a *pillarbox*. **SEE 14.9**

Interestingly enough, some programs make a virtue out of this unavoidable handicap. You may have seen MTV presentations or commercials that are letterboxed, with black borders at the top and the bottom of the screen. This is to imply that they were originally shot for wide-screen movie presentation rather than television distribution, which supposedly lends more prestige to the program. Also, many producers are quite pleased to have this additional screen space. They consider the side bars anything but "dead" space and fill it with additional program information and advertisements. The side bars are also a timesaver: often the previous show's credits are shown on a side bar while the new program segment is already under way. We as viewers seem to accept quite readily the stretching or fattening effect of digital manipulation.

INFORMATION DENSITY AND READABILITY

Taking a cue from overcrowded Web pages, there is a tendency to load the screen with a great amount of information. And in our quest to squeeze as much information as possible onto the relatively small television screen, the print used for on-the-air copy gets smaller and smaller.

Unless you have a large, high-resolution monitor, such information is virtually unreadable.

INFORMATION DENSITY

There is some justification for crowding the screen if the data simultaneously displayed are related and add relevant information. For example, if in a home-shopping program you show a close-up of an item and simultaneously display the retail price, the sale price, and the telephone number to call, you are providing the viewer with a valuable service. On the other hand, if you show a newscaster reading the news in one corner of the screen, display the weather report in another, run stock market numbers and sports scores across the top and the bottom, and show station logos and ads all at the same time, you run the risk of information overload in addition to excessive screen clutter. **SEE 14.10**

When the elements are properly arranged according to the principles of composition, however, such additional information can add significantly to the basic communication. With thoughtfully arranged secondary frames, we are less likely to be overwhelmed and can pick and choose among the information presented. **SEE 14.11**

READABILITY

In television graphics readability means that you should be able to read the words that appear on-screen without straining. As obvious as this statement is, it seems to have eluded many a graphic artist. Sometimes titles explode onto and disappear from the screen so quickly that only video game champs and people with superior perceptive abilities can actually see and make sense out of them; or the letters

14.11 PROPER STRUCTURE OF MULTIPLE SCREEN ELEMENTS

The arrangement of these secondary frames and information areas makes it relatively easy to seek out the desired information.

are so small and detailed that you can't read them without a magnifying glass.

Such readability problems occur regularly when motion picture credits are shown on a traditional 4 × 3 television screen. First, as already pointed out, the titles generally extend beyond the essential area, so you can see only parts of them. Second, the credit lines are so small that they are usually impossible to read on the low-resolution STV screen. Third, the letters themselves are not bold enough to show up well on television, especially if the background is busy. These problems are greatly minimized on an HDTV screen but are greatly magnified when watching a small cell-phone display. In consideration of the many viewers watching standard television and the ever-growing number of mobile multimedia users, you need to aim for a

high degree of readability. What, then, makes for optimal readability? Here are some recommendations:

■ Keep all written information within the essential area.

■ Choose fonts that have a bold, clean contour. Thin-lined fonts are hard to read, even on an HDTV screen. Also, the fine strokes and serifs of the letters are susceptible to breakup when keyed. Sometimes even bold, sans serif fonts can get lost in the background and need to be reinforced with a drop shadow or color outline.

■ Limit the amount of information. The less information that appears on-screen, the easier it is to comprehend. Some television experts suggest a maximum of seven lines per page. It is more sensible to prepare a series of titles on several C.G. "pages," each displaying a small amount of text, than a single page with an overabundance of information. As you well know from text messaging, even brief messages gain by their own visual shorthand. When programming for the small screen of mobile multimedia, keep the words short and the letters bold.

■ Format all lettering into blocks for easily perceivable graphical units. **SEE 14.12** This block layout is often used in well-designed Web pages. If the titles are scattered, they look unbalanced and are hard to read. **SEE 14.13** Scattered information is a typical characteristic of a poorly designed Web page, where bits of text, little secondary screens, and pop-ups randomly drop onto the screen.

■ Avoid keying lettering into a busy background. If you must add lettering, select a simple, bold font. **SEE 14.14**

14.12 BLOCK ORGANIZATION OF TITLES

When titles are arranged in blocks, related information is graphically organized for easy perception.

Terry   Craig   Ray   Muscat
Mark   Cummings   Ric   Panizo
Vic   Jones   Susan   Tyler
Tony   Klemens   Wayne   Weeks
Frank   Logan   Ben   Wong
Al   Bowens

14.13 SCATTERED TITLES
When titles are scattered, the information is difficult to read.

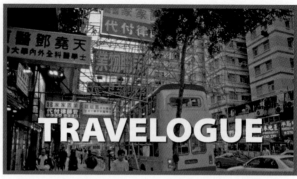

14.14 BOLD LETTERS OVER A BUSY BACKGROUND
This title reads well despite the busy background. The letters are bold and differ sufficiently in brightness from the background.

The same principles apply when you animate a title using special effects. In fact, if the title twists and tumbles around the screen, the letters must be even more legible than if they were used for a static, straightforward title.

Bear in mind that whenever you use printed material as on-air graphics, including reproductions of famous paintings, professional photographs, illustrated books, and similar matter, you must obtain copyright clearance. If you have subscribed to a stock image service, ask whether it holds the copyright to those images. Your copyright limits normally depend on the amount of user fees you pay.

COLOR

You read in chapter 5 about the attributes of color and the technical aspects of additive color mixing. In general, the difference between HDTV and HDV (high-definition video) is not the relative sharpness of the picture—they look pretty much the same—but the fidelity of the color. Because color is an important design element, you need to learn more about its aesthetics—that is, how various colors influence design and how the television system reacts to them.

COLOR AESTHETICS

The recognition and the application of color harmony cannot be explained in a short paragraph; they require experience, practice, sensitivity, and taste. Rather than try to dictate which colors go with what other colors, you can more easily divide the colors into "high-energy" and "low-energy" and then balance their energies.

The high-energy colors include bright, highly saturated hues, such as rich reds, yellows, and blues. The low-energy group contains more-subtle hues with a low degree of saturation, such as pastels. Normally, you should keep the colors of the background low-energy and the foreground high-energy. In a set (as in your home), the background (walls) is usually less colorful than the set pieces and dressings, such as rugs, sofas, pictures, and pillows. **SEE 14.15 AND 14.16** Titles work on the same principle:

14.15 HIGH-ENERGY COLORS
The energy of a color is determined mainly by its saturation. High-energy colors are highly saturated hues, usually at the red and yellow end of the spectrum. They are especially effective when set against a low-energy background.

14.16 LOW-ENERGY COLORS

Low-energy colors are desaturated hues. Most pastels are low-energy.

you will find that an easily readable title has high-energy lettering on a low-energy background.

Of course, the colors must also be appropriate for the event. For example, if the titles are intended to announce a high-energy show, such as a vivacious dance program, high-energy colors are certainly fitting. If, however, you use the same high-energy colors to introduce a discussion on the perils and the benefits of atomic energy, the choice is inappropriate even if the title has good readability.

Independent of aesthetics, only top-of-the-line television cameras can handle highly saturated reds. Unless there is an abundance of baselight, the video camera "sees red" when looking at red—at best, distorting the red color or, in some cases, making red areas in the shot vibrate (excessive video noise) or bleed into adjacent areas. This color bleeding is not unlike the bleeding of one sound track into another. When working with lesser-quality camcorders, suggest that the talent not wear highly saturated red clothing and that scene designers not paint large areas with saturated reds. This problem becomes especially noticeable in electronic field production (EFP), where you generally work in less-than-optimal lighting conditions.

GRAYSCALE

Besides the low- and high-energy determinants of color, its differences in brightness are equally important to the readability of lettering and the color contrast. As you recall, the relative brightness of a color is usually measured by how much light it reflects. The television system is not capable of reproducing pure white (100 percent reflectance) or pure black (0 percent reflectance); at best it can reproduce an off-white (about 70 percent reflectance for monochrome television and only about 60 percent for color) and an off-black (about 3 percent reflectance). We call these brightness extremes TV white and TV black. If you divide the brightness range between TV white and TV black into distinct steps, you have the television **grayscale**. Black-and-white

14.17 NINE-STEP GRAYSCALE

The nine-step grayscale shows nine different grays, ranging from TV white on the left to TV black on the right.

images are mainly discernible because of their brightness differences—their grayscale (the other factor being the outline of objects). The most common number of brightness steps between TV white and TV black on a grayscale is nine. **SEE 14.17**

The new HDTV systems not only produce superior resolution (picture sharpness) but their brightness range is considerably larger, one of the major factors in achieving the "film look" of HDTV. Like film, HDTV can display many more subtle steps of gray between TV white and TV black. Note that the middle value of the grayscale is not 30 percent but 18 percent. This means that you need more light to get from the very bright step 3 to an even brighter step 2 than when moving from the darker 8 to the slightly lighter 7. This principle is the same as using a flashlight at night and in daylight. At night, a flashlight can illuminate a room; in bright sunlight, you need to look at the lamp to tell whether it is even turned on.

Compatible color   Technically, *color compatibility* means that a graphic is equally readable on a black-and-

14.18 **TITLE WITH INCOMPATIBLE COLORS**
Although these colors show up prominently on a color monitor, their brightness is almost the same; they are illegible on a black-and-white monitor.

white television set as on a color one. In production it simply means that a color picture shows up well and with enough brightness contrast. For titles there should be a significant brightness contrast between the background and the foreground lettering. When you use exclusively high-energy colors for a title, such as red lettering on a green or blue background, the difference in hue is so obvious that you might be tempted to neglect the grayscale difference. As different as they seem on a color monitor, if they have the same brightness they are unreadable on a monochrome monitor. **SEE 14.18**

Even if the colors you use are not intended for reproduction on a black-and-white television set, good brightness contrast is also important for color rendition. It aids the picture's resolution and three-dimensionality and helps separate the colors. With a little experience, you will find that just by squinting your eyes while looking at the set, you can determine fairly well whether two colors have enough brightness contrast to ensure compatibility.

STYLE

Style, like language, is animate and nonstatic. It changes according to the specific aesthetic demands of a given time and location. To ignore it means to communicate less effectively. You learn style not from a book but primarily through being sensitive to your environment—by experiencing life with open eyes and ears and, especially, an open heart. The way you dress now compared with the way you dressed 10 years ago is an example of a change in style.

Some people not only sense the prevailing style but also manage to enhance it with a personal, distinctive flair.

Sometimes it is the development of television equipment that influences presentation styles more than personal creativity or social need. As emphasized in chapter 13, DVE equipment contributed not only to a new graphical awareness but also to an abuse of style. Often animated titles are generated not to reflect the prevailing aesthetic taste or to signal the nature of the upcoming show but simply because it is fun to see letters dance on-screen. Although flashy graphics in news may be tolerated because they express and intensify the urgency of the message, they are inappropriate for shows that explore a natural disaster or plays that delve into an intense relationship between two people.

You may have noticed that contemporary television graphics are imitating the colors and the layout of computer Web pages. Some television graphics even parrot the shortcomings of the computer image, such as the aliasing ("jaggies") of diagonals or curves in lines and letters, differently colored horizontal strips that contain lettering and small product icons, or the scattering of tiny secondary frames on the main television screen (see figure 14.10). One of the reasons for such emulation is to be hip and on the cutting edge. More often than not, however, such screen clutter works against a distinctive style and, unfortunately, against effective communication.

Regardless of whether you are a trendsetter, you should try to match the style of the artwork with that of the show. But do not go overboard and identify your guest from China with Chinese-like lettering or your news story about the devastating flood with titles that bob across the screen. Do not abandon good taste for effect. In a successful design, all images and objects interrelate and harmonize with one another—from the largest, such as the background scenery, to the smallest, such as the fruit bowl on the table. Good design displays a continuity and a coherence of style.

SYNTHETIC IMAGES

Synthetic images refer to pictures that are created entirely with the computer. Most desktop imaging software offers millions of different colors, thin and thick lines, shapes, and various brush strokes and textures for creating digital art. A television weathercast is a good example of the many capabilities of a large-scale *graphics generator*. The lettering, basic geographic map, temperature zones and numbers, high- and low-pressure zones, symbols for sunshine and precipitation, and moving clouds and falling rain—all are generated and animated by the digital graphics generator. **SEE 14.19**

Depending on the storage capacity and the sophistication of the software, you can create and store complex graphical sequences, such as clips of animated three-

14.19 DIGITALLY GENERATED WEATHER MAP
This weather map is entirely computer-generated. Some of the multilevel effects are animated.

dimensional titles that unfold within an animated 3D environment, or multilevel mattes that twist within a 3D video space.[3] **SEE 14.20 AND 14.21**

---

3. *Zettl's VideoLab* has many 2D and 3D animated renderings, which you can control interactively.

14.20 3D RENDERING
Software specifically for graphics generators can create a variety of three-dimensional titles and moving images.

14.21 DIGITAL RENDERING: PIAZZA SAN PIETRO
This animated fly-by sequence shows the Piazza San Pietro in Vatican City from various points of view.

14.22 FRACTAL LANDSCAPE
Most painting software allows you to "paint" irregular images using mathematical formulas.

Some computer programs, based on complex mathematical formulas, allow you to paint irregular shapes, called fractals, which are used to create realistic and fantasy landscapes and countless abstract patterns. **SEE 14.22**

MAIN POINTS

▶ Design is an overall concept that includes such elements as the fonts for titles, the station logo, the look of the news set, and even the office furniture.

▶ The major purposes of television graphics are to give you specific information, to tell you something about the nature of the event, and to grab your attention.

▶ The scanning area is what the camera viewfinder and the preview monitor show. The essential, or safe title, area is the portion seen by the viewer regardless of transmission loss or slight misalignment of the receiver.

▶ Out-of-aspect-ratio graphics need special consideration to make them fit the STV (standard television) or HDTV (high-definition television) screen.

▶ Making the entire frame of a wide-screen movie fit into the 4 × 3 aspect ratio of STV results in empty (black) space at the top and the bottom of the frame. The resulting horizontal aspect ratio is called a letterbox.

▶ To show a standard 4 × 3 television frame on the 16 × 9 screen, empty dead zones, or side bars, are added on both sides of the frame. The resulting vertical aspect ratio is called a pillarbox.

▶ To avoid information overload when showing unrelated information simultaneously on a single screen, arrange the elements in easy-to-read secondary frames or text blocks.

▶ Good readability results when the written information is within the essential area, the letters are relatively large and have a clean contour, the background is not too busy, and there is good color and brightness contrast between the lettering and the background.

▶ Color compatibility means that the color image translates into distinct brightness values (grayscale steps) when seen on a monochrome receiver. Most STV systems reproduce at best nine separate brightness steps, ranging from TV white (1) to TV black (9). These steps make up the television grayscale. HDTV delivers a much wider grayscale.

▶ Synthetic images are generated entirely by computer graphics. They can be still or animated.

14.2

Scenery and Props

Although you may never be called upon to design or build scenery, you will likely set up scenery in the studio or rearrange an interior at a remote location. Setting up even a small interview set requires that you know what the pieces of scenery are called and how to read a floor plan. Your ability to see an existing on-location interior as a "set" will not only speed up camera placement and lighting but also help you determine if it needs redecorating for maximally effective camera shots. Knowing how to manage studio space through scenery and properties will also help you structure screen space in general.

▶ **TELEVISION SCENERY**
   Standard set units, hanging units, platforms and wagons, and set pieces

▶ **PROPERTIES AND SET DRESSINGS**
   Stage props, set dressings, hand properties, and the prop list

▶ **ELEMENTS OF SCENE DESIGN**
   Floor plan, set backgrounds, and virtual sets

TELEVISION SCENERY

Because the television camera looks at a set both at close range and at a distance, scenery must be detailed enough to appear realistic yet plain enough to prevent cluttered pic-

tures. Regardless of whether it's a simple interview set or a realistic living room, a set should allow for optimal camera angles and movement, appropriate lighting, microphone placement and occasionally boom movement, and maximum action by performers. Fulfilling these requirements are four types of scenery: standard set units, hanging units, platforms and wagons, and set pieces.

STANDARD SET UNITS

Standard set units consist of softwall and hardwall *flats* and a variety of set modules. Both are used to simulate interior or exterior walls. Although television stations and nonbroadcast production houses use hardwall scenery almost exclusively, softwall scenery is more practical for rehearsals as well as high-school and college television operations.

Softwall flats   The flats for standard softwall set units are constructed of a lightweight wood frame covered with muslin or canvas. They have a uniform height but various widths. The height is usually 10 feet (about 3 meters) or 8 feet (about 2½ meters) for small sets or studios with low ceilings. Width ranges from 1 to 5 feet (30 centimeters to 1½ meters). When two or three flats are hinged together, they are called twofolds (also called a book) or threefolds. Flats are supported by jacks, wood braces that are hinged or clamped to the flats and weighted down by sandbags or metal weights. **SEE 14.23**

Softwall scenery has numerous advantages: it is relatively inexpensive to construct and can usually be done in the scene shops of theater departments; it lends itself to a great variety of set backgrounds; it is easy to move and store; it is simple to set up, brace, and strike; and it is relatively easy to maintain and repair. The problems with softwall scenery are that it is difficult to hang pictures on the flats, and they often shake when someone closes a door or a window on the set or when something brushes against them.

Hardwall flats   Hardwall flats are much sturdier than softwall flats and are preferred for more-ambitious television productions. Hardwall scenery does have a few drawbacks: hardwall units do not always conform to the standard set dimensions of softwall scenery, and the flats are heavy and difficult to store. (In the interest of your—and the flats'—well-being, do not try to move hardwall scenery by yourself.) Hardwall flats also reflect sound more readily than do softwall flats, which can interfere with good audio pickup. For example, if a set design requires that

14.23 SOFTWALL FLATS
Softwall flats consist of a wood frame covered with muslin or canvas.

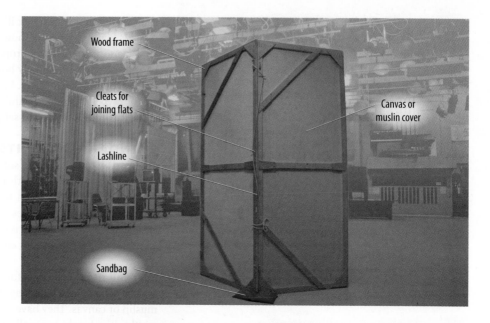

Wood frame

Cleats for joining flats

Canvas or muslin cover

Lashline

Sandbag

14.24 HARDWALL SET
This set was constructed with hardwall flats for a specific television drama. Note the specific set props that give the set its character.

two hardwall flats stand opposite and in close proximity to each other, the talent operating in this space will most likely sound as though they are speaking inside a barrel.

Most hardwall scenery is built for specific shows—such as newscasts, interview areas, and soap operas—and remains set up for the length of the series. Carefully constructed hardwall scenery is a must for HDTV or any other form of digital television that has a higher picture resolution than STV. **SEE 14.24**

Set modules   For small television stations or educational institutions, where you do not have the luxury of building new sets for every show, you may consider versatile set modules that can be used in a variety of configurations. A set module is a series of flats and three-dimensional set pieces whose dimensions match, whether they are used vertically (right side up), horizontally (on their sides), or in combinations. A wide variety of set modules are commercially available.

The muslin cyc runs on overhead tracks and normally covers three sides of the studio.

HANGING UNITS

Whereas flats stand on the studio floor, hanging units are supported from overhead tracks, the lighting grid, or lighting battens. They include the cyclorama, drops, and drapes and curtains.

Cyclorama   The most versatile hanging background is a cyclorama, or cyc, a continuous piece of muslin or canvas stretched along two, three, and sometimes even all four studio walls. **SEE 14.25**

A fairly light color (light gray or beige) is more advantageous than a dark cyc. You can always make a light cyc dark by keeping the light off it, and you can colorize it easily using floodlights (scoops or softlights) with color gels attached. A dark cyc will let you do neither. Some studios have hardwall cycs, which are not actually hanging units but are built solidly against the studio wall. **SEE 14.26**

Drops   A chroma-key drop is a wide roll of chroma-key blue or green cloth that can be pulled down, and even stretched over part of the studio floor, for chroma keying.

You can make a simple and inexpensive drop by suspending a roll of seamless paper (9 feet wide by 36 feet long), which comes in different colors. Seamless paper hung from a row of flats provides a continuous cyclike background. Simply roll it sideways and staple the top edge to the flats. You can paint it for a more detailed background or use it for a cookie projection. **SEE 14.27**

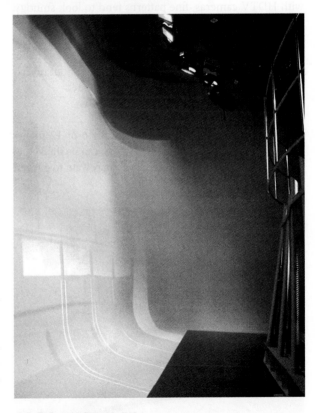

14.26 HARDWALL CYC
This cyc is made of hardwall material and is permanently installed on two sides of the studio.

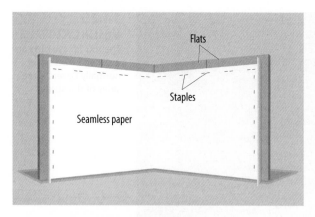

14.27 SEAMLESS PAPER DROP
A simple yet effective backdrop can be constructed by hanging a roll of seamless paper from a row of flats.

Drapes and curtains   Stay away from detailed patterns and fine stripes when choosing drapes. Unless you shoot with HDTV cameras, fine patterns tend to look smudgy, and contrasting stripes often cause moiré interference. Drapes are usually stapled to 1 × 3 battens and hung from the tops of the flats. Most curtains should be translucent enough to let the back light come through without revealing scenic pieces that may be in back of the set.

PLATFORMS AND WAGONS
Platforms are elevation devices, typically 6 or 12 inches (roughly 15 or 30 centimeters) high, that can be stacked. If you use a platform for interviews, you may want to cover it

with carpeting. This cover not only will look good on camera but will also absorb the hollow sounds of people moving on the platform. You can further dampen this sound by filling the platform interior with foam rubber.

Some 6-inch platforms have four casters so that they can be moved around. Such platforms are called wagons. **SEE 14.28** You can mount a portion of a set, or even a whole set, on a series of wagons and, if the doors are big enough, move these sections with relative ease in and out of the studio. Once in place, wagons should be secured with wood wedges and/or sandbags so that they do not move unexpectedly.

Larger platforms and hardwall scenery are often supported by a slotted-steel frame, which works like a big erector set.

SET PIECES
Set pieces are important scenic elements. They consist of freestanding three-dimensional objects, such as pillars, pylons (which look like thin, three-sided pillars), sweeps (curved pieces of scenery), folding screens, steps, and periaktoi (pronounced "pear-ee-*ack*-toy"; plural for periaktos) a three-sided standing unit that looks like a large pylon. Most periaktoi move and swivel on casters and are painted differently on each side to allow for quick scene changes. **SEE 14.29**

There are numerous advantages to using set pieces: you can move them easily, they are self-supporting, and they quickly and easily establish three-dimensional space. Although set pieces are freestanding and self-supporting

14.28 PLATFORMS AND WAGONS
Platforms are usually 6 or 12 inches high. When equipped with sturdy casters, they are called wagons.

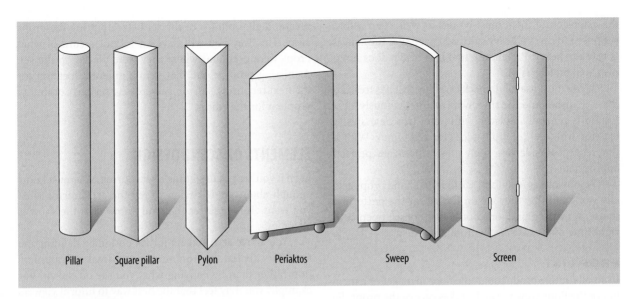

Pillar   Square pillar   Pylon   Periaktos   Sweep   Screen

14.29 SET PIECES
Set pieces are freestanding scenic elements that roll on casters for quick and easy repositioning.

(which are, after all, their major advantages), always check whether they need additional bracing. At a minimum they must be able to withstand bumps by people and cameras.

As a general rule, *it is always better to overbrace than to underbrace a set.* As in all other aspects of television production, do not forsake safety for convenience or speed.

PROPERTIES AND SET DRESSINGS

After having struggled with softwall and hardwall scenery, you will find that it is really the properties and the set dressings that give the environment a specific look and style. Much like decorating your room, it is primarily the furniture and what you hang on the walls that distinguish a particular environment, rather than the walls themselves. Because good television has more close-ups than medium and long shots, the three types of *props*—stage props, set dressings, and hand props—must be realistic enough to withstand the close scrutiny of the camera.

STAGE PROPS

Stage props include common furniture and items constructed for a specific purpose, such as news desks, panel tables, and chairs. You should also have enough furniture to create settings for a modern living room, a study, an office, a comfortable interview area, and perhaps some type of outdoor area with a patio table and chairs. For an interview set, relatively simple chairs are more useful than large, upholstered ones. You don't want the chairs to take on more prominence than the people sitting on them. Try to get chairs and couches that are not too low so that sitting and rising gracefully is not problematic, especially for tall people.

SET DRESSINGS

Set dressings are a major factor in determining the style and the character of a set. Although the flats may remain the same from one show to another, the dressings help give each set individual character. They include such items as draperies, pictures, lamps and chandeliers, fireplaces, flowerpots, plants, candleholders, and sculptures. Secondhand stores provide an unlimited source for these things. In an emergency you can always raid your own home or office.

HAND PROPERTIES

Hand properties consist of all items that are actually handled by the talent during a show. They include dishes, silverware, telephones, radios, and desktop computers. In television the hand props must be realistic: use only real objects. A papier-mâché chalice may look regal and impressive on-stage, but on the television screen it looks dishonest if not ridiculous. Television is very dependent on human action. Think of hand props as extensions of gestures. If you want the actions to be sincere and genuine, the extension of them must be real as well. If an actor is supposed to carry a heavy suitcase, make sure the suitcase is actually heavy. Pretending that it is heavy does not go over well on television.

If you must use food, check carefully that it is fresh and that the dishes and the silverware are meticulously clean. Liquor is generally replaced with water (for clear spirits), tea (for whiskey), or fruit juice (for red wine). With all due respect for realism, such substitutions are perfectly appropriate.

As obvious as it sounds, see to it that hand props actually work and that they are on the set for the performers to use. A missing prop or a bottle that doesn't open at the right time may cause costly production delays.

PROP LIST

In small routine productions, the floor manager or a member of the floor crew normally takes care of the props. For elaborate productions, however, have a person assigned exclusively to the handling of props—the property manager. To procure the props and ensure that they are available at the camera rehearsal and taping sessions, you need to prepare a prop list. **SEE 14.30**

If you need to strike a set and set it up again for subsequent recording sessions, mark all the props and take

five outside bushes	6' blue sofa
two rubber plants	set of eight family photos
potted palm	sunflower painting
transparent curtains	Picasso print
low 8' cabinet	magazines
square end table	newspaper
small chest of drawers	books
two bookcases	stereo
chair (with armrests)	tea set
blue wing chair	lamp for end table
coffee table	Indian sculpture
round end table	louvered screen

14.30 PROP LIST
This prop list contains all set props, set dressings, and hand properties shown in the set in figure 14.32.

several digital photos of the set before putting the props away. This way you will have an instant record of what props were used and where they were placed on the set. A missing prop or one that is in a different location for the next recording session can create a serious continuity problem for the editor.

ELEMENTS OF SCENE DESIGN

Even if you are not designing a set yourself, you must know enough about scene design to tell the art director what you want. This requires that you know what the show is all about.

You arrive at a concept for set design by defining the necessary spatial environment for optimal communication rather than by copying what you see on the air. For example, you may feel that the best way to inform viewers is not by having an authoritative newscaster read stories from a pulpitlike contraption but by moving the cameras into the newsroom itself or out into the street where events are happening. If the show is intended to be shot with a single camera for heavy postproduction editing, it may be easier to take the camera to the street corner rather than to re-create the street corner in the studio.

But even if the show is slated for studio production, you can often streamline the set design by taking some time to visualize the entire show in screen images and work from there. For example, even if the interview guest is a famous defense lawyer, you don't automatically have to set up a typical lawyer's office complete with antique desk, leather chairs, and law books in the background. Ask about the nature of the interview and its intended communication objective. This is where a clear process message proves immensely helpful. If, for example, the process message is to probe the conscience and the feelings of the defense lawyer rather than hear about future defense strategies, you could visualize the entire interview being conducted in intimate close-ups of the guest. Does this interview require an elaborate lawyer's set? Not at all. Considering the shooting style that includes a majority of tight close-ups, two comfortable chairs in front of a simple background will do just fine.

When the show is sketched out on a detailed storyboard, the set design is frequently predetermined. Nevertheless, speak to the producer and the director if you think you have a much better idea.

There are three major elements of scene design: the floor plan, set backgrounds, and virtual sets.

FLOOR PLAN

A set design is drawn on the ***floor plan pattern***, which is literally a plan of the studio floor. It shows the floor area, the main studio doors, the location of the control room, and the studio walls. The lighting grid or batten locations are normally drawn on the floor area to give a specific orientation pattern according to which the sets can be placed. In effect, the grid resembles the orientation squares of a city map. **SEE 14.31**

The completed ***floor plan*** should convey enough information that the floor manager and the crew can put up the set and dress it, even in the absence of the director or set designer. You may find that both the floor plan pattern and the finished floor plan that shows the scenic design are called "floor plan."

The scale of the floor plan pattern varies, but it is normally ¼ inch = 1 foot. All scenery and set properties are then drawn on the floor plan pattern in the proper position relative to the studio walls and the lighting grid. For simple setups you may not need to draw the flats and the set properties to scale; you can approximate their size and placement relative to the grid. **SEE 14.32**

Floor plan functions   The floor plan is an important tool for all production and engineering personnel. The director uses it to visualize the show and to block the major actions of performers, cameras, and microphone booms. It is essential to the floor crew, who must set up the scenery and place the major properties. The LD (lighting director) needs it for designing the general light plot. The audio technician can become familiar with specific microphone placement and possible audio problems.

Set positioning   Whenever possible, try to locate the set where the lights are. Position it so that the back lights, key lights, and fill lights hang in their approximate positions. Sometimes an inexperienced designer will place a set in a studio corner, where most of the lighting instruments have to be rehung for proper illumination, whereas in another part of the studio the same set could have been lighted with the instruments already in place.

As you can see once again, you cannot afford to specialize in a single aspect of television production. Everything interrelates, and the more you know about the various production techniques and functions, the better your coordination of those elements will be.

Problem areas   When drawing a floor plan, watch for potential problem areas. Many times a carelessly drawn floor plan will indicate scenery backing, such as the

Control room door

Studio door

Lighting grid

Studio door

Studio

Control room

Big doors for scene storage and props

14.31 FLOOR PLAN PATTERN

The floor plan pattern shows the dimensions of the studio floor, which is further defined by the lighting grid or similar pattern. The set is drawn on this basic studio grid.

14.32 SIMPLE FLOOR PLAN
This floor plan shows all the necessary scenery, set props, and dressings as well as the more prominent hand props.
It is usually not drawn precisely to scale.

walls of a living room, that's not wide enough to provide adequate cover for the furniture or other items placed in front of it. One way to avoid such design mistakes is to draw the in-scale furniture on the floor plan first, then add the flats for the backing. Limit the set design to the actual space available.

Always place active furniture (used by the performers) at least 6 feet (roughly 2 meters) from the set wall so that the back lights can be directed at the performance areas at not too steep an angle. Also, the director can use the space between wall and furniture for camera placement and talent movement.

SET BACKGROUNDS

The background of a set helps unify a sequence of shots and places the action in a single continuous environment. It can also provide visual variety behind relatively static foreground action. Although set continuity is an important element in scene design, a plain background is not the most

interesting scenic background. You need to "dress" the set by hanging artwork, posters, or other objects on the wall to break it up into smaller yet related areas. When you dress a plain background with pictures or other objects, place them so that they are in camera range. For example, if you hang a picture between two interview chairs, it will show only in the straight-on two-shot but not in the individual close-ups. If you want more background texture in the close-up shots, position pictures so that they are seen by the cameras during cross shooting. **SEE 14.33**

VIRTUAL SETS

Virtual sets are computer-generated and keyed into a chroma-key area behind the talent, much like a weather map. Such a technique, however, rarely saves time and money. The major problem is actually for the talent, who have to work in an often disorienting blue or green environment. Parts of virtual sets, such as keying in ceilings and floors in postproduction, are an effective technique to skirt potentially difficult design problems.

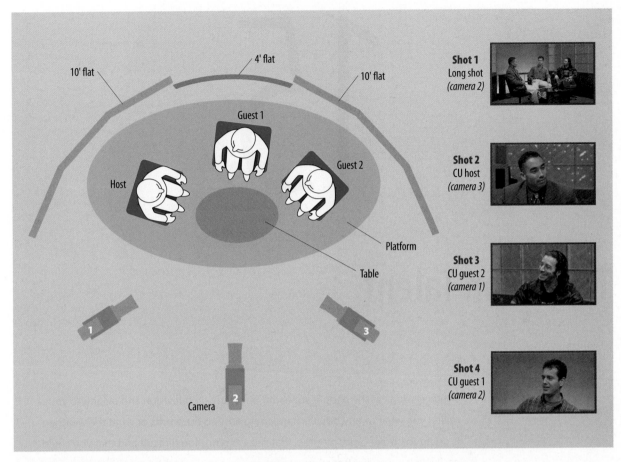

Shot 1
Long shot
(camera 2)

Shot 2
CU host
(camera 3)

Shot 3
CU guest 2
(camera 1)

Shot 4
CU guest 1
(camera 2)

14.33 BACKGROUND DRESSING
The establishing (long) shot of this interview set shows that the background flats provide some visual texture and interest for the host (camera-left) and guest 2 (far right), but not for guest 1 in the middle. The subsequent close-ups confirm this design problem.

M A I N   P O I N T S

▶ Television scenery encompasses the three-dimensional aspects of design.

▶ There are four types of scenery: standard set units, that is, hardwall and softwall flats and set modules; hanging units, such as cycloramas (cycs), drops, and curtains; platforms and wagons; and set pieces, such as pillars, screens, and periaktoi.

▶ The three basic types of properties are stage props, such as furniture, news desks, and chairs; set dressings, such as pictures, draperies, and lamps; and hand props—items such as dishes, telephones, and computers that are actually handled by the talent.

▶ To procure the props and ensure that they are available at the camera rehearsal and recording sessions, you need to prepare a prop list.

▶ When a set must be struck and set up again for a subsequent taping session, take digital photos of all set details to ensure consistency of the setup.

▶ A floor plan is drawn on a floor plan pattern and shows the exact location of the scenery and the set properties relative to the lighting grid. The floor plan is essential for the director to prepare the preliminary blocking of talent, cameras, and microphone booms; for the floor crew to set up the scenery and place the major set properties; and for the lighting director to design the basic light plot.

▶ The background of a set helps unify a sequence of shots and places the action in a single continuous environment. It can also provide visual variety behind relatively static foreground action.

▶ Virtual sets are technically complicated and difficult for the talent to move within. They are, however, quite successfully used to key in ceilings and floors.

CHAPTER

15

Television Talent

When you look at the people appearing regularly on television and talking to you—telling you what to buy, what is happening around the world, or what the weather is going to be like—you may feel that the job is not too difficult and that you could easily do it yourself. After all, most of them are simply reading copy that appears on a teleprompter. But when you actually stand in front of the camera, you quickly learn that the job is not as easy as it looks. Appearing relaxed on-camera, and pretending that the camera lens or the teleprompter is a real person to whom you are talking, takes hard work and a good amount of talent and skill. This is why we call all people appearing regularly on television *talent*. Although television talent may have varied communication objectives—some seek to entertain, educate, or inform; others seek to persuade, convince, or sell—all strive to communicate with the television audience as effectively as possible.

Section 15.1, Television Performers and Actors, concerns the major on-camera performance and acting techniques. Section 15.2, How to Do Makeup and What to Wear, briefly describes the makeup performers and actors use and what type of clothing looks good on-camera.

actor A person (male or female) who appears on-camera in dramatic roles. Actors always portray someone else.

blocking Carefully worked-out movement and actions by the talent and for all mobile television equipment.

cake A makeup base, or foundation makeup, usually water-soluble and applied with a sponge. Also called *pancake*.

cue card A large, hand-lettered card that contains copy, usually held next to the camera lens by floor personnel.

foundation A makeup base over which further makeup such as rouge and eye shadow is applied.

makeup Cosmetics used to enhance, correct, or change appearance.

pan stick A foundation makeup with a grease base. Used to cover a beard shadow or prominent skin blemish.

performer A person who appears on-camera in nondramatic shows. Performers play themselves and do not assume someone else's character.

talent Collective name for all performers and actors who appear regularly on television.

teleprompter A prompting device that projects the moving (usually computer-generated) copy over the lens so that the talent can read it without losing eye contact with the viewer. Also called *auto-cue*.

Television Performers and Actors

PERFORMANCE TECHNIQUES

The performer speaks directly to the camera, plays host to television guests, and or communicates with other performers or the studio audience; he or she is also fully aware of the presence of the television audience at home. This latter audience, however, is not the large, anonymous, and heterogeneous television audience that modern sociologists study. For the television performer, the audience is an individual or a small, intimate group who have gathered in front of a television set.

If you are a performer, try imagining your audience as a family of three, seated in their favorite room, about 10 feet away from you. With this picture in mind, you have no reason to scream at the "millions of viewers out there in videoland"; a more successful approach is to talk quietly and intimately to the family who were kind enough to let you into their home.

When you assume the role of a television performer, the camera becomes your audience. You must adapt your performance techniques to its characteristics and to other production aspects such as audio and timing. In this section we discuss the performer and the camera, the performer and audio, the performer and timing, the floor manager's cues, prompting devices, and maintaining continuity.

You can divide television talent into two categories: performers and actors. The difference between them is fairly clear-cut. Television ***performers*** are engaged basically in nondramatic activities: they play themselves and do not assume roles of other characters; they sell their own personalities to the audience. Television ***actors***, on the other hand, always portray someone else: they project a character's personality rather than their own, even if the character is modeled after their own experience. Their stories are always fictional.

Although there are distinct differences between television performers and television actors, the groups do share several functions. All talent communicate with the viewers through the television camera and must keep in mind the nuances of audio, movement, and timing. And all talent interact with other television personnel—the producer, the director, the floor manager, the camera operator, and the audio technician.

In section 15.1, Television Performers and Actors, you will read about the basics of working in front of the camera.

PERFORMER AND CAMERA

The camera is not simply an inanimate piece of machinery; it sees everything you do or don't do. It sees how you look, move, sit, and stand—in short, how you behave in a variety of situations. At times it looks at you much more closely and with greater scrutiny than a polite person would ever dare to do. It reveals the nervous twitch of your mouth when you are ill at ease and the expression of mild panic when you have forgotten a name. The camera does not look away when you scratch your nose or ear. It faithfully reflects your behavior in all pleasant and unpleasant details. As a television performer, you must carefully control your actions without letting the audience know that you are conscious of doing so.

Camera lens   Because the camera represents your audience, you must look directly into the lens (or the prompting device in front of it) whenever you intend to establish eye contact with the viewer. As a matter of fact, you should try to look *through* the lens, rather than at it, and keep eye contact much more than you would with an actual person. If you merely look at the lens instead of looking through it, or if you pretend that the camera operator is your audience and therefore glance away from the lens ever so slightly, you break the continuity and the intensity of the communication between you and the viewer; you break, however temporarily, television's magic.

Camera switching   If two or more cameras are used, you must know which one is on the air so that you can remain in direct contact with the audience. When the director switches cameras, you must follow the floor manager's cue (or, when working with robotic cameras, the change of tally lights) quickly but smoothly. Do not jerk your head from one camera to the other. If you suddenly discover that you have been talking to the wrong one, look down as if to collect your thoughts and then casually look up and glance into the "hot" camera. Continue talking in that direction until you are again cued to the other camera. This method works especially well if you work from notes or a script, as in a newscast or an interview. You can always pretend to be looking at your notes when, in reality, you are changing your view from the wrong camera to the right one.

    If the director has one camera on you in a medium shot (MS) and the other camera in a close-up (CU) of the object you are demonstrating, such as the guest's book during an interview, it is best to keep looking at the host (medium-shot) camera during the whole demonstration, even when the director switches to the close-up camera. You will not be caught looking the wrong way because only the medium-shot camera is focused on you. **SEE 15.1** You will also find that it is easier to read the copy off of a single teleprompter rather than switch from one to another in midsentence.

Close-up techniques   The tighter the shot, the harder it is for the camera to follow movement. If a camera is on a close-up, you must restrict your motions severely and move with great care. While you're performing a song, for example, the director may want to shoot very closely to intensify an especially emotional passage. Try to stand as still as possible, and do not wiggle your head. The close-

15.1 PERFORMER CAMERA

When one camera (camera 1) is on a close-up of the product (the book), and the other (camera 2) is on a medium shot of the host, the host should continue looking into camera 2 during the close-up.

up itself is intensification enough. All you have to do is sing well.

    When demonstrating small objects on a close-up, hold them steady. If they are arranged on a table, do *not* pick them up. You can either point to them or tilt them a little to give the camera a better view. There is nothing more frustrating to the camera operator and the director than a performer who snatches the product off the table just when the camera has a good close-up of it. A quick look at the studio monitor usually tells you how to hold the object for maximum visibility on-screen. If two cameras are used, "cheat" (orient) the object somewhat toward the close-up camera, but do not turn it so much that it looks unnaturally distorted on the medium-shot camera.

Warning cues   In most nondramatic shows—lectures, demonstrations, interviews, and the like—there is generally not enough time to work out a detailed blocking scheme. The director usually just walks the performers through some of the most important crossovers from one performance area to the other and through a few major actions, such as complicated demonstrations. During the on-the-air performance, you as a performer must therefore give the director and the studio crew visual and audible warnings of your unrehearsed actions. Before you stand up, for instance, first shift your weight and position your arms and legs; this signals the camera operator as well as the microphone boom operator to prepare for your move. If you pop up unexpectedly, the camera may stay in one position, focusing on the middle part of your body, which won't make for the most interesting shot to say the least, and the boom microphone will be clearly visible on-screen.

If you intend to move from one set area to another, you may use audio cues. For instance, you can warn the production crew by saying: "Let's go over to the children and ask them..." or "If you will follow me over to the lab area...." Such cues sound natural to the viewer, who is generally unaware of the fast reactions these seemingly innocuous remarks actually trigger. You must be specific when you cue unrehearsed visual material. For example, you can alert the director to the upcoming visuals by saying: "The first picture shows..." This cueing device should not be used too often, however. If you can alert the director more subtly yet equally directly, do so.

Do not try to convey the obvious. The director, not the talent, runs the show. Don't tell the director to bring the cameras a little closer to get a better view of a small object, especially if the director has already obtained a good close-up through a zoom-in. Also, avoid walking toward the camera to demonstrate an object. You may walk so close to the camera that it has to tilt up into the lights to keep your face in the shot or so close that the zoom lens can no longer focus. The zoom lens allows the camera to get to you much faster than you can get to the camera.

PERFORMER AND AUDIO

As a television performer, besides looking natural and relaxed, you must speak clearly and effectively; it rarely comes naturally. Don't be misled into believing that a resonant voice and affected pronunciation are the two prime requisites for a good announcer or other performer. On the contrary: first, you need to have something important to say; second, you need to say it with conviction and sincerity; third, you must speak clearly so that everyone can understand you. Thorough training in television announcing is an important prerequisite for any performer. Most novices speak much too fast, as though they wanted to get through the on-camera torture as quickly as possible. Don't speed up when you come to the end of a sentence or paragraph. Take a deep breath and slow down. You will be amazed how much more relaxed you will be.

Microphone technique   The following summarizes the main points about handling microphones and assisting the audio technician. (See chapter 8 for a detailed discussion of the basic microphone techniques.)

■ Most often you will work with a lavalier microphone. Once it is properly fastened, you do not have to worry about it, especially if you are relatively stationary during the performance. If you have to move from one set area to another on-camera, watch that the mic cord does not get tangled up with the set or props. Gently pull the cable behind you to keep the tension off the mic itself. A wireless lavalier will enable you to move within the performance area without having to worry about a cable.

■ When using a hand mic, check that you have enough cable for your planned actions. Speak across it, not into it. If you are interviewing someone in noisy surroundings, such as a downtown street, hold the microphone close to your mouth when you are talking, then point it toward the person as he or she responds to your questions.

■ When working with a boom mic (including a handheld shotgun or one that is mounted on a fishpole), be aware of the boom movements without letting the audience know. Give the boom operator enough warning so that he or she can anticipate your movements. Move slowly so that the boom can follow. In particular, do not make fast turns because they involve a great amount of boom movement. If you have to turn fast, try not to speak until the boom has been repositioned.

■ Do not move a desk mic, unless it is pointing in the opposite direction. Even if the microphone is pointing more toward another performer than at you, it was probably placed that way by the audio technician to achieve better audio balance.

In all cases, treat microphones gently. Mics are not intended to be hand props, to be tossed about or twirled by their cords like a lasso, even if you see such misuse occasionally in a rock performance.

Audio level   A good audio technician will ask you for an audio level before you go on the air. Many performers have the bad habit of rapidly counting to 10 or mumbling and speaking softly while the level is being taken, then, when they go on the air, blasting their opening lines. If a level is taken, speak as loudly as you will in your opening remarks and as long as required for the audio technician to adjust the volume to an optimal level.

Opening cue   At the beginning of a show, all microphones are dead until the director gives the cue for audio. You must therefore wait until you receive the opening cue from the floor manager or through the I.F.B. (interruptible foldback, or feedback) system. If you speak beforehand, you will not be heard. Do not take your opening cue from the red tally lights on the cameras unless you are so instructed. When waiting for the opening cue, look into the camera that is coming up on you and not at the floor manager.

PERFORMER AND TIMING

Live and live-recording television operate on split-second timing. Although it is ultimately the director's responsibility to get the show on and off the air as scheduled, you as the performer have a great deal to do with successful timing. Aside from careful pacing throughout the show, you must learn how much program material you can cover after you have received a 3-minute, a 2-minute, a 1-minute, a 30-second, and a 15-second cue. You must, for example, still look comfortable and relaxed although you may have to cram a lot of program material into the last minute while at the same time listening to the director's or producer's I.F.B. On the other hand, you must be prepared to fill an extra 30 seconds without appearing to grasp for words and things to do. This presence of mind, of course, is achieved through practical experience and cannot be learned solely from a textbook. It also requires that you are at least somewhat familiar with the news stories that you read off the teleprompter.

FLOOR MANAGER'S CUES

Unless you are connected with the producer and the director via I.F.B., it is the floor manager who provides the link between the director and you, the performer.

With the use of robotic cameras, the floor manager may be the only other human being in the studio besides you. The floor manager can tell you whether your delivery is too slow or too fast, how much time you have left, and whether you are speaking loudly enough or holding an object correctly for a close-up shot.

Although stations and production houses may use slightly different cueing signals and procedures, they normally consist of time cues, directional cues, and audio cues. If you are working with an unfamiliar production crew, ask the floor manager to review the cues before you go on the air. **SEE 15.2**

React to each cue immediately, even if you think it is not appropriate at that particular time. The director would not give the cue if it were not necessary. A truly professional performer is not one who never needs cues but rather one who can react to all signals quickly and smoothly. Do not look nervously for the floor manager if you think you should have received a cue; he or she will find you and draw your attention to the signal. When you receive a cue, do not acknowledge it in any way; the floor manager will know whether you noticed it.

You will find that receiving and reacting to I.F.B. information during a performance is no easy task. We all know how difficult it can be to continue a telephone conversation when someone close by is trying to tell us what else to communicate to the other party. But when reporting news in the studio or in the field, such simultaneous communication is common. You must learn to listen carefully to the I.F.B. instructions of the director or producer without letting the audience know that you are listening to someone else while talking to them. Do not interrupt your communication with the audience when getting I.F.B. instructions, even if the transmission is less than perfect. If during a live remote you can't understand what is being said on the I.F.B. channel, however, you may have to stop your narration to tell the audience that you are getting some important information from your director. Listen carefully to the I.F.B. instructions, then go on with what you were saying. Try not to adjust your earpiece while on the air. If at all possible, wait until the camera cuts away from you to do an adjustment.

PROMPTING DEVICES

Prompting devices have become an essential production tool, especially for news and speeches. The audience has come to expect the newscaster to talk directly to them rather than read the news from a script, although we all know that the newscaster cannot possibly remember the entire news copy. We expect speakers to deliver copious and complicated information without having to think about what to say next. Prompting devices are also helpful to performers who fear they may suddenly forget their lines or who have no time to memorize a script.

15.2 FLOOR MANAGER'S CUES

The floor manager uses a set of standard hand signals to relay the director's commands to the on-the-air talent.

CUE	SIGNAL	MEANING	SIGNAL DESCRIPTION
TIME CUES			
Standby		Show about to start.	Extends hand above head.
Cue		Show goes on the air.	Points to performer or live camera.
On time		Go ahead as planned (on the nose).	Touches nose with forefinger.
Speed up		Accelerate what you are doing. You are going too slowly.	Rotates hand clockwise with extended forefinger. Urgency of speed-up is indicated by fast or slow rotation.
Stretch		Slow down. Too much time left. Fill until emergency is over.	Stretches imaginary rubber band between hands.

15.2 FLOOR MANAGER'S CUES (continued)

CUE	SIGNAL	MEANING	SIGNAL DESCRIPTION
TIME CUES			
Wind up		Finish up what you are doing. Come to an end.	Similar motion to speed-up but usually with arm extended above head. Sometimes expressed with raised fist, good-bye wave, or hands rolling over each other as if wrapping a package.
Cut		Stop speech or action immediately.	Pulls index finger in knifelike motion across throat.
5 (4, 3, 2, 1) minute(s)		5 (4, 3, 2, 1) minute(s) left until end of show.	Holds up five (four, three, two, one) finger(s) or small card with number on it.
30 seconds (half minute)		30 seconds left in show.	Forms a cross with two index fingers or arms. Or holds card with number.
15 seconds		15 seconds left in show.	Shows fist (which can also mean wind up). Or holds card with number.
Roll VR (and countdown) 2, 1, take VR		Video recorder is rolling.	Holds extended left hand in front of face, moves right hand in cranking motion. Extends two, one finger(s); clenches fist or gives cut signal.

15.2 FLOOR MANAGER'S CUES *(continued)*

CUE	SIGNAL	MEANING	SIGNAL DESCRIPTION
DIRECTIONAL CUES			
Closer		Performer must come closer or bring object closer to camera.	Moves both hands toward self, palms in.
Back		Performer must step back or move object away from camera.	Uses both hands in pushing motion, palms out.
Walk		Performer must move to next performance area.	Makes a walking motion with index and middle fingers in direction of movement.
Stop		Stop right here. Do not move any more.	Extends both hands in front of body, palms out.
OK		Very well done. Stay right there. Do what you are doing.	Forms an O with thumb and forefinger, other fingers extended, motioning toward talent.

15.2 FLOOR MANAGER'S CUES (continued)

CUE	SIGNAL	MEANING	SIGNAL DESCRIPTION
AUDIO CUES			
Speak up		Performer is talking too softly for current conditions.	Cups both hands behind ears or moves hand upward, palm up.
Tone down		Performer is too loud or too enthusiastic for the occasion.	Moves both hands toward studio floor, palms down, or puts extended forefinger over mouth in shhh-like motion.
Closer to mic		Performer is too far away from mic for good audio pickup.	Moves hand toward face.
Keep talking		Keep on talking until further cues.	Extends thumb and forefinger horizontally, moving them like a bird's beak.

Prompting devices must be totally reliable, and the performer must be able to read the copy without appearing to lose eye contact with the viewer. Two devices have proved especially successful: cue cards and the teleprompter.

Cue cards　Used for relatively short pieces of copy, there are many types of *cue cards*, and the choice depends largely on what the performer is used to and what he or she prefers. Usually, they are fairly large posterboards on which the copy is hand-lettered with a felt-tipped marker. The size of the cards and the lettering depends on how well the performer can see and how far away the camera is. Even the handling of cue cards is easier said than done. A good floor person holds the cards as close to the lens as

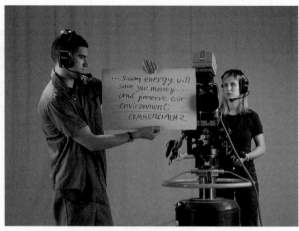

15.3 HANDLING CUE CARDS

A This is the wrong way to hold a cue card: the card is too far away from the lens, and the hands cover part of the copy. The floor person cannot see the copy and does not know when to change the card.

B This is the correct way to hold a cue card: the floor person does not cover the copy, holds the card close to the lens, and reads along with the talent.

Glass plate reflecting image from monitor

Flat panel or monitor displaying copy

Copy as it appears to talent

15.4 TELEPROMPTER DISPLAY OF COPY

The monitor or flat-panel display reflects the copy onto a glass plate directly over the lens. The lettering remains invisible to the camera, but the talent can read the copy while keeping eye contact with the audience.

possible, the hands do not cover any of the copy, and he or she follows the performer's lines so that the changes from one card to the next are smooth. **SEE 15.3**

As a performer you must learn to read by peripheral vision so that you will not lose eye contact with the lens. Get together with the floor person handling the cards to double-check their correct order. If the floor person forgets to change the card at the appropriate moment, snap your fingers to attract his or her attention; in an emergency you may have to ad-lib until the system is functioning again. You should study the topic long before the show begins, enabling you to improvise sensibly at least for a short time. If your performance is shot for postproduction, ask the director to stop the recording so that the cards can be put in the correct order.

Studio teleprompter   The most effective prompting device is the *teleprompter*, or auto-cue, which normally uses a flat-panel video display upon which the copy scrolls. The video display is then reflected onto a glass angled over the camera lens. You can read the copy, which now appears in front of the lens but which remains invisible to the camera. This way you do not have to glance to the side but can maintain eye contact with the viewer at all times. **SEE 15.4**

Most often the copy is typed into a computer that acts as a combination word processor and character generator. It can produce the text in several font sizes and scroll (often referred to as crawl) the copy up and down the screen at various speeds. The copy is then sent to the teleprompter flatbed screen mounted on the camera. All cameras used in the production display the same copy.

In newscasts the anchorperson should have the text as it appears on the teleprompter also printed out as hard copy. This script serves as backup in case the prompting device fails. Such copy also gives the anchor a reason to glance down to indicate a story transition, to change cameras, or to see during a commercial break what is coming up next.

When using a teleprompter, the distance between you and the camera is no longer arbitrary. The camera must be close enough for you to read the copy without squinting but not so close that the home viewer can see your eyes moving back and forth. If the minimum camera distance is too far to see the teleprompter copy comfortably, have the font enlarged.

Field prompter   Have you ever wondered how some correspondents can stand on a busy city street and report a well-written story without ever stumbling or searching for words? Although some certainly have that skill, others use some kind of prompting device. If the copy is brief, handheld cue cards or even some notes will do. Longer copy calls for a field prompter.

There are several models of field prompters, including a miniature version of the studio teleprompter. The flat-panel video displays are so lightweight that they can be attached to a tripod. Most high-end field prompters can be hooked up to a laptop computer with prompting software. **SEE 15.5** You can adjust the size of the font and scroll the copy at different speeds. Low-end prompters use a paper roll mounted immediately below or to one side of the lens. Similar units can be used independent of the camera and held by a floor person or mounted on a tripod directly above or below the camera lens. Regardless of the quality of the teleprompter, you should always be familiar enough with the subject matter to be able to talk about it intelligently if the prompting device fails. If you don't have a prompter, read the package intro or story from a regular news script. If it is windy, use a clipboard or a piece of foam core as backing for the script. This is especially important when you need the other hand to hold a hand mic.

CONTINUITY

When you work on a brief commercial or announcement that presents a continuous event but that is shot film-style over a period of several days or even weeks for postproduction, you must look the same in all the video-recording sessions. Obviously, you must wear the same clothes. You

15.5 FIELD PROMPTER
A lightweight prompter with a flat-panel video display can be mounted on any type of field camera. Like a studio prompter, it projects the text directly over the lens.

must also wear the same jewelry, scarf, and tie from one recording session to the next. You cannot have your coat buttoned on one take and unbuttoned on the next one. Makeup and hairstyle too must be identical for all sessions. Have digital photos taken of yourself from the front, sides, and back immediately after the first recording session for an easy and readily available reference.

Most important, you must maintain the same level of energy throughout the recording sessions. For example, you cannot end one session full of energy and then be very low-key the next day when the video recording resumes, especially when the edited version does not suggest any passage of time between takes. On repeat takes, try to maintain identical energy levels.

ACTING TECHNIQUES

In contrast to the television performer, the television actor assumes someone else's character and personality. (In this discussion the term *actor* refers to both male and female talent.) To become a good television actor, you obviously must first master the art of acting, a subject beyond the scope of this chapter. This discussion focuses on how to adapt your acting to the peculiarities of the television medium. Many excellent actors consider television the most difficult medium in which to work. They must function effectively within an environment crowded with confusing and impersonal technical gear, and they often get less attention from the director than do the camera operator and the sound technician.

AUDIENCE

The biggest difference between stage acting and screen acting is that you are not playing for a stationary live audience but for a constantly moving camera that never blinks or offers feedback on your performance. Worse, your performance is chopped up into short takes that rarely, if ever, allow you to work up to a memorable performance pitch. Each of the little performance segments must be on the mark.

In most takes the camera moves around you, looking at you at close range and from a distance as well as from above and below. It may look at your eyes, your feet, your hands, your back—whatever the director selects for the audience to see. And at all times you must look completely convincing and natural; the character you are portraying must appear on-screen as a believable human being. Keep in mind that you are playing to a virtual audience that is almost always standing right next to you, looking at you from very close up and from all angles. You need not (and should not) project your motions and emotions as you would when acting on-stage. The television camera does the projecting—the communicating—for you. Be aware of the camera or cameras, but don't ever acknowledge their presence.

Internalization of your role, as opposed to externalization, is a key factor in your performance. You must attempt to become as much as possible the person you are portraying, rather than act out the character. Because of the close scrutiny of the camera and the intimacy of the close-up, keep your gestures minimal. Also, your reactions become as important as your actions. You can often communicate feelings more readily by reacting to a situation than by being a part of it.

BLOCKING

You must be meticulous in following rehearsed *blocking*— where you should move and what you should do in relation to the set, the other actors, and the television equipment. Sometimes inches are significant, especially if the show is shot primarily in close-ups. Precise television lighting and the limited microphone radius when booms are used also force you to adhere strictly to the established blocking.

Once the show is on the air, you have an obligation to follow the rehearsed action. This is not the time to innovate just because you have a sudden inspiration. If the director has not been warned of your change, the new blocking will always be worse than the previously rehearsed one. The camera has a limited field of view; if you want to be seen, you must stay within it.

Some directors have the floor manager mark the exact spots for you to stand or the paths of movement. This is called spiking your position. Look for these tape or chalk marks and follow them without being too obvious. If such spike marks are not used, establish a mental blocking map by remembering where you stand for specific shots in relation to the set and the props. For example, for your scene with the office manager you stand to the left of the file cabinet; for the scene in the doctor's office, you walk counterclockwise around the desk and stop at the camera-right corner of the desk.

In over-the-shoulder and cross-shots, you need to see the camera lens if you are to be seen by the camera. If you cannot see the lens, the camera cannot see you. Even the lighting instruments can help you with blocking. For example, to be sure you're in the light when coming through a door, move forward until you feel the warmth of the lights on your forehead.

Sometimes the director will position you in a way that seems entirely wrong to you, especially in relation to the other actors. Don't try to correct this on your own by arbitrarily moving away from the designated spot. A certain camera angle and zoom lens position may very well warrant unusual blocking to achieve a certain effect. Do not second-guess the director.

When you are handling props, the camera is often on a close-up. This means that you must remember all the rehearsed actions and execute them in exactly the same way and with the same speed as they were initially rehearsed. Don't appear nervous when using props (unless the director calls for it); handle them routinely as extensions of your gestures. The way you handle props, such as taking off your glasses, cleaning them, and putting them on again, can often sharpen your character.

MEMORIZING LINES

As a television actor, you must be able to learn your lines quickly and accurately. If, as is the case in soap operas, you have only one evening to learn a great number of lines for the next day, you must indeed be a quick study. You cannot ad-lib during such performances simply because you have played the role for so long. Most of your lines are important not only from a dramatic point of view but also because they serve as video and audio cues for the whole production team. Your last line of a speech is often a trigger for several key actions in the control room: to switch to another camera, to roll a video-recorded insert, or to call up a special effect.

For a single-camera EFP (electronic field production) or digital cinema studio production, each shot is set up and recorded separately. Such a production approach often gives you a chance to read over your lines for each take. Although this approach may make it easier to remember lines, it is harder to maintain continuity of action and emotion. Good screen actors do not rely on prompting devices; after all, you should live, not read, your role. Nevertheless, many good actors like to have all their lines backed up by cue cards, just in case. Most of the time, they never look at them. But even if the cue cards function only as a safety net, their contribution to a good performance more than justifies their use.

TIMING

Like the television performer, as an actor you must have an acute sense of timing. Timing matters for pacing your performance, for building to a climax, for delivering a punch line, and for staying within a tightly prescribed clock time. Even if a play is video-recorded scene-by-scene or even shot-by-shot, you still need to carefully observe the stipulated running times for each take. You may have to stretch a scene without making it appear to drag, or you may need to gain a few seconds by speeding up a scene without destroying its solemn mood. You must be flexible without stepping out of character.

Always respond immediately to the floor manager's cues. Do not stop in the middle of a scene simply because you disagree with a specific cue; you're not privy to all the goings-on in the control room. Play the scene to the end and then speak up. Minor timing errors are usually corrected in postproduction.

MAINTAINING CONTINUITY

As you know, digital cinema and television plays are video-recorded piecemeal, which means that you are not able to perform a play from beginning to end as in a theater production. You cannot be upbeat during the first part of the video recording and then, a few days later when the scene is continued, project a low-energy mood because you didn't sleep well the previous night. Often scenes are shot out of sequence for production efficiency and, ultimately, to save money, so it is not possible to have a continuous and logical development of emotions, as is the case in a continuous live or live-recording pickup. Scenes are inevitably repeated to make them better or to achieve various fields of view and camera angles. This means that, as an actor, you cannot psych yourself up for a single show-stopping performance. Rather, you need to maintain your energy and motivation for each take. Television unfailingly detects subtle nuances and levels of energy and the accompanying acting continuity—or lack thereof.

One of the most important qualities to watch for when continuing a scene that was started some days before is the tempo of your performance. If you moved slowly in the first part of the scene, do not race through the second part unless the director wants such a change. It usually helps to watch a recording of your previous performance so that you can continue the scene with the same energy level and tempo.

DIRECTOR/ACTOR RELATIONSHIP

As a television actor, you cannot afford to be temperamental; the director has too many people and elements to coordinate. You may sometimes feel utterly neglected by the director, who seems to worry more about a camera shot than advising you on how to play a difficult scene. The problem is that often you will, indeed, be neglected by the director in favor of some technical detail. You need to realize that you are not the only significant element in the production; other production people are too—the camera operators, the technical director, the audio technician, the recording technician, and the lighting director, to name but a few.

Even if you have no intention of becoming a television actor, you should make an effort to learn as much about acting as possible. An able actor is generally an effective television performer; a television director with training in acting is generally better equipped to deal with talent than one who has no knowledge of the art.

AUDITIONS

All auditions are equally important, whether you are trying out for a one-line off-camera utterance or a principal role in a dramatic series. Whenever you audition give your best. You can prepare yourself even if you don't know beforehand what you will be reading. Wear something appropriate that looks good on-camera and be properly groomed. Keep your energy up even if you have to wait half a day before you are called to deliver your line.

When you get the script beforehand, study it carefully. For example, if you are doing a commercial for a soft drink, become as familiar as possible with the product, the company that makes it, and the advertising agency producing the commercial. Knowing about the product gives you a certain confidence that inevitably shows up in your delivery. Listen carefully to the instructions given to you before and during the audition. Remember that television is an intimate medium.

When instructed to demonstrate a product, practice before you are on-camera to make sure you know how, for example, to open the easy-to-open package. Ask the floor crew to help you prepare a product for easy handling. Also find out how close the majority of shots will be so that you can keep your actions within camera range.

As an actor be sure to understand thoroughly the character you are to portray. If the script does not tell you much about the character, ask the director or producer to explain how he or she perceives it. You should be able to sense the specifics of the character even when given only minimal cues. Decide on a behavior pattern and follow it, even if your interpretation may be somewhat off base. If the director's perceptions run counter to your interpretation, do not argue. Most important, do not ask the casting director to provide you with the "proper motivation" as you may have learned in acting school. At this point it is assumed that you can analyze the script and motivate yourself for the reading. Realize that you are auditioned primarily on how well and how quickly you perceive the script's image of the character and how close you can come to it in speech and sometimes also in looks and actions.

Be creative without overdoing it. When auditions were held for the male lead in a television play about a lonely woman and a rather crude and unscrupulous man who wanted to take advantage of her, one of the actors auditioning added a little of his own interpretation of the character that eventually got him the part. While reading an intimate scene in which he was supposed to persuade the leading lady to make love to him, he manicured his fingernails with slightly rusty fingernail clippers. In fact, this aggravating fingernail clipping was later written into the scene.

Finally, when auditioning—as when participating in athletics or any competitive activity—be aware, but not afraid, of the competition. Innate acting talent is not always the deciding factor in casting a part. Sometimes the director may have a particular image in mind of the physical appearance and the behavior of the actor—heavy and awkward, light and agile, or lean and muscular—that overrides acting skill. Sometimes a well-known actor who can guarantee a large audience may win out. As an actor you need to be prepared to take it repeatedly on the chin.

MAIN POINTS

▶ Television talent refers to all persons who perform regularly in front of the camera. They are classified into two large groups: performers and actors.

▶ Television performers are basically engaged in nondramatic shows, such as newscasts, interviews, and game shows. They portray themselves. Television actors portray someone else.

▶ The television performer must adapt his or her techniques to the characteristics of the camera and the other production elements, including audio, timing, the floor manager's cues, prompting devices, and continuity.

▶ Because the camera lens represents the audience, performers must look *through* the lens to establish and maintain eye contact with the viewer. If cameras are switched, performers must transfer their gaze to the hot camera smoothly and naturally.

▶ Timing is an important performance requirement. A good performer must respond quickly yet smoothly to the floor manager's time, directional, and audio cues.

▶ Prompting devices have become essential in television production. The two most frequently used devices are cue cards and the teleprompter.

▶ Television acting requires that the actor overcome the lack of an actual audience and internalize the role, restrict gestures and movements because of close-ups, follow exactly the rehearsed blocking, memorize lines quickly, have a good sense of timing, maintain continuity in physical appearance and energy level over a series of takes, and keep a positive attitude despite occasional neglect by the director.

▶ Performers and actors should prepare as much as possible for auditions, dress properly for the occasion (role), and sharpen the character through some prop or mannerism.

15.2

How to Do Makeup and What to Wear

When you hear of makeup, you may think of movies in which actors are transformed into monsters or odd-looking aliens or of how to fake a variety of wounds. But most television makeup is done not so much to transform appearance as to make someone look as good as possible on-camera. The same goes for clothing. Unless you act in a period play, most actors wear clothes that fit the role, and performers choose clothes that make them look attractive on-camera.

The aim of section 15.2 is to help you choose makeup, clothing, and costumes that not only fit but also add to the overall production values and communication intent.

▶ **MAKEUP**
  Materials, application, and technical requirements

▶ **CLOTHING AND COSTUMING**
  Line, texture and detail, and color

MAKEUP

All *makeup* is used for three basic reasons: to enhance appearance, to correct appearance, and to change appearance. Standard over-the-counter makeup is used daily by many women to accentuate and improve their features. Minor skin blemishes are covered up, and the eyes and lips are emphasized. Makeup can also be used to correct closely or widely spaced eyes, sagging flesh under the chin, a short or long nose, a slightly too prominent forehead, and many similar minor "flaws." If a person is to portray a specific character in a play, a complete change of appearance may be necessary. Dramatic changes of age, ethnicity, and character can be accomplished through creative makeup techniques. Make-up artists working for crime show or medical series have a field day. Their grisly renderings of all sorts of bodily harm or close-ups of bloody operations are often so realistic that they border on the repulsive; somehow we seem to have lost the respect for the miracle of life and go to any extreme to capture the audience's attention. Nevertheless, these effects are testimony to the high artistic skills of the makeup artists.

The various purposes for applying cosmetics require different techniques, of course. Enhancing someone's appearance calls for the most straightforward procedure; correcting someone's appearance is slightly more complicated; and changing an actor's appearance may require involved and complex makeup techniques. Making a young actor look 80 years old is best left to the professional makeup artist. You need not learn all about corrective and character makeup methods, but you should have some idea of the basic materials, techniques, and technical requirements of television makeup.

MATERIALS

A great variety of excellent television makeup material is available. Most makeup artists in the theater arts department of a college or university have up-to-date product lists. In fact, most large drugstores can supply you with the basic materials for enhancing a performer's appearance. Women performers are generally experienced in cosmetic materials and techniques; men may, at least initially, need some advice.

The most basic makeup item is a *foundation* that covers minor blemishes and cuts down light reflections on oily skin. Water-based *cake* makeup foundations are preferred over the more cumbersome cream-based foundations, often called *pan-stick*. Any one of the Kryolan Aqua Color Cake and Supracolor Cream Foundation line, the Maybelline EverFresh cake series, or the Max Factor cake and pan-stick selection is probably all you need for most makeup jobs. The colors range from a warm, light ivory to dark shades for dark-skinned performers.

Women can use their own lipsticks so long as the reds do not contain too much blue. For dark-skinned talent, a warm red, such as coral, is often more effective than a darker red that contains a great amount of blue. Other materials, such as eyebrow pencil, mascara, and eye shadow, are generally part of every woman performer's makeup kit.

Materials such as hairpieces or even latex masks are part of the professional makeup artist's inventory. They are of little use in most nondramatic productions.

APPLICATION

It is not always easy to persuade nonprofessional performers, especially men, to put on necessary makeup. You may do well to look at the guests on-camera before deciding whether they need any. If they do, you must be tactful in suggesting its application. Try to appeal not to the performer's vanity but to his or her desire to contribute to a good performance. Explain the necessity for makeup in technical terms, such as color and light balance.

All makeup rooms have large mirrors so that talent can watch the entire makeup procedure. Adequate, even illumination is critical. The color temperature of the light in which the makeup is applied must match, or at least closely approximate, that of the production illumination. Most makeup rooms have two illumination systems that can be switched from the indoor (3,200K) standard to the outdoor (5,600K) standard. Ideally, makeup should be applied under the lighting conditions in which the production is recorded. This is because each lighting setup has its own color temperature. Reddish light (low color temperature) may require cooler, more bluish makeup than would higher-color-temperature lighting. In higher-color-temperature lighting (more bluish light), you need to use warmer (more reddish) makeup. (For a review of color temperature, see chapter 11.) **ZVL1** ▶LIGHTS→ Color temperature→ light sources

When makeup is applied in the studio, have a small mirror on hand. Most women performers are glad to apply the more complicated makeup themselves—lipstick and mascara, for instance. In fact, most professional television talent prefer to apply their makeup themselves; they usually know what kind they need for a specific television show.

When using a water-based cake makeup, apply it evenly with a wet sponge over the face and adjacent exposed skin areas. Get the base right up into the hairline, and have a towel ready to wipe off the excess. If close-ups of hands are shown, apply cake base to them and the arms. This is especially important for performers who demonstrate small objects on-camera. If an uneven suntan is exposed (especially when women performers wear backless dresses or different kinds of bathing suits), all bare skin areas must be covered with cake makeup. Bald men need a generous

amount of cake foundation to tone down inevitable light reflections and to cover up perspiration.

Be careful not to give male performers a baby-face complexion through too much makeup. It is sometimes desirable to have a little beard area show. Frequently, a slight covering up of the beard with a pan-stick is all that is needed. If additional foundation is necessary, a pan-stick around the beard area should be applied first and then set with powder. A very light application of yellow or orange greasepaint satisfactorily counteracts the blue of a heavy five-o'clock shadow (much like the backlight for the blue chroma-key area). There are professional beard covers available.

Because your face is the most expressive communication agent, try to keep your hair out of your face as much as possible.

TECHNICAL REQUIREMENTS

Like so many other production elements, makeup must yield to the demands of the television camera. These limitations include color distortion, color balance, and close-ups.

Color distortion   As mentioned, skin tones are the only real color references the viewer has for color adjustment on a home receiver. Their accurate rendering is therefore of the utmost importance. Because cool colors (hues with a blue tint) have a tendency to overemphasize bluishness, especially in high-color-temperature lighting, warm colors (warm reds, oranges, browns, and tans) are preferred for television makeup. They usually provide more sparkle, especially when used on a dark-skinned face.

The color of the foundation makeup should match the natural skin tones as closely as possible, regardless of whether the face is naturally light or naturally dark. Again, to avoid bluish shadows, warm rather than cool foundation colors are preferred. Be careful, however, that light-colored skin does not turn pink. As much as you should guard against too much blue in a dark face, you must watch for too much pink in a light face.

The skin reflectance of a dark face can produce unflattering highlights. These should be toned down by a proper cake foundation or a translucent powder. Otherwise the video operator will have to compensate for the highlights through shading, making the dark picture areas unnaturally dense.

Color balance   Generally, the art director, scene designer, makeup artist, and costume designer coordinate in production meetings all the colors in a scene. In non-broadcast productions, where freelance people are usually hired for scene design and makeup, such coordination is not always easy. In any case try to communicate the color requirements to these people as best you can. Some attention beforehand to the coordination of the colors used in the scenery, costumes, and makeup certainly facilitates the production process.

Sometimes the surrounding colors reflect on the performer's clothing or face, which the camera shows as noticeable color distortions. One way of avoiding such reflections is to have the talent step far enough away from the reflecting surfaces. When such a move is not possible, apply an adequate amount of cake makeup and additional powder to the discolored skin areas. The viewer will tolerate to some extent the color distortion on clothing but not on skin unless the colors are purposely distorted for dramatic effect.

Close-ups   Makeup must be smooth and subtle enough that the talent's face looks natural even in an extreme close-up with a high-definition television (HDTV) camera. The skin should have a normal sheen, neither too oily (high reflectance) nor too dull (low reflectance but no brilliance—the skin looks lifeless). The subtlety of television makeup goes directly against theater makeup techniques, in which features and colors are greatly exaggerated for the benefit of the spectators in the back row. Good television makeup remains largely invisible, so a close-up of a person's face under actual production lighting conditions is the best criterion for judging the necessity for and the quality of makeup. If the performer or actor looks good on-camera without makeup, none is needed. If the performer needs makeup and the close-up of his or her finished face looks normal, the makeup is acceptable. If it shows, the makeup must be toned down.

CLOTHING AND COSTUMING

In small-station operations and most nonbroadcast productions, you are mainly concerned with clothing the performer rather than costuming the actor. The performer's clothes should be attractive and stylish but not too conspicuous or showy. Television viewers expect a performer to be well dressed but not overdressed. After all, a television performer is a guest in the viewer's home, not a nightclub entertainer.

CLOTHING

The type of clothing you wear as a performer depends largely on your personal taste. It also depends on the type of program or the setting and the occasion. Obviously, you dress differently when reporting live in the field during a snowstorm than when taking part in a panel discussion on the homeless in your city. Whatever the occasion, some types of clothing look better on television than others. Because the camera may look at you both from a distance and at close range, the lines, texture, and details are as important as the overall color scheme.

Line   Television has a tendency to add a few extra pounds to the performer, even if they are not digitally stretched to make a 3 × 4 picture fit the 16 × 9 screen. Clothing cut to a slim silhouette helps combat this problem. Slim dresses and closely tailored suits look more attractive than do heavy, horizontally striped fabrics and baggy styles. The overall silhouette of the clothing should look pleasing from a variety of angles and should appear slim-fitting yet comfortable.

Texture and detail   Whereas line is especially important in long shots, the texture and the detail of clothing become important on close-ups. Textured material often looks better than plain, but avoid patterns that have too much contrast or are too busy. Closely spaced geometric patterns such as herringbone weaves and checks cause a moiré effect, which looks like superimposed vibrating rainbow colors. **SEE 15.6**

Such moiré patterns are caused when the scanning lines of the camera literally bump into the lines of the optical pattern. HDTV does not help and in fact frequently makes it worse. One proven technique is to defocus the camera somewhat, which will render the optical lines less precise. Note that most high-quality studio monitors have moiré suppression circuits built-in, but most home receivers do not. You may not always be aware of the moiré problem a herringbone jacket or checked tie causes when watching yourself in the mirror or on a high-end monitor. If you suspect possible moiré problems, view the attire on a television set that does not contain such preventive circuits.

Stripes may also cause problems. They sometimes extend beyond the garment and bleed through surrounding sets and objects. Unless you have a high-quality HDTV camera, extremely fine detail in a pattern will either look too busy or appear smudgy.

15.6 MOIRÉ PATTERN
Clothing with thinly striped patterns can cause an undesirable artifact, called moiré pattern. The pattern usually vibrates and sometimes produces rainbow colors.

Make your clothing more interesting on-camera not by choosing a detailed cloth texture but by adding decorative accessories, such as scarves and jewelry. Although jewelry style depends, of course, on the performer's taste, in general he or she should limit it to one or two distinctive pieces. The sparkle of rhinestones can become an exciting visual accent when dressing for a special occasion, such as the televised fund-raising dinner or a concert by the community symphony, but they are obviously out of place when interviewing a crime victim.

Color The most important consideration for choosing colors is that they harmonize with the set. If the set is lemon yellow, do not wear a lemon yellow dress. As mentioned before, avoid saturated red, unless you are working with very good studio cameras. If you are taking part in blue chroma keying (such as in weathercasting), don't wear a similar blue unless you want to become transparent during the chroma key. Even a blue scarf or tie may give you trouble. The same goes for wearing green if you work in front of a green chroma-key backdrop.

You can wear black or a very dark color, or white or a very light color, so long as the material is not glossy and highly reflective. But avoid wearing a combination of the two, even if the high-end digital camera can handle such a contrast. If the set is very dark, avoid a starched white shirt. If the set colors are extremely light, do not wear black. As desirable as a dramatic color contrast is, extreme brightness variations cause difficulties for even the best cameras and video operators. Stark white, glossy clothes can turn exposed skin areas dark on the television screen or distort the more subtle colors, especially when the cameras are on

auto-iris. Dark-skinned performers should avoid highly reflecting white or light-yellow clothes. If you wear a dark suit, reduce the brightness contrast by wearing a pastel shirt. Light blue, pink, light green, tan, or gray—all show up well on television. As always, when in doubt as to how well a certain color combination photographs, preview it on-camera on the set and under the actual lighting conditions.

If two prospective weathercasters—a man and a woman—were now to ask you for advice on what to wear, what would you tell them?

Both should wear something comfortable that does not look wide or baggy. Because of chroma keying, avoid wearing anything blue (or green, if the chroma-key backdrop is green). If possible, tell them the color of the set background so that they can avoid wearing the same hue. The woman might wear a slim suit or dress of plain, simple colors. Avoid black-and-white combinations, such as a black jacket over a highly reflecting white blouse. She should avoid highly contrasting narrow stripes or checks and wear as little jewelry as possible, unless she wants to appear flashy. The man might wear a slim suit or slacks and a plain coat, with a plain tie or one with a simple pattern. He should avoid wearing a white shirt under a black or dark blue suit, as well as clothes or accessories with checkered or herringbone patterns.

COSTUMING
For most normal productions in nonbroadcast, or non-network, operations, you do not need costumes. If you do a play or a commercial that involves costumed actors, you can always rent the necessary articles from a costume company or borrow them from the theater arts department

of a local high school or college. Theater departments usually have a well-stocked costume room from which you can draw most standard uniforms and period costumes. If you use stock costumes on television, they must look convincing even in a tight close-up. The general construction and, especially, the detail of theater accessories are often too coarse for the television camera.

The color and pattern restrictions for clothing also apply for costumes. The total color design—the overall balance of colors among scenery, costumes, and makeup—is important in some television plays, particularly in musicals and variety shows, where long shots often reveal the total scene, including actors, dancers, scenery, and props. As pointed out before, rather than try to balance all the hues, it is easier to balance the colors by their relative aesthetic energy. You can accomplish this balance by keeping the set relatively low-energy (colors with low saturation) and the set accessories and costumes high-energy (high-saturation colors).

ZETTL'S VIDEOLAB

For your reference or to track your work, the *Zettl's VideoLab* program cue in this chapter is listed here with its corresponding page number.

ZVL1 LIGHTS→ Color temperature→ light sources   **330**

MAIN POINTS

▶ Makeup and clothing are important aspects of the talent's preparation for on-camera work.

▶ Makeup is used for three basic reasons: to enhance, to correct, and to change appearance.

▶ Warm colors generally look better than cool colors because the camera tends to emphasize the bluishness of cool colors; but avoid wearing red unless you work with high-end cameras.

▶ Makeup must be smooth and subtle to appear natural in the actual production lighting and on extreme close-ups. The most basic makeup item is a foundation that covers minor blemishes. Water-based cake foundations, which come in a variety of skin tones, are generally used for television makeup.

▶ The techniques of television makeup do not differ drastically from applying ordinary street makeup, especially if the purpose is to enhance or correct appearance.

▶ These factors are important when choosing clothing: line, whereby a slim cut is preferred; texture and detail, which must not make the clothing appear too busy; and color, which should harmonize yet contrast with the dominant color of the set.

▶ Tightly striped or checkered patterns and herringbone weaves, as well as highly saturated reds and a combination of black-and-white fabrics, should be avoided.

16

The Director in Production: Preparation

As a director you tell talent and the entire production team what to do before, during, and after the actual production. But before you can tell *them* what to do, you obviously need a clear idea of what *you* need to do: think about what the program should look like and how to get from the idea to the television image.

More specifically, as a director you must be able to translate an idea, a script, or an actual event (such as an interview, a parade, or a basketball game) into effective television pictures and sound. You translate the defined process message (the expected outcome of the program—the program objective) into the various medium requirements and then combine them through the production process into a specific television program. You must decide on the people (talent and crew) and the technical production elements (cameras, mics, sets, lighting, and so forth) that will produce the intended effect—the process message—and coordinate all these elements with maximum efficiency and effectiveness. And you must do so with style. Because you may have to accomplish some of these preparation tasks on a moment's notice, it counts more as production preparation than a meticulous preproduction activity. **ZVL1** PROCESS→ Process introduction

Section 16.1, How a Director Prepares, looks at the director's roles, how to make sure the director knows what the show is all about, and some essential steps in preparing for the show. Section 16.2, Communication and Scheduling, addresses the functions of the support staff, the need to double-check on the producer's facilities requests and schedules, and how to communicate with talent and crew.

The director's activities in the production and postproduction phases are the focus of chapter 17.

KEY TERMS

AD Stands for *associate* or *assistant director*. Assists the director in all production phases.

DP Stands for *director of photography*. In major motion picture production, the DP is responsible for the lighting (similar to the LD in television). In smaller motion picture productions and in EFP, the DP will operate the camera. In television it refers to the camera operator, or shooter.

facilities request A list that contains all technical facilities needed for a specific production.

locking-in An especially vivid mental image—visual or aural—during script analysis that determines the subsequent visualizations and sequencing.

medium requirements All content elements, production elements, and people needed to generate the defined process message.

process message The message actually received by the viewer in the process of watching a television program.

production schedule The calendar that shows the preproduction, production, and postproduction dates and who is doing what, when, and where.

sequencing The control and the structuring of a shot series during editing.

storyboard A series of sketches of the key visualization points of an event, with the corresponding audio information.

time line A breakdown of time blocks for various activities on the actual production day, such as crew call, setup, and camera rehearsal.

visualization Mentally converting a scene into a number of key video images and sounds, not necessarily in sequence. The mental image of a shot.

16.1

How a Director Prepares

As a television director, you are expected to be an artist who can translate ideas into effective pictures and sounds, a psychologist who can encourage people to give their best, a technical adviser who can solve problems the crew would rather give up on, and a coordinator and a stickler for detail who leaves nothing unchecked. You must be skilled in multitasking but also able to pay full attention to every single production element. Not an easy job by any means! Although some directors think that their profession requires a divine gift, most good directors acquired and honed their skills through painstaking study and practice.

▶ **THE DIRECTOR'S ROLES**
   Artist, psychologist, technical adviser, and coordinator

▶ **WHAT THE SHOW IS ALL ABOUT**
   Process message and production method

▶ **SCRIPT ANALYSIS**
   Locking-in point and translation

▶ **VISUALIZATION AND SEQUENCING**
   Formulating the process message and determining the medium requirements

▶ **PREPARING FOR THE SHOW**
   Floor plan, location sketch, storyboard, and marking the script

THE DIRECTOR'S ROLES

The various roles you must assume as a director are not as clear-cut as you will see them described in this section. They frequently overlap, and you may have to switch from one to another several times just in the first five minutes of rehearsal. Even when pressed for time and pressured by people with a variety of problems, always pay full attention to the task at hand before moving on to the next one.

DIRECTOR AS ARTIST

In the role of an artist, a director is expected to produce pictures and sound that not only convey the intended message clearly and effectively but that do so with flair. You need to know how to look at an event or a script, quickly recognize its essential quality, and select and order those elements that help interpret it for a specific audience. Flair and style enter when you do all these things with a personal touch—when, for example, you shoot a certain scene very tightly to heighten its energy or when you select unusual background music that helps convey a specific mood. But unlike the painter, who can wait for inspiration and can retouch the painting until it is finally right, the television director is expected to be creative by a specific clock time and to make the right decisions the first time around.

DIRECTOR AS PSYCHOLOGIST

Because you deal with a variety of people who approach television production from different perspectives, you need to also assume the role of psychologist. For example, in a single production you may have to communicate with a producer who worries about the budget, technicians who are primarily concerned with the technical quality of pictures and sound, temperamental talent, a designer who has strong ideas about the set, and the mother of a child actor, who thinks your close-ups of her daughter are not tight enough.

Not only must you get everyone to perform at a consistently high level, you also have to get them to work as a team. Although there is no formula for directing a team of such diverse individuals, the following are some basic guidelines to help you exercise the necessary leadership.

■ Be well prepared and know what you want to accomplish. You cannot possibly get people to work for a common goal if you do not know what it is.

■ Know the specific functions of each team member. Explain to all the individuals what you want them to do before holding them accountable for their work.

■ Be precise about what you want the talent to do. Do not be vague with your instructions or intimidated by a celebrity. The more professional the talent, the more readily they will follow your direction.

■ Project a secure attitude. Be firm but not harsh when giving instructions. Listen to recommendations from other production staff but do not yield your decision-making to them.

■ Do not ridicule someone for making a mistake. Point out the problems and suggest solutions. Keep the overall goal in mind.

■ Treat the talent and all members of the production team with respect and compassion. A good director knows no hierarchy of importance among the team members. All have equal responsibility for getting the production done.

DIRECTOR AS TECHNICAL ADVISER

Although you do not have to be an expert in operating the technical equipment, as a director you should still be able to give the crew helpful instructions on how to use it to achieve your communication goal. In the role of technical adviser, you are acting much like a conductor of a symphony orchestra. The conductor may not be able to play all the instruments in the orchestra, but he or she certainly knows the sounds that the various instruments can generate and how they ought to be played to produce good music. The preceding chapters were designed to give you a satisfactory background in technical production.

DIRECTOR AS COORDINATOR

In addition to your artistic, psychological, and technical skills, you must be able to coordinate a great many production details and processes. The role of coordinator goes beyond directing in the traditional sense, which generally means blocking the talent and helping them give peak performances.

Especially when directing nondramatic shows, you must expend most of your effort on cueing members of the production team (both technical and nontechnical) to initiate certain video and audio functions, such as getting appropriate camera shots, rolling the video recorder, riding audio levels, switching among cameras and special effects, retrieving electronically generated graphics, and switching to remote feeds. You still need to pay attention to the talent, who sometimes (and rightly so) feel that they play second fiddle to the television machine. You also need to coordinate productions within a rigid time frame in which every

second has a hefty price tag attached. Such coordinating requires practice, and you should not expect to be a competent director immediately after reading this chapter.

WHAT THE SHOW IS ALL ABOUT

Before you can shout "lights, camera, action" or even mark the script properly for your live or video-recorded show, you need to find out what the show you are to direct is all about. As obvious as this may sound, you will find that as a staff director (who directs a daily variety of shows that happen in a particular time slot) you don't always have the time to carefully inquire about every detail of each show. You normally don't have time to do much preparing for a daily news show, except for marking the script at the last minute. Nor do you have to do a thorough script analysis of a daily postgame sports segment that is part of a routine morning show. This does not mean, however, that you should "wing" a show or step into the control room or a remote truck unprepared.

If you have to direct a show that is not part of a daily routine, you must try to formulate the process message and decide on the most effective production method.

PROCESS MESSAGE

Before you do anything, revisit the ***process message***—the purpose of the show and its intended effect on a specific audience (see chapter 1). If you are not quite sure what the show is to accomplish, check with the producer. Only then can you make all the other personnel understand what the show is about and the expected outcome of the production. An early agreement between producer and director about specific communication goals and production type and scope can prevent many frustrating arguments and costly mistakes. Keep the producer apprised of your plans, even if you have been given responsibility for all creative decisions. Keep a record of telephone calls, save your e-mail, and follow up on major verbal decisions with memoranda.

PRODUCTION METHOD

If you thoroughly understand the process message, the most appropriate production method becomes clear—that is, whether the show is best done in the studio or in the field, live or live-recorded, single-camera or multicamera, and in a sequential or nonsequential event order.

If, for example, the process message is to help the viewer participate in the excitement of watching a Thanksgiving Day parade, you need to do a live, multicamera remote in the field. A traffic safety segment on observing stop signs may require a single-camera approach and plenty of postproduction time. To help the audience gain a deeper insight into the thinking and the work habits of a famous painter, you might observe the painter in her studio over several days with a single camcorder and then edit the video-recorded material in postproduction. If the viewer is to share the excitement of the participants in a new game show and is encouraged to call in while the game is in progress, the show must obviously be a live, multicamera studio production.

But a clear process message might also suggest whether your approach should be a "looking-at" or "looking-into" one. Looking *at* in this context means that you observe an event as best you can, such as covering a city council meeting; on the other hand, perhaps you need to have the camera look *into* an event, that is, reveal the emotional impact through a series of close-ups and a close sound presence.[1]

If you are also the writer, such considerations must happen while writing the script. If you get a script for a show from the producer, you need to learn what to look for to make your directing as effective as possible.

SCRIPT ANALYSIS

Because explaining the intricacies of analyzing and interpreting nondramatic and dramatic scripts is beyond the scope of this book, the following list offers some basic guidelines on reading a script as a director. This technique is especially useful when reading and visualizing a dramatic script.

LOCKING-IN POINT AND TRANSLATION

Locking-in means that you conjure up a vivid visual or aural image while reading the script. This locking-in may well occur at the very opening scene, at the closing scene, or at any particularly striking scene in between. Do not try to force this locking-in process. It may well occur as an audio rather than a video image. If the script is good, the locking-in is almost inevitable. Nevertheless, there are a few steps that will expedite the process.

■ Read the script carefully—don't just glance at it. The video and audio information provide an overview of the show and how complex the production will be.

■ Try to isolate the basic idea behind the show. Better yet, try to formulate an appropriate process message, if it isn't already stated in the original proposal.

■ Try to lock-in on a key shot, a key action, or some key technical maneuver. This may give you some idea of how to translate the images into concrete production requirements, such as camera positions, specific lighting and audio setups, video recording, and postproduction activities.

Analyzing a dramatic script is, of course, more complicated than translating the video and audio instructions of a nondramatic script into the director's production requirements. A good dramatic script operates on many conscious and unconscious levels, all of which need to be interpreted and made explicit. Above all, you should be able to define the theme of the play (the basic idea—what the story is all about), the plot (how the story moves forward and develops), the characters (how one person differs from the others and how each reacts to the situation at hand), and the environment (where the action takes place). In general, television drama emphasizes theme and character rather than plot, and inner, rather than outer, environment. Isolate all points of conflict.[2]

After the locking-in, further analysis depends greatly on what production method you choose: whether you shoot the play in sequence with multiple cameras and a switcher or with a single camera in discontinuous, out-of-sequence takes. Regardless of the method, you will need to visualize the script before deciding on location and equipment.

VISUALIZATION AND SEQUENCING

Directing starts with the visualization of the key images. *Visualization* means seeing the script in pictures and hearing the accompanying sounds. There is no sure-fire formula for this translation process; it requires a certain amount of imagination and artistic sensitivity and lots of practice. The best way to practice is to carefully observe the events around you—how people behave in a classroom or a restaurant or on a bus or an airplane—and mentally note what makes one event so different from the others. When you read a description of some happening in a newspaper, magazine, or novel, try to visualize it as screen images and sound.

Because we see only what the camera sees, you need to carry the initial visualization further and translate it into

---

1. See Herbert Zettl, *Sight Sound Motion: Applied Media Aesthetics,* 5th ed. (Belmont, Calif.: Thomson Wadsworth, 2008), pp. 101–3.

2. See Zettl, *Sight Sound Motion,* pp. 272–73.

such directing details as where people and things should be placed relative to the camera and where the camera should be positioned relative to the event (people and things). You must then consider the *sequencing* of the portions of this visualized event through postproduction editing or switching. Concurrently, you must hear the individual shots and the sequence.

FORMULATING THE PROCESS MESSAGE

As mentioned, a carefully defined process message facilitates the visualization process and, especially, makes it more precise. After deciding on what the target audience is to see, hear, feel, or do, you can follow the effect-to-cause model and determine just how the key shots should look and how to accomplish them.

Here is an example: You are to direct three segments of a program series on teenage driving safety. The first assignment is an interview, consisting of a female interviewer who regularly hosts the weekly half-hour community service show, a male police officer who heads the municipal traffic safety program, and a female student representative of the local high school. The second assignment is an interview with a male high-school student who has been confined to a wheelchair since a serious car accident. The third is a demonstration of some potential dangers of running a stop sign.

The scripts available to you at this point are very sketchy and look more like fact sheets than partial two-column A/V scripts. **SEE 16.1–16.3**

Because the producer has an unusually tight deadline for the completion of the series, she asks that you get started with the production preparation despite the lack of more-detailed scripts. She can give you only a rough idea of what each show is supposed to accomplish: segment 1 should inform the target audience (high-school and college students) of the ongoing efforts by the police department to cooperate with schools to teach traffic safety to young drivers; segment 2 should shock the viewers into an awareness of the consequences of careless driving; and segment 3 should make the audience aware of the potential dangers of running a stop sign.

Let's apply the effect-to-cause model and see how these scripts can be translated into video programs. (To refresh your memory of the effect-to-case model, see chapter 1.) **ZVL2** PROCESS→ Effect-to-cause→ basic idea | desired effect | cause

Despite the sketchy scripts and process messages, many images have probably entered your head already: the police officer in his blue uniform sitting next to the high-school student; a young man straining to move his wheelchair up a ramp to his front door; a car almost hit in an intersection by another car running a stop sign. Before going any further, you may want to define more-precise process messages.

Process message 1: The interview with the traffic safety officer and the student representative should demonstrate to high-school and college students a 10-point traffic safety program to help teenagers become more-responsible drivers. It should also demonstrate how police and students could cooperate in this effort.

Process message 2: The interview with the student in the wheelchair should make viewers (in the desired target audience) gain a deeper insight into his feelings and attitudes since his accident and empathize with him.

Process message 3: The program should show viewers at least four different accidents caused by running a stop sign and demonstrate how to avoid them.

A careful reading of these objectives should make your visualization a little more precise. For example, just how do you see the three people (host, officer, and student representative) interacting in the interview? What shots and shot sequences do you feel would best communicate the interview to the audience? Do you visualize a different approach to the interview with the student in the wheelchair? The demonstration of running a stop sign probably triggers some stereotypical Hollywood video and audio images (such as glass shattering, tires squealing, and cars spinning, some subjective driver's points-of-view, and so forth).

DETERMINING THE MEDIUM REQUIREMENTS

Without trying to be too specific, you can now proceed from some general visualizations to the *medium requirements*: certain key visualizations and sequencing, production method (multicamera studio show or single-camera EFP), necessary equipment, and specific production procedures.

Here is how you might arrive at specific medium requirements for each segment (process message).

Segment 1   The interview is strictly informational. What the people say is more important than getting to know them. The student may not always agree with the officer's views, so the two may not only answer the interviewer but also talk to each other. According to the sketchy script, the

```
TRAFFIC SAFETY SERIES

Program No: 2 Interview (Length: 26:30)
VR Date: Saturday, March 16, 4:00-5:00 P.M. STUDIO 2
Air Date: Tuesday, March 19

Host:          Yvette Sharp
Guests:        Lt. John Hewitt, head of traffic safety program,
               City Police Department
               Rebecca Child, senior and student representative,
               Central High School

-----------------------------------------------------------------

        VIDEO                        AUDIO

STANDARD OPENING
CU of host (faces camera)      HOST INTRODUCES SHOW
2-shot of guests               HOST INTRODUCES GUESTS
CU of host                     HOST ASKS FIRST QUESTION


-----------------------------------------------------------------

INTERVIEW: Lieutenant John Hewitt is the officer in charge of the
traffic safety program. Is a 20-year veteran of the City Police Department.
Has been in traffic safety for the past eight years.

NOTE: HE WILL REFER TO A 10-POINT PROGRAM (DISPLAY VIA C.G.).

Rebecca Child is the student representative of Central High.
She is an A student, on the debate team, and on the championship
volleyball team. She is very much in favor of an effective traffic
safety program but believes that the city police are especially
tough on high-school students and are out to get them.


-----------------------------------------------------------------

STANDARD CLOSE

CU of host                     HOST MAKES CLOSING REMARKS
LS of host and guests          THEME
C.G. credits
```

16.1 TRAFFIC SAFETY STUDIO INTERVIEW

This script is written as a show format. It is simply intended to give some information about the guests appearing on the show.

TRAFFIC SAFETY SERIES

Program No: 5 Location Interview (Length: 26:30)
EFP Date: Friday, March 29, 9:00 A.M.—all day
Postproduction to be scheduled
Air Date: Tuesday, April 9

Interviewer: Yvette Sharp
Interviewee: Jack Armstrong
Address: 49 Baranca Road, South City
                Tel.: 990 555-9990

OPENING AND CLOSING ARE TO BE DONE ON-LOCATION

Jack is a high-school senior. He has been confined to a wheelchair
since he was hit by a car running a stop sign. The other driver was
from his high school. Jack was an outstanding tennis player and is
proud of the several trophies he won in regional tournaments.
He is a good student and coping very well. He is eager to participate
in the traffic safety program.

NOTE: EMPHASIS SHOULD BE ON JACK. GET GOOD CUs.

16.2 TRAFFIC SAFETY FIELD INTERVIEW
The location interview is also sketched out in a show format, which simply gives information about the guest to be interviewed.

```
TRAFFIC SAFETY SERIES

Program No: 6 Running Stop Signs (Length: 26:30)
EFP Date: Tuesday, April 7, 7:00 A.M.—all day
VR Date: Saturday, May 2, 4:00 P.M.—4:30 P.M.
Postproduction to be scheduled
Air Date: Saturday, May 16

EFP Location:        Intersection of West Spring Street and
                     Taraval Court

Contact:             Lt. John Hewitt, head of traffic safety
                     program, City Police Department
                     Tel.: 990 555-8888

-------------------------------------------------------------

OPENING AND CLOSING (YVETTE) ARE TO BE DONE ON-LOCATION

EFP: Program should show car running a stop sign at
intersection and the consequences: almost hitting a
pedestrian, jogger, bicycler; running into another car,
etc. Detailed script will follow.

-------------------------------------------------------------

STUDIO: Lt. Hewitt will briefly demonstrate some typical
accidents, using toy cars on a magnetic board.

NOTE: LT. HEWITT WILL PROVIDE ALL VEHICLES AND DRIVERS AS
WELL AS TALENT. HE WILL TAKE CARE OF ALL TRAFFIC CONTROL,
VEHICLE PARKING, AND COMMUNICATIONS. CONFIRM EFP APRIL 5.

ALTERNATE POLICE CONTACT: Sgt. Fenton McKenna (same telephone)
```

16.3 TRAFFIC SAFETY STOP SIGN SCENE
This show format gives basic information about the major events to be recorded at the electronic field production (EFP). All three traffic formats must eventually be scripted in a partial A/V format before the actual studio and field productions.

officer's 10-point program on traffic safety and other items should be shown on-screen as C.G. (character generator) graphics, unless he brings an easel card.

The show is obviously best done as a live recording in the studio. There you can put the guests in a neutral environment, have good control over the lighting and the audio, switch among multiple cameras, and use the C.G.

The lighting should be normal, that is, fairly high-key, slow-falloff lighting so the viewer can see everyone well. There is no need for dramatic shadows. Perhaps you can persuade the police officer to take off his cap to avoid annoying shadows on his face. How about cameras? Three or two? Even a lively exchange of ideas between the officer and the student will not require terribly fast cutting. Assuming that the host and the guests sit across from one another, you really need only two cameras. We will guide you through a possible camera setup as soon as we get a rough sketch of the set from the art director.

Segment 2   In contrast to segment 1, the segment 2 interview is much more private. Its primary purpose is not to communicate specific information but to have an emotional impact on the audience. The communication is intimate and personal; viewers should strongly empathize with the young man in the wheelchair. These aspects of the process message suggest quite readily that we visit him in his own environment—his home—and that, except for the opening shots, we should see him primarily in close-ups and extreme close-ups rather than in less intense medium and long shots. Again, you will inevitably visualize certain key shots that you have called up from your personal visual reservoir.

Considering the major aspects of the process message (revealing the student's thoughts and feelings and having the audience develop empathy with him), the general production type and the specific medium requirements become fairly apparent. It is best done single-camera style in the student's home. First, the single camera and the associated equipment (lights and mics) cause a minimum intrusion into the environment. Second, the interview itself can be unhurried and stretch over a considerable period of time. Third, the interview does not have to be continuous; it can slow down, be briefly interrupted, or be stopped and then picked up at any time. The production can be out of sequence. Here are some of the specific (and modest) medium requirements: camcorder, recording media, batteries, tripod, playback monitor, two lavalier mics, shotgun mic, and portable lighting kit. Compared with segment 1, this production needs considerably more editing time.

To facilitate your visualization and sequencing, try to visit the student in his home prior to the EFP. Meeting the student and getting to know him will give you a sense of the atmosphere, enable you to plan the shots more specifically, and more accurately determine the specific medium requirements.

Segment 3   This production is by far the most demanding of you as a director. It requires the coordination of different people, locations, and actions. Start with some key visualizations. Running a stop sign is obviously best shown by having a car actually do it. To demonstrate the consequences of such an offense, you may need to show the car going through the stop sign, barely missing a pedestrian and a bicyclist who happen to be in the intersection, or even crashing into another car.

Now is the time to contact the producer again and ask her some important questions: Who will provide the vehicles for this demonstration? Who drives them? What about insurance? You may not need Hollywood stunt drivers for these demonstrations, but in no way should you have students perform these feats. Perhaps the police can assist you and the producer by furnishing both cars and experienced drivers. Who will play the harassed pedestrian and bicyclist? You should also ask the producer whether the actors are insured and whether they are subject to union pay scales and other regulations. Will the police close portions of the street and the intersection for the shoot? For how long?

At this point you would be better off abandoning the project and asking the producer to have it done by a company that specializes in such productions. In any case, it looks as though this is something you and your station may not be prepared to do.

You could, however, suggest simulating these close-call actions by concentrating on the reaction of an onlooker rather than by showing the actual close calls or the crash itself. You can build up to the crash by showing the car going through the stop sign (provided you have the police controlling the traffic) and then showing the frightened pedestrian jumping back onto the curb and the bicyclist trying to get out of the way (of the imagined oncoming car). A fast zoom-in on the car while it is moving toward the camera will definitely lead to an intensification of the shot and an exciting sequence when intercut with progressively closer shots of the pedestrian's frightened face. The crash itself is implied by the close-up (CU) of the frightened onlooker and a good dose of crash sounds from a sound-effect library.

In any case, you would need several camcorders in iso positions, capturing the same event from different points of view. Although most of the sound effects will be added in postproduction, you should still record the ambient sounds with the camera mic during the outdoor shoot.

As you can see, even the "simple" version of the crash is quite complicated. Perhaps you should simply skip this portion and ask the producer to get some stock footage of a car accident. If not, you can intercut the police officer's magnetic board demonstrations with portions of Jack's description of what he felt during the crash.

PREPARING FOR THE SHOW

Once you know what the show is all about and have a fairly well-defined process message, you can move to the next production step for the director: interpreting the floor plan or location sketch. Studying the floor plan or location sketch will help you determine the talent's principal movements, place the cameras and the microphones, and mark the script accordingly.

INTERPRETING A FLOOR PLAN

Unless you direct a routine studio production that occurs on the same set, such as a news, interview, or game show, you need a floor plan to visualize the shots and translate them into camera positions and traffic patterns. It also influences, and sometimes dictates, how you block the talent.

With some practice you can do almost all the talent blocking and the camera positioning simply by looking at the floor plan or location sketch. You will also be able to spot potential production problems. Let's look at a simple interview floor plan and the location sketch for the stop sign segment and see whether we can isolate some potential production problems before they actually occur.

Interview floor plan   Let's go back to the first segment—the studio interview with the police officer and the high-school representative. The art director has given you a rough sketch of the interview set and has asked you to approve it before he has his assistant prepare the final version. **SEE 16.4**

This interview setup seems quite workable. You can have camera 2 take care of the establishing three-shot and then move it to the right for CUs of the host. Camera 1 can be used on the guests. The line monitor is oriented toward the host so that the guests are not tempted to admire themselves on TV during the recording.

When the assistant art director hands you the final, neat version of the floor plan and the attached prop list, however, you detect some serious production problems. **SEE 16.5** What are they?

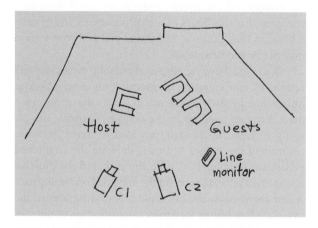

16.4 TRAFFIC SAFETY INTERVIEW: ROUGH SKETCH
This rough sketch for a studio interview set shows the approximate locations of the chairs and the cameras.

16.5 INTERVIEW SET: FLOOR PLAN AND PROP LIST
This floor plan and prop list, based on the rough sketch of an interview set, reveal serious production problems.

Take another look at the floor plan and try to visualize some of the key shots, such as opening and closing three-shots, two-shots of the guests talking to the host and to each other, and individual CUs of the three people. Visualize the foreground as well as the background because the camera sees both. You may surmise that there are some definite camera problems with this floor plan. **SEE 16.6**

■ Given the way the chairs are placed, an opening three-shot would be difficult to achieve. If camera 2 shoots from straight on, the chairs are probably too far apart. Even in a 16×9 aspect ratio, the host and the guests would seem glued to the screen edges, placing undue emphasis on the painting in the middle. Also, you would probably overshoot the set on both ends. The guests would certainly block each other in this shot.

■ When you shoot from the extreme left (camera 1) to get an over-the-shoulder shot from the host to the guests, you will overshoot the set. On a close-up you would run the risk of the rubber plant's seeming to grow out of the guest's head.

■ When switching to camera 2, you will again overshoot the set, and the second rubber plant would most likely appear to grow out of the host's head (see figure 16.6).

■ If you pulled the cameras more toward the center to avoid overshooting, you would get nothing but profiles.

Aside from issues with camera shots, there are additional production problems:

■ White hardwall panels hardly create the most interesting background. The surface is too plain, and its color is too bright for the foreground scene, rendering skin tones unusually dark. Because the host is an African American woman, the contrast problem with the white background is even more extreme—and you cannot correct the problem by putting more light on her.

■ See how close the chairs are to the background flats? Any key light and fill light will inevitably strike the background too, adding to the silhouette effect. The back lights would also function as front (key) lights, causing fast falloff (dense attached shadows) toward the camera side. If you were now to lighten up the shadows on the faces with additional fill light coming from the front of the set (roughly from camera 2's position), it would inevitably hit the white flats, further aggravating the silhouette effect.

16.6 INTERVIEW SET: CAMERA POSITIONS
The camera positions reveal some of the production problems caused by this setup.

■ The acoustics may also prove to be less than desirable because the microphones are very close to the sound-reflecting hardwall flats.

■ The prop list signals yet more problems. The large upholstered chairs are definitely not appropriate for an interview. They look too pompous and would practically engulf their occupants.

■ Because most of the setup requires cross shooting from extreme angles, the painting is useless. If you want to break up the plain background with a picture, hang it so that it serves as a background in most of the shots.

■ If you happen to know something about art history, you may suspect that the tight, contrasting patterns of Brigit Riley's paintings would probably cause a moiré effect.

■ Finally, with the chairs directly on the studio floor, the cameras would have to look down on the performers, or the camera operators would have to pedestal all the way down and stoop for the entire interview.

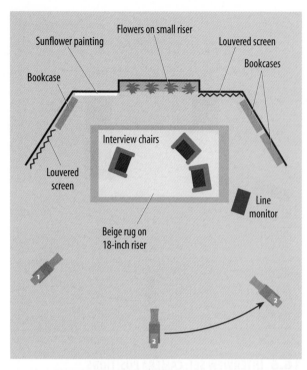

16.7 REVISED INTERVIEW SET

The revised floor plan for the interview provides for adequate background cover and interesting shots.

We went into this detail to illustrate how a careful reading of a floor plan can uncover production problems that, if not discovered until the actual recording, would eat up valuable studio time. As you can see, even this simple floor plan and prop list reveal important clues to a variety of production problems.

The figure at left shows one possible solution to the aforementioned problems. You can probably come up with several more suggestions for an improved interview set. **SEE 16.7**

INTERPRETING A LOCATION SKETCH

There is no time for resting on your laurels. Just when you have fixed the interview set, the associate director comes back from a location survey for the segment on running the stop sign and shows you her location sketch. **SEE 16.8** She feels that there may be several potential production problems. See if you can identify some of them.

■ The intersection is obviously downtown. You can therefore expect a great deal of traffic to pass through, and the police would not close such a busy intersection for anything but a real accident.

■ Even if the intersection were not in the middle of downtown, the proximity of the bank and the supermar-

16.8 LOCATION SKETCH FOR STOP SIGN SEGMENT

This location sketch points to several major problems that make the field production infeasible.

ket would make closing the intersection, even for a little while, infeasible.

■ A schoolyard is very noisy during recess. Unless you do not mind the laughing and yelling of children during the production, every school recess means a forced recess for the production crew.

■ The four-way stop signs make the intersection less hazardous, even if someone runs one of them. The demonstration is much more effective if one of the streets has through traffic.

The solution to these problems is relatively simple: have the producer contact the police department and find an intersection in a quiet neighborhood that has very little traffic. There should be sufficient alternate routes so that a temporary closure of the intersection will not cause traffic delays or prevent neighbors from getting to and from their homes.

USING THE STORYBOARD

In a complicated assignment like the one just described, or in any directing undertaking that goes beyond a routine show, you will be greatly aided in your visualization by a good storyboard. A *storyboard* is a sequence of visualized shots; it contains key visualization points and audio information. **SEE 16.9**

A storyboard is usually drawn on preprinted storyboard paper, which has areas that represent the television screen. Another area, usually below the screen, is dedicated to audio and other information. A storyboard can also be drawn on plain paper or created by computer. Storyboard software programs offer a great many stock images (houses, streets, cars, living rooms, and offices, for example) into which you can place figures and move them into position in the storyboard frame. **SEE 16.10**

Most commercials are carefully storyboarded shot-by-shot before they ever go into production. Storyboards help people who make decisions about the commercial see the individual shots and their intended sequence.

Storyboards are also used for other types of single-camera productions that contain a great number of especially complicated discontinuous shots or shot sequences. A good storyboard offers immediate clues to certain production requirements, such as general location, camera position, approximate focal length of the lens, method of audio pickup, cutaways, amount and type of postproduction, talent actions, set design, and hand props.

MARKING THE SCRIPT

Proper marking of a script will aid you greatly in multi-camera directing from the control room or on-location. In control room directing, you need to coordinate many people and machines within a continuous time frame. The marked script becomes a road map that guides you through the intricacies of a production. Although there is no single correct way of marking a script, certain conventions and standards have been developed. Obviously, a fully scripted show requires more precise cueing than does an interview that is directed from a simple show format. Live productions or uninterrupted recordings of live productions (live-recorded) directed from the control room in a continuous time frame need a more carefully marked script than do shows that are recorded for postproduction editing. But even in discontinuous single-camera productions, a well-marked script will help you remember camera and talent positions and make your directing more exacting.

Script marking for instantaneous editing (switching)
Whatever system of script marking you choose or develop, it must be clear, readable, and above all consistent. Once you arrive at a working system, stick with it. As in musical notation, where you can perceive whole passages without reading each individual note, the script-marking system permits you to interpret and react to the written cues without having to consciously read each one. The three figures on pages 350–52 provide examples of script marking. **SEE 16.11–16.13** Take a look at the markings in figure 16.11 again and compare them with those in figures 16.12 and 16.13. Which script seems cleaner and more readable to you?

The script in figure 16.11 shows information that is more confusing than helpful. By the time you've read all the cue instructions, you will certainly have missed part or all of the action and perhaps even half of the talent's lines. You do not have to mark all stand-by cues or any other obvious cues that are already implied. For example, "ready" cues are always given before a cue, so they need not be part of your script markings.

In contrast, the markings in figures 16.12 and 16.13 are clean and simple. They are kept to a minimum, and there is little writing. You are able to grasp all the cues quickly without actually reading each word. As you can see, the cues in figure 16.12 provide the same information as those in figure 16.11, but they allow you to keep track of the narration, look ahead at upcoming cues, and especially watch the action on the preview monitors. Let us now

THE RETURN OF AGENT 12
DETONATION FILMS

Shot: 327

CU – Agent 12

AGENT 12
Jetpack! Maximum burn!

Shot: 328

FAST CU – JETPACK rises
As the thruster IGNITES!

Audio: ROAR of jets.

Shot: 329

DRAMATIC DOWNSHOT ON AGENT 12
As he ROCKETS into the air, the ground dropping
below as he streaks UP and PAST CAM, trailing flame.

Audio: ROAR of jets, pitch drops in Doppler effect.

Shot: 330

TRACKING LS – Agent 12 continues ascent.
This shot appears on-screen in following shot.

Shot: 331

ON DR. VENGEANCE
Reacting to what he's seeing on-screen.
He can't believe it.

DR. VENGEANCE
Awww, MAN! Who gave him a *jetpack*?

Shot: 332

CU
SCOTT about to speak up . . .

Shot: 333

CU
. . . but thinks better of it.

Shot: 334

MLS TIGHTEN and CANT to CU
Dr. Vengeance shouts into radio handset.
Audio: KLAXON horn sounds.
DR. VENGEANCE
Tiger! Gameboy! *Scramble!*

Shot: 335

ANGLE ON THE ROOF – Showing TIGER and GAMEBOY
sprinting for the howitzer controls. The massive
cannons overshadow the entire roof.

DR. VENGEANCE (ON RADIO)
Ready the roof guns!

16.9 HAND-DRAWN STORYBOARD
The hand-drawn storyboard shows the major visualization points and sometimes lists the key audio sections or the shot sequence.

Careful Roadways PSA

1   00:00:05:00

VO: The amazing function between the eyes and the brain is called the "sense of vision."

2   00:00:10:00

VO: The human vision system processes information faster than a Cray supercomputer.

3   00:00:13:00

VO: The human eye outperforms our best video.

4   00:00:20:00

VO: Human vision updates images, including the details of motion and color, on a time scale so rapid . . .

5   00:00:23:00

VO: . . . that a "break in the action" is almost never perceived.

6   00:00:28:00

VO: The Cray supercomputer can process more than a hundred million arithmetic operations per second.

16.10 COMPUTER-GENERATED STORYBOARD

The computer-generated storyboard has 3D graphics that can be used to create a variety of exterior and interior environments in which images of people can be placed.

VIDEO	AUDIO
Effects	
Wipe to: VTR (SOT) (showing a series of paintings from realism to expressionism)	AUDIO IN-CUE: "ALL THE PAINTINGS WERE DONE BY ONE ARTIST . . . PICASSO"
	OUT-CUE: ". . . PHENOMENAL CREATIVE FORCE"
MS Barbara by the easel	But even Picasso must have had some bad days and painted some bad pictures. Take a look. The woman's hands are obviously not right. Did Picasso deliberately distort the hands to make a point? I don't think so.
CU of painting	Look at the outline. He obviously struggled. The line is unsure, and he painted this section over at least three times. Because the rest of the
Key effects	painting is so realistically done, the distorted hands seem out of place. This is quite different from his later period, when he distorted images to intensify the event.
VTR SOT *Insert time* *4:27 min*	IN-CUE: "DISTORTION MEANS POWER. THIS COULD HAVE BEEN PICASSO'S FORMULA . . ."
	OUT-CUE: ". . . EXPRESSIVE POWER THROUGH DISTORTION IN HIS LATER PAINTINGS."
CU Barbara	But the formula "distortion means power" does not always apply. Here again it seems to weaken the event. Take a look at . . .

Handwritten margin notes:

Ready on effects
Take effects
Ready to wipe to VTR
Roll VTR and take VTR 4
Track up on VTR 4
Ready camera 2
Cue Barbara and take camera 2

Ready camera 3 on the easel — closeup
Take camera 3

Ready to roll VTR 4 Segment 2
Roll VTR 4 and take VTR 4

Ready camera 2
Cue Barbara and take camera 2

16.11 BAD SCRIPT MARKING
This script is marked with too much unnecessary information that makes it hard to read.

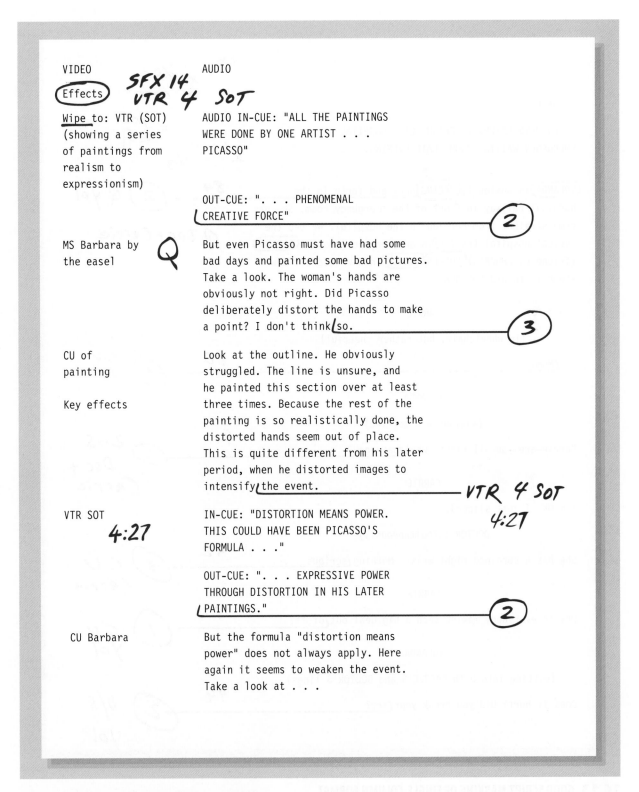

```
VIDEO                      AUDIO
                  SFX 14
(Effects)         VTR 4  SOT

Wipe to: VTR (SOT)         AUDIO IN-CUE: "ALL THE PAINTINGS
(showing a series          WERE DONE BY ONE ARTIST . . .
of paintings from          PICASSO"
realism to
expressionism)
                           OUT-CUE: ". . . PHENOMENAL
                           CREATIVE FORCE"                          (2)

MS Barbara by        Q     But even Picasso must have had some
the easel                  bad days and painted some bad pictures.
                           Take a look. The woman's hands are
                           obviously not right. Did Picasso
                           deliberately distort the hands to make
                           a point? I don't think so.                (3)

CU of                      Look at the outline. He obviously
painting                   struggled. The line is unsure, and
                           he painted this section over at least
Key effects                three times. Because the rest of the
                           painting is so realistically done, the
                           distorted hands seem out of place.
                           This is quite different from his later
                           period, when he distorted images to
                           intensify the event.                — VTR 4 SOT
                                                                  4:27
VTR SOT                    IN-CUE: "DISTORTION MEANS POWER.
      4:27                 THIS COULD HAVE BEEN PICASSO'S
                           FORMULA . . ."

                           OUT-CUE: ". . . EXPRESSIVE POWER
                           THROUGH DISTORTION IN HIS LATER
                           PAINTINGS."                               (2)

CU Barbara                 But the formula "distortion means
                           power" does not always apply. Here
                           again it seems to weaken the event.
                           Take a look at . . .
```

16.12 GOOD SCRIPT MARKING OF A/V FORMAT
This script is clearly marked and can be easily read by the director.

SCENE 6

A FEW DAYS LATER. INTERIOR. CITY HOSPITAL
EMERGENCY WAITING ROOM. LATE EVENING.

↑ x doc
x carrie

yol

2 ✓   ✓ 3

(YOLANDA) is anxiously (PACING) back and forth in the
hospital hallway in front of the emergency room. She has
come straight from her job to the hospital. We see the
typical hospital traffic in an emergency room. A (DOCTOR)
(friend of CHUCK'S) (PUSHES) (CARRIE) in a wheelchair down
the hall toward YOLANDA.

89   ② *Q yol*

Q Doc + Carrie

                    CARRIE

          (in wheelchair, but rather cheerful)

Hi, Mom!

90   ① *CU yol*

                    YOLANDA

          (anxious and worried)

Carrie—are you all right? What happened?

91   ② *2-S Doc + Carrie*

                    CARRIE

I'm OK. I just slipped.

            DOCTOR (simultaneously)

She has a sprained right wrist. Nothing serious . . .

92   ③ *CU Carrie*

                    CARRIE

Why is everybody making such a big deal out of it?

93   ① *CU yol*

                    YOLANDA

      (cutting into both CARRIE'S and DOCTOR'S lines)

Does it hurt? Did you break your arm?

94   ② *O/S yol*

16.13 GOOD SCRIPT MARKING OF SINGLE-COLUMN FORMAT
The marking on this multicamera single-column drama script shows the cameras used, the shot number, the type of shot, and the major actions. Note the blocking sketch at the beginning of this scene.

highlight some of the qualities of a well-marked script from a director's point of view (refer to figure 16.12).

■ All action cues are placed *before* the desired action.

■ If the shots or camera actions are clearly described in the video column (page-left), or the audio cues in the audio column (page-right), simply underline or circle the printed instructions. This keeps the script clean and uncluttered. If the printed instructions are hard to read, do not hesitate to repeat them with your own symbols.

■ If the script does not indicate a particular transition from one video source to another, it is always a cut. A large handwritten *2* next to a cue line means that the upcoming transition is a cut to camera 2. It also implies a "ready 2" before the "take 2" call.

■ If the show requires rehearsals, do preliminary script marking in pencil so you can make quick changes without creating a messy or illegible script. Once you are ready for the dress rehearsal, however, you should have marked the script in bold letters. Have the associate director and the floor manager copy your markings onto their own scripts.

■ Mark the cameras by circled numbers all in one row. This allows you to see quickly which camera needs to be readied for the next shot.

■ In addition to the camera notation, number each shot in consecutive order, starting with 1, regardless of the camera you use for the shot. These numbers will not only help you ready the various shots for each camera but also make it easy to create a shot sheet for each camera. **SEE 16.14** You can now easily delete or add shots for the cameras. All you need to do is say, "delete shot 89," and camera 2 will delete the shot with Yolanda pacing back and forth.

■ You may want to devise a symbol that signifies action, such as someone coming through the door, walking over to the map, sitting down, or getting up. In figure 16.13 this cue is a handwritten arrow (↗).

■ If there are several moves by the talent, draw little maps (see figure 16.13). Such blocking sketches are usually more helpful for recalling talent moves, camera positions, and traffic than are storyboard sketches of shot compositions.

Script marking for postproduction editing　The marking of the script for discontinuous takes consists of a careful breakdown and indication of the various scenes, their locations (hospital, front entrance), and principal

16.14　SHOT SHEET FOR CAMERA 2

visualizations (camera point of view, field of view). You then number the scenes in the proposed production sequence, ending up with a list of scenes that refers to the original script by page number. Here is an example:

LOCATION	SCENE	SCRIPT PAGES
Hospital	6	41–47
corridor	7	48–55
Emergency	3	5–7
room entrance	14	102–10
Yolanda's kitchen	14	2–4

In the script itself, you are free to use whatever markings you prefer. When video-recording discontinuous takes for postproduction, you obviously have more time to consult the script than during a live or live-recorded production. For discontinuous taping it may help to mark the talent movements on the script as well as draw next to the dialogue small storyboard sketches that show unusual shot framings. Such sketches assist in recalling what you had in mind when preparing the script. Some film directors (such as Steven Spielberg) storyboard almost every shot of the entire movie before ever shooting a single frame of film.

As you can see, the more time and effort you devote to such production details ahead of time, the less time and effort you will have to expend during the actual video-recording sessions. Production efficiency does not mean to hurry through a production regardless of quality; it means extensive preparation.

MAIN POINTS

▶ As a television director, you must be an artist who can translate a script or an event into effective television pictures and sound, a psychologist who can work with people of different temperaments and skills, a technical adviser who knows the potentials and the limitations of the equipment, and a coordinator who can initiate and keep track of myriad production processes.

▶ A clear understanding of the process message (desired effect) will help you decide on the most appropriate type of production (single-camera or multicamera, studio or field,

recorded or live, continuous or discontinuous takes for postproduction) and the medium requirements.

▶ A careful script analysis should lead to a locking-in point—an especially vivid visual or aural image—that determines the subsequent visualizations and sequencing.

▶ Visualization (mentally seeing and hearing key images) is crucial for the successful translation of script to screen event.

▶ The floor plan or location sketch enables the director to plan camera and talent positions and traffic.

▶ The storyboard shows drawings or computer-generated images of key visualization points of an event with accompanying audio information as well as the proper sequencing of shots.

▶ When preparing the show for the actual production day, you must interpret the floor plan or a location sketch, and mark the script,

▶ The important aspects of good script marking are readability and consistency.

▶ Precise and easy-to-read script markings help you and other production personnel anticipate and execute a great variety of cues.

16.2

Communication and Scheduling

This section deals with the functions of the director's support staff and the necessity of working with the producer on facilities requests, schedules, and communication with talent and production personnel. **ZVL3** PROCESS→ People→ nontechnical | technical

▶ **SUPPORT STAFF**
Floor manager, production assistant, and associate director

▶ **FACILITIES REQUESTS, SCHEDULES, AND COMMUNICATION**
Facilities request, production schedule, time line, and the director's communication

SUPPORT STAFF

The director's support staff depends on the size of the production company. Some documentaries are done by a three-person team: the producer/director; the *DP* (director of photography), who runs the camera and does the lighting; and the audio person. Many field productions are run with only a two-person team—the videographer and the talent—whereby either one or both act as director. In a television station or a larger independent production company, a director will have the support of at least two or three people: the floor manager, the production assistant, and, in larger productions, an associate or assistant director.

FLOOR MANAGER

The floor manager is also called the floor director, stage manager, or unit manager, even though the unit manager functions more like a production manager or line producer who takes care of the daily production and budgetary details. The floor manager's primary functions are to coordinate all activities on the "floor" (studio or on-location site) and relay the cues from the director to the talent.

Before the production the floor manager needs to oversee and help the floor crew set up scenery, place set and hand props, dress the set, and put up displays. During rehearsals and the production, the floor manager must coordinate the floor crew and the talent and relay the director's talent cues. After the production he or she is responsible for striking the set and the props or restoring the remote production site to its original condition.

The following are some points to keep in mind when managing the floor.

■ Unless you are doing a routine show that is produced on a permanent set (one that is not struck after each show), you as floor manager need to obtain a detailed floor plan and prop list. Check with the art director and the director about any specific features or changes. Get a marked script from the director so that you can anticipate talent and camera traffic. Have the director look at the set before fine-tuning the lighting. Once the lighting is complete, even minor set changes can require major lighting adjustments. When the set is put up and dressed, take a digital photo of it. Such a record is much more readily accessible than a video recording.

■ You are responsible for having all hand props on the set and in operating condition. For example, if the show involves a studio demonstration of a new laptop computer, run the specific series of computer programs a few times to see how it works. Hard-to-open jars or bottles are a constant challenge to the performer. Twist the lid of a jar slightly or loosen the bottle cap so that the talent can remove it without struggling. This small courtesy can prevent retakes and frayed nerves and is usually a quick way of establishing trust between you and the talent.

■ Check that the teleprompter works and that the correct copy is displayed.

■ If you use an on-camera slate in the field, have it ready and filled out with the essential information. Have several pens available as well as a rag to erase the writing.

■ For complex productions study the marked script before the rehearsal and add your own cues, such as talent entrances and exits and prop, costume, or set changes. In case of doubt, ask the director for clarification.

■ Introduce yourself to the talent and the guests and have a designated place for them to sit while waiting in the studio. Because most production people are quite busy (including the director and the producer), you are the one who must establish and maintain a rapport with the talent and the guests throughout the production. Verify that they have signed the proper release forms and other necessary papers. Ask them periodically if they would like some water or coffee, whether they are comfortable, and if you can be of assistance. When working with outside talent, review your major cues with them (see chapter 15).

■ When using a teleprompter, ask the performers whether the font size is big enough and if its distance from the camera is tolerable.

■ During the rehearsal of a fully scripted show, follow the script as much as possible and anticipate the director's cues. Keep notes on especially difficult camera travels and talent actions. If the production is shot in segments for postproduction editing, pay particular attention to continuity of the talent's appearance, positions, and major moves.

■ Always carry a pen or pencil, a broad marking pen, rolls of masking and gaffer's tape, and a piece of chalk (for taping down props and equipment and for spiking—marking—talent and camera positions). Also have a large pad ready so that you can write out messages for the talent in case the I.F.B. system breaks down or is not used.

■ During rehearsal deliver all cues as though you were on the air, even if the director stands right next to you. You do not always have to remain next to the camera when cueing. As much as possible, position yourself so that you can see the talent's eyes. This is one of the reasons why you should not be tied to a studio camera's intercom outlet.

■ During the show do not cue on your own, even if you think the director has missed a cue. Rather, ask the director on the intercom whether you should give the cue as marked and rehearsed. If there are interruptions in the video recording because some technical problems are being discussed in the control room, inform the talent about what is going on. Tell the talent that they did a good job but that the director has to work out some technical details. If there are extended problem-solving interruptions, invite the talent to get out from under the lights and relax in the

small studio area you have set up for them—but don't let them wander off.

■ After the show thank the talent or guests and show them out of the studio. You then need to supervise the strike of the set in the studio or of the items set up on-location. Be careful not to drag scenery or prop carts across cables that might still be on the studio floor. Locate objects that were brought in by a guest and see to it that they are returned. If you shot indoors on-location, put things back as you found them. A small location sketch or digital photo will be of great help when trying to return things to the way they were. When shooting on-location remember that you are a guest operating in someone else's space.

PRODUCTION ASSISTANT

As a production assistant (PA), you must be prepared to do a variety of jobs—from duplicating and distributing the script, looking for a specific prop, and welcoming the talent to getting coffee, calling a cab, and taking notes for the producer and the director (unless the AD is taking notes). Usually, note taking is the PA's most important assignment. You simply follow the producer and/or director with a pad and pen and record everything they mumble to themselves or tell you to write down. During the "notes" breaks, you read back your notes item by item. When in the field, you may also have to keep a field log of all the production takes, which helps the postproduction editor locate shots on the recording media. **ZVL4** ▶EDITING→ Production guidelines→ field log

ASSOCIATE, OR ASSISTANT, DIRECTOR

As an **AD** (associate, or assistant, director), you mainly assist the director in the production phase—the rehearsals and the on-the-air performance or recording sessions. In complex studio shows, a director may have you give all standby cues (for example: "Ready to cue Mary, ready 2 CU of John") and preset the cameras by telling the camera operators on the intercom the upcoming shots or camera moves. This frees up the director somewhat to concentrate more on the preview monitors or the talent's performance. Once preset by you, the director then initiates the action by the various action cues: "Ready 2, take 2," or, in fast dialogue, simply by snapping fingers.

In elaborate EFPs or complicated studio productions, you may have to direct the run-throughs (rehearsals) for each take, which enables the director to stand back and observe the action on the field or line monitor.

The AD in digital cinema productions may also function as a second-unit director. The second unit consists of a smaller crew whose job it is to capture various inserts, such as establishing shots, certain close-ups, special-effects sequences, or other small scenes that do not involve major dialogue portions.

As an AD you are also responsible for the timing of the show segments and the overall show during rehearsals as well as during the actual production.

FACILITIES REQUESTS, SCHEDULES, AND COMMUNICATION

Now is the time for you, as the director, to double-check with the producer about various important tasks that should have been done in the preproduction period, such as requesting the necessary facilities and scheduling.

FACILITIES REQUEST

Even if in your operation it is the producer who requests and schedules the equipment and the facilities, you still need to check with him or her whether the *facilities request* actually includes all the equipment and technical facilities you may have added during your production preparations. Ask the TD (technical director) whether the final facilities request is meeting all the show's technical demands.

PRODUCTION SCHEDULE

Unless you are directing a routine show, such as the morning news, check with the producer about the *production schedule*—the calendar that shows the preproduction, production, and postproduction dates and who is doing what, when, and where. Most likely, the producer will have taken care of the production schedule, but you as the director will have to prepare the time line.

TIME LINE

In larger operations the daily *time line* is worked out by the production manager or the producer. In smaller production companies, the director establishes the time line for a specific production day. Assuming that you as the director are responsible for the time line, verify with the producer whether the production schedule was actually delivered to the talent and all members of the production team. A simple telephone call by the PA will confirm this distribution and make you sleep better. **ZVL5** PROCESS→ Phases→ preproduction | production

As with every other aspect of television production, each production day is governed by strict time limits. Time lines differ considerably, depending on how complex a

studio show or a remote telecast is going to be. On a difficult remote, such as a parade through a narrow downtown street, you may need a whole day for the setup. The following examples are typical time lines for an interview and a one-hour soap opera segment.

Time line: interview   This time line is prepared for a half-hour interview (actual length: 23 minutes), featuring two folk singers who have gained world fame because of their socially conscious songs. The singers, who accompany themselves on acoustic guitars, are scheduled to give a concert the following day on the university commons. Their contract does not allow the presence of television cameras during the actual concert, but they, their manager, and AFTRA (the talent union) agreed that the singers could come to the studio for a brief interview and play a few short selections.

The process message is relatively simple: to give viewers an opportunity to meet the two singers, learn more about them as artists and concerned human beings, and watch them perform.

To save time and money, the show is scheduled for a live-on-tape production (the recording media being videotape). This means that the director will direct the show as though it were going on the air live, or at least with as few stop-downs (interruptions whereby the videotape is stopped) as possible.

TIME LINE: INTERVIEW (JULY 15)

11:00 a.m.	Crew call
11:10–11:30 a.m.	Tech meeting
11:30 a.m.–1:00 p.m.	Setup and lighting
1:00–1:30 p.m.	Lunch
1:30–1:45 p.m.	Production meeting: host and singers
1:45–2:30 p.m.	Run-through and camera rehearsal
2:30–2:40 p.m.	Notes and reset
2:40–2:45 p.m.	Break
2:45–3:30 p.m.	Recording
3:30–3:45 p.m.	Spill
3:45–4:00 p.m.	Strike

As you can see from this time line, a production day is divided into blocks of time during which certain activities take place.

11:00 a.m.   **Crew call**   This is the time the crew must arrive at the studio.

11:10–11:30 a.m. **Tech meeting**   You start the day with a technical meeting during which you discuss with the crew the process message and the major technical requirements. One of these requirements is the audio setup because the singers are obviously interested in good stereo sound. You need different mics for the interview and for the performance area. You should also explain what camera shots you want. The sincerity of the artists and their guitar-playing skills are best conveyed by CUs and ECUs (extreme close-ups), and you may want to shift the attention from one singer to the other through a rack focus effect. The audio technician may want to discuss the specific mic setup with you, such as stand mics for the performance and wireless lavaliers for the singers' crossover. The TD (acting as studio crew chief) may ask about the desired lighting and confirm the simultaneous recording of the show on DVD, which can be given to the guests right after the taping as a small thank-you.

11:30 a.m.–1:00 p.m. **Setup and lighting**   This should be sufficient time to set up the standard interview set and light the interview and performance areas. Although as director you are not immediately involved in this production phase, you might want to keep an eye on the setup so that you can make minor changes before the lighting is done.

1:00–1:30 p.m. **Lunch**   Tell everyone to be back by 1:30 sharp—not 1:32 or 1:35—which means that everyone has to be able to leave the studio at exactly 1:00, even if there are still some technical details left undone. Minor technical problems can be solved during the production meeting with the host and the singers.

1:30–1:45 p.m. **Production meeting: host and singers**   When the singers and their manager arrive at this meeting, they have already been introduced to the host by the producer or PA. Nevertheless, check on whether they have signed all the necessary papers. In this meeting confirm their musical selections and the running time for each. Discuss the opening, the closing, and the crossover to the performance area. Tell them some of your visualization ideas, such as shooting very tightly during especially intense moments in their songs and for intricate guitar sections.

1:45–2:30 p.m. **Run-through and camera rehearsal**   Although the setup is relatively simple and there will be little camera movement during the songs, you need to rehearse the crossovers from the interview set to the performance area and back. You may also want to rehearse some of the unusually tight shots or the rack focus shots from one

singer to the other. Then go through the opening and the closing with all facilities (theme music, credits, and name keys). Dictate to the PA any production problems you may discover during this rehearsal for the notes segment. This rehearsal is especially important for the audio engineer, who is trying to achieve an optimal sound pickup. Do not get upset when the audio technician repositions mics during the camera rehearsal. If all goes well, you may be done before 2:30 p.m.

2:30–2:40 p.m. **Notes and reset**   You now gather the key production people—producer, AD, TD, audio technician, LD (lighting director), floor manager, and host—to discuss any production problems that may have surfaced during the camera rehearsal. Ask the PA to read the notes in the order written down. Direct the production team to take care of the various problems. At the same time, the rest of the crew should get the cameras into the opening positions, reset the pages of the C.G., ready the VTR and the DVD recorder, and make minor lighting adjustments.

2:40–2:45 p.m. **Break**   This short break will give everyone a chance to get ready for the taping. Don't tell the crew to "take five" but rather when to be back in the studio (exactly at 2:45).

2:45–3:30 p.m. **Recording**   You should be in the control room and start the recorder at exactly 2:45 p.m.—not 2:50 or 3:00. If all goes well, the half-hour show should be "in the can," or finished, by 3:30, including the stop-down time for the first crossover.

3:30–3:45 p.m. **Spill**   This is a grace period because we all know that television is a complex, temperamental machine that involves many people. For example, you may have to redo the opening or the closing because the C.G. did not deliver the correct page for the opening credits or because the host gave the wrong time for the upcoming concert.

3:45–4:00 p.m. **Strike**   During the strike time, you can thank the singers and their manager, the host, and the crew. Arrange for a playback in case they want to see and especially listen to the video recording right away. Play back the audio track through the best speaker system you have. All the while keep at least one eye on the strike, but do not interfere with it. Trust the floor manager and the crew to take down the set and clean the studio for the next production in the remaining 15 minutes.

One of the most important aspects of a time line is sticking to the time allotted for each segment. You must learn to get things done within the scheduled time block and, more important, to jump to the next activity at the precise time shown on the schedule regardless of whether you have finished your previous chores. Do not use up the time of a scheduled segment with the preceding activity. A good director terminates an especially difficult blocking rehearsal at midpoint to meet the scheduled notes and reset period. Inexperienced directors often spend a great amount of time on the first part of the show or on a relatively minor detail, then go on the air without having rehearsed the rest of the show. The time line is designed to prevent such misuse of valuable production time.

Time line: soap opera   Here is an example of a time line for a more complicated one-hour soap opera. Assume that the setup and the lighting were accomplished the night before (from 3 to 6 a.m.) and that some set changes will happen after 6 p.m. for the following day.

AS THE SUN RISES   SEGMENT 987

6:00–8:00 a.m.	Dry run—rehearsal hall
7:30 a.m.	Crew call
8:00–8:30 a.m.	Tech meeting
8:30–11:00 a.m.	Camera blocking
11:00–11:30 a.m.	Notes and reset
11:30 a.m.–12:30 p.m.	Lunch
12:30–2:30 p.m.	Dress rehearsal
2:30–3:00 p.m.	Notes and reset
3:00–5:30 p.m.	Recording
5:30–6:00 p.m.	Spill

As you can see, this time line leaves no time for you to think about what to do next. You need to be thoroughly prepared to coordinate the equipment, technical people, and talent within the tightly prescribed time frame. There is no time allotted for striking the set because the set stays up for the next day's production.

DIRECTOR'S COMMUNICATION

Although the producer is responsible for maintaining the contact information of the talent and the technical and nontechnical production personnel, you as the director are responsible for getting the show done on time. You should therefore establish a routine procedure for communicating efficiently with all personnel involved in a day's production. Note that such a double-check is necessary only when you work on onetime studio and field productions. If you do a routine show, you need to trust the producer or production manager to handle crew changes or substitutions for talent. Still you should have ready access to the same personnel

information so that your PA can verify last-minute crew and talent substitutions. If you use e-mail for your communication, request an immediate response from the recipient and always copy the producer.

Such communication verification is especially important if you are to direct a field production that needs access to restricted areas, such as a sports stadium. You will learn more about communicating with the contact person in chapter 18. **ZVL6** PROCESS→ People→ nontechnical

M A I N   P O I N T S

▶ The director's immediate support staff normally comprises a floor manager, a PA (production assistant), and, in larger productions, an AD (associate or assistant director).

▶ The facilities request is an essential communication device for procuring the necessary production facilities and equipment.

▶ The production schedule shows the preproduction, production, and postproduction dates and who is doing what, when, and where.

▶ The time line shows a breakdown of time blocks for various activities on the actual production day.

▶ To facilitate communication between the director and the technical and nontechnical personnel, the director must establish a specific routine and stick to it. E-mail messages must be immediately acknowledged by the recipient.

Z E T T L ' S   V I D E O L A B

For your reference or to track your work, the *Zettl's VideoLab* program cues in this chapter are listed here with their corresponding page numbers.

ZVL1 PROCESS→ Process introduction   **334**

ZVL2 PROCESS→ Effect-to-cause→ basic idea | desired effect | cause   **339**

ZVL3 PROCESS→ People→ nontechnical | technical   **355**

ZVL4 EDITING→ Production guidelines→ field log   **356**

ZVL5 PROCESS→ Phases→ preproduction | production   **357**

ZVL6 PROCESS→ People→ nontechnical   **359**

17

The Director in Production: Directing

Now that you have prepared yourself so well for the production day, it's time to step into the television control room, or go on-location, and direct. In fact, all the meticulous preparation means little if you cannot direct or coordinate the various elements during the production phase. Section 17.1, Multicamera Control Room Directing, gives an overview of what is required when directing various multicamera studio and remote productions.

In section 17.2, Single-camera and Digital Cinema Directing, you will read about so-called film-style shooting: using a high-definition television (HDTV), or digital cinema, camera for the acquisition of the video scenes.

camera rehearsal Full rehearsal with cameras and other pieces of production equipment. Often identical to the dress rehearsal.

dress rehearsal Full rehearsal with all equipment operating and with talent in full dress. The dress rehearsal is often video recorded. Often called *camera rehearsal* except that the camera rehearsal does not require full dress for talent.

dry run Rehearsal without equipment, during which the basic actions of the talent are worked out. Also called *blocking rehearsal*.

intercom Short for *intercommunication system*. Used by all production and technical personnel. The most widely used system has telephone headsets to facilitate voice communication on several wired or wireless channels. Includes other systems, such as I.F.B. and cell phones.

multicamera directing Simultaneous coordination of two or more cameras for instantaneous editing (switching). Also called *control room directing*.

running time The duration of a program or program segment.

schedule time The time at which a program starts and ends.

single-camera directing Directing method for a single camera. For digital cinema it may mean moving from an establishing long shot to medium shots, then to close-ups of the same action. Also called *film-style shooting*.

walk-through Orientation session with the production crew *(technical walk-through)* and the talent *(talent walk-through)* wherein the director walks through the set and explains the key actions.

17.1

Multicamera Control Room Directing

Like so many other production activities, directing has its own language. Your first task in becoming a director is, of course, to learn to speak this lingo with clarity and confidence. Only then can you fulfill your difficult task as master juggler of schedules, equipment, people, and artistic vision. Section 17.1 takes you through the major steps of multicamera, or control room, directing, and the use of multiple cameras for digital cinema.

▶ **THE DIRECTOR'S TERMINOLOGY**

Terms and cues for visualization, sequencing, special effects, audio, video recording, and the floor manager

▶ **MULTICAMERA DIRECTING PROCEDURES**

Directing from the control room, and control room intercom systems

▶ **DIRECTING REHEARSALS**

Script reading; dry run, or blocking rehearsal; walk-through; camera and dress rehearsals; and walk-through/camera rehearsal combination

▶ **DIRECTING THE SHOW**

Standby procedures and on-the-air procedures

▶ **CONTROLLING CLOCK TIME**

Schedule time and running time, back-timing and front-timing, and converting frames into clock time

THE DIRECTOR'S TERMINOLOGY

As does any other human activity in which many people work together at a common task, television directing demands a precise and specific language. This jargon, which must be understood by all members of the team, is generally called the director's language or, more specifically, the director's terminology. It is essential for efficient, error-free communication between the director and the production team.

By the time you learn television directing, you will probably have mastered most production jargon in general and perhaps even the greater part of the director's specific lingo. Like any language the director's terminology is subject to habit and change. Although the basic vocabulary is fairly standard, you will hear some variations among directors. And as new technology develops, the director's language changes accordingly. For example, we still don't have a standard terminology for an entirely tapeless operation. Some directors still call for "SOT" (sound on tape) even if the clips are delivered by a server; or they refer to "live-on-tape" when they record a show on a hard drive during a live telecast.

The terminology listed here reflects primarily multicamera directing from the studio or remote truck control room—the type of directing that requires the most precise terminology. A single inaccurate call can cause a number of serious mistakes. You can also use most of these terms in single-camera directing, regardless of whether the production happens in the studio or in the field.

Whatever terminology you use, it must be consistently precise and clear and it must be understood by everyone on the production team; there is little time during a show to explain. The shorter and less ambiguous the signals, the better the communication. The following tables list the director's terminology for visualization, sequencing, special effects, audio, video recording, and cues to the floor manager. **SEE 17.1–17.6**

MULTICAMERA DIRECTING PROCEDURES

When *multicamera directing* you direct and coordinate various production elements simultaneously from a television control room in the studio or the remote truck (see chapter 18). You generally try to create as finished a product as possible, which may or may not need some postproduction editing. When doing a live telecast, you have no chance to fix anything in postproduction; your directing is the final cut. Multicamera directing involves the coordination of many technical operations as well as the actions of the talent. You will find that, at first, managing the complex machinery—cameras, audio, graphics, video recorder (VR), remote feeds, and the clock—provides the greatest challenge. But once you have mastered the machines to some extent, the most difficult job will be dealing with people—those in front of the camera (talent) as well as those behind it (production people). **ZVL1** ›PROCESS→ Methods→ multicamera

DIRECTING FROM THE CONTROL ROOM

In multicamera directing you need to be concerned with not only the visualization of each shot but also the immediate sequencing of the various shots. It includes the directing of live shows, live-recorded (formerly live-on-tape) productions, and longer show segments that are later assembled but not otherwise altered in relatively simple postproduction. Multicamera directing always involves the use of a control room, regardless of whether it is attached to the studio, inside a remote truck, or temporarily assembled in the field for digital cinema. Because the control room is designed specifically for multicamera productions and for the smooth coordination of all other video, audio, and recording facilities and people, multicamera directing is often called control room directing.

Your lifeline during camera rehearsals and on-the-air directing is a reliable and flawlessly working intercommunication system that connects you with the rest of the control room personnel, the studio crew, and, if necessary, the talent.

CONTROL ROOM INTERCOM SYSTEMS

The control room *intercom* systems provide immediate voice communication among all production and technical

17.1 DIRECTOR'S VISUALIZATION CUES

The visualization cues are directions for the camera to achieve optimal shots. Some of these visualizations can be achieved in postproduction (such as an electronic zoom through digital magnification), but they are much more easily done with proper camera handling.

FROM	DIRECTOR'S CUE	TO
	Headroom, or tilt up	
	Tilt down	
	Center it, or pan left	

17.1 DIRECTOR'S VISUALIZATION CUES *(continued)*

FROM	DIRECTOR'S CUE	TO
	Pan left	
	Pan right	
	Pedestal up, or crane up	
	Pedestal down, or crane down	
	Dolly in	

17.1 DIRECTOR'S VISUALIZATION CUES *(continued)*

FROM	DIRECTOR'S CUE	TO
	Dolly out	
	Zoom in, or tighter	
	Zoom out, or looser	
	Truck right	
	Arc left	

17.2 DIRECTOR'S SEQUENCING CUES

The sequencing cues help get from one shot to the next. They include the major transitions.

ACTION	DIRECTOR'S CUE
Cut from camera 1 to camera 2	**Ready two — take two.**
Dissolve from camera 3 to camera 1	**Ready one for dissolve — dissolve.**
Horizontal wipe from camera 1 to camera 3	**Ready three for horizontal wipe [over 1] — wipe.** *or:* **Ready effects number** *x* **[the number being specified by the switcher program] — effects.**
Fade in camera 1 from black	**Ready fade in one — fade in one.** *or:* **Ready up on one — up on one.**
Fade out camera 2 to black	**Ready black — go to black.**
Short fade to black between cameras 1 and 2	**Ready cross-fade to two — cross-fade.**
Cut between camera 1 and clip 2 from server	**Take clip two.** [Sometimes you simply call the server number. If, for example, the server is labeled 6, you say: **Ready six — take six.**]
Cut between VR and C.G.	**Ready C.G. — take C.G.** *or:* **Ready effects on C.G. — take effects.**
Cut between C.G. titles	**Ready change page — change page.**

personnel. The most common systems are the P.L., the I.F.B., and the S.A. systems.

P.L. intercom Most small stations and independent production studios use the telephone intercommunication, or P.L. (private line or phone line), system. All production and technical personnel who need to be in voice contact with one another wear standard telephone headsets with an earphone and a small microphone for talkback. Although most studio P.L. systems are wireless, you still should have a wired system for backup.

Most production studios have several intercom outlets for plugging in the headsets for the floor manager, floor crew, and microphone boom operator. In addition, each camera has at least two intercom outlets: one for the camera operator and the other for a member of the floor crew. It is best, however, to have the floor crew connect their headsets to the wall outlets rather than the extra camera outlet. A tie to the camera not only limits their operation radius but also interferes with the camera's flexibility. There is always the danger of the floor manager's yanking the camera while trying to catch the talent's attention.

Some shows require a simultaneous feed of program sound and control room signals to other production personnel, such as the microphone boom operator or studio musicians (usually the band or orchestra leader), who have to coordinate their actions with both the program sound and the director's cues. In such cases you can use a double

17.3 DIRECTOR'S SPECIAL-EFFECTS CUES

Special-effects cues are not always uniform, and, depending on the complexity of the effect, directors may invent their own verbal shorthand. Whatever cues are used, they need to be standardized among the production team members.

ACTION	DIRECTOR'S CUE
To super camera 1 over 2	**Ready super one over two — super.**
To return to camera 2	**Ready to lose super — lose super.** *or:* **Ready to take out one — take out one.**
To go to camera 1 from the super	**Ready to go through to one — through to one.**
To key the C.G. over the base picture on camera 1	**Ready key C.G. [over 1] — key.**
To key the studio card title on camera 1 over the base picture on camera 2	**Ready key one over two — key.**
To fill the keyed-out title from the studio card on camera 1 with a yellow hue over the base picture on camera 2	**Ready matte key one, yellow, over two — matte key.**
To have the title from the C.G. appear in drop-shadow outline over the base picture on camera 1	**Ready C.G. drop shadow over one — key C.G.** [Sometimes the director may use the name of the C.G. manufacturer, such as Chyron. Thus you would say: **Ready Chyron over one — key Chyron.** Because the C.G. information is almost always keyed, the "key" is usually omitted in the ready cue.] *or:* **Ready effects, drop shadow — take effects.** [Some directors simply call for an "insert," which refers to the downstream keyer. Usually the lettering mode (drop shadow or outline) is already programmed into the C.G., so you just say: **Ready insert seven — take insert.**]
To have a wipe pattern appear over a picture, such as a scene on camera 2, and replace a scene on camera 1 through a circle wipe	**Ready circle wipe two over one — wipe.** [Any other wipe is called for in the same way except that the specific wipe pattern is substituted for "circle wipe." If you need a soft wipe, simply call for "Ready soft wipe" instead of "Ready wipe."]
To have an insert (video B) grow in size in a zoomlike motion, replacing the base picture (video A)	**Ready squeeze out — squeeze.** *or:* **Ready effect sixteen — squeeze out.**
To achieve the reverse squeeze (video B getting smaller)	**Ready squeeze in — squeeze.**
To achieve a great many transitions through wipes	**Ready wipe effect twenty-one — wipe.**

Many of the complicated effects are preset and stored in the computer program. The retrieval goes by numbers. All you do to activate a whole effects sequence is call for the number: **Ready effects eighty-seven — take effects.**

17.4 DIRECTOR'S AUDIO CUES

Audio cues involve cues for microphones, starting and stopping audio sources such as CD players, and integrating or mixing those sources.

ACTION	DIRECTOR'S CUE
To activate a microphone in the studio	**Ready to cue talent.** [Or something more specific, like **Mary — cue her.** The audio engineer will automatically open her mic.] *or:* **Ready to cue Mary — open mic, cue her.**
To start music	**Ready music — music.**
To bring the music under for an announcer	**Ready to fade music under — music under, cue announcer.**
To take the music out	**Ready music out — music out.** *or:* **Fade music out.**
To close the microphone in the studio (announcer's mic) and switch over to the sound on source, in this case, a clip from the server	**Ready SOS** [sound on source] **— close mic, track up.** *or:* **Ready SOS — SOS.**
To roll an audio recording (such as a clip or CD)	**Ready audio recorder, clip two** [or **CD two**]**.** **Roll audio.** *or:* **Ready audio clip two — play.**
To fade one sound source under and out while simultaneously fading another in (similar to a dissolve)	**Ready cross-fade from** *[source]* **to** *[other source]* **— cross-fade.**
To go from one sound source to another without interruption (usually two pieces of music)	**Ready segue from** *[source]* **to** *[other source]* **— segue.**
To increase program speaker volume for the director	**Monitor up, please.**
To play a sound effect from a CD	**Ready CD cut** *x* **— play.** *or:* **Ready sound effect** *x* **— play.**
To put slate information on the recording media (either open floor manager's mic or talkback patched to the VR)	**Ready to read slate — read slate.**

17.5 DIRECTOR'S VIDEO-RECORDING CUES

The video-recording cues are used to start and stop the video recorder, to slate a video recording, and to switch to the VR output.

ACTION	DIRECTOR'S CUE
To start recording a program	**Ready to roll VR one — roll VR one.** [Now you have to wait for the "in-record" or "speed" confirmation from the VR operator.]
To "slate" the program after the VR is in the record mode. The slate is on camera 2 or on the C.G.; the opening scene is on camera 1. (We are assuming that the color bars and the reference level audio tone are already on the recording media.)	**Ready two [or C.G.], ready to read slate — take two [or C.G.], read slate.**
To put the opening 10-second beeper on the audio track and fade in on camera 1. (Do not forget to start your stopwatch as soon as camera 1 fades in.)	**Ready black, ready beeper — black, beeper.** **Ten — nine — eight — seven — six — five —** **four — three — two — cue Mary — up on one.** [Start your stopwatch.]
To stop the recording on a freeze-frame	**Ready freeze — freeze.**
To roll the recording out of a freeze-frame	**Ready to roll VR three — roll VR three.**
To roll the recording for a slow-motion effect	**Ready VR four slo-mo — roll VR four.** *or:* **Ready VR four slo-mo — slo-mo four.**
To roll a VR as a program insert while you are on camera 2; sound is on source. Assuming a 2-second roll.	**Ready to roll VR three, SOS — roll VR three.** **Two — one, take VR three, SOS.** If you do not use a countdown because of instant start, simply say: **Ready VR three, roll and take VR three.** [Start your stopwatch for timing the VR insert.]
To return from VR to camera and Mary on camera 1. (Stop your watch and reset it for the next insert.)	**Ten seconds to one, five seconds to one.** **Ready one, ready cue Mary — cue Mary, take one.**

headset wherein one of the earphones carries the intercom signals and the other carries the program sound.

Sometimes when you work in noisy surroundings or near a high-volume sound source, such as a rock band, you may need a double-muff headset, which filters out the high-volume sounds at least to some degree. The mic in such headsets does not transmit the ambient sound and is activated only when you speak into it.

In most television operations, production and technical crews use the same intercom channel, which means that everyone can be heard by everyone else. Most of these systems also have provisions for separating the lines for different functions. For example, while the TD (technical director) confers with the video operator on one channel, the director may simultaneously give instructions to the floor crew. Larger studios and remote trucks provide a dozen or more separate intercom channels.

I.F.B. system   You use an I.F.B. (interruptible foldback or interruptible feedback) system in shows with highly flexible formats or when program changes are likely to occur while on the air. The I.F.B. system connects the

17.6 DIRECTOR'S CUES TO THE FLOOR MANAGER

The directional cues are always given from the camera's point of view, not the talent's. "Left" means camera-left; "right" means camera-right.

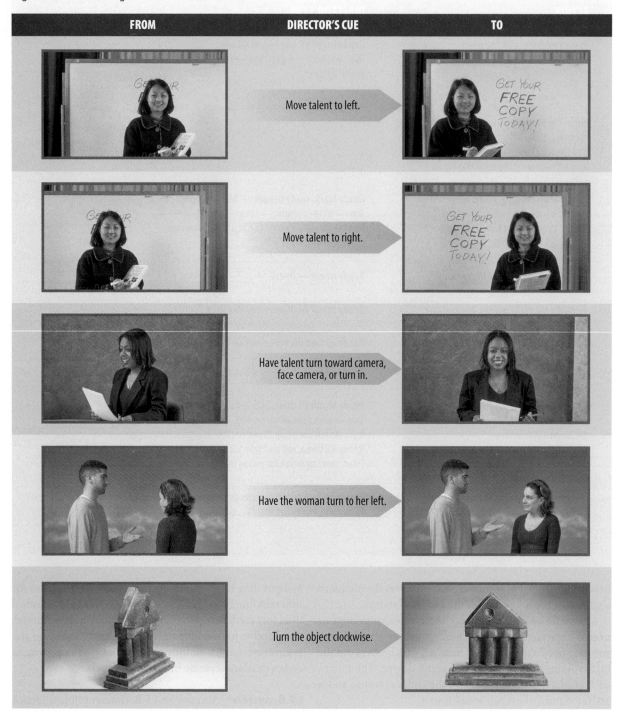

FROM	DIRECTOR'S CUE	TO
	Move talent to left.	
	Move talent to right.	
	Have talent turn toward camera, face camera, or turn in.	
	Have the woman turn to her left.	
	Turn the object clockwise.	

control room (director and producer) directly with the performers, bypassing the floor manager. The performer wears an earpiece that carries the total program sound (including his or her own voice) unless the director, the producer, or any other member of the control room team connected with the system interrupts the program sound with instructions.

For example, an on-camera field reporter in Washington who is describing the arrival of foreign dignitaries can hear herself until the director cuts in and says, "Throw it back to New York"—that is, for the talent to tell the viewers that the program is returning to the origination center in New York. But while the director is giving these instructions, the viewer still hears the field reporter's continuous description of the event. Relaying such messages through an off-camera floor manager would be much too slow and inaccurate in as tight a show as a newscast or a live telecast of a special event. The producer also uses I.F.B. to supply the host with follow-up questions while interviewing a guest. Needless to say, such a system works only with experienced talent and producer or director. There are countless occasions when the I.F.B. system unfortunately acts as a performer-interrupt device because the inexperienced performer cannot maintain effective commentary while listening simultaneously to the producer's instructions.

S.A. system   The S.A. (studio address) system is used by the control room personnel, primarily the director, to give instructions to people in the studio not connected by the P.L. system. Also called studio talkback, the S.A. system uses a studio loudspeaker similar to a public address system, helping communicate directly with everyone in the studio. For example, you may use it to give some general instructions to everybody, especially at the beginning of a rehearsal, or to inform talent and production personnel of a temporary delay. Also, if most personnel happen to be off the P.L. headsets, as is frequently the case during a short break, you can use the talkback system to call them back to work.

Considering the importance of the intercom systems, you should include them in routine facilities checks. If you discover faulty headsets or a noisy intercom line, report it to the maintenance crew and have it fixed right away. A faulty intercom can be more detrimental to a multicamera production than a defective camera.

DIRECTING REHEARSALS

Unless you are directing routine shows or doing a live remote pickup of a special event, you need to rehearse as much as possible. Rehearsals not only give you and the rest of the production team practice in what to do during the recording session but they also readily reveal any major and minor flaws or omissions in your production preparation.

Ideally, you should be able to rehearse everything that goes on the video recorder or on the air. Unfortunately, in practice this is hardly the case. Because the amount of scheduled rehearsal time always seems insufficient, the prerehearsal preparations (discussed in chapter 16) become extremely important. To make optimal use of the available time during scheduled rehearsals, you might try the following methods: script reading; dry run, or blocking rehearsal; walk-through; camera and dress rehearsals; and walk-through/camera rehearsal combination.

Note, however, that you rarely go through all these steps. Many nondramatic shows are rehearsed simply by walking the talent through certain actions, such as moving to a display table and holding items properly for close-ups, or walking to the performance area to greet the guest.

SCRIPT READING

Under ideal conditions every major production should begin with a script-reading session. Even for a relatively simple show, you should meet at least once with the talent, the producer, the PA (production assistant), and the key production personnel—AD (assistant director), TD, and floor manager—to discuss and read the script. Bring the floor plan along; it will help everyone visualize just where the action takes place and may reveal some potential production problems. In such a session, which normally doubles as a production meeting, you should address these points:

- Explain the process message, including the purpose of the show and its intended audience.

- Outline the major actions of the performers, the number and the use of hand props, and the major crossovers (walking from one performance area to another while on-camera).

- Discuss the performer's relationship to the guests, if any. In an interview, for example, discuss with the host the key questions and what he or she should know about the guest. Normally, such talent preparation is done by the producer before rehearsal time.

The script-reading sessions are, of course, particularly important if you are rehearsing TV specials or a television drama. You will find that the time you invest in thorough script interpretation is regained during subsequent rehearsals.

In the script-reading sessions for onetime plays, you should discuss the process message, the structure of the play (theme, plot, and environment), and the substance of each character. An extremely detailed analysis of the characters is probably the most important aspect of the dramatic script-reading session. The actor who really understands his or her character, role, and relationship to the event has mastered the principal part of his or her performance. After this analysis the actors tend to block themselves (under your careful guidance, of course) and move and "act" naturally. You no longer need to explain the motivation for each move. More than any other, the television actor must understand a character so well that he or she is no longer acting out but rather living the role. The internalization of the character, which can be readily achieved through extensive script-reading sessions, will almost always enhance the actor's performance.

When you direct a daily daytime serial or a weekly situation comedy with an ensemble cast, such intense and repeated character explorations are obviously superfluous. By the second or third episode, the actors will have a firm grip on their roles and how to relate to the rest of the cast.

DRY RUN, OR BLOCKING REHEARSAL

In the *dry run*, also called blocking rehearsal, the basic actions of the talent are worked out. By that time you must have a very good idea of where the cameras should be in relation to the set and where the actors should be in relation to the cameras and to one another.

The dry run presupposes a detailed floor plan and thorough preparation by the director. It also presumes that the actors have pretty much internalized their characters and roles. Tell them where the action should take place (the approximate location in the imagined set area—the actual set is rarely available at this point) and let them block as naturally as possible. Watch their actions as screen images, not from the point of view (POV) of a live audience. Adjust their blocking and your imagined camera positions so that you are reasonably assured that you will achieve the visualized screen image in the actual camera rehearsal. Do not fuss about specially framed shots at this time; you can always make such adjustments during the camera rehearsal. Be ready to give precise directions to the actor who is asking what to do next. Rather than always knowing what to do without the director's help, a good actor asks what to do and then does it convincingly and with precision.

Generally, try to observe the following in a dry run:

■ Hold the dry run in the studio or a rehearsal hall. In an emergency any room will do. Use tables, chairs, and chalk marks on the floor for sets and furniture.

■ Work out the blocking problems. Use a director's view-finder or a small consumer camcorder, bearing in mind that a studio camera is not as flexible. Have the PA take notes of the major blocking maneuvers. Allow time later for reading back these notes so that you can correct the blocking.

■ Try to block according to the actors' most natural movements, but keep in mind the camera and microphone positions and moves. Some directors walk right to the spot where the active camera will be and watch the proceedings from the camera's POV. If you block nondramatic action, observe first what the performers would do without the presence of a camera. As much as possible, try to place the cameras to suit the action rather than the other way around.

■ If it will help, call out all major cues, such as "cue Lisa," "ready two, take two," and so forth.

■ Run through the scenes in the order in which they are to be recorded. If you do the show live or live-recorded, try to go through the whole script at least once. If you cannot rehearse the whole script, pick the most complicated parts for rehearsal. In a nondramatic show, rehearse the opening as much as time allows. Inexperienced talent often stumble over the opening lines, with the show going downhill from there.

■ Time each segment and the overall show. Allow time for long camera movements, music bridges, announcer's intro and closing, opening and closing credits, and so forth.

■ Reconfirm the times and dates for the upcoming rehearsals.

WALK-THROUGH

The *walk-through* is an orientation session that helps the production crew and the talent understand the necessary medium and performance requirements. You can have both a technical walk-through and a talent walk-through. When pressed for time, or when doing a smaller production, combine the two.

The walk-throughs as well as the camera rehearsals occur shortly before the actual on-the-air performance or recording session. Walk-throughs are especially important when you are shooting on-location. The talent will get a feel for the new environment, and the crew will discover possible obstacles to camera and microphone moves.

Technical walk-through   Once the set is in place, gather the production crew—AD, floor manager, floor personnel, TD, LD (lighting director), camera operators, audio engineer, and boom or fishpole operator—for the technical walk-through. Explain the process message and your basic concept of the show. Then walk them through the set and explain these key factors: basic blocking and actions of talent, camera locations and traffic, specific shots and framings, mic locations and moves, basic cueing, scene and prop changes (if any), and major lighting effects.

The technical walk-through is especially important for electronic field production (EFP) and big remotes. Have the AD or PA take notes of all your major decisions; then have the notes read back and discussed so that the technical crew can take care of the problems.

Talent walk-through   While the production people go about their tasks, take the performers on a talent walk-through—a short excursion through the set or location; explain once again their major actions, positions, and crossovers. Tell them where the cameras will be in relation to their actions and whether they are to address the camera directly. Here are some of the more important aspects of the talent walk-through:

■ Point out to each performer his or her major positions and walks. If the performer is to look directly into the camera, indicate which camera it is and where it will be positioned.

■ Explain briefly where and how the talent should work with specific props. For example, tell the actor that the coffeepot will be here and how he should walk with the coffee cup to the couch—in front of the table, not behind it. Explain your blocking to the talent from the POV of the camera. Have the performer go through part of the demonstration, and watch this simulation from the camera's POV. Watch that the performer does not block close-ups of the product he is demonstrating.

■ Have all the talent go through their opening lines, then have them skip to the individual cue lines (often at the end of their dialogue). If the script calls for ad-lib commentary, ask the talent to ad-lib so that everyone will get an idea of what it sounds like.

■ Allow enough time for makeup and dressing before the camera rehearsal. During the talent walk-through, try to stay out of the crew's way as much as possible. Again, have the AD or PA take notes. Finish the walk-through early enough so that you can have a "notes" session before everyone takes a break before the camera rehearsal.

Try to rehearse by yourself the opening and closing of a show prior to camera rehearsal. Sit in a quiet corner with the script and start calling out the opening shots: "Roll VR [video recorder]. Ready slate—take slate. Ready black, ready beeper. Black, beeper. Ready to cue Lynne. Ready to fade up on two. Open mic. Cue Lynne, up on two," and so

on. By the time you enter the control room, you will practically have memorized the opening and closing of the show and will be able to pay full attention to the control room monitors and the audio.

CAMERA AND DRESS REHEARSALS

The following discussion of camera rehearsals is primarily for studio productions and big multicamera remotes that are directed from a control room. (Camera rehearsals for EFPs are discussed in section 17.2.)

Essentially, the *camera rehearsal* is a full rehearsal that includes all cameras and other production equipment. In minor productions the camera rehearsal and final *dress rehearsal*, or dress, are almost always the same, the only difference being that the talent is already properly dressed and made-up for the final taping. Frequently, the camera rehearsal time is cut short by technical problems, such as lighting or mic adjustments. Do not get nervous when you see most of the technical crew working frantically on the intercom system or audio console five minutes before airtime. Be patient and stay calm. Realize that you are working with a highly skilled group who know just as well as you do how much depends on a successful performance. Like all other systems, the television system sometimes breaks down. Be ready to suggest alternatives should the problem prevail.

The two basic methods of conducting a camera rehearsal for a live or recorded live production are the stop-start method and the uninterrupted run-through. A stop-start rehearsal is usually conducted from the control room, but it can also be done, at least partially, from the studio floor. An uninterrupted run-through rehearsal is always conducted from the control room.

In both types of rehearsals you should call for a "cut" (stop all action) only when a grave mistake has been made—one that cannot be corrected later. All minor mistakes and fumbles are corrected after the run-through. Dictate notes of all minor problems to the AD or PA and have them read back at scheduled "notes" sessions; provide enough time for following up on the items listed (reset).

In larger productions camera rehearsals and the dress rehearsal are conducted separately. Whereas in camera rehearsals the actors are not yet dressed and you may stop occasionally to correct some blocking or technical problem, dress rehearsals are normally done in full costume and are run straight through. You stop only when major production problems arise. Many times, as in the video recording of a situation comedy before a live audience, the recording of the dress rehearsal is combined with that of the "on-the-air" performance to make the final edit master recording that is then broadcast.

WALK-THROUGH/CAMERA REHEARSAL COMBINATION

As necessary as the preceding rehearsal procedures seem, they are rarely possible in smaller operations. First, most directing chores in nonbroadcast or nonnetwork productions are of a nondramatic nature, demanding less rehearsal effort than dramatic shows. Second, because of time and space limitations, you are lucky to get rehearsal time equal to or slightly more than the running time of the entire show; 45 or even 30 minutes of rehearsal time for a half-hour show is not uncommon. In some cases you have to jump from a cursory script reading to a camera rehearsal immediately preceding the on-the-air performance or recording session. In these situations you have to resort to a walk-through/camera rehearsal combination.

Because you cannot rehearse the entire show, you simply rehearse as well as possible the most important parts. Usually, these are the transitions rather than the parts between them. Always direct this rehearsal from the studio floor. If you try to conduct it from the control room, you will waste valuable time explaining shots and blocking over the intercom system.

Here are some of the major points for conducting a walk-through/camera rehearsal combination:

■ Get all production people into their respective positions: all camera operators at their cameras (with the cameras uncapped and ready to go); the fishpole mic ready to follow the sound source; the floor manager ready for cueing; and the TD, the audio console operator, and, if appropriate, the LD ready for action in the control room.

■ Have the TD feed the studio monitor with a tripart or quad-split screen, with each of the three or four mini-screens showing a respective camera feed. This split-screen display will serve as your preview monitors. If you don't have a wireless intercom system, use a wireless lavalier to relay your directing calls from the studio floor to the control room. If you cannot do such a split-screen display for your studio monitor, have the TD execute all your switching calls and feed the line-out pictures to the studio monitor. This way everybody can see the shots and the sequence you selected.

■ Walk the talent through all the major parts of the show. Rehearse only the critical transitions, crossovers, and specific shots. Watch the action on the studio monitor.

■ Give all cues for music, sound effects, lighting, video-recording rolls, slating procedures, and so forth to the TD via the open studio mic, but do not have them executed (except for the music, which can be easily reset).

■ Even if you are on the floor yourself, have the floor manager cue the talent and mark the crucial spots on the studio floor with chalk or masking tape.

If everything goes well, you are ready to go to the control room. Do not allow yourself or the crew to get hung up on some insignificant detail.

Once you are in the control room, contact the cameras by number and verify that the operators can communicate with you. Then briefly rehearse once more from the control room the most important parts of the show: the opening, closing, major talent actions, and camera movements.

When in the control room, the only way you can see the floor action is via the preview monitors. You should therefore develop a mental map of the major talent and camera movements and of where the cameras are in relation to the primary performance areas. To help you construct and maintain this mental map, always try to position the cameras counterclockwise, with camera 1 on the left and the last camera on the far right.

As pressed for time as you may be, try to remain cool and courteous to everyone. This is not the time to make drastic changes; there will always be other ways in which the show might be directed and even improved, but the camera rehearsal is not the time to try them out. Reserve sudden creative inspirations for your next show. Stick as closely as possible to the time line. Do not rehearse right up to videotaping or airtime. Give the talent and the crew a brief break before the actual taping. As mentioned earlier, don't just say, "Take five"; tell them the exact time to be back in the studio.

DIRECTING THE SHOW

Directing the on-the-air performance or the final taping session is, of course, the most important part of your job as a director. After all, the viewers do not sit in on the rehearsals—all they see and hear is what you finally put on the air. This section gives some pointers about standby procedures and on-the-air directing. Again, we assume that you are doing a live or uninterrupted recording of a multicamera show or at least the video recording of fairly long, uninterrupted show segments that require a minimum of postproduction editing. You will notice that you can transfer multicamera-directing skills much more readily to single-camera direction than the other way around.

STANDBY PROCEDURES

Here are some of the most important standby procedures to observe immediately preceding the recording session or on-the-air telecast.

■ Call on the intercom every member of the production team who needs to react to your cues—TD, camera operators, mic operator, floor manager and other floor personnel, VR operator, LD or lighting technician, audio technician, and character generator (C.G.) operator. Ask them if they are ready.

■ Check with the floor manager to make sure that everyone is in the studio and ready for action. Tell the floor manager who gets the opening cue and which camera will be on first. From this point, the floor manager is an essential link between you and the studio.

■ Announce the time remaining until the telecast or recording. If you are directing a video-recorded show or show segments, have the TD, C.G. operator, and audio engineer ready for the opening slate identification. You can save time by having the AD or TD direct the recording of the video leader (bars and tone) before airtime. Check that the slate shows the correct information. Verify the spelling of names that you will use as key inserts and credit crawl.

■ Again, alert everyone to the first cues.

ON-THE-AIR PROCEDURES

Assuming you direct an uninterrupted recording, such as the interview with the singers described in chapter 16, you must first go through the usual VR rolling procedures (see figure 17.5).

Directing from the control room Once the video recorder is rolling and the scene and take are slated, you can begin the actual recording. You are now on the air. Imagine the following opening sequence:

> Ready to come up on three [CU of Lynne, the interview host]. Ready to cue Lynne. Open mic, cue Lynne, up on [or "fade in"] three [Lynne addresses camera 3 with opening sentence]. Ready C.G. opening titles— take C.G. Cue announcer. Change page. Change page. Ready three [which is still on Lynne]. Cue Lynne—take three [introduces guests]. One, two-shot of singers. Two, cover [wide shot of all three]. Ready one—take one. Ready two, open mics [guest mics in the interview set]—take two. Ready three—take three [Lynne is asking her first question]. One, on Ron [CU of one of the singers]. Ready one—take one. Two, on Marissa [the other singer]. Ready two—take two.

By now you are well into the show. Listen carefully to what is being said so that you can anticipate the proper shots. Have the floor manager stand by to give Lynne time cues to the crossover. When you stop down for the cross-over, wait until the singers leave the frame before stopping down. This way you can logically cut from a close-up (CU) of Lynne introducing the singers to an establishing shot of the performance area. After the singers have returned to the interview set, watch the time carefully and give closing time cues to Lynne. After the one-minute cue, you must prepare for the closing. Are the closing credits ready? Again, watch the time.

> Thirty seconds. Wind her up. Wind her up [or "give her a wrap-up"]. Fifteen [seconds]. C.G. closing credits. Two, zoom in on Ron's guitar. Ready two, ready C.G. Cut Lynne. Cut mics. Roll credits. Take two. Key C.G. [over camera 2]. Lose key. Ready black—fade to black. Hold. Stop VR.

> OK, all clear. Good job, everyone.

Unfortunately, not every show goes this smoothly. You can contribute to a smooth performance, however, by paying attention to the following on-the-air directing procedures.

■ Give all signals clearly and precisely. Be relaxed but alert. If you are too relaxed, everyone will become somewhat lethargic, thinking that you don't really take the show too seriously.

■ Cue talent *before* you come up on him or her with the camera. By the time he or she speaks, the TD will have faded in the picture.

■ Indicate talent by name. Do not tell the floor manager to cue just "him" or "her," especially if the talent consists of several "hims" or "hers" anticipating a cue sooner or later.

■ Do not give a ready cue too far in advance or the TD or camera operator may have forgotten it by the time your take cue finally arrives. Repeating the same ready cue may trigger a take by the TD.

■ Do not pause between the take and the number of the camera. Do not say, "Take [pause] two." Some TDs may punch up the camera before you say the number.

■ Keep in mind the number of the camera already on the air, and do not call for a take or dissolve to that camera. Watch the preview monitors as much as possible. Do not bury your head in your script or fact sheet.

■ Do not ready one camera and then call for a take to another. In other words, do not say, "Ready one—take two." If you change your mind, nullify the ready cue—"No" or "Change that"—then give another.

■ Talk to the cameras by number, not by the name of the operator.

■ Call the camera first before you give instructions. For example: "One, stay on the guitar. Two, give me a close-up of Ron. Three, CU of Marissa. One, zoom in on the guitar."

■ After you have put one camera on the air, immediately tell the other camera what to do next. Do not wait until the last second; for example, say, "Take two. One, stay on this medium shot. Three, tight on Ron's guitar." If you reposition a camera, give the operator time to recalibrate the zoom lens; otherwise, the camera will not stay in focus during subsequent zooms.

■ If you make a mistake, correct it as well as you can and go on with the show. Do not meditate on how you could have avoided it while neglecting the rest of the show. Pay full attention to what is going on.

■ If you record each take separately, spot-check the video recording after each take to make sure that the take is actually recorded and technically acceptable. Check the audio. Then go on to the next one. It is always easier to repeat a take one right after the other than to go back at the end of a strenuous recording session and try to recapture the mood and the energy level of the original take.

■ If there is a technical problem that you must solve from the control room, tell the floor manager about it on the intercom or use the S.A. system to inform the whole studio about the delay. The talent then know that there is a technical delay and that it was not caused by them. The people on the floor can use this time to relax, however busy it may be for you in the control room.

■ During the show speak only when necessary. If you talk too much, people will stop listening and may miss important instructions. Worse, the crew will follow your example and start chatting on the intercom.

■ When you have the line in black (your final fade to black), call for a VR stop and give the all-clear signal. Thank the crew and the talent for their efforts. If something went wrong, do not storm into the studio to complain. Take a few minutes to catch your breath, then talk calmly to the people responsible for the problem. Be constructive in your criticism to help them avoid the mistake in the future. Just telling them that they made a mistake helps little at this point.

CONTROLLING CLOCK TIME

In commercial television, time is indeed money: each second of broadcast time has a monetary value. Salespeople sell time to their clients as though it were a tangible commodity. One second of airtime may cost much more than another, depending on the potential audience an event may command. As director, you are ultimately responsible for getting a program on and off the air on time and for the proper timing of segments, such as news packages.

SCHEDULE TIME AND RUNNING TIME

Schedule time is the clock time at which a program starts and ends. When doing a live show, you need to start and stop exactly according to the start and end schedule times as indicated in the daily program log. When video-recording a show, you don't have to worry about its schedule time, but you are still responsible for the accurate *running time*—the actual duration of a program or program segment—so that it can fit the prescribed time slot in the day's programming.

When directing a live show such as a newscast, you use the control room clock for meeting the schedule times (the switch to network news) and the stopwatch for measuring the running times of the program inserts (the individual video-recorded stories).

BACK-TIMING AND FRONT-TIMING

Although the master control computer calculates almost all the start and end times of programs and program inserts, and pocket calculators help you add and subtract clock times, you should nevertheless know how to do time calculations even in the absence of electronic devices. For example, a performer may request at the last minute specific time cues, which you then have to figure by hand. Note that you need to convert the seconds and the minutes on a scale of 60 rather than 100.

Back-timing   One of the most common time controls involves cues to the talent so that he or she can end the program as indicated by the schedule time. In a 30-minute program, the talent normally expects a 5-minute cue and subsequent cues with 3 minutes, 2 minutes, 1 minute, 30 seconds, and 15 seconds remaining in the show. To figure out such time cues quickly, you simply back-time from the scheduled end time or the start time of the new program segment (which is the same thing). For example, if the program log shows that your live *What's Your Opinion?* show is followed by a Salvation Army public service announcement (PSA) at 4:29:30, at what clock times do you give the talent the standard time cues, assuming that the recorded close takes 30 seconds?

You should start with the end time of the panel discussion, which is 4:29:00, and subtract the various time segments. (You do not back-time from the end of the program at 4:29:30 because the standard video-recorded close will take up 30 seconds.) When, for example, should the moderator get her 3-minute cue or the 15-second wind-up cue?

Let's proceed with back-timing this program:

4:24:00	5 minutes to VTR	*Back-time to here*
4:26:00	3 minutes	
4:27:00	2 minutes	
4:28:00	1 minute	
4:28:30	30 seconds	
4:28:45	15 seconds	
4:29:00	Cut moderator for prerecorded close	*Start here*
4:29:30	PSA (Salvation Army)	

Front-timing   To keep a show—such as a live newscast with many recorded inserts—on time, you need to know more than the start and end times of the program and the running times of the inserts. You also need to know when (using clock time) the inserts are to be run; otherwise you cannot figure whether you are ahead or behind with the total show.

To figure out the additional clock times for each break or insert, simply add the running times to the initial schedule time as shown on the program log or show format.

CONVERTING FRAMES INTO CLOCK TIME

Because in the NTSC system we figure that 30 frames make up 1 second, the frames roll over after 29, with the thirtieth frame starting the new second. But seconds and minutes roll over after 59. You must therefore convert frames into seconds, or seconds into frames, when front- or back-timing time code numbers. Again, you need to compute the frames, seconds, minutes, and hours individually, then convert the frames on the 30 scale and the seconds and the minutes on the 60 scale.

For example:

$$00:01:58:29$$
$$+ 00:00:03:17$$
$$00:01:61:46 \longrightarrow 00:01:62:16 \longrightarrow 00:02:02:16$$

Note that you simply added the frames, then subtracted 30 for the additional second.

Fortunately, the time code will do this for you automatically. There are also computer programs and handheld calculators available that take care of the rollovers of clock time as well as frame time.

MAIN POINTS

▶ A precise directing terminology is essential for the proper coordination of talent and crew and the instantaneous editing during a show.

▶ Multicamera directing involves the simultaneous use of two or more cameras and instantaneous editing with a switcher. It is done from the control room.

▶ Directing from the control room involves not only the proper visualization of shots but also their immediate sequencing.

▶ Properly functioning intercom systems—P.L. (private line or phone line), I.F.B. (interruptible foldback or interruptible feedback), and S.A. (studio address)—are essential for successful control room directing.

▶ The different types of rehearsals include script reading; dry run, or blocking rehearsal; walk-through; camera and dress rehearsals; and walk-through/camera rehearsal combination.

▶ The two important clock times are schedule time (start and end of a program) and running time (program length).

▶ Back-timing means figuring specific clock times (usually for cues) by subtracting the running time from the schedule time at which the program ends.

▶ Front-timing means starting at the schedule time that marks the beginning of a program and then adding specific running times.

▶ When converting frames into clock time, you must have the frames roll over to the next second after 29, but seconds and minutes after 59.

In **single-camera directing** you are concerned primarily with directing individual takes for later assembly in post-production. The big difference between directing multi-camera and single-camera productions is that multicamera productions are continuous and single-camera productions are discontinuous. *Continuous* in this context means that you do not stop after each shot but rather sequence a series of shots through instantaneous editing (switching) with a minimum of interruption or none at all. In single-camera studio productions, the video recording is discontinuous: you no longer intend to video-record a finished product that needs little or no postproduction for broadcast but rather to produce effective source material that can be shaped into a continuous program through extensive postproduction.

Digital cinema is mentioned because it is mostly single-camera but can also be done with a multicamera setup.

▶ **SINGLE-CAMERA DIRECTING PROCEDURES**
 Visualization, script breakdown, rehearsals, and video recording

▶ **DIRECTING DIGITAL CINEMA**
 Directing from the studio floor and directing on-location

SINGLE-CAMERA DIRECTING PROCEDURES

This section focuses on the following major aspects of single-camera studio directing: visualization, script break-down, rehearsals, and video recording. **ZVL2** PROCESS→ Methods→ single-camera

VISUALIZATION

Even if you are video-recording a production discontinu-ously—shot-by-shot—your basic visualization is not much different from what it would be when continuous-shooting with multiple cameras and instantaneous editing. As de-scribed in chapter 16, the first reading of a script may con-jure up some locking-in points—key visualizations that set the style for the entire production. This process is intuitive and depends a great deal on your own perception of the environment and the situation. It also depends on how you perceive the people in a documentary or the development of characters in a scripted drama.

Once you have established locking-in points that determine your general shooting style, you must go back to the script and break it down for discontinuous video recording. The order in which you video-record the shots is no longer guided by the script context, the narrative, or even aesthetic continuity but strictly by convenience and efficiency. For example, you may want to video-record all the scenes in the hospital corridor, then the waiting-room scenes, then all the operating-room scenes, then all the scenes in the patient's room, and so forth, irrespective of when they actually occur in the story.

To give you an idea of how script preparation for multicamera shooting differs from the single-camera approach, take another look at figure 16.13, showing the director's markings of a brief multicamera drama script. How would you break down the very same script segment for a single-camera shoot? Write down a series of shots that show Yolanda meeting Carrie in the hospital hallway, then compare it with the breakdown in figure 17.7. **SEE 17.7**

SCRIPT BREAKDOWN

As you can see, the breakdown is more detailed and not necessarily in the order of the action. Note that this script breakdown is just one of many possibilities.

Some script breakdowns list the corresponding page numbers to the master script and some continuity infor-mation, such as the time of day. Also, if you are shooting several scenes in the same location, you may want to video-record the scenes involving specific characters first, and then move on to the next set of characters. This way they can be scheduled at different times of the day. Shooting a scene piecemeal requires that the actors repeat their lines

RECEPTION ROOM AND HALLWAY

1. Yolanda in the reception room

2. Hallway: Yolanda pacing up and down the hallway in the vicinity of the emergency room

3. Hallway: Typical hospital traffic--nurses, a gurney, a wheelchair, visitors with flowers, a doctor and a nurse, a physical therapist protecting a person on crutches

4. Hallway: Doctor pushes Carrie in wheelchair

5. POV Carrie: Yolanda

6. CU Yolanda

7. POV Yolanda: Doctor and Carrie

YOLANDA RUSHING TOWARD DOCTOR AND CARRIE

1. Hallway: Yolanda rushes toward Doctor and Carrie

2. Reverse-angle shot (POV Carrie): Yolanda

3. Same shots with gurney traffic interfering with Yolanda's approach (Steadicam)

CARRIE AND YOLANDA

1. CU Carrie: "Hi, Mom!"

2. CU Yolanda: "Carrie--are you all right? What happened?"

3. CU swish pan from Carrie to Yolanda: "Carrie--are you all right? What happened?"

4. CUs and ECUs of Carrie

5. CUs and ECUs of Yolanda

6. CUs and ECUs of doctor

17.7 SINGLE-CAMERA SCRIPT BREAKDOWN
Takes are grouped for convenience and efficiency, not for narrative order.

and actions several times identically; you must watch carefully that the individual shots will eventually cut together into a seamless scene. This means that you must also connect the various visualization points so that the scene and the sequences have both narrative (story) continuity and continuity of aesthetic energy.

Continuity   All the shots in a sequence must connect seamlessly so that they are no longer recognized by the audience as individual shots but as a single scene. As explained in chapter 16, a detailed storyboard will aid you greatly in seeing individual shots as a sequence. Even if you don't have the time or resources to design storyboards for each sequence, you must try to visualize how well the shots cut together and watch for continuity errors during the video recording. If, for example, Yolanda kisses her daughter on the left cheek in the medium shot, do not let her switch to the right cheek during the close-ups of the same scene.

Close-ups and cutaways   Whatever breakdown you have, be sure to get some close-ups and extreme close-ups (ECUs) of all the people in the scene for intensification and possible cutaways. You can assign the AD or second-unit director to take care of such pickups. How you start and finish a specific take can make the postproduction editor's job a delight or a nightmare. As a director you are responsible for providing the editor with shots that can eventually be assembled into a continuous and sensible sequence.

REHEARSALS
As mentioned before, in single-camera directing you rehearse each take immediately before video-recording it. Walk the talent and the camera and microphone operators through each take, explaining what they should and should not do. Have the single camera connected to a monitor so that you can watch the action on-screen and, if necessary, make necessary corrections before the video recording. When on-location, you can set up small, battery-powered monitors on a simple card table and relay your directions to the camera operators via a P.L. system.

VIDEO RECORDING
Slate each take. When on-location use a simple handheld slate or clapstick. If you're in a hurry, you can audio-slate the takes (have the floor manager read the next take number and title into the hot mic). Have the VR operator or the PA keep an accurate field log. Always watch for continuity mistakes, but be careful not to wear out talent and crew with too many retakes; there is a point where

retakes become counterproductive because of talent and crew fatigue. Finally, have the VR operator or the PA label all recording media and boxes and verify that the labels correspond with the field log.

DIRECTING DIGITAL CINEMA
When using a multicamera setup for digital cinema or a complex EFP, and assuming that you have a competent AD, you can direct some fully scripted scenes from the studio floor, very much like doing a walk-through/camera rehearsal combination, or from a temporary control room that is set up on-location.

DIRECTING FROM THE STUDIO FLOOR
In this case, all cameras are functioning as iso cameras that also feed the switcher. You rehearse each take from the floor and then watch the performance on a studio monitor while the AD is calling the shots from the control room. One camera is usually on an establishing shot, another with a Steadicam mount gets the CUs and more-fluid shots, with the rest of the cameras assigned to different-angle shots. Much like in a walk-through/camera rehearsal combination, you can have the studio monitor show a quad-split that acts like small preview monitors of the various cameras.

DIRECTING ON-LOCATION
When on-location you need to set up a control center on the set unless you use a remote truck (see chapter 18). This "control room" usually consists of a large flat-panel display with preview images (smaller screens for each camera preview, and larger preview and line monitor displays), a portable switcher, and intercom systems that connect the control center with the cameras and the floor manager.

Much like in the studio setup, each HDTV camcorder is placed in an iso position but also feeds into the switcher. You can then either call for the various shots on the intercom or have the AD conduct the instantaneous editing while you watch the performance. Such a setup is especially helpful when covering onetime-only events, such as complicated stunts, explosions, and the like. If all goes well, the customary repeats for close-ups and different-angle shots are no longer necessary.

The advantage of such a multicamera setup is that you end up with a director's cut through instantaneous editing in addition to the recordings of the various cameras that can be used for postproduction editing. You can then watch the flow of the scene or scenes and, if necessary, do some retakes right then and there.

M A I N   P O I N T S

▶ Like multicamera directing, single-camera directing starts with the visualization of key shots.

▶ The script breakdown in single-camera directing is guided more by production convenience and efficiency than by visualization and sequencing. The production sequence is dictated not by the event sequence but by such production factors as location and getting various points of view or close-ups of the same action.

▶ Each take is normally rehearsed immediately before it is recorded.

▶ When video-recording the separate takes, always slate each with a handheld slate or clapstick, or at least do a verbal audio slate. Label the boxes and the recording media.

▶ When using a multicamera setup for digital cinema or a complex EFP, you can direct some fully scripted scenes from the studio floor or from a temporary control room that is set up on-location.

Z E T T L ' S   V I D E O L A B

For your reference or to track your work, the *Zettl's VideoLab* program cues in this chapter are listed here with their corresponding page numbers.

ZVL1 PROCESS→ Methods→ multicamera   **363**

ZVL2 PROCESS→ Methods→ single-camera   **378**

18

Field Production and Big Remotes

When you see one of those big television trailer rigs pull up and production crews start unloading cameras, microwave and satellite uplink dishes, miles of cable, and other pieces of television equipment, you know that a big remote is in the offing. Why undergo such an effort when you could simply grab a few small camcorders to shoot the same field event? This chapter provides some answers.

Section 18.1, Field Production, takes a closer look at each of the three field production methods: ENG (electronic news gathering), EFP (electronic field production), and big remotes. Section 18.2, Covering Major Events, offers further information about standard television setups of sports remotes and other field events, interpreting location sketches, major field communication systems, and signal transport.

big remote A production outside of the studio to televise live and/or live-record a large scheduled event that has not been staged specifically for television. Examples include sporting events, parades, political gatherings, and studio shows that are taken on the road. Also called *remote*.

broadband A high-bandwidth standard for sending information (voice, data, video, and audio) simultaneously over cables.

direct broadcast satellite (DBS) Satellite with a relatively high-powered transponder (transmitter/receiver) that broadcasts from the satellite to small, individual downlink dishes; operates on the Ku-band.

downlink The antenna (dish) and equipment that receive the signals coming from a satellite.

field production All productions that happen outside of the studio; generally refers to electronic field production.

instant replay Repeating for the viewer, by playing back a key play or an important event immediately after its live occurrence. In drama it is used as a visualized recall of a prior event.

iso camera Stands for *isolated camera*. Feeds into the switcher and into its own separate video recorder.

Ku-band A high-frequency band used by certain satellites for signal transport and distribution. The Ku-band signals can be influenced by heavy rain or snow.

live recording The uninterrupted video recording of a live show for later unedited playback. Formerly called *live-on-tape,* live recording includes all recording devices.

location sketch A rough map of the locale of a remote telecast. For an indoor remote, it shows the room dimensions and the furniture and window locations. For an outdoor remote, it indicates the location of buildings, the remote truck, power sources, and the sun during the time of the telecast.

microwave relay A transmission method from the remote location to the station and/or transmitter involving the use of several microwave units.

mini-link Several microwave setups that are linked together to transport the video and audio signals past obstacles to their destination (usually the television station and/or transmitter).

remote survey A preproduction investigation of the location premises and event circumstances. Also called *site survey*.

remote truck The vehicle that carries the program control, the audio control, the video-recording and instant-replay control, the technical control, and the transmission equipment.

uplink Earth station transmitter used to send video and audio signals to a satellite.

uplink truck A truck that sends video and audio signals to a satellite.

VJ Stands for *video journalist*. A television news reporter who shoots, edits, and writes his or her own material.

18.1

Field Production

When a television production happens outside the studio, it is known as a *field production*. We normally distinguish among electronic news gathering that covers daily news events, electronic field production that deals with smaller scheduled events, and big remotes that are done for major events, such as sports, parades, and political conventions.

There are advantages to taking a production out of the studio and into the field:

■ You can place or observe an event in its real setting or select a specific setting for a fictional event.

■ You can choose from an unlimited number and a variety of highly realistic settings.

■ You can use available light and background sounds so long as they accomplish your technical and aesthetic production requirements.

■ You can save on production people and equipment because many EFP productions require less equipment and crew than similar studio productions (unless you do a complex EFP or a big remote).

■ You avoid considerable rental costs for studio use and, if you work for a station, studio scheduling problems.

There are disadvantages as well:

■ You do not have the production control the studio affords. Good lighting is often difficult to achieve in the field, in both indoor and outdoor locations, as is high-quality audio.

■ On outdoor shoots the weather always presents a hazard. For example, rain or snow can cause serious delays simply because it is too wet or too cold to shoot outside. A few clouds may give you considerable continuity problems when the preceding takes showed clear skies.

■ You are always location-dependent, which means that some locations require the close cooperation of nonproduction people. For example, if you shoot on a busy downtown street, you will need the help of the police to control traffic and onlookers.

■ When shooting on city, county, or federal property, you may need a permit from these agencies plus additional insurance stipulated by them.

■ Field productions also normally require crew travel and lodging as well as equipment transportation.

As a television professional, you need to cope with these disadvantages. After all, you can't squeeze a football field into a studio. With ENG and relatively simple EFP, the production efficiency of shooting in the field usually outweighs the lack of production control. Although ENG and EFP have been discussed throughout this book, the focus here is on their specific field production requirements.

▶ **ELECTRONIC NEWS GATHERING**
ENG production features and satellite uplink

▶ **ELECTRONIC FIELD PRODUCTION**
EFP preproduction; production with equipment check, setup, rehearsals, video recording, and strike and equipment check; and postproduction

▶ **BIG REMOTES**
Preproduction remote survey and production procedures by director, floor manager, and talent

ELECTRONIC NEWS GATHERING

Electronic news gathering is the most flexible remote operation. As pointed out in previous chapters, one person with a camcorder can handle a complete ENG assignment. Even if the signal must be relayed back to the station or transmitter, ENG requires only a fraction of the equipment and the people of a big remote. Sometimes the shooter, or videographer (news camera operator), or even the *VJ* (video journalist) will also take care of the signal feed from the news vehicle to the station. With WiFi access the video clips can be uploaded and sent to the station much like e-mail.

ENG PRODUCTION FEATURES

The major production features of ENG are the readiness with which you can respond to an event, the mobility possible in the coverage of an event, and the flexibility of ENG equipment and people. Because ENG equipment is compact and self-contained, you can get to an event and video-record or broadcast it faster than with any other type of television equipment. An important operational difference between ENG and EFP or big remotes is that ENG requires no standard preproduction. ENG systems are specifically designed for immediate response to a breaking story. In ENG you exercise no control over the event but merely observe it with your camcorder and microphone as best you can.

Even when working under extreme conditions and time restrictions, experienced VJs and shooters can quickly analyze an event, select its most important parts, and video-record pictures that edit together well. For important events the ENG team normally consists of two people—the videographer and the field reporter; but many ENG stories are covered by a single VJ or shooter and narrated later by the anchor during the newscast. ENG equipment can go wherever you go. It can operate in a car, an elevator, a helicopter, or a small kitchen. Your shoulder or arms usually substitute for a heavy tripod.

With ENG equipment you can either video-record an event or transmit it live. Note that video recording includes a variety of recording methods, such as videotape, hard drives, optical discs, and flash memory devices (flash drives). The transmission equipment has become so compact and flexible that a single camera operator can accomplish even a live transmission. Most ENG vehicles (usually vans) are equipped with a microwave transmitter, which, when extended, can establish a transmission link from the remote location to the station. **SEE 18.1** Some ENG camcorders have a transmitter attached to them for signal transmission over relatively short distances.

When doing a live transmission, you connect the camera cable to the microwave transmitter. You can also use such a microwave link to quickly transmit to the station

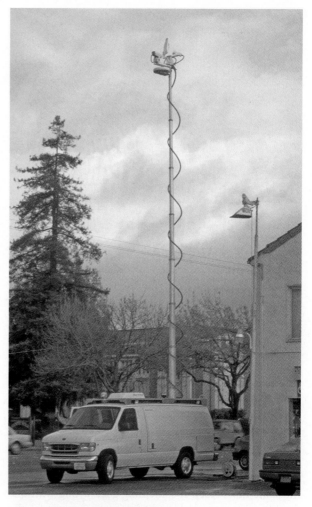

18.1 ENG VAN WITH EXTENDED MICROWAVE TRANSMITTER
This regular-sized van houses the extendible microwave transmission device and a variety of recording and inter-communications equipment.

the unedited video recording directly from the camcorder or the video recorder (VR) in the ENG van.

SATELLITE UPLINK

If you cannot establish a signal connection between your ENG location and the station, you need to request a satellite uplink van. This van looks like a small remote truck and contains computer-assisted uplink equipment and, when used for news, one or two VRs as well as editing equipment (often laptops). You can also play back the captured footage directly from the camcorder. When time permits, you

18.2 SATELLITE UPLINK VAN
The satellite news vehicle is a portable earth station. It sends television signals to the Ku-band satellites.

should transfer the video from the camcorder to the video recorder in the van. **SEE 18.2**

Newspeople prefer uplinking "hot" video recordings (those made moments before the transmission) to live transmission because it permits repeated transmission in case the satellite feed is temporarily interrupted or lost altogether. To further safeguard against signal loss, two VRs are sometimes used for the recording and the playback of the same news story. If something goes wrong with one machine, you can quickly switch over to the next for the same material.

Such uplinks are pressed into service whenever big and especially newsworthy events are scheduled, such as a presidential election, a summit meeting of heads of state, a high-profile criminal trial, or the world soccer finals. But the uplink truck is also used locally for the distribution of news stories, national and international teleconferencing, and whenever a signal cannot be sent readily by microwave or cable.

ELECTRONIC FIELD PRODUCTION

As you already know, EFP uses both ENG and studio techniques. From ENG it borrows its mobility and flexibility; from the studio it borrows its production care and quality control. The following discussion of some fundamental steps of preproduction, production, and postproduction

in the field assumes that you are still functioning as the director. This way you have to deal with production detail that is important for each member of the EFP team regardless of the specific jobs assigned. **ZVL1** PROCESS→ Methods→ location | studio

PREPRODUCTION

Compared with ENG, in which you simply respond to a situation, EFP requires careful planning. In general, the preproduction steps are almost the same for EFP as for a studio production. As a first step, you need to study the script and formulate a workable process message, which you then need to translate into the most effective and efficient production method—whether to shoot it indoors or outdoors, single- or multicamera, in the normal sequence of events or shot-by-shot.

PRODUCTION PREPARATION

The preparation for the actual production starts with deciding on the medium requirements—equipment and people. Assuming that you have practiced this translation of process message into production requirements (see chapter 1), we jump to the production phase and the initial production steps: location survey, initial production meeting, and field production time line.

Location survey   To get to know the environment in which the production will take place, make an accurate *location sketch*—a map of the locale of a remote telecast. For an indoor remote, the sketch shows the room dimensions and the furniture and window locations. For an outdoor remote, it indicates the location of buildings, the EFP vehicle, power sources, and the sun during the time of the telecast.

Take a look at the location sketch of an artist's studio. **SEE 18.3** This sketch gives important information about lighting and audio requirements, camera positions, and shooting sequences. Although technical preparations may not be your immediate concern, check on the availability of power (wall outlets), the acoustics (small room, reflective walls and floor, and traffic noise from nearby freeway), and potential lighting problems (large windows).

If the production is literally in a field, are the most basic conveniences available? (Location surveys are discussed further in the context of big remotes later in this chapter.)

Initial production meeting   The initial production meeting ideally involves all key personnel, including the

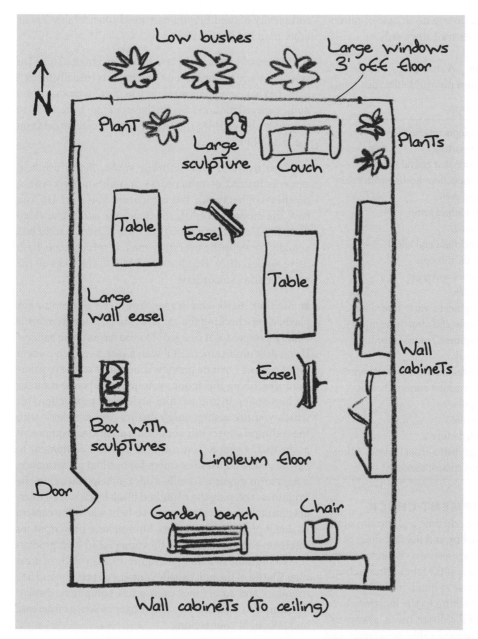

Low bushes

Large windows
3' off floor

PlanT

Large
sculpTure

Couch

PlanTs

Table

Easel

Table

Large
wall easel

Easel

Wall
cabineTs

Box with
sculpTures

Linoleum floor

Door

Garden bench

Chair

Wall cabineTs (To ceiling)

18.3 INDOOR LOCATION SKETCH: ARTIST'S STUDIO
This location sketch of an artist's studio shows the basic dimensions and the doors, windows, and furnishings.

PA (production assistant), the floor manager, and the DP or camera operator. For more-complex field productions that involve several indoor locations, you may want to include the LD (lighting director). At a minimum you should meet with the PA (who may double as the audio/ recording operator) and the camera operator. Explain the process message and what you hope to accomplish. Distribute the location sketch and discuss the major production steps.

It is critical that everyone knows the exact location of the production and how to get there. Can everyone fit into the EFP van? Who is riding with whom? Who needs to come first to the station for equipment check-out, and who will go directly to the location? Who will drive the van? Hand out the time line and ask the PA to distribute it (via fax and/or e-mail) to all other crewmembers who may not be at the meeting. As you can see, transportation to and from the location is an essential scheduling issue. If the field production is outdoors, what do you do in case of rain or snow? Always have an alternate time line ready.

Field production time line A shooting schedule for a fairly elaborate field production may look like this:

TIME LINE: FIELD PRODUCTION

7:30–8:15 a.m.	Equipment check-out
8:15 a.m.	Departure
9:15 a.m.	Estimated arrival time
9:30–10:00 a.m.	Production meeting with talent and crew
10:00–11:00 a.m.	Technical setup
11:00–11:30 a.m.	Lunch
11:30 a.m.–12:00 p.m.	Technical and talent walk-through
12:00–12:20 p.m.	Notes and reset
12:20–12:30 p.m.	Break
12:30–1:00 p.m.	Segment 1 video recording
1:00–1:15 p.m.	Notes and reset for segment 2
1:15–1:45 p.m.	Segment 2 video recording
1:45–1:55 p.m.	Break
1:55–2:10 p.m.	Notes and reset for segment 3
2:10–2:40 p.m.	Segment 3 video recording
2:40–3:00 p.m.	Spill
3:00–3:30 p.m.	Strike
3:30 p.m.	Departure
4:30 p.m.	Estimated arrival time at station
4:30–4:45 p.m.	Equipment check-in

PRODUCTION: EQUIPMENT CHECK

Again, apprise the crew of the schedule and the aim of the production. Go over the time line and the fact sheet of the major locations and recording sessions. Be extracareful when loading the equipment. Unlike studio productions, where all the equipment is close at hand, in field productions you need to bring everything to the location. Even if you have done the same EFP a dozen times, always use an equipment checklist. A wrong cable or adapter can cause undue delays or even the cancellation of the entire production.

Before loading equipment onto a vehicle, check each item to see that it works properly. At a minimum do a test recording of picture and sound before leaving for the location shoot.

Equipment checklist The following equipment checklist is intended as a general guide and may not include all the items you need to take along. Depending on the relative complexity of the EFP, you may need considerably less or more than the items listed.

■ *Cameras.* How many? Have they been checked out? Do you have the appropriate lens attachments (usually filters), if any? What camera mounts do you need: tripods, tripod dollies, special mounts? Do you have enough batteries? Are they fully charged? Do they fit the specific camcorders you use in the EFP?

■ *Video recorders and recording media.* If you use field cameras instead of camcorders or additional recorders, do they connect with the camcorder you use? Do you have the proper recording media for the additional video recorder? Do you have enough of them? Check that the box actually contains the necessary media (specific tape, flash drive, optical disc). Do all audio cables fit the jacks on the recorder and camcorders?

■ *Monitor, RCU, and scopes.* You need a monitor for playback or checking the camera's shots. If the monitor is battery-powered, is it charged? Do you have a spare battery? If you do a multicamera EFP with a switcher, each camera input needs a separate preview monitor. If you have a narrator describing the action, you need a separate monitor for him or her. In critical (film-style) field productions for which you use a single high-quality camera, check with the technical supervisor about such additional equipment as an RCU (remote control unit) and test equipment to enable you to adjust the camera for optimal performance; a waveform monitor (oscilloscope) to help you adjust the brightness (keeping the white and black levels within tolerable limits); and a vector scope to help adjust the camera so that it produces true colors. Do you have provisions for intercom and tally lights for the cameras? In such productions a portable switcher (see figure 13.18) will be of great help. The lid of the unit usually contains all preview and line monitors and sometimes even a test-equipment display. The unit also contains an audio mixer as well as intercom and tally light connections.

■ *Audio.* If you have not checked out the acoustics of the location, take several types of mics. Check your wireless lavaliers. Do you have enough batteries for the wireless mic transmitters? Do the portable mics fit the channel frequency of the receiver? All remote mics, including the lavaliers, should have windscreens. Shotgun mics need additional wind jammers. Choose the most appropriate mounting equipment, such as clamps, stands, and fishpoles. Do you need a small field mixer? Does it work? If you use a separate audio recorder, check it out before taking it on-location. Don't forget headsets for the fishpole operator and the audio-recording technician.

■ *Power supply.* Do you have the right batteries for the monitors, camcorders or field cameras, and audio equipment? Are they fully charged? If using alternating current (AC), do you have the right AC/DC adapters? Do you have enough AC extension cords to reach the AC outlet? Unless they are battery-driven, you also need AC power and extension cords for the monitors. Take a few power strips along, but be careful not to overload the circuits.

■ *Cables and connectors.* Do you have enough camera cables, especially if there is a long run between the camera and the RCU or portable switcher? Are there enough coax and AC cables for monitor feeds? Always take a sufficient number of mic cables along, even if you plan to use wireless mics. The mic cables may save a whole production day if the wireless system breaks down or is unusable on-location. Do you have the right audio connectors for the mic cables and jacks (usually XLR connectors, but sometimes RCA phono)? Bring some adapters for video and audio cables (BNC to RCA phono, and XLR to RCA phono and vice versa). Although you should avoid adapters as much as possible, bring some along that fit the cables and a variety of input jacks, just for insurance.

■ *Lighting.* You can light most interiors with portable lighting instruments. Bring several lighting kits. Check that the kits actually contain the standard complement of lights, stands, and accessories. Do the lights work? Always pack a few spare lamps. Do the lamps actually fit the lighting instruments? Do they burn with the desired color temperature (3,200K or 5,600K)? Do you have enough reflectors (white foam core), umbrella reflectors, diffusion material (scrims, screens, diffusion gels), and color gels for regulating color temperature? The color gels most often needed are the amber or light-orange ones for lowering the color temperature and the light-blue ones for raising it.

Other important items to take along are: a light meter, light stands and clamps, sandbags to secure the portable light stands, some pieces of 1×3 lumber to construct a light bridge for back lights, a roll of aluminum foil for heat shields, extra barn doors, flags, and a dozen or so wood clothespins to attach scrims or color gels to barn doors.

■ *Intercom.* If the single-camera EFP is taking place in a confined area, you don't need elaborate intercom systems; you can call your shots right from the production area. But if the event covers a large outdoor area, you need a small power megaphone and walkie-talkies and cell phones to communicate with the widely dispersed crew and the station, if necessary. If you use the portable switcher for a live or *live-recording* pickup, such as for the high-school state championship basketball game, you need headsets and intercom (often regular audio) cables.

■ *Miscellaneous.* There are a few more items that are often needed for a field production: extra scripts and time lines; field log sheets; slate and dry-erase markers; regular rain umbrellas and "raincoats" (plastic covers) for cameras; white cards for white-balancing; a teleprompter (flat-panel display and laptop), if applicable; blank cue cards or large newsprint pad and marker; an easel; and several rolls of gaffer's tape and masking tape. You also need white chalk, extra sandbags, wood clothespins, rope, makeup kit and bottled water, towels, flashlights, trash bags, and a first-aid kit.

PRODUCTION: SETUP

Once everyone knows what is supposed to happen, the setup will be relatively smooth and free of confusion. Although as director you may not be responsible for the technical setup, you should watch carefully that the equipment is put in the right places.

For example, when shooting indoors, will the lights be out of camera range? Are they far enough away from combustible materials (especially curtains) and properly insulated (with aluminum foil, for example)? Are the back lights high enough so that they will be out of the shot? Is there a window in the background that might cause lighting problems? (The window in the artist's studio in figure 18.3 would certainly present a problem if you had to shoot the large sculpture.) Does the room look too cluttered? Too clean? Are there any particular audio problems you can foresee? If the talent wears a wired lavalier mic, does the mic cord restrict talent mobility? If you use a shotgun mic, can the fishpole operator get close enough to the talent and, especially, move with the talent without stumbling over furniture? Are pictures hung where the camera can see them? Look behind the talent to see whether the background will cause any problems (such as lamps or plants seeming to extend from the talent's head).

When outdoors check for obvious obstacles that may be in the way of the camera, fishpole operators, and talent. Look past the shooting location to see whether the background fits the scene. Are there bushes, trees, or telephone poles that may, again, appear to extend from the talent's head? Large billboards are a constant background hazard. What are the potential audio hazards? Although the country road may be quiet now, will there be traffic at certain times? Are there any factory whistles that may go off in the middle of your scene? Is there any air traffic near your location?

PRODUCTION: REHEARSALS

Most often rehearsals are limited to a quick walk-through. But you may need more rehearsals if the EFP requires the interaction of more than one or two persons.

Walk-through   Before you start with the actual rehearsal and video recording, you should have a brief walk-through first with the crew and then with the talent to explain the major production points, such as camera positions, specific shots, and principal actions. In relatively simple productions, you can combine the technical and talent walk-throughs. Always follow the walk-through with the "notes" session, then have the crew take care of the remaining problems. Don't forget to give the talent and the crew a short break before starting with the rehearsal and recording sessions.

Rehearsal   As pointed out earlier, single-camera field directing has its own rehearsal technique. Basically, you rehearse each take immediately before recording it. You walk the talent and the camera and fishpole operators through the take, explaining what they should and should not do. Record some of the critical scenes and watch and listen to the playback. You may want to change the mic or the mic position for a better, less noisy pickup.

PRODUCTION: VIDEO RECORDING

Just before the actual recording, ask the DP (director of photography) and/or the camera operator whether the camera is properly white-balanced for the scene location. Sometimes clouds or fog move in between the rehearsal and the taping, changing the color temperature of the light. Slate all takes and have the PA or the video-record operator record them on the field log.

Watch the background action as well as the main foreground action. For example, curious onlookers may suddenly appear out of nowhere and get in your shot, or the talent may stop her action exactly in line with a distant power pole that then appears to grow out of her head. Listen carefully to the various foreground and background sounds during the take. Do not interrupt the taping because there was a faint airplane noise. Most likely, such noise will get buried by the main dialogue or the additional sounds added in postproduction (such as music). But the noise of a nearby helicopter that interrupts a Civil War scene definitely calls for a retake.

At the end of each take, have the talent stand quietly and let the camera record a few seconds of additional material. This cushion will be of great help to the editor in postproduction. Always record some usable cutaways and location sounds and room ambience for each location. The recorded "silence" will help bridge possible audio drops at edit points in postproduction.

When you feel that you have a series of good takes, play them back on the field monitor to see whether they are indeed acceptable for postproduction. If you detect gross problems, you can still do some retakes before moving on to the next scene or location. But watch your time line.

PRODUCTION: STRIKE AND EQUIPMENT CHECK

Have the location reset (furniture, curtains, and the like) the way you found it and the place cleaned before you leave. Pick up all scripts, shot sheets, and log sheets. Do not leave pieces of gaffer's tape stuck on floors, doors, or walls, and take away your trash. When loading the EFP vehicle, the floor manager, crew chief, or PA should run down the equipment checklist to see that everything is back in the vehicle before leaving or changing locations. Check that the source media are all properly labeled and—most important—loaded onto the vehicle. Some directors insist on carrying the source media personally.

POSTPRODUCTION

EFP postproduction activities are, for all practical purposes, identical to those of single-camera studio productions: making protection copies and window dubs, logging all takes on the source media, capturing the various takes on the hard drive of the editing computer, doing a rough-cut, and finally doing an on-line edit that is transferred to the edit master tape or DVD.

BIG REMOTES

A *big remote*, or simply remote, is done to televise live or live-record large scheduled events that have not been staged specifically for television. Examples are sporting events, parades, and political gatherings. All big remotes use high-quality field cameras (studio cameras with high-zoom-ratio lenses) in key positions, a number of ENG/EFP cameras, and an extensive audio setup. The cameras and the various audio elements are coordinated from a mobile control center—the *remote truck*. Remote trucks are usually powered by a portable generator, with a second one standing by in case the first one fails. If there is enough power available at the remote site, the truck is connected to the available power, with a single generator serving as backup.

The remote truck represents a compact studio control room and equipment room. It contains the following control centers:

- *Program control,* also called production, with preview and line monitors, a switcher with special effects, a character generator (C.G.), and various intercom systems: P.L., P.A. (public address), and elaborate I.F.B. systems

- *Audio control* with a fairly large audio console, digital recording media, monitor speakers, and intercom systems

- *Video-recording control* with several high-quality VRs that can do regular recordings, do instant replays, and play in slow-motion and freeze-frame modes

- *Technical control* with CCUs (camera control units), line monitors, patchboards, a generator, and signal transmission equipment **SEE 18.4 AND 18.5**

In very big remotes, one or more additional trailers may be used for supplemental production and control equipment.

Because the telecast happens away from the studio, some production procedures are different from those for studio productions. We therefore examine the following production aspects specific to the field: remote survey, equipment setup and operation, and floor manager and talent procedures.

REMOTE SURVEY

Like any other scheduled production, a big remote requires thorough preparation—only more so. One problem with preparing for big remotes is that the event you cover is normally a onetime happening that you cannot rehearse. It would be ridiculous to ask two national hockey teams to repeat the whole game for you, or to ask political leaders to restate their lively debate verbatim just so you can have your rehearsal. A remote of an award ceremony, however, allows some limited rehearsals; you can rehearse with stand-ins filling in for the master of ceremonies and the award recipients. Still, you have no control over the event itself but must follow it as best you can. Your production preparations must take these, and several other such considerations, into account. Yet another problem is that you can truck only the control room and the technical facilities to the site—not the studio itself. Cameras, microphones, and often lighting need to be brought to the remote location and made operational.

One of the key preparations is the remote survey. Many of the survey items for big remotes are equally applicable to other EFPs, such as an MTV segment or a visit to a car manufacturing plant. As the name implies, a ***remote survey,*** or site survey, is an investigation of the location premises and the event circumstances. It should provide you with

18.4 REMOTE TRUCK
The remote truck is a complete control center on wheels. It contains program, audio, video, and technical control centers as well as C.G. and recording facilities.

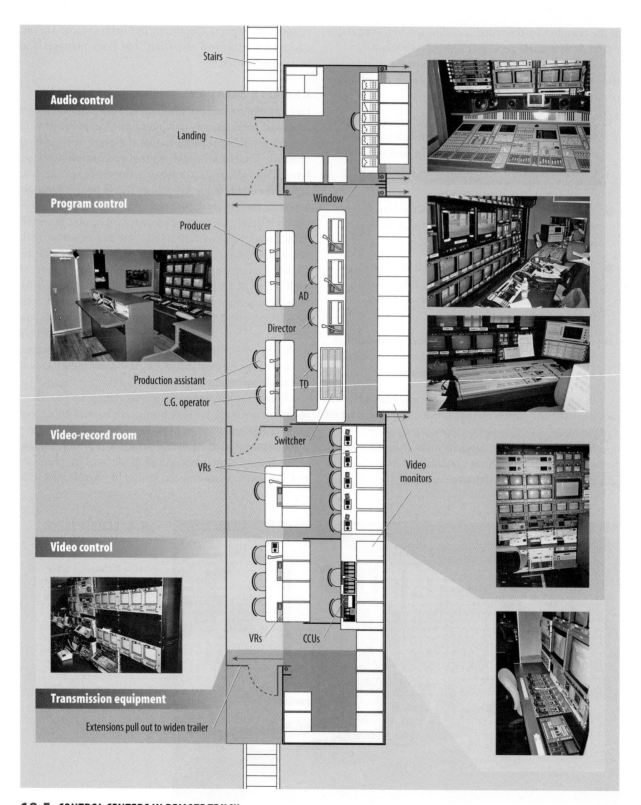

18.5 CONTROL CENTERS IN REMOTE TRUCK

The remote truck carries the audio control, the program control, the video-recording and instant-replay control, the video control, and the transmission equipment.

answers to some key questions about the nature of the event and the technical facilities necessary to televise it.

Contact person   Your first concern is to talk to someone who knows about the event. This person, called the contact person, or simply contact, may be the public relations officer of an institution or someone in a supervisory capacity. Call the contact to find out what he or she knows about the event and whether he or she can refer you to others who might answer your questions. In any case, get the contact's full name and position, business and e-mail addresses, and business, home, fax, cell, and pager numbers. Then make an appointment for the actual remote survey.

Ideally, the time of day of the survey should be the same as that of the scheduled remote telecast because the location of the sun is extremely important for outdoor remotes as well as for indoor remotes where windows will be in the shots. Arrange to have the contact person with you during the production. Establish an alternate contact and copy him or her on information you send to the primary contact. Sometimes the contact person comes down with a cold on your production day.

Survey party   The remote survey itself is concerned with production and technical considerations. The survey party therefore includes people from production and engineering. The minimum party usually comprises the producer, the director, and the technical director (TD) or technical supervisor of the remote. Additional production and technical supervisory personnel, such as the production manager and the chief engineer, may join the survey party, especially if the remote covers an important event and includes such elements as complex microwave or satellite links.

In general, the production requirements are first determined, and then the technical people try to make the planned production procedures technically possible. Depending on the complexity of the telecast, extensive compromises must often be made by production people as well as by technical personnel.

As director you can make such compromises only if you know what the particular technical setup and pickup problems are and what changes in procedures will help overcome them. You should therefore familiarize yourself with the production as well as the engineering requirements of television remotes. Although many production and technical survey questions overlap, for better clarification we consider them separately here.

Production survey   The table on the following pages lists the key questions you should ask during the production survey. **SEE 18.6** A good location sketch can help you prepare for the production and anticipate major problems (see figures 18.15 through 18.18).

Technical survey   The technical survey shown on page 396 lists only those items that directly influence the production procedures and, ultimately, your portion of the remote survey. **SEE 18.7** Technical points that have already been mentioned in the production survey, such as cameras and microphones, are not listed again.

EQUIPMENT SETUP AND OPERATION

There is no clear-cut formula for setting up equipment for a remote telecast. As with a studio production, the number of cameras, the type and the number of microphones, the lighting, and so forth depend entirely on the event or, more precisely, on the process message as defined in the preproduction meetings. Employing a great number of cameras, microphones, and other types of technical equipment does not necessarily guarantee a better telecast than when using less equipment. In fact, one or two camcorders are often more flexible and effective than a cumbersome remote truck with the fanciest VRs, audio-recording, and switching gear. Even for multicamera EFPs, a portable switcher is usually easier to set up and operate than using large trucks. For such big-remote operations as the live coverage of major sporting events, however, which may use 20 or more cameras, the remote truck provides essential equipment and production control.

Once set up, many of the production routines of big remotes do not differ significantly from studio productions. There are nevertheless some procedures in big-remote operations, such as instant replays, that you will not find in normal studio productions. For the following discussion, let's assume that you are functioning first as a director of a big remote, then as a floor manager, and finally as talent.

Directing the setup   Because the actual on-the-air telecast of big remotes is usually live, the directing procedures bear little resemblance to the other field production methods; they more closely resemble live or live-recorded studio productions.

■ As soon as the remote truck is in position, conduct a thorough technical walk-through. Tell the technical staff where you want the stationary cameras located and what field of view you require (how close or wide a shot you need to get with each camera). Get the cameras as close to the action as possible to avoid overly narrow-angle zoom lens positions. Apprise the crew of the approximate moves and ranges of mobile cameras and what audio needs you

18.6 REMOTE SURVEY: PRODUCTION

These are the key questions you should ask during the production survey.

SURVEY ITEM	KEY QUESTIONS
Contact	Who are your principal and alternate contacts? Title; business and e-mail addresses; business, home, and cell phone numbers; and fax and pager numbers.
Place	Where is the exact location of the telecast? Street address, telephone number. If you need traffic control, have the police been notified?
Time	When is the remote telecast? Date, time. What is the arrival time of the truck? Who is meeting you at the site for positioning the truck?
Nature of event	What is the exact nature of the event? Where does the action take place? What type of action do you expect? The contact person should be able to supply the necessary information.
Cameras (stationary)	How many cameras do you need? Use as few as possible. Where will you place the cameras? Do not place cameras on opposite sides of the action. In general, the closer together they are, the easier and less confusing the cutting will be. Shoot with the sun, not against it. Try to keep it behind or to the side of the cameras for the entire telecast. The press boxes of larger stadiums are generally located on the shadow side.
	If possible, survey the remote location during the exact time of the scheduled telecast. If it is not a sunny day, determine the position of the sun as closely as possible.
	Are there any large objects blocking the camera view, such as trees, telephone poles, or billboards? Will you have the same field of view during the actual telecast? A stadium crowd, for instance, may block the camera's field of view, although the view is unobstructed during the survey.
	Can you avoid large billboards in the background of shots, especially if the advertising competes with your sponsor's product?
	Do you need camera platforms? Where? How high? Can the platforms be erected at a particular point? Can you use the remote truck as a platform? If competing stations are also covering the event, have you obtained exclusive rights for your camera positions? Where do you want iso cameras positioned?
Cameras (mobile)	Do you need to move certain cameras? What kind of floor is there? Can the camera be moved on a field dolly, or do you need remote dollies (usually with large, inflatable rubber tires)? Will the dolly with the camera fit through narrow hallways and doors? Can you use ENG/EFP cameras instead of large studio/field cameras? What is their action radius? Can you connect them to a remote truck by cable (less chance of signal interference or signal loss), or do you have to send the signal back to the remote truck via microwave?
Lighting	Do you need additional lighting? Where and what kind? Can the instruments be hung conveniently, or do you need light stands? Do you need to make arrangements for back lights? Will the lights be high enough so that they are out of camera range? Do you have to shoot against windows? If so, can they be covered or filtered to block out undesirable daylight? Can you use reflectors?

18.6 REMOTE SURVEY: PRODUCTION *(continued)*

SURVEY ITEM	KEY QUESTIONS
Audio	What type of audio pickup do you need? Where do you need to place the mics? What is the exact action radius so far as audio is concerned? How long must the mic cables be? Which are stationary mics and which are handled by the talent? Do you need long-distance mics, such as shotgun or parabolic mics? Do you need wireless mics? Can their signals reach the wireless receivers?
	Do you need such audio arrangements as audio foldback or a speaker system that carries the program audio to the location? Can you tie into the "house" public address system? Do you need long-distance mics for sound pickups over a long range?
Intercommunications	What type of intercom system do you need? Do you have to string intercom lines? How many I.F.B. channels and/or stations do you need and where do they go? Is there a need for a P.A. talkback system? In case cell phones do not work in this area, are there enough telephone lines available?
Miscellaneous production items	Do you need a clock? Where? Do you need line monitors, especially for the announcer? How many? Where should they be located? Will the announcer need a preview monitor to follow iso playbacks? Do you have a camera slate in case the C.G. cannot be used?
Permits and clearances	Have you (or the producer, if you do not act as producer-director) secured clearances for the telecast from police and fire departments? Do you have written clearances from the originators of the event? Do you have parking permits for the remote truck and other production vehicles?
	Do you have passes and parking for all technical and production personnel, especially when the event requires entrance fees or has some kind of admission restrictions?
Other production aids	Does everyone have a fact sheet of the approximate order of events? These sheets are essential for the director, floor manager, and announcer and are extremely helpful to the camera operators, audio engineer, and additional floor personnel. Does the director have a spotter who can identify the major action and the people involved? In sports remotes, spotters are essential.

have. Unless they will be in a booth, specify where the announcers are going to be so that their monitors, mics, and intercom can be properly routed.

■ While the technical crew is setting up, hold a production meeting with the contact person, the producer, the AD (associate director), the floor manager, the PA, the talent, and, if not directly involved in the setup, the TD or technical supervisor. Have the contact describe the anticipated event. Explain how you intend to cover it. Although it is the producer's job to alert the talent to the prominent features of the event, such as a prize-winning float in the parade, be prepared to take over in case the producer is sidetracked by some other problem. Delegate the setup

supervision to the AD, floor manager, and TD. Do not try to do everything yourself.

■ Pay attention to all communication systems, especially the intercom. During the telecast you will have no chance to run in and out of the remote truck to the actual site; all your instructions will come via voice communication from the truck. Discuss the coverage of the event in detail with the floor manager, who holds one of the most critical production positions during a remote.

■ Usually, you as director have no control over the event itself; you merely try to observe it as faithfully as possible. Once again, check with the contact person and the announcer on the accuracy of the fact sheet and the specific

18.7 REMOTE SURVEY: TECHNICAL

The technical survey lists only those items that directly influence the production procedures.

SURVEY ITEM	KEY QUESTIONS
Power	Assuming you do not work from a battery pack or your own generator, is enough electricity available on-site? Where? Does the contact person have access to the power outlets? If not, who does? Make sure the contact is available during the remote setup and the actual production. Do you need extensions for the power cables? If you use a generator, do you have a second one for backup?
Location of remote truck and equipment	Where should the remote truck be located? Its proximity to the available power is critical if you do not have a power generator. Are you then close enough to the event location? Keep in mind that there is a maximum length for camera cables beyond which you will experience video loss. Watch for possible sources of video and audio signal interference, such as nearby X-ray machines, radar, or any other high-frequency electronic equipment. Does the remote truck block normal traffic? Does it interfere with the event itself? Reserve parking for the truck. Have you asked the police for assistance?
Recording devices	If the program is recorded, do you have the necessary video recorders in the truck? Do you need additional VRs for instant replays? If you have to feed the audio and video signals back to the station separately, are the necessary phone lines cleared for the audio feed? Do you have enough media to cover the full event? Have you made provisions for switching media without losing part of the event? Are the iso cameras properly patched into the switcher and into separate VRs?
Signal transmission	If the event is fed back to the station for video recording or directly to the transmitter for live broadcasting, do you have a good microwave or satellite uplink location? Do you need microwave mini-links? Double-check on the requirements for feeding the satellite uplink.
Cable routing	How many camera cables do you need? Where do they have to go? How many audio cables do you need? Where do they have to go? How many intercom lines do you need? Where do they have to go? How many AC (power) lines do you need? Where do they go? Route the cables in the shortest possible distance from remote truck to pickup point, but do not block heavily traveled hallways, doors, walkways, and so on. Do the cables have to cover a great span? If so, string a rope and tie the cable to it to relieve the tension.
Lighting	Are there enough AC outlets for all lighting instruments? Are the outlets fused for the lamps? Do not overload ordinary household circuits (usually 15 amps). Do you have enough extension cords and power strips (or simple multiple wall plugs) to accommodate all lighting instruments and the power supply for monitors and electric clocks?
Communication systems	What are the specific communication requirements? P.L.s? I.F.B. channels? Telephone lines? Cell phones? P.A. systems? Long-range walkie-talkies? Two-way radios?

information concerning the event. Ask the talent to double-check on the pronunciation of the names of participants and places.

■ Walk through the site again and visualize the event from the cameras' perspectives. Are they in the optimal shooting positions? Are they all on one side of the principal vector line so that you will not reverse the action on-screen when cutting from one to another? If shooting outdoors, will any of the cameras be blinded by the sun? Will the sun be directly behind the cameras (which, in effect, will wash out the viewfinder images)? Experienced camera operators will use an umbrella or flags attached to the camera to prevent the sun from washing out their viewfinders.

■ Keep in mind that you are a guest while covering a remote event. Unless television is an integral part of the event, such as in most sports, try to work as quickly and as unobtrusively as possible. Do not make a big spectacle of your production. Realize that you are basically intruding on an event and that the people involved are usually under some stress.

Directing the on-the-air telecast Once you are on the air, try to keep on top of the event as well as possible. If you have a good spotter (the contact person, event expert, or the AD), you will be able to anticipate certain happenings and be ready for them with the cameras. The following are some general points to remember.

■ Speak loudly and clearly. Usually, the site is noisy and the camera operators and the floor crew may not hear you very well. Put your headset mic close to your mouth. Yell if you have to, but do not get frantic. Tell the crewmembers to switch off their headset talkbacks to prevent the ambient sound from entering the intercom system.

■ Listen to the floor manager and the camera operators. They may help spot event details and report them to you as they occur.

■ Watch the monitors carefully. Often the off-air cameras will get especially interesting shots, but do not be tempted by cute yet meaningless or even event-distorting shots. If, for example, the great majority of an audience listens attentively to the orchestra, do not single out the one person who is conducting in the back row, as colorful a shot as this may be.

■ Listen to the audio. A good announcer will give you clues as to the development of the event and sometimes direct your attention to a significant event detail.

■ If things go wrong, stay calm. For example, if a spectator blocks the key camera or if the camera operator swish-pans to another scene because he thinks his camera is off the air, don't scream at the camera operator that he is still "hot" or at the floor manager to "get this jerk out of the way." Simply cut to another camera.

■ Exercise propriety and good taste in what you show the audience. Avoid capitalizing on accidents (especially during sporting events) or situations that are potentially embarrassing to the person on-camera, even if such situations might appear hilarious to you and the crew at the moment.

Instant replay In an *instant replay*, a key play or event segment is repeated for the viewer. Instant-replay operations usually use *iso cameras*, which feed into the switcher and into their own separate video recorders. Some large sports remotes employ a second, separate switcher that is dedicated exclusively to inserting instant replays.

During the replay digital video effects (DVE) are often used to explain a particular play. The screen may be divided into several squeezed boxes or corner wipes, each displaying a different aspect of the play; or it may function as an electronic blackboard that shows simple line drawings over the freeze-frame of an instant replay, very much like the sketches on a traditional blackboard. Game and player statistics are displayed using the C.G. Some of the information is preprogrammed and stored on disk, but up-to-date statistics are continuously entered by a C.G. operator. The whole instant-replay and C.G. operation is usually guided by the producer or the AD. The director is generally much too occupied with the real-time coverage to worry about instant replays and special effects.

When watching an instant replay of a key action, you may notice that the replay either duplicates exactly the sequence you have just seen or, more frequently, shows the action from a slightly different perspective. In the first case, the picture sequence of the regular game coverage—that is, the line output—has been recorded and played back; in the second case, it is the pickup of an iso camera that has been recorded and played back. In sports the principal function of the iso cameras is to follow key plays or players for instant replay. Iso cameras are also used in remote productions such as rock concerts or orchestra performances with a multicamera setup. When covering an orchestra, you may want to have an iso camera on the conductor at all times, which provides a convenient cutaway in postproduction.

When a remote production is done for postproduction rather than live, all cameras may be used in iso positions, with each camera's output recorded by a separate VR. The output of all iso cameras is then used as source material for extensive postproduction editing.

Postshow activities   The remote is not finished until all the equipment is struck and the site is restored to its original condition. As a director of big remotes, you should pay particular attention to the following postshow procedures.

■ If something went wrong, do not storm out of the remote truck, accusing everyone, except yourself, of making mistakes. Cool off first.

■ Thank the crew and the talent for their efforts. Nobody ever wants a remote to look bad. Especially thank the contact person and others responsible for making the event and the remote telecast possible. Leave as good an impression as you can of you and your team. Remember that when you are at a remote location, you are representing your company and, in a way, the whole of "the media."

■ Thank the police for their cooperation in reserving parking spaces for the remote vehicles, controlling the spectators, and so forth. Remember that you will need them again for your next remote telecast. See to it that the floor manager returns all the production equipment to the station.

PRODUCTION: FLOOR MANAGER AND TALENT PROCEDURES

As the floor manager, you play a key role in big remotes. The "floor" activities you have to manage have increased considerably in size and complexity.

Floor manager's procedures   As a floor manager (also called stage manager or unit manager on big remotes), you have, next to the director and the TD, the major responsibility for the success of the remote telecast. Because you are close to the scene, you often have a better overview of the event than does the director, who is isolated in the remote truck. The following points will help you make the big-remote production a successful one.

■ Familiarize yourself with the event ahead of time. Find out where it is taking place, how it will develop, and where the cameras and the microphones are positioned relative to the remote truck. Make a sketch of the major event developments and the equipment setup (see section 18.2).

■ Triple-check all intercom systems. Find out whether you can hear the instructions from the remote truck and if

you can be heard there. Check that the intercom is working properly for the other floor personnel. Check all wireless headsets, I.F.B. channels, walkie-talkies, cell-phone connections, and any other field communication devices.

■ Be aware of the traffic in the production area. Try to keep onlookers away from the equipment and the action areas. Be polite but firm. Work around the crews from other stations. Be especially aware of reporters from other media. It would not be the first time that a news photographer snapping pictures just happens to stand right in front of your key camera. Appeal to the photographer's sense of responsibility: say that you too have a job to do in trying to inform the public.

■ If the telecast is to be video-recorded, have the slate ready, unless the C.G. is used for slating.

■ Check that all cables are properly secured to minimize potential hazards to the people in the production area. If it has not been done by the technical crew, tape cables to the floor or sidewalk and put a mat over the cables at major pedestrian traffic areas.

■ Introduce yourself to the police officers assigned to the remote and fill them in on the major event details. Introduce them to the talent. The police are generally more cooperative and helpful when they get to meet on-the-air personalities and feel that they are part of the remote operation.

■ Help the camera operators with spotting key event details. Discuss with the cable pullers (floor personnel) the action radius of the portable cameras. These people are often the key to getting good shots with a portable EFP camera or a camcorder that is also attached to an RCU.

■ Relay all director's cues immediately and precisely. Position yourself so that the talent sees the cues without having to look for you. (Most of the time, talent are hooked up to the I.F.B. via small earphones, so the director can cue them directly without the floor manager as an intermediary.)

■ Have several 3 × 5 cards handy so you can write cues and pass them to the talent, just in case you lose the I.F.B. channel.

■ When the talent are temporarily off the air, keep them informed about what is going on. Help keep their appearance intact for the next on-the-air performance and offer encouragement and positive suggestions.

■ After the telecast pick up all the production equipment for which you are directly responsible—easels, platforms, sandbags, slates, and headsets. Double-check whether you have forgotten anything before you leave the remote site. Make use of the director's or TD's equipment checklist.

Talent procedures   The general talent procedures (as discussed in chapter 15) also apply to remote operations, but there are some points that are especially pertinent for you as talent.

■ Familiarize yourself thoroughly with the event and your specific assignment. Know the process message and do your part to effect it. Review the event with the producer, the director, and the contact person.

■ Test your microphone and your intercommunication system. If you work with an I.F.B. system, check it out with the director or producer.

■ Verify that your monitor is working. Ask the floor manager to have the TD punch up the line-out picture as soon as the cameras are uncapped. Ask for at least color bars to be put on-line.

■ If you have the help of a contact person or a spotter to identify the players in a particular event, discuss again the major aspects of the event and the communication system between the two of you once you're on the air. For example, how is the spotter going to tell you what is going on while the microphone is hot?

■ Verify the pronunciation of names and places. Little is more embarrassing for all involved than when names of locally well-known people are mispronounced by the television commentators.

■ When you're on the air, tell the audience what they cannot see for themselves. Do not report the obvious. For example, if you see the celebrity stepping out of the airplane and shaking hands with the people on the tarmac, do not say, "The celebrity is shaking hands with some people"; tell who is shaking hands with whom. If a football player lies on the field and cannot get up, do not tell the audience that the player apparently got hurt—they can see that for themselves; tell them who the player is and what might have caused the injury. Also, follow up this announcement periodically with more-detailed information on the injury and how the player is doing.

■ Do not get so involved in the event that you lose your objectivity. On the other hand, do not remain so detached that you appear to have no feelings whatsoever.

■ If you make a mistake in identifying someone or something, admit it and correct it as soon as possible.

■ Do not identify event details solely by color, as colors are often distorted on home receivers. For instance, refer to the runner not only as the one in the red trunks but also as the one on the left side of the screen.

■ As much as possible, let the event itself do the talking. Keep quiet during extremely tense moments. For example, do not talk during the intense pause between the starter's "Get set" command and the firing of the starter's pistol in the 100-meter track finals.[1]

---

1. For a more detailed description of announcing a remote, see Stuart W. Hyde, *Television and Radio Announcing*, 10th ed. (Boston: Houghton Mifflin, 2004).

M A I N   P O I N T S

▶ The three types of remotes are ENG (electronic news gathering), EFP (electronic field production), and big remotes.

▶ ENG is the most flexible remote operation. It offers speed in responding to an event, maximum mobility while on-location, and flexibility in transmitting the event live or in recording it with camcorders for immediate transmission by the station or for postproduction editing.

▶ Unlike ENG, which has little or no preparation time for covering a breaking story, EFP must be carefully planned. In this respect it is similar to big remotes.

▶ EFP is normally done with an event that can be interrupted and restaged for video-recording various event segments. It is most often done with a single camera or sometimes with multiple iso (isolated) cameras that shoot an event simultaneously.

▶ A big remote televises live, or live-records, a large scheduled event that has not been staged specifically for television, such as a sporting event, parade, political gathering, or congressional hearing.

▶ All big remotes use high-quality cameras in key positions and ENG/EFP cameras for more-mobile coverage. Big remotes usually require extensive audio setups.

▶ Big remotes are coordinated from the remote truck, which contains a program control, an audio control, video-recording and instant-replay control, and a technical control with CCUs and transmission equipment.

▶ Big remotes require extensive production and technical surveys as part of the production activities.

▶ In sports remotes instant replay is one of the more complicated production procedures. It is normally handled by an instant-replay producer or an AD.

18.2

Covering Major Events

As you know by now, EFP and especially big remotes require meticulous planning. Such careful preparation is particularly important for onetime happenings, such as sporting events. No two remotes are exactly the same, and there are always unique circumstances that require adjustments and compromises. This section includes some typical setups for sports remotes, how to read location sketches and some examples of typical indoor and outdoor remote setups, and an overview of field communication systems and signal transport.

▶ **SPORTS REMOTES**
Pickup requirements for baseball, football, soccer, basketball, tennis, boxing or wrestling, and swimming

▶ **LOCATION SKETCH AND REMOTE SETUPS**
Reading location sketches, indoor remotes, and outdoor remotes

▶ **COMMUNICATION SYSTEMS**
ENG, EFP, and big-remote communication systems

▶ **SIGNAL TRANSPORT**
Microwave transmission, cable distribution, and communication satellites

SPORTS REMOTES

Many big remotes are devoted to the coverage of sporting events. The number of cameras used and their functions depend almost entirely on who is doing the remote. Networks use a great amount of equipment and many personnel for the average sports remote. For especially important games, such as the Super Bowl or World Cup soccer, a crew of a hundred or so people set up and operate 20 or more cameras, countless mics, multiple monitors, and intercom and signal-distribution systems. There are several large trailers that house the control room and the production equipment. For the coverage of a local high-school game, however, you must get by with far less equipment. You may have only two cameras and three mics to do the pickup. Local stations or smaller production companies usually supply only the key production and technical personnel (producer, director, AD, PA, floor manager, TD, engineering supervisor, and audio technician) and hire a remote service that includes a remote truck, all equipment, and extra technical personnel.

The following figures illustrate the minimum video and audio pickup requirements for baseball, football, soccer, basketball, tennis, boxing or wrestling, and swimming. **SEE 18.8–18.14** Sometimes small ENG/EFP cameras are used in place of the larger high-quality studio/field cameras or are added to the minimal setups described here.[2]

LOCATION SKETCH AND REMOTE SETUPS

To simplify preproduction you as the director, or your AD, should prepare a location sketch. Like the studio floor plan, the location sketch shows the principal features of the environment in which the event takes place (stadium and playing field, street and major buildings, or hallways and rooms). This location sketch will help you decide on the placement of cameras, it will help the audio technician decide on the type and the possible location of microphones, and it will give the TD some idea about the location of the remote truck and the cable runs. Finally, if indoors, it will help the LD determine the type and the placement of lighting instruments.

---

2. For detailed miking setups of multiple sporting events, see Stanley R. Alten, *Audio in Media,* 8th ed. (Belmont, Calif.: Thomson Wadsworth, 2008), pp. 213–24.

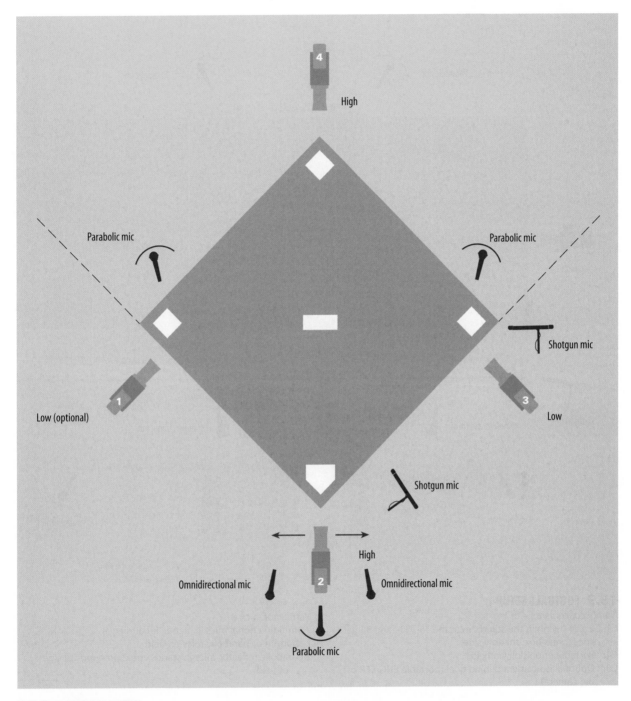

18.8 BASEBALL SETUP

Number of cameras: 3 or 4

C1: Near third base; low, optional

C2: Behind home plate; high

C3: Near first base; low; watch for action reversal when intercutting with C1

C4: Opposite C2 in center field; high; watch for action reversal

Number of mics: 6 or 7

2 omnidirectional mics high in stands for audience

2 shotgun mics or a parabolic (mobile) mic behind home plate for game sounds

2 or 3 parabolic mics for field and audience sounds

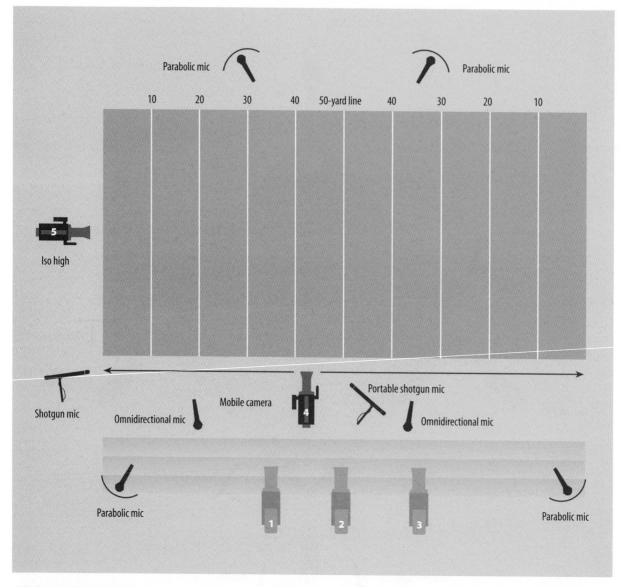

18.9 FOOTBALL SETUP

Number of cameras: 4 or 5

C1, C2, C3: High in the stands, near the 35-, 50-, and 35-yard lines (press box, shadow side)

C4: Portable or on dolly in field

C5: Optional iso camera behind goal (portable ENG/EFP or big camera)

Number of mics: 8

2 omnidirectional mics in stands for audience

2 shotgun or parabolic mics on field

2 parabolic reflector mics in stands and 2 on opposite side of field

18.10 SOCCER SETUP

Number of cameras: 3 or 4

C1: Left of centerline (high)
C2: Right of centerline (high)
C3: Mobile on field
C4: Optional, left corner; may be used as iso camera and
     mobile camera on field

All four cameras are on shadow side of field.

Number of mics: 7

1 omnidirectional mic in stands for audience
4 shotgun mics on field
2 parabolic mics on opposite side of field

18.11 BASKETBALL SETUP

Number of cameras: 4

C1: High in stands, left of centerline—follows game
C2: Lower (2 rows down) in stands, right of centerline (fairly close to C1)—gets close-ups
C3: In left corner (mobile)
C4: In right corner (mobile)

Number of mics: 6

1 omnidirectional mic in stands for audience
2 PZM or parabolic mics in stands for audience
2 shotgun mics behind each basket for game sounds
1 shotgun mic at center court

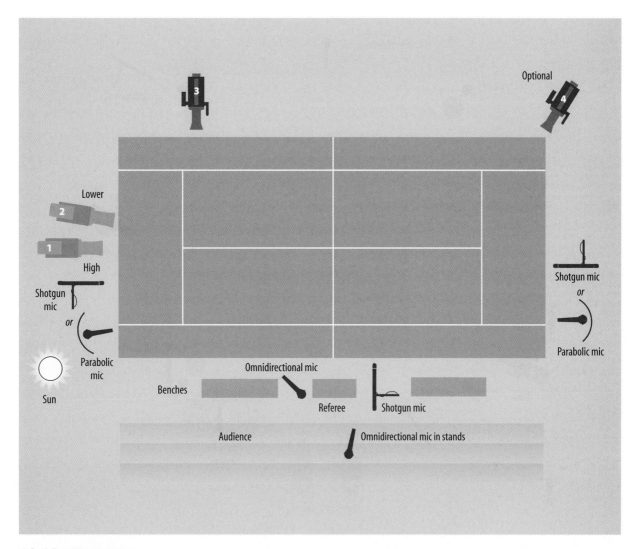

18.12 TENNIS SETUP

Number of cameras: 3 or 4

C1: At end of court, high enough so that it can cover total court, shooting with the sun

C2: Next to C1, but lower

C3: At side of court, opposite officials or where players rest between sets (mobile); also shoots CUs of players

C4: If four cameras are used, C3 shoots CUs of left player, C4 of right player

Number of mics: 5

1 omnidirectional mic in stands for audience

1 omnidirectional mic for referee's calls

3 shotgun mics at center court and on each end of court for game sounds, or 2 parabolic mics on the ends of the court

18.13 BOXING OR WRESTLING SETUP

Number of cameras: 3 or 4

C1: High enough to overlook the entire ring
C2: About 10' feet to the side of C1; high, slightly above
     ropes; used for replays
C3: ENG/EFP mobile camera carried on floor, looking
     through the ropes
C4: ENG/EFP mobile camera carried on floor, looking
     through the ropes

All mobile cameras have their own camera shotgun mics.

Number of mics: 5

1 omnidirectional mic for audience
2 shotgun mics for boxing sounds and referee
1 lavalier for bell
1 desk mic for announcer

18.14 SWIMMING SETUP

Number of cameras: 2 or 3

C1: High in stands, about at center of pool—follows swimmer
C2: Next to C1—gets close-ups
C3: Optional ENG/EFP mobile camera on side and ends of pool

Number of mics: 3

1 omnidirectional mic in stands for audience
1 shotgun mic at pool level for swimmers
1 omnidirectional mic on stand

READING LOCATION SKETCHES

The location sketch for indoor events should show the general dimensions of the room or hallway and the location of windows, doors, and furniture. Ideally, it should also indicate the principal action (where people are seated or where they will be walking) and such details as power outlets; actual width of especially narrow hallways, doors, and stairs; direction the doors open; and prominent thresholds, rugs, and other items that may present problems for the movement of cameras mounted on tripod dollies. The following two examples show a location sketch for a public hearing room and an outdoor location sketch for a parade.

Public hearing   The occasion is a newsworthy public hearing at city hall. **SEE 18.15** Assuming that you are the director of the remote, what can you tell from this sketch? How much preparation can you do? What key questions

does the sketch generate? Limiting the questions to the setup within this hearing room, what are the camera, lighting, audio, and intercom requirements?

Parade   The outdoor remote is intended for a Sunday afternoon live multicamera telecast. The estimated time of the telecast is from 3:30 to 5:30 p.m. The location sketch in figure 18.16 shows the action area as well as the major facilities. What setup and production clues can you devise from this location sketch? **SEE 18.16**

Before continuing, study the indoor location sketch (figure 18.15) and the outdoor location sketch (figure 18.16) and list as many production requirements as you can determine, then pencil in the type and the placement of cameras and microphones. In the following section, you'll compare your lists and equipment placement with subsequent figures in the context of the production requirements discussion.

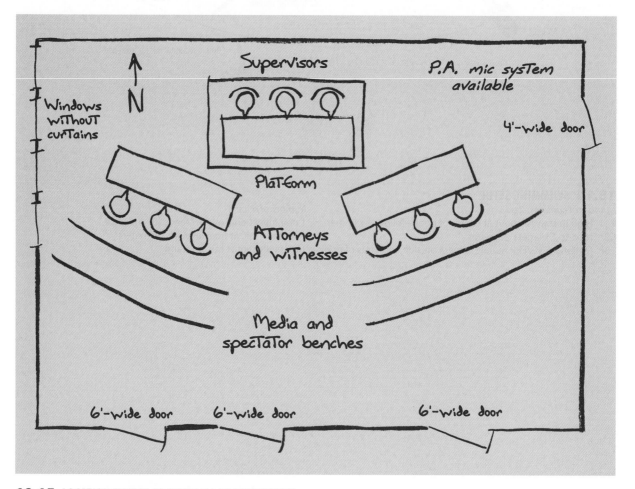

18.15   LOCATION SKETCH OF CITY HALL HEARING ROOM

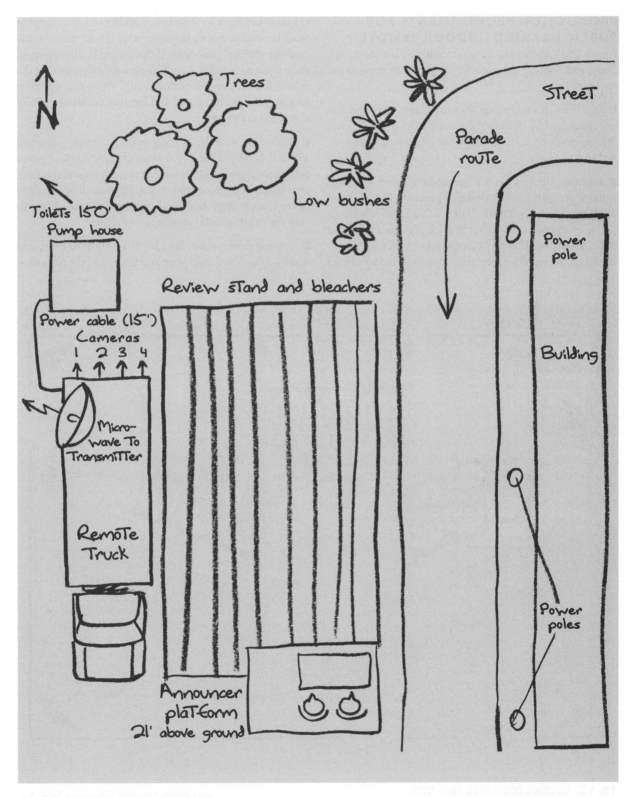

18.16 LOCATION SKETCH OF PARADE

PRODUCTION REQUIREMENTS FOR PUBLIC HEARING (INDOOR REMOTE)

Figure 18.17 shows the possible camera placement, mic setup, and lighting solutions for the public hearing room.
SEE 18.17

■ *Cameras.* This setup requires two cameras on tripod dollies connected by cable to the remote truck. C1 will cover the supervisors; C2 will cover the attorneys, witnesses, and spectators.

■ *Lighting.* The hearing is scheduled for 3 p.m. The large window presents a definite lighting problem. There are two solutions: (1) cover it with drapes and add floodlights or (2) have camera 2 truck closer to the supervisors' table and try to avoid shooting the window when covering the attorneys at the window-side table. Now the window can act

as a large key light. In this case, all additional floodlighting must have blue gels to raise the color temperature to the outdoor (5,600K) standard. If the ceiling is high enough, place some back lights. Are there enough AC outlets for the lights? Are they on different circuits? There may be some access problems if the mic and lighting cables are strung across the doorways.

■ *Audio.* Because the hearing room is already equipped with a P.A. system, tie into the existing mics. If the system is not operational, desk mics are the most logical solution. One additional mic should be placed on each of the three tables (supervisors' table and two witness tables) just in case the existing audio system malfunctions.

■ *Intercommunications.* Because there is little or no cueing involved (usually for the start and the end of the recording

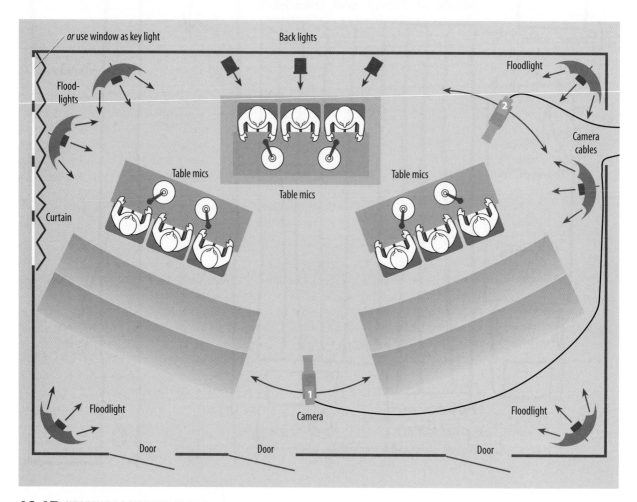

18.17   HEARING ROOM WITH FACILITIES

only), the floor manager can plug the headsets into one of the cameras. If ENG/EFP cameras are used, separate intercom cables may have to be strung for the floor manager and each camera operator.

■ *Other considerations.* Camera cables can be routed through the side door. If the room has a hardwood floor, the cameras could dolly into various positions for optimal shots. Because there is much traffic in the room, all cables must be taped to the floor and covered by rubber mats. Camera 1 will be in heavy traffic because of the public access doors.

PRODUCTION REQUIREMENTS FOR PARADE (OUTDOOR REMOTE)

Now compare your list and sketch for the parade with the setup shown in the next figure. **SEE 18.18**

■ *Location of remote truck.* The truck is in a good location. It's fairly close to a power source (pump house) and the camera positions, minimizing cable runs.

■ *Cameras.* You'll need a minimum of four cameras: C1 and C2 (studio/field cameras) on top of the bleachers, and C3 and C4 (ENG/EFP) on the street. C2 can also cover talent. C4 could also be mounted on a field jib at street level.

■ *Lighting.* Because the videotaping is scheduled for 3:30 to 5:30 p.m., there is sufficient light throughout the telecast. Because the sun is mostly behind the cameras, you may need a device to prevent the sun from washing out the viewfinders of cameras 1 and 2.

■ *Audio.* There are three types of audio pickup: (1) the voice pickup of the two announcers, (2) the bands in the parade, and (3) the sounds of the spectators. Use lavalier mics with windscreens or headset mics for the talent. Use two shotgun or parabolic mics (one high in the stands, the other just above ground level) for the bands. Use one omnidirectional mic near the announcer platform for the crowd noise. All mics need windscreens, and the shotgun mics need wind jammers.

■ *Intercommunications.* The camera operators are connected to the normal P.L. lines of the camera cables. You'll need a separate intercom line for the floor manager's headset. Use I.F.B. for the talent. At least two telephone lines for intercommunication come from the truck: a direct line to the station and the transmitter and another line for general voice communication.

■ *Signal transmission.* You'll use a direct microwave link to the transmission tower (and from there to the station). Audio is sent via telephone lines (independent of microwave). This separation ensures audio continuity if the microwave link fails.

■ *Other considerations.* Cameras 1 and 2 need a field lens to catch close-ups of the action around the bend (40×). You will need a large monitor for the talent and a second monitor for backup. Shade the monitors from the sun. Route the cables underneath the platform to reduce the potential tripping hazard. The ENG/EFP cameras (C3 and C4) need cable pullers in addition to the camera operators. Toilet facilities are fairly close to the pump house. Raincoats and umbrellas may be needed for crew, talent, and cameras just in case the weather report predicting a beautiful day is wrong.

COMMUNICATION SYSTEMS

Well-functioning communication systems are especially important for production people in the field, regardless of whether the "field" is the street corner across from the station or one in London. These systems must be highly reliable and must enable the people at home base to talk with the field personnel, and the field personnel to talk with one another. When doing ENG you must be able to receive messages from the newsroom as well as the police and fire departments. As a producer or director, you need to reach the talent directly with specific information, even while the talent is on the air.

We have come to expect the relatively flawless transporting of television pictures and sound, regardless of whether they originate from the mayor's downtown office or the orbiting space station. Although communication systems and signal distribution are the province of the technical crew, you should still be familiar with them so that you will know what is available to you. This section provides a brief overview of ENG, EFP, and big-remote communication systems.

ENG COMMUNICATION SYSTEMS

Electronic news gathering has such a high degree of readiness not only because of the mobile and self-contained camera/recorder/audio unit but also because of elaborate communication devices. Most ENG vehicles are equipped with cell phones, scanners that continuously monitor the frequencies used by police and fire departments, a paging system, and two-way radios. Scanners lock in on a certain

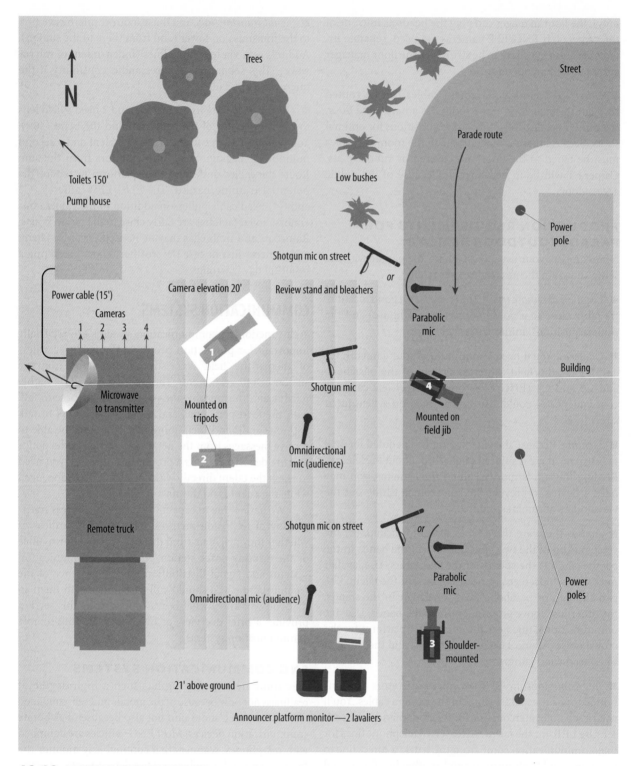

18.18 LOCATION SETUP FOR PARADE

frequency as soon as they detect a signal and let you hear the conversation on that frequency.

These communication systems also make it possible for your station's newsroom to contact you while you are on the road and give you a chance to respond immediately to police and fire calls. Sometimes news departments use codes to communicate with their "cruising" field reporters to prevent the competition from getting wind of a breaking story.

EFP COMMUNICATION SYSTEMS

A single-camera EFP needs the least sophisticated communication system. Because the director is in direct contact with the crew and the talent at the shoot location, no intercom system is needed. Generally, widely dispersed crewmembers keep in touch with one another via walkie-talkies or cell phones. As pointed out earlier, a small power megaphone might save your voice when giving directions collectively to talent and crew.

The EFP van is normally equipped with phone jacks for regular phone connections, but cell phones will usually suffice. If the EFP uses multiple cameras that are coordinated from a central location, a headset intercom system must be set up for the communication among director, TD, and crew. When doing a live telecast from the field, an I.F.B. system is added.

BIG-REMOTE COMMUNICATION SYSTEMS

Big remotes need communication systems between the remote truck (or any other remote control room) and the production people and crew, between the truck and the station, and between the truck and the talent. The truck and the production crew communicate through a regular P.L. (private line or phone line) system, which uses the P.L. channels in the camera cable, separately wired P.L. lines, or wireless P.L.s. During a complicated setup in which the crew is widely scattered (such as when covering a downhill ski race), walkie-talkies are also used. If necessary, the P.L. communication can be carried by telephone lines from truck to station.

The I.F.B. (interruptible foldback or feedback) system is one of the most important lines of communication between the producer or director and the talent during a big remote. If several reporters or commentators are involved in the same event, you can switch among several I.F.B. channels so that, if necessary, you can address the field reporters and the commentators individually. If needed, your I.F.B. instructions to the talent can be transmitted via satellite over great distances. Realize, however, that there is inevitably a slight delay before the talent receives your instructions. In sports remotes the talent occasionally wear headsets through which they receive instructions from the truck.

The remote truck is, of course, equipped with several wired telephone lines, two-way radios, cell phones, paging systems, and walkie-talkies.

SIGNAL TRANSPORT

Signal transport refers to the systems available to you when transmitting the video and audio signals from their origin (microphone and camera) to the recording device or transmitter, and from the point of origin to various reception points. Signal transport includes microwave transmission, cable distribution, and communication satellites.

MICROWAVE TRANSMISSION

If you need to maintain optimal camera mobility during a live pickup, such as when shooting interviews from a convention floor, you cannot use a camera cable but must send the signal to the remote truck via microwave.

From camera to remote truck   There are small, portable, battery-powered transmitters that can be mounted on the camera. If the distance from camera to receiving station is not too great, you can use this system to relay the camera video and audio signals to the remote truck without too much difficulty. To minimize interference by other stations covering the same event, you can transmit on several frequencies, a practice called frequency agility.

If you need a more powerful microwave transmitter, you can mount the small microwave dish on a tripod and place it close to the camera action radius. That way you can work at a considerable distance from the remote truck while using only a relatively short cable run from camera to dish. This type of link is especially useful if a cable run would create potential hazards, such as when strung from a building across high-tension wires or across busy streets. **SEE 18.19**

The main problem with camera-to-truck microwave links is interference, especially if several television crews are covering the same event. Even if you use a system with relatively great frequency agility, your competition may be similarly agile and overpower you with a stronger signal.

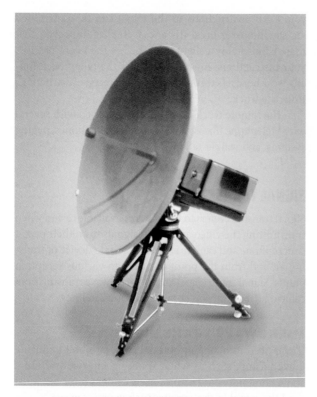

18.19 TRIPOD-MOUNTED MICROWAVE TRANSMITTER
This small tripod-mounted microwave transmitter can relay camera signals over a considerable distance.

From remote van to station or transmitter   The longer, and usually much more complex, signal link is from the remote van to the television station. (Although sometimes the signal is sent directly to the transmitter, we will call the end point of this last link before the actual broadcast the "station.") You can send the signals from the remote van directly to the station only if you have a clear, unobstructed line of sight. **SEE 18.20**

Because the microwave signal travels in a straight line, tall buildings, bridges, or mountains that are in the line of sight between the remote van and the station may block the signal transmission. In such cases several microwave links, called *mini-links*, have to be established to carry the signal around these obstacles. **SEE 18.21**

Television stations in metropolitan areas have permanent *microwave relays* installed in strategic locations so that remote vans can send their signals back from practically any point in their coverage area. If these permanent installations do not suffice, helicopters are used as microwave relay stations (see figure 18.21). Permanent microwave relays are also used for transmitting the video of permanently installed cameras that monitor the weather or traffic.

There are several other ways to transmit signals from the remote location to the station. Although this is not your responsibility unless you are a broadcast engineer, you should nevertheless have some idea of what is available.

18.20 DIRECT MICROWAVE LINK
You can transmit the signal via microwave from the remote van back to the station only if there is a clear, unobstructed line of sight.

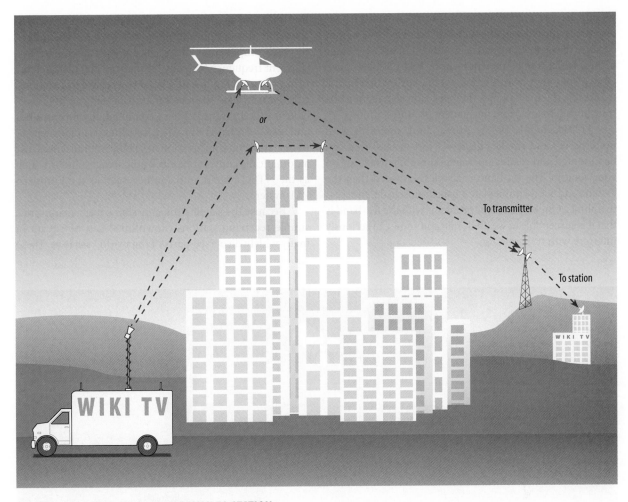

18.21 MINI-LINK FROM REMOTE VAN TO STATION
If there is no clear line of sight between the remote location and the station, the microwave signal must be transported via mini-links.

CABLE DISTRIBUTION

The telephone companies can provide broadband high-definition digital cable service (coax or fiber-optic) that transports all video and audio signals, including HDTV 1080i signals. *Broadband* is a high-bandwidth standard for sending information (voice, data, video, and audio) simultaneously over cables.

COMMUNICATION SATELLITES

The communication satellites used for broadcast are positioned in a geosynchronous orbit 22,300 miles above the earth. In this orbit the satellite moves synchronously with the earth, thereby remaining in the same position relative to it.

Communication satellites operate on two frequency bands: the lower-frequency C-band and the higher-frequency *Ku-band* (pronounced "kay-*you*-band"). Some satellites have transponders for C-band as well as Ku-band transmission and can convert internally from one to the other.

A *direct broadcast satellite (DBS)* has a relatively high-powered transponder (transmitter/receiver) that broadcasts from the satellite to small individual downlink dishes (which you can buy in larger electronic stores and install yourself). A DBS operates on the Ku-band.

The C-band is a highly reliable system that is relatively immune to weather interference. Because the C-band works with microwave frequencies, it may interfere with ground-based microwave transmission. To avoid such interference, the C-band operates with relatively low power; because of the low power, the ground stations need large dishes, which range anywhere from 15 to 30 feet. Such large dishes are obviously not suitable for mobile uplink trucks. To use the C-band, the television signals must be transported to and from permanent ground stations.

The Ku-band, on the other hand, operates with more power and smaller dishes (3 feet or less) that can be mounted and readily operated on mobile trucks or on your rooftop. The Ku-band is also less crowded than the C-band and allows immediate, virtually unscheduled access to uplinks. One of the major problems with the Ku-band is that it is susceptible to weather; rain and snow can seriously interfere with transmission.

Uplinks and downlinks   Television signals are sent to a satellite through an *uplink* (earth station transmitter), received, amplified by the satellite, and beamed back at a different frequency (actually rebroadcast) by the satellite's own transmitter to one or several receiving earth stations, called *downlinks*. The receiver-transmitter unit in the satellite is called a transponder, a combination of *trans*mitter and res*ponder* (receiver). Many satellites used for international television transmission have built-in translators that automatically convert one electronic signal standard, such as the NTSC system, into another, such as the European PAL system.

Because the satellite transmission covers a large area, simple receiving stations (downlinks) can be set up in many widely dispersed parts of the world. **SEE 18.22** These

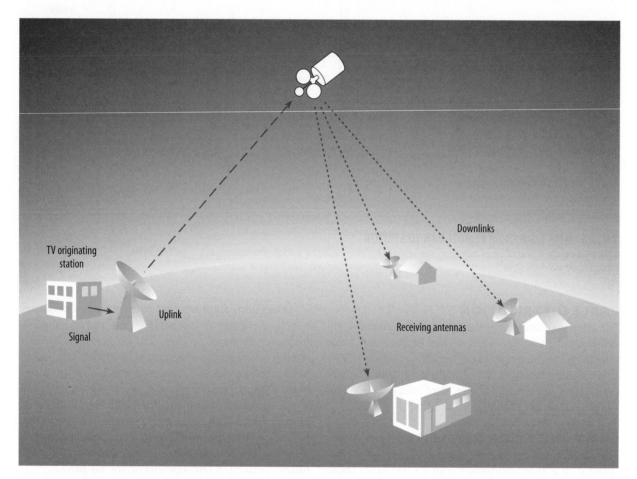

18.22 SATELLITE UPLINK AND DOWNLINKS
The uplink sends television signals to the satellite. The downlinks receive television signals from the satellite.

strategically placed satellites can spread their footprint (coverage area) over the whole earth.

Specialized vans can provide mobile uplinks for the transport of television signals. These ***uplink trucks*** operate on the very same principle as a microwave van except that they send the television signals to a satellite rather than to a receiving microwave dish. As noted in section 18.1, satellite uplink vans usually contain additional equipment, such as video recorders and editing computers.

MAIN POINTS

▶ Many big remotes are devoted to the coverage of sporting events. Networks typically use a great amount of equipment and many personnel for sports remotes, but good coverage is also possible with less equipment.

▶ There are standard setups for most sporting events, which can be augmented with more cameras and audio equipment.

▶ Location sketches are a valuable preproduction aid for big remotes. For an indoor remote, they may show the general dimensions of a room or hallway; the locations of windows, doors, and furniture; and the principal action areas. Outdoor location sketches may show buildings, remote truck location, power source, steep inclines or steps, the path of the sun, and the location and/or direction of the main event.

▶ A good location sketch can aid the director and the technical supervisor in deciding on camera locations, focal lengths of zoom lenses, lighting and audio setups, and intercommunication systems.

▶ Remote operations depend heavily on reliable intercommunication systems, including the P.L. system, walkie-talkies, pagers, cell phones, and multichannel I.F.B. systems. The I.F.B. information can be transmitted via telephone lines and/or satellite to widely scattered talent in remote locations.

▶ Remote signals are usually transported via microwave, cable, or satellite.

▶ Communication satellites used for broadcast operate in the lower-frequency C-band and the higher-frequency Ku-band.

ZETTL'S VIDEOLAB

For your reference or to track your work, the *Zettl's VideoLab* program cue in this chapter is listed here with its corresponding page number.

ZVL1 PROCESS→ Methods→ location | studio   **386**

PART

IV

Postproduction

19

Postproduction Editing: How It Works

Almost all programs you see on television have been edited in some way, either during or after the actual production. When editing is done after (*post* in Latin), it is known as postproduction editing. Its processes differ considerably from switching, the instantaneous editing done during production. In postproduction you have more time to deliberate just which shot to include in your masterpiece and which to discard, but you also have the responsibility to select the one that tells the story most effectively.

Today most postproduction editing is done with a computer and editing software rather than with videotape recorders (VTRs), whereby you copy the selected shots from one videotape to another. When using a computer for editing, you are engaged in nonlinear editing. When transferring shots in a particular order from one VTR to another, you are doing linear editing.

Regardless of the system you are using, your aesthetic choices are the most important aspect of the postproduction phase. You must now apply everything you have learned about television production to identify the most impressive shots and sequence them so that they will tell your story with clarity and impact.

Section 19.1, How Nonlinear Editing Works, examines the basic components and procedures of the nonlinear editing system and describes some pre-editing tasks. Section 19.2, How Linear Editing Works, gives an overview of the basic linear editing process.

AB-roll editing Creating an edit master tape by combining the A-roll, which contains a set of shots (such as long and medium shots), and the B-roll, which contains different but related shots (such as cutaways or close-ups of the same scene).

assemble editing Adding shots in linear editing on videotape in consecutive order without first recording a control track on the edit master tape.

automated dialog replacement (ADR) The synchronization of speech with the lip movements of the speaker in postproduction.

batch capture Having the computer use the logging information to capture all the selected clips for editing.

capture Transferring video and audio information to a computer hard drive for nonlinear editing. Also called *importing*.

clip A shot or brief series of shots as captured on the hard drive and identified by a file name.

control track system Editing system that counts the control track sync pulses and translates that count into elapsed time and frame numbers. It is not frame-accurate. Also called *pulse-count system*.

edit controller Machine that assists in editing functions, such as marking edit-in and edit-out points, rolling source and record videotape recorders, and activating effects equipment. Often a desktop computer with specialized software. Also called *editing control unit*.

edit decision list (EDL) Consists of edit-in and edit-out points, expressed in time code numbers, and the nature of transitions between shots.

edit master recording The recording of the final edit on videotape or other media. Used for broadcast or duplication.

insert editing Requires the prior laying of a control track on the edit master tape. The shots are edited in sequence or inserted into an already existing recording. Necessary mode for editing audio and video tracks separately.

linear editing Analog or digital editing that uses tape-based systems. Selection of shots is nonrandom.

nonlinear editing (NLE) Allows instant random access to shots and sequences and easy rearrangement. The video and audio information is stored in digital form on computer hard drives or read/write optical discs.

off-line editing In linear editing it produces an edit decision list or a videotape not intended for broadcast. In nonlinear editing the selected shots are captured in low resolution to save computer storage space.

on-line editing In linear editing it produces the final high-quality edit master recording for broadcast or program duplication. In nonlinear editing it can mean recapturing the selected shots at a higher resolution.

record VTR The videotape recorder that edits the program segments as supplied by the source VTR(s) into the final edit master tape. Also called *edit VTR*.

shot The smallest convenient operational unit in video and film, usually the interval between two transitions. In cinema it may refer to a specific camera setup.

slate (1) Visual and/or verbal identification of each videotaped segment. (2) A small blackboard or whiteboard upon which essential production information is written. It is recorded at the beginning of each take.

SMPTE/EBU time code Stands for *Society of Motion Picture and Television Engineers/European Broadcasting Union time code*. Electronic signal recorded on the cue or address track of a videotape or a track of a multitrack audiotape to give each frame a specific address. The time code reader translates this signal into a specific number (hour, minutes, seconds, and frames) for each frame.

source media The media (videotape, hard disk, optical disc, or flash memory device) that holds the recorded camera footage.

source tape The videotape with the original camera footage.

source VTR The videotape recorder that supplies the program segments to be assembled by the record VTR. Also called *play VTR*.

split edit Technically, the audio of a shot is substituted with related sounds or narration. In common practice the audio precedes the shot or bleeds into the next one. Viewers hear the audio of the next shot before seeing it, or they still hear the audio of the previous shot at the beginning of the new one.

take Any one of similar repeated shots taken during video recording or filming. Usually assigned a number. A *good take* is the successful recording of a shot. A *bad take* is an unsuccessful recording, requiring another take.

time code Gives each television frame a specific address (number that shows hours, minutes, seconds, and frames of elapsed tape).

vector Refers to a perceivable force with a direction and a magnitude. Vector types include graphic vectors, index vectors, and motion vectors.

video recorder (VR) All devices that record video and audio. Includes videotape, hard disks, read/write optical discs, and flash memory devices.

VR log A list of all takes—both good (acceptable) and no good (unacceptable)—in consecutive order by scene number and time code address. Often done with computerized logging programs. A vector column facilitates shot selection.

window dub A "bumped-down" copy of all source media that has the time code keyed over each frame.

19.1

How Nonlinear Editing Works

▶ **PREPARATION PHASE**
Time code, capture, and audio transcription

▶ **EDITING PHASE: VIDEO**
Editing video to audio, editing audio to video, and transitions and effects

▶ **EDITING PHASE: AUDIO**
Linear audio editing, nonlinear audio editing, condensing, correcting, mixing, controlling quality, and automated dialogue replacement

NONLINEAR EDITING

As indicated in the introduction to this chapter, the fundamental difference between linear and nonlinear editing systems is that linear systems copy selected portions from the source tapes to another videotape—the edit master (see section 19.2). Nonlinear editing, on the other hand, does not copy anything. All that the computer really does is mark the files that contain specific *clips* and play the clips back in a particular order. Instead of editing one shot next to another, with NLE you are engaged in file management.

Nonlinear editing allows you to try, compare, and keep as many editing versions as you like, without being committed to any one. All you do is create *edit decision lists (EDLs)*, which the computer remembers and applies when recalling the clips. Once you decide on a particular arrangement, you can output that version to the edit master recorder, which may use videotape or another digital storage media.

WHY NONLINEAR?

Why are these editing modes called linear and nonlinear? When editing film and videotape, you need to start with shot 1, then add shot 2, then shot 3, and so forth until you have added the last shot. The whole process is a linear affair that starts at the beginning title and ends with the closing credits. Even when looking for a particular clip in the source tapes, you cannot jump to it directly but must patiently roll through the footage until you find it. This procedure is especially trying if the clip happens to be buried in the middle of the tape. Once the final cut is done and you change your mind, or if the director or client wants you to replace a shot or scene in the middle of the final cut, you may have to re-edit everything that follows the insert.

On the other hand, the nonlinear editing system allows random access. There is no need to roll through a videotape until the desired shot finally shows up. Once the source material is stored on the hard drive of the editing system, you can access any frame or clip randomly and almost

The operational principle of *nonlinear editing (NLE)* is selecting video and audio data files and making the computer play them back as a specific sequence. All nonlinear editing is done by selecting and sequencing shots that have been transferred from a camcorder to the computer hard drive of an editing system. Once you use editing software to transfer the source footage in the camcorder to the hard drive of the computer, you are engaged in nonlinear editing.

During the transfer, it does not matter whether the digital camcorder used videotape, a hard disk, an optical disc, or some kind of flash memory device to record the event for postproduction. If, however, the editing system uses VTRs for supplying the selected shots and another VTR for the recording them in the desired sequence, you are doing linear editing. **ZVL1** EDITING→ Editing introduction

This section explains the nonlinear editing system and its use in postproduction editing.

▶ **NONLINEAR EDITING**
Why nonlinear?

▶ **NONLINEAR EDITING SYSTEM**
Computer hardware and software, source media, audio/video capture, and exporting the final edit

▶ **PRE-EDIT PHASE**
Thinking about shot continuity, recordkeeping, and reviewing and ordering the source footage

instantly. You can also insert or delete a shot anywhere in the edited sequence without affecting the footage preceding or following the change. There is no linearity in storing the source material, in retrieving it, or even in assembling the selected clips. Because even the final cut is nonlinear, you can accommodate the director's or client's request for a change in the middle of the production as easily as changing the opening title or last credit line. Learning this type of file management is just a bit more difficult than a simple word-processing program, however.

Because there are so many nonlinear systems on the market, we concentrate on how a basic nonlinear system works rather than go into detail about a particular software program. If you want to learn a specific NLE system, you need to study the often-voluminous instructions and tutorials.

NONLINEAR EDITING SYSTEM

A nonlinear editing system consists of a playback facility for the source material; a high-speed computer and software for the capture, storage, and manipulation of video and audio clips; and a *video recorder (VR)* that produces the final *edit master recording* for broadcast or distribution. **SEE 19.1** **ZVL2** EDITING→ Nonlinear editing→ system

Let's take a closer look at each element and the major processes of the NLE system: computer hardware and

software, source media, audio/video capture, and exporting the final edit.

COMPUTER HARDWARE AND SOFTWARE

All nonlinear editing systems are basically computers that store digital video and audio information on high-capacity hard drives and compatible software that allows the selection and the sequencing of video and audio clips. An important factor in the choice of an editing computer is that it has a large storage capacity and a fast enough processor to ensure smooth playback even if the video and audio files are only slightly compressed. Some NLE systems have their own computer configuration, and some have keyboards whose keys are marked with the various edit commands, but most editing software supplies stickers with symbols that you can apply to a standard keyboard.

Although you may have a relatively large flat-panel monitor that can be divided into two screens, you will find that a second, separate monitor greatly facilitates editing. You can use the large one for the editing display, and the second one as a playback monitor of the edited segments. Sometimes you may want to mix sound before importing it into the computer. In this case you will need a small audio mixer that feeds into the computer. **SEE 19.2**

Thanks to readily available and sophisticated editing software, even a laptop computer can be a powerful nonlinear editing system. In fact, you will find that some

19.1 NONLINEAR EDITING SYSTEM
The components of a nonlinear editing system are: playback facility for the source footage, computer with software, and video recorder that produces the final edit.

19.2 BASIC NONLINEAR EDITING SETUP

The nonlinear setup normally has a high-speed, high-capacity computer; a keyboard; a display for the editing interface and one for viewing the edited sequences; a small audio mixer; and speakers for stereo sound.

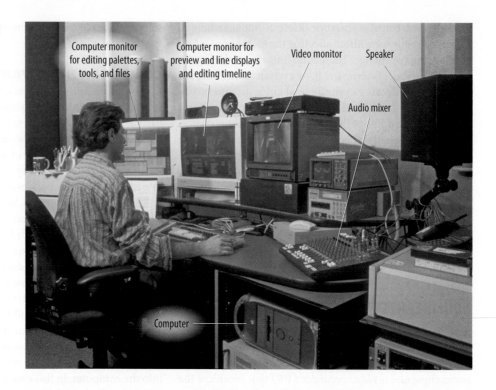

Computer monitor for editing palettes, tools, and files

Computer monitor for preview and line displays and editing timeline

Video monitor

Speaker

Audio mixer

Computer

of the simpler editing software, such as Apple's iMovie, offers more than you need for the average editing job. When watching the final edit, nobody can tell whether you used iMovie software or the latest version of Final Cut Pro for a cut from one shot to another. The major drawback of the simple editing software is its relatively limited audio and special-effects capabilities.

It would be futile to describe a specific nonlinear editing program. Although most editing programs have similar features, they differ enough to require study and especially practice. Even the simpler nonlinear programs offer so many features that you will definitely need to consult the manual and the tutorials. Nevertheless, there are features that are common to most editing software. **SEE 19.3** As you can see, the terminology differs from one system to another as do the functions. Once you are familiar with one NLE program, however, you will find it easier to learn the others.

If you plan to do extensive color correction or a great variety of transitions and effects in a high-definition television (HDTV) production, high-end editing and special-effects software is a must. Nonlinear editing lets you manipulate audio clips and create a great variety of transitions and digital video effects (DVE)—all with relative ease.

For example, with Adobe's After Effects you can build even complex animated effects in a short rendering time.

A final caveat: The ease with which you can create DVE might tempt you to pay more attention to the special effects than to the story. Use such knock-your-socks-off effects only if they are appropriate to the content of the story and energize the message.

SOURCE MEDIA

All the footage you shot with a camcorder or received from a camera team constitutes the source material, regardless of whether it was recorded on a mini- or full-sized video-cassette, a portable hard drive, an optical disc, or a flash memory device like a P2 card. When using digital *source media*, you can connect the camcorder directly to the editing computer via FireWire (IEEE 1394) or High-Definition Multimedia Interface (HDMI) cable. Some systems let you plug flash media (such as a P2 card) directly into the editing computer for easy capture.

You can also use older analog tapes so long as you digitize them before or during the capture phase. Most computers have a built-in digitizing card that enables you to convert analog to digital signals. You can also use an external digitizing unit or bridge, a peripheral with RCA phono

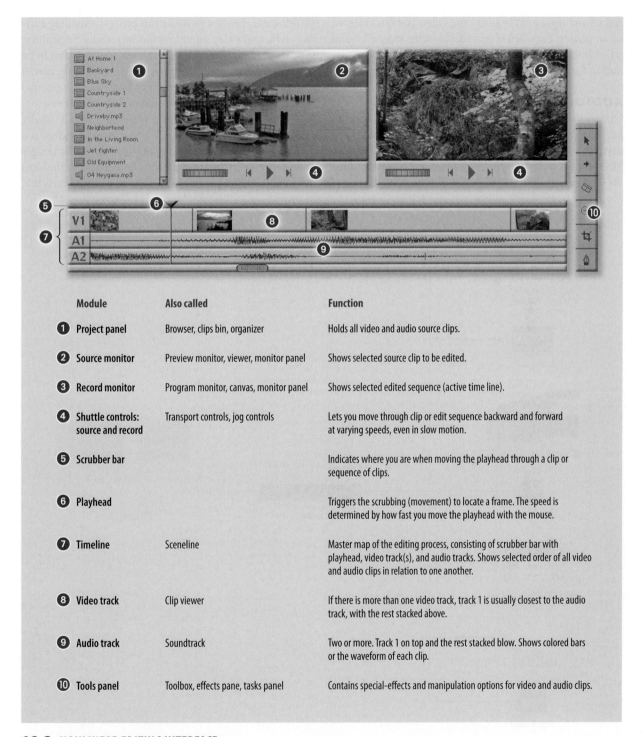

Module	Also called	Function
① Project panel	Browser, clips bin, organizer	Holds all video and audio source clips.
② Source monitor	Preview monitor, viewer, monitor panel	Shows selected source clip to be edited.
③ Record monitor	Program monitor, canvas, monitor panel	Shows selected edited sequence (active time line).
④ Shuttle controls: source and record	Transport controls, jog controls	Lets you move through clip or edit sequence backward and forward at varying speeds, even in slow motion.
⑤ Scrubber bar		Indicates where you are when moving the playhead through a clip or sequence of clips.
⑥ Playhead		Triggers the scrubbing (movement) to locate a frame. The speed is determined by how fast you move the playhead with the mouse.
⑦ Timeline	Sceneline	Master map of the editing process, consisting of scrubber bar with playhead, video track(s), and audio tracks. Shows selected order of all video and audio clips in relation to one another.
⑧ Video track	Clip viewer	If there is more than one video track, track 1 is usually closest to the audio track, with the rest stacked above.
⑨ Audio track	Soundtrack	Two or more. Track 1 on top and the rest stacked blow. Shows colored bars or the waveform of each clip.
⑩ Tools panel	Toolbox, effects pane, tasks panel	Contains special-effects and manipulation options for video and audio clips.

19.3 NONLINEAR EDITING INTERFACE

This generic nonlinear editing interface shows the major components of an NLE system. Note that it does not show or list the various items accessible through the menus.

jacks for plugging in the audio and video cables connected to an analog camcorder or videocassette recorder (and an additional S-video jack for video only) and a FireWire output for connecting to the computer.

AUDIO/VIDEO CAPTURE

Once you have selected the source material you want to have available for the edit, you must deliver it to the hard drive of the computer you are using for the NLE system. This process, called *capture*, or importing, is usually done via FireWire (IEEE 1394 400 and 800 versions) or the newer

HDMI cable. Bridges facilitate this process, enabling various audio and video inputs, including standard definition (SD), high-definition (HD), and even analog video to be converted to the capture standards of the NLE computer. If you use such a bridge, you obviously don't need the external digitizing unit for converting analog footage. **SEE 19.4**

When importing the source material, you can usually select a specific codec that will compress the video to a certain degree. Recall from chapter 4 that the more images are compressed, the less space the files occupy on the hard disk and the faster the import will be. The downside is that

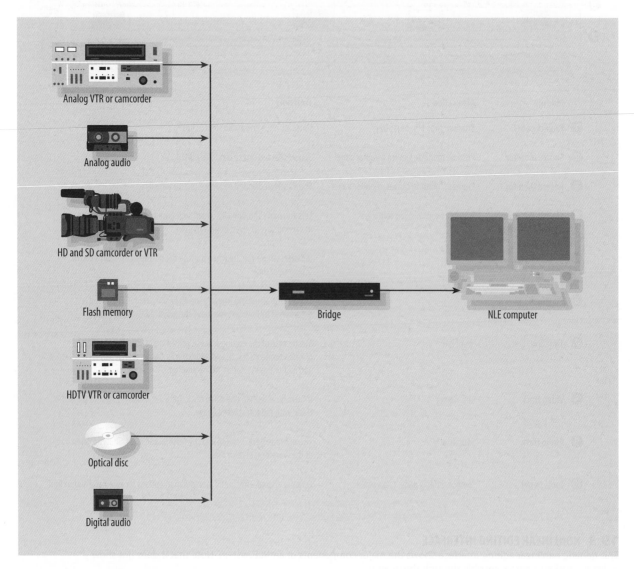

Analog VTR or camcorder

Analog audio

HD and SD camcorder or VTR

Flash memory

HDTV VTR or camcorder

Optical disc

Digital audio

Bridge

NLE computer

19.4 SOURCE MEDIA CONNECTION

The source footage is usually delivered via FireWire to the NLE computer. A bridge connects a variety of video and audio inputs to the computer, enabling the signals to be converted to the capture standards of the NLE system.

the pictures look worse (lower definition and color fidelity) with higher compression.

Unless you have already logged the source material, you can do it during the capture phase. You will read more about logging later in this chapter.

EXPORTING THE FINAL EDIT

When you are all done with the actual editing, you need to export the final edit version and record it on videotape or other media. When slated for broadcast, the final edit must be converted to the NTSC scanning standard.

PRE-EDIT PHASE

Editing starts with turning on the camcorder. Although this may seem strange, it means that experienced videographers are already thinking about postproduction editing when video-recording during the production phase. The actual editing will also be greatly facilitated if you spend some time looking over the source footage and ordering the videocassettes or other media according to the intended event sequence. Specifically, the pre-edit phase includes thinking about shot continuity, keeping accurate records, and reviewing and ordering the source footage.

THINKING ABOUT SHOT CONTINUITY

Much of the editing is predetermined by the way the material is shot. Some novice directors or camera operators stop one shot or scene and begin the next without any pads (overlapping action) or consideration for continuity. Others have the ability and the foresight to visualize transitions between shots and scenes and to provide images that cut together well in postproduction. The key is to visualize not just individual shots but shot sequences. Imagining a shot sequence will help you compose shots that join together well to form seamless transitions. Here are a few pointers:

■ When recording an event, such as a standup field report, start recording a few seconds both before the cue and after the reporter has finished speaking. These pauses will give you a video pad, called trim handles, to cut to the next shot at just the right moment. A change in the angle and the field of view (moving the camera nearer or farther away from the event) between shots will also help make the cuts look organic and smooth. **ZVL3** ▸EDITING→ Production guidelines→ pickup

■ Always get some cutaway shots. A *cutaway* is a brief shot that establishes continuity between two shots; provides the necessary video pad when editing according to sound bites

(portion of video-recorded interview in which we see and hear the person talk); and, in more-ambitious productions, helps connect jumps in time and/or location. The cutaway may or may not be part of the principal action, but it must be thematically related to the actual event. Good cutaways are relatively static and neutral as to screen direction. Examples are straight-on shots of onlookers, reporters with still cameras or camcorders, buildings that show the location, house numbers, or objects that are part of the story (such as the book the guest has written). **ZVL4** ▸EDITING→ Production guidelines→ cutaways

■ When on an ENG assignment, try to get some cutaway shots that identify the location of the event. For example, after covering the downtown fire, get a shot of the street signs of the nearest intersection, the traffic that has backed up, and some close-ups of onlookers and exhausted firefighters. For good measure also get several wide shots of the event location. You will then have cutaways that not only facilitate transitions but also show exactly where the fire occurred.

■ Always record the ambient (background) sound with the cutaways. The sound is often as important as the pictures for smooth transitions. The continuity of ambient sound can also help immensely in preserving shot continuity, even if the visuals do not cut together too well.

■ Record a minute or two of "room tone" or any other kind of environmental sound, even if the camera has nothing interesting to shoot.

■ Whenever possible during electronic news gathering (ENG), verbally *slate* (identify) the various takes or at least the shot series. You can do this by simply calling out the name of the event and the take number, such as: "Market Street police station, take 2." You can do the slating on the camera mic or the portable (reporter's) mic. After saying the take number, count backward from five or three to one. This counting is similar to the beeper after the slate in studio productions. Although not essential, it helps locate the take and cue it up during editing, especially if no address code is used.

RECORDKEEPING

Entering data in a field log or labeling the recording media seems like an unnecessary interruption of your creative fervor while in the middle of a production. This is true until you have to organize the source footage for postproduction editing. At that point you may recollect certain scenes, especially when they didn't go well, but you might have a hard time remembering just where in the various source material they are buried. This is why accurate record-keeping during the production is such an important aid to postproduction.

Field log   As you recall from chapter 12, you need to slate and log all takes unless you are engaged in ENG. You should write on the field log the number of the tape reel or other recording media; the scene and take number; and in and out time code numbers for all takes. If the time code numbers are not available, you should nevertheless write down the scene title and number, the take numbers, and whether the takes are OK or NG (no good).

In a pinch you can audio-slate each take. If you are operating the camera, quickly call out "scene 3, take 5" and record it on the camera-mic track. The slating and the logging of takes are especially important when the camcorder uses an internal hard drive as the recording media and records all the source material on the same drive. The field log will save you a considerable amount of time when constructing the VR log in postproduction.

Labeling the recording media   Even if it seems like a waste of time and effort when you video-record some especially difficult scenes for a documentary, you must nevertheless take the time to label each recording media as you extract it from the camcorder. Be sure to label the box *and* the media it contains. Cross-reference the information with your field log entry. A good system is to consecutively number (starting with 1) the boxes and the media they contain and note the title of the production.

REVIEWING AND ORDERING THE SOURCE FOOTAGE

Basically, this means looking at what you've got. If you were actively involved in the field shoot or studio production, you start with source media 1 through however many recordings you made. This is to check that all takes were properly recorded, regardless of the quality of the individual takes. This process is much like looking at the series of still shots you took on your vacation, to get some idea of which ones you may want to keep.

If you are handed a stack of videotape cassettes or other recording media from a news videographer or a producer of a documentary or drama series, your first-impression review is even more important than if you were part of the production team. Not only will you get an overall impression of the quality of the shots but it's also your first chance to get a feel for the story line.

Getting to know the story   If you are editing a fully or partially scripted show, the script will be your primary editing guide. Otherwise, the first quick review will usually give you some idea of what the story or process message is all about.

When you work in corporate television, where many of the productions have specific instructional objectives, the process message may not reveal itself even after several viewings of the source material. In this case, ask someone who knows. After all, the story and the communication objective will greatly influence your selection of shots or scenes and their sequencing. Read the script and discuss the communication objectives with the writer or producer/director. Discussions about overall story, mood, and style are especially important when editing documentaries and plays. When reviewing the source footage, look for the content but also for vector continuity. Will the shots cut together relatively well, or will you need to insert cutaways?

When editing ENG footage, you rarely get a chance to learn enough about the total event. Worse, you have to keep to a rigid time frame ("Be sure to keep this story to 20 seconds!") and work with limited footage ("Sorry, I just couldn't get close enough to get good shots" or "The mic was working when I checked it"). Also, you have precious little time to get the job done ("Aren't you finished yet? We go on the air in 45 minutes!"). Very much like an ENG videographer or an emergency-room doctor, the ENG editor has to work quickly yet accurately and with little preproduction preparation. While shot continuity is still important, it clearly plays second fiddle to telling the story.

Unless you were the VJ (video journalist) who did the videography and is now doing the editing, you must get as much information as you can about the story before you start editing. Ask the reporter, the camera operator, or the producer to fill you in. After some practice you will be able to sense the story and edit it accordingly.

In all editing, you will also find that it is often the audio that gives you quicker clues to the story than looking at the pictures.

Ordering the recording media   Once you are done with this cursory review of the source material, you can refer to the field logs while you stack the cassettes, discs, or flash drives in the order in which you will tell the story. This order may be different from the numbers the media were assigned during the production. Is this necessary if the NLE system gives you random access anyway? Yes. The main reason is for convenience when you start logging the footage. Not only will you save time with such a basic ordering of shots, but it will also help with searching for a specific shot and keeping track of the overall story continuity.

PREPARATION PHASE

Before you can engage in the actual editing, you need to take care of a few items and operational procedures: time code, logging, and capture.

TIME CODE

A **time code** marks each frame of a video recording with a specific numeric address, which represents elapsed recording time: hours, minutes, seconds, and frames. For example, if you see a time code read-out of 00:45:16:29, this means the recording contains 45 minutes, 16 seconds, and 29 frames of footage. If you had recorded one more frame, you would end up with a time code reading of 00:45:17:00. Because there are roughly 30 frames per second in the NTSC system, the time code counter rolls over to the next second after 29 frames, to the next minute after 59 seconds, and to the next hour after 59 minutes.[1] **SEE 19.5** `ZVL5` EDITING→ Postproduction guidelines→ time code

---

1. In countries that use the 25-frame-per-second PAL system, the roll-over occurs, of course, after the twenty-fourth frame instead of the twenty-ninth as in the 30-frame NTSC system.

Hours   Minutes   Seconds   Frames

Plus one frame:

Hours   Minutes   Seconds   Frames

19.5 TIME CODE
The time code gives each television frame a specific address— a number that shows hours, minutes, seconds, and frames of elapsed video and audio.

But, true to all things in television production, even time code gets a bit more complicated. One of the most widely used time codes, called **SMPTE/EBU time code** (for Society of Motion Picture and Television Engineers/European Broadcasting Union), lets you select from two modes: non–drop frame and drop frame.

Non–drop frame mode In this mode the time code will dutifully stamp every frame with a unique address, but it will be a little off for longer pieces when compared with the actual elapsed clock time. For example, when non–drop frame time code tells you that a show is exactly one hour long (01:00:00:00), your stopwatch will tell you that the show is actually about 3½ seconds over. The reason for this time discrepancy is that the actual NTSC frame rate is not exactly 30 frames per second (fps) but only 29.97 fps. The missing 0.03 second per frame does not cause any conflict in shorter clips but does became an issue in longer programs when you use the time code as an accurate indicator of real time.

Drop frame mode To synchronize exactly the time code read-out with actual time, you need to switch the camcorder to the drop frame mode. This causes the counter to skip a few frames at regular intervals so that the time code window shows the same time as your stopwatch. Note that the drop frame mode does not drop any actual frames but simply skips a few during counting.

The DV code, which is normally used instead of the SMPTE code in DV camcorders, is automatically in the drop frame mode; it starts with 00:00:00:00 for the first frame with all MiniDV cassettes.

All of this means that unless you need to identify every single frame, you should use the drop frame mode. That way you will know how long the clips actually are no matter how long they run.[2]

Time code use Time code is routinely recorded with each take. The time code helps you mark the precise spots where a clip starts and ends. This is important for logging the clips and also for locating them. Time code is especially useful for matching audio with video. Because the audio portion of your source material shows up as clips on the editing screen much like the video portion,

---

2. Because the refresh rate in PAL is a true 25 fps, there is no need for the drop-frame or non–drop frame mode.

the audio and video time codes can be synchronized for a perfect marriage.

Synchronized time code   A synchronized time code is especially helpful when you shoot a scene with several cameras simultaneously. To synchronize the time code, you need to start the cameras at approximately the same time and have them all point at a clapboard, somebody clapping with outstretched arms, or—best of all—at a still camera triggering a flash. The first frame that is overexposed will serve as the synchronization point for the time code even if the cameras were not all started at the exact same moment.

Logging   Haven't we done a log already? Yes. Can't we use the field log for editing? No. The field log is only a rough guide to where the shots are on specific source media, but it is usually not accurate enough for editing. The **VR log** (formerly VTR log) takes the field log as a rough guide but then lists all takes—both good (OK) and no good (NG)—in consecutive order by scene number and time code address. **SEE 19.6**

As you can see in figure 19.6, this log is similar to the field log except that it contains the scene numbers and the in and out time code numbers of each take as actually recorded on the source media. It also contains additional information that is especially useful in editing. **ZVL6** EDIT-ING→ Postproduction guidelines→ VTR log

Let's take a closer look at each of the VR log columns.

■ *Source media numbers.* These numbers refer to the ones you or somebody else wrote on each source media and box, such as S1 (source 1), S2 (source 2), et cetera.

PRODUCTION TITLE: Traffic Safety				PRODUCTION NO: 114			DATE: 07/15	
PRODUCER: Hamid Khani				DIRECTOR: Elan Frank				
MEDIA NO.	SCENE/ SHOT	TAKE NO.	IN	OUT	OK/ NG	SOUND	REMARKS	VECTORS
4	2	1	04 44 21 14	04 44 23 12	NG		mic problem	
		②	04 44 42 06	04 47 41 29	OK	car sound	car A moving through stop sign	
		③	04 48 01 29	04 50 49 17	OK	brakes	car B putting on brakes (toward camera)	
		④	04 51 02 13	04 51 42 08	OK	reaction	pedestrian reaction	
5	5	1	05 03 49 18	05 04 02 07	NG	car brakes ped.yelling	ball not in front of car	
		2	05 05 02 29	05 06 51 11	NG	"	Again, ball problem	
		③	05 07 40 02	05 09 12 13	OK	car brakes ped.yelling	car swerves to avoid ball	
	6	①	05 12 03 28	05 14 12 01	OK	ped.yelling	kid running into street	
		②	05 17 08 16	05 21 11 19	OK	car	cutaways car moving	
		3	05 22 15 03	05 26 28 00	NG	street	lines of sidewalk	

19.6 VR LOG

The VR log contains all the necessary information about the video and audio recorded on the source media. Notice the notations in the Vectors column: g, i, and m refer to graphic, index, and motion vectors. The arrows show the principal direction of the index and motion vectors. Z-axis index and motion vectors are labeled with ⊙ (toward the camera) or • (away from the camera).

■ *Scene/shot and take numbers.* If you have properly slated the scenes, shots, and takes, copy the numbers from the slates. Otherwise, simply list all shots as they appear on the source media in ascending order. A *shot* refers to the smallest convenient operational unit in video and film, usually the interval between two transitions. In cinema it may mean a specific camera setup. A *take* is any one of similar repeated shots taken during video-recording or filming. It is usually assigned a number. A good take is the successful completion of a shot. A bad take is an unsuccessful recording, requiring another take.

■ *Time code.* Enter the time code number of the first frame of the shot in the In column and the last frame of the shot in the Out column, regardless of whether the shot is OK or no good.

■ *OK or no good.* Mark the acceptable shots by circling the shot number and/or by writing "OK" or "NG" (no good) in the appropriate column. Unless you have already eliminated all shots that were labeled "NG" on the field log, you can now see if you agree with previous assessments of whether a take was OK.

When evaluating shots look for obvious mistakes—but also look for whether the shot is suitable in the context of the defined process message and the overall story. An out-of-focus shot may be unusable in one context but quite appropriate if you try to demonstrate impaired vision. Look behind the principal action: Is the background appropriate? Too busy or cluttered? It is often the background rather than the foreground that provides the necessary visual continuity. Will the backgrounds facilitate continuity when the shots are edited together?

■ *Sound.* Here you note in- and out-cues for dialogue and sound effects that need attention during editing. Listen carefully not only to the foreground sounds but also to the background sounds. Is there too much ambience? Not enough? Note any obvious audio problems, such as trucks going by, somebody hitting the microphone or kicking the table, intercom chatter of the crew, or talent flubs in an otherwise good take. Write down the nature of the sound problem and its time code address.

■ *Remarks.* Use this column to indicate what the shot is all about, such as "CU of watch," and to record the audio cues (unless you have a designated audio column).

■ *Vectors.* **Vectors** indicate the major directions of lines or motions within a shot. Noting such directional vectors will help you locate specific shots that continue or purposely oppose a principal direction.

There are three types of vectors: graphic, index, and motion. A graphic vector is created by stationary elements that guide our eyes in a specific direction, such as a line formed by the window frame or the edge of a book. An index vector is created by something that points unquestionably in a specific direction, such as an arrow or a person's gaze. A motion vector is brought about by something moving. Take another look at the Vectors column in figure 19.6. The *g*, *i*, and *m* refer to the vector type (graphic, index, or motion); the arrows indicate the principal direction. The circled-dot symbol indicates movement or pointing toward the camera; the dot alone indicates movement or pointing away from the camera. **ZVL7** EDITING→ Continuity→ vectors

Logging method You can do this log by hand or with the editing software.

When logging by hand, you take each source media as ordered by the scene number, review it, and fill in the pertinent information. Do not use the camcorder for this logging process. Except for flash drives, which don't have moving parts, the drive mechanisms of camcorders are not designed for the stop-and-go torture of constant shuttling. It is better to dub the source material onto a sturdier recording device such as a VTR, hard drive, or server before doing any logging or editing.

You can now play each take through the monitor you normally use for your video display and enter by hand on the logging sheet the media number, scene number, in and out time code numbers, and additional remarks for each desired clip (see figure 19.6). A better way is to enter the information on a basic spreadsheet (without using any editing software), which you can then save as a text file and later use as a guide for the capture phase—transferring the selected clips onto the hard drive of the editing system.

Most high-end editing software allows you to log your source footage before the actual capture. When using the logging function, you can import the footage from the source device (camcorder hard drive, server, VTR, disc, or flash drive) and log it by media and scene number, the in and out time code numbers, and remarks. The only category missing is the vector information, but you can devise your own symbols for the three types of vectors and enter them in the log notes section.

CAPTURE

Once you have logged the source material, you can proceed with the video and audio capture. This means that you must now import the selected clips into the actual editing file on your NLE system hard drive. Again, there are different ways of capture. One is to use the VR log and import one clip after another from the original media or from the copy of the footage you used for logging. Another is to use your log information (clip names and time code numbers per the spreadsheet or computer log) and let the computer perform a **batch capture**, whereby it will do the work for you: reading your log and importing the clips as specified by name and time code. This requires that you have everything set up just right for such an operation. For smaller projects, you will find that importing each clip is often faster than initiating a batch capture. **ZVL8** EDITING→ Non-linear editing→ capture

Off-line and on-line capture Some editors who are engaged in large editing projects prefer to perform the original capture in low resolution to save disk space, do the editing in low resolution, and then recapture the clips in high resolution for the final cut. The low-resolution import is called off-line, and the high-resolution import, on-line. These designations are a holdover from linear editing, where off-line editing was done with less expensive equipment, and, when everybody was satisfied with the off-line version, the edit was repeated with top-of-the-line equipment. This linear editing version, which produces the edit-master tape, is called on-line. In nonlinear editing, the off-line editing usually results in the EDL (edit decision list) that specifies which clips need to be imported again at a higher resolution. **ZVL9** EDITING→ Non-linear editing→ off-line and on-line

AUDIO TRANSCRIPTION

There's one more chore to do before indulging in sorting out pictures and sound. Unless you are editing sports, fully scripted plays, or routine daily news, you still need to transcribe the audio. A transcription is an essential aid when editing interviews and documentaries. Transcribing audio involves typing every word that is on the recorded clips. You will find that reading words will let you scan the content much more quickly than listening to them. A printed page is not linear like an audio recording and enables you skip over sections without having to listen to the recording over and over again.

If, for example, you need to cut down a 64-minute interview to 30 seconds, it would take you hours to go back and forth in the recording to find the most significant moments, even if you have a good memory. When looking at the page, you can grasp the important quotes more quickly and simply mark them with a highlighter.

EDITING PHASE: VIDEO

Just how you edit depends entirely on the NLE software you are using. Despite some major operational differences, the basic editing principles and the approach to the actual editing phase as described here are basically common to all programs. Just keep in mind that there is no need for the latest complex editing system if all you do is order your shots and join them mostly with cuts and a few dissolves. If, however, you include a great number of special effects, perform extensive color correction, and engage in elaborate audio mixing and audio/video matching, you need a high-end editing system that will provide the tools to go beyond the cut-and-paste approach.

Whatever system you use, don't expect to become a master editor overnight. Good editing takes patience and especially practice, much like learning to play a musical instrument. Once you are adept at using the software, you will realize that the real editing skill lies in making the right decisions in selecting and sequencing the most effective shots. Just how to do this is discussed in chapter 20.

EDITING VIDEO TO AUDIO

Whenever you deal with speech, you must match the video to the audio. This is where an audio transcription can save you hours of tedious listening. The transcribed audio lets you quickly locate a specific part of an interview without having to run the audio track over and over again. If you have provided the audio clips with time code, you can locate the audio clips as easily as the video clips.

The audio—the spoken text—is your primary editing guide. Although you ordinarily cut at the end of a sentence, whoever is uttering it, in this type of **split edit** you can cut in midsentence to the interviewer listening, or to the interviewee listening to the questions, to capture the all-important reaction shots.

If somebody gives a speech, you can save time by replacing the speaker's audio with a voice-over narration by the news anchor while showing the speaker for a while longer. **SEE 19.7**

If you do a feature story that is primarily advanced by voice-over (off-camera) narration, or even brief news features, it is best to first lay down the audio track of the narration and match it with the appropriate video. In effect, the audio becomes the A-roll and the video becomes the B-roll. In this way you establish a guide for the length of the video clips and the sequence rhythm much more

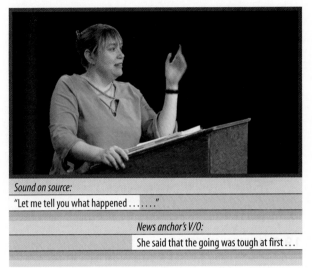

Sound on source:

"Let me tell you what happened . . . ."

News anchor's V/O:

She said that the going was tough at first . . .

19.7 VOICE-OVER NARRATION

The voice-over narration replaces from time to time the speaker's comments and summarizes what she said.

easily than when trying to match the narration to the video sequence. **SEE 19.8**

Obviously, when editing video to music, the sound track becomes the primary editing guide regardless of whether you are matching video with a classical piece or a hard rock song. Although you normally cut on the beat, you may also decide to place the video edits just a little before or after the beat. When not overdone, such "cutting-around-the-beat" can greatly intensify the scene.[3]

---

3. For a lucid treatment of editing video to audio, see Nancy Graham Holm, *Fascination: Viewer Friendly TV Journalism* (Århus, Denmark: Ajour Danish Media Books, 2007), pp. 43–46. See also Herbert Zettl, *Sight Sound Motion: Applied Media Aesthetics,* 5th ed. (Belmont, Calif.: Thomson Wadsworth, 2008), pp. 372-84.

EDITING AUDIO TO VIDEO

When the video drives the narrative, such as in a recording of a football game, the video becomes the A-roll, and the audio is the B-roll. This means that the editing of the game's highlights is guided by what happened on the field, not by what the play-by-play announcer said. The editing of a fully scripted drama is guided primarily by its dramatic development, the story's inherent conflict, and the director's visualization rather than by the dialogue or background music. The music is *added* to the edited play rather than used as the principal guide for the video edit.

TRANSITIONS AND EFFECTS

All that remains to do is select the transitions between shots and the special effects, if any. Editing software offers a generous number of transitions and effects, and you can always add to the effects arsenal by using additional effects software, but recall the warning from chapter 13: any effect that does not intensify the scene or is in the wrong place will most certainly degrade your shot if not your whole effort. A cut is still the least obtrusive transition if the preceding and following shots have good continuity. All other transitions occupy screen time and therefore slow down the edited sequence. More often they also introduce a new element which, if not in line with the feel of the show, will look out of place or, worse, ridiculous and amateurish.

But the ease of generating transitions and effects in nonlinear editing is also blessing: you can try any number of them without affecting your overall edit. Just click on the transition or effects menu and preview the choices. If you don't like what you see, try something else, or go back to what you had in the first place. In the old days of film editing, such experimentation was not possible. Each transition or special effect had to be rendered in the processing lab, which added considerably to production time

A-roll audio   "...and one house...   after another...   was engulfed in flames..."

B-roll: four shots cut in the rhythm of the V/O comments

Shot 1   Shot 2   Shot 3   Shot 4

19.8 EDITED VOICE-OVER A-ROLL AND B-ROLL VISUALS

In this sequence the audio track represents the A-roll (edited voice-over), and the video track represents the B-roll (video clip sequence as guided by the audio A-roll). The video edit is guided by the voice-over track.

and cost. Even if you didn't like the effect, you were pretty much stuck with it.

EDITING PHASE: AUDIO

Think back to chapter 9 and the brief description of the audio postproduction room and equipment. Much like the video postproduction systems, the audio postproduction systems can be relatively simple but can also get quite complex.

Even if you had the money, a large audio postproduction room is unnecessary if all you need to do is select some key phrases from an interview. If, however, your audio editing usually involves the mixing of dialogue and sound effects, you obviously need a more sophisticated setup.

Generally, audio production tasks involve condensing, correcting, mixing, and controlling sound quality. As in video there are considerable differences between linear and nonlinear audio editing. Although you may be editing almost exclusively with nonlinear systems, you should nevertheless have some idea of how to approach linear sound editing.

LINEAR AUDIO EDITING

When editing the audio track of a videotape, you need to select the video and audio portions from the source VTR that contains the original footage, then copy the video and the audio (or the audio only) onto the edit master tape of the record VTR. You can adjust the record VTR so that it reads the audio track independent of the video track. To accomplish this split, the video-editing system must be in the insert mode. If you want to add audio that is not on the source tape, you need to feed the new audio to the record VTR via a small mixer.

NONLINEAR AUDIO EDITING

If you work with a nonlinear video-editing system, all the audio files—much like the video files—are stored on the hard drive of the editing system. Like video editing, audio editing resembles cutting and pasting words and sentences with a word-processing program. The great advantage of nonlinear audio editing is that you can not only hear the sounds but also see them as a waveform graphic on-screen. Such a visual representation of sound makes it possible for you to cut the sound at exactly the right frame. Another advantage is that you can synchronize specific sounds with

19.9 AUDIO WAVEFORM
All nonlinear editing systems show a visual representation—a waveform—of the sound tracks.

the selected video or move them from place to place with relative ease.[4] **SEE 19.9**

CONDENSING

You will find that the most common postproduction audio assignment is making sense of what somebody says, even though that particular person's comments are drastically cut. You may see in a newscast a political candidate speaking behind a lectern but not hear her actual words. Instead the news anchor summarizes what she has said so far before we hear her actual sound bite about lowering taxes (synchronized video and audio of her statement). Or, we start with the sound bite and then, while the camera still shows her behind the lectern, switch the audio to the anchor's summary of her numerous other promises (see figure 19.7).

To dramatize the danger of children playing with matches, you may sneak in the sound of a fire engine while the kids, playing in the attic, laugh and strike the first match, and then cut to the actual fire engine racing to the resulting fire. You could also show the fire engine racing to the fire while we still hear the children talking about the fun of striking one match after another. Both examples are versions of a split edit. The most common split edit is when

---

4. For a detailed discussion of nonlinear audio editing, see Stanley R. Alten, *Audio in Media*, 8th ed. (Belmont, Calif.: Thomson Wadsworth, 2008), p. 386–411.

the audio of a shot precedes its pictures or bleeds into the next one. This means that viewers hear the audio of the next shot before seeing it, or they still hear the audio of the previous shot at the beginning of the new one.

As simple as it looks when watching television, such audio-editing tasks can get complicated and require practice. Whenever you have to condense a speech to a few sound bites, you will be thankful for the audio transcription. Instead of playing the audiotapes over and over again to search for the appropriate sound bites, you can identify them quickly by skimming the written pages.

CORRECTING

Fixing a seemingly simple mistake, such as the talent's mispronouncing a word or giving the wrong address, can become a formidable if not impossible postproduction task. When a politician says "I am not a *cook*" instead of "crook" in the middle of video-recording his defense, "fixing it in post" can be very labor-intensive. It is much easier to correct the problem right away and have the politician repeat his comments a few sentences before he made the mistake. Such problems become almost impossible to fix if you have to try to lip-sync the new word or words in postproduction. **ZVL10** EDITING→ Functions→ correct

Filtering out the low rumble of wind during an outdoor shoot or the hum of a lighting instrument in the studio is possible with sophisticated equipment but is nevertheless difficult and time-consuming. Even experienced audio production people labor long hours correcting what may seem like a relatively simple problem. The more care you take during the audio acquisition, the more time you save in the postproduction phase.

MIXING

Postproduction mixing is not much different from live mixing except that you remix separately recorded sound tracks instead of live inputs. Because you mix recorded sound tracks, you can be much more discriminating in how to combine the various sounds for optimal quality. In digital cinema, sound designers and engineers can spend weeks if not months on audio postproduction. But don't worry—nobody will ask you to do complicated audio postproduction for video right away, but if audio is your main interest in television production, try to participate in as many mixing sessions as possible, even if you can only watch and listen.

CONTROLLING QUALITY

The management of sound quality is probably the most difficult aspect of audio control. You must be thoroughly familiar with signal-processing equipment (such as equalizers, reverberation controls, and filters), and, most important, you must have a trained ear. As with the volume control in live mixing, you must be careful how you use these quality controls. If there is an obvious hum or hiss that you can filter out, by all means do, but do not try to adjust the quality of each input before you've done at least a preliminary mix.

For example, you may decide that the sound effect of a police siren sounds much too thin, but when mixed with the traffic sounds, the thin and piercing siren may be perfect for communicating mounting tension. Before making any final quality judgments, listen to the audio track in relation to the video. An audio mix that sounds warm and rich by itself may lose those qualities when juxtaposed with a high-impact video scene. As in all other aspects of television production, the communication goal and your aesthetic sensitivity, not the availability and production capacity of the equipment, should determine your quality control. No volume meter or equalizer in the world can substitute for aesthetic judgment.

AUTOMATED DIALOGUE REPLACEMENT

Some large postproduction houses have a room specifically for *automated dialogue replacement (ADR)*. Technically, ADR refers to the postdubbing of dialogue, but it sometimes refers to the synchronization of sound effects as well. This audio-dubbing process is borrowed directly from motion pictures. Many sounds, including dialogue, that are recorded simultaneously with pictures do not always live up to the expected sound quality, so they are replaced by dialogue and sounds re-created in the studio. Most of the time, ADR requires painstaking re-creations and mixing of dialogue, sound effects, and ambient sounds.

Elaborate ADR has the actors repeat their lines while watching footage of themselves on a large-screen projection. Recording sound effects is usually done with the *Foley stage,* which consists of a variety of props and equipment that are set up in a recording studio to produce common sound effects, such as footsteps, opening and closing of doors, and so forth. The Foley stage uses sound-effects equipment much like that of traditional radio and film productions. Foley offers this equipment in efficiently packaged boxes so that it can be transported by truck, sound-effect artists included.

MAIN POINTS

▶ Nonlinear editing allows random access to all source material, multiple editing versions, and any number of transitions and special effects.

▶ The nonlinear editing (NLE) system consists of a playback facility for the source media; a high-speed computer with software for the capture, storage, and manipulation of audio and video clips; and a video recorder for the final edit master recording.

▶ Nonlinear editing enables you to create edit decision lists (EDLs), which the computer remembers and applies when recalling the clips.

▶ The pre-edit phase includes thinking about shot continuity during the production, labeling the source media and keeping accurate records by entering each take into the field log, reviewing the source footage, and ordering the various media (videocassettes, hard disks, optical discs, flash drives) according to the sequence of the story.

▶ The preparation phase includes using and synchronizing the time code, creating a VR log, capturing the source footage, and transcribing the audio track.

▶ The time code shows the elapsed time of a recording in hours, minutes, seconds, and frames. The SMPTE/EBU time code has two modes: drop frame and non–drop frame.

▶ The VR log lists the source media numbers, the scene/shot numbers, and all takes by the time code in- and out-numbers. It usually shows additional information such as shot evaluation (OK or no good), audio instructions, vector directions, and general remarks.

▶ All footage recorded by the camcorder must be imported in digital form by the editing computer—a process called capture.

▶ Audio and video capture is usually done by FireWire or HDMI cables. When flash drives are used as recording media, they can usually be directly inserted into the editing computer for capture.

▶ In some cases, all speech on the audio track is transcribed into readable form, which facilitates editing.

▶ Editing can be done by editing the audio track first and then matching the video to it, or the other way around.

▶ Transitions and special effects are added as the last editing task, before the final edit is exported to the edit master video recorder.

▶ The audio editing phase includes linear and nonlinear editing, condensing, correcting, mixing, controlling quality, and automated dialogue replacement (ADR).

19.2

How Linear Editing Works

Because there are still linear editing systems in operation and some of their techniques also apply to nonlinear editing, this section outlines the major elements and practices of linear editing.

▶ **BASIC AND EXPANDED LINEAR EDITING SYSTEMS**
Single-source system, edit controller, multiple-source system, AB-roll editing, and time code and window dub

▶ **CONTROL TRACK AND TIME CODE EDITING**
Finding a clip or frame

▶ **ASSEMBLE AND INSERT EDITING**
The two principal modes of linear editing

▶ **LINEAR OFF- AND ON-LINE EDITING**
Creating a rough cut and the final edit master tape

BASIC AND EXPANDED LINEAR EDITING SYSTEMS

The basic principle of *linear editing* is selecting shots from one videotape and copying them in a specific order onto another tape. It is called linear because once the footage is recorded on tape, you can no longer retrieve it randomly.

To locate shot 25 on a videotape, for example, you need to roll through the previous 24 shots before reaching shot 25. You cannot simply jump to shot 25, skipping all preceding shots. All tape-based editing systems are linear, regardless of whether the tapes contain analog or digital video and audio information.

However complex tape-based linear editing systems may be, they all work on the same basic principle: one or several VTRs play back portions of the tape with the original source footage, and another VTR records on its own tape the selected material from the source tape. The different tape-based systems fall into two categories: the single-source system and the multiple-source systems. **ZVL11** EDITING→ Linear editing→ system

SINGLE-SOURCE SYSTEM

A basic system that has only one VTR supplying the material to be edited is called a single-source, or cuts-only, editing system. The machine that plays back the tape with the original footage is called the *source VTR* or play VTR. The machine that copies the selected material is called the *record VTR* or edit VTR. In the same manner, the videotape with the original footage is the *source tape*, and the one onto which the selected portions are recorded in a specific editing sequence is the *edit master tape*. To see what is on both the source and edit master tapes, you need monitors for both VTRs. **SEE 19.10**

When doing the actual editing, you use the source VTR to find the exact in- and out-points of the source footage you want to copy to the edit master tape. The record

Source (play)
VTR monitor shows first
frame of new shot
Shot 3

Record (edit)
VTR monitor shows last
frame of previous shot
Shot 2

Source (play) VTR
and monitor

Record (edit) VTR
and monitor

19.10 BASIC SINGLE-SOURCE SYSTEM
The source VTR supplies specific sections of the source tape (displayed on the source VTR monitor). The record VTR copies in a particular sequence and adds each new shot to the previously recorded shot (displayed on the record VTR monitor).

VTR does the actual copying of the material supplied by the source VTR and joins the frames at predetermined points—the edit points. You have to tell the record VTR when to start recording (copying) the source material and when to stop recording. An in-cue (or entrance cue) tells the record VTR when to start recording the source material; an out-cue (or exit cue) tells it when to stop.

Edit controller   Assisting you in this task is a piece of equipment called the ***edit controller,*** or editing control unit. This unit automates editing to a certain extent. It memorizes your commands and executes them with precision and reliability. **SEE 19.11**

A basic edit controller performs the following functions:

- Controls VTR search modes (variable forward and reverse speeds) separately for the source and record VTRs to locate scenes

- Reads and displays elapsed time and frame numbers or time code (frame address) for accurate cueing of the source and edit master tapes

- Marks and remembers precise edit-in and -out points (cues)

- Backs up, or "backspaces," both VTRs to precisely the same preroll point (on some edit controllers, a switch gives you several preroll choices, such as a 2-second or a 5-second preroll; preroll helps the VTRs achieve optimal speed for jitter-free recording)

- Simultaneously starts both machines and synchronizes their tape speeds

- Makes the record VTR perform in either the assemble- or the insert-edit mode (discussed later in this section)

Most single-source system edit controllers can also do additional editing tasks, such as letting you do a trial run before performing the actual edit, performing separate edits for video and audio tracks without one affecting the other, and producing intelligible sounds at fast-forward tape speeds.

Source VTR time code

Record VTR time code

Source VTR controls

Record VTR controls

19.11 EDIT CONTROLLER
The edit controller is an interface between the source and record VTRs. It displays elapsed tape time and frames, controls source and record VTR rolls, stores edit-in and edit-out points and tells the VTRs to locate them on the tape, and offers previewing before the edit and reviewing after the edit.

MULTIPLE-SOURCE SYSTEM

The tape-based multiple-source editing system consists of two or more source VTRs (generally labeled with letters *A, B, C,* etc.), a single record VTR, and a computer-assisted edit controller. Multisource systems can, and usually do, include an audio mixer, a switcher, and special-effects equipment. The computerized edit controller directs the functions of the source A and B VTRs, the character generator (C.G.) or effects generator (unless part of the software program), the audio mixer, and the edit and record functions of the record VTR. **SEE 19.12**

The multiple-source editing system allows you to synchronously run two or more source VTRs and combine the shots and/or audio tracks from any of them quickly and effectively through a variety of transitions or other special effects. The big advantage of this system is that it facilitates a great variety of transitions (such as cuts, dissolves, and wipes) and allows the mixing of audio tracks from two or more source tapes. Another advantage is that you can arrange all even-numbered shots on the A-roll (the tape used for the source A VTR) and all odd-numbered shots on the B-roll (the tape for the source B VTR). By switching from

19.12 MULTIPLE-SOURCE SYSTEM

The multiple-source linear editing system has two or more source VTRs (A and B) and interfaces special effects, audio, and switcher equipment or functions.

the A-roll to the B-roll during editing, you can quickly assemble the "pre-edited" shots.

AB-ROLL EDITING

Here is an example of an editing assignment that lends itself well to *AB-roll editing*: Assume that one of the source tapes—the A-roll—contains primarily long and medium shots of a rock band. The second source tape—the B-roll—has various close-ups (CUs) of the band members. Assuming that the source tapes have a common time code and, in this case, a common audio track (the band playing), you can tell the edit controller when to switch from the A-roll long shots and medium shots to the B-roll CUs at certain edit points. **SEE 19.13**

TIME CODE AND WINDOW DUB

Once the videotape is striped with time code, for convenient logging you can make a window dub and log the time code of the A and B rolls, showing when to switch from one to the other. A *window dub* is a "bumped-down" (lower-quality, such as VHS) copy of all source tapes, which has the time code keyed over each frame. The window dub also helps when establishing a preliminary EDL for linear editing. **SEE 19.14**

19.13 AB-ROLL EDITING TO COMMON SOUND TRACK
In this AB-roll editing example, the A-roll consists of long and medium shots of the band; the B-roll contains CUs of the individual members. Because both source VTRs are synchronized, you can use the A-roll sound track to insert the B-roll video.

19.14 TIME CODE DISPLAY IN WINDOW DUB
The window dub shows the unique time code number keyed over each frame.

CONTROL TRACK AND TIME CODE EDITING

All linear editing systems are guided by the control track or the time code. Recall from chapter 12 that the control track is the area of the videotape used for recording the synchronization information (sync pulse), providing a reference for the running speed of the VTR and for counting the number of frames. The ***control track system*** counts the sync pulses and translates this count into elapsed time and frames, similar to the time code. Unlike time code, however, no frame is given a unique address.

CONTROL TRACK EDITING

The control track on a videotape marks each frame of recorded material. It therefore takes 30 control track pulses to mark each second of tape play. **SEE 19.15**

Any one of the individual sync pulses of the control track can become an actual edit-in or edit-out point (frame). By counting the number of pulses, you can locate specific edit-in and edit-out points with greater accuracy than by simply looking at the video pictures. Control track editing is also called pulse-count editing because the edit controller counts the number of control track pulses. **ZVL12** ⟩EDITING→
Postproduction guidelines→ tape basics

The edit controller counts the pulses of both the source and the edit master tapes from the beginning and displays—just like the time code—the count as elapsed time: hours, minutes, seconds, and frames.

Finding the right address   Although the control track system can identify a specific frame with a pulse-count number, it is not frame-accurate. This drawback means that you may get different frames when advancing repeatedly to the same pulse-count number. Realize that when you advance the tape by only 2 minutes, the edit controller must count 3,600 pulses. If you were to back up the tape to the beginning and again run it for 2 minutes, you would probably end up at a different frame, mainly because during high-speed shuttles or repeated threading and unthreading, the tape may stretch or slip, or the unit may simply skip some pulses when counting thousands of them.

TIME CODE EDITING

As you recall, whenever more-precise editing is required, such as when editing video to the beat of music or when synchronizing dialogue or specific sound effects to the video track, you need to edit with time code. Because each frame has its own time code address, you can locate a specific frame relatively quickly and reliably, even if it is buried in hours of recorded program material or despite occasional tape slippage during repeated high-speed shuttles. Once the edit controller is told which frame to use as an edit point, it will find it again no matter how many times you shuttle the tape back and forth, and it will not initiate an edit until the right address is located.

Most studio VTRs, portable professional VTRs, and camcorders have a built-in time code generator for writing time code during the production and reading it during playback. Otherwise you need a time code generator that can be connected to the camcorder, and a time code reader when playing back the tapes. Although you may encounter various types of time codes, they all work on the same principle.

Control track

15 pulses = ½ second

30 pulses = 1 second

19.15 CONTROL TRACK PULSES

The control track, or pulse-count, system counts the sync pulses to mark a specific spot on the videotape. Every 30 pulses mark one second of elapsed tape time.

ASSEMBLE AND INSERT EDITING

Most professional VTRs let you switch between two editing modes: assemble editing and insert editing.

ASSEMBLE EDITING

When in the assemble mode, the record VTR erases everything on its tape (video, audio, control, and address tracks) just ahead of copying the material supplied by the source VTR. When you use a tape that has last year's vacation pictures on it to chronicle your new adventures, the camcorder will, in effect, use *assemble editing* every time you shoot a new scene: it will simply erase what was there before and replace it with the new video and audio.

The same thing happens in a more sophisticated editing system. Even if the edit master tape has a previous recording on it (not recommended by the way), the assemble mode will clear the portion of the tape that is needed for the new first shot. When editing shot 2 onto shot 1, the record VTR will erase everything on the edit master tape following shot 1 to make room for copying the new video and audio information. The record VTR will then supply a new control track that is modeled exactly after the control track information contained in shot 2 of the source tape.

The same happens when you assemble the subsequent shots. **SEE 19.16**

If you can simply select and connect some shots from the source tapes in the order in which they were recorded, assemble editing is quite fast and efficient. The problem with assemble editing, however, is that the control track on the edit master tape, as reconstructed by the record VTR from the bits and pieces of the source tapes, is not always smooth and evenly spaced. A slight mismatch of sync pulses will cause some edits to "tear," causing a sync roll, which, as you recall from chapter 12, causes the picture to break or roll momentarily at the edit point.

The primary advantage of assemble editing is that it is fast. You do not have to prepare the edit master tape by first recording a continuous control track as you do when editing in the insert mode.

INSERT EDITING

For *insert editing*, you need first to record a continuous control track on the edit master tape. The simplest way to do this is to record "black," with the video and audio inputs in the *off* position. Some editors prefer to record color bars as a continuous color reference. As though it

Shot 2
Source tape

Shot 1

Control track of edit master tape

Control track sync pulses must align at the edit point

19.16 ASSEMBLE EDITING

In assemble editing, the record VTR produces the control track in bits and pieces. The record VTR copies from the source VTR all video and audio information of shot 2. The control track for shot 2 stays with the source VTR but is regenerated and attached to the shot 1 control track by the record VTR.

were recording an important event, the VTR faithfully lays down a control track in the process. The "blackened" tape has now become an empty edit master, ready to receive the momentous scenes from your source tapes. Note that you do not have to blacken any of the source tapes you use in the camcorder but only the tape onto which your selected shots are copied. **SEE 19.17**

The recording of black or color bars (and thereby laying a control track) happens in real time, which means that you cannot speed up the process but must take 30 minutes to lay a 30-minute control track. Though this may seem like wasted time, it has the following advantages:

- All insert edits are roll-free and tear-free.

- You can easily insert new video and/or audio material anywhere in the tape without affecting anything preceding or following the insert (hence the name).

- You can edit the video without affecting the sound track, or you can edit the audio without affecting the pictures. This is especially important when you want to edit the sound track first and then insert the pictures to match the sound track. The process

is the same as AB-roll editing, discussed earlier in this chapter.

Most professional editing is, therefore, done in the insert mode.

LINEAR OFF- AND ON-LINE EDITING

Off- and on-line editing mean quite different things in linear and nonlinear editing environments. *Off-line editing* with a nonlinear system refers to a low-resolution import of clips, whereas in linear editing it means a preliminary edit with a lower-quality editing system to produce an EDL or a rough-cut—an edit not intended for broadcast or duplication. *On-line editing* in nonlinear environment refers to the recapture of high-resolution images for the final cut; in linear editing it means to use a high-end editing system to produce the final edit master tape.

OFF-LINE EDIT

The linear off-line edit will give you a rough idea of how the intended shot sequence looks and feels. It is a sketch, not the final painting. It gives you a chance to check the rhythm of the shot sequence, decide on various transitions

Shot 2

Shot 1

Prerecorded control track of edit master tape

19.17 INSERT EDITING
In insert editing, the source material is transferred without its control track and placed according to the prerecorded continuous control track of the edit master tape.

and effects, and get some idea of the audio requirements. You could even use two VHS recorders for an off-line rough-cut: one feeds the source tapes, and the other records the selected shots in the desired sequence. Never mind the sloppy transitions or audio—all you want to see is whether the sequences make sense, that is, tell the intended story. The most valuable by-product of off-line editing is a final edit decision list that you can then use for on-line editing.

Paper-and-pencil edit   When you edit a longer and more complex production, such as a documentary or drama, your main concern is picking the shots that most effectively fulfill the story and contribute to a smooth shot sequence. You can save a great amount of actual editing time by simply watching the window dubs (in linear editing) or the clips (in nonlinear editing) and making a list of the edit-in and edit-out points for each selected shot. This list will be your preliminary EDL. Because this list is usually written by hand, this decision-making activity is called paper-and-pencil editing, or paper editing for short. **SEE 19.18** **ZVL13** EDITING→ Linear editing→ paper edit

ON-LINE EDIT

Much like in nonlinear editing, the on-line edit in linear editing results in the final edit master tape. It is actually a re-edit according to the EDL created in the off-line process. It contains all the transitions and effects as well as a clean audio track. You obviously use the best equipment available to produce the on-line version.

PRODUCTION TITLE: Traffic Safety					PRODUCTION NO: 114 DATE: 07/15		
PRODUCER: Hamid Khani					DIRECTOR: Elan Frank		
TAPE NO.	SCENE/ SHOT	TAKE NO.	IN	OUT	TRANSITION	SOUND	REMARKS
1	2	2	01 46 13 14	01 46 15 02	cut	car	
		3	01 51 10 29	01 51 11 21	cut	car	
	3	4	02 05 55 17	02 05 56 02	cut	ped. yelling—brakes	
		5	02 07 43 17	02 08 46 01	cut	brakes	
		6	02 51 40 02	02 51 41 07	cut	ped. yelling—brakes	

19.18 HANDWRITTEN EDIT DECISION LIST

Paper-and-pencil off-line editing normally yields a handwritten EDL containing information similar to that generated by a computerized system.

MAIN POINTS

▶ All linear systems are tape-based and do not allow random access of information.

▶ The basic single-source editing system consists of a source (or play) VTR and a record (or edit) VTR. The basic principle of linear editing is selecting shots from the source VTR and copying them onto the record VTR in a specific order.

▶ The edit controller facilitates marking the in- and out-points of the selected shots on the source VTR and copying of the shots in a specific order to the record VTR.

▶ The multiple-source editing system consists of two or more source VTRs, a single record VTR, and a computer-assisted edit controller. Multisource systems can also include an audio mixer, a switcher, and special-effects equipment, enabling a variety of transitions between shots.

▶ The control track, or pulse-count, linear editing system uses sync pulses for locating specific edit-in and edit-out points. It does not supply a unique frame address, however, and is not frame-accurate.

▶ Time code editing uses a specific code that gives each frame a unique address. It is frame-accurate.

▶ In assemble editing, all video, audio, control, and address tracks on the edit master tape are erased to make room for the shot to be copied over from the source tape (containing its own video, audio, and control track information for the record VTR). If the newly assembled control track is not perfectly aligned, the edits will cause brief video break-ups—or sync rolls—at the edit points.

▶ In insert editing, the entire control track is prerecorded continuously on the edit master tape before any editing takes place. It prevents breakups at the edit points and allows separate video and audio editing.

▶ In linear editing, off-line means to use lower-quality equipment for the rough cut. It can be used to produce an edit decision list (EDL). On-line means to use high-end equipment to prepare the final edit master tape.

ZETTL'S VIDEOLAB

 For your reference or to track your work, the *Zettl's VideoLab* program cues in this chapter are listed here with their corresponding page numbers.

20

Editing Functions and Principles

You have practiced enough with the new editing software to help your friend edit his short documentary on water conservation. He likes your postproduction job and is especially impressed by the special effects you used to "liven things up a little." But when you show your masterpiece to a family friend, who happens to be a professional video editor, she shows much less enthusiasm. All she initially says is: "Well, nice—but..." When you press her for a frank evaluation, she tells you that she likes your seamless cuts in the first part but dislikes the occasional jump cuts. She thinks you should do away with the many dissolves that destroy the rhythm of the otherwise pretty good montage in the second part. She then adds that there is a general problem with index vector continuity that works against forming a mental map. Finally, she warns about using so many effects transitions that they become too obvious and draw attention away from the story. Besides, they make the whole edit look amateurish.

What in the world is she talking about? You will find out in this last chapter. In fact, you will soon realize that the hardest part of editing is not running the equipment but making the right aesthetic decisions—which shot to include and which to leave out to tell an effective story. This is what the editor meant when she said that editing, like most other television production activities, requires a mix of technical skills and creative aesthetics.

Section 20.1 addresses the major editing functions and the basic principles of continuity editing—how to make editing look seamless. Section 20.2 describes complexity editing—how to use editing to intensify a story. **ZVL1** EDITING→ Editing introduction

K E Y   T E R M S

complexity editing The juxtaposition of shots that primarily, though not exclusively, helps intensify a screen event. Editing conventions as advocated in continuity editing are often purposely violated.

continuity editing The establishment of a visual flow from shot to shot—to make the series appear seamless.

cutaway A shot that is thematically connected with the overall event. When inserted between the jump-producing shots, will camouflage the position shift. Used to facilitate continuity.

graphic vector A vector created by lines or by stationary elements in such a way as to suggest a line.

index vector A vector created by someone looking or something pointing unquestionably in a specific direction.

jump cut Cutting between shots that are identical in subject yet slightly different in screen location, or any abrupt transition between shots that violates the established continuity.

mental map Tells viewers where things are or are supposed to be in on- and off-screen space.

montage The juxtaposition of two or more separate event details that combine into a larger and more intense whole—a new gestalt.

motion vector A vector created by an object actually moving or perceived as moving on-screen.

vector Refers to a perceivable force with a direction and a magnitude. Vector types include graphic vectors, index vectors, and motion vectors.

vector line A dominant direction established by two people facing each other or through a prominent movement in a specific direction. Also called the *line,* the *line of conversation and action,* and the *hundredeighty.*

20.1

Editing Functions and Continuity Editing

As an editor, you have to work with the footage you shot or, more often, the footage that is handed to you. In some rare cases, such as in digital cinema production, you may be able to gather some missing material even in the postproduction stage, but usually you need to work with the footage you've got. As indicated in the introduction to this chapter, the shots you chose must not only create story continuity but also sequence continuity. This section is designed to help you in this task.

▶ **EDITING FUNCTIONS**
Combine, shorten, correct, and build

▶ **EDITING FOR CONTINUITY**
Story continuity, subject continuity, vectors and mental map, screen position continuity, motion continuity, light and color continuity, and sound continuity

EDITING FUNCTIONS

Editing is done for different reasons. Sometimes you need to arrange shots so that they tell a story. Other times you may have to eliminate extraneous material to make a story fit a given time slot, or you may want to cut out the shot where the talent stumbled over a word or substitute a close-up for an uninteresting medium shot. These different reasons are all examples of the four basic editing functions:

combine, shorten, correct, and build. **ZVL2** EDITING→ Functions→ select

COMBINE

The simplest editing is combining program portions by hooking the video-recorded pieces together in the proper sequence. The more care that was taken during the production, the less work you have to do in postproduction. For example, most soap operas are shot in long, complete scenes or in even longer sequences with a multicamera studio setup; the sequences are then combined in postproduction. Or, you may select various shots taken at a friend's wedding and simply combine them in the order in which they occurred.

SHORTEN

Many editing assignments involve cutting the available footage to make the final edit fit a given time slot or to eliminate extraneous material. As an ENG (electronic news gathering) editor, you will find that you often have to tell a complete story in an unreasonably short amount of time and that you have to pare down the available material to its bare minimum. For example, the producer may give you only 20 seconds to tell the story of a rescue scene of a car stuck on a flooded bridge, although the ENG team had proudly returned with 30 minutes of exciting footage.

Paradoxically, when editing ENG footage, you will discover that although you have an abundance of similar material, you may lack certain shots to tell the story coherently. For example, when screening the flood footage you may find that there are many beautiful shots of the flood waters creeping higher and higher to window-level but no pictures of the child who was pulled to safety on the opposite side. **ZVL3** EDITING→ Functions→ condense

CORRECT

Much editing time is spent on correcting mistakes, either by eliminating unacceptable portions of a scene or by replacing them with better ones. This type of editing can be simple—merely cutting out the part during which the talent coughed and replacing it with a retake. But it can also be challenging, especially if the retake does not match the rest of the recording. You may find, for example, that some of the corrected scenes differ noticeably from the others in color temperature, sound quality, or field of view (shot too close or too loose in relation to the rest of the footage). In such cases the relatively simple editing job becomes a formidable postproduction challenge and, in some cases, a nightmare.

Although most nonlinear editing (NLE) software includes remarkably powerful color correction features, applying them is often a tedious and highly time-consuming affair. This is one reason why you should pay particular attention to color matching (white-balancing) during the production phase. Even if you can fix many mistakes in postproduction, editing should never be regarded as a convenient magic bullet for sloppy production practices. **ZVL4** EDITING→ Functions→ correct

BUILD

The most difficult, but also the most satisfying, editing assignments are those on which you can build a show from a great many takes. Postproduction is no longer ancillary to production but constitutes a crucial phase in the production process. For example, when a play or documentary is shot film-style, you need to select those shots that reveal not only the basic process message but also the major action. Film-style refers to the established motion picture technique whereby you repeat a brief scene several times and shoot it from a variety of angles and fields of view, irrespective of the scripted event sequence. When editing these shots, you cannot simply select some and combine them in the sequence in which they were recorded; rather, you have to go back to the script and rearrange the shots to fit the story line. The story is literally built shot-by-shot. **ZVL5** EDITING→ Functions→ combine | try it

EDITING FOR CONTINUITY

Continuity editing refers to the achievement of story continuity despite the fact that great chunks of the story are actually missing, and to assemble the shots in such a way that viewers are largely unaware of the edits. These are the major points to consider: story continuity, subject continuity, vectors and mental map, screen position continuity, motion continuity, light and color continuity, and sound continuity.[1]

STORY CONTINUITY

The overriding factor in making editing decisions is telling a story. Most of the time, your editing will probably not involve a major motion picture but rather commercials, documentaries, news features, or your personal footage. You will then find that some of the most difficult assignments are not the longer projects but the ones in which you have to tell your story in 30 seconds or less.

For example, if the story for the five out-of-order clips in figure 20.1 is a young woman getting into her car to drive home after work, how would you sequence the shots? **SEE 20.1** Without peeking ahead, renumber the shots in the order you would sequence them to tell the story. Now look at the three edited versions. **SEE 20.2–20.4** Identify the one you think is the best combination of shots.

---

1. For a more detailed discussion of continuity editing, see Herbert Zettl, *Sight Sound Motion: Applied Media Aesthetics,* 5th ed. (Belmont, Calif.: Thomson Wadsworth, 2008), pp. 289–313.

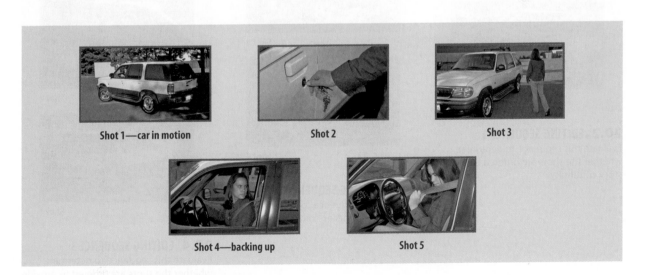

Shot 1—car in motion   Shot 2   Shot 3

Shot 4—backing up   Shot 5

20.1 SOURCE RECORDING SHOT SEQUENCE

The story is about a woman getting into her car and driving home after work. This is the sequence in which the event was restaged and recorded.

20.2 EDITING SEQUENCE 1

Evaluate this sequence to determine whether the shots are ordered to provide story continuity.

20.3 EDITING SEQUENCE 2

Evaluate this sequence to determine whether the shots are ordered to provide story continuity.

20.4 EDITING SEQUENCE 3

Evaluate this sequence to determine whether the shots are ordered to provide story continuity.

If you selected sequence 3, you made the right choice. Here's why: Obviously, the driver needs to walk to the car (shot 3) and unlock the door (shot 2) before fastening the seat belt (shot 5). The next action is to back the car out (shot 4). Finally, we see the car driving off (shot 1).

If you now had to reduce the edit to three clips, which ones would you select? You can certainly cut her walking to the car (shot 3). Then you could use either shot 2 (key) or shot 5 (seat belt) to qualify the story requirement of "getting into the car." The better sequence would probably be to drop shot 4, keeping this sequence: shot 2 (key), shot 5 (seat belt), and shot 1 (long shot of car driving off). **SEE 20.5** **ZVL6** EDITING→ Continuity→ try it

SUBJECT CONTINUITY

The viewer should be able to recognize a subject or an object from one shot to the next. Therefore avoid editing between shots of extreme changes in distance. **SEE 20.6** If it is available, you can intercut a medium shot (MS) from a different angle or use a slow zoom-in. **ZVL7** EDITING→ Continuity→ subject ID

VECTORS AND MENTAL MAP

Learning about vectors and the mental map will help you greatly not only in continuity editing but also in the pre-editing production phase, when visualizing the proper framing of shots or how they will edit together as well as the blocking of talent.

Vectors   Think of *vectors* as graphic forces with a direction and a magnitude (strength). In video and film, we work with three types of vectors: graphic, index, and motion.

A *graphic vector* is created by lines or by stationary elements that are positioned in such a way as to suggest a line. Look around you and you see nothing but graphic vectors: the doorframe, the lines of the desk, the computer screen. The red cones that are lined up at a construction site also form a graphic vector. **SEE 20.7**

Shot 2   Shot 5   Shot 1

20.5 EDITING SEQUENCE 4
There are several possibilities, one of which is the following sequence: shot 2 (unlocking the car), shot 5 (getting ready to drive), and shot 1 (driving off).

20.6 EXTREME CHANGES IN DISTANCE
When you cut from an extreme long shot (ELS) to a tight close-up (CU), viewers may not recognize exactly whose close-up it is.

20.7 GRAPHIC VECTORS
The lines of the ceiling lights, the curved edge and the slanted lines of the baggage carousel, the vertical lines of the pillars, the lines of the vertical baggage carousel, and the lines on the floor—all are strong graphic vectors

20.8 INDEX VECTOR
An index vector points in a specific direction. The camera lens and the microphone point unquestionably screen-right.

Shot 1

Shot 2

20.9 GRAPHIC VECTOR CONTINUITY
The prominent graphic vectors of a horizon line must match from shot to shot.

An **index vector** is formed by someone looking or something pointing unquestionably in a specific direction. **SEE 20.8**

A **motion vector** is generated by something actually moving or perceived to be moving on the screen. You can illustrate this type of vector with a video camera but not in a book. **ZVL8** EDITING→ Continuity→ vectors

Mental map   Like when we drive from our house to our favorite restaurant, when watching a screen event we automatically establish a **mental map** that shows where things are and where they should be on the screen. Because even the large flat-panel television screen is relatively small compared with a movie screen, we normally see little of a total scene in the on-screen space. Rather, the many close-

ups suggest, or should suggest, that the event continues in the off-screen space. What you show in the on-screen space defines the off-screen space as well. All vector types play a significant role in achieving and preserving shot continuity and keeping the viewer's mental map of on- and off-screen space intact.

For example, if you show a horizon line in subsequent shots rather than by panning, the strong graphic vector of the horizon must continue at approximately the same screen height. **SEE 20.9** If the horizon jumps from shot to shot, the graphic vector is no longer seen as continuing but rather suggests a new scene.

Proper handling of index vectors during editing plays a major role in preserving the mental map. If, for example, the screen shows person A looking screen-right in a close-

20.10 MENTAL MAP SHOT 1
Here person A's screen-right gaze (his index vector)
suggests that person B must be located in the off-screen
space to the right.

20.11 MENTAL MAP SHOT 2
When we now see person B in a close-up looking screen-left,
we assume person A to be in the left off-screen space.

up, obviously talking to an off-screen person (B), the viewer
would expect person B to look screen-left on a subsequent
close-up. **SEE 20.10 AND 20.11**

Once the mental map is established, the viewer expects the subsequent screen positions to adhere to it. The
mental map is so strong that if the subsequent shot showed
person B also looking screen-right, the viewer would think
that both persons A and B are talking to a third party.
SEE 20.12 **ZVL9** EDITING→ Continuity→ mental map

As you can see, the on-screen index vectors have a
considerable influence on how we perceive the off-screen
vectors. If you were to apply the index vectors to the example in figures 20.10 and 20.11 of on-screen person A
talking to off-screen person B, the screen-right index vector of A needs to be edited to the screen-left index vector

of B. Although the index vectors of the two persons are
converging in off-screen space, they indicate that A and
B are talking with each other rather than away from each
other. Obviously, if you were to cut to a two-shot of the two
people, their index vectors would have to converge much
like the ones on the individual close-ups.

SCREEN POSITION CONTINUITY

According to the mental map we established in figures
20.10 and 20.11 of A and B talking to each other, we expect
A to remain on screen-left and B on screen-right in the follow-up on-screen two-shot. A switch of A to screen-right
and B to screen-left would not make A and B unrecognizable but would certainly disturb the viewer's mental map
and, with it, inhibit rather than facilitate communication.

| Shot 1 | Shot 2 | Imagined third person |

20.12 MENTAL MAP SHOT 3

When both A and B look screen-right in successive shots, we conclude that they both are looking at somebody in the right off-screen space.

20.13 MAINTAINING SCREEN POSITIONS IN REVERSE-ANGLE SHOOTING

In this over-the-shoulder reverse-angle shot sequence, the interviewer and the interviewee maintain their basic screen positions.

Motion vector line

Index
vector line

20.14 VECTOR LINE

The vector line is formed by extending converging index vectors or a motion vector.

Maintaining screen positions is especially important in over-the-shoulder shots. If, for example, you show a reporter interviewing somebody in an over-the-shoulder two-shot, the viewer expects the two people to remain in their relative screen positions and not switch places during a reverse-angle shot. SEE 20.13

Vector line   One important aid in maintaining the viewer's mental map and keeping the subjects in their expected screen locations in reverse-angle shooting is the vector line. The *vector line* (also called the line, the line of conversation and action, and the hundredeighty) is an extension of converging index vectors or of a motion vector in the direction of object travel. SEE 20.14

When doing reverse-angle switching from camera 1 to camera 2, you need to position the cameras on the same side of the vector line. SEE 20.15 Crossing the line with one of the two cameras will switch the subjects' screen positions and make them appear to be playing musical chairs, thus upsetting the mental map. SEE 20.16 **ZVL10** EDITING→ Continuity→ mental map | try it

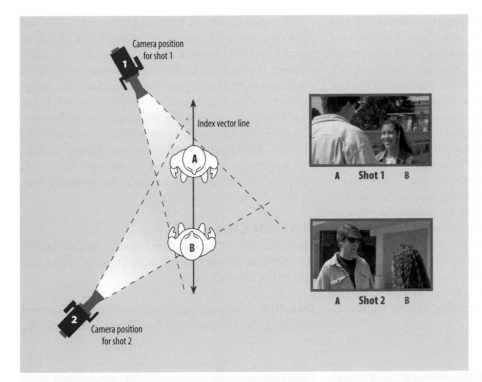

20.15 VECTOR LINE AND PROPER CAMERA POSITIONS

To maintain the screen positions of persons A and B in over-the-shoulder shooting, the cameras must be on the same side of the vector line.

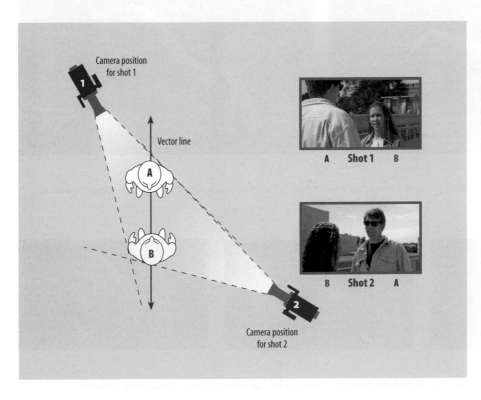

20.16 CROSSING THE VECTOR LINE

When one of the cameras crosses the vector line, persons A and B will switch positions every time you cut between the two cameras.

Jump cut   A small position change of an object from one shot to the next can cause an even bigger problem—the *jump cut*. If the director stops a dance routine because of a lighting problem and then tries to have the dancer pick it up exactly where she left off, her positions in the two succeeding shots will rarely match exactly. **SEE 20.17** When cutting the two shots together, you will see her arm suddenly jerk up as if yanked by an unseen force. Even though the position change is relatively small, the cut produces an obvious position jump—hence its name.

You will also get an undesirable jump cut if you are shooting on a set or location where props are moved from one shooting day to the next. If, for example, the vase on the background dresser had been moved sideways even a few inches, you may see the vase jump left or right even when the person in the foreground is framed in the same way as on the previous production day.

Generally, anything that is caused by a cut to bounce from one screen position to another without motivation is considered a jump cut.

To avoid a jump cut, try to find a succeeding shot that shows the object from a different angle or field of view or insert a cutaway. **SEE 20.18** Recall from chapter 19 that a *cutaway* is a shot that is thematically connected with the overall event and that when inserted between the jump-producing shots will camouflage the position shift. If you don't have a cutaway available, you don't have much choice. You can either let it jump or use a dissolve to muddle the problem. **ZVL11** EDITING→ Production guidelines→ cutaways

Sometimes a jump cut is intentional to get the viewer's attention. We discuss this technique in the context of complexity editing in section 20.2.

MOTION CONTINUITY

Motion continuity is determined not only by maintaining the principal direction in which an object is moving but also by the movement itself.

Direction   Crossing the motion vector line with cameras (shooting the moving object from both sides or placing

20.17 JUMP CUT
If the size, screen position, or shooting angle of an object is only slightly different in two succeeding shots, the object seems to jump within the screen.

20.18 CUTAWAY
You can avoid a jump cut by changing image size and/or angle of view or by separating the two shots with a cutaway, as shown here.

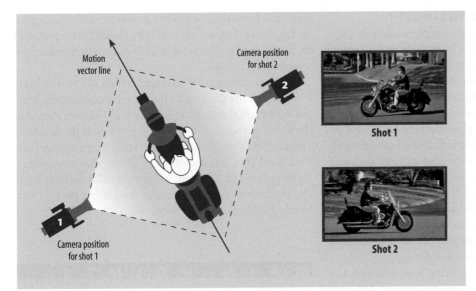

20.19 CROSSING THE MOTION VECTOR LINE
When crossing the motion vector line with cameras, the object motion will be reversed in each shot.

Motion vector line

Camera position for shot 2

Camera position for shot 1

Shot 1

Shot 2

cameras on both sides of the line) will reverse the direction of object motion every time you cut. **SEE 20.19** In a multi-camera setup, you would also see the opposite camera in the background. To continue a screen-left or screen-right object motion, you must keep both cameras on the same side of the motion vector line.

Movement To preserve motion continuity, cut during the motion of the subject, not before or after it. For example, if you see in a long shot a man walking to a park bench and sitting down, cut to the medium shot of the man as he is still in the act of sitting. This way the motion appears quite seamless. If you wait until he is seated, the medium shot draws attention to his next actions rather than connecting the two shots. If you cut too early, you will be repeating some of the sitting action. **ZVL12** EDITING→ Continuity→ cutting on motion

To trim the shots for a seamless cut, select the in-point of the second (closer) shot so that it matches exactly the out-point of the first (wider) shot. **ZVL13** EDITING→ Continuity→ cutting on motion | try it

If one shot contains a moving object, do not follow it with a shot that shows the object stationary. Similarly, if you follow a moving object in one shot with a camera pan, do not cut to a stationary camera in the next shot. Equally jarring is a cut from a stationary object to a moving one. You need to have the subject or camera move in both the preceding and the subsequent shots.

When working with footage in which the action has been shot from both sides of the motion vector line (resulting in a reversal of screen direction), you must separate the two shots with a cutaway or a head-on shot so that the reversed screen direction can be perceived as continuing. **SEE 20.20**

20.20 CUTAWAY FOR MOTION VECTOR REVERSAL
If you want to suggest a continuing motion vector of two diverging shots (the Jeep going in opposite directions), you need to insert a cutaway that has some connection to the event (in this case, the Jeep's rearview mirror).

LIGHT AND COLOR CONTINUITY

When editing indoor events, you must obviously watch that day doesn't change to night and back again in subsequent shots, especially when the action shows nothing but a brief conversation in the living room. A more subtle change may occur during an outdoor field production. The director may have shot both the greeting and good-bye scenes at the front entrance of a house during morning hours and the rest of the show in different locations under a progressively denser cloud cover. So long as the gradual lighting change from sunlight to overcast sky is coinciding with the time progression of the story, it poses no editing problem. But when the final good-byes at the doorstep happen in bright sunlight again, you have a big continuity problem. If too obvious, the good-bye scene needs to be reshot. In any case, consult the director about possible solutions.

Despite careful white-balancing, you will find that the colors don't always match from shot to shot. Although viewers are generally tolerant of minor color shifts, seeing a bride's white wedding dress turn blue when she steps from the church into the sunlight is simply unacceptable, and you must resort to color correction using high-end editing software. Keep in mind, however, that color correction requires skill that goes way beyond the routine editing described in this text.

SOUND CONTINUITY

When editing dialogue or commentary, take extra care to preserve the general rhythm of the speech. The pauses between shots of a continuing conversation should be neither much shorter nor much longer than those in the unedited version. In an interview the cut (edit or switcher-activated) usually occurs at the end of a question or an answer. Reaction shots, however, are often smoother when they occur during rather than at the end of phrases or sentences. But note that action is generally a stronger motivation for a cut than dialogue. If somebody moves during the conversation, you must cut on the move, even if the other person is still in the middle of a statement. **ZVL14** EDIT-ING→ Continuity→ sound

As discussed in chapter 9, ambient (background) sounds are very important in maintaining editing continuity. If the background noise acts as environmental sounds, which give clues to where the event takes place, you need to maintain those sounds throughout the scene, even if it was built from shots actually taken from different angles and at different times. You may have to supply this continuity by mixing in additional sounds in the postproduction sweetening sessions.

When editing video to music, try to cut with the beat. Cuts determine the beat of the visual sequence and keep the action rhythmically tight, much as the bars measure divisions in music. If the general rhythm of the music is casual or flowing, dissolves are usually more appropriate than hard cuts, but do not be a slave to this convention. Cutting "around the beat" (slightly earlier or later than the beat) on occasion can make the cutting rhythm less mechanical and intensify the scene.

MAIN POINTS

▶ The four basic editing functions are: to combine—to hook various video-recorded pieces together pretty much in the sequence in which they were recorded; to shorten—to make the program fit a given time slot and to eliminate extraneous material; to correct—to cut out bad portions of a scene and replace them with good ones; and to build—to select and sequence shots that will advance a specific story.

▶ Editing for continuity includes story continuity, subject continuity, vectors and the mental map, screen position continuity, motion continuity, light and color continuity, and sound continuity.

▶ Graphic, index, and motion vectors are pictorial forces that play an important part in establishing and maintaining continuity from shot to shot.

▶ Paying attention to vector continuity facilitates the viewer's mental map of where things are or move in on- and off-screen space.

▶ A small position change of an object from one shot to the next is known as a jump cut.

▶ Motion continuity is determined not only by maintaining the principal direction in which an object is moving but also by the movement itself.

▶ Crossing the vector line with cameras will reverse object positions and the direction of object motion every time you cut; you must keep both cameras on the same side of the motion vector line.

▶ To preserve motion continuity, cut during the motion of the subject, not before or after it.

20.2

Complexity Editing

Complexity editing goes beyond the seamless sequencing of shots and is more concerned with the intensification of the screen event. Your selection and sequencing of shots is guided no longer by the need to maintain visual and aural continuity but by ways of getting and keeping viewers' attention and increasing their emotional involvement. To increase the complexity and the intensity of a scene, such editing often makes a deliberate break with the conventions discussed in section 20.1. Although by no means exhaustive, this discussion should give you some idea of what complexity editing involves.

▶ **TRANSITIONS IN COMPLEXITY EDITING**
  Cut, dissolve, fade, wipe, and animated transitions

▶ **CROSSING THE VECTOR LINE**
  Background shift, position shift, and motion vector reversal

▶ **SPECIAL COMPLEXITY EFFECTS**
  Flashback and flashforward, instant replays, and multiple screens

▶ **MONTAGE**
  Filmic shorthand, complexity, meaning, and structure

▶ **ETHICS**
  Objectivity and honesty in editing

TRANSITIONS IN COMPLEXITY EDITING

The wide choice of readily available transitions may be as bewildering as they are tempting. Your choice of transitions will be less arbitrary if you know their functions and the importance of context in complexity editing. We'll first look at the cut, dissolve, wipe, and fade; then we'll focus on how animated transitions are perceived in various contexts.

Recall the discussion in chapter 13 of the more common digital video effects (DVE). We'll revisit some of these DVE to see how they might be perceived by viewers when used as transitions.

CUT

The most common transition, the cut, is invisible. It does not occupy any screen time because it does not actually exist. It gets its name from film editors, who literally cut the film apart at certain frames, sort the pieces, and glue them back together again in a specific order. How "visible" a cut is, that is, how much we are aware of the change from one shot to another, depends entirely on the pictures, sounds, and general vector structures of the preceding and following shots. Much like the bars in music, the cut is primarily responsible for the basic rhythm of a shot sequence. **ZVL15** SWITCHING→ Transitions→ cut | try it

DISSOLVE

The dissolve, or lap dissolve, is a gradual transition from shot to shot, with the two images overlapping temporarily. Whereas the cut itself cannot be seen on-screen, the dissolve is a clearly visible transition. Dissolves are often used to provide a smooth bridge for action or to indicate the passage of time. Depending on the overall rhythm of an event, you can use slow or fast dissolves. A very fast one functions almost like a cut but makes the transition a little softer. It is therefore called a soft cut. For an interesting and smooth transition from a wide shot of a dancer to a close-up, for instance, simply dissolve from one camera to the other. When you hold the dissolve in the middle, you will create a superimposition, or super. A slow dissolve will indicate a relatively long passage of time; a fast dissolve, a short one.

Because dissolves are so readily available in NLE software, you may be tempted to use them more often than is necessary or even desirable. A dissolve will inevitably slow down the transition and, with it, the scene. If dissolves are overused, the presentation will lack precision and accent and will bore the viewer. **ZVL16** SWITCHING→ Transitions→ mix/dissolve | try it

FADE

In a fade the picture either goes gradually to black (fadeout) or appears gradually on-screen from black (fade-in). You use the fade to signal a definite beginning (fade-in) or end (fade-out) of a scene. Like the curtain in a theater, it defines the beginning or end of a portion of a screen event. As such the fade is technically not a true transition, although some directors and editors use the term *cross-fade,* or *dip-to-black,* for a quick fade to black followed immediately by a fade-in to the next image to separate one story from the next. Here the fade acts as a transition device, decisively distinguishing the preceding and following images from each other. But do not go to black too often—the program continuity will be interrupted too many times by fades that all suggest final endings. **ZVL17** SWITCHING→ Transitions→ fade | try it

WIPE

There are a great variety of wipes available, the simplest of which is when the base picture is replaced by another one that moves conspicuously from one screen edge to the other. The wipe is such an unabashed transition device that it is normally classified as a special effect. Wipes are pushy and show up especially prominently on the large 16 × 9 HDTV screen.

Vertical wipe   Both horizontal and vertical wipes bully us into entering a new scene. This is almost like having someone change channels on us while watching television. The wipe signals a new theme. If it happens within a story, it disrupts continuity rather than establishes it.

Circle wipe   Both the expanding and shrinking circle wipes are, for some reason, funny. Don't use them in a serious documentary. When we fade in with an expanding circle wipe, you certainly don't expect to see a scene of an accident. A shrinking circle wipe signals "The End" even if you have never seen it used in silent movies. **ZVL18** SWITCHING→ Transitions→ wipe | try it

Sawtooth wipe   Any kind of sawtooth wipe has a cutting effect. It has no place in the context of subtle and intimate scenes. Using it to spice up a series of mom-and-baby shots is not good idea; the teeth of the wipe seem to cut right into the tranquil scene.

ANIMATED TRANSITIONS

Beware of animated transitions and use them only in the right context. For example, the computer rendering of a photo album in which the various clips appear may be fitting for family videos, but it is certainly inappropriate for showing a series of flag-draped coffins.

Peels   In a peel transition, the first image curls up as though it were torn off a pad of paper images, revealing the new one underneath. Such a transition may accentuate the different locations you visited when showing how kids play soccer around the world, but it is certainly out of place when showing children in various big-city slums.

Flips   These are extended peel effects that imitate a stack of still pictures or clips that slide off the pile and then flip and tumble through the air. You may have seen them used to introduce upcoming news stories. Unless the newscast consists entirely of flippant reports, don't use such animated transitions. They may catch our attention, but they also suggest, however subconsciously, that even the most grievous events shown are merely pictures. Because the images flip through the air as though they were disposable, the effect tends to distance us psychologically from the events shown; we will watch them but not empathize with them in any way.

Even a simple NLE program offers a wide array of such transition effects. Before using any of them, ask yourself whether the transition is appropriate in the context of your show. The advantage of nonlinear editing is that you can try a variety of effects before realizing that, perhaps, the "nonexistent" cut is the most fitting after all.

CROSSING THE VECTOR LINE

In section 20.1 you learned how to use the vector line in continuity editing; you will now be teased with breaking the rules of the line for event intensification. The idea is to cross the vector line on purpose to create a break in background continuity, cause a position change, and disrupt motion vector continuity.

BACKGROUND SHIFT

Some directors like to indicate a person's confused state of mind by shooting him or her from both sides of the vector line and by canting the camera. Crossing the line causes a noticeable and disrupting background shift. Tilting the horizon line makes the event less stable. When edited into a sequence of brief shots, the shifts of POV (points of view) and the tilting horizon line emphasize the person's mental instability. **SEE 20.21**

20.21 INSTABILITY THROUGH COMPLEXITY EDITING
Here the shooting from both sides of the vector line creates a disturbing flip-flop of index vectors and backgrounds, conveying the subject's confusion.

20.22 INTENSIFICATION BY CROSSING THE VECTOR LINE
Converging motion vectors of a prominent moving object will intensify its power. The head-on shot acts as a connecting cutaway.

POSITION SHIFT

Although not the result of crossing the line, the most jarring position shift—the jump cut—has been exonerated from the accusation of being an inexcusable editing error and has become a popular intensification device. You have probably seen commercials where the featured product is suddenly yanked a little to the left or right. Didn't the editor, director, and client see that this was a jump cut? Of course they did. In fact, they placed it there to draw attention to the product and to shake the viewers out of their perceptual complacency.

MTV productions use jump cuts routinely, sometimes out of ignorance but mostly by design. Although hardly necessary, the jarring position shift and the discontinuity of shots intensify the high energy of the music and its performers. Although this is often an effective intensification technique for music videos, I wouldn't use it for a college president's monthly campus video address. In such a context, the jump cut would certainly be perceived as an editing mistake.

MOTION VECTOR REVERSAL

As you well know, shooting a moving object from one side of the vector line and then from the opposite side will cause the object to reverse its direction. But this vector reversal is sometimes used to intensify the power of the moving object. If you had to magnify the raw power of a truck, for example, you can shoot the moving truck from both sides of the vector line and then show the sequence with converg-

ing motion vectors—the truck moving screen-right in shot 1 and screen-left in shot 2. Using a cutaway of a head-on shot of the truck between the converging motion vectors will make it easier to perceive the reversed screen directions (converging motion vectors) as continuing without detriment to the intensification factor. **SEE 20.22**

SPECIAL COMPLEXITY EFFECTS

By watching just one night's television programming, you can come across a great selection of complexity effects. Among the more popular ones are the flashback and the flashforward, instant replays, and multiple screens.

FLASHBACK AND FLASHFORWARD

You are certainly familiar with crime shows that have the victim recall parts of a dramatic experience through flashbacks. The screen flashes, and we see a re-creation of the scene the victim is describing to the authorities. The flashes are usually accompanied by *whooosh* sounds just to make sure we get the point that this is what the victim remembers. A similar technique is employed in flashforward scenes, where a character foresees an upcoming event. Such complexity effects are generally color-distorted to distinguish them from the "real" event in progress.

INSTANT REPLAYS

In sports, instant replays are usually done to show again an especially exciting moment in the live coverage of a game or to check on whether a player has violated a rule. In complexity editing, the instant replay is similar to the flashback except that the recall is almost immediately after the actual event. For example, it can show how two people perceive the same statement or situation in different ways. You must be careful, however, that such replays do not turn into unplanned comedy routines. Of course, it works great for Woody Allen–type bits of introspection.

MULTIPLE SCREENS

You can use multiple screens to show the complexity of a moment. A well-known technique is to show on multiple screens related events that occur in different locations simultaneously. You can also use multiple screens to show an event from different points of view or how we perceive the identical event over time. You should realize, however, that when you show a secondary frame on the actual television display, the image in the second-order space will more likely be perceived as a picture rather than the primary event happening in the first-order space of the television display.[2]

MONTAGE

Montage in its original French means "assembly." It can refer to assembling the parts of an automobile, but in a media context it usually means a deliberate assemblage of shots. In fact, **montage**—the juxtaposition of two or more separate event details that combine into a larger and more intense whole—is considered the basic building block of complexity editing.

Montage was essential to express specific ideas in the days of silent movies but has now become a filmic shorthand to lead up to an event or describe the complexity of a moment, similar to multiple screens. Montage can also be used as a structural device to give a series of shots rhythmic unity. Many commercials are built on the montage principle.

FILMIC SHORTHAND

If, for example, you need to edit the footage for a public service announcement in which a drunk driver hits a bicyclist, you can use a montage to tell the story in a very short time: man sitting at bar having still another drink, having trouble inserting ignition key, can't see the road well in the rain, wet bicyclist struggling uphill on a curve, extremely quick CU cuts of driver-bicycle-driver-bicycle-

driver, police and ambulance next to a twisted bicycle. What happened to the accident?

In this type of montage, the main event is often left to the viewer's imagination.

COMPLEXITY

To describe the complexity and the tension of the moment when the judge reads the jury's decision, you can use the montage principle to look around the courtroom, using quick CU cuts of the principals involved. You can intensify the tension by making the shots progressively shorter up to the guilty verdict. Such a montage is often used in sports coverage just ahead of the decisive action.

MEANING

You can also engender new meaning by juxtaposing two different shots. For example, you can intensify the anguish of a veteran in a wheelchair by showing a young girl skipping happily past him. Such collision montages were quite popular and effective in the days of silent movies, but today they are often so blunt that we tend to be alienated rather than moved by them. Also beware of unintentional juxtapositions. To follow a commercial for laxatives with one for toilet paper is not a good idea.

STRUCTURE

A montage is often determined not so much by its content as by its length and rhythm. All montages are relatively brief and the shots are cut to equal lengths or, as in the accident and courtroom examples, grow shorter toward the climax.

You should be able to clap rhythmically to the edits in a montage.

ETHICS

Because as an editor you have even more power than the cameraperson over what and what not to show and the ability to construct different meanings of the basic event footage, this section ends with a brief discussion of ethics, or principles of right conduct.

The willful distortion of an event through editing is not a case of poor aesthetic judgment but a question of ethics. The most important principle for the editor, as for all production people working with the presentation of nonfictional events (news and documentaries rather than drama), is to remain as true to the actual event as possible. For example, if you were to add applause simply because your favorite political candidate said something you happen to support, although in reality there was dead silence,

---

2. For a more thorough discussion of multiple screens, see Zettl, *Sight Sound Motion*, pp. 145–150, 186–189.

you would definitely be acting unethically. It would be equally wrong to edit out all the statements that go against your convictions and leave only those with which you agree. If someone gives pro and con arguments, be sure to present the most representative of each. Do not edit out all of one side or the other to meet the prescribed length of the segment.

Be especially careful when juxtaposing two shots that may generate by implication a third idea not contained in either of the two shots. To follow a politician's plea for increased armaments with the explosion of an atomic bomb may unfairly imply that this politician favors nuclear war. These types of montage shots are as powerful as they are dangerous.

Montage effects between video and audio information are especially effective; they may be more subtle than the video-only montages but are no less potent. For example, adding the penetrating and aggravating sounds of police sirens to the footage of "for sale" signs of several houses in a wealthy neighborhood would probably suggest that the neighborhood is changing for the worse. The implied message is to not buy any houses in this "crime-ridden" neighborhood.

Do not stage events just to get exciting pictures. For example, if a police officer made a successful rescue but the only footage you got was the rescued person on a stretcher, do not ask the officer to return to the scene of the accident to simulate the daring feat. Although reenactments of this sort have become routine for some ENG teams, stay away from them. There is enough drama in all events if you look closely enough and take effective pictures. You do not have to stage anything.

Finally, you are ultimately responsible to the viewers for your choices as an editor. Do not violate the trust they put in you. As you can see, there is a fine line between intensifying an event through careful editing practices and distorting an event through careless or unethical ones. The only safeguard the viewers have against irresponsible persuasion and manipulation is your responsibility as a professional communicator and your basic respect for your audience.

MAIN POINTS

▶ Complexity editing is a deliberate break with editing conventions to reveal the stratification of a scene and increase its intensity.

▶ Any one of the many available transitions—cut, dissolve, fade, wipe, and animated—can enhance a complexity edit so long as the transition fits the story content and context.

▶ In complexity editing, the vector line is sometimes deliberately crossed. The resulting background and position shifts as well as motion vector reversals can intensify the scene.

▶ Special complexity effects such as the flashback and flashforward, instant replays, and multiple screens have become widely used techniques in complexity editing.

▶ The montage is a filmic shorthand that uses a series of rhythmic cuts to advance a story, show various points of view, create new meaning through juxtapositions, and help establish a beat.

▶ Because as editor you have power over what the audience will see in the final edit, you must make your decisions in not only an aesthetic context but an ethical one as well.

ZETTL'S VIDEOLAB

For your reference or to track your work, the *Zettl's VideoLab* program cues in this chapter are listed here with their corresponding page numbers.

ZVL1 EDITING→ Editing introduction   **447**

ZVL2 EDITING→ Functions→ select   **448**

ZVL3 EDITING→ Functions→ condense   **448**

ZVL4 EDITING→ Functions→ correct   **449**

ZVL5 EDITING→ Functions→ combine | try it   **449**

ZVL6 EDITING→ Continuity→ try it   **451**

ZVL7 EDITING→ Continuity→ subject ID   **451**

ZVL8 EDITING→ Continuity→ vectors   **452**

ZVL9 EDITING→ Continuity→ mental map   **453**

ZVL10 EDITING→ Continuity→ mental map | try it   **454**

ZVL11 EDITING→ Production guidelines→ cutaways   **456**

ZVL12 EDITING→ Continuity→ cutting on motion   **457**

ZVL13 EDITING→ Continuity→ cutting on motion | try it   **457**

ZVL14 EDITING→ Continuity→ sound   **458**

ZVL15 SWITCHING→ Transitions→ cut | try it   **459**

ZVL16 SWITCHING→ Transitions→ mix/dissolve | try it   **459**

ZVL17 SWITCHING→ Transitions→ fade | try it   **460**

ZVL18 SWITCHING→ Transitions→ wipe | try it   **460**

Epilogue

You are now in command of one of the most powerful means of communication and persuasion. Use it wisely and responsibly.

Treat your audience with respect and compassion. Whatever role you play in the production process—pulling cables or directing a network show—you influence many people. Because they cannot communicate back to you very readily, they must—and do—trust your professional skills and judgment.

Do not betray that trust.

Glossary

480i The number of visible, or active, lines (out of 525 total scanning lines) in the standard television (STV) system. The *i* stands for *interlaced*, which means that a complete frame is formed from two fields, each carrying half of the picture information.

480p The lowest-resolution scanning system of digital television. The *p* stands for *progressive*, which means that each complete television frame consists of 480 visible, or active, lines that are scanned one after the other (out of 525 total scanning lines).

720p A progressive scanning system of high-definition television. Each frame consists of 720 visible, or active, lines (out of 750 total scanning lines).

1080i An interlaced scanning system of high-definition television. The *i* stands for *interlaced,* which means that a complete frame is formed from two fields, each carrying half of the picture information. Each field consists of 540 visible, or active, lines (out of 1,125 total scanning lines). Just like the standard NTSC television system, the digital HDTV 1080i system produces 60 fields, or 30 complete frames, per second.

AB-roll editing Creating an edit master tape by combining the A-roll, which contains a set of shots (such as long and medium shots), and the B-roll, which contains different but related shots (such as cutaways or close-ups of the same scene).

AC Stands for *alternating current*. Electric energy as supplied by normal wall outlets.

actor A person (male or female) who appears on-camera in dramatic roles. Actors always portray someone else.

AD Stands for *associate* or *assistant director*. Assists the director in all production phases.

additive primary colors Red, green, and blue. Ordinary white light (sunlight) can be separated into the three primary light colors. When these three colored lights are combined in various proportions, all other colors can be reproduced. The process is called *additive color mixing*.

address code An electronic signal that marks each frame with a specific address. *See* **SMPTE/EBU time code**.

ad-lib Speech or action that has not been scripted or specially rehearsed.

ADR *See* **automated dialogue replacement**

advanced television *See* **digital television (DTV)**

AFTRA Stands for *American Federation of Television and Radio Artists*. A broadcasting talent union.

AGC *See* **automatic gain control**

ambience Background sounds.

analog A signal that fluctuates exactly like the original stimulus.

analog recording systems Record the continually fluctuating video and audio signals generated by the video and/or audio source.

aperture Iris opening of a lens, usually measured in *f*-stops.

arc To move the camera in a slightly curved dolly or truck.

aspect ratio The width-to-height proportions of the standard television screen and therefore of all standard television pictures: 4 units wide by 3 units high. For HDTV the aspect ratio is 16 × 9. The small portable media (cell-phone) screens have various aspect ratios.

assemble editing Adding shots in linear editing on video-tape in consecutive order without first recording a control track on the edit master tape.

ATR *See* **audiotape recorder**

ATV Stands for *advanced television. See* **digital television (DTV).**

audio The sound portion of television and its production. Technically, the electronic reproduction of audible sound.

audio control booth Houses the audio, or mixing, console; analog and digital playback machines; a turntable; a patchbay; a compute display; speakers; intercom systems; a clock; and a line monitor.

audio monitor *See* **program speaker**

audio postproduction room For postproduction activities such as sweetening; composing music tracks; adding music, sound effects, or laugh tracks; and assembling music bridges and announcements.

audiotape recorder (ATR) A reel-to-reel audiotape recorder.

audio track The area of the videotape used for recording the sound information.

auto-cue *See* **teleprompter**

auto-focus Automated feature whereby the camera focuses on what it senses to be the target object.

auto-iris Automatic control of the lens diaphragm.

automated dialogue replacement (ADR) The synchronization of speech with the lip movements of the speaker in postproduction.

automatic gain control (AGC) Can regulate sound volume or video brightness and contrast levels.

auto-transition An electronic device that functions like a fader bar.

A/V format Another name for the two-column AV (audio/video) script.

background light Illumination of the set, set pieces, and backdrops. Also called *set light.*

back light Illumination from behind the subject and opposite the camera.

back-timing The process of figuring additional clock times by subtracting running times from the schedule time at which the program ends.

balanced mic or line Professional audio wiring with three connectors or wires: two that carry substantially the same audio signal out of phase and one that is a ground shield. Relatively immune to hum and other electronic interference.

barn doors Metal flaps mounted in front of a lighting instrument that control the spread of the light beam.

base *See* **baselight**

baselight Even, nondirectional (diffused) light necessary for the camera to operate optimally. Normal baselight levels are 150 to 200 foot-candles (1,500 to 2,000 lux) at $f/8$ to $f/16$. Also called *base.*

baselight level *See* **operating light level**

batch capture Having the computer use the logging information to capture all the selected clips for editing.

batten A horizontal metal pipe that supports lighting instruments in a studio.

beam splitter Compact internal optical system of prisms within a television camera that separates white light into the three primary colors: red, green, and blue (RGB). Also called *prism block.*

big boom *See* **perambulator boom**

big remote A production outside of the studio to televise live and/or live-record a large scheduled event that has not been staged specifically for television. Examples include sporting events, parades, political gatherings, and studio shows that are taken on the road. Also called *remote.*

binary A number system with the base of 2.

binary digit (bit) The smallest amount of information a computer can hold and process. A charge is either present, represented by a *1,* or absent, represented by a *0.* One bit can describe two levels, such as on/off or black/white. The standard decimal system has 10 digits: 0–9. The binary system has only two: 0 and 1.

bit *See* **binary digit**

black Darkest part of the grayscale, with a reflectance of approximately 3 percent; called *TV black*. "To black" means to fade the television picture to black.

blocking Carefully worked-out movement and actions by the talent and for all mobile television equipment.

blocking rehearsal *See* **dry run**

BNC Standard coaxial cable connector for professional video equipment.

book Two flats hinged together. Also called *twofold*.

boom (1) *Audio:* microphone support. (2) *Video:* part of a camera crane. (3) To move the camera via the boom of the camera crane; also called *crane*.

boundary microphone Microphone mounted or put on a reflecting surface to build up a pressure zone in which all the sound waves reach the microphone at the same time. Ideal for group discussions and audience reaction. Also called *pressure zone microphone (PZM)*.

brightness The color attribute that determines how dark or light a color appears on the monochrome television screen or how much light the color reflects. Also called *lightness* and *luminance*.

broad A floodlight with a broadside, panlike reflector.

broadband A high-bandwidth standard for sending information (voice, data, video, and audio) simultaneously over cables.

bump-down Dubbing (copying) picture and sound information from a higher-quality VTR format to a lower-quality one.

bump-up Dubbing (copying) picture and sound information from a lower-quality videotape format to a higher-quality one.

burn-in A permanent trace of an image in a video display.

bus (1) A row of buttons on the switcher. (2) A common central circuit that receives electrical signals from several sources and that feeds them to a common or several separate destinations.

bust shot Framing of a person from the upper torso to the top of the head.

byte Eight bits. Can define 256 discrete levels (2^8 bits), such as shades of gray between black and white. *See also* **binary digit (bit)**.

cake A makeup base, or foundation makeup, usually water-soluble and applied with a small sponge. Also called *pancake*.

calibrate (1) *Audio:* To make all VU meters (usually of the audio console and the video recorder) respond in the same way to a specific audio signal. (2) *Video:* to preset a zoom lens to remain in focus throughout the zoom.

camcorder A portable camera with the videotape recorder or some other recording device built into it to form a single unit.

cameo lighting Foreground figures are lighted with highly directional light, with the background remaining dark.

camera The general name for the *camera head,* which consists of the lens (or lenses), the main camera with the imaging device and the internal optical system, electronic accessories, and the viewfinder.

camera chain The television camera (head) and associated electronic equipment, including the camera control unit, sync generator, and power supply.

camera control unit (CCU) Equipment, separate from the camera head, that contains various video controls, including color fidelity, color balance, contrast, and brightness. The CCU enables the video operator to adjust the camera picture during a show.

camera head The actual television camera, which is at the head of a chain of essential electronic accessories. It comprises the imaging device, lens, and viewfinder. In ENG/EFP cameras, the camera head contains all the elements of the camera chain.

camera light Small spotlight mounted on the front of the camera, used as an additional fill light. (Frequently confused with tally light.) Also called *eye light* or *inky-dinky*.

camera mounting head A camera mounting device that permits smooth tilts and pans. Also called *pan-and-tilt head*.

camera pickup device *See* **imaging device**

camera rehearsal Full rehearsal with cameras and other pieces of production equipment. Often identical to the dress rehearsal.

camera stabilizing system Camera mount whose mechanism holds the camera steady while the operator moves.

cant Tilting the shoulder-mounted or handheld camera sideways.

capacitor microphone *See* **condenser microphone**

capture Transferring video and audio information to a computer hard drive for nonlinear editing. Also called *importing.*

cardioid Heart-shaped pickup pattern of a unidirectional microphone.

cassette A video- or audiotape recording or playback device that uses tape cassettes. A cassette is a plastic case containing two reels—a supply reel and a takeup reel.

C-band A frequency band for certain satellites. It is relatively immune to weather interference. *See also* **Ku-band**.

CCD *See* **charge-coupled device**

C-clamp A metal clamp with which lighting instruments are attached to the lighting battens.

C channel *See* **chrominance channel**

CCU *See* **camera control unit**

CD *See* **compact disc**

C.G. *See* **character generator**

character generator (C.G.) A dedicated computer system that electronically produces a series of letters, numbers, and simple graphic images for video display. Any desktop computer can become a C.G. with the appropriate software.

charge-coupled device (CCD) The imaging sensor in a television camera. It consists of horizontal and vertical rows of tiny image-sensing elements, called *pixels,* that translate the optical (light) image into an electric charge that eventually becomes the video signal.

chip A common name for the camera's imaging device. *See* **imaging device**.

chroma-key backdrop A well-saturated blue or green canvas backdrop that can be pulled down from the lighting grid to the studio floor as a background for chroma keying.

chroma keying Effect that uses color (usually blue or green) for the backdrop, which is replaced by the background image during a key.

chrominance channel Consists of the three color (chroma) signals in a video system. The chrominance channel is responsible for each of the basic color signals: red, green, and blue (RGB). Also called *C channel.*

classical dramaturgy The technique of dramatic composition.

clip (1) To compress the white and/or black picture information or prevent the video signal from interfering with the sync signals. (2) A shot or brief series of video frames as captured on the hard drive and identified by a file name.

clip control *See* **key-level control**

clip light Small internal reflector spotlight that is clipped to pieces of scenery or furniture with a gator clip. Also called *PAR (parabolic aluminized reflector) lamp.*

clipper *See* **key-level control**

close-up (CU) Object or any part of it seen at close range and framed tightly. The close-up can be extreme (extreme or big close-up—*ECU*) or rather loose (medium close-up—*MCU*).

closure Short for *psychological closure.* Mentally filling in spaces of an incomplete picture. *See also* **mental map**.

CMOS A camera imaging sensor similar to a CCD but which operates on a different technology. It translates light into an electronic video charge that eventually becomes the video signal.

codec Short for *compression/decompression.* A specific method of compressing and decompressing digital data.

coding To change the quantized values into a binary code, represented by 0's and 1's. Also called *encoding.*

color bars A color standard used by the television industry for the alignment of cameras and videotape recordings. Color bars can be generated by most professional portable cameras.

color compatibility Color signals that can be perceived as black-and-white pictures on monochrome television sets. Generally used to mean that the color scheme has enough brightness contrast for monochrome reproduction with a good grayscale contrast.

color media *See* **gel**

color temperature The standard by which we measure the relative reddishness or bluishness of white light. It is measured on the Kelvin (K) scale. The standard color temperature for indoor light is 3,200K; for outdoor light it is 5,600K. Technically, the numbers express Kelvin degrees.

compact disc (CD) A small, shiny disc that contains information (usually sound signals) in digital form. A CD player reads the encoded digital information using a laser beam.

complexity editing The juxtaposition of shots that primarily, though not exclusively, helps intensify a screen event. Editing conventions as advocated in continuity editing are often purposely violated.

component system A process in which the luminance (Y, or black-and-white) signals and color (C) signals, or all three color signals (RGB), are kept separate throughout the recording and storage process. *See also* **Y/C component system**, **Y/color difference component system**, and **RGB component system**.

composite system A process in which the luminance (Y, or black-and-white) signal and the chrominance (C, or color) signal as well as sync information are encoded into a single video signal and transported via a single wire. Also called *NTSC signal*.

compression (1) *Data:* reducing the amount of data to be stored or transmitted by using coding schemes (codecs) that pack all original data into less space (*lossless* compression) or by throwing away some of the least important data (*lossy* compression). (2) *Optical:* The crowding effect achieved by a narrow-angle (telephoto) lens wherein object proportions and relative distances seem shallower.

condenser microphone A mic whose diaphragm consists of a condenser plate that vibrates with the sound pressure against another fixed condenser plate, called the *backplate*. Also called *electret* or *capacitor microphone*.

contact A person, usually a public relations officer, who knows about an event and can assist the production team during a remote telecast.

continuity editing The establishment of a visual flow from shot to shot—to make the series appear seamless.

continuous-action lighting Overlapping triangle lighting for all major performance areas. Also called *zone lighting*.

contrast ratio The difference between the brightest and the darkest portions in the picture (often measured by reflected light in foot-candles). The contrast ratio for low-end cameras and camcorders is normally 50:1, which means that the brightest spot in the picture should be no more than 50 times brighter than the darkest portion without causing loss of detail in the dark or light areas. High-end digital cameras can greatly exceed this ratio and can tolerate a contrast ratio of 1,000:1 or more.

control room A room adjacent to the studio in which the director, the technical director, the audio engineer, and sometimes the lighting director perform their various production functions.

control room directing *See* **multicamera directing**

control track The area of the videotape used for recording the synchronization information (sync pulse). Provides reference for the running speed of the videotape recorder, for the reading of the video tracks, and for counting the number of frames.

control track system An editing system that counts the control track sync pulses and translates this count into elapsed time and frame numbers. It is not frame-accurate. Also called *pulse-count system*.

cookie A popularization of the original term *cucoloris*. Any pattern cut out of thin metal that, when placed inside or in front of an ellipsoidal spotlight (pattern projector), produces a shadow pattern. Also called *gobo*.

crab Sideways motion of the camera crane dolly base.

crane (1) Motion picture camera support that resembles an actual crane in both appearance and operation. The crane can lift the camera from close to the studio floor to more than 10 feet above it. (2) To move the boom of the camera crane up or down. Also called *boom*.

crawl The horizontal movement of electronically generated copy (the vertical movement is called a *roll*). Can also refer to the program that activates such a movement.

cross-fade (1) *Audio:* transition method whereby the preceding sound is faded out and the following sound is faded in simultaneously; the sounds overlap temporarily. (2) *Video:* transition method whereby the preceding picture is faded to black and the following picture is faded in from black.

cross-keying The crossing of key lights for two people facing each other.

cross-shot (X/S) Similar to the over-the-shoulder shot except that the camera-near person is completely out of the shot.

CU *See* **close-up**

cucoloris *See* **cookie**

cue card A large, hand-lettered card that contains copy, usually held next to the camera lens by floor personnel.

cue-send *See* **foldback**

cue track The area of the videotape used for such information as in-house identification or SMPTE address code. Can also be used for an additional audio track.

cut (1) The instantaneous change from one shot (image) to another. (2) Director's signal to interrupt action.

cutaway A shot that is thematically connected with the overall event. When inserted between the jump-producing shots, will camouflage the position shift. Used to facilitate continuity.

cuts-only editing system *See* **single-source editing system**

cyc *See* **cyclorama**

cyc light *See* **strip light**

cyclorama A U-shaped continuous piece of canvas or muslin for backing of scenery and action. Also called *cyc*.

DAT *See* **digital audiotape**

DBS *See* **direct broadcast satellite**

DC Stands for *direct current*.

decoding The reconstruction of a video or an audio signal from a digital code.

definition How sharp an image appears. In television, the number and size of pixels that make up the screen image. *See also* **resolution**.

delegation controls Buttons on the switcher that assign specific functions to a bus.

demographics Audience research factors concerned with such data as age, gender, marital status, and income.

depth of field The area in which all objects, located at different distances from the camera, appear in focus. Depth of field depends on the focal length of the lens, its *f*-stop, and the distance between the object and the camera.

depth staging Arrangement of objects on the television screen so that foreground, middleground, and background are each clearly defined.

diaphragm (1) *Audio:* the vibrating element inside a microphone that moves with the air pressure from the sound. (2) *Video: See* **iris**.

dichroic filter A mirrorlike color filter that singles out from the white light the red light (red dichroic filter) and the blue light (blue dichroic filter), with the green light left over. Also called *dichroic mirror*.

dichroic mirror *See* **dichroic filter**

diffused light Light that illuminates a relatively large area with an indistinct light beam. Diffused light, created by floodlights, produces soft shadows.

diffusion filter Filter that attaches to the front of the lens, which gives a scene a soft, slightly out-of-focus look.

digital Usually means the binary system—the representation of data in the form of binary digits (on/off pulses).

digital audiotape (DAT) The sound signals are encoded on audiotape in digital form. Includes digital recorders as well as digital recording processes.

digital cart system A digital audio system that uses built-in hard drives, removable disks, or read/write optical discs to store and access audio information almost instantaneously. It is normally used for the playback of brief announcements and music bridges.

digital cinema camera A high-definition television camera that has a native frame rate of 24 frames per second and a variable frame rate for slow and accelerated motion. Most digital cinema cameras use high-quality CCDs or CMOS sensors, state-of-the-art lenses, and high-definition viewfinders.

digital recording systems Sample the analog video and audio signals and convert them into discrete on/off pulses. These digits are recorded as 0's and 1's.

digital television (DTV) Digital television systems that generally have a higher image resolution than STV (standard television). Also called *advanced television (ATV)*.

digital versatile disc (DVD) The standard DVD is a read-only, high-capacity (4.7 gigabytes or more) storage device of digital audio and video information.

digital video effects (DVE) Visual effects generated by computer or digital effects equipment in the switcher.

digital zooming Simulated zoom by cropping the center portion of an image and electronically enlarging the cropped portion. Digital zooms lose picture resolution.

digital zoom lens A lens that can be programmed through a built-in computer to repeat zoom positions and their corresponding focus settings.

digitize To convert analog signals into digital (binary) form or to transfer information in a digital code.

dimmer A device that controls the intensity of light by throttling the electric current flowing to the lamp.

direct broadcast satellite (DBS) Satellite with a relatively high-powered transponder (transmitter/receiver) that broadcasts from the satellite to small, individual downlink dishes; operates on the Ku-band.

direct bus See **program bus**

direct input See **direct insertion**

direct insertion Recording technique wherein the sound signals of electric instruments are fed directly to the mixing console without the use of speaker and microphone. Also called *direct input*.

directional light Light that illuminates a relatively small area with a distinct light beam. Directional light, produced by spotlights, creates harsh, clearly defined shadows.

director of photography See **DP**

disk-based video recorder All digital video recorders that record or store information on a hard disk or read/write optical disc. All disk-based systems are nonlinear.

dissolve The gradual replacement of one image by another through a temporary double exposure. Also called *lap dissolve*.

distortion Unnatural alteration or deterioration of sound.

diversity reception Setup for a single wireless microphone wherein more than one receiving station is established, so one can take over when the signal from the other gets weak.

dolly (1) Camera support that enables the camera to move in all horizontal directions. (2) To move the camera toward (dolly in) or away from (dolly out or back) the object.

double headset A telephone headset (earphones) that carries program sound in one earphone and the P.L. information in the other. Also called *split intercom*.

downlink The antenna (dish) and equipment that receive the signals coming from a satellite.

downloading The transfer of files that are sent in data packets. Because these packets are often transferred out of order, the file cannot be seen or heard until the downloading process is complete. *See also* **streaming**.

downstream keyer (DSK) A control that allows a title to be keyed (cut in) over the picture (line-out signal) as it leaves the switcher.

DP Stands for *director of photography*. In major motion picture production, the DP is responsible for the lighting (similar to the LD in television). In smaller motion picture productions and in EFP, the DP will operate the camera. In television it refers to the camera operator, or shooter.

drag Degree of friction needed in the camera mounting head to allow smooth panning and tilting.

dramaturgy The technique of dramatic composition.

dress (1) What people wear on-camera. (2) Decorating a set with set properties. (3) Dress rehearsal.

dress rehearsal Full rehearsal with all equipment operating and with talent in full dress. The dress rehearsal is often video recorded. Often called *camera rehearsal* except that the camera rehearsal does not require full dress for talent.

drop Large, painted piece of canvas used for scenery backing.

drop frame A video recording mode in which single frames are periodically overlooked (dropped) by the SMPTE time code to make it match the actual elapsed clock time.

dropout Loss of part of the video signal, which shows up on-screen as white or colored glitches. Caused by uneven videotape iron-oxide coating (bad tape quality or overuse) or dirt.

dry run Rehearsal without equipment, during which the basic actions of the talent are worked out. Also called *blocking rehearsal.*

DSK *See* **downstream keyer**

DTV *See* **digital television**

dual-redundancy The use of two identical microphones for the pickup of a sound source, whereby only one of them is turned on at any given time. A safety device that permits switching over to the second microphone in case the active one becomes defective.

dub The duplication of an electronic recording. Dubs can be made from tape to tape, or from disc to tape and vice versa. The dub is always one generation away from the recording used for dubbing. In analog systems each dub shows increased deterioration. Digital dubbing produces copies almost identical in quality to the original.

DVCAM Digital videotape recording system developed by Sony.

DVCPRO Digital videotape recording system developed by Panasonic.

DVD *See* **digital versatile disc**

DVE *See* **digital video effects**

dynamic microphone A mic whose sound pickup device consists of a diaphragm that is attached to a movable coil. As the diaphragm vibrates with the air pressure from the sound, the coil moves within a magnetic field, generating an electric current. Also called *moving-coil microphone.*

echo A sound that is reflected from a single surface and perceived as consecutive, rapidly fading, and repetitious. *See also* **reverberation**.

ECU *See* **extreme close-up**

edit controller Machine that assists in editing functions, such as marking edit-in and edit-out points, rolling source and record videotape recorders, and activating effects equipment. Often a desktop computer with specialized software. Also called *editing control unit.*

edit decision list (EDL) Consists of edit-in and edit-out points, expressed in time code numbers, and the nature of transitions between shots.

editing The selection and assembly of shots in a logical sequence.

editing control unit *See* **edit controller**

edit master recording The recording of the final edit on videotape or other media. Used for broadcast or duplication.

edit master tape The videotape on which the selected portions of the source tapes are edited. Used with the record VTR.

edit VTR *See* **record VTR**

EDL *See* **edit decision list**

effects buses Program and preview buses on the switcher, assigned to perform effects transitions.

effect-to-cause model Moving from idea to desired effect on the viewer, then backing up to the specific medium requirements to produce such an effect.

EFP Stands for electronic field production. Television production outside of the studio that is normally shot for postproduction (not live). Part of *field production.*

EFP camera High-quality portable, shoulder-mounted field production camera that must be connected to an external video recorder.

electret microphone *See* **condenser microphone**

electron gun Produces the electron (scanning) beam in a television receiver.

electronic field production *See* **EFP**

electronic still store (ESS) system An electronic device that can grab a single frame from any video source and store it in digital form. It can retrieve the frame randomly in a fraction of a second.

ellipsoidal spotlight Spotlight that produces a very defined beam, which can be shaped further by metal shutters.

ELS *See* **extreme long shot**

electronic news gathering *See* **ENG**

encoding *See* **coding**

ENG Stands for *electronic news gathering.* The use of portable camcorders, lights, and sound equipment for the production of daily news stories. ENG is usually not planned in advance and is often transmitted live or immediately after postproduction.

ENG/EFP camcorder High-quality portable field production camera with the recording device built-in.

environment General ambience of a setting.

equalization Controlling the quality of sound by emphasizing certain frequencies while de-emphasizing others.

essential area The section of the television picture, centered within the scanning area, that is seen by the home viewer regardless of masking or slight mis-

alignment of the receiver. Also called *safe title area* and *safe area.*

ESS system *See* **electronic still store (ESS) system**

establishing shot *See* **extreme long shot (ELS)** and **long shot (LS)**

event order The way event details are sequenced.

extender *See* **range extender**

external key The cutout portion of the base picture is filled by the signal from an external source, such as a second camera.

extreme close-up (ECU) Shows the object with very tight framing.

extreme long shot (ELS) Shows the object from a great distance. Also called *establishing shot.*

eye light *See* **camera light**

facilities request A list that contains all technical facilities needed for a specific production.

fact sheet Lists the items to be shown on-camera and their main features. May contain suggestions of what to say about the product. Also called *rundown sheet.*

fade The gradual appearance of a picture from black (*fade-in*) or its disappearance to black (*fade-out*).

fader A sound-volume control that works by means of a button sliding horizontally along a specific scale. Identical in function to a pot. Also called *slide fader.*

fader bar A lever on the switcher that activates preset transitions, such as dissolves, fades, and wipes, at different speeds. It is also used to create superimpositions.

falloff (1) The speed with which light intensity decays. (2) The speed (degree) with which a light picture portion turns into shadow area. *Fast falloff* means that the light areas turn abruptly into shadow areas and there is a great brightness difference between light and shadow areas. *Slow falloff* indicates a very gradual change from light to dark and a minimal brightness difference between light and shadow areas.

fast lens A lens that permits a relatively great amount of light to pass through at its maximum aperture (relatively low *f*-stop number at its lowest setting). Can be used in low-light conditions.

fc *See* **foot-candle**

feed Signal transmission from one program source to another, such as a network feed or a remote feed.

feedback (1) *Audio:* piercing squeal from the loudspeaker, caused by the accidental reentry of the loudspeaker sound into the microphone and subsequent overamplification of sound. (2) *Communications:* reaction of the receiver of a communication back to the communication source. (3) *Video:* wild streaks and flashes on the monitor screen caused by reentry of a video signal into the switcher and subsequent overamplification.

fiber-optic cable Thin, transparent fibers of glass or plastic used to transfer light from one point to another. When used in broadcast signal transmission, the electrical video and audio signals use optical frequencies (light) as the carrier wave to be modulated.

field (1) A location away from the studio. (2) One-half of a complete scanning cycle, with two fields necessary for one television picture frame. There are 60 fields, or 30 frames, per second in standard NTSC television.

field log A record of each take during the video recording. *See also* **VR log**.

field of view The portion of a scene visible through a particular lens; its vista. Expressed in symbols, such as *CU* for close-up.

field production All productions that happen outside of the studio; generally refers to electronic field production.

figure/ground (1) *Audio:* emphasizing the most important sound source over the general background sounds. (2) *Video:* objects seen in front of a background; the ground is perceived to be more stable than the figure.

fill light Additional light on the opposite side of the camera from the key light to illuminate shadow areas and thereby reduce falloff. Usually done with floodlights.

film-style shooting *See* **single-camera directing**

fishpole A suspension device for a microphone; the mic is attached to a pole and held over the scene for brief periods.

fixed-focal-length lens A lens whose focal length cannot be changed (contrary to a zoom lens that has a variable focal length). Also called *prime lens.*

flag A thin, rectangular sheet of metal, plastic, or cloth used to block light from falling on specific areas. Also called *gobo.*

flash drive *See* **flash memory device**

flash memory card *See* **flash memory device**

flash memory device A read/write portable storage device that can download, store, and upload very fast (in a flash) a significant amount of digital information. Also called *flash drive, stick flash, flash stick,* and *flash memory card.*

flash stick *See* **flash memory device**

flat (1) *Lighting:* even illumination with minimal shadows (slow falloff). (2) *Scenery:* a piece of standing scenery used as a background or to simulate the walls of a room.

flat response Measure of a microphone's ability to hear equally well over its entire frequency range. Is also used as a measure for devices that record and play back a specific frequency range.

floodlight Lighting instrument that produces diffused light with a relatively undefined beam edge.

floor plan A diagram of scenery and properties drawn on a grid pattern. *See also* **floor plan pattern**.

floor plan pattern A plan of the studio floor, showing the walls, main doors, location of the control room, and lighting grid or battens. *See also* **floor plan**.

floor stand Heavy stand mounted on a three-caster dolly, designed specifically to support a variety of lighting instruments. An extension pipe lets you adjust the vertical position of the lighting instrument to a certain degree.

fluorescent Lamps that generate light by activating a gas-filled tube to give off ultraviolet radiation, which lights up the phosphorous coating inside the tube.

focal length The distance from the optical center of the lens to the front surface of the camera's imaging device at which the image appears in focus with the lens set at infinity. Focal lengths are measured in millimeters or inches. *Short-focal-length* lenses have a wide angle of view (wide vista); *long-focal-length (telephoto)* lenses have a narrow angle of view (close-up). In a *variable-focal-length (zoom)* lens, the focal length can be changed continuously from wide-angle (zoomed out) to narrow-angle (zoomed in) and vice versa. A *fixed-focal-length (prime)* lens has a single designated focal length.

focus A picture is in focus when it appears sharp and clear on-screen (technically, the point at which the light rays refracted by the lens converge).

foldback The return of the total or partial audio mix to the talent through headsets or I.F.B. channels. Also called *cue-send.*

Foley stage A variety of props and equipment set up in a recording studio to produce common sound effects, such as footsteps, doors opening and closing, and glass breaking.

follow focus Maintaining the focus of the lens in a shallow depth of field so that the image of an object is continuously kept sharp and clear even when the camera or object moves.

follow spot Powerful special-effects spotlight used primarily to simulate theater stage effects. It generally follows action, such as dancers, ice skaters, or single performers moving in front of a stage curtain.

foot-candle (fc) The amount of light that falls on an object. One foot-candle is the amount of light from a single candle that falls on a 1-square-foot area located 1 foot away from the light source. *See also* **lux**.

format Type of television script indicating the major programming steps; generally contains a fully scripted show opening and closing.

foundation A makeup base over which further makeup such as rouge and eye shadow is applied.

fps Stands for *frames per second. See* **frame rate**.

frame (1) The smallest picture unit in film, a single picture. (2) A complete scan from top to bottom of all picture lines by the electron beam, or one single frame of a motion series. *See* **interlaced scanning** and **progressive scanning**.

frame rate The number of complete video frames the video system is producing each second. Also expressed as *fps*. The NTSC standard of traditional American television is 30 fps. The 480p and 720p scanning systems normally have a frame rate of 60 fps. Some HD digital cinema cameras have a frame rate of 24 fps and/or variable frame rates. The standard 1080i HDTV system has a frame rate of 30 fps.

framestore synchronizer Image stabilization and synchronization system that stores and reads out one complete video frame. Used to synchronize signals from a variety of video sources that are not genlocked.

freeze-frame Continuous replaying of a single frame, which is perceived as a still shot.

frequency Cycles per second, measured in hertz (Hz).

frequency response Measure of the range of frequencies a microphone can hear and reproduce.

Fresnel spotlight One of the most common spotlights, named after the inventor of its lens. Its lens has step-like concentric rings.

front-timing The process of figuring out clock times by adding given running times to the clock time at which the program starts.

f-stop The calibration on the lens indicating the aperture, or iris opening (and therefore the amount of light transmitted through the lens). The larger the *f*-stop number, the smaller the aperture; the smaller the *f*-stop number, the larger the aperture.

full shot *See* **long shot**

fully scripted format A complete script that contains all dialogue or narration and major visualization cues.

gain (1) *Audio:* level of amplification for audio signals. "Riding gain" means keeping the sound volume at a proper level. (2) *Video:* electronic amplification of the video signal, boosting primarily picture brightness.

gel Generic term for color filters put in front of spotlights or floodlights to give the light beam a specific hue. *Gel* comes from *gelatin,* the filter material used before the invention of more-durable plastics. Also called *color media.*

generating element The primary part of a microphone. It converts sound waves into electric energy.

generation The number of dubs away from the original recording. A first-generation dub is struck directly from the source tape. A second-generation tape is a dub of the first-generation dub (two steps away from the original tape), and so forth. In analog recordings, the greater the number of nondigital generations, the greater the quality loss. Digital recordings remain virtually the same through many generations.

genlock The synchronization of two or more video sources (such as cameras and video recorders) or origination sources (such as studio and remote) to prevent picture breakup during switching. A house sync will synchronize all video sources in a studio.

gigabyte 1,073,741,824 bytes (2^{30} bytes); usually figured as roughly 1 billion bytes.

gobo In television, a scenic foreground piece through which the camera can shoot, thus integrating the decorative foreground with the background action. In film a gobo is an opaque shield used for partially blocking a light, or the metal cutout that projects a pattern on a flat surface. *See also* **cookie** and **flag**.

goal-directed information Program content intended to be learned by the viewer.

graphics generator Dedicated computer or software that allows a designer to draw, color, animate, store, and retrieve images electronically. Any desktop computer with a high-capacity RAM and a hard drive can become a graphics generator with the use of 2D and 3D software.

graphic vector A vector created by lines or by stationary elements in such a way as to suggest a line.

grayscale A scale indicating intermediate steps from TV white to TV black. Usually measured with a nine-step scale for standard television.

hand props Objects, called *properties,* that are handled by the performer.

hard drive A high-capacity computer storage disk. Often called *hard disk.*

HDMI Stands for *High-Definition Multimedia Interface.* A high-speed cable of great bandwidth that can carry a great number of digital video and audio signals, and connect with a variety of audio/video equipment.

HDV *See* **high-definition video**

HDTV *See* **high-definition television**

head assembly (1) *Audio:* small electromagnets that erase the signal from the tape (erase head), put the signals on the tape (record head), and read (induce) them off the tape (playback head). (2) *Video:* small electromagnets that put electrical signals on the videotape or read (induce) the signals off the tape. Video heads, as well as the tape, are in motion.

headroom The space left between the top of the head and the upper screen edge.

headset microphone Small but good-quality omni- or unidirectional mic attached to padded earphones; similar to a telephone headset but with a higher-quality mic.

helical scan The diagonally slanted path of the video signal when recorded on the videotape. Also called *helical VTR* or *slant-track.*

high-definition television (HDTV) Has at least twice the picture detail of standard (NTSC) television. The 720p uses 720 visible, or active, lines that are normally scanned progressively each $\frac{1}{60}$ second. The 1080i standard uses 60 fields per second, each field consisting of 540 visible, or active, lines. In interlaced scanning, a complete frame consists of two scanning fields of 540 visible lines. The *refresh rate* (complete scanning cycle) for HDTV systems can vary.

high-definition television (HDTV) camera Video camera that delivers pictures of superior resolution, color fidelity, and light-and-dark contrast; uses high-quality imaging sensors and lenses.

high-definition video (HDV) A recording system that produces images of the same resolution as high-definition television (720p and 1080i) with equipment that is similar to standard digital video camcorders. The video signals are much more compressed than those of HDTV, however, which results in lower overall video quality.

high-key Light background and ample light on the scene. Has nothing to do with the vertical positioning of the key light.

high-Z High impedance. *See also* **impedance**.

HMI light Stands for *hydragyrum medium arc-length iodide*. Uses a high-intensity lamp that produces light by passing electricity through a specific type of gas. Needs a separate ballast.

horizontal blanking The temporary starvation of the electron beam when it returns to write another scanning line.

hot (1) A current- or signal-carrying wire. (2) A piece of equipment that is turned on, such as a hot camera or a hot microphone.

hot spot Undesirable concentration of light in one spot.

house number The in-house system of identification for each piece of recorded program material. Called the *house number* because the code numbers differ from station to station (house to house).

hue One of the three basic color attributes; hue is the color itself—red, green, yellow, and so on.

hundredeighty *See* **vector line**

HUT Stands for *households using television*. Used in calculating share, the HUT figure represents 100 percent of all households using television. *See also* **share**.

Hz Hertz, which measures cycles per second.

IATSE Stands for *International Alliance of Theatrical Stage Employees, Moving Picture Technicians, Artists and Allied Crafts of the United States, Its Territories and Canada*. Trade union.

IBEW Stands for *International Brotherhood of Electrical Workers*. Trade union for studio and master control engineers; may include floor personnel.

I.F.B. *See* **interruptible foldback or interruptible feedback**

I-F lens *See* **internal focus (I-F) lens**

imaging device The imaging element in a television camera. Its sensor (CCD or CMOS) transduces light into electric energy that becomes the video signal. Also called *camera pickup device, chip,* and *sensor*.

impedance Type of resistance to signal flow. Important especially in matching high- or low-impedance microphones with high- or low-impedance recorders.

impedance transformer Device allowing a high-impedance mic to feed a low-impedance recorder or vice versa.

importing *See* **capture**

incandescent The light produced by the hot tungsten filament of ordinary glass-globe or quartz-iodine light bulbs (in contrast to fluorescent light).

incident light Light that strikes the object directly from its source. An incident-light reading is the measure of light in foot-candles (or lux) from the object to the light source. The light meter is pointed directly into the light source or toward the camera.

index vector A vector created by someone looking or something pointing unquestionably in a specific direction.

inky-dinky *See* **camera light**

input overload distortion Distortion caused by a microphone when subjected to an exceptionally high-volume sound. Condenser microphones are especially prone to input overload distortion.

insert editing Requires the prior laying of a control track on the edit master tape. The shots are edited in sequence or inserted into an already existing recording. Necessary mode for editing audio and video tracks separately.

instant replay Repeating for the viewer, by playing back a key play or an important event immediately after its live occurrence. In drama it is used as a visualized recall of a prior event.

instantaneous editing *See* **switching**

intercom Short for *intercommunication system*. Used by all production and technical personnel. The most widely used system has telephone headsets to facilitate voice communication on several wired or wireless channels. Includes other systems, such as I.F.B. and cell phones.

interframe compression A compression technique that borrows recurring pixels from previous frames, thus reducing the number of pixels.

interlaced scanning In this system the electron beam skips every other line during its first scan, reading only the odd-numbered lines. After the beam has scanned half of the last odd-numbered line, it jumps back to the top of the screen and finishes the unscanned half of the top line and continues to scan all even-numbered lines. Each such even- or odd-numbered scan produces a *field*. Two fields produce a complete *frame*. Standard NTSC television operates with 60 fields per second, which translates to 30 frames per second.

internal focus (I-F) lens A mechanism of an ENG/EFP lens that allows focusing without having the front part of the lens barrel extend and turn.

interruptible foldback or interruptible feedback (I.F.B.) Communication system that allows communication with the talent while on the air. A small earpiece worn by on-the-air talent carries program sound or instructions from the producer or director.

in-the-can A term borrowed from film, which referred to when the finished film was literally in the can. It now refers to a finished television recording; the show is preserved and can be broadcast at any time.

intraframe compression A compression method that looks for and eliminates redundant pixels in each frame.

inverse square law The intensity of light falls off as $1/d^2$ from the source, where d is distance from the source. It means that light intensity decreases as distance from the source increases. Valid only for light sources that radiate light isotropically (uniformly in all directions) but not for light whose beam is partially collimated (focused), such as from a Fresnel or an ellipsoidal spot.

ips Stands for *inches per second*. An indication of tape speed.

iris Adjustable lens-opening that controls the amount of light passing through the lens. Also called *diaphragm* and *lens diaphragm*.

iso camera Stands for *isolated camera*. Feeds into the switcher and into its own separate video recorder.

jack (1) A socket or phone-plug receptacle. (2) A brace for scenery.

jib arm Similar to a camera crane. Permits the jib arm operator to raise, lower, and tongue (move sideways) the jib arm while titling and panning the camera.

jogging Frame-by-frame advancement of videotape with a VTR. *See also* **stop-motion**.

JPEG A video compression method mostly for still pictures, developed by the Joint Photographic Experts Group.

jump cut Cutting between shots that are identical in subject yet slightly different in screen location, or any abrupt transition between shots that violates the established continuity.

Kelvin (K) Refers to the Kelvin temperature scale. In lighting it is the specific measure of color temperature—the relative reddishness or bluishness of white light. The higher the K number, the more bluish the white light. The lower the K number, the more reddish the white light.

key An electronic effect. *Keying* means cutting with an electronic signal one image (usually lettering) into a different background image.

key bus A row of buttons on the switcher, used to select the video source to be inserted into a background image.

key-level control Switcher control that adjusts the key signal so that the title to be keyed appears sharp and clear. Also called *clip control* and *clipper*.

key light Principal source of illumination.

kicker light Usually directional light that is positioned low and from the side and the back of the subject.

kilobyte 1,024 bytes (2^{10} bytes); usually figured as roughly 1,000 bytes.

kilowatt (kW) 1,000 watts.

knee shot Framing of a person from approximately the knees up.

Ku-band A high-frequency band used by certain satellites for signal transport and distribution. The Ku-band signals can be influenced by heavy rain or snow. *See also* **C-band**.

kW *See* **kilowatt**

lag Smear that follows a moving object or motion of the camera across a stationary object under low light levels.

lap dissolve *See* **dissolve**

lavalier microphone A small mic that can be clipped onto clothing.

layering Combining two or more key effects for a more complex effect.

LCD Stands for *liquid crystal display*. A flat television display screen that uses an electric charge to activate liquid crystals. These in turn filter colors from white light for each pixel.

LD Stands for *lighting director*.

leader numbers Numerals used for the accurate cueing of the videotape and film during playback. The numbers from 10 to 3 flash at 1-second intervals and are sometimes synchronized with short audio beeps.

leadroom The space left in front of a person or an object moving toward the edge of the screen. *See also* **nose-room**.

lens Optical lens, essential for projecting an optical (light) image of a scene onto the film or the front surface of the camera pickup device. Lenses come in various fixed focal lengths or in variable focal lengths (zoom lenses) and with various maximum apertures (iris openings).

lens diaphragm *See* **iris**

lens prism A prism that, when attached to the camera lens, produces special effects, such as the tilting of the horizon line or the creation of multiple images.

letterbox The aspect ratio that results from fitting the full width of a 16×9 image onto a 4×3 screen by blocking the top and bottom screen edges with stripes. *See also* **pillarbox**.

level (1) *Audio:* sound volume. (2) *Video:* signal strength (amplitude).

libel Written or televised defamation.

lighting The manipulation of light and shadows: to provide the camera with adequate illumination for technically acceptable pictures; to tell us what the objects on-screen actually look like; and to establish the general mood of the event.

lighting triangle The triangular arrangement of key, back, and fill lights. Also called *triangle lighting*. *See also* **photographic lighting principle**.

light level Light intensity measured in lux or foot-candles. *See also* **foot-candle (fc)** and **lux**.

lightness *See* **brightness**

light plot A plan, similar to a floor plan, that shows the type, size (wattage), and location of the lighting instruments relative to the scene to be illuminated and the general direction of the beams.

light ratio The relative intensities of key, back, and fill. A 1:1 ratio between key and back lights means that both light sources burn with equal intensities. A 1:½ ratio between key and fill lights means that the fill light burns with half the intensity of the key light. Because light ratios depend on many production variables, they cannot be fixed. A key:back:fill ratio of 1:1:½ is often used for normal triangle lighting.

limbo Any set area that has a plain, light background.

line *See* **vector line**

linear editing Analog or digital editing that uses tape-based systems. Selection of shots is nonrandom.

line monitor The monitor that shows only the line-out pictures that go on the air or on videotape. Also called *master monitor* and *program monitor*.

line of conversation and action *See* **vector line**

line-out The line that carries the final video or audio output for broadcast.

line producer Supervises daily production activities on the set.

lip-sync Synchronization of sound and lip movement.

live recording The uninterrupted video recording of a live show for later unedited playback. Formerly called *live-on-tape*, live recording includes all recording devices.

location sketch A rough map of the locale of a remote telecast. For an indoor remote, it shows the room dimensions and the furniture and window locations. For an outdoor remote, it indicates the location of buildings, the remote truck, power sources, and the sun during the time of the telecast.

location survey Written assessment, usually in the form of a checklist, of the production requirements for a remote.

locking-in An especially vivid mental image—visual or aural—during script analysis that determines the subsequent visualizations and sequencing.

lockup time The time required by a videotape recorder for the picture and sound to stabilize once the tape has been started.

log The major operational document: a second-by-second list of every program aired on a particular day. It carries such information as program source or origin, scheduled program time, program duration, video and audio information, code identification (house number, for example), program title, program type, and additional pertinent information.

long-focal-length lens *See* **narrow-angle lens**

long shot (LS) Object seen from far away or framed loosely. Also called *establishing shot* and *full shot*.

lossless compression Rearranging but not eliminating pixels during storage and transport. *See also* **compression**.

lossy compression Throwing away redundant pixels during compression. Most compression methods are of the lossy kind. *See also* **compression**.

low-angle dolly Dolly used with high hat to make a camera mount for particularly low shots.

low-key Dark background and illumination of selected areas. Has nothing to do with the vertical positioning of the key light.

low-Z Low impedance. *See also* **impedance**.

LS *See* **long shot**

lumen The light intensity power of one candle (light source radiating isotropically, i.e., in all directions).

luminaire Technical term for a lighting instrument.

luminance The measured brightness (black-and-white) information of a video signal (reproduces the gray-scale). Also called *Y signal*.

luminance channel A separate channel within color cameras that deals with brightness variations and allows them to produce a signal receivable on a black-and-white television. The luminance signal is usually electronically derived from the chrominance signals. Also called *Y channel*.

luminant Lamp that produces the light; the light source.

lux European standard unit for measuring light intensity: 1 lux is the amount of 1 lumen (one candlepower of light) that falls on a surface of 1 square meter located 1 meter away from the light source; 10.75 lux = 1 fc; usually roughly translated as 10 lux = 1 fc. *See also* **foot-candle (fc)**.

macro position A lens setting that allows it to be focused at very close distances from an object. Used for close-ups of small objects.

makeup Cosmetics used to enhance, correct, or change appearance.

master control Nerve center for all telecasts. Controls the program input, storage, and retrieval for on-the-air telecasts. Also oversees technical quality of all program material.

master monitor *See* **line monitor**

matte key Keyed (electronically cut-in) title whose letters are filled with shades of gray or a specific color.

MCU Medium close-up.

MD *See* **mini disc**

M/E bus Short for *mix/effects bus*. A row of buttons on the switcher that can serve a mix or an effects function.

medium requirements All content elements, production elements, and people needed to generate the defined process message.

medium shot (MS) Object seen from a medium distance. Covers any framing between a long shot and a close-up. Also called *waist shot*.

megabyte 1,048,576 bytes (2^{20} bytes); usually figured roughly as 1 million bytes.

megapixel A CCD or digital image containing about 1 million pixels. The higher the number of pixels, the higher the picture resolution. Generally used to indicate the relative quality of digital still cameras.

mental map Tells viewer where things are or are supposed to be in on- and off-screen space. *See also* **closure**.

mic Stands for *microphone*.

microwave relay A transmission method from the remote location to the station and/or transmitter involving the use of several microwave units.

MIDI *See* **musical instrument digital interface**

mini-cassette A small (2½ × 1⅝ inch or 65mm × 47mm) ¼-inch tape cassette used in digital cameras. It allows one hour of recording with standard recording speed.

mini disc (MD) Optical 2½-inch-wide disc that can store one hour of CD-quality audio.

mini-link Several microwave setups that are linked together to transport the video and audio signals past obstacles to their destination (usually the television station and/or transmitter).

minimum object distance (MOD) How close the camera can get to an object and still focus on it.

mix bus (1) *Audio:* a mixing channel for audio signals. The mix bus combines sounds from several sources to produce a mixed sound signal. (2) *Video:* rows of buttons on the switcher that permit the mixing of video sources, as in a dissolve or super.

mixdown Final combination of sound tracks on a single or stereo track of an audio- or videotape.

mix/effects bus *See* **M/E bus**

mixing (1) *Audio:* combining two or more sounds in specific proportions (volume variations) as determined by the event (show) context. (2) *Video:* creating a dissolve or superimposition via the switcher.

mix-minus Type of multiple audio feed missing the part that is being recorded, such as an orchestra feed with the solo instrument being recorded. Also refers to a program sound feed without the portion supplied by the source that is receiving the feed.

mm Millimeter, one-thousandth of a meter: 25.4mm = 1 inch.

MOD *See* **minimum object distance**

moiré effect Color vibrations that occur when narrow, contrasting stripes of a design interfere with the scanning lines of the television system.

monitor (1) *Audio:* speaker that carries the program sound independent of the line-out. (2) *Video:* high-quality television set used in the television studio and control rooms. Cannot receive broadcast signals.

monochrome One color. In television it refers to a camera or monitor that reads only various degrees of brightness and produces a black-and-white picture.

monopod A single pole onto which you can mount a camera.

montage The juxtaposition of two or more separate event details that combine into a larger and more intense whole—a new gestalt.

mounting head A device that connects the camera to the tripod or studio pedestal to facilitate smooth pans and tilts. Also called *pan-and-tilt head*.

motion vector A vector created by an object actually moving or perceived as moving on-screen.

moving-coil microphone *See* **dynamic microphone**

MP3 A widely used compression system for digital audio. Most Internet-distributed audio is compressed in the MP3 format.

MPEG A compression technique for moving pictures, developed by the Moving Picture Experts Group.

MPEG-2 The compression standard for motion video.

MPEG-4 The compression standard for Internet streaming.

MS *See* **medium shot**

multicamera directing Simultaneous coordination of two or more cameras for instantaneous editing (switching). Also called *control room directing*.

multiple-microphone interference The canceling out of certain sound frequencies when two identical microphones close together are used to record the same sound source on the same tape.

multiple-source editing system Editing system having two or more source VTRs.

musical instrument digital interface (MIDI) A standardized protocol that allows the connection and interaction of various digital audio equipment and computers.

NAB Stands for *National Association of Broadcasters.*

NABET Stands for *National Association of Broadcast Employees and Technicians.* Trade union for studio and master control engineers; may include floor personnel.

narrow-angle lens Gives a close-up view of an event relatively far away from the camera. Also called *long-focal-length* and *telephoto lens.*

ND filter *See* **neutral density filter**

neutral density (ND) filter Filter that reduces the incoming light without distorting the color of the scene.

news production personnel People assigned exclusively to the production of news, documentaries, and special events.

noise (1) *Audio:* unwanted sounds that interfere with the intentional sounds, or unwanted hisses or hums inevitably generated by the electronics of the audio equipment. (2) *Video:* electronic interference that shows up as "snow."

NLE *See* **nonlinear editing**

non–drop frame mode A video-recording mode in which the slight discrepancy between actual frame count and elapsed clock time is ignored by the SMPTE time code.

nonlinear editing (NLE) Allows instant random access to shots and sequences and easy rearrangement. The video and audio information is stored in digital form on computer hard drives or read/write optical discs.

nontechnical production personnel People concerned primarily with nontechnical production matters that lead from the basic idea to the final screen image.

normal lens A lens or zoom lens position with a focal length that approximates the spatial relationships of normal vision.

noseroom The space left in front of a person looking or pointing toward the edge of the screen. *See also* **leadroom**.

NTSC Stands for *National Television System Committee.* Normally designates the composite television signal, consisting of the combined chroma information (red, green, and blue signals) and the luminance information (black-and-white signal). *See also* **composite system**.

NTSC signal *See* **composite system**

off-line editing In linear editing it produces an edit decision list or a videotape not intended for broadcast. In nonlinear editing the selected shots are captured in low resolution to save computer storage space.

omnidirectional Pickup pattern in which the microphone can pick up sounds equally well from all directions.

on-line editing In linear editing it produces the final high-quality edit master recording for broadcast or program duplication. In nonlinear editing it can mean recapturing the selected shots at a higher resolution.

operating light level Amount of light needed by the camera to produce a video signal. Most high-end cameras still need from 100 to 250 foot-candles of illumination for optimal performance at a particular f-stop, such as $f/8$. Also called *baselight level.*

optical disc A digital storage device whose information is recorded and read by laser beam.

O/S *See* **over-the-shoulder shot**

oscilloscope *See* **waveform monitor**

over-the-shoulder shot (O/S) Camera looks over a person's shoulder (shoulder and back of head included in shot) at another person.

PA Stands for production assistant.

P.A. Stands for public address. Loudspeaker system. Also called studio talkback or S.A. (studio address) system.

pace Perceived duration of the show or show segment. Part of subjective time.

pan To turn the camera horizontally.

pan-and-tilt head *See* **camera mounting head**

pancake *See* **cake**

pan-stick A foundation makeup with a grease base. Used to cover a beard shadow or prominent skin blemish.

pantograph Expandable hanging device for lighting instruments.

paper-and-pencil editing The process of examining window-dubbed, low-quality (VHS) source tapes and creating a preliminary edit decision list by writing down edit-in and edit-out numbers for each selected shot. Also called *paper editing*.

PAR (parabolic aluminized reflector) lamp *See* **clip light**

parabolic reflector microphone A small parabolic dish whose focal center contains a microphone. Used for the pickup of faraway sounds.

partial two-column A/V script Describes a show for which the dialogue is indicated but not completely written out. *See also* **two-column A/V script**.

patchbay *See* **patchboard**

patchboard A device that connects various inputs with specific outputs. Also called *patchbay* and *patch panel*.

pattern projector An ellipsoidal spotlight with a cookie (cucoloris) insert, which projects the cookie's pattern as a cast shadow.

peak program meter (PPM) Meter in an audio console that measures loudness. Especially sensitive to volume peaks, it indicates overmodulation.

pedestal (1) Heavy camera dolly that permits raising and lowering the camera while on the air. (2) To move the camera up and down via a studio pedestal. (3) The black level of a television picture; can be adjusted against a standard on the waveform monitor.

pencil mic A short condenser shotgun mic normally used on a fishpole boom. It has exchangeable heads for omnidirectional or cardioid pickup patterns.

perambulator boom Mount for a studio microphone. An extension device, or boom, is mounted on a dolly, called a *perambulator,* that permits rapid and quiet relocation anywhere in the studio. Also called *big boom*.

performer A person who appears on-camera in nondramatic shows. Performers play themselves and do not assume someone else's character.

periaktos A triangular piece of scenery that can be turned on a swivel base.

phantom power The power for preamplification in a condenser microphone, supplied by the audio console rather than a battery.

phone plug A ¼-inch plug most commonly used at both ends of audio patch cords. These plugs are also used to route sound signals over relatively short distances from various musical instruments, such as electric guitars or keyboards.

photographic lighting principle The triangular arrangement of key, back, and fill lights, with the back light opposite the camera and directly behind the object, and the key and fill lights on opposite sides of the camera and to the front and the side of the object. Also called *triangle lighting*.

pickup (1) Sound reception by a microphone. (2) Reshooting parts of a scene for postproduction editing.

pickup pattern The territory around the microphone within which the mic can "hear equally well," that is, has optimal sound pickup.

picture element *See* **pixel**

pillarbox The aspect ratio that results from fitting a 4 × 3 image onto a 16 × 9 screen by blocking the sides with stripes. *See also* **letterbox**.

pipe grid Heavy steel pipes mounted above the studio floor to support lighting instruments.

pixel Short for *picture el*ement. (1) A single imaging element (like the single dot in a newspaper picture) that can be identified by a computer. The more pixels per picture area, the higher the picture quality. (2) The light-sensitive elements on a CCD that contain a charge.

P.L. Stands for *private line* or *phone line*. Major intercommunication system in television production.

plasma display A flat-panel television screen whose RGB pixels are activated by specific gases.

playhead In nonlinear editing, can be moved with the mouse to various locations on the scrubber bar. Helps to locate a frame within a clip or sequence.

play VTR *See* **source VTR**

plot How a story develops from one event to the next.

point of view (POV) As seen from a specific character's perspective. Gives the director a clue to camera position.

polar pattern The two-dimensional representation of a microphone pickup pattern.

polarity reversal The reversal of the grayscale; the white areas in the picture become black, and the black areas become white. Color polarity reversal in colors results in the complementary color.

pop filter A bulblike attachment (either permanent or detachable) on the front of a microphone, which filters out sudden air blasts, such as plosive consonants (*p, t,* and *k*) delivered directly into the mic.

ports (1) Slots in the microphone that help achieve a specific pickup pattern and frequency response. (2) Jacks on the computer for plugging in peripheral hardware.

posterization Visual effect that reduces the various brightness values to only a few (usually three or four) and gives the image a flat, posterlike look.

postproduction Any production activity that occurs after the production. Usually refers to either video editing or audio sweetening (a variety of quality adjustments of recorded sound).

postproduction editing The assembly of recorded material after the actual production.

pot Short for *potentiometer*. A sound-volume control.

POV *See* **point of view**

PPM *See* **peak program meter**

preamp Short for *preamplifier*. Strengthens weak electrical signals produced by a microphone or camera pickup device before they can be further processed (manipulated) and amplified to normal signal strength.

preproduction The preparation of all production details.

preroll To start a videotape and let it roll for a few seconds before it is put in the playback or record mode so that the electronic system has time to stabilize.

preset/background bus *See* **preview/preset bus**

preset monitor (PST) Allows previewing of a shot or an effect before it is switched on the air. Its feed can be activated by the *CUT* button. Similar to or the same as the preview monitor.

pressure zone microphone (PZM) *See* **boundary microphone**

preview/preset bus Rows of buttons on the switcher used to select the upcoming video (preset function) and route it to the preview monitor (preview function) independent of the line-out video. Also called *preset/background bus*.

preview (P/V) monitor (1) Any monitor that shows a video source, except for the line (master) and off-the-air monitors. (2) A color monitor that shows the director the picture to be used for the next shot.

prime lens *See* **fixed-focal-length lens**

prism block *See* **beam splitter**

process message The message actually received by the viewer in the process of watching a television program.

producer Creator and organizer of television shows.

production The actual activities in which an event is recorded and/or televised.

production schedule The calendar that shows the preproduction, production, and postproduction dates and who is doing what, when, and where.

production switcher Switcher located in the studio control room or remote truck, designed for instantaneous editing.

program (1) A specific television show. (2) A sequence of instructions, encoded in a specific computer language, to perform predetermined tasks.

program/background bus *See* **program bus**

program bus The bus on a switcher whose inputs are directly switched to the line-out. Allows cuts-only switching. Also called *direct bus* and *program/background bus*.

program monitor *See* **line monitor**

program proposal Written document that outlines the process message and the major aspects of a television presentation.

program speaker A loudspeaker in the control room that carries the program sound. Its volume can be controlled without affecting the actual line-out program feed. Also called *audio monitor*.

progressive scanning In this system the electron beam starts with line 1, then scans line 2, then line 3, and so forth, until all lines are scanned, at which point the beam jumps back to its starting position to repeat the scan of all lines.

project panel A folder in nonlinear editing that holds all video and audio source clips. Also called *browser* or *clips bin*.

props Short for *properties*. Furniture and other objects used for set decoration and by actors or performers.

PSA Public service announcement.

PST *See* **preset monitor**

psychographics Audience research factors concerned with such data as consumer buying habits, values, and lifestyles.

psychological closure *See* **closure**

pulse-count system *See* **control track system**

P/V *See* **preview monitor**

pylon Triangular set piece, similar to a pillar.

PZM Stands for *pressure zone microphone*. *See* **boundary microphone**.

quad-split Switcher mechanism that makes it possible to divide the screen into four quadrants and fill each one with a different image.

quantization *See* **quantizing**

quantizing A step in the digitization of an analog signal. It changes the sampling points into discrete values. Also called *quantization*.

quartz A high-intensity incandescent light whose lamp consists of a quartz or silica housing (instead of the customary glass) that contains halogen gas and a tungsten filament. Produces a very bright light of stable color temperature (3,200K). Also called *TH (tungsten-halogen) lamp*. *See also* **tungsten-halogen (TH)**.

quick-release plate A mounting plate used to attach camcorders and ENG/EFP cameras to the mounting head.

rack focus To change focus from one object or person closer to the camera to one farther away or vice versa.

radio frequency (RF) Broadcast frequency divided into various channels. In an RF distribution, the video and audio signals are superimposed on the radio frequency carrier wave. Usually called *RF*.

radio mic *See* **wireless microphone**

range extender An optical attachment to the zoom lens that extends its focal length. Also called *extender*.

rating Percentage of television households tuned to a specific station in relation to the total number of television households. *See also* **share**.

RCA phono Video and audio connector for consumer equipment.

RCU *See* **remote control unit**

rear projection (R.P.) Translucent screen onto which images are projected from the rear and photographed from the front.

record VTR The videotape recorder that edits the program segments as supplied by the source VTR(s) into the final edit master tape. Also called *edit VTR*.

reel-to-reel A tape recorder that transports the tape past the heads from one reel (the supply reel) to the other reel (the takeup reel).

reference black The darkest element in a set, used as a reference for the black level (beam) adjustment of the camera picture.

reference white The brightest element in a set, used as a reference for the white level (beam) adjustment of the camera picture.

reflected light Light that is bounced off of the illuminated object. A reflected-light reading is done with a light meter held close to the illuminated object.

refresh rate The number of complete digital scanning cycles (frames) per second. *See also* **frame**.

remote *See* **big remote**

remote control unit (RCU) (1) The CCU control separate from the CCU itself. (2) A small, portable CCU that is taken into the field with the EFP camera. *See also* **camera control unit (CCU)**.

remote survey A preproduction investigation of the location premises and event circumstances. Also called *site survey*.

remote truck The vehicle that carries the program control, the audio control, the video-recording and instant-replay control, the technical control, and the transmission equipment.

resolution The measurement of picture detail, expressed in the number of pixels per scanning line and the number of visible scanning lines. Resolution is influenced by the imaging device, the lens, and the television set that shows the camera picture. Often used synonymously with *definition*.

reverberation Reflections of a sound from multiple surfaces after the sound source has ceased vibrating. Generally used to liven sounds recorded in an acoustically "dead" studio. *See also* **echo**.

RF *See* **radio frequency**

RF mic *See* **wireless microphone**

RGB Stands for *red, green, and blue*—the basic colors of television.

RGB component system Analog video-recording system wherein the red, green, and blue (RGB) signals are kept separate throughout the entire recording and storage process and are transported via three separate wires.

ribbon microphone A mic whose sound pickup device consists of a ribbon that vibrates with the sound pressures within a magnetic field. Also called *velocity mic*.

riser (1) Small platform. (2) The vertical frame that supports the horizontal top of the platform.

robotic *See* **robotic pedestal**

robotic pedestal Remotely controlled studio pedestal and mounting head. It is guided by a computerized system that can store and execute a great number of camera moves. Also called *robotic*.

roll (1) Graphics (usually credit copy) that move slowly up the screen; *see also* **crawl**. (2) Command to start the videotape recorder.

rough-cut The first tentative arrangement of shots and shot sequences in the approximate order and length. Done in off-line editing.

R.P. *See* **rear projection**

rundown sheet *See* **fact sheet**

running time The duration of a program or program segment.

runout signal The recording of a few seconds of black at the end of each videotape recording to keep the screen in black for the video changeover or editing.

run-through Rehearsal.

S.A. Stands for *studio address*. Loudspeaker system. *See also* **studio talkback**.

safe area *See* **essential area**

safe title area *See* **essential area**

sampling The process of reading (selecting and recording) from an analog electronic signal a great many equally spaced, tiny portions (values) for conversion into a digital code.

saturation The color attribute that describes a color's richness or strength.

scanning The movement of the electron beam from left to right and from top to bottom on the television screen.

scanning area Picture area that is scanned by the camera pickup device; in general, the picture area usually seen in the camera viewfinder and the preview monitor.

scene Event details that form an organic unit, usually in a single place and time. A series of organically related shots that depict these event details.

scenery Background flats and other pieces (windows, doors, pillars) that simulate a specific environment.

schedule time The time at which a program starts and ends.

scoop A scooplike television floodlight.

scrim (1) *Lighting:* a spun-glass material that is put in front of a lighting instrument as an additional light diffuser or intensity reducer. (2) *Scenery:* loosely woven curtain hanging in front of a cyclorama to diffuse light, producing a soft, uniform background.

script Written document that tells what the program is about, who says what, what is supposed to happen, and what and how the audience should see and hear the event.

script marking A director's written symbols on a script to indicate major cues.

scrubber bar Guide for the playhead when moving through a clip or sequence of clips to locate a frame.

SDTV Standard digital television.

secondary-frame effect Visual effect in which the screen shows several images, each of which is clearly contained in its own frame.

SEG (1) Stands for *Screen Extras Guild.* Trade union. (2) *See* **special-effects generator**.

selective focus Emphasizing an object in a shallow depth of field through focus while keeping its foreground and/or background out of focus.

sensor The CCD or CMOS imaging device in a video camera.

sequencing The control and the structuring of a shot series during editing.

servo zoom control Zoom control that activates motor-driven mechanisms.

set Arrangement of scenery and properties to indicate the locale and/or mood of a show.

set light *See* **background light**

set module Series of flats and three-dimensional set pieces whose dimensions match, whether they are used vertically, horizontally, or in various combinations.

shader *See* **video operator (VO)**

shading Adjusting picture contrast to the optimal contrast range; controlling the color and the white and black levels.

share Percentage of television households tuned to a specific station in relation to all households using television (HUT); that is, all households with their sets turned on. *See also* **rating**.

shooter An ENG/EFP camera operator. Sometimes called *DP (director of photography)* in EFP.

shot The smallest convenient operational unit in video and film, usually the interval between two transitions. In cinema it may refer to a specific camera setup.

shot list *See* **shot sheet**

shot sheet A list of every shot a particular camera has to get. It is attached to the camera to help the camera operator remember the shot sequence. Also called *shot list.*

shotgun microphone A highly directional mic for picking up sounds from a relatively great distance.

show format Lists the show segments in order of appearance. Used in routine shows, such as daily game or interview shows.

shuttle Fast-forward and fast-rewind movement of videotape to locate a particular address (shot) on the tape.

side light Usually directional light coming from the side of an object. Acts as additional fill light or a second key light and provides contour.

signal processing The various electronic adjustments or corrections of the video signal to ensure a stable and/or color-enhanced picture. Usually done with digital equipment.

signal-to-noise (S/N) ratio The relation of the strength of the desired signal to the accompanying electronic interference (the noise). A high S/N ratio is desirable (strong video or audio signal relative to weak noise).

silhouette lighting Unlighted objects or people in front of a brightly illuminated background.

single-camera directing Directing method for a single camera. For digital cinema it may mean moving from an establishing long shot to medium shots, then to close-ups of the same action. Also called *film-style shooting.*

single-column drama script Traditional script format for television and motion picture plays. All dialogue and action cues are written in a single column.

single-source editing system Basic editing system that has only one source VTR. Also called *cuts-only editing system.*

site survey *See* **remote survey**

slander Oral defamation.

slant-track *See* **helical scan**

slate (1) Visual and/or verbal identification of each videotaped segment. (2) A small blackboard or whiteboard upon which essential production information is written. It is recorded at the beginning of each take.

slide fader *See* **fader**

sliding rod Steel pipe that supports a lighting instrument and can be moved into various vertical positions. It is attached to the lighting batten by a modified C-clamp.

slow lens A lens that permits a relatively small amount of light to pass through at its maximum aperture (relatively high *f*-stop number at its lowest setting). Can be used only in well-lighted areas.

SMPTE/EBU time code Stands for *Society of Motion Picture and Television Engineers/European Broadcasting Union time code.* Electronic signal recorded on the cue or address track of a videotape or a track of a multitrack audiotape to give each frame a specific address. The time code reader translates this signal into a specific number (hour, minutes, seconds, and frames) for each frame.

S/N *See* **signal-to-noise ratio**

snow Electronic picture interference; looks like snow on the television screen.

softlight Television floodlight that produces extremely diffused light.

soft wipe Transition in which the demarcation line between two images is softened so the images blend into each other.

solarization A special effect produced by a partial polarity reversal of an image. In a monochrome image, thin black lines are sometimes formed where the positive and negative image areas meet. In a color image, the reversal results in a combination of complementary hues.

SOS Stands for *sound on source.* The video is played back with pictures and sound. Formerly called *SOT.*

SOT Stands for *sound on tape.* The videotape is played back with pictures and sound. *See also* **SOS.**

sound bite Brief portion of someone's on-camera statement.

sound perspective Distant sound must go with a long shot, close sound with a close-up.

source media The media (videotape, hard disk, optical disc, flash memory device) that holds the recorded camera footage.

source tape The videotape with the original camera footage.

source VTR The videotape recorder that supplies the program segments to be assembled by the record VTR. Also called *play VTR.*

special-effects controls Buttons on a switcher that regulate special effects. They include buttons for specific wipe patterns, the joystick positioner, DVE, color, and chroma-key controls.

special-effects generator (SEG) An image generator built into the switcher that produces special-effects wipe patterns and keys.

spiking To mark on the studio floor with chalk or gaffer's tape critical positions of talent, cameras, or scenery.

split edit Technically, the audio of a shot is substituted with related sounds or narration. In common practice the audio precedes the shot or bleeds into the next one. Viewers hear the audio of the next shot before seeing it, or they still hear the audio of the previous shot at the beginning of the new one.

split intercom *See* **double headset**

split screen Multi-image effect caused by stopping a directional wipe before its completion, each screen portion therefore showing a different image within its own frame.

spotlight A lighting instrument that produces directional, relatively undiffused light with a relatively well-defined beam edge.

spreader A triangular base mount that provides stability and locks the tripod tips in place to prevent the legs from spreading.

standard television (STV) A system based on the NTSC scanning system of 525 (480 visible) interlaced lines.

stand-by A warning cue for any kind of action in television production.

star filter Filter that attaches to the front of the lens; changes prominent light sources into starlike light beams.

Steadicam Camera mount whose built-in springs hold the camera steady while the operator moves.

stick flash *See* **flash memory device**

stock shot An image of a common occurrence—clouds, storm, traffic, crowds—that can be repeated in a variety of contexts because its qualities are typical. There are stock-shot libraries from which any number of such shots can be obtained.

stop-motion A slow-motion effect in which one frame jumps to the next, showing the object in a different position. *See also* **jogging**.

storyboard A series of sketches of the key visualization points of an event, with the corresponding audio information.

streaming A way of delivering and receiving digital audio and/or video as a continuous data flow that can be listened to or watched while the delivery is in progress. *See also* **downloading**.

strike To remove certain objects; to break down scenery and remove equipment from the studio floor after the show.

striped filter Extremely narrow, vertical stripes of red, green, and blue filters attached to the front surface of the single pickup device (single chip). They divide the incoming white light into the three light primaries without the aid of a beam splitter. More-efficient filters use a mosaic-like pattern instead of stripes to generate the light primaries.

strip light Several self-contained lamps arranged in a strip; used mostly for illumination of the cyclorama or chroma-key area. Also called *cyc light*.

studio camera High-quality camera with a large zoom lens that cannot be maneuvered properly without the aid of a pedestal or some other camera mount.

studio monitor A video monitor located in the studio, which carries assigned video sources, usually the video of the line-out.

studio pan-and-tilt head A camera mounting head for heavy cameras that permits extremely smooth pans and tilts.

studio talkback A public address loudspeaker system from the control room to the studio. Also called *S.A. (studio address)* or *P.A. (public address) system*.

STV *See* **standard television**

subtractive primary colors Magenta (bluish red), cyan (greenish blue), and yellow. When mixed these colors act as filters, subtracting certain colors. When all three are mixed, they filter out one another and produce black.

super Short for *superimposition*. A double exposure of two images, with the top one letting the bottom one show through.

supply reel Reel that holds film or tape, which it feeds to the takeup reel.

surround sound Sound that produces a soundfield in front of, to the sides of, and behind the listener by positioning loudspeakers either to the front and the rear or to the front, sides, and rear of the listener.

S-video *See* **Y/C component system**

sweep Curved piece of scenery, similar to a large pillar cut in half.

sweetening A variety of quality adjustments of recorded sound in postproduction.

switcher (1) Technical crewmember doing the video switching (usually the technical director). (2) A panel with rows of buttons that allow the selection and the assembly of various video sources through a variety of transition devices, and the creation of electronic special effects.

switching A change from one video source to another during a show or show segment with the aid of a switcher. Also called *instantaneous editing*.

sync generator Part of the camera chain; produces an electronic synchronization signal.

sync pulses Electronic pulses that synchronize the scanning in the various video origination sources (studio cameras and/or remote cameras) and various recording, processing, and reproduction sources (videotape, monitors, and television receivers). *See also* **control track**.

sync roll Vertical rolling of a picture caused by switching among video sources whose scanning is out of step. Also noticeable on a bad edit in which the control tracks of the edited shots do not match.

system microphone Mic consisting of a base upon which several heads can be attached that change its sound pickup characteristic.

take (1) Signal for a cut from one video source to another. (2) Any one of similar repeated shots taken during video recording or filming. Usually assigned a number. A *good take* is the successful recording of a shot. A *bad take* is an unsuccessful recording, requiring another take.

takeup reel Reel that receives (takes up) film or tape from the supply reel. Must be the same size as the supply reel to maintain proper tension.

talent Collective name for all performers and actors who appear regularly on television.

tally light Red light on the camera and/or inside the viewfinder, indicating when the camera is on the air.

tape-based video recorder All video recorders (analog and digital) that record or store information on videotape. All tape-based systems are linear.

tape cassette *See* **cassette**

tapeless system Refers to the recording, storage, and playback of audio and video information via digital electronic recording devices other than videotape.

tapeless video recorder All digital video recorders that record or store digital information on media other than videotape.

target audience The audience selected or desired to receive a specific message.

TBC *See* **time base corrector**

TD Stands for *technical director*.

technical production personnel People who operate the production equipment.

telephoto lens *See* **narrow-angle lens**

teleprompter A prompting device that projects the moving (usually computer-generated) copy over the lens so that the talent can read it without losing eye contact with the viewer. Also called *auto-cue*.

television system Equipment and people who operate the equipment for the production of specific programs. The basic television system consists of a television camera and a microphone, which convert pictures and sound into electrical signals, and a television set and a loudspeaker, which convert the signals back into pictures and sound.

test tone A tone generated by the audio console to indicate a 0 VU volume level. The 0 VU test tone is recorded with the color bars to give a standard for the recording level.

theme (1) What the story is all about; its essential idea. (2) The opening and closing music in a show.

TH (tungsten-halogen) lamp *See* **quartz**

threefold Three flats hinged together.

three-shot Framing of three people.

tilt To point the camera up or down.

time base corrector (TBC) Electronic accessory to a video recorder that helps make playbacks or transfers electronically stable.

time code Gives each television frame a specific address (number that shows hours, minutes, seconds, and frames of elapsed tape). *See also* **SMPTE/EBU time code**.

time cues Cues to the talent about the time remaining in the show.

time line (1) *Production:* a breakdown of time blocks for various activities on the actual production day, such as crew call, setup, and camera rehearsal. (2) *Nonlinear editing:* shows all video and audio tracks of a sequence and the clips they contain. Each track has individual controls for displaying and manipulating the clips.

tongue To move the boom or jib arm with the camera from left to right or right to left.

track Another name for *truck* (lateral camera movement).

tracking (1) An electronic adjustment of the video heads so that in the playback phase they match the recording phase of the tape. It prevents picture breakup and misalignment, especially in tapes that have been recorded on a machine other than the one used for playback. (2) Another name for *truck* (lateral camera movement).

transponder A satellite's own receiver and transmitter.

treatment A brief narrative description of a television program.

triangle lighting *See* **photographic lighting principle**

triaxial cable Thin camera cable in which one central wire is surrounded by two concentric shields.

trim (1) *Audio:* to adjust the signal strength of mic or line inputs. (2) *Video:* to lengthen or shorten a shot by a few frames during editing; also to shorten a video-taped story.

tripod A three-legged camera mount. Can be connected to a dolly for easy maneuverability.

truck To move the camera laterally by means of a mobile camera mount. Also called *track*.

tungsten-halogen (TH) The kind of lamp filament used in quartz lights. The tungsten is the filament itself; the halogen is a gaslike substance surrounding the filament enclosed in a quartz housing. *See also* **quartz**.

two-column A/V script Traditional script format with video information on page-left and audio information on page-right for a variety of television scripts, such as for documentaries and commercials. Also called *A/V (audio/video) format*.

twofold Two flats hinged together. Also called *book*.

two-shot Framing of two people.

unbalanced mic or line Microphone or other audio-producing source that has as output two wires: one that carries the audio signal and the other acting as ground. Susceptible to hum and electronic interference.

unidirectional Pickup pattern in which the microphone can pick up sounds better from the front than from the sides or back.

uplink Earth station transmitter used to send video and audio signals to a satellite.

uplink truck A truck that sends video and audio signals to a satellite.

variable-focal-length lens *See* **zoom lens**

vector Refers to a perceivable force with a direction and a magnitude. Vector types include graphic vectors, index vectors, and motion vectors. *See also* **graphic vector**, **index vector**, and **motion vector**.

vector line A dominant direction established by two people facing each other or through a prominent movement in a specific direction. Also called the *line,* the *line of conversation and action,* and the *hundredeighty*.

vector scope A test instrument for adjusting color in television cameras.

velocity mic *See* **ribbon microphone**

vertical blanking The return of the electron beam to the top of the screen after each cycle of the basic scanning process.

vertical key light position The relative distance of the key light from the studio floor, specifically with respect to whether it is above or below the eye level of the performer. Not to be confused with *high-* and *low-key lighting,* which refer to the relative brightness and contrast of the overall scene.

VHS Stands for *video home system.* A consumer-oriented ½-inch VTR system. Used extensively in all phases of television production for previewing and off-line editing.

video Picture portion of a television program.

videocassette A plastic container in which a videotape moves from a supply reel to a takeup reel, recording and playing back program segments through a videotape recorder.

video leader Visual material and a control tone recorded before the program material. Serves as a technical guide for playback.

video operator (VO) In charge of initial camera setup (white-balancing the camera and keeping the brightness contrast within tolerable limits) and for picture control during the production. Also called *shader.*

video recorder (VR) All devices that record video and audio. Includes videotape, hard disks, read/write optical discs, and flash memory devices.

videotape recorder (VTR) Electronic recording device that records video and audio signals on videotape for later playback or postproduction editing.

videotape tracks Most videotape systems have a video track, two or more audio tracks, a control track, and sometimes a separate time code track.

video track The area of the videotape used for recording the picture information.

viewfinder Generally means electronic viewfinder (in contrast to the optical viewfinder in a film or still camera); a small television set that displays the picture as generated by the camera.

visualization Mentally converting a scene into a number of key television images, not necessarily in sequence. The mental image of a shot.

VJ Stands for *video journalist.* A television news reporter who shoots, edits, and writes his or her own material.

VO *See* **video operator**

volume The relative intensity of the sound; its relative loudness.

volume-unit (VU) meter Measures volume units, the relative loudness of amplified sound.

VR *See* **video recorder**

VR log A list of all takes—both good (acceptable) and no good (unacceptable)—in consecutive order by scene number and time code address. Often done with computerized logging programs. A vector column facilitates shot selection. *See also* **field log**.

VTR *See* **videotape recorder**

VU meter *See* **volume-unit meter**

W Watt.

wagon A platform with casters, which can be moved about the studio.

waist shot *See* **medium shot**

walk-through Orientation session with the production crew *(technical walkthrough)* and the talent *(talent walk-through)* wherein the director walks through the set and explains the key actions.

waveform monitor Electronic measuring device showing a graph of an electrical signal on a small CRT (cathode-ray tube) screen. Also called *oscilloscope.*

wedge mount Wedge-shaped plate attached to the bottom of a studio camera; used to attach the heavier cameras to the mounting head.

white balance The adjustments of the color circuits in the camera to produce a white color in lighting of various color temperatures (relative reddishness or bluishness of white light).

wide-angle lens A short-focal-length lens that provides a broad vista of a scene.

window dub A "bumped-down" copy of all source media that has the time code keyed over each frame.

windscreen Material (usually foam rubber) that covers the microphone head or the entire microphone to reduce wind noise.

wipe Transition in which a second image, framed in some geometric shape, gradually replaces all or part of the first image.

wireless microphone A system that transmits audio signals over the air rather than through mic cables. The mic is attached to a transmitter, and the signals are received by a receiver connected to the audio console or recording device. Also called *RF (radio frequency) mic* or *radio mic.*

workprint (1) A dub of the original videotape recording for viewing or off-line editing. (2) In film a dub of the original footage for doing a rough-cut.

wow Sound distortions caused by a slow start or variations in speed of an audiotape.

XLR connector Three-wire audio connector used for all balanced audio cables.

X/S *See* **cross-shot**

Y channel *See* **luminance channel**

Y/C component system Analog video-recording system wherein the luminance (Y) and chrominance (C) signals are kept separate during signal encoding and transport but are combined and occupy the same track when actually laid down on videotape. The Y/C component signal is transported via two wires. Also called *S-video.*

Y/color difference component system Video-recording system in which three signals—the luminance (Y) signal, the red signal minus its luminance (R–Y) signal, and the blue signal minus its luminance (B–Y)—are kept separate throughout the recording and storage process.

Y signal *See* **luminance**

z-axis An imaginary line representing an extension of the lens from the camera to the horizon—the depth dimension.

zone lighting *See* **continuous-action lighting**

zoom To change the lens gradually to a narrow-angle position (zoom-in) or to a wide-angle position (zoom-out) while the camera remains stationary.

zoom lens A variable-focal-length lens. It can gradually change from a wide shot to a close-up and vice versa in one continuous move.

zoom range The degree to which the focal length can be changed from a wide shot to a close-up during a zoom. The zoom range is often stated as a ratio; a 20:1 zoom ratio means that the zoom lens can increase its shortest focal length 20 times.

Index